Praise for

UNTO THE SONS

A *New York Times* Notable Book of the Year

"*Unto the Sons* is a triumph. . . . Place and and time are summoned directly and sensuously out of the memory of Gay Talese, who begins this story as a first-person narrator, creating a voice, an entirely trustworthy witness. But soon he vanishes gracefully into the telling of the tale, a tale of others. . . . The story begins as a personal account but ends as a communal one, a shared experience."

—*Chicago Tribune Book World*

"Richly human . . . [Talese] interweaves the history of [his family's] private lives with the public history of contemporary Italy, the wars and leaders and economic forces that sent so many Italians across the sea to work hard and suffer the indignities of prejudice in a new land. . . . Talese is able to make this all-important personal story—where he came from—significant for the rest of us as well."

—*USA Today*

"Brilliantly evoked . . . The book is a sweeping saga tracing the fate of the Taleses and their far-flung family during World War II. . . . extremely moving."

—*Vogue*

"A dazzling self-examination on a large canvas. Perhaps nobody but Talese, a demon for research and a natural storyteller, could have pulled it off. . . . *Unto the Sons* is thick with revealing incident and colorful character."

—*People*

"A wonderful and unforgettable book and I think the finest work he's produced in his remarkable career. Mr. Talese has taken the raw material of his own family's migration to America and turned it into epic dimensions. He turns the story of his Italian family into one of the most quintessentially American stories ever told. *Unto the Sons* is a love song to the courage of immigrants and the continuing power of the American dream."

—PAT CONROY

"Gay Talese has spoken often of his debt to Fitzgerald, Cheever, and other modern masters of fiction; and in this book he makes a grand leap into the form, bringing the characters of his father, himself as a boy, and their ancestors in Italy to vividly dramatic life with novelistic storytelling. It is a compelling use of the form by Talese, who, as he has proven again and again with his books, is a master of the narrative art. With this new work he delves into the souls of his people to tell a universal story we haven't heard before; and the consequence is a wonderful book."

—WILLIAM KENNEDY

"Masterful . . . a story that will resonate for parents and children of every nationality."

—*Publishers Weekly*

"A magnificent multigenerational saga . . . *Unto the Sons* demonstrates every bit of the talent and industry that established and kept Talese a star. . . . A work of literature, a nonfiction novel, a tone poem from the first paragraph."

—*The Philadelphia Inquirer*

"Gay Talese has produced a work that is part fiction, part history, part biography and part autobiography. . . . [He] has written an entertaining, valuable and insightful book that will appeal to all Americans today of Italian ancestry."

—*Chicago Sun-Times*

ALSO BY GAY TALESE

UNTO THE SONS

RANDOM HOUSE

TRADE PAPERBACKS

NEW YORK

Gay Talese

UNTO THE
SONS

2006 Random House Trade Paperback Edition

Copyright © 1992 by Gay Talese

All rights reserved.

Published in the United States by
Random House Trade Paperbacks,
an imprint of The Random House Publishing Group,
a division of Random House, Inc., New York.

RANDOM HOUSE TRADE PAPERBACKS and
colophon are trademarks of Random House, Inc.

Originally published in hardcover in the
United States by Alfred A. Knopf, a
division of Random House, Inc., in 1992.

This edition published by arrangement with
Alfred A. Knopf, a division of Random House, Inc.

ISBN 978-0-8129-7606-9

www.atrandom.com

Book design by Barbara M. Bachman

For my daughters,

Pamela Frances

and

Catherine Gay

The ambitions of people who never became very rich, who founded no dynasty or long-lasting company, and who lived in the middle and lower ranks of the business world, are difficult to write about, because they are seldom recorded.

But the character of a society is greatly influenced by the form the ambitions of such men take, and by the extent to which they are satisfied or frustrated.

—Theodore Zeldin,
France, 1848–1945: Ambition and Love

UNTO THE SONS

THE BEACH IN WINTER was dank and desolate, and the island dampened by the frigid spray of the ocean waves pounding relentlessly against the beachfront bulkheads, and the seaweed-covered beams beneath the white houses on the dunes creaked as quietly as the crabs crawling nearby.

The boardwalk that in summer was a festive promenade of suntanned couples and children's balloons, of carousel tunes and colored lights spinning at night from the Ferris wheel, was occupied in winter by hundreds of sea gulls perched on the iron railings facing into the wind. When not resting they strutted outside the locked doors of vacated shops, or circled high in the sky, holding clams in their beaks that they soon dropped upon the boardwalk with a splattering *cluck*. Then they zoomed down and pounced on the exposed meat, pecking and pulling until there was nothing left but the jagged, salty white chips of empty shells.

By midwinter the shell-strewn promenade was a vast cemetery of clams, and from a distance the long elevated flat deck of the boardwalk resembled a stranded aircraft carrier being attacked by dive-bombers—and oddly juxtaposed in the fog behind the dunes loomed the rusting remains of a once sleek four-masted vessel that during a gale in the winter of 1901 had run aground on this small island in southern New Jersey called Ocean City.

The steel-hulled ship, flying a British flag and flaunting hundred-fifty-foot masts, had been sailing north along the New Jersey coast toward New York City, where it was scheduled to deliver one million dollars' worth of Christmas cargo it had picked up five months before in Kobe, Japan. But during the middle of the night, while a number of crewmen drank rum and beer in a premature toast to the long journey's end, a fierce storm rose and destroyed the ship's sails, snapped its masts, and drove it into a sandbar within one hundred yards of the Ocean City boardwalk.

Awakened by the distress signals that flared in the night, the alarmed residents of Ocean City—a conservative community founded in 1879 by Methodist ministers and other Prohibitionists who wished to establish an island of abstinence and propriety—hastened to help the sailors, who were soon discovered to be battered but unharmed and smelling of sweat, salt water, and liquor.

After the entire thirty-three-man crew had been escorted to shore, they were sheltered and fed for days under the auspices of the town's teetotaling elders and ministers' wives; and while the sailors expressed gratitude for such hospitality they privately cursed their fate in being shipwrecked on an island so sedate and sober. But soon they were relocated by British nautical authorities, and the salvageable cargo was barged to New York to be sold at reduced prices. And the town returned to the tedium of winter.

The big ship, however, remained forever lodged in the soft white sand—unmovable, slowly sinking, a sight that served Ocean City's pious guardians as a daily reminder of the grim consequences of intemperate guidance. But as I grew up in the late 1930s, more than three decades after the shipwreck—when the visible remnants at low tide consisted only of the barnacle-bitten ridge of the upper deck, the corroded brown rudder post and tiller, and a single lopsided mast—I viewed the vessel as a symbol of adventure and risk; and during my boyhood wanderings along the beach I became enchanted with exotic fantasies of nights in foreign ports, of braving the waves and wind with wayward men, and of escaping the rigid confines of this island on which I was born but never believed I belonged.

I saw myself always as an alien, an outsider, a drifter who, like the shipwrecked sailors, had arrived by accident. I felt different from my young friends in almost every way, different in the cut of my clothes, the food in my lunch box, the music I heard at home on the record player, the ideas and inner thoughts I revealed on those rare occasions when I was open and honest.

I was olive-skinned in a freckle-faced town, and I felt unrelated even to my parents, especially my father, who was indeed a foreigner—an unusual man in dress and manner, to whom I bore no physical resemblance and with whom I could never identify. Trim and elegant, with wavy dark hair and a small rust-colored moustache, he spoke English with an accent and received letters bearing strange-looking stamps.

These letters sometimes contained snapshots of soldiers wearing uniforms with insignia and epaulets unlike any I had seen on the recruitment posters displayed throughout the island. They were my uncles and cousins, my father explained to me quietly one day early in World War II, when I was ten; they were fighting in the Italian army, and—it was unnecessary for him to add—their enemy included the government of the United States.

I became increasingly sensitive to this fact when I sat through the newsreels each week at the local cinema; next to my unknowing classmates, I watched with private horror the destruction by Allied bombers of mountain villages and towns in southern Italy to which I was ancestrally linked through a historically ill-timed relationship with my Italian father. At any moment I half expected to see up on the screen, gazing down at me from a dust-covered United States Army truck filled with disheveled Italian prisoners being guarded at gunpoint, a sad face that I could identify from one of my father's snapshots.

My father, on the other hand, seemed to share none of my confused sense of patriotism during the war years. He joined a citizens' committee of shore patrolmen who kept watch along the waterfront at night, standing with binoculars on the boardwalk under the stanchioned lights that on the ocean side were painted black as a precaution against discovery by enemy submarines.

He made headlines in the local newspaper after a popular speech to the Rotary Club in which he reaffirmed his loyalty to the Allied cause, declaring that were he not too old for the draft (he was thirty-nine) he would proudly join the American troops at the front, in a uniform devotedly cut and stitched with his own hands.

Trained as an apprentice tailor in his native village, and later an assistant cutter in a prominent shop in Paris that employed an older Italian cousin, my father arrived in Ocean City circuitously and impulsively at the age of eighteen in 1922 with very little money, an extensive wardrobe, and the outward appearance of a man who knew exactly where he was going, when in fact nothing was further from the truth. He knew no one in town, barely knew the language, and yet, with a self-assurance that has always mystified me, he adjusted to this unusual island as readily as he could cut cloth to fit any size and shape.

Having noticed a "For Sale" sign in the window of a tailor shop in the center of town, my father approached the asthmatic owner, who was desperate to leave the island for the drier climate of Arizona. After a brief negotiation, my father acquired the business and thus began a lengthy, spirited campaign to bring the rakish fashion of the Continental boulevardier to the comparatively continent men of the south Jersey shore.

But after decorating his windows with lantern-jawed mannequins holding cigarettes and wearing Borsalino hats, and draping his counters with bolts of fine imported fabrics—and displaying on his walls such presumably persuasive regalia as his French master tailor's diploma bordered by cherubim and a Greek goddess—my father made so few sales during his first year that he was finally forced to introduce into his shop a somewhat undignified gimmick called the Suit Club.

At the cost of one dollar per week, Suit Club members would print their names and addresses on small white cards and, after placing the cards in unmarked envelopes, would deposit them into a large opaque vase placed prominently atop a velvet-covered table next to a fashion photograph of a dapper man and woman posing with a greyhound on the greensward of an ornate country manor.

Each Friday evening just prior to closing time, my father would invite one of the assembled Suit Club members to close his eyes and pick from the vase a single envelope, which would reveal the name of the fortunate winner of a free suit, to be made from fabric selected by that individual; after two fittings, it would be ready for wearing within a week.

Since as many as three or four hundred people were soon paying a dollar each week to partake in this raffle, my father was earning on each free suit a profit perhaps three times the average cost of a custom-made suit in those days—to say nothing of the additional money he earned when he enticed a male winner into purchasing an extra pair of matching trousers.

But my father's bonanza was abruptly terminated one day in 1928, when an anonymous complaint sent to City Hall, possibly by a rival tailor, charged that the Suit Club was a form of gambling clearly outlawed under the town charter; thus ended for all time my father's full-time commitment to the reputable but precarious life of an artist with a needle and thread. My father did *not* climb down from an impoverished mountain in southern Italy and forsake the glorious lights of Paris and sail thousands of miles to the more opportunistic shores of America to end up as a poor tailor in Ocean City, New Jersey.

So he diversified. Advertising himself as a ladies' furrier who could alter or remodel old coats as well as provide resplendent new ones (which he obtained on consignment from a Russian Jewish immigrant who resided in nearby Atlantic City), my father expanded his store to accommodate a refrigerated fur storage vault and extended the rear of the building to include a dry-cleaning plant overseen by a black Baptist deacon who during Prohibition operated a small side business in bootlegging. Later, in the 1930s, my father added a ladies' dress boutique, having as partner and wife a well-tailored woman who once worked as a buyer in a large department store in Brooklyn.

He met her while attending an Italian wedding in that borough in December 1927. She was a bridesmaid, a graceful and slender woman of twenty with dark eyes and fair complexion and a style my father immediately recognized as both feminine and prepossessing. After a few dances at the reception under the scrutiny of her parents, and the frowns of the saxophone player in the band with whom she had recently gone out on a discreet double date, my father decided to delay his departure from Brooklyn for a day or two so that he might ingratiate himself with her. This he did with such panache that they were engaged within a year, and married six months later, after buying a small white house near the Ocean City beach, where, in the winter of 1932, I was born and awoke each morning to the smell of espresso and the roaring sound of the waves.

My first recollection of my mother was of a fashionable, solitary figure on the breezy boardwalk pushing a baby carriage with one hand while with the other stabilizing on her head a modish feathered hat at an unwavering angle against the will of the wind.

As I grew older I learned that she cared greatly about exactness in appearance, preciseness in fit, straightness in seams; and, except when positioned on a pedestal in the store as my father measured her for a new suit, she seemed to prefer standing at a distance from other people, conversing with customers over a counter, communicating with her friends via telephone rather than in person. On those infrequent occasions when her relatives from Brooklyn would visit us in Ocean City, I noticed how quickly she backed away from their touch after offering her cheek for a kiss of greeting. Once, during my preschool days as I accompanied her on an errand, I tried to hold on to her, to put my hand inside the pocket of her coat not only for the warmth but for a closer feeling with her presence. But when I tried this I felt her hand, gently but firmly, remove my own.

It was as if she were incapable of intimate contact with anyone but my father, whom she plainly adored to the exclusion of everyone else; and the impression persisted throughout my youth that I was a kind of orphan in the custody of a compatible couple whose way of life was strange and baffling.

One night at the dinner table when I casually picked up a loaf of Italian bread and placed it upside down in the basket, my father became furious and, without further explanation, turned the loaf right side up and demanded that I never repeat what I had done. Whenever we attended the cinema as a family we left before the end, possibly because of my parents' inability or unwillingness to relate to the film's content, be it drama or comedy. And although my parents spent their entire married life living along the sea, I never saw them go sailing, fishing, or swimming, and rarely did they even venture onto the beach itself.

In my mother's case I suspect her avoidance of the beach was due to her desire to prevent the sun from scorching and darkening her fair skin. But I believe my father's aversion to the sea was based on something deeper, more complex, somehow related to his boyhood in southern Italy. I suggest this because I often heard him refer to his region's coastline as foreboding and malarial, a place of piracy and invasion; and as an avid reader of Greek mythology—his birthplace is not far from the renowned rock of Scylla, where the Homeric sea monster devoured sailors who had escaped the whirlpool of Charybdis—my father was prone to attaching chimerical significance to certain bizarre or inexplicable events that occurred during his youth along the streams and lakes below his village.

I remember overhearing, when I was eleven or twelve, my father complaining to my mother that he had just experienced a sleepless night during which he had been disturbed by beachfront sounds resembling howling wolves, distant but distinct, and reminiscent of a frightful night back in 1914 when his entire village had been stirred by such sounds; when the villagers awoke they discovered that the azure water of their lake had turned a murky red.

It was a mournful precursor of things to come, my father explained to my mother: his own father would soon die unexpectedly of an undiagnosed ailment, and a bloody world war would destroy the lives of so many of his young countrymen, including his older brother.

I, too, had sometimes heard in Ocean City at night what sounded like wolves echoing above the sand dunes; but I knew they were really stray dogs, part of the large population of underfed pets and watchdogs abandoned each fall by summer merchants and vacationers during the peak years of the Depression, when the local animal shelter was inadequately staffed or closed entirely.

Even in summertime the dogs roamed freely on the boardwalk during the Depression, mingling with the reduced number of tourists who strolled casually up and down the promenade, passing the restaurants of mostly unoccupied tables, the soundless bandstand outside the music pavilion, and the carousel's riderless wooden horses.

My mother loathed the sight and smell of these dogs; and as if her disapproval provoked their spiteful nature, they followed her everywhere. Moments after she had emerged from the house to escort me to school before her mile walk along deserted streets to join my father at the store, the dogs would appear from behind fences and high-weeded yards and trail her by several paces in a quiet trot, softly whimpering and whining, or growling or panting with their tongues extended.

While there were a few pointers and terriers, spaniels and beagles, they were mostly mongrels of every breed and color, and *all* of them seemed unintimidated by my mother, even after she abruptly turned and glared at them and tried to drive them away with a sweeping gesture of her right arm in the air. They never attacked her or advanced close enough to nip at her high heels; it was mainly a game of territorial imperative that they played each morning with her. By the winter of 1940, the dogs had definitely won.

At this time my mother was caring for her second and final child, a daughter four years my junior; and I think that the daily responsibility of rearing two children, assisting in the store, and being followed, even when we children accompanied her, by the ragged retinue of dogs—a few of which often paused to copulate in the street as my sister and I watched in startled wonderment—drove my mother to ask my father to sell our house on the isolated north end of the island and move us into the more populated center of town.

This he unhesitatingly did, although in the depressed real estate market of that time he was forced to sell at an unfavorable price. But he also benefitted from these conditions by obtaining at a bargain on the main street of Ocean City a large brick building that had been the offices of a weekly newspaper lately absorbed in a merger. The spacious first floor of the building, with its high ceiling and balcony, its thick walls and deep interior, its annex and parking lot, provided more than enough room for my father's various enterprises—his dress shop and dry-cleaning service, his fur storage vaults and tailoring trade.

More important to my mother, however, was the empty floor of the building, an open area as large as a dance hall that would be converted into an apartment offering her both a convenient closeness to my father and the option of distance from everyone else when she so desired. Since she also decorated this space in accord with her dictum that living quarters should be designed less to be lived in than to be looked at and admired, my sister and I soon found ourselves residing in an abode that was essentially an extended showroom. It was aglow with crystal chandeliers and sculpted candles in silver holders, and it had several bronze claw-footed marble-topped coffee tables surrounded by velvet sofas and chairs that bespoke comfort and taste but nonetheless conveyed the message that should we children ever take the liberty of reclining on their cushions and pillows, we should, upon rising, be certain we did not leave them rumpled or scattered or even at angles asymmetrical to the armrests.

Not only did my father not object to this fastidiously decorative ambience, he accentuated it by installing in the apartment several large mirrors that doubled the impression of almost everything in view, and also concealed in the rear of the apartment the existence of three ersatz bedrooms that for some reason my parents preferred not to acknowledge.

Each bed was separately enclosed within an L-shaped ten-foot-high partition that on the inside was backed by shelves and closets and on the outside was covered entirely with mirrors. Whatever was gained by this arrangement was lost whenever a visitor bumped into a mirror. And while I never remember at night being an unwitting monitor of my parents' intimacy, I do know that otherwise in this domestic hall of mirrors we as a family hardly ever lost sight of one another.

Most embarrassing to me were those moments when, on entering the apartment unannounced after school, I saw reflected in a mirror, opposite a small alcove, the bowed head of my father as he knelt on the red velvet of a prie-dieu in front of a wall portrait of a bearded, brown-robed medieval monk. The monk's face was emaciated, his lips seemed dry, and as he stood on a rock in sandals balancing a crosier in his right arm, his dark, somber eyes looked skyward as if seeking heavenly relief from the sins that surrounded him.

Ever since my earliest youth I had heard again and again my father's astonishing tales about this fifteenth-century southern Italian miracle worker, Saint Francis of Paola. He had cured the crippled and revived the dead, he had multiplied food and levitated and with his hands stopped mountain boulders from rolling down upon villages; and one day in his hermitage, after an alluring young woman had tempted his celibacy, he had hastily retreated and leaped into an icy river to extinguish his passion.

The denial of pleasure, the rejection of worldly beauty and values, dominated the entire life of Saint Francis, my father had emphasized, adding that Francis as a boy had slept on stones in a cave near my father's own village, had fasted and prayed and flagellated himself, and had finally established a credo of punishing piety and devotion that endures in southern Italy to this day, almost six hundred years after the birth of the saint.

I myself had seen other portraits of Saint Francis in the Philadelphia homes of some of my father's Italian friends whom we occasionally visited on Sunday afternoons; and while I never openly doubted the veracity of Francis's achievements, I never felt comfortable after I had climbed the many steps of the private staircase leading to the apartment and opened the living room door to see my father kneeling in prayer before this almost grotesque oil painting of a holy figure whose aura suggested agony and despair.

Prayer for me was either a private act witnessed exclusively by God or a public act carried out by the congregation or by me and my classmates in parochial school. It was not an act to be on exhibition in a family parlor in which I, as a nonparticipating observer, felt suddenly like an interloper, a trapped intruder in spiritual space, an awkward youth who dared not disturb my father's meditation by announcing my presence. And yet I could not unobtrusively retreat from the room, or remain unaffected or even unafraid as I stood there, stifled against the wall, overhearing during these war years of the 1940s my father's whispered words as he sought from Saint Francis nothing less than a miracle.

2.

QUITE APART FROM his patriotic activities with the Ocean City shore patrol throughout World War II, and his pro-American speeches to the local Rotary Club, which would soon elect him its president, my father was silently terrified by the Allied forces' successful invasion of Sicily in 1943 and their inevitable plan to move north up the Italian peninsula against the Nazi and Fascist troops who were encamped in and around the southern region of his birth.

His widowed mother still occupied the Talese family's ancient stone house in the hills with most of my father's kinfolk, except those who were soldiers at the front, associated with the Germans against the advancing Allied ground units and bombers.

The southernmost part of Italy was virtually indefensible, my father conceded to me at breakfast after reading in *The New York Times* about the fall of Sicily; it was the fragile toe of the Italian boot, an exposed area where the slanted farmlands and jagged hills descended from the higher northern peaks and were surrounded almost entirely by unguarded bodies of water. To the east was the Ionian Sea, to the west the Tyrrhenian, and to the southwest was the Strait of Messina, which scarcely separated the southern tip of Italy from the island of Sicily.

Although my father's village—Maida—was sixty-five miles northeast of Messina, it was precariously situated. The curving coastlines of the Ionian and Tyrrhenian seas cut deeply into the mainland, so deeply that Maida's population of thirty-five hundred people was clustered in beige stone houses on the rocky interior of the narrowest part of Italy. The distance between the two coastlines here could be traversed by a motorist in little more than an hour; and adding to Maida's vulnerability to invasion, my father said, was a wide plateau below its western slope that could serve as a passageway or attacking ground for great numbers of troops traveling with heavy equipment. Indeed, this land had already been the scene of a brutal battle between the soldiers of France and Britain during the era of Napoleon Bonaparte.

It happened on a hot July morning in 1806, said my father, whose recounting of history was always accompanied by precise details; it happened after the surprise landing of more than five thousand British troops on the shingly shore of the Tyrrhenian Sea along the outer edge of Maida's plateau.

The British troops were led by a bold American-born officer who was a native of Georgia—General John Stuart, whose property-owning parents in the American South had remained loyal to the crown during the American Revolution. After they had returned to England, young Stuart received a commission as a British officer in 1778. In 1780 he participated in the siege of Charleston, South Carolina; then the invasion of North Carolina and, finally, Virginia, where, severely wounded, he and other red-coated units under Lord Cornwallis surrendered to the Americans at Yorktown in 1781.

After recovering his health and returning to England, Stuart resumed a military career that during the following decades would see him leading British regiments, brigades, and divisions between Flanders and Alexandria in almost constant conflict with the French—culminating, after sailing with his troops from Sicily past the rock of Scylla northward toward that plateau, in the battle of Maida in 1806.

The Italian mainland in 1806 was largely influenced by the Emperor Napoleon Bonaparte, a fact that was not displeasing to a large percentage of Italians. As my father often said, the Italians considered Napoleon more Italian than French because he was descended from a family that had emigrated from northern Italy to Corsica when that island was ruled by the Italian republic of Genoa—which, over the protests of many Corsicans, ceded it to the French shortly before Napoleon's birth in Corsica in 1769.

Among the anti-French Corsican agitators during this time was Napoleon's father, who became resigned to the French occupation of the island only after the leader of the Corsican resistance movement had been forced to flee. As a result of his father's subsequent cooperation and politicking with the French administrators, the younger Napoleon was able to leave Corsica and receive the benefits of a higher education in continental France. And yet during his school years and swift rise through the ranks of the French army, Napoleon continued to spell his surname in the Italian style, "Buonaparte," even after he had been appointed a brigadier general at the age of twenty-four in 1793.

It was in this same year that the British officer John Stuart became a lieutenant colonel at thirty-four; but as my father pointed out, it was much more difficult to move up within the British officer corps than the French because France was then involved with its Reign of Terror, and there were frequent vacancies created at the top of the French military establishment because of the many defections, expulsions, and even executions of aristocratic French officers.

It was during this very same year of 1793, in fact, that the French beheaded King Louis XVI and his wife, Marie Antoinette. The act shocked royal rulers around the world, but it was mourned with more personal passion in the palace at Naples, the capital city of the southern Italian kingdom, where the throne was occupied by Queen Marie Caroline (sister of the guillotined Marie Antoinette) and the Bourbon king Ferdinand, a member of a branch of the same dynasty as the fallen French king.

In addition to the sadness and anger in Naples there were grave feelings of insecurity among the ruling elite throughout the Kingdom of Southern Italy, because they were aware that in Maida, as in dozens of other villages, secret revolutionary societies were scheming to overthrow the privileged families who had ruled over the hills and farmlands since the Norman conquerors had brought feudalism into southern Italy in the eleventh century.

A Norman castle built in Maida in that century was still standing in the early twentieth, my father told me; and despite its decrepit condition, it was sometimes used when he was a child as a place of incarceration while the accused awaited transfer to a larger prison elsewhere. But the castle's dungeon also served to remind my father how deep-rooted was the medieval mentality of his native land, how enduring were certain of its archaic methods. Indeed, the Maida valley that would be the battle-

ground between Napoleon's musketeers and Stuart's invaders in 1806—
the British won the conflict after four ferocious days, and subsequently
memorialized it by naming a West London district Maida Vale, after my
father's village—had undoubtedly absorbed the blood of two thousand
years of warfare, going back to the days of Roman chariots and Hannibal's
elephants, of savage Magyar horsemen and Saracen pirates who, sailing
toward southern Italy with clarions and trumpets blaring, filled the sunny
sky with darts of poison.

While I was always impressed with my father's vivid depiction of history, my attention sometimes wandered during these long and frequently
repetitive lectures conducted after dinner amid the soft but often distract-
ing sounds of Puccini and Verdi rising from the scratchy glass records of
my father's old Victrola. And yet his intensity made me aware of his almost obsessive need to tell me about himself, to explain and perhaps justify himself as he described his past and traced his odyssey along the
Tyrrhenian Sea to Paris and later across the Atlantic Ocean to the Jersey
shore, where he now had me as his captive audience. To me he could confess his anxiety and, possibly, guilt, or at the very least expose a side of
himself that his tailor's taste for appearances would prevent him from revealing beyond the walls of this mirrored apartment.

Ironically, while I was failing an American history course in parochial
school—where I was also subjected to ethnic slurs hurled by a few Irish
Catholic boys whose older brothers had just participated in the conquest
of Sicily—I was becoming, under my father's tutelage, a reluctant scholar
of the history of the southern tip of Italy, which, if my father's worst fears
materialized, would soon be blown off the map.

Perhaps that accounted for his determination to enlighten me about
it, so that I might survive, as he had, to keep its obscure history alive in the
retelling—and to take pride, as well as solace, in associating Italy with the
rich chronology preceding its alliance with Nazi Germany.

3.

To HEAR MY father tell it, and I have heard it often, the south of Italy
flourished long before the rise of the Roman Empire and the birth of
Christ, and in his native village of Maida and its surrounding region—

which extends south of Naples down through ancient hills and valleys to form the toe and heel of the Italian boot—there occurred historical spectacles and scenes that constituted many centuries of human experience at its worst and best, its most barbaric and aesthetic, its most destitute and luxurious.

A word synonymous with luxury and sensual gratification—*sybaritic*—derives, my father told me, from a pre-Christian city north of Maida called Sybaris, which was founded in 720 B.C. by enterprising Greek colonists who combined a thriving economy with a penchant for self-indulgence and comfort: Sybaris's bright streets were shaded with awnings; its leading citizens regularly bathed in saunas tended by slaves; and its women appeared at sumptuous banquets wearing gold circlets in their hair, high-heeled shoes imported from Persia, and low-cut gowns that revealed part of their breasts.

South of Sybaris on the eastern shore of southern Italy was the more cerebral city of Crotone, populated by such intellectuals as Pythagoras and by a restrictive administration that became so envious and contemptuous of Sybaris that in 510 B.C. it attacked and looted it, set it afire, and, after diverting the course of the Crati River, submerged the entire city under water and mud.

My father's own hillside village was assaulted and plundered several times during the pre-Christian era, once by the Greek king Pyrrhus of Epirus—a man best remembered for annihilating many thousands of Romans in the Pyrrhic victories that destroyed most of his own troops as well. Spartacus also passed through the territory of Maida in his clashes with the Romans, and the anti-Roman campaigns and rebellions joined by most southern Italians later brought about cruel Roman retaliation upon the south: temples were demolished, women were raped, farms were torched, and so many trees were cut down for Roman shipbuilding and other purposes that the southern hills were eventually denuded. Rocks and mud began to slide, lakes became stagnant, and the water became malarial.

The water was *still* malarial at the time of my father's birth in Maida in 1903, and this fact, in addition to the villagers' eternal fear of seafaring invaders, probably contributed to the hydrophobic tradition that persists in my family and was transferred to the New World by my immigrant father, who, oddly, settled along the south Jersey shore near the sea that he shunned. And it was there that I grew up in the late 1930s, watching the waves with trembling fascination, but never in my entire life did I dare learn how to swim.

That my father had crossed the Atlantic Ocean to come to America had at first seemed to me an extraordinary triumph of courage over timidity, until he confessed one day that he had been terrified and seasick during the turbulent voyage and had prayed constantly to Saint Francis for survival. Although none of my father's three brothers had followed him to America—they remained in Maida with their hydrophobic mother and sister—my father's father, Gaetano Talese (whose name I inherited after my birth in 1932, in the anglicized form "Gay"), *was* an atypically fearless traveler, although his five trans-Atlantic voyages had less to do with his love of the sea than with his contempt for the land he was doomed to inherit in Maida.

Gaetano Talese, according to my father—who rarely saw him, knew him only slightly, but idealized him always—was a handsome, wandering man of six feet with a lean, sensitive face, large brown eyes resembling my own, and a slight scar over his right temple that was inflicted during his bachelorhood in Maida. One night while he stood under a young woman's balcony, he engaged in a conversation that seemed perhaps too intimate by the standards of her jealous suitor who, after eavesdropping in the shadows, suddenly leaped upon Gaetano from behind, slashed him with a knife, and escaped into the night.

While such fierce possessiveness of women had long been a male custom in Maida—as it was in other southern villages with a history of invasion by foreign men, and domination at times by feudal barons who presumed first-night privileges with the brides of villagers beholden to the barony—Gaetano Talese abhorred this lingering manifestation of primitive emotion, regarding it as symptomatic of a backward society in which he saw no future for himself. All that he saw in his village seemed impervious to change, too deeply rooted in rock, as stagnant as the malarial lakes left by the Romans.

In Maida the countrywomen still walked with clay pots balanced on their heads, and the dust rising along the sun-scorched roads of the valley behind the horse-drawn carriages and farmers' oxen was possibly the same dust kicked up ages before by Hannibal's elephants, by the Norman knights who galloped through the eleventh century, and by the elaborate caravan of King Frederick II, the thirteenth-century German conqueror of Italy, whose traveling retinue included Arab dancers, acrobatic jesters, and black eunuchs who hoisted curtained palanquins containing the reclining figures and veiled faces of his royal harem.

Most of Maida's hillside homes leaned against one another at bizarre angles, standing crookedly on oblique foundations, and the narrow cobblestone roads leading up and down the hill between the irregular rows of houses and shops were so curved and jagged that they could be traversed gracefully only by mules and goats.

The people of Maida usually walked as if they had drunk too much wine, and yet despite their lurching, listing, and shifting of weight as they walked, their facial expressions never suggested that they were discomforted by the difficult footing. Perhaps they did not even know that they lived in a lopsided town; it was, after all, the only town most of them had ever seen.

And so except for such adventurous young men as Gaetano, who frequently rode off on horseback down to the sea to watch the ships sailing back and forth between Naples and Messina, and dreamed of his escape, Maida's citizenry seemed content to remain perched up in the village where they were accustomed to all that was awry—although they *did* hope and pray they would be spared another earthquake that might further alter the deformed shape of their hill town, which in the past had often been subjected to God's fickle nature.

Maida exists in Italy's seismic center of uncertainty. Situated between two great volcanoes—Mount Vesuvius to the north and Mount Etna to the south—the inhabitants of Maida and its neighboring villages were ever aware that they might at any moment be flung into obscurity by a calamitous convulsion. Perhaps this is one reason why southern Italians have always been very religious, dwelling, as most of them do, on perilously high ground dependent for its stability on the goodwill of the omnipotent force that periodically reasserts its power by shaking people up and bringing them to their knees.

One day, many decades before Gaetano's birth, as dark clouds and cliffside vibrations moved along Italy's southwesterly coastline toward the village of Paola, north of Maida, it appeared that a vengeful God might be anticipating the desecration of the shrine of southern Italy's most idolized native son, Saint Francis of Paola—a prospect that panicked the villagers and led the priests to guide them to the hill site of the large statue of Saint Francis and urge them to prostrate themselves and beg God for mercy.

Within an hour, as the desperate crowd remained huddled in prayer around the trembling base of the towering statue, the black clouds began to lift, the sky became brighter, and the earth tremors seemed to subside and then to expire entirely—having finally no effect on the landscape except that the statue of Saint Francis, which had overlooked the sea, had been slowly spun around by vibrations and now faced the village.

The large beige stone house in which Gaetano was born in 1871 had cracked walls, slanted floors, an eroding façade, an exterior staircase that was almost scallop-shaped as a result of the countless contorting eruptions that had struck Maida through the centuries. This house, and the two tottering lodges that flanked it, were remnants of a sixteenth-century feudal estate purchased from an impoverished nobleman by Gaetano's father, Domenico Talese, who, by the modest standards of Maida in the late 1800s, was a relatively affluent and influential figure.

In addition to his large farm in the valley—which contained part of another man's olive plantation that had flown through the sky during an earthquake and, having landed intact, was successfully acquired by Domenico after a court dispute in which he argued that the airborne olive trees had been entrusted to him by the will of the Almighty—Domenico owned a wheat mill and a percentage of the local aqueduct, and operated a thriving business on the side as a moneylender. Strained by Domenico's high interest rates, the people of Maida equated the occupation of moneylender with that of middling cutthroat—or, to use their word for it, *strozzino.*

Although Domenico was married to a genteel woman named Ippolita who was descended from a large titled family in a neighboring village, her parents' branch of that family was almost destitute; yet in Maida the people continued to address her, with a respectful bow, as "Donna Ippolita," whereas her husband, the moneylender and new owner of an old barony, was never approached deferentially as "Don Domenico" but was referred to instead, behind his back, as "Domenico the Strozzino."

His awareness of such an unflattering appellation greatly rankled Domenico's prickly pride. He smoldered within himself while maintaining his stringent business standards, and remained remote from his fellow villagers except for his once-a-year walk with them on the feast day of Saint Francis of Paola, when he helped carry the heavy statue through the narrow winding roads down toward the sloping stone sanctuary which, four centuries before, the saint himself had blessed.

Other than this annual procession, and his attendance each Sunday at Mass—wearing a flowing cape and polished boots, and carrying his feathered felt hat with his missal—Domenico always appeared alone in public, whether on foot or horseback, coming or going from his row of stone houses on the hill that he occupied in baronial presumptuousness with his large extended family, whose affection for him rarely exceeded their sense of indebtedness. All of them worked for him—on the farm, or at the wheat mill, or at the aqueduct—and he ran his family as he did his businesses, in the autocratic tradition of a medieval lord. The fact that the feudal system of masters and serfs was now outlawed in postrevolutionary Italy did not discourage Domenico Talese from trying to extend the past into the present for whatever advantage he could take of it; and much advantage could still be taken in isolated places like Maida, where the distant past and the present were barely distinguishable.

Here the ancient superstitions and religious traditions extended through timeless days and nights, and my grandfather Gaetano— Domenico's first son—grew up often feeling as rootless and displaced as the trees and rocks of his village. Each morning he awakened to the blacksmith's thrice clanging anvil that beseeched the Blessed Trinity, and he half believed, as everyone claimed, that the moths fluttering through the early-evening air were representatives of the souls in purgatory. On certain holy days, and on Tuesdays and Fridays, which were days of bad luck, Gaetano watched the flagellants in crowns of thorns as they crawled up the rocky roads on bleeding knees. He was also affected, much as he sought to be different from his antiquated father, by such superstitions as the dreaded *jettatura*.

The *jettatura* was a vengeful power said to exist within the eyes of certain strangers who, although they journeyed through the countryside with words of goodwill and courteous manners, possessed within their mesmerizing glance the glint of a curse that presaged disaster, or death itself, or some unimaginable vexation that would surely victimize the villager unless he carried an amulet to neutralize the threat of *jettatura*. The women of Maida, in addition to always wearing protective charms, would attempt to thwart *jettatura* when they perceived it in a stranger's eyes, by placing their hands within the folds of their long skirts and pointing their thumbs, which they would tuck under their forefingers, toward any potentially perilous individual. When the men of Maida sensed the closeness of curse-carrying strangers, they would usually place their hands deep into their pockets and quickly touch their testicles.

If the farmlands were under attack by locusts or other crop-threatening pests, the village priest was summoned to read from a book containing certain prescriptive conjuring words that constituted a curse, and if the spring rains were excessively late, or during any prolonged period of treacherous drought, the statue of Saint Francis of Paola was taken from the church by the farmers and paraded slowly through the fields.

In this hazardous hill country, ruled for centuries by a remote aristocracy that seemed too often irresponsible and inadequate if not always evil, the villagers were conditioned to petition heaven for comfort and support. From elderly fanatics like Domenico to younger skeptics like Gaetano—and to Gaetano's son Joseph, my father, who made the transition from the Old World to the New—there existed a bond of belief in the God-appointed prowess of Saint Francis of Paola, the fifteenth-century mystical monk credited by eyewitnesses with resuscitating the dead, giving voice to the mute, realigning the malformed, multiplying food for the famished, and, during droughts, creating rain.

One day, after discovering a parched valley south of Maida that demanded irrigation, Saint Francis was said to have walked a mile to the nearest spring and, with his staff, traced a line along the ground that led back to the acres of dryness. Soon a stream of water was following him along the line that he had drawn.

On another occasion, after a ferryboat captain at the Strait of Messina, along the southernmost tip of Italy, had refused the saint's request for a ride to Sicily, Francis had simply removed his large cloak and laid it flat on the sandy shore. Then, after hooking one end of the fabric to the edge of his staff and holding it up in the air like a sail, he was suddenly thrust forward by a gust of wind and placed softly on the sea, atop his raftlike cloak with its billowing improvised bow, which he then guided calmly across the four-mile strait onto the island of Sicily.

Two hundred years earlier, in Sicily and southern Italy, the guiding force over the people was a papal loyalist named Charles d'Anjou, who had been urged by the Pope to eradicate from the land the last vestiges of the irreverent influence of the thrice excommunicated German ruler of Italy, Frederick II, whose hedonistic involvement with his harem, and half-hearted participation in the Church's Crusades against Muhammadanism in the Middle East, had established him in Rome as a spiritual outcast.

Brother of the devout King Louis IX of France (later canonized as Saint Louis), Charles d'Anjou came to Italy with pious credentials, which are exemplified in the large heroic painting of him that my father as a boy saw hanging in the Maida church where the Talese family worshipped. In the portrait, Charles is presented as a benign figure, almost enshrined in heavenly sunlight, being blessed by the Pope. According to my father, however, Charles d'Anjou's thirteenth-century invasion and conquest of Frederick II's dominions in southern Italy and Sicily was—quite apart from Charles's building many splendid churches that pacified the papacy—more accurately characterized by the activities of his soldiers, who burned the crops of farmers, extorted money from men whom they later murdered, and abducted and raped women.

Several years of such behavior finally led to a people's rebellion, an eruption of such magnitude that it culminated in the death of two thousand French soldiers of occupation and quickly diminished the size and influence of Charles d'Anjou's dynasty in the Kingdom of Southern Italy.

The spark of the insurrection was ignited in Sicily during a quiet afternoon in a park on the outskirts of Palermo. The year was 1282. It was Easter Monday, a sunny day on which many Sicilian men, women, and children wore holiday clothes and strolled or relaxed in the park, or sat on the grass surrounded by baskets filled with fruit, cheese, and wine.

French soldiers were also in the park, patrolling the area in pairs, and they would occasionally join the picnickers without being invited and help themselves to the wine and make personal comments that, while embarrassing to the women, the Sicilian men tried to ignore.

But as the drinking continued and the soldiers' remarks became more bold and crude, some Sicilians began to express their resentment. When two men stood up to address the soldiers more directly, a drunken French officer appeared on the scene and ordered his soldiers to search the men to determine whether they carried knives or other dangerous objects. When nothing was discovered, the officer demanded that the search be extended to include the women in the area; as this was being done, the officer saw walking along a path a beautiful young woman, accompanied by the man she had married earlier that morning.

Pointing to the woman, the officer announced that he would search her himself, and as her husband was held back by soldiers, the officer proceeded to move his hands up under her skirts and then into her blouse, where he fondled her breasts, causing her to faint. Her anguished husband was provoked to yell out to the crowd: "Death to all the French!"

Suddenly from behind trees and bushes came Sicilians armed with knives which they thrust into the backs of the officer and his soldiers. After confiscating the dead Frenchmen's weapons, they formed a mob armed mostly with knives, sticks, and stones, and rushed out of the park in a rampageous spirit exacerbated as they were joined by hundreds of other Sicilians who were eager to attack and kill every Frenchman they could find.

By sheer numbers they overwhelmed the French garrisons on the island, killing not only soldiers but also French women and children—anyone who was French faced the likelihood of a brutal death. The method the mob used to identify the French occupants of Sicily was to force them at knifepoint to pronounce one word: *ciceri*. This is the name for a small vegetable, a beige bean about the size of a pea, and its proper pronunciation (*chi*-che-ri) was so beyond the mastery of the French tongue that its mere mispronunciation provided the mob with ample evidence for a throat-slashing death sentence. When news of this massacre reached Charles d'Anjou, who was then traveling near Rome, he immediately dispatched one hundred thirty armed ships toward Sicily, while he himself led the charge of five thousand cavalry officers down the coast through the Maida valley toward the seething southernmost tip of Italy.

But before Charles d'Anjou could fight his way across the Strait of Messina to reconquer Sicily, the rebels had gained the support of the Spanish king, Peter of Aragon, who sailed with ten thousand soldiers from his African campaign against the Moors toward the western shore of Sicily. From there he crossed the island and contributed to the destruction of the French cavalry and fleet.

In addition to King Peter's army, many of the noble families of Sicily and southern Italy supported the cause of the mob, which had meanwhile organized itself into secret groups led by underground chieftains who, according to my father, were the first "godfathers" of the Mafia. This, my father insisted, is how the Mafia began—as a revolutionary resistance dedicated to the overthrow of such tyrannical foreign despots as Charles d'Anjou. And while these goals were later corrupted and replaced by ones that were entirely self-serving, the Mafia's underground network, which was first operational in the anti-French massacre of 1282 (which became popularly known as the Sicilian Vespers and inspired a Verdi opera that I often heard played on my father's Victrola during my boyhood in Ocean City), continued to exist as a vengeful force in Sicily and southern Italy for years eternal.

Among other things, the Mafia *organized* crime as a political weapon in a largely peasant society that was apolitical, my father explained. It catered to a need for power among a powerless class of people whose ever-changing foreign rulers and invaders were unaware of or unconcerned with their poverty and misery.

The Mafia filled the vacuum, my father said. Where the underclass lacked influence, the Mafia imposed its own influence. Where there was an impoverished economy controlled by an exploitative aristocracy, the Mafia introduced a lively trade in larceny, smuggling, extortion, and kidnapping for ransom. When a baron excessively taxed a farmer's land or produce, a *mafioso* offered to negotiate for the farmer and, for a price, drive a hard bargain. And the *mafioso* drove an equally hard bargain, my father added, if hired by the baron to negotiate with the farmer.

Gradually, in this backward land, the Mafia leaders became middlemen, brazen functionaries whose roles would remain largely unchanged from medieval to modern times. And like the old ruling class from which it learned its methods, the Mafia shifted its manner easily and quickly from courtliness to violence. When an innocent woman was molested by a foreign officer or soldier of occupation, the Mafia conveyed to her family their words of condolence—and provided them the satisfaction of revenge with the knife.

While my father never condoned the Mafia, he always said he could well understand its continued existence. In lighter moments of exaggeration, he even suggested that were it not for the retaliatory threat of the Mafia in these places that were constantly disrupted by invaders and turmoil—and were it not also for the moral influence of the Church at its best, as personified by Saint Francis of Paola—the social and sexual history of Sicily and southern Italy, and indeed his own village of Maida, might well have been centuries of unrequited suffering and one-night stands.

4.

MY MOTHER HAD a cousin in Brooklyn who was a member of the Mafia, or so I always assumed, because, although he never held a job, he invariably arrived at the Brooklyn home of my mother's parents for holiday dinners driving a big new car and wearing silk suits and shirts adorned with diamond cuff links and stickpins—and tilted forward on his head was a black bulletproof hat, a bowler, that was lined with steel.

I *knew* it was lined with steel because one weekend, after I had accompanied my mother and father to a large wedding reception in Brooklyn and was sitting on the edge of the dance floor near this cousin, he accidentally dropped his hat on my left foot while attempting to doff it—and my toe was swollen with pain for several days.

When I questioned my mother about him she explained that he was only a "distant" cousin who habitually visited her parents uninvited, and she added that since her marriage to my father, and her resettlement in Ocean City, she was relieved and pleased to be dwelling more than a hundred miles away from her Brooklyn cousin's unwelcome appearances.

Then, on a very hot day in late August 1941, as I was roller-skating near my parents' dress shop on the main street of Ocean City, I saw cruising slowly along the avenue, in search of a parking space, a large black automobile driven by a man wearing a dark jacket and a rounded black hat. The jaunty men of Ocean City wore straw hats on sunny days, and their suits usually were made of white flannel or beige linen; and since the vacationers at this summer resort were almost exclusively from Philadelphia or elsewhere in Pennsylvania, it was most uncommon to see an out-of-state automobile license plate, as I just had, bearing the stencil of New York.

Having little doubt about the driver's identity, I skated as quickly as I could toward my parents' store, then toe-hopped across the showroom rug with clattering awkwardness, past the disapproving glances of the salesladies, and impatiently waited to speak with my mother, who was then preoccupied with a customer. My mother had told me that I should *never* interrupt her when she was busy with a customer, and so now I watched quietly as she removed a dress from a hanger and handed it to a girdled, buxom woman who stood peeking through a half-opened door of a fitting room.

It was the final day of the big summer sale, and the racks still contained much unsold merchandise that my mother was eager to replace with the autumn stock, which was already uncrated but unpaid for, in the annex. It had been a slow season at the seashore, where the local economy was still in a slump from the paucity of vacation dollars caused by the Great Depression of the 1930s. Earlier, on the avenue, I had seen my father walking toward the bank, where, I knew from his breakfast conversation with my mother, he was hoping to improve the terms of an unfavorable loan. He had still not returned to the store when I stood waiting to forewarn my mother about her cousin. But before I could speak with her, I saw her cousin standing in front of the store window, a portly, black-hatted figure silhouetted in the sunlight, his eyes looking up at the sign above the door to confirm that he had arrived at his desired location.

Before he could get a glimpse of me, I skated into one of the empty fitting rooms and watched from behind a curtain, as curious as I was frightened. He walked slowly through the crowd along the counters and clothes racks back toward my mother, his broad face forming a smile, his hat clutched firmly in one hand while his other hand (extended beyond a gleaming cuff link) reached out in anticipation of a warm embrace.

When my mother saw him, she smiled with none of the enthusiasm she bestowed upon her customers. Although she offered her cheek for a light kiss, she quickly took his arm and guided him toward the far side of the showroom, away from the shoppers and salesclerks, and near the fitting room whose curtain I hid behind, fidgeting on motionless roller skates.

"Cousin Catherine," I heard him say, "I was in the area on business, and since I was so close, I thought I'd drop by and spend the weekend with you, and maybe get a little sun."

Immediately my mother shook her head. "I am sorry," she said, "but I cannot have houseguests at this time of year."

Stunned by her response, he was suddenly transformed, and with a frown and a raised eyebrow he said solemnly: "Catherine, I'm your cousin."

Unaffected, my mother lifted her right hand and, with a pointed finger, directed his attention to the rows of unsold dresses extending the length of the store.

"In summertime," she said, "only *these* are my cousins."

Much as he tried to convince her to change her mind, my mother refused to accommodate him, and before my father had returned to the store, her cousin was gone.

I remained in the fitting room, not yet ready to abandon my place of concealment; and sitting carefully on the cushioned bench, I began with some difficulty to free my feet from the metal skates that were tightly clamped to the soles of my Buster Brown shoes. While I twisted and jiggled the warped skate key, I noticed that my father had arrived and my mother had now gone forward to speak with him. Although I was too far away to hear what was being said, I could see from the expression on my father's face that he was not happy with what my mother was telling him.

A serious man by nature, he stood looking almost mournfully at the floor, his head nodding slowly as my mother spoke, his arms folded tightly across the front of his chest in a way that bunched up the material of the new gabardine jacket he had recently designed and tailored for himself—a jacket with narrow, sharply cut, high-pointed lapels that now seemed to rise slightly like the ears of an alerted rabbit. My mother had been inhospitable to a *mafioso,* a cousin no less—it was a serious social insult that in my father's native southern Italy might well have induced a vendetta.

But as I watched my mother, there was no indication that she shared my father's concern. She was *American*-born, after all; even though her parents in Brooklyn had come from the same part of Italy as my father, she had somehow separated herself from their old customs and fears— had created with her modish clothes and detached manner the modern woman that she appeared to be on this day, standing firmly in her high-heeled white shoes, as cool and unruffled as the slender window mannequins that she stylishly dressed and which she resembled. If she were concerned about anything after disposing of her cousin, it was probably that the transactions on this final day of the summer sale had not yet met her highest expectations.

My mother was betrothed to the dress business. As a young girl growing up in Brooklyn, she had outfitted her dolls with a varied wardrobe that she changed with the seasons, and she never permitted these pampered idols to be played with, or even touched, by any of her four sisters—my aunts, who, in recalling this fact to me years later, conveyed the suggestion of a slight yet everlasting sense of resentment toward the unsharing, aloof little girl my mother perhaps once was.

After high school she sold dresses in a large department store in Brooklyn, where she later became the assistant buyer; I think that had she not met my father, she would have been content to remain in that store for the rest of her working life. It provided my mother, who might otherwise have been restricted by the insularity of her Italian neighborhood and the prosaic expectations of her parents, with a passport to a larger America, to the grand bazaar of business and new ideas, of wishful thinking and whimsy, of temptation in a variety of colors, shapes, and sizes. Here she learned about marketing and money, and befriended fellow employees whose backgrounds and lives were different from her own—she often had lunch with the decorator and his boyfriend—and here she also studied the manners and moods of inveterate browsers and frugal consumers, impulse buyers and lavish spenders, bargain hunters and kleptomaniacs.

The store was a substitute for the travel opportunities and college education she lacked; within its gilded and spacious multistoried interior, she felt like a princess in a castle aglow with crystal chandeliers, surrounded by freshly cut flowers and serenaded by music. It contained countless gowns and robes and negligees and cocktail dresses and elegant gift boxes and also glass jewelry counters, which each day reflected the faces of promenading customers united in their avidity for what was desirable, enhancing, and fashionably contemporary.

But when she returned home in the early evening, wearing the colorful frocks that she had obtained from the store on her employee's discount, she readjusted to the cloistered ambience of her family's home, where the walls were hung with crucifixes and holy pictures, and where her parents were usually dressed in black. Before their marriage to each other, both of them had experienced tragic marriages during their younger years, and their early habit of wearing the color of mourning had outlasted the pain they had felt for those once mourned.

The first husband of my mother's mother, Angelina, died of malaria in Maida during the early months of the marriage, and Angelina was left childless at nineteen and uncourted for three years—until she received in the mail a snapshot from Brooklyn of a willing widower who was a friend of her American immigrant uncle and his enterprising son, not yet distinguished for wearing black steel-lined bowlers.

Although the widower in the photograph appeared to be somewhat severe and at least ten years her senior, Angelina's matchmaking relatives in America favorably described him as an energetic man who would be a most able provider. He worked for a real estate tycoon as a coachman and personal attendant in lower Manhattan and Brooklyn, and because of his reddish moustache and full head of red hair, he was known to all as Rosso.

So Angelina agreed to leave Maida and visit her relatives in Brooklyn for two months in order to become acquainted with Rosso. During that time Rosso came to dinner every Sunday night, sometimes bringing flowers, rarely saying very much, but often suggesting impatience by his mood or manner.

If dinner was late he would remove his gold watch on a chain from his black vest pocket and look at it, and five minutes later he would look at it again. His coachman's compulsion for punctuality was matched by his coachman's manner of sitting rigidly and straight-spined in his chair and holding his utensils firmly and upright, as if gripping the reins of a team of ill-tempered horses, and there was always in his expression a sense of intensity, the narrow-eyed look of a man who was accustomed to traveling into the wind, the fog, the rain, the sleet, and endless unseen but clearly imagined adversities.

Yet there was a redeeming stubbornness and strength about this man that Angelina found comforting, and it was also true that gentility, sensitivity, and a flair for romance were not quintessential requisites among Italian courting couples in America at the turn of the century. Life to them was a very practical matter—and it certainly was to this widow and widower who were getting no younger in Brooklyn in 1902. Angelina wanted children. Rosso wanted a wife. Her relatives wanted relief from the responsibility of finding her a husband. And so it was done. Angelina married Rosso, and thus began a lengthy relationship during which Angelina resigned herself, with the help of prayers and her own perseverance, to the burden of being Rosso's wife.

He indeed proved to be a man of severity—the very quality that Angelina had perceived in him after first seeing his image in the photograph sent to her in Maida. And while he always maintained a formal air of courtesy toward her, she began to worry after the birth of their first child that his harshness, his temper that matched the fiery color of his hair, would sooner or later cost him his job—especially after she overheard him one morning screaming insults in the street at the stout, monocled Prussian real estate magnate who was his boss.

Much to her relief, however, the Prussian responded only by shrugging his shoulders and shaking his head slowly while he meekly climbed into his carriage. Then, after Rosso had hoisted himself vigorously up onto his seat and pulled his top hat down hard on his head, the carriage bolted forward jerkily as he cracked the horses' hides twice with his whip.

With Rosso's continued employment came a second child, then a third, and then three more in the next decade—a total of five daughters and one son, none of whom bore any physical resemblance to the others. The first child was an emerald-eyed brunette with olive complexion. The next was a florid-toned, brown-eyed redhead. The third, my mother, had auburn hair, very dark eyes, and fair skin. The fourth child was a tall, freckle-faced boy with light chestnut hair. The fifth was a plumpish, rosy-cheeked blonde who resembled a Wagnerian soprano. The sixth was a lissome, sallow-skinned girl with nut-brown hair and almond-shaped Eastern eyes who required only a silken veil and a snake to charm a sultan.

It was as if the genes and bloodlines of Rosso and Angelina had been interfused with the hybrid history of those southern Italians who for centuries had been invaded, conquered, reconquered, and partly absorbed by competing Greeks and Romans, Goths and Saracens, Normans and Franks; by the fleeing Albanians and their Turkish pursuers; by the Waldensian heretics and their papist inquisitors; by the Jacobin sympathizers and their cutthroat assailants led by the brigand-rostered army of Cardinal Fabrizio Ruffo; by the Spanish Bourbon musketeers who were driven through southern Italy into Sicily by Napoleon's rampaging cavalry, itself harassed by Lord Nelson's gunboats, which controlled the Mediterranean and soon landed British troops on the besieged beachfront of Maida itself.

As the eyes of Angelina's offspring reflected the assorted tints and tones of a Byzantine mosaic, so did her children's different personalities and conduct represent the heterogeneity of southern Italy.

The first daughter was a born domestic who clung to her mother's apron strings as a child and remained close to Angelina until the latter's death, by which time the devoted, aging daughter, having recently been married for the first time (to a widower), was too old to bear children of her own.

The red-haired second daughter grew up as a rebel and agnostic who defied her father's will in accepting a nighttime job as a telephone operator (Rosso claimed that most of the Brooklyn operators moonlighted as prostitutes), then defied him again by dating a politicized factory worker who subscribed to Communist periodicals and played trombone on weekends in Broadway orchestras; finally she became an art student who carefully studied, and tried to improve upon, Leonardo da Vinci's Mona Lisa.

The next child, my mother, was the family escapist and fantasist, who covered her bedroom walls with film posters of young Lillian Gish, and invariably kept her door closed to avoid contact with her family and their guests; when she was not sewing dresses for her dolls or modeling her own clothes in front of the mirror, she sat rocking slowly in her white wicker chair, listening to her music box, and imagining that she was somewhere else.

Her brother, the fourth child in the family, became a Golden Gloves boxer before graduating from high school—he drifted prematurely into the sport after being banished from class for hitting a teacher who had called him "dago." When not in the boxing ring, he was employed by his father's boss, the Prussian, as an attendant in a large garage in which were parked several delivery trucks, and also a black automobile owned by the cousin who wore the steel-lined bowler. Rosso also worked there. One day, on instructions from the boss, Rosso told his son to drive a laundry truck to a certain Brooklyn pier, where men would be waiting to unload its contents. After arriving at the pier, the young man noticed that concealed under stacks of tablecloths and bed linen were several cases of whiskey, which were surreptitiously loaded into an awaiting motorboat.

The fifth child in the family, the Teutonic-looking blonde, was the resident glutton and practical joker, a young woman of earthy humor and an indulgent nature. She smoked; she drank; she generously colored her face with rouge and lipstick; and on weekends, when she also helped her eldest sister and mother with the grocery shopping, she served as the kitchen's pasta taster and tester before the food was placed on the table for the big Sunday dinner.

Angelina's final daughter, as the baby of the family, grew up accustomed to being pampered and adored, was spared most domestic chores, and ventured through life with a blithesome disposition. A teenaged flapper during the 1920s and always a bit of a coquette, she was the most attractive of Angelina's daughters, the best dancer by far, the most sought after by men, the most socially liberated and politically liberal. After divorcing her husband, she befriended a man who was black.

If Angelina and Rosso's six children had anything in common, it was probably an enduring affection for their mother and a disaffection for their father, a man whose support of them was primarily financial (and even that proffered in a begrudging manner) and who preferred taking his evening meals alone in the kitchen, served by his wife *precisely* at seven o'clock, and without any commotion or conversation coming from the children with whom he never learned to communicate.

Part of his problem was language itself. Rosso insisted on speaking his brand of south Italian dialect in the home, a dialect that his children never fully understood, or wanted to understand, for in their ignorance of his words they more easily avoided the responsibility of dealing with him directly. What was clearly needed in this family was someone to serve as an interpreter between the children and their parents, and also to translate for Rosso certain business letters or documents that, because written in formalized English, were beyond his comprehension.

Since Rosso would not trust an outsider to perform this function, and since none of his children would voluntarily do it, he ordered my more obedient mother one day to assume the role of his interpreter and intermediary with the English-speaking world. She had learned to speak and write English perfectly in primary school, and now, after returning home each afternoon from high school, she would be tutored in Italian by a white-bearded language professor who had been born in Maida but lived in the neighborhood.

Within a year, my mother spoke and read Italian with sufficient competence to clarify all the family problems of communication, if not to solve the problems themselves. One interesting result of this experience for her, however, was that in becoming her father's domestic secretary and confidante, in dealing with him each day in his own dialect, my mother began to understand this contentious and estranged individual. From her perusal of his old letters, foreign documents, and mementos— and from what he occasionally told her during uncharacteristically candid moments—he emerged as a wounded, vulnerable man who was much more of an escapist than she: he was a fugitive from some dark center in his soul, a helpless misanthrope who had fled the austere foundling home into which he had been placed by vaguely remembered relatives.

As a teenager he joined a boatload of illegal aliens and was employed as a laborer's apprentice in Brazil, but he loathed the life in South America and returned to Italy two years later with enough savings to purchase two horses and begin working as a teamster and carriage driver. The economy of southern Italy was then at a starvation level, however, and most of his passengers in the 1880s were men abandoning the dry soil and horizon-less hills, bearing heavy valises made of wood: they were en route to the rail terminal to await the Naples-bound train that would take them to the trans-Atlantic ships headed for the promised land of the United States.

In the town square of Maida, as in villages throughout the peninsula, there were billboards declaring that good jobs awaited healthy, hardwork-ing men in America. The signs noted that steamship tickets would be paid in advance by American employers, who would later be recompensed by deductions drawn from the workers' salaries.

And so from the hill towns and fishing villages of Italy, young men planned their departures, and Rosso carried many of them in his wagon along the dusty roads away from aging parents and newly wed brides and small children who waved until the wagon faded from view. Rosso heard their final words, saw their tears, observed their embraces and kisses, but, a stranger to intimacy, he had no idea how they truly felt during these parting moments. He knew only that when he returned to the village, life seemed to be changing.

There was one change in particular that he watched with mixed plea-sure each Sunday in the town square. This had always been a male pre-serve, a place where the village men gathered (while their wives attended Mass or were occupied at home) to drink liquored coffee and argue over local politics, or to stroll around, arm in arm, showing off their best suits, and smoking cigarettes or small cigars as they talked business or exchanged bawdy jokes, or casually admitted things to one another that women would confess most reluctantly to a priest.

This procession around the square was called the *passeggiata*. And al-though it took place in the village's most public place, it was nonetheless a private affair. Except now, as Rosso was becoming aware, a certain num-ber of younger women were flouting the once accepted exclusion of fe-males and, without invitation or explanation, were joining in the path of the *passeggiata*.

Like the men, these women walked arm in arm and spoke animatedly among themselves. While they kept their distance from male couples who walked in front or behind, and avoided making eye contact, they were in no way deferential, nor did they seem to be intimidated by the other men who sat almost leering in the cafés, saying nothing but sometimes making sibilant sounds as they forcefully exhaled the cigarette smoke through their teeth.

This new development in the square did not, of course, escape the insatiable curiosity of Maida's more traditional women—including those elderly, dark-clad ladies who missed nothing even while they sat outside their houses facing the wall, adhering to the discreet style of the ancient Greek and Arab women who once basked in this same sunlight. Nor did it go unnoticed by the village's nubile young virgins who, wearing white linen blouses and festive skirts, stood on the balconies overlooking the *passeggiata* as they arranged flowers and furtively exchanged quick glances with the unmarried men of their age who gathered around the fountain on Sundays, singing songs and playing guitars.

The walking women were other men's women; they were the wives of the ambitious young men who had left the village to make money in America. They were therefore women who were worthy of respect, and in church on Sundays they were often seen lighting candles at the altar and, presumably, praying for the safe and speedy return of their spouses, who were sometimes known to remain away from the village for two years or even longer. Yet very few of these women who were long deprived of their husbands appeared to be suffering from grief or depression. While they may occasionally have felt in private some kinship to widowhood, in public they radiated gaiety and confidence, and they often dressed in the same light colors of the hopeful village maidens. Which was why they were called "white widows."

There was, to be sure, a certain amount of gossip about them, and all that it took to activate the village's most tireless tale-bearing tongues was for one of the white widows to be observed in church not receiving the holy sacrament with the regularity of the other female communicants. Envy, of course, circulated as freely as the ever-present flies through the pews and high-vaulted naves, and even the most secure of traditional women felt at times threatened by these relatively free, semi-married *signore* who, thanks to the profitable efforts of their husbands overseas, had more money to spend on themselves and their children than did the wives of the local men who had chosen to remain on the farms or to struggle as vendors or artisans.

Still, the money sent to the white widows from America bolstered the local economy. The widows spent it at the food market, invested it in farm improvements, and shared it with their parents or in-laws or other relatives in whose homes they often dwelled, providing the primary means of support. Such a position of economic power had never before been held by women of ordinary families, and with this new power the white widows personified an evolving matriarchy, a sorority of sorts composed of strong-willed individuals who would assume in their husbands' absence full responsibility for the rearing of children and the managing of matters of proprietary interest. They also decided how they would spend the idle hours of the day and perhaps part of the night.

During this period there was considerable marital stress because a majority of Italy's pioneering migratory workers were not yet able or willing to transfer their families to America. Despite the money earned there, the workmen during the 1880s and 1890s usually lived in teeming boardinghouses or in railway boxcars or in the grim barracks of cold and remote company towns where, instead of rising each morning to such soothing village sounds as the ringing of church bells or the crowing of roosters, they were aroused at dawn by harsh factory whistles that summoned them into coal mines, steelyards, stone quarries, or gravel pits, from which they emerged exhausted at twilight, covered with dust and dirt and sweat, and infected with a foul temper.

So most of these men wisely kept their wives and children in the familiar surroundings of the village, convinced that the sunny poverty of Italy was much more habitable and healthful than the polluted prosperity of America. While the men were often made aware through letters of their wives' loneliness and feelings of abandonment, they assumed the women knew that these years of separation would cease as soon as enough money had been earned and saved to achieve economic solvency in southern Italy.

Most of the men sent expressions of affection and reassurance through the mail, along with money, American-made dresses and shoes, and toys for the children. Sometimes, on impulse, the men themselves sailed across the sea, arriving at the Maida station to pay a surprise visit to their families on the occasion of a wedding anniversary, or a birthday, or to attend the annual festival of Saint Francis of Paola, which throughout southern Italy was regarded as a joyful day of spiritual solidarity.

My maternal grandfather, Rosso, was often the first person to greet these arriving men at the station, and during the forty-minute ride uphill in his wagon, laden with luggage and parcels containing gifts, he would inform the men of the latest local happenings and hear their tales of overseas adventures and experience vicariously their pleasure in returning home.

One morning at the terminal, however, Rosso was approached by a man who stepped off the train without luggage. Seeming sullen and impatient, he asked that Rosso immediately transport him to the inn located at the crossroads near the Norman wall that bordered the western edge of Maida. Rosso had never before seen this man, who was neatly dressed in what Rosso assumed to be an American-made suit; while the man said little during the ride, he did confide that a recent family quarrel had forced his return to Italy. But, he added, he was sure that he could solve the problem within a day's time, and he asked that Rosso pick him up at the crossroads on the following morning so that he could board the noon train back to Naples.

Rosso was there the next day, as requested, and during the ride back to the station the man sat quietly on the bench, gazing pensively at the countryside and at times touching his eyes with his fingers as if wiping away tears.

Upon arrival at the terminal Rosso received his payment, and, after nodding in thanks, he watched the man board the dust-covered train that slowly edged forward to the sound of hissing steam and the clanging of bells. Rosso then returned to the village, where later that evening he was approached by the police and questioned about the man he had taken to the train.

Two people in Maida had been fatally shot with pistol bullets during the night, the police told Rosso. One was a woman who had been married to a worker in America. The other victim was a man who resided in Maida and was presumed to be her lover. Rosso told the police the little that he knew, and the desk clerk at the inn could add nothing of significance because the man had entered the inn only for a drink at the bar, then had left without registering to spend the night.

The police did not appear irritated or disappointed by this insufficient information, nor did they say that they planned to continue their investigation. It was, after all, a crime of familial passion that was hardly uncommon in southern Italy, where there had long existed a tradition of understanding, if not respect, for a cuckold who sought revenge by killing his wife—in this case, a white widow—and her illicit lover. So the police released Rosso and the desk clerk from further questioning, and soon the case was closed without great inconvenience to anyone except the couple who had perhaps once been in love.

Rosso himself was in love at this time—not with one of the public ladies who paraded in the *passeggiata,* but with a modest and dainty young woman whom he had often seen as she sat in her balcony and whom he had recently been honored to escort home from church in his carriage.

Her name was Rosaria. Her father, whom Rosso knew slightly, was an elderly, gimp-gaited widower who had been injured decades earlier while serving as a soldier in the army of General Giuseppe Garibaldi, the hero whose triumphs during the 1860 revolution had finally unified the peninsula and liberated southern Italy from more than a decade of severe rule under the Spanish Bourbon kings.

Rosaria's father was now inebriated much of the time, and, except for his soldier's pension that he irregularly received, he relied, for his livelihood, on the money his only daughter earned as a housekeeper in a deteriorating palazzo owned by one of Maida's last noble families.

The speed with which her father accepted Rosso's marriage proposal both surprised and piqued Rosaria, who might well have wondered if her father had been influenced by the fancied convenience of having a carriage-owning chauffeur for a son-in-law. But she herself welcomed the opportunity to quit her job at the palazzo. Working as an outside housekeeper in southern Italy was deemed a degrading occupation for a young woman—the assumption being that a housekeeper was sometimes expected to provide, and was sometimes agreeable to providing, sexual favors in secret to the head of the household or perhaps to one of his sons.

In Rosaria's case, such intimacies had indeed occurred between herself and the baron's second son. But later, as her feelings of guilt increased along with her concern that a public scandal would nullify her chances of marriage to an eligible suitor of her class, she became more amenable than she otherwise would have been to her father's urgings that she marry Rosso.

Rosaria married Rosso in the winter of 1884. Within a year she gave birth to a son and two years later had a second son, both of them with Rosso's red hair. Rosso was happy with his life, but in the years ahead it seemed impossible with his earnings as a carriage driver adequately to support his household, which included not only his wife and young sons but also his father-in-law.

While complaining of his financial difficulties one day to a friend visiting Maida from America—a man who worked as a construction foreman for a wealthy Prussian realtor in New York—Rosso was told that the realtor was expanding his business and would soon be needing additional help. Rosso's friend volunteered to speak to the boss about arranging Rosso's ship passage. Months later, Rosso received a job offer from New

York, and after promising to send for his family as soon as he could manage it, he sailed to America.

He spent the next year working first as a laborer in his friend's construction gang and then as the boss's carriage driver and the superintendent of a large building that his employer owned on Hester Street in lower Manhattan.

A spacious, empty apartment in this building was made available to Rosso, who quickly sent word to his wife to prepare the family for the move to America. But her response to his letter was unenthusiastic, and she continued in polite but evasive ways to delay the departure from Italy for more than a year. Her excuses were attributed at times to the illness of her father, or to the fact that her sons were yet too young for the trip. Or she complained of various household complications, or of her own mild but endless ailments. The date of the passage seemed to fade further and further away.

And then one day in New York, Rosso heard from a friend who had just returned from visiting Maida that Rosaria was having an affair with the baron's son. It was more than an affair, the man quickly corrected himself, for she was now pregnant with this other man's child.

Rosso was overwhelmed by astonishment and grief. For days he could barely eat or speak. He could hardly believe what he had been told. It was a betrayal so insulting that, rather than inspiring him to a violent revenge, it made him internalize his pain, so that it soon became a poison that was to circulate within his system for the rest of his life. It poisoned not only his memory of his wife but his affection for his sons as well. His wife and sons became dead to him—destroyed, gone forever from his life; and in private he disowned them, vowing never again to see them, or desire to see them, even if they came crawling to his door. They were all as dead to him as they would have been had he taken a gun and shot them himself.

From that time on, in Brooklyn, Rosso wore the dark clothes of mourning, bearing in private this anguish and bitterness through his second marriage, to my grandmother Angelina, and the birth of his six American children.

When my mother told me this story, and often elaborated upon it in ways that presented her upbringing—and that of her siblings—as hopelessly connected to Rosso's forlorn and unforgettable past, she left little doubt in my mind as to why she was eager to leave her father's home as soon as she could find someone to whom she could give her love unreservedly. In 1929 she married the man who would become my father, and she immediately dissociated herself from Brooklyn as she resettled along the Jersey shore, near the boardwalk, where it was the custom for American women to dwell in a modern world in the brightly colored dresses of their choice, with the men of their choice. She left the long shadow that was cast on Brooklyn sidewalks for a place where she hoped to remain forever distant from the conspicuous mourning of her father for a white widow, and the unwelcome visits of a cousin who wore a steel-lined black hat.

5.

WHILE MY MOTHER gained through marriage a kind of liberation she never could have known in her father's house, it was my destiny to become the dutiful only son of an exacting tailor who presumed to possess the precise measure of my body and soul; and it was my unavoidable birthright to wear the customized clothes that reflected his taste, advertised his trade, and reaffirmed his talent with a needle and thread.

I became my father's miniature mannequin soon after I learned to walk, and during winter I was draped in sturdy worsted coats and jackets with squarish shoulders and hand stitching on the edges of my lapels; and on my head was a feathered felt fedora—slanted at an angle favored by my father—that was occasionally knocked off by the rowdy students with whom I rode the bus to parochial school.

Nearly all of my classmates were the children of the Irish Catholic families who lived in white bungalows along the south Jersey marshlands on the other side of the bay; and although Catholicism was still a minority religion on the island, the Irish Catholics brandished absolute authority over my early education and my often flattened fedora.

Each night I went to bed dreading the next morning's ride on the bus, a rusting vehicle of a purplish black that precisely matched the robes worn by the nuns who dominated the classrooms. The school's bus driver, Mr. Fitzgerald, was a crusty Dublin-born janitor who wore a tweed cap and whose breath exuded a sour blend of oatmeal and whiskey. In addition to his weekday job as driver and school janitor, he appeared each Sunday morning in the vestry of the church to help the elderly pastor dress for Mass and to help himself surreptitiously to the sacramental wine that the pastor stored in a closet stacked high with white altar linen.

One Sunday morning in the vestry, before the ten-fifteen Mass, as I was buttoning up my cassock in preparation for my duties as an altar boy, I watched, riveted, while Mr. Fitzgerald (after lifting a lace-trimmed gown over the pastor's head and shoulders) took quick, squint-eyed swallows from a tiny silver flask that he slipped in and out of his jacket. He assumed that his furtive drinking was observed by no one—until he turned to catch me staring at him from the far corner of the room.

Mr. Fitzgerald glared at me with fury in his bloodshot blue eyes; then his pale lips began to form words that, although I could not hear them, I took to be curses in response to my indiscreet curiosity.

Although I was momentarily stunned, I knew immediately that I should convey some gesture of apology. But as I took a step toward him, Mr. Fitzgerald signaled with an upraised palm that I should keep my distance. Then he jabbed his index finger toward me and pointed toward a wall hook from which was hung a thin, six-foot-long wooden pole topped by a taper. It was used to light the tall candles that stood above the altar. I realized that I had forgotten to light the candles. It was nearly ten-fifteen, and the pastor was now fully dressed and placing holy wafers in a gold receptacle. Mass was about to begin.

Quickly I moved through the doorway and, after lighting the taper at the end of the pole, entered the main body of the church. Among the waiting parishioners were my mother and father, sitting close to each other in the third row, two well-tailored Italians in a humble Irish Catholic parish on a Protestant island, a minority within a minority.

Holding the front of my cassock above my ankles, I climbed five steps to the base of the altar. I could barely see the highest points of the six towering candles, and I had no view whatsoever of the wicks because they were concealed within heavy gold rings that encircled the candle tips, to prevent the wax from dripping.

Standing on my toes, I extended the long pole above my head toward the gold ring that rimmed the first candle. I waited resolutely, expectantly, gazing up at the burning end of the pole and watching as it emitted black wisps of smoke. But the obstinate wick failed to ignite. I stood there for what seemed like several minutes, stretching higher as my arms ached and my eyes watered. Less cautiously I now pressed the end of the pole harder against the ring, but still there was no sign of light—and I heard the rustle of the congregation. Rather than feel self-conscious, I began to take a perverse satisfaction in commanding the attention of the entire church.

No longer the bumbling acolyte who could not light a candle, I imagined myself a graceful exemplar of perseverance and fortitude, a circus performer who played with fire and soared to daring heights; and, just as suddenly, I envisioned the elusive little wick as a poisonous spider lodged in the head of the candle whose long white neck I wanted to choke and singe, to torture as I had seen conspirators coerced in war films.

But before I could further indulge my fantasies, I was startled by a loud snap behind me. Lowering the pole and turning toward my audience, I saw eight dark-robed nuns in the front row tilted forward in their seats, frowning. Standing above them was the Mother Superior, snapping her fingers and leaning over the altar rail, trying with her upraised eyes and jutting chin to direct my attention to the candle that held the spider of my imagination.

I moved back a few paces on the platform and looked up to see that the wick was burning brightly above the candle's ring—and perhaps it had been burning the entire time I had stood daydreaming under the pole. I heard someone snicker and glanced back toward the Mother Superior. But she had now taken her seat, and her eyes were rigidly focused straight ahead into space. Behind the nuns were dozens of parishioners who sat with their faces pinched in expressions of pique, or with their mouths open as they yawned—except for my parents, who sat with their heads slightly bowed, their eyes lowered as if in prayer.

Aware that I had lost my audience as well as whatever might have passed for my aplomb, I turned to the five other candles—but not before noticing Mr. Fitzgerald at the vestry door, pointing frenetically at his wristwatch. Mass was now ten minutes late, thanks to my incompetence, and seeing Mr. Fitzgerald in such agitation caused me to panic; in haste, I began to swipe the fiery black pole back and forth through the air, perilously close to each of the five unlit candle wicks. Twice I clanged against the gold rings that encircled the wicks, and each time it appeared that a reeling candle-holder might topple. Had it not been for the intensified sighs of the alarmed audience that prompted me to regain my composure, I might well have desecrated the entire altar with the wayward oscillations of my pole.

Finally, having grazed the sixth and final candle, I waited for my hands to stop shaking. Then I turned and climbed down the red carpeted steps, and, without looking up to see whether or not I had ignited the wicks, I headed toward the side door into the vestry. But as I disappeared through the doorway, my curiosity made me turn at the final moment to peer over my shoulder and sneak a peek at the upper ledge of the altar. The wicks of the candles were all miraculously aglow.

As Father Blake feebly picked up his chalice and readjusted his tri-cornered black cap, I took my place in front of him and walked out to the altar—to begin the Mass that was now almost twenty minutes late.

For most of the next hour I performed my functions by rote. I held the hem of Father Blake's long vestments as he climbed the altar steps. I genuflected at the proper times. And I adroitly handled and poured from the cut-glass cruets the consecration water and the red wine that Mr. Fitzgerald had mercifully not consumed. I did not fail to ring the bell three times when the priest raised the host—nor did I forget my liturgical responses to the priest, even though, like most altar boys in the parish, I could translate hardly a word of the Latin I had been forced to memorize.

But at the point of the Mass when I was to lift a heavy, cumbersome prayer book with its wooden stand and carry it from the right side of the altar to the left, I tripped on the hem of my cassock. I fell heavily across the book and its stand, and I heard the sharp sound of splintered wood—and heard as well the groans of the congregation as my chin hit the floor behind the black heels of Father Blake.

Gallantly he did not turn around, possibly because of his partial deaf-ness; and as I slowly rose to my feet hoisting the book on its fractured stand, and carefully placed it atop the altar—where it rested at a lopsided angle—the old priest closed his eyes and made the sign of the cross, while I slinked down the steps, prepared to occupy my rightful place in the purgatory of errant altar boys.

How I continued to serve out the rest of the Mass on that most mis-erable Sunday of my young life I will never know. For years, the mere rec-ollection of the morning could bring blood rushing to my face. But I remained on the altar to complete my chores, oblivious of the people, aloof from the spirit of the Mass, my body like a piece of flotsam pushed back and forth along the shore by the tide. When Mass finally ended, I felt relief but no escape from my humiliation.

Ignoring the dour glances of Mr. Fitzgerald as he stood behind Father Blake removing the priestly gowns, I pulled off and hung up my short white surplice and my cassock, then quickly put on my topcoat and fe-dora, and departed through the side door of the church without saying good-bye to anyone.

Cold gusts of salty ocean air met me as I raced along the sidewalk toward my parents' car, which was parked a block away. It was a two-year-old 1941 blue Buick coupe that my father had bought one month before the government stopped automobile production. I climbed into the backseat, slumped low, and pulled my hat forward, hoping to avoid the notice of passersby who might have witnessed my pathetic performance in church.

Through the windshield I spotted my parents a half-block away approaching with my seven-year-old sister, Marian. After a few paces they stopped and turned to face the church, expecting to see me leaving from the side entrance. They stood close together near a large leafless tree, seeking shelter from the wind, watching the church; they continued to wait as I observed them, distantly, without moving. I did not want to be with them now. I did not want to talk to them, did not want them to invade the quiet enclosure of the car.

My mother, I noticed, was wearing a beaver coat that my father had recently made slimmer and remodeled with a mink collar and cuffs—the coat had hung unclaimed for years in the fur storage vault of my parents' store and had once been worn by a portly Philadelphia dowager who had died in Ocean City without heirs during the summer of 1937. This was one of several fur coats that my mother had, some having been purchased on discount from a designer friend of my father's in Atlantic City; others had been inherited, more or less, from storage customers who had died without claimants, or who had bartered their furs in exchange for new dresses and suits during the Depression, or who had long abandoned them in the vault because the coat or cape or boa, with head and tails, had now become outmoded and was no longer considered worth the cost of several years of unpaid storage bills.

Thus did my family's legacy become festooned with fur pieces of every size and shape, texture and tint, and during sweltering summer afternoons I liked nothing better than to unlock the frosty vault that extended along one side of the store and to sidle swiftly down the rows of coats while nuzzling my face into the variegated pelts: the luxurious mink, the curly broadtail, the bristly raccoon, the deep, incredibly cool softness of chinchilla.

Hundreds of them were hung in the alphabetical order of their owner's names within the vault's lunar blue light and camphor-scented air; and here I imagined myself in almost spiritual communication with the wildlife of the world—African leopards and Persian lambs, Alaskan seals and Scandinavian foxes, Canadian badgers and Russian lynxes, Siberian squirrels and Asian cheetahs. And here I also contemplated many animals' being mangled in metal traps, or being fatally shot during safaris.

At my age I was not so far removed from my illustrated childhood books in which animals were invariably personalized, and even humanized, that I could be dispassionate about the final destiny of these animals in my parents' vault, a gray stone-walled confinement that suggested an extermination factory if one focused on the rows and rows of hanging heads, feet, and tails of the fox boas. The boas were formed by the remains of three foxes linked in a loop—with the tip of each fox's tail locked in the jaws of the fox behind it. It was a grotesque pretense to realism that both demeaned and mocked those once sly creatures which now adorned suited shoulders with their claws clipped, their eyes replaced by glass, their noses flattened, and their upraised ears long deaf to the horns and hounds of the hunt.

There was one coat in the vault, a long leopardskin with a brown leather belt, that hung apart from the others and bore no name tag. It had last been worn by a woman who had herself been hunted. She was a blond waitress who worked in a luncheonette around the corner from my parents' store, and she had been given the coat by her lover, a balding entrepreneur who had a few shops on the boardwalk and a jealous wife whose doubts about his fidelity prompted her to hire a private detective.

One night the detective, accompanied by a photographer, followed the husband by car across the bridge and up the coast to Atlantic City. There, in a hotel lobby, he was seen meeting his lady friend wearing the leopard coat, and then walking arm in arm with her toward one of the elevators. But before the detective and the photographer could catch the couple in a compromising position, the concierge had called their room from the house phone and warned the couple—and immediately the blond woman fled down a back staircase, leaving her coat in the hotel room closet.

Later, and more casually, the man left the room carrying the coat concealed in a hotel laundry bag; and, after strolling through the lobby with affectations of nonchalance, he locked the coat in the trunk of his car and drove home. The news of this incident soon circulated throughout Ocean City, and in my parents' store I overheard numerous versions from the town gossips who were friendly with my mother—who, to be sure, always pretended to be hearing about the incident for the first time.

There was a touch of the thespian in my mother, and it served her admirably when the man himself arrived at the counter carrying the leopardskin coat, still in the hotel laundry bag, and asked her to place it in the vault. This she did, without raising an eyebrow; and there the coat hung through the rest of the winter and the entire following year, and through the subsequent changing seasons of my adolescence in Ocean City—an isolated coat, exiled in the vault, spotted with scandal.

The car door opened, and my mother in her beaver coat got into the front seat with my little sister ahead of her.

"We were outside all this time looking for you," my mother began, seeming more concerned than irritated. "Why didn't you wait for us along the side of the church?"

"I was too cold," I replied.

She said nothing as we all waited for my father to finish wiping the windshield with the classified-advertising section of the Sunday edition of the Atlantic City *Press,* a paper he sometimes purchased after Mass at the newsstand across from the church. The dim sunlight that had shone through the glass was now subdued by clouds, and a sudden strong breeze blew dust and sand across the hood of the car, causing my father to close his eyes and hold on to his hat. He tucked the newspaper tightly under his arm, opened the door, and glanced toward me in the backseat, as if assessing my mood.

"We could drive to Philadelphia and have a good dinner, if we had the gas," he said, alluding to the wartime fuel shortage. "But instead we'll go tonight to Atlantic City."

"They have homework to do," my mother said promptly.

"They have all afternoon to do their homework," my father said. "We'll go early enough, and be back before ten." Smiling at me in the rearview mirror, he seemed to understand my desire to escape, however briefly, the narrow boundaries of this island.

My mother unbuttoned my sister's snowsuit as my father started up the Buick. We began the ten-minute ride to our apartment above the store in the midtown business district. I gazed at my family in the front seat— my father in a tweed overcoat and brown fedora, my mother with her fur coat and black leather curve-brimmed hat, and my sister in a pink snow-suit trimmed with pieces of white rabbit fur that had been left over from one of my father's alteration jobs.

He wasted nothing. The fur scraps left on his cutting table after he had shortened one customer's coat would later reappear to decorate the pocket flaps or the collar or the hem of another customer's cloth coat he had been paid to remodel. The creative skill he had once exhibited as a designer and cutter of men's custom-made suits, a skill that in the current economy was reduced to a pauper's art, was now put to profit in the repair and restyling of ladies' wear.

Earlier that year, when fabric of every kind was rationed because of the war, I had watched my father one afternoon tear about one hundred small swatches of woolen material out of several sample books; then, after he had laid out the swatches on a table and arranged them into an interesting mosaic, he sewed the varicolored pieces together to form a large section of material from which he created a most uncommon hacking jacket. After lining it with satin, he proceeded to wear it around town with a vivid silk handkerchief sprouting immediately from his breast pocket.

The Buick continued slowly uptown past several small white hotels and large rooming houses that were closed for the winter. Most of the houses had turrets topped by finials that sea gulls stood on, dormered roofs, and spacious porches cluttered with upturned wicker sofas and deck chairs tied down against the whip of the wind. Hardly anyone was walking along the sidewalks, and there were entire blocks in which not a single car was parked at the curb. Except for the pharmacy and cigar store, there was a Sabbath ban on all businesses, including the town's single cinema, where the marquee's lettering read: THE HUNCHBACK OF NOTRE DAME . . . CHARLES LAUGHTON, MAUREEN O'HARA.

I listened absently while my parents exchanged shoptalk over my sister's head as she snuggled between them reading the Sunday comics. The radio was tuned to a Philadelphia station that specialized in classical music, but there was so much static that the music was barely audible. Still, I knew that my father's commitment to that kind of music would prevent him from switching to one of the clearer stations featuring such popular bands as Benny Goodman's and Tommy Dorsey's, or the modern vocalists I liked to hear, such as Bing Crosby, Nat King Cole, and Frank Sinatra.

That Sinatra was an Italo-American gained no concession from my father, who seemed irrationally resistant to any and all performers who appealed primarily to a youthful spirit or exemplified the latest fad. The objects of his displeasure included not only crooners but also the most celebrated new stars of Hollywood and the heralded figures of the sports world.

Among athletes, he regarded baseball players as the most excessively praised and the sport itself as the most tediously time-consuming, and his weary response to the game escalated to an active dislike of it after I became, at the age of nine, a baseball addict. I became hooked on baseball during the summer of 1941, as the New York Yankees' center fielder, Joe DiMaggio, was breaking a major-league record by hitting in fifty-six successive games. Even on my provincial island, where the fans were partial to the teams from Philadelphia, the New York slugger was admired by the crowds that gathered on the boardwalk or under the green-striped awning of a midtown grocery market, where a radio loudly played a new song recorded by Les Brown's band:

From Coast to Coast, that's all you hear
Of Joe the One-Man Show
He's glorified the horsehide sphere,
Jolting Joe DiMaggio . . .
Joe . . . Joe . . . DiMaggio . . .
We want you on our side . . .

One day as I strolled into my parents' store whistling that tune, my father, who recognized it immediately, turned away and walked back to the cutting room, slowly shaking his head. I continued with my whistling, albeit less forcefully, throughout the day; and I recognize this as perhaps my first sign of rebellion against my father, a rebellion that would intensify during the next two years to the point that now, in December 1943, as my agitated mind wandered in the backseat of my father's Buick, I was planning my escape from parochial school when the Yankees began spring training the following March.

I would not have to go far. It had recently been announced on the local sports page that, as a result of wartime restrictions on long-distance travel, the Yankees would forgo Florida to train in Atlantic City. After reading this, I secretly marked the passage of each grim, cold day, anticipating a glorious spring in which I would travel by trolley across the marshlands to the rickety little stadium that would be ennobled by the presence of baseball's World Champions. I revealed none of these plans to my father, of course, and I vowed that my rendezvous with the Yankees would be realized no matter what he said or did to justify his abnormal aversion to the national pastime.

If truth be told, however, I would one day understand my father's lack of appreciation of sports. When he was a boy growing up in his village during World War I, there were no games to be played, no opportunities for leisure or relaxation—it was a time and place in which child labor was not only accepted but demanded by the destitute conditions of the day; and my father passed through his adolescent years without knowing what it was like to be young.

As he was quick to remind me whenever I complained about having to help out in the store, *he* had been forced to hold down two demanding jobs while attending grammar school. He rose at dawn to serve as a tailor's apprentice in his uncle's shop in the village; later, after school, he toiled in the valley on his grandfather's farm, which was short of workers because increased numbers of men had been conscripted by the Italian army.

Among those summoned was my father's older brother, Sebastian, who would return from the front in 1917 crippled and mentally disturbed from inhaling poison gas and being bombarded by artillery shells during the trench warfare against the Germans. Since Sebastian never fully recovered, and since my father's father, Gaetano, had died three years earlier of asbestosis soon after returning to Italy from his factory job in America, my father became prematurely responsible for the welfare of his widowed mother and her three younger children.

Two of these children (my father's brothers Nicola and Domenico) were Italian infantrymen, united with the Germans against the Allied armies attacking Italy. Almost every night after I went to bed, I could overhear my father's whispered prayers as he knelt before the portrait of Saint Francis, begging the monk to save his brothers from death or the fate that had befallen Sebastian, and pleading also for the protection of his mother and other family members who were now trapped in the war. Sicily had surrendered by this time, but the Allies had not yet conquered all of southern Italy, and throughout 1943, in our apartment and in the store, I was aware of my father's volatile behavior, his moods abruptly shifting between resignation and peevishness, tenderness and aloofness, openness and secrecy. On this flag-waving island where my father wished to be publicly perceived as a patriotic citizen, I instinctively understood and sympathized with his plight as a kind of emotional double agent.

After returning from school, I would see his uneasiness when the postman walked into the store to drop a pack of mail on the counter. When the postman had left, my father would approach the mail tentatively and sift through it to see whether it contained any of those flimsy gray envelopes sent from overseas. If he found any, he would place them unopened next to the cash register in my mother's dress department for her to open later and read.

My mother, who was candid and direct in ways antithetical to my circuitous father, had earlier confided to me that most of these letters were from a prisoner-of-war camp in North Africa where one of my father's relatives was imprisoned. This relative had been captured with several hundred other Italian soldiers after the British victory over the

Germans at El Alamein; but this imprisonment did not prevent him from forwarding to my father information that he had somehow learned inside the camp about the welfare of the people in and around my father's village.

After the doors of the store were closed and locked, my mother would open and silently read each overseas letter, while my father watched her face for any sign of shock or sadness. If she showed neither, he would be reassured that there had been no disaster and would quietly take the letter from her and read it himself.

Perhaps what I was witnessing was a superstitious stratagem on his part, an idiosyncrasy that could be traced back to some strange turn of mind that had shaped the occult character of his ancient, isolated village. Or maybe he was simply using my mother as a crutch in this period of uncertainty and anxiety—a guarantee against the possibility that he would be the sole recipient of the news of death.

But whatever the reason, I was disturbed by these scenes and wanted to remain as detached as possible from the complex reality that embraced my life. There were many times when I wished that I had been born into a different family, a plain and simple family of impeccable American credentials—a no-secrets, nonwhispering, no-enemy-soldiers family that never received mail from POW camps, or prayed to a painting of an ugly monk, or ate Italian bread with pungent cheese.

I would have preferred having a mother who spent less time in the store with the island's leading Protestant ladies, to whom she sold dresses, and more time playing parish politics with the nuns and the mainland Irish women who invaded our school on PTA evenings and Bingo Nights. And I would have welcomed a father who could have become more relaxed and casual, and who on weekends would have removed his vest and tie and played ball with me on the beach or in the small park across from the Methodist Tabernacle church. But this last wish, I knew, was pure fantasy on my part—I had made the discovery the summer before, after I had spent a half-hour bouncing a red rubber ball against a brick wall in the parking lot behind our shop. I was supposed to be working in the store at the time, affixing long thin cardboard guards to the bottom of wire hangers, then lining up these hangers on a pipe rack within reach of two black men who were pressing trousers and jackets. But after I had hung up about fifty hangers with the guards attached, I disappeared through the clouds of steam rising from the pressing machines and, with the ball in my pocket, slipped out the back door into the cool breeze of the parking lot. There I began to fling the ball against the wall and practice fielding it on the short hop in imitation of the Yankees' star second baseman, the acrobatic, dark-eyed Joe Gordon, to whom I fancied I bore a resemblance.

I assumed that my father was away from the store having lunch, as he always did in the middle of Saturday afternoons; I was therefore suddenly shaken by the sight of him opening the back door, then walking toward me with a frown on his face. Not knowing what to do, but nonetheless compelled by nervous energy to do *something,* I quickly took the ball in my right hand, cocked my arm, and threw it at him.

The ball soared forty feet in a high arc toward his head. He was so startled to see it coming that he halted his step and stared skittishly up at the sky through his steel-rimmed glasses. Then—as if not knowing whether to block the ball or try to catch it—he extended his arms upward and cupped his soft tailor's hands, and braced himself for the impact.

I stood watching anxiously from the far corner of the lot, no less shocked than he that I had chosen this moment to confront him—perhaps for the first time in his life—with the challenge of catching a ball. I cringed as I saw the ball hit him solidly on the side of the neck, carom off a shoulder, rebound against the wall behind him, and come rolling slowly back to his feet, where it finally stopped.

As I waited, holding my breath, he lowered his head and began to rub his neck. Then, seeing the ball at his feet, he stooped to pick it up. For a moment he held the rubber ball in his right hand and examined it as if it were a strange object. He squeezed it. He turned it around in his fingers. Finally, with a bashful smile, he turned toward me, cocked his arm awkwardly, and tried to throw the ball in my direction.

But it slipped from his grip, skidded weakly at an oblique angle, and rolled under one of his dry-cleaning trucks parked along the edge of the lot.

As I hastened to retrieve it, I saw him shrug his shoulders. He seemed to be very embarrassed. He who cared so much about appearances had tried his best, and yet the results were pitiful. It was a sorrowful moment for both of us.

But I heard my father make no excuses as I crawled under the truck to get the ball. And when I got up again, I saw that he was gone.

The Buick turned the corner and drove past the bank into the business district and stopped in front of our store. It was almost twelve-fifteen, and I should have been hungry when my father announced cheerfully, "I'm making pancakes—who wants some?" My sister jumped and cheered, but I remained silent.

I followed behind as Marian skipped up the steep carpeted indoor staircase with its beige stone walls, which ascended past two landings to an arched entrance. A black cast-iron chandelier hung above the entrance, and the outer wall at each landing contained a four-foot niche encasing a holy statue and an ever-burning red votive candle.

In one niche was the serene figure of the Virgin Mary, who stood exquisitely unruffled while under her bare feet a snake squirmed. In the other niche was a brown-robed statuette of Saint Francis who, although his sandaled feet were free from snakes, possessed a characteristically grim and sulky facial expression—just as depressing as that in his wall portrait in our apartment and in the living room of most of my father's Philadelphia friends. This wretched-looking monk was the leading spoilsport in all of sainthood, a horror since my earliest childhood; and today he reminded me somewhat of myself, and I loathed him more than usual.

In the apartment I hung up my hat and coat, and, after politely refusing my mother's offer to bring me lunch while I did my homework, I closed my bedroom door—to resume working on one of my model airplanes. It was a Lockheed P-38 fighter with a twin fuselage. While carefully pasting crisp, thin sections of tissue paper onto the balsa-wood frame, I could hear the musical sounds of Puccini rising softly from my father's Victrola. I pictured him seated in his favorite chair reading the newspaper—and also my mother, at the other end of the apartment, in her usual seat at the dining room table, helping my sister with her spelling, reading, and arithmetic.

A typical Sunday. So different from the rest of the week because there were no bell sounds heard in the apartment every time a customer opened or closed the main door of the shop; and the upstairs telephone extension was not ringing every minute with business calls; and if I turned on my small bedside radio there would not be the usual static that existed whenever the electric sewing machines were zipping along in the cutting room and the spotlights were burning in the dress department for the enhancement of my mother's wooden mannequins. Often on summery Saturday afternoons, when the Yankees' games were being broadcast from New York, I would sneak down the side staircase into the front of the store and turn off the spotlights that caused most of the static, then quickly go back upstairs to press my right ear against the warm radio and hope that the voice of the Yankees, Mel Allen, would fill me in on whatever action I had missed.

When my father became aware of my gamesmanship with the lights, he would quietly enter the apartment and sometimes catch me hunched against the radio—and after snapping off the dial, he would furiously shove me by the shoulders down the rear steps into the back of the store, near the pressing machines and the sweating men partly obscured by the clouds of steam. There on the floor were huge boxes of cardboard guards waiting to be hooked to new wire hangers. Or *worse,* there were piles of rusty, used hangers that my father had bought cheaply from customers (to offset the limited supply of metal hangers produced in wartime). These entangled hangers that clung together like crabs in a basket had to be separated, bent into proper shape, scraped clear of rust, then outfitted one by one with a cardboard guard. The game upstairs proceeded without me, its eventual conclusion unknown to me until, on the following day, I eagerly reached for the sports section of the Sunday paper.

But on this static-free Sunday in December, since the broadcasts of professional football held little appeal, I concentrated on my model airplanes—I razor-cut the wood, fit it to the pattern, and slowly succumbed to the etherlike effect of the powerful glue that soon put me to sleep.

Hours passed before my mother, with a soft nudge, whispered so that my father could not hear: "Hurry, dress—we're leaving for Atlantic City."

The Buick moved through the darkened streets along an interior route toward the bay bridge, avoiding the coastline. All lighting was prohibited along the ocean. Houses within view of the ocean had their window shades pulled down, and the beach was occupied only by mounted Coast Guardsmen, whose horses could move in water reaching up to their necks and were trained not to become alarmed by the sight of the phosphorus flashes that sometimes jumped above the waves.

Over the marshlands, past the pine trees, beyond the frosted farmlands and country roads that barely reflected the blue-tinted headlights of our car, we finally reached the circular boulevard with its central granite monument that marked the entrance, away from the coast, into Atlantic City. After a few blocks on the main avenue, over which a silvery span of Christmas decorations devoid of lights framed the night, my father turned into a side street where there were bars and nightclubs with black men and women standing in front. Two blocks beyond, without a black person in sight, we were in the Italian neighborhood, with its locally renowned restaurant The Venice.

Men wearing overcoats and wide-brimmed hats, and smoking cigarettes and cigars, stood outside The Venice guiding the cars in and out of the parking lot. One of them nodded toward my father, who had been coming here for years; inside, the headwaiter shook my father's hand and escorted us through the crowd at the bar to our table against the wall in the middle of the room. Nearly every table was occupied by Italo-American families, some with babies in high chairs (I recognized a red chair that I had once occupied); and the waiters, wearing tuxedos and clip-on bow ties, moved swiftly up and down the aisles with their trays, conversing with their customers and with one another in a dialectal blend of English and Italian. Although the restaurant was called The Venice, there was little about it that was Venetian; the aroma of cooking was clearly Neapolitan, and prominently displayed behind the bar was a mural of the Bay of Naples—the last view of Italy that many of these people had had before embarking years earlier for America.

My father took our orders, as he always did, then conveyed them in Italian to one of the waiters, who never wrote anything down. As usual, my first plate was spaghetti with clam sauce—and my usual way of consuming this was with a fork and a round tablespoon, which I held like a catcher's mitt to scoop up the fallen bits of clam and to stabilize my fork as I attempted to twirl the spaghetti strands into a tight and tidy mouthful.

My father, I'd noticed, never ate spaghetti in this fashion. He used only the fork, with which he masterfully twirled the strands without letting any of them dangle as he lifted them to his mouth. But on this occasion, after my plate had arrived and I had begun in my customary style with the spoon, he sat watching with an almost pained look on his face. Then he said, patiently:

"You know, I think you're old enough now to learn how to do it right."

"To do what right?"

"To eat spaghetti right," he said. "Without the spoon. Only people without manners eat spaghetti that way—or people who are ignorant; or those Italians who are *cafoni* [country bumpkins]. But in Italy the *refined* Italians would never be seen in public using the spoon."

Putting aside the spoon, I tried three or four times to spin the spaghetti around the fork, but each time the strands either slipped off and splashed into the sauce, or skipped off the plate and fell onto the floor.

"Forget it," my father said finally. "Forget it for today—but from now on, practice. One day you'll learn to get it right."

Soon the second course arrived, then dessert and the black coffee in the small cup that my father drank. My parents talked business, and my sister and I shifted restlessly.

My wandering attention was drawn to a large table near the bar, around which a festive crowd of middle-aged men and women were laughing and applauding, raising their wineglasses toward a young soldier who was with them. The soldier sat very tall in his khaki uniform. His hair was shiny black and precisely parted. His shoulders were huge, his long face lean and hard, and his brown eyes were alert. He seemed to be fully aware of how special he was.

The people around him could hardly stop watching him, or touching him, or patting him gently on the back as he bent forward to eat. Only *he* was eating. The others ignored their plates to concentrate on watching him, applauding and toasting his every move with his knife and fork.

As the waiter arrived with our check, I held his sleeve before he left, and asked: "Who's that soldier over there?"

The waiter's eyebrows rose with a slight flutter, and he leaned into my ear and replied: *"That's Joe DiMaggio!"*

Bolting to my feet, I stared at the tall soldier who continued to eat, and I imagined in the distance the solid sound of the bat, the roar of the crowd, the spirited rhythm of Les Brown's band.

I tapped my father's shoulder and said: *"That's Joe DiMaggio!"*

My father looked up from the check he had been scrutinizing for any sign of error and glanced casually at the big table. Then he turned back to me and replied: "So?"

Ignoring my father, I remained standing, in prolonged appreciation. And before we left the restaurant I took a final look, closer this time, and noticed that on the table in front of my hero was a steaming plate of spaghetti. Then his head leaned forward, his mouth opened, and everybody around him smiled—including me—as he twirled his fork unabashedly against a large silver spoon.

6.

THE AURA OF the great DiMaggio that had brought an exhilarating conclusion to my dismal Sunday was rudely interrupted on the following morning by the rattling sound of my metal alarm clock. It was Monday, a school day. Within a half-hour I was expected to be standing at the bus stop, at the corner near the bank, awaiting the eight-fifteen arrival of

Mr. Fitzgerald. Usually he was five or ten minutes late. But on this day I suspected he would be precisely on time, hoping that *I* would be late, so that he could leave me at the curb and thus add tardiness to my list of peccadilloes—misdeeds and mental lapses for which the nuns had conditioned me to expect, in this life or the next, appropriate punishment. Although I was not yet twelve years of age, I was developing a precocious sense of paranoia.

As I dressed I could hear rising from the store the hissing sounds of the pressing machines, and the ringing of the doorbell that signaled the early arrival of the employees who were assisting my parents during this busy period before Christmas. Since my sister Marian was still in bed, benefitting from an early holiday vacation that the school allowed the lower grades, I sat alone at the breakfast table in the rear of the apartment, eating the fruit and cereal my mother had left for me. Also on the table, packed in a brown paper bag, was my lunch—a soggy ham-and-egg sandwich made with Italian bread that my father had gotten the night before from our waiter at The Venice.

After hastily tossing the sandwich into my schoolbag, and grabbing my hat and coat, I skipped down the side staircase onto the sidewalk and waited at the bus stop almost ten minutes before the arrival of Mr. Fitzgerald. Shivering, I stood against a granite wall of the bank watching the activity along the avenue: shopkeepers unlocking their front doors, truckers unloading merchandise, sanitation men sweeping the streets. On the sidewalk of every block, chained to lampposts, were large wire baskets filled with corded bundles of cardboard and newspapers that people had deposited during the weekend to be collected later in the day by volunteer workers affiliated with a wartime recycling agency; and in the windows of shops were signs reminding citizens to conserve on household fats, to turn in old toothpaste tubes as new ones were purchased, and also to remit all tin cans, flattened, to grocery stores.

Ever since a tanker had been torpedoed a year before by a German submarine ten miles down the coast from Ocean City, the resort had been smitten by patriotic fervor. Middle-aged men and women, like my father, volunteered as air-raid wardens and auxiliary beach patrollers; and most draft-age men who had been found physically unfit for the military took jobs in Philadelphia defense plants, or at the bayside boat factory on the south end of the island, where barges and towboats were being constructed for the War Department.

With so many people in military work or the army, there was an acute shortage of help on the island—which was why I was expected to assist in the store after school, and why my parents were burdened by inept or unreliable personnel whom in better days they would have replaced. My mother's salesladies were either garrulous or absentminded older women who preferred exchanging gossip with the customers to ringing up sales, or aggressive younger women who were impatient with the customers and even rude to those who did not buy; and most of the saleswomen also chain-smoked and occasionally burned holes in the merchandise.

My father's dry-cleaning trucks were driven by high school seniors whose inexperience and recklessness led to frequent accidents and countless traffic violations; my father's assistant in the cutting room was a seventy-seven-year-old retired tailor from Philadelphia, who, because of failing eyesight and frayed nerves, was not renowned for his flawless measuring and cutting of cloth. But even more of a problem for my father were his pressing machines and the men who operated them.

These machines were jawlike monstrosities with elongated padded white lips that voraciously compressed clothes in boisterous heads of steam—and then, with a sudden malfunctioning of one of their many recondite and irreplaceable parts, they would choke, sizzle, and stall to a halt, breaking down most often on those afternoons when the back-room tables were stacked highest with wrinkled suits and overcoats that had been promised for delivery to customers before nightfall.

These antiquated machines that my father had purchased during the late 1920s were not only confounding to fix but enfeebling to use; the workers were forced to stretch and strain as they pulled down on the levers of the long iron padded flatbeds that pressed the clothes against the lower flatbeds; and since the imperfectly repaired boilers of the machines leaked excessive amounts of steam, the men at work quickly became drowsy and debilitated, like weightlifters in a sauna.

Even on the coldest day of winter, when all the overhead fans were vibrating at top speed, the men would sometimes wilt and faint from prostration; and no doubt they sometimes wondered if the military life for which they had been found physically unfit could have been as taxing as their labors behind these enervating hulks of metal.

There was one young man, however, who was more than a match for the machines. He was a tall, sinewy black man with an agile, bony face and lively eyes, and a shiny mass of wiry black bronze-tinted peroxided hair that he combed dramatically over his head back to the gaudy shoulders of the tropical shirts he always wore. He was called "Jet," and he had come up from the South as a saxophone player with a jazz band before the war; but he had been forced to quit after developing a tuberculous lung—which he claimed he was now slowly curing through the inhalation of steam and the snorting of white powder that he carried in a tiny bag in his shirt pocket.

Although Jet was afflicted as well with severely infected feet—his toes were gnarled with carbuncles and corns that popped out under his socks through the leather straps of the sandals he even wore in winter—he was by far the most vigorous and productive employee in the store, pressing clothes faster and better than anybody else; and when his machine blew a gasket or otherwise fizzled out, he played with its valves and keys as with a musical instrument, and soon he and his steam machine were back in harmonious rhythm.

Bedazzled by Jet and totally dependent on him, my father never complained about his loud radio that was tuned all day to a jazz station, and he pretended not to notice when Jet appeared at eight-thirty each morning, a half-hour late, or left an hour or two early, because Jet's speed could always compensate for any temporary slowdown in the flow of the load of pressing.

But on those days when Jet did not show up even by nine a.m. (as he was now doing with increased frequency), my worried father would put on his hat and coat, leave the shop through the back door, and begin his cautious stroll in the direction of the black ghetto, which was a largely dilapidated row of white shanties and small frame structures two blocks beyond the rear of the store, built along a stretch of railroad tracks within view of the bay.

If it was a Saturday, the one day I worked full-time at the store, my father would insist that I accompany him, reasoning perhaps that the presence of a young boy would make his surveillance in a black area seem less officious, less foreboding or punitive. Since my father was never certain of Jet's exact address, the latter constantly shifting from one rental space to another, we would begin arbitrarily at one of the places where Jet was known to have dwelled in the past, hoping that some tenant would provide a lead that would help my father locate his truant presser.

But we often arrived so early in the neighborhood on Saturdays that we woke people up and irritated them so much that they told us nothing. One morning as my father stood on the loose boards of a rotting porch, tapping on the slats of a torn screen door and calling to Jet by name, an elderly woman wearing a bathrobe leaned out of an upstairs window and hurled down a metal pot at my father. Although it missed him, it caused such a clatter as it bounced off the sidewalk that the dogs barked in the house next door, and children began to cry, and a large black man from across the street abruptly opened his front door and glared.

"Hey," he said, after a pause, "what the hell you want?"

"I'm looking for Jet," my father replied.

"Jet *who?*" the man asked, challengingly.

Surprised, confused, my father did not respond. Momentarily he held his breath. It had apparently occurred to him for the first time that he did not know Jet's last name. The man across the street, his heavy arms folded, stood waiting; and I feared that he might leave his porch and come over to us. But as my father remained silent and kept his eyes downward, the man merely sneered as he said: "We don't know no Jet around here!"—and, upon reentering his house, slammed the door behind him.

My father turned toward me slowly, forcing a smile. Then, firmly taking my hand, he led me down the icy steps. I assumed that we were on our way home. But after we had walked a half-block in silence, he said: "Let's try one more place, that house on the corner." I protested; but he pulled me toward a two-story clapboard house that, like the other peeling buildings on the block, had brown stains streaking down the white walls beneath the drainpipes, and rusty dented automobiles parked in the driveway, and a muddy yard littered with broken bottles, punctured tires, and assorted household rubbish soundly stuck in the frosty, weed-strewn earth.

"Let's go home," I pleaded. But my father moved toward the corner house, where he soon was knocking on the door and, with somewhat less force than before, calling out to Jet. This time, however, there was no response whatsoever. No one came to a window, there was no barking of dogs; it was as if it were a totally abandoned house. My persistent father knocked louder, rapping his gloved knuckles against the white door patched with plywood, causing a hollow echo that rose in the harsh morning air. But from the house, continuing silence.

"Okay," he said finally, "let's go." Relieved, I followed him down the path, then toward the street in the direction of the store. I had seen enough of Jet's world. But a sense of sadness lingered within me as we walked, for I knew that after we had gotten back to the store on this Saturday, as on other Saturdays when Jet was adrift, I would see my father in the back room remove his jacket and tie, and strip to his undershirt, and then begin on this busiest day of the week to labor as long as he could in the steam of Jet's machine.

And not only my father, but I as well would be confined—until Jet's unpredictable return—to the hot and hazy atmosphere where no conversation could be heard above the pounding and hissing of the machines, and where time always passed slowly as my father sharpened the front creases of other men's pants (while his own tailored trousers became sodden and baggy-kneed), and where I, sitting near him as he expressly wished, listlessly affixed hundreds of cardboard guards onto wire hangers before hooking them along the pipes within reach of the perspiring men.

My father, I unavoidably noticed, lagged behind even the portly gray-haired semi-retired presser whose leisurely pace at other times he had repeatedly criticized; and while this man was at least twenty years my father's senior, he possessed an enduring stamina that my father clearly lacked. After a half-hour in the steam, my father was a lamentable figure. His eyeglasses were fogged over. His neck seemed to have shrunk within the soaked, sagging noose of his knotted white handkerchief. And after he had extended his slender arms above his head to grip the levers of the machine, he would heave as he pulled downward, straining under the flat-iron's weight, and his face suddenly bore the agonized expression of his favorite saint.

I sometimes wondered, many years later, if there was not a part of him that almost reveled in these moments, these humbling efforts that perhaps put him in touch spiritually with those flagellants he had once described watching intently as a boy, a bedraggled but tenacious multitude crawling uphill on bleeding knees—or those ascetic village elders, among them his grandfather Domenico, who vied for the honor of hoisting on their shoulders the weighty statue of the monk who had extolled the virtues of mortification.

In this period of World War II, with citizens everywhere receptive to sacrificing—and with my father's widowed mother existing vulnerably in the hills of southern Italy and his brothers in enemy trenches—it was possible that he was experiencing in his discomfort a kindred comfort with his primal concerns. Or at the very least, he was imposing upon me, his only son, a lasting awareness of how hard his life could be, and how little right I had, by comparison, to complain about the minimal obligations required of me in the store.

Still, I did complain, and sulk in silence; and in the back room, when I thought my father was not watching, I would sometimes try to slip away. But he always caught me, and scolded me; and with his feet he pushed in my direction another large box filled with cardboard guards for the hangers. As I kneeled to pry open the box, and as he turned and raised his hands to the lever of the white matted machine, I submitted to my role as

methodically as I served the priest at Mass; and yet, in the store, I sometimes prayed with uncharacteristic fervor and faith, hoping and believing
that within a miraculous few seconds the back door would open, and I
would hear the shuffling sounds of Jet's sandaled feet that would soon replace my father's wing-tipped shoes on the iron pedals—and thus I would
gain at least temporary relief from a stifling and wistful Saturday.

7.

THE SCHOOL BUS screeched to a halt, two minutes before it was scheduled to arrive; and after the door swung open, I saw the stern profile of
Mr. Fitzgerald. He wore his gray peaked cap pointed straight forward
toward the windshield, and along the edges of the steering wheel his fingers tapped impatiently.

As I climbed the two steps, holding my bulky schoolbag close to my
body to avoid brushing it against the grease-coated rod that held the door
securely open, I observed that Mr. Fitzgerald's eyes did not shift even
slightly in my direction. He seemed determined to avoid all personal contact; and so I accommodated him by not saying good morning—a social
slight to which he might have been responding a second later when he
clangorously slammed the door closed and hurtled the bus to a quick start
before I had settled into a seat.

Although the bus was less crowded than usual because the primary
schoolers were already on holiday, there was actually an increased amount
of noise and disorder generated in the back of the bus by some older boys
who, relieved of all concern for the physical well-being of the young,
were now less inhibited as they hurled spitballs wildly back and forth, and
scuffled with one another in the aisles, and took turns pinching and squeez-
ing the arms of the squealing, frolicsome girls who seemed to be enjoying their company. These middle school boys in their early teens were
dressed in hooded plaid mackinaws and thick corduroy pants that made
whipping sounds when they walked; and under their hunting caps they
wore colorful fuzzy earmuffs that I sometimes envied but, for reasons
presumably aesthetic, was prohibited by my father from owning. The
items of clothing envied by most other male students in my school were
the U.S. Army belts that a few boys had obtained from their older soldier

brothers—khaki canvas belts that, in the schoolyard during recess, they would extract from their pants loops and twirl like lassos feverishly above their heads, daring anyone to stand close to the bright menacing blur of the belts' brass buckles.

The girls in the back of the bus also wore hooded mackinaws, or navy blue pea jackets patriotically complemented by red mufflers and white tasseled caps; and, together with the boys, they would sometimes duck their heads behind the seats to smoke cigarettes. Most of the girls and boys were bused in each day from the agricultural areas, the rustic pinelands, and a small community directly across the bay that had a honky-tonk strip; they were the progeny of rural housewives and truck farmers, hospital nurses and boatyard repairmen, file clerks and firemen, and waitresses and bartenders who worked at night in the neon-lit waterfront establishments that were viewed disapprovingly, if dimly through the fog, by the Prohibitionist standard-bearers of dry Ocean City. The lights blazing above the taverns and dance halls were seen as beacons of indulgence that had a depreciating effect not only on the property values but also on the moral values of the entire Back Bay region—which was perhaps why many conscientious Catholic families in that region sent their children miles away each day to receive a regimental education under the tutelage of the island's authoritarian nuns.

But whatever positive effect the nuns were having over the mainland children was not evident on the bus this morning. And while I would have preferred sitting as far as possible from Mr. Fitzgerald, I did not want to be within easy target range of the spitball shooters. So I sat near the front, in the third row, among a dozen students who were my own age or a bit younger—individuals whom I knew by name but who, because of the hours I spent in the store, were mainly classroom acquaintances.

When the bus stopped again, we were joined by a student I knew better. She sometimes came into the store with her parents, who were steady patrons. She was Rosemary Kurtz, the genial daughter of the local Ford dealer, a loquacious, rotund, balding man who was the island's preeminent Catholic parishioner, the foremost financial supporter of the church, and the sponsor of the parish's annual Altar Boy Award, which I entertained no foolish expectation of ever winning.

Although Rosemary was already showing some tendency toward inheriting her father's large-boned, plump body, she had a delicately shaped face with radiant eyes and pink complexion that was uncommonly attractive. Whenever the nuns were looking for someone to wear a halo in a school play, or to represent the Madonna in the nativity scene, Rosemary was usually their first choice; and she played the role equally well offstage. She was serene, considerate, poised, although socially distant. She seemed to have no close friends and belonged to no clique. She came to school dressed each day in primly fashioned coats of pastel shades and matching hats that were sometimes trimmed with my father's fur pieces; and while she conversed with everyone on the bus, and occasionally even took a seat close to the hooded-mackinaw crowd in the rear, she nonetheless conveyed the impression that she expected to be treated at all times with the respect and dignity that the parishioners at Sunday Mass bestowed upon her magnanimous parents. And insofar as I could tell, she did indeed receive such treatment even from the school's rowdier students, who refrained from cursing in her presence, or blowing cigarette smoke in her direction, or firing spitballs in her general vicinity. She was therefore the ideal traveling companion when riding the parochial school bus, and I was comforted by this when she chose to sit near me on this Monday morning—and consequently I was more astonished than upset when, suddenly, while we chatted as the bus moved uptown, a small flying object nearly grazed my cheek, caromed high off the empty seat in front of me, and hit hard against the windshield close to the face of Mr. Fitzgerald.

It was a chunk of rubber eraser. And as it bounced along the floor, Mr. Fitzgerald slammed on the brakes, spun around, and, his bloodshot eyes examining us with wrath and suspicion, bellowed: "Okay, who's the wise guy?"

More than two dozen students in the front and middle rows all turned immediately toward the back, where the disruptive older group now sat motionless in a posture of innocence, their white faces and unfurrowed brows under the hoods of their mackinaws making them seem almost as guileless as a gathering of monks at prayer. I, too, turned and waited for some admission of guilt, some twitch that would betray the malefactor—until it occurred to me, as I scrutinized the older faces, that I was doubtless making eye contact at this very moment with the mysterious culprit; and quickly I turned away, not wanting to risk offending the offender with an accusatory stare that could provoke retaliation later in the schoolyard from someone who possibly owned a brass-buckled U.S. Army belt.

As I turned around I noted that Rosemary Kurtz was the only student who had not looked back to examine the others. She had kept facing the front—uninterested, uninvolved, and thereby untainted by the back-bus boorishness. Mr. Fitzgerald soon lost interest, realizing that there would be no confessions of wrongdoing today. And so, after a kind of face-saving admonition—"If you don't cut it out, I'll throw you out!"—he pressed the gas pedal, and we resumed our journey along a damp black macadam road that ran parallel to the beach, passing foggy white rows of vacant apartment houses with gingerbread verandas and boarded-up windows.

In summertime, the sidewalks were crowded with sandaled sun-bathers carrying wood-framed canvas chairs and long-poled umbrellas, and wearing straw hats and cotton robes over their modestly designed bathing suits—which included tops for men, who were prohibited by local law from exposing their bare chests on the avenue, on the beach, or even in the sea. Since in summer the number of Catholics on the island increased significantly, overcrowding the parish's single church down-town, auxiliary Masses were offered on Sundays in the chapel of our school. No Masses were said there during the rest of the year, however, although the architecture of the school was unmistakably ecclesiastic—the familiar outlines of which I could now see through the rising mist as the bus turned inland from the ocean.

It was a chunky brick building with a gray peaked roof and a stunted, cross-topped steeple that rose above a white double-doored entranceway. Along the sides of the building, which extended a half-block behind a wide newly paved sidewalk, were tall clear-glass windows that looked into the classrooms, providing added light for brighter students and vague vistas of escape for daydreamers like me. Two smaller windows in the rear of the building, stained-glass, marked the location of the chapel. On the far side of the building, and behind it, was a weedless acre of isolated land composed of steamrolled light gravel and windblown sand that, in the gray light of the morning, resembled snow. As the bus slowly cruised to within half a block of the school, I could also see, emerging beyond the windshield, a stark white-and-black-clad figure. She was standing on the stone steps of the entranceway, awaiting our arrival. She was Sister Rita, the mistress of discipline.

She was the youngest of the school's eight nuns, and as a result she perhaps inherited the mundane duties that the older sisters had risen above—such as standing like a sentry each morning in the cold weather to await Mr. Fitzgerald's imprecise arrivals, and then lining up the students along the sidewalk in two sexually segregated files to be marched into school, a routine that she often hastened by lightly prodding the backs of stragglers with a rubber-tipped blackboard pointer that she held in her right hand like a whip.

Once she was alleged to have lashed the buttocks of an errant boy with the metal crucifix that hung from the large rosary beads she wore around her waist; and while I could not testify to the accuracy of that tale, I did personally observe Sister Rita on two occasions rapping with a ruler the knuckles of older boys who had lingered at the urinals, touching their forbidden parts for periods of time she deemed excessive.

She seemed to be obsessed with what took place in the boys' rest room, and she was forever banging in and out of that place, grabbing by the scruff of the neck any youth who sought refuge there. It was she who instructed students on how they should sleep each night: on their backs, with their arms crossed on their chests, hands on opposite shoulders—a presumably holy posture that, not incidentally, made masturbation impossible. Masturbation, or even the thought of it, apparently represented one of the great anathemas to Sister Rita. One morning while I sat in her geography class, looking down at a book of maps and listening to her lecture, I was aware all at once of her sudden silence. Looking up, I saw that she was staring at me, or more precisely, at the way I was sitting, with my right leg in the aisle and my right hand in my pants pocket.

"What are you *doing* with your hand?" she demanded. Everyone in the classroom turned toward me. I felt myself redden with embarrassment and confusion—I was being reviled, precipitately, for committing some indefinable act that was inscrutably deviant. Slowly, I removed my hand. With my eyes focused on the floor, I waited.

"Never," she said, in a trembling voice, "*never* put your hands in your pockets!"

Now Mr. Fitzgerald turned off the bus engine, and—with what sounded like a sigh of relief—pushed the metal handle that forced the greasy rod to open the door. I could hear Sister Rita calling up from the sidewalk: "All right, girls and boys—*straight lines, straight lines,* and be quick about it!" As she held the pointer in the folds of her long skirt, I hopped off the bus behind some younger boys and took my place within an emerging line that began in front of the school steps and was soon backed up almost to the curb. Parallel to us, but three feet away, was a line formed by girls—headed, I noticed, by Rosemary Kurtz. In all, there were fewer than forty of us. But dozens of other students were now arriving on foot, or by bicycle, or in parental car pools; complying with Sister Rita's instructions, they joined the lengthening lines that soon bent at right angles near the curb and extended along the edge of the sidewalk.

Cold as it was, we were detained for a few minutes to be ventilated, more or less, by the frosty ocean air; and then, with our schoolbags on the ground, Sister Rita began to count aloud—"One-two, three-four" signaling us to begin our daily ritual of calisthenics. This consisted of stretching our arms above our heads, taking deep breaths, and leaning forward with our fingertips toward our toes. Although Sister Rita did not join us in these exercises—being less than ideally attired in her towering headdress, flowing veils, and starched white, half-moon-shaped clerical collar that encircled her neck like a yoke—she did zestfully tap her feet in time with her counting, and she moved her pointer back and forth like a metronome. And as she shouted to us from the top step of the entranceway, urging us to accelerate our movements on this bone-chilling morning, vaporous clouds floated out of her mouth, blurring and briefly transforming her image into that of an ascending apparition, a cloaked and nebulous figure commanding us with transcendent force and clarity—calisthenics *ex cathedra.*

For nearly ten minutes the workout continued along the sidewalk; and while it was intended to circulate our blood and heighten our sensibilities for the schoolwork ahead, it merely made me dizzy and opened up my mind to aimless wandering. Still, this class represented the only organized sports activity conducted by the school, which lacked the interior space or financial resources for a gymnasium, and which otherwise offered, later in the day, only two fifteen-minute recess periods in the school's gravel yard. At one end of the yard stood a Maypole painted a purplish black— the paint having been left over from a recent retouching job to the school bus; and hanging from the spinning top of the Maypole were six long pieces of hemp, each with a knotted end that was supposed to keep—but did not succeed in keeping—children from slipping off the rope as they gripped its lower end and glided in a circular arc around the pole.

At the other end of the yard was a wide open area on which was played a provisional form of cold-weather baseball. The sphere was a hard rubber ball; the hitter used his mittened fist instead of a bat (which Sister Rita disallowed as a potentially dangerous weapon), and the boundary lines for the infield and outfield were scratched into the earth with the sharp ends of tree branches or sticks, which were constantly in use since the lines were forever being obscured by the wind or the footprints of the players. Not so eradicable were the pitcher's mound and home plate, which were marked by pieces of rock or brick.

Because we did not have enough players or time during the luncheon and afternoon recess periods to play baseball properly, our version of the game had ten or twelve boys scattered at random through the infield and outfield forming a defense against a single self-appointed hitter—

who, swinging his fist at a ball tossed underhand by a self-appointed pitcher, slapped it hither and yon until someone in the field caught it before it touched the ground. At that point, the person who caught the ball changed places with the hitter; and this system normally produced such a quick rotation of hitters that everyone had a chance to hit before the recess period ended—unless Billy Maenner was at bat.

Billy was a freckled, sorrel-haired boy whose father owned a tavern on the other side of the bay. He was my only friend among the mainland students. During Sister Rita's calisthenics class on this morning, as I reached to touch my toes, I saw Billy wink at me from his upside-down position near the curb. Then he shook his head slowly and raised his eyebrows, indicating that he was as bored as I was with these exercises; the gesture belied the fact that he was the closest thing our school had to an athlete. Although he was no larger than I, and was also a sixth-grader not yet in his teens, Billy Maenner could hit a ball harder and farther than any of the older boys; and he was adept at punching the ball into places where no one could reach it. For five or ten minutes, or even longer, he would cock his fist at each of forty or fifty pitches served to him high or low, inside or outside, and solidly pop each one beyond the infielder's outstretched fingers, or between the converging outfielders or over their heads entirely, the ball rolling all the way to the Maypole.

Such prowess earned him sufficient status to sit as an equal among the older boys in the back of the bus. But unlike them, he was never mischievous or discourteous—not the type to hurl rubber erasers through the air; and with me he was always very cordial. In the yard one day during autumn he gave me hitting tips that subsequently improved my never spectacular performances at the plate; and sometimes after I had boarded the bus and sat alone, he would leave his friends and come up to join me; and with his modest and pensive demeanor he gave the impression of being a lonely person, intrinsically an outsider like me.

According to my father, there was some German blood in Billy's family, which, if that was true, may have been a factor in our kindred feeling. We were both, to a degree, on the wrong side of the war. And like me, he received mediocre grades; in fact, academically we both ranked near the bottom of our class. And yet he seemed far less upset than I about the report cards that were mailed to our homes each month, perhaps because our fathers reacted in different ways to the somber news.

My sensitive and protective father, who cared greatly about the reputation of his family in this town of few secrets, saw my inferior grades as demeaning to himself, an affront to his pride and dignity as a parent and leading Catholic layman—who, incidentally, contributed more money to the church than anyone except the Ford dealer. My father had also cultivated an intimate relationship with the venerable pastor, Father Blake, whom he had finally persuaded to hang a picture of Saint Francis along the side wall of the church, and it went without saying that my father always dry-cleaned gratis the pastor's black suits, coats, and priestly apparel, as well as the long black habits of the nuns.

When scrutinizing my report card, my father often wondered aloud if there was not something wrong with the school's grading system rather than with my diligence as a student; and, despite my objections, he would telephone the Mother Superior for an appointment, and days later, through the windows of my classroom, I would see my moustachioed father stepping out of his Buick, walking with a dour expression on his face as he entered the side door, his homburg in hand, looking like a foreign diplomat en route to discuss one of the pricklier issues of the long-disputed Lateran Treaty. As far as I could see, none of these dialogues ever accrued to my benefit, for when the next report card arrived the nuns seemed to have judged me with more severity than before.

Billy's father, on the other hand, never appeared at the school. As a tavern owner who worked until the early hours of the morning, he perhaps had the habit of sleeping through the entire school day. Whatever the situation, Billy never showed any stress as his lowly marks each month matched my own; if anything, his morale seemed only to improve as time transpired—and despite their downgrading him, the nuns often smiled at him in the corridor between classes, and even allowed him to cut a class on occasion.

"Straight lines!" Sister Rita called from the steps, her breath trailing through the air like the words of a sky-writer, her pointer waving toward the pathway in front of the entrance. Calisthenics was finally over on this Monday, and now we were to proceed in an orderly manner into the building. It was almost eight forty-five. Unenthusiastically I picked up my bag and took my place in line. Billy Maenner slipped in behind me.

"Hi," he said, "how'd you like that eraser flying past your nose in the bus?"

"I didn't. Who threw it?"

"I did," he said, gleefully. I was dumbfounded.

"Well," I said, finally, "you missed."

Just then Sister Rita directed her pointer toward us, demanding our silence; but not before Billy had whispered back: "Yes. I was trying to miss."

Up the steps we marched, girls and boys in separate files, into the warm corridor, not stopping until we reached the assembly room. Along the way we passed the classrooms, their doors closed to retain the heat, and inhaled a blended fragrance of incense, candles, and floor wax. In the assembly room were ten rows of wooden folding chairs, all facing a wide, green-carpeted platform in the back of which was a small altar. In summers this was where Masses were said, but during winter the room served varied purposes: it was the students' dining hall at lunchtime, it was the PTA's meeting room on certain weeknights (often followed by bingo parties), and each morning before class it was where the Mother Superior, seated in a high-backed chair, greeted the students and led them in prayer.

She was tall and slender, and she was waiting on the platform with authoritative ease as we settled along the rows, schoolbags near our feet. She waited and said nothing until the room was quiet, so intensely quiet that we could hear the clicking sounds of the rosary beads she held dangling in her long fingers. Her hands were abnormally white, as if the chalk she used for writing at the blackboard each day had become permanently ingrained in her skin. Her eyes were a pale shade of indefiniteness—indefinite to me because I had never once looked closely into them. Nor had I ever had a private conversation with her. My father did enough talking for both of us; and the dubious results of his intercessions on my behalf convinced me that it was better for all involved if I remained far from her sight.

Finally, standing and bowing her head, the Mother Superior began a decade of the Rosary: "Our Father, who art in heaven . . ."; and her reedy voice immediately became lost in the murmurous response of the entire room, with the other nuns' voices rising higher as they stood together in the outer aisles, their lofty bonnets tilted so far forward that it seemed they might soon topple off their heads to the floor.

Indeed, no sight would have been more welcomed by most of the students in this room, who speculated endlessly on what exactly was beneath the nuns' bonnets. Were the nuns' heads completely shaven? Was their hair cut short, like boys'? Which nun's hair was blond, or brunette, or gray, or white? These women who hovered over *our* heads all day in school, who conditioned our minds, who regulated our hours, who invaded our rest rooms, remained for us shrouded in mystery, dark brides of Christ, elusive and aloof. Few of us ever saw them arrive at school in the morning, or leave in the afternoon; nor did we have any idea where they spent their nights.

I, however, was an exception. Not only did I know where they lived—my father's dry-cleaning trucks often made deliveries there—but

I myself had recently accompanied the driver to that quiet residence on the other end of town from the school; and while helping him carry packages onto the porch, I looked through the open doorway where the housekeeper stood, and caught a brief glimpse of something in the house that was perplexing and exciting.

The house was a spacious but simple three-story frame residence located in the middle of a street lined with similar-looking buildings that in wintertime were mostly unoccupied. It was two blocks from the church. On the house there was no religious symbol or sign that identified it as the domicile of the nuns. Draperies were pulled closed behind all the first-floor windows, and when the driver and I arrived in the truck in the late afternoon we saw no lights burning in the front of the house.

But soon after the driver had rung the bell, a soft beam of light streamed down from a bulb within a black tin can that hung from the porch ceiling—a fixture installed in conformity with the wartime dim-out policies of the island—and then the door was opened wide by a cheerful black woman. She accepted the packages one by one as the driver carefully checked off the items on his inventory slips. I stood behind him, holding the two final packages, while gazing into a large living room that was revealed faintly in the light of small candles on the wainscoting ledges and larger candles that stood on the refectory table in the dining room. Hanging from one wall above a sofa was a large ebony cross on which was nailed a silver figure of Christ, and on another wall within a gilt frame was an oil painting of the Virgin Mary.

Behind the dining room was a small room sharply outlined in light. There, I suddenly saw a moving shadow, and then a woman's naked back and extended arms, and a delicately shaped head with dark hair cropped high above the ears. From behind, another pair of hands touched her neck, massaging it; and as her head tilted back, I turned away, holding my breath.

The housekeeper closed the door, and I followed the driver to the truck, telling him nothing of what I had seen. Certainly I did not mention it to any of the students with whom I was now praying in the assembly room. But as the recitation continued, I shifted my eyes toward the cluster of nuns who stood with bowed heads in the aisles, and I wondered, as I had repeatedly, which one I had seen.

When the prayer session ended, there was the sound of shuffling feet along the rows and the clacking of chair slats; but the Mother Superior, silencing the students with her raised hand, said, "One moment, please— Sister Rita has today's announcements."

Sister Rita ascended the platform and, in an imperious tone of voice, said: "There will be a fire drill later today, replacing the midafternoon recess period. . . ." There was soft hissing from the boys, especially from Billy Maenner standing next to me.

"And after the fire drill," she continued, "all altar boys are to report to the sacristy, where you'll receive your Mass assignments for Christmas week. . . ." I hoped I would be included among those to serve the ceremonious Christmas Midnight Mass, which would allow me to sleep late on Christmas morning. "As you know, all Masses this season are dedicated to the welfare and personal safety of our Holy Father the Pope, who must live in the midst of the terrible war in Italy. . . ." The students were more than aware of this august figure, for a picture of Pius XII hung in every classroom: a brooding man with a long face and thin nose who wore a white skullcap, and steel-rimmed glasses exactly like my father's.

"And finally," Sister Rita went on, "and *this* is important: I want each and every one of you to clean out your lockers before the final day of school tomorrow. Your lockers *must* be aired out during the Christmas holidays. Am I making myself clear?" Everyone stood in silence, some quietly bending to pick up their schoolbags. "All right, then," she concluded, looking at her watch—it was eight fifty-five—"you may proceed to your homerooms."

This gave us five minutes to hang up our coats and, if necessary, use the bathrooms. The girls' and boys' rest rooms were behind two large metal doors along the far wall of the assembly room. The boys' room, which had six urinals and six enclosed toilets, had its stone floor hosed and mopped twice daily by a custodian who applied such liberal amounts of ammonia that anyone entering the place felt his eyes burn. This was Sister Rita's method of achieving sanitary conditions as well as discouraging boys from using the room as a center for fraternization. On those frequent occasions when she entered, she invariably carried a handkerchief in front of her face.

The homerooms to which we reported were eight in number—the four lower grades along the western side of the building, and the four higher grades along the eastern side, which was exposed to the ocean breezes and had misty classroom windows. We remained in our respective homerooms all day, while the various teaching nuns rotated every hour from room to room. After a fifty-five-minute session, there was a five-minute interim during which students were permitted to stand and talk in the aisles, or to pay hasty visits to the rest rooms.

When a loud clang from the corridor's wall clock signaled the start of a new hour, order was immediately reimposed in each room by the arriving nun, and the students returned to their desks for another fifty-five minutes of exposure to the curriculum. Since we sat in alphabetical order, arranged in four rows from left to right, I occupied what I considered a desirable position in the rear of the room—on the fringe of the nun's purview, and frequently concealed behind the incessantly raised hand of a studious mainland student named Mary Steelman, whose avidity for answering questions relieved me of what little desire I ever had for being heard.

But as I walked toward my homeroom on this morning, I knew that I would be unable to hide behind Mary Steelman: a written examination was scheduled for our first hour, an American history test that dealt with the territorial expansion of the United States during the nineteenth and early twentieth centuries. Our teacher was Sister Irma, a kindly but shy individual who spoke in a singsong manner and presented history as a series of impersonal episodes and precise dates that were largely devoid of the passions and vagaries of the human spirit. History as she related it was unrelievedly monotonous; and during those evenings when I sought help from my father, whose favorite subject was history, I would receive an interpretation of American history from an Italian viewpoint that, while interesting at times, was entirely irrelevant to Sister Irma's class and contributed nothing to my elevation in her grading system.

For example, on the question of the Louisiana Purchase—about which Sister Irma cared only that it was bought from France in 1803 for $15,000,000 and added 827,987 square miles to American territory—my father saw in the land deal the "fine Italian hand" of his adopted fellow ethnic, Napoleon Bonaparte, who, in selling a distant possession that was reachable only via the ocean on which the British fleet was preeminent, wisely enriched his war chest and shifted his priorities toward battling the British in a place closer to home; indeed, my father continued, the French forces in 1803 were massed along the English Channel, prepared for a British invasion, and among Napoleon's troops were six thousand Italian soldiers. . . .

"But," I interrupted, "this has nothing to do with *American* history!" To this he emphatically responded: "You'll never properly understand American history unless you understand the history of Europe, including Italy. . . . Don't ever forget that America was discovered by an Italian, was named after an Italian, and that the American Declaration of

Independence—those words about mankind being born free and equal—were taken by Jefferson from the writings of Philip Mazzei! Have you ever heard of Philip Mazzei?"

"No," I said, wishing I had never gotten involved in this conversation.

"Do they ever mention Mazzei in your school?"

"No, but I'm being tested on the Louisiana Purchase, and the Panama Canal, and how the United States got to own Florida, and Texas, and whatever else. . . . *That's* what I'm worried about for my test!"

And I was still worried about it as I walked into Sister Irma's classroom on this morning of the examination, and took my place behind Mary Steelman and in front of a skinny, ebullient boy named Jackie Walsh, and across the aisle from Billy Maenner—who seemed not to have a worry in the world. As Sister Irma began to walk up and down the aisles handing copies of the test to each student, Billy sat casually at his desk, with a hand under his chin, staring at the blackboard with a smile on his face. He turned toward me and winked. Then, with a finger, he directed my attention to the blackboard, on the top of which were drawn, in vari-colored chalk, small figures of flying angels, and cherubs, and a reindeer leaping through the clouds toward what I assumed was supposed to be the Star of Bethlehem. The top of the adjacent blackboard was also decorated like a Christmas card, with colored chalk drawings of the Madonna and Child in a manger, surrounded by cattle and Wise Men, and more angels fluttering above—and under it all, in neat printing, was the artist's signature: "B. Maenner."

Within a moment I understood why Billy had been treated so courteously by the nuns at the end of the previous week, and had received permission to cut certain classes. He had probably been busy planning these sketches, which he must have drawn on the blackboards during the weekend. I wondered if similar drawings by him were in other classrooms. I did not know. I knew only that there had been no art on our blackboards when I left school on Friday.

And suddenly the incident just before Thanksgiving, in the Mother Superior's religion class, made sense. Billy had been sitting at his desk paying no attention to her lecture; his head was down, and he was doodling with his pencil across his notepad. Twice the Mother Superior had glared at him, but he did not notice her until her shadow was nearly upon him, and she was seeing on his pad what at first appeared to be a sensuous female figure, a woman with her arms tossed high in the air in the frisky manner of a magazine pinup.

"And what is *this?*" the Mother Superior had asked, grabbing his pad.

But before he could reply, the Mother Superior's eyes softened and the tense lines around her mouth diffused into a demure smile. And as she held the pad close to her face and studied it, she saw that Billy had been drawing an angel.

It was a copy of the angel that adorned the cover of our religion textbook—it was, on one level, a line-for-line imitation, *except,* as the Mother Superior could see, Billy's version had an ethereal quality that surpassed the stylized work of the professional illustrator. Billy's angel floated across the page. It was as if his pencil had received guidance from above.

The Mother Superior had turned the drawing in our direction, holding it high so that we might examine it and share her admiration for it. I was as impressed as everyone else seemed to be by his deft strokes, his charismatic curlicues; and while I had conveyed complimentary words to him across the aisle, and was sincere in my sentiments, I also felt rising within myself a pang of envy. Not only did Billy possess the hardest-hitting fist in the schoolyard, but now he was being hailed for his hand's artistic touch. It was no wonder that the nuns had been treating him with such deference. They were conforming to the beneficent tradition that the Church throughout the ages had always bestowed on favored artists. Billy was our Michelangelo, a unique personage whose academic short-comings were being ignored because of the exquisite way he drew celestial creatures; and before the Mother Superior had concluded her religion class on the day of Billy's discovery, I had watched with mixed feelings as she summoned him to her desk, spoke with him briefly in private, and then placed in his hands a small cardboard box containing chalk of eight different colors. It was more than a gift, I had thought as I stood watching on that day; it was an augury of his rising status, and it seemed at that moment to separate Billy Maenner from us, his classmates, and from me, his friend.

And now as Sister Irma placed a copy of the history test on his desk, my feelings about our separateness came back and were confirmed by the way he was reacting to the tension of this moment: we were jittery in our seats; he seemed as calm as a clam. When he lowered his eyes to look at the examination that was spread before him, I watched closely, hoping to get some indication of how difficult it was—for I still believed, in a scholastic sense, that he belonged in the low category that had always been basic to our compatibility. But his face told me nothing. Within a moment he looked up, glanced toward the blackboard, and seemed to be very contented.

I turned to my test. Automatically I wrote "J/M/J" on the top of the left margin, as the nuns required on all classroom papers, in reverential remembrance of Jesus, Mary, and Joseph. On the upper right corner of the page I printed my name. Then I proceeded to confront the first question, which contained three parts; and at once I knew I was in trouble.

It concerned the Louisiana Purchase, and we were asked to identify the nation from which France had purchased the territory before France had sold it to the United States in 1803, and it also asked that we include the date of this earlier transaction and the price of the sale. To this three-pronged question, I could barely hazard a guess. While I doubted that France had gotten Louisiana from Britain—not after the way my father had described the French-British rivalry—I also knew that in written tests the answer that you think is the most definitely wrong is often the most definitely right. Teachers often enjoyed tricking students with such questions. Still, I hesitated, knowing that France could as easily have obtained Louisiana from Spain, or Portugal, or—was it possible?—from Mexico. Was Mexico *Mexico* then? And if so, was it doing business with the United States? When *was* that Mexican-American War?

Aware that I was wasting time on this first question, and even more aware that there was a long list of other questions awaiting my wisdom, I edged up in my seat and stretched my neck slightly so that I might peek over Mary Steelman's shoulder. On the paper of that bright student, if I could get a look at it, would be the solution to my problem. After first making sure that Sister Irma would not catch me in this compromising position, I leaned forward and, squinting with all my focused power, I saw that Mary Steelman had replied to the first part of the first question: "Spain." Casually, I wrote "Spain" on my page. But as I leaned forward again, trying to see the rest of her answer, she suddenly covered her test with her arm. All at once I felt resentful, *insulted*—and abandoned. I was now on my own.

I decided to skip the rest of the first question and move down to the second, planning to go back and complete the first later with some wild guessing—and perhaps some inspired help from "J/M/J." But the second question, also in three parts, offered no relief. It dealt with the United States' involvement with the Republic of Panama, a complicated relationship that I had never really understood even after I had carefully read the section about it in our textbook, and then reread it almost a dozen times. About Panama I knew only that, unlike Louisiana, it was not owned by the United States. The United States did not own the Panama Canal, either, but as the book explained, our nation did possess the "perpetual right of occupation, use, and control" of the canal, for which the United

States had paid the Republic of Panama $10,000,000, plus an added $250,000 annually to use it. When I had looked at the map and seen how small Panama was (when compared with Louisiana, for instance), I was bewildered by the terms of the deal. But I was even more bewildered by the three parts to the second question on the test: (a) By what treaty did the United States gain use of the Panama Canal? (b) When? (c) How wide is the Canal?

Since I had not a clue about the first two parts of the question, I ignored them summarily and moved to the third part: How wide? Here I felt somewhat more confident, having spent my entire life around the water. Knowing that the bay separating the island of Ocean City from the liquor-selling mainland, where Billy Maenner's father had his bar, was two miles wide—and imagining no reason why the Panama Canal should be wider (despite all the money the United States had, incredibly, invested there)—I wrote down, to be on the generous side, "Three miles."

Looking at my watch, and realizing that I had only twenty minutes left in which to answer the six remaining questions, I began to panic. Quickly I gave a sweeping glance at the rest of the test, eager to salvage whatever I could from this disaster, and was relieved to discover that many of the questions sought information about which I was not totally unaware. For example, in the third through sixth questions—which concerned, respectively, the acquisition of Florida in 1819, and Texas in 1845, and Oregon in 1846, and Alaska in 1867—I had fortunately memorized most of the isolated facts and other minutiae that now qualified me to respond knowingly to the questions posed by Sister Irma.

The seventh question, however, concerned the so-called Gadsden Purchase, a procurement about which I was completely ignorant. I had no idea where Gadsden was located in the United States, *if* it indeed was; and until this examination, in fact, I had never ever heard of Gadsden. So in response to the questions about Gadsden—from whom had the United States purchased it? When? And for what amount?—I repeated the same financial figure and date that I had used earlier for the Oregon Purchase (reasoning that this perhaps doubled my chances of getting *something* right), and I cited "France" as the selling nation because I had an inkling that I had overused "Spain" in my replies to previous questions.

As I moved down to the eighth and final question, there was a sudden uplifting of my morale. Here I was confident, having carefully memorized this material with some inadvertent assistance from my father. The eighth question was: "From which nation did the U.S. obtain the Philippines, Guam, and Puerto Rico? By what treaty was this ratified? In what year?" I had been reading about this in my bedroom, seated at my desk, when my father had looked in and asked: "How are you doing?"

"I'm reading about the Spanish-American War," I said, "and how Spain lost it, and then had to give up the Philippines, Guam, and Puerto Rico to the United States." With my finger on the paragraph of my textbook, I continued irrefutably: "These were ceded to the United States in 1898 by terms of the Treaty of Paris." At the mention of Paris, my father's interest increased, his eyes twinkled, and he began to recall in detail his youthful days in Paris as an apprentice tailor in 1920, and how he had worked in a shop near the Rue de la Paix.

As my father reminisced about Paris, and as I kept my finger pressed on the paragraph about the treaty, I could almost *feel* the mental connection clicking in my head: Paris, my father, the Philippines, Guam, Puerto Rico, and the official termination of the Spanish-American War by the terms of the Paris Treaty of 1898. And as I now incorporated this information into my answers, it brought my examination to an auspicious conclusion—and I still had five minutes left to fill in the blank spaces of the earlier questions.

Racing toward what I hoped would be a worthy finish, jotting down whatever seemed plausible in these frantic final moments, I found myself looking around the room every few seconds to see how my classmates were faring. In the first row I observed that two of the smarter students were idling comfortably at their desks, apparently having completed the examination and handed it in to Sister Irma. They were Bobby Becotte, the son of a local policeman, and Mary Chester, a realtor's daughter who gradually was becoming even prettier than Rosemary Kurtz. Mary Chester's family fortunes seemed to be rising, too, for word had gotten around town that her father had bought a secluded mainland mansion that had a private tennis court and had once belonged to a flamboyant scion of Ocean City's founding family of Methodist ministers—Harvey Lake, who during the 1920s drove around the island in a flashy Duesenberg. Behind Mary Chester sat three mainland boys who wore brass Army buckles and were still struggling with the examination; and across from me, I could see that Rosemary Kurtz was reading over her answers with a composed expression. And behind *her*, with his sharp copyist corneas blazing down on her paper, reproducing her answers on *his* paper as quickly as possible before the bell rang, was Billy Maenner.

I could not believe how blatant he was. He sat with his neck stretched forward and, seemingly unconcerned that he might be caught in the act by Sister Irma, he forthrightly filled in the blanks of his paper with Rosemary's responses. I watched with amazement as he concentrated with hawklike attention on Rosemary's page, zooming in over her shoulder to consume piece by piece the content of her intellect and then, with dizzying speed, to appropriate all that he saw. As the bell rang and I put my pencil down, I furtively leaned across the aisle to scrutinize more closely what Billy had copied. In addition to her answers, I noticed that he had neatly printed, in the upper right corner of his page, her name—"Rosemary Kurtz."

Stupefied, I said nothing. Should I whisper to him to erase her name? It occurred to me to do that, but before I could act, he walked quickly up the aisle behind Rosemary to place his examination paper on the pile in the center of Sister Irma's desk. As I followed with my paper, I looked to see whether Sister Irma had observed anything unusual, but her attentions were devoted only to how neatly the students were placing their exams on her desk. She wanted all the papers to be stacked in a straight pile, with the edges even; if the edges were infinitesimally askew, she would immediately tidy them up with the tips of her chalky white fingers. Then, after all the students had delivered their papers, Sister Irma carefully tucked them into her black leather briefcase. After the Christmas holidays, she would return them to us with her grades. Between now and then, I could only wonder what her reaction would be when she saw the same student's name on two examinations in distinctly different handwriting. Perhaps it would amuse her. Perhaps it would make her furious.

After returning to my desk to await the start of Sister Helen's geography class, I sat gazing up at the blackboard, admiring the flying row of what might be the last flight of Billy Maenner's guardian angels.

I drifted through the rest of the school day peacefully and inattentively, relieved that the examination was behind me and that I had a vacation to look forward to, starting the next afternoon. For me it would not be a real vacation—I would be helping out in the store during the busy holiday season; but, except for the task of putting cardboard guards on the hangers, the time I spent in the store was usually diverting and pleasant.

I did not mind dusting the glass cases or cleaning the mirrors in my mother's dress department, and I enjoyed accompanying the drivers in the trucks that traveled the length of the island, stopping at small midtown hotels or at customers' homes to deliver ticketed garments in boxes or brown paper bags, and at the same time collect rumpled trousers, jackets, and overcoats, which we took back to the store to be dry-cleaned—or, as my father insisted on calling it, "French dry-cleaned."

While there was absolutely nothing Gallic or special about the process used at my father's plant—the clothes were spun around in a large standard circular basin afloat with naphtha, then tossed into a drying machine, then conveyed to the pressers—my father liked to embellish his business with a certain socially acceptable foreign éclat whenever possible. Which was why his newspaper advertising in the local weekly always specified "French dry-cleaning"; and why he prominently hung on the wall of the store his grandiloquent French tailor's diploma (signed in Paris in 1920 with the flourishing hand of his cousin Antonio); and why the side panels of the trucks displayed, in addition to the store's name in Gothic lettering, my father's coat of arms in the shape of an opened pair of scissors and crossed needles, and under it his motto in Latin: *Pro vobis optimum,* For you the best.

The white-and-black-trimmed trucks, Fords purchased from Rosemary Kurtz's father, were such spacious, high-roofed vans that a grown man could stand inside without stooping and I could swing from the overhead clothes pipes as if I were in my own private gym.

My job during these outings was to assist the driver when necessary in carrying large quantities of clothing in or out of the truck, and to write up the voucher slips on all the clothing that we collected to be cleaned— this latter chore being one that I especially relished, for it allowed me to pick through other people's pockets with impunity and with a thrilling sense of anticipation.

It was remarkable how careless men in particular were about leaving things in the pockets of their jackets and pants, and after a single day's excursion my booty often included fountain pens, nail clippers, toll tickets for the bridge to Atlantic City, love letters, cigarettes, unopened packages of chewing gum, tubes of Chap Stick, Trojan condoms, keys, matchbooks with women's names and phone numbers written on the inside cover, handkerchiefs, and countless other things, including, of course, money. One day I found five twenty-dollar bills that had been folded into a small rectangular shape and tucked into the watch pocket of a man's vest.

All the paper money I found, along with any object of more than a dollar's value (I chewed the gum, threw away the Trojans), I later relinquished to my mother, who then notified the customer and arranged for the items to be returned. But I never felt obligated to report the discovery of change, which, while never a sizable amount on any given day, added up to cover my cinema and soda fountain expenses during the weekend.

As I stood in the school corridor after my last class waiting for the bell that would signify it was our homeroom's turn to get our coats in the cloakroom, I was trying to remember what film would be playing in town this weekend—was it the revival of *The Hunchback of Notre Dame*? or was it *The Phantom of the Opera,* which starred one of my mother's favorites, Nelson Eddy?—when suddenly my classmate Bobby Becotte came over and asked: "Why weren't you at the altar boy meeting this afternoon?"

I groaned; and after cursing my lapsed memory and chronic capacity for daydreaming, I raced down the hall toward the sacristy, hoping that I would find Sister Rita and might offer her some acceptable excuse that I planned to concoct along the way. When I arrived, however, the sacristy was empty. But on a table in the middle of the room I did see a small white envelope addressed to me. These envelopes were given to the altar boys every week, and they contained a card notifying us of what Masses we were scheduled to serve. But on this occasion it would also list the names of those altar boys who had been chosen for Midnight Mass, the service that most of the parish, including my parents, would attend, and that I yearned to be a part of.

Slowly I opened the envelope. Then, reading the card, I felt all at once a surge of anger and the agony of being left out. I was not on the list. Instead, I had received the least desirable assignment: Christmas Day at seven a.m.

Mr. Fitzgerald had delivered his message.

8.

AFTER SCHOOL I decided to walk home, avoiding the bus. It was a fourteen-block walk in the cold, but the light drizzle that had fallen through most of the day had stopped, and I wanted to spend some time alone before tending to my obligations in the store. I left the school building through a side door, then hastened across the damp gravel yard past the Maypole toward a concrete path that cut between two vacated apartment houses and led to a side street. Twice I heard a boy's voice calling out to me from the front of the building, where moments before I had noticed a line of students waiting to board the bus.

I headed toward Wesley Avenue, which in winter was the quietest street in this town of quiet winter streets. It extended through the center of the island, midway through the bay and the ocean, and was flanked by once grand Victorian houses now deteriorating with age and neglect; too expensive to heat, they were occupied only in summertime, by people who were attracted to their low rent. Although I could hear the pounding of the waves as I walked, I knew from the complaints of summer customers in the store that Wesley Avenue was an inconvenient walk to the beach when the sidewalks were burning hot, and that on sweltering August evenings the ocean breeze barely was felt on the verandas of these spacious old homes. Our dry-cleaning trucks did scant winter business along this wide street, for which I was most grateful—nothing could have appealed to me less at this moment than seeing a familiar face and, as I did with customers in the store, feeling an obligation to be convivial.

Not for this reason alone did I proceed with a certain ease and reposeful contentment along Wesley Avenue. This was the route my mother had always taken, with me in a baby carriage, when she strolled on mild afternoons during the 1930s from her bridal cottage on the north end of the island to visit my father at the store downtown. In our photo album I have studied snapshots that she had paused to take along the way, of me sitting in the carriage, a rattle in my hand, the familiar houses of Wesley Avenue in the background, showing early signs of abandonment.

The Depression had already debased the resort economy; the town's leading bank had gone into receivership, dollars had been replaced by scrip, and these homes, which the leading Methodist families had proudly occupied at the turn of the century, were soon in foreclosure or were forced to open their doors to monthly boarders or to frugal vacationers who in summer would complain about the ten-minute walk to the beach.

Still, as I walked along carrying my schoolbag, feeling in my surroundings a remoteness from my disappointment, it seemed to me that with coats of bright paint and the repair of a few filigreed fences, this tattered part of town could once again reflect the better times of the past, an age of splendor and innocence, of women in frilly long dresses carrying parasols through the park I was now approaching.

In the center of the park, surrounded by trees that rose as high as possible in a community founded on sand, was the Methodist Tabernacle, a large frame building with a cupola that was completed in 1881 by the devotees of John Wesley. Leading the settlers who spiritually shaped the island, and who were ministers in the Tabernacle, were the three Lake brothers, one of whom, the Reverend Wesley Lake, sired the tennis-playing son who in the 1920s would drive the Duesenberg. Near the Tabernacle's main entrance was a cedar tree with a bronze tablet that memorialized the founding ministers' first meeting here in 1881; and at the other end of the park, pointed toward the business district that was two blocks to the west, was a Revolutionary War cannon that had been washed ashore with a wrecked British warboat in 1777.

As I walked along the path near the cannon, I saw three young soldiers in trench coats bent in front of the cannon reading its inscription. There were many soldiers in town now, some of them daytime visitors from the military hospital in Atlantic City, but most of them local men on home leave for the holidays. Their photographs had been appearing frequently in the town newspaper since the war began, and in the past week I had recognized some of them as they strolled up and down the main street in their uniforms, waving at the pretty girls who worked in the small shops and the five-and-dime; and in the last year I had heard several stories about such young women suddenly quitting their jobs to run off with servicemen. Even the older blond waitress at the luncheonette who had been romantically involved with the married entrepreneur on the boardwalk, and whose leopard coat still hung unclaimed in my parents' cold storage vault, had abruptly left town after Thanksgiving with a Coast Guard officer who was stationed in Camden. Since then, in the window of the luncheonette, there had been a sign to which there had apparently been little response: "Waitress Wanted."

If none of my mother's salesladies had yet disappeared with a serviceman, it was not for lack of opportunities; for every day there were military men in the store, leaving off their uniforms to be cleaned and pressed, or requesting to have insignias or stripes sewn on in a hurry. The men seemed *always* to be in a hurry, wanting overnight service for cleaning and pressing, and insisting that their new military stripes be sewn on their sleeves while they sat waiting, jacketless, on the delicate chairs my mother had placed near the fitting rooms of her dress department. It was understandable to my parents, of course, that these proud young men, having just been promoted from private to corporal, or from corporal to sergeant, would want to exhibit promptly the symbols of their elevation, but there were insufficient numbers of tailors and seamstresses in the workroom to do these jobs—for which my parents patriotically accepted no money. Yet the slowness of the work often resulted in unpleasant exchanges between the impatient soldiers and my frustrated father.

It was the demanding manner of many of these young men that most aggravated my father, whose Italian village upbringing had always stressed respect for one's elders. And yet the exigencies of the war, and the jingoism that now prevailed on this flag-waving island—in which the latest recruitment posters displayed a fat and ranting Mussolini even more villainous than Hitler or Tojo—seemed to heighten my father's sensitivity to his Italian accent and force him to repress his emotions.

In the store even I at times perceived him as a citizen of questionable status, an alien surrounded by soldiers of occupation. Indeed, his entire business often appeared to be under military supervision, with soldiers blocking the aisle to the dry-cleaning counter while others sat near the dressing rooms, smoking and exchanging barracks talk. Occasionally one of the soldiers, impatient to receive his uniform, on which chevrons were being sewn, would walk boldly back into the workroom, an area that had always been off-limits to customers. As if on an inspection tour, he would wander among the employees seated along the benches with their needles and thread. Spotting his chevrons and seeing that they had not all been sewn on, the soldier would ask, loudly, "How much longer is this going to take?" All the workers would look up, expressionless, their needles pointed into olive drab jackets or sailors' blue blouses or the high-collared greenish uniforms of the Marine Corps; and my father, from his table in the rear of the room, would reply: "Just a few minutes more." Then the heads of the men and women would again be bent, and their needles would continue to worm their way through the fabric—including a needle sometimes held in the unsteady hand of Jet, the presser, who in emergency situations was recruited to help sew on chevrons, while a mounting pile of unpressed civilian clothes remained untouched on his table.

Supporting the military seemed to be the mission of all the shopkeepers along the avenue (many had banners in their windows, with stars indicating that they had family members in the service); and the town newspaper constantly reminded its readers to write letters often to those GIs who were unable to be home. In a recent editorial the paper urged the residents of Ocean City not to complain about the fighter planes that "shave our rooftops," awakening babies and elderly invalids, because the town's tiny airstrip on the south end of the island was being used for a worthy cause: it was where naval pilots were undergoing accelerated training in carrier landing.

Shortly after this editorial, the newspaper published a front-page story with a photograph announcing the death of the first local man in the war. Lieutenant Edgar Ferguson, who had worked in the post office and had graduated from Ocean City High School, was a veteran of the North African and Sicilian campaigns. He had died on the battlefield in Italy, not far from my father's birthplace.

My father had attended the memorial service with other members of the Rotary Club, had expressed his sympathies to the lieutenant's family, and then had left early to return to the store, where, I recall, he was both distracted and short-tempered as he gave me my list of duties for the afternoon. This was in mid-November, shortly before Thanksgiving, and my mother later explained to me that my father had just received word from someone overseas who had connections with the Italian army that his youngest brother, Domenico, assigned to the Italian infantry, was listed as missing somewhere in the Balkans or Russia.

I had seen my father tuck the overseas envelope into the drawer of his desk in his small balcony office. He always kept the drawer locked, and it was packed with the letters that had been sent from overseas and had been read by my mother. It also contained photographs of our Italian relatives, including several snapshots of the now missing Domenico Talese, about whom my father had spoken to me so often and emotionally in the recent past. My uncle Domenico was the only foreign relative whom I envisioned in terms beyond snapshots, mostly because Domenico's life, or his life as it was recounted to me by my mother, seemed to be filled with great drama and danger.

Eleven years younger than my father, Domenico was born in Maida in 1914, a few months after their father, Gaetano, had returned to the village to die of his disease. When Domenico was six years old, my father left Maida, and the two brothers had not seen each other in more than twenty years—which was probably why Domenico had written so frequently and descriptively, usually with photographs enclosed: he did not want to be forgotten by his older brother in America, or to be remembered merely as the shy six-year-old who had stood waving good-bye with the other Talese relatives at the Maida train station in the spring of 1920.

In 1937, Domenico had been drafted by the Italian army; and because Mussolini was supporting General Franco's cause in the Spanish Civil War, Domenico was dispatched along with many Italian troops to Cádiz, where during the next year he was assigned to battle units and twice was hospitalized with bullet wounds. But the most frightening moment that he wrote about from Spain occurred on a day when he was unscathed in battle.

Crouched in the trenches, my uncle Domenico overheard a conversation between two Italian soldiers nearby in which one was saying: "I was born and raised in a time of war, and I'm *still* in a war!" The other soldier asked, "When were you born?" To which the first soldier moaned, as if the day carried a curse: "April 16, 1914." On hearing this, my uncle Domenico's interest perked up, for he *too* had been born on that day, in the same year!

"Hey," my uncle yelled over the trench, "what's your name?" "Domenico Talese," came the reply. *"Domenico Talese!"* my uncle exclaimed. "That's *my* name!" My uncle immediately poked his head up, and, seeing that his namesake had also risen above the trench, he examined a dark-eyed helmeted man with similar facial features—who, smiling and holding up a flask, said: "I'm Domenico Talese of Naples! Come over, let's drink!"

"Yes," my uncle said. "I'll tell the lieutenant." Edging his way toward the lieutenant, who stood yards away in the other direction, my uncle was requesting permission for the visit, when suddenly he was jolted by an explosion behind him. Moments after the dirt had settled and the smoke had cleared, my uncle turned to see that the trench in which his namesake and the other soldier had stood was now completely gone. It had been eliminated by a direct hit from an artillery shell. Domenico Talese of Naples had been blown out of sight, plucked from the earth and carried into oblivion before my uncle could learn exactly where in Naples he had lived, or how they were related.

Shortly after the end of the Spanish Civil War, Domenico was recalled into the army for World War II; and in the autumn of 1942 he had been on a troopship bound for Crete when a British submarine torpedoed the vessel. With five hundred other Italian soldiers, Domenico sank into the sea. My uncle did not know how to swim. But he grabbed on to a large piece of floating lumber and was able to remain afloat for six hours, and was then rescued by an Italian cruiser. After eight days in the hospital, he was sent on to Crete.

For many months my father heard nothing of Domenico's whereabouts, except that his unit had been transported by German planes to the European theater. And then, just before the memorial service in Ocean City for Lieutenant Ferguson, my father learned that Domenico was officially listed as missing.

It had never been easy for me to think of Domenico Talese as my uncle—not only because I had never seen him (and now perhaps never would), but because in all of his photographs he looked so different from my father: there was in his pose an almost careless disregard for what people might think of him, a rough-hewn audacity that bordered on bravado and was antithetical to everything I had been taught at home; and the way he wore his peaked military cap, pushed back on his head, revealing a tuft of dark hair above his forehead, was an affectation that my father would have considered roguish. Certainly Domenico's uniform contributed to my sense of dissociation: there was a small star on each lapel, a royal crown and crossed rifles on the insignia of his hat, and the chevron stripes on his sleeve pointed downward, opposite from the upward-pointed stripes of American soldiers.

But I liked my uncle's looks, and what made him most appealing to me was the lighthearted, mildly mischievous hint of the bachelor conscript-adventurer, a man with a live-today, die-tomorrow attitude that was totally at odds with my father's measured demeanor. It was as if my father's unlived youth had been inherited by Domenico, who was enjoying it to the fullest if he had not already taken it to his grave. My father, on the other hand—even in those photos taken of him as a teenager in Paris—was always pictured in the sartorial style of a middle-aged man, and with a posture that exuded serious purpose. For my father *was* a serious man, a man who listened to serious music, and who at dinner expressed serious thoughts, and who complained that many contemporary American films, plays, and radio programs were too juvenile, unsuitable for the serious mind.

This most serious self had only increased as the war added to his anxiety, and it had now reached such a point that I was reluctant to express an opinion, fearing that I might provoke him to anger with my opposing view. Sensing that he might explode at any moment, I kept my distance, or trod lightly in his presence, and kept secret as best I could my own tribulations at parochial school.

As I approached the shop on this late Monday afternoon, and watched the trolley from Atlantic City pause at the corner near the bank before clanging on toward the boardwalk, I knew that I would reveal nothing of the decision that had excluded me from the list of altar boys who would be serving Mass on Christmas Eve. To mention this would only invite questions and perhaps prompt my father to make another in the series of futile telephone calls on my behalf to the Mother Superior. Instead, I intended to ride with my parents to Midnight Mass, and go with them through the front door of the church, where it would be inappropriate— and also too late—for a lengthy explanation or discussion of why I was not in the sacristy with the other altar boys. On the following morning, I would resignedly ride my bicycle to the seven-o'clock Mass.

This at least was what I had in mind as I swung my schoolbag off my shoulder and opened the plate-glass door to the shop—and saw, much to my amazement, that my usually controlled father was standing behind the dry-cleaning counter engaged in an animated dispute with a woman wearing a silver fox coat. Trying to slip past unnoticed, I tiptoed along the aisle of the dress department. My mother, who was occupied with customers near the fitting rooms, smiled at me uneasily as I passed; and then with a raised eyebrow she acknowledged the contretemps in a way that indicated she was as bewildered by it as I was.

I climbed the steps to my father's balcony office and seated myself behind a potted palm that provided camouflage. Now I could eavesdrop on the scene below and see spread out on the counter between my father and the lady a red silk cocktail dress. All at once I recognized this dress from having seen it during the previous week, when this same woman had brought it in to have it cleaned, and had made a point of requesting quick service because she wished to wear it to a party on Monday night, which was this evening. I remember that the counter clerk had taken the dress back to my father in the workroom, to ask if it could be properly cleaned in the allotted time. When he examined the dress my father noticed a small spot on the bodice, which was perhaps a stain that would require special, time-consuming treatment. For this reason he was reluctant to accept the dress, and I remember that he himself had walked out to the main room of the store to explain the problem to the woman.

"I'm sorry," I had heard my father say, "but I doubt we can get this back to you by Monday. This spot might be a liquor stain that can't be removed by dry-cleaning, and if we try washing it there's a good chance the dress will shrink. . . ."

"But can't you at least try?" she had pleaded; to which my father had said, "We can try, but we cannot guarantee it. I definitely wouldn't wash this dress, and yet if we dry-clean it—without taking the extra time to analyze that spot and have it specially treated—you'll only get the dress back on Monday looking no better than it does now."

"Oh, just do the best you can," the woman had said, shrugging her shoulders. And as she left the dress and walked toward the door, she said: "I'll see you on Monday."

Now she was back, and it seemed obvious that the cleaning of the red silk dress had brought happiness neither to the woman nor to my father. As they stood practically nose to nose across the counter, with the dress spread out on white tissue paper between them, I heard my father saying over and over, "I told you, I told you, but you wouldn't listen. . . ."

"I *was* listening," she replied, "but I didn't expect you people to make the dress worse."

"How did we make it worse?"

"You made the spot bigger!"

"Look, madam," my father said, sharply, "I've been in business in this town for more than twenty years, and I didn't stay in business that long by making spots bigger!"

"You not only made it bigger," she insisted, "but there is a spot in the back that wasn't there when I left it."

"*Now* you're saying that we not only make spots bigger, but we add spots also, is that right?" His face was taut with tension, anger.

"What I *am* saying," she replied firmly, "is what I said at the beginning. You have *ruined* my dress!"

"*You ruined your own dress!*" My father was now shouting. "You spilled liquor on it, and—"

"I want a *new* dress," she interrupted. "You've ruined my dress, and I want it replaced. . . ."

Suddenly my father slammed his fist against the counter and shouted: "I want you out of my store!"

"Not until we settle this," she replied; but then my mother, who had been watching all this time silently, undoubtedly embarrassed in front of her customers, walked over and said, "*Please,* can't we discuss this quietly. Perhaps tomorrow . . ."

"I have a party to go to tonight, and I want to settle this now!"

"*Out!*" my father said, pointing to the door. "I want you out of here, or I'm calling the cops."

"Well, you can call the cops," she said, glaring at him. "I'm getting my husband, and I'll be right back!"

Watching from behind the palms, my hands perspiring, I saw the woman stride out of the store, leaving the door open. My mother placed a hand on my father's arm, whispering something into his ear, but he began to shake his head. Across the room I could see the salesladies and their customers standing along the dress counters, speaking quietly among themselves. Everyone was waiting; and within a few moments, the husband appeared—a large man in a brown hat and a tan camel's-hair coat, smoking a cigar.

Heading straight for my father, he bellowed: "So you're the man who just insulted my wife!"

"I did *not* insult your wife," my father replied, in a steady voice. "I told her to get out of my store. And now I'm telling *you* to get out of my store!"

"Who do you think *you* are?" the man asked, getting closer to my father, who, standing behind the counter, now quickly took off his steel-rimmed glasses and handed them to my startled mother. Then the man paused and said something in a softer tone, so soft that I am not sure I heard it precisely; but my father surely heard it, because he suddenly left my mother's side, went back into the workroom while everybody in the store stood frozen in position as my mother called out, "Joe . . . Joe . . ."

Perhaps what the man had said—I *may* have heard it—was "dago." There was no other explanation for the fury that now possessed my father as he reappeared, a transformed figure carrying a long, heavy pair of scissors that were customarily used for cutting thick material or fur skin.

"*Out!*" he said, in a voice now coldly calm. "*Out!*" he repeated, as the man in the camel's-hair coat retreated, walking backward, not taking his eyes off my father, who repeated the word "Out!" as he walked, until the man had pushed the door open and stumbled into the wintry air. But before he left, he took one final look at my father and said: "You haven't seen the last of me yet! You'll soon be hearing from me again—with my *lawyer.* And we'll sue you for every dime you have. . . ."

My father showed no reaction, except the scissors in his right hand began to shake. My mother gently took the scissors and handed it to the white-haired seventy-seven-year-old tailor, who during the commotion had followed my father out of the workroom. Behind this tailor stood Jet and another presser from the workroom, shaking their heads. I left my hiding place behind the palm and walked down the steps to join the others. The salesladies and the two customers still left in the store slowly turned and began to look over some of the new dresses hung along the racks.

With my mother speaking to him softly, my father seemed to have regained his composure. But then, as he turned toward the dry-cleaning counter, the fury flared once more within him. There, on the counter, was the red dress. The couple had forgotten it, perhaps intentionally. Without saying a word, my father grabbed the silk dress, crumpled it into a ball, and quickly headed out the door.

"Follow him," my mother urged me; and I did, trailing a few paces behind as my father looked along the sidewalk for the couple, who were nowhere to be seen on the avenue crowded with Christmas shoppers. But then, near the corner, my father saw the man in the camel's-hair coat, climbing into a car. He ran in that direction, and I followed; but before my father could reach the car, it had pulled away from the curb. I could see that the man behind the wheel had turned his head and spotted my father—and, perhaps thinking that he still carried the scissors, had accelerated into the lane, with my father in swift pursuit.

When my father realized that he could not catch up and perhaps wrap the dress around the car's aerial, as I suspect was his intention, I saw him tighten his grip around the balled-up dress, cock his arm, and aim the dress toward the taillights of the moving car. And in that awkward pitching motion, he rocked back and heaved the garment with all his might; and I watched as it sailed through the air, suddenly catching a gust of ocean breeze that swept across the avenue—a breeze that took the dress higher into space and blew it in the direction of an oncoming trolley.

Then, like a magnet, the sparkling overhead wires and prongs atop the trolley seemed to suck the dress into the spinning wheel on the roof; and as my father and I watched, breathlessly, the dress was transformed into a flapping, torn flag and began its long, windy ride across the bay toward Atlantic City.

9.

THERE IS A certain type of mild mental disorder that is endemic in the tailoring trade, and it began to weave its way into my father's psyche during his apprentice days in Italy, when he worked in the shop of a volatile craftsman named Francesco Cristiani, whose male forebears had been tailors for four successive generations and had, without exception, exhibited symptoms of this occupational malady.

Although it has never attracted scientific curiosity and therefore cannot be classified by an official name, my father once described the disorder as a form of prolonged melancholia that occasionally erupted into cantankerous fits—the result, my father suggested, of excessive hours of slow, exacting, microscopic work that proceeds stitch by stitch, inch by inch, mesmerizing the tailor in the reflected light of a needle flickering in and out of the fabric.

A tailor's eye must follow a seam precisely, but his pattern of thought is free to veer off in different directions, to delve into his life, to ponder his past, to lament lost opportunities, create dramas, imagine slights, brood, exaggerate—in simple terms, the tailor when sewing has too much time to think.

My father, who served as an apprentice each day before and after school, was aware that certain tailors could sit quietly at the workbench for hours, cradling a garment between their bowed heads and crossed knees, and sew without exercise or much physical movement, without any surge of fresh oxygen to clear their brains—and *then,* with inexplicable suddenness, my father would see one of these men jump to his feet and take wild umbrage at a casual comment of a coworker, a trivial exchange that was not intended to provoke. And my father would often cower in a corner as spools and steel thimbles flew around the room—and, if goaded on by insensitive colleagues, the aroused tailor might reach for the workroom's favorite instrument of terror, the sword-length scissors.

There were also confrontations in the front of the store in which my father worked, disputes between the customers and the proprietor—the diminutive and vainglorious Francesco Cristiani, who took enormous pride in his occupation and believed that he, and the tailors under his supervision, were incapable of making a serious mistake; or, if they were, he was not likely to acknowledge it.

Once when a customer came in to try on a new suit but was unable to slip into the jacket because the sleeves were too narrow, Francesco Cristiani not only failed to apologize to the client but behaved as if insulted by the client's ignorance of the Cristiani shop's unique style in men's fashion. "You're not supposed to put your arms *through* the sleeves of this jacket!" Cristiani informed his client, in a superior tone. "This jacket is designed to be worn only *over the shoulders!*"

On another occasion, when Cristiani paused in the town square after lunch to listen to the Maida band during its midday concert, he noticed that the new uniform that had been delivered the day before to the third trumpeter showed a bulge behind the collar whenever the musician lifted the instrument to his lips.

Concerned that someone might notice it and cast aspersions on his status as a tailor, Cristiani dispatched my father, then a skinny boy of seven, to sneak up behind the bunting of the bandstand and, with furtive finesse, pull down on the end of the trumpeter's jacket whenever the bulge appeared. When the concert was over, Cristiani contrived a subtle means by which he was able to reacquire and repair the jacket.

But around this time, in the spring of 1911, there occurred a catastrophe for which there seemed no possible solution. The problem was so serious, in fact, that Cristiani's first reaction was to leave town for a while rather than remain in Maida to face the consequences. The incident that provoked such panic had taken place in Cristiani's workroom on the Saturday before Easter, and it centered around the damage done by an apprentice, accidentally but irreparably, to a new suit that had been made for one of Cristiani's most demanding customers—a man who was among the region's renowned *uomini rispettati,* men of respect, popularly known as the Mafia.

Before Cristiani became aware of the accident, he had enjoyed a prosperous morning in his shop collecting payment from several satisfied customers who had come in for the final try-on of their attire, which they would wear on the following day at the Easter *passeggiata,* the most exhibitionistic event of the year for the men of southern Italy. While the modest women of the village—except for the bolder wives of immigrants in America—would spend the day after Mass discreetly perched on their balconies, the men would stroll in the square, chatting with one another as they walked arm in arm, smoking and shiftily examining the fit of each other's new suits. Despite the poverty in southern Italy, or perhaps because of it, there was excessive emphasis on appearances—it was part of the region's syndrome to put on a good show, *fare una bella figura,* and most of the men who assembled in the piazza of Maida, and in dozens of similar squares throughout the south, were uncommonly knowledgeable about the art of fine tailoring.

They could assess in a few seconds the craft of another man's suit, could appraise each dexterous stitch, could appreciate the mastery of a tailor's most challenging task, the shoulder, from which more than twenty individualized parts of the jacket must hang in harmony and allow for fluidity. Almost every prideful male, when entering a shop to select fabric for a new suit, knew by heart the twelve principal measurements of his tailored body, starting with the distance between the neckline and the waist of the jacket, and ending with the exact width of the cuffs above the shoes. Among such men were many customers who had been dealing with the Cristiani family firm all of their lives, as had their fathers and grandfathers before them. Indeed, the Cristianis had been making men's clothes in southern Italy since 1806, when the region was controlled by Napoleon Bonaparte; and when Napoleon's brother-in-law Joachim Murat, who had been installed on the Naples throne in 1808, was assassinated in 1815 by a Spanish Bourbon firing squad in the village of Pizzo, twelve miles southwest of Maida, the wardrobe that he left behind included a suit made by Francesco Cristiani's great-grandfather.

But now, on this Holy Saturday in 1911, Francesco confronted a situation that could not benefit from his family's long tradition in the trade. In his hands he held a new pair of trousers that had an inch-long cut across the left knee, a cut that had been made by an apprentice who had been idling with a pair of scissors atop the table on which the trousers had been laid out for Cristiani's inspection. Although apprentices were repeatedly reminded that they were not to handle the heavy scissors—their main task was to sew on buttons and baste seams—some young men unwittingly violated the rule in their eagerness to gain tailoring experience. But what magnified the youth's delinquency in this situation was that the damaged trousers had been made for the *mafioso,* whose name was Vincenzo Castiglia.

A first-time customer from the nearby city of Cosenza, Vincenzo Castiglia was so blatant about his criminal profession that, while being measured for the suit one month before, he had asked Cristiani to allow ample room inside the jacket for the holstered pistol that he wore strapped around his chest. On that same occasion, however, Mr. Castiglia had made several other requests that elevated him in the eyes of his tailor as a man who had a sense of style and knew what might flatter his rather corpulent figure. For example, Mr. Castiglia had requested that the suit's shoulders be cut extra wide so that it would give his hips a more narrow appearance; and he sought to distract attention from his protruding belly by ordering a pleated waistcoat with wide pointed lapels, and also a hole in the center of the waistcoat through which a gold chain could be looped and linked to his diamond pocket watch.

In addition, Mr. Castiglia specified that the hems of his trousers be turned up, in accord with the latest Continental fashion; and as he peered into Cristiani's workroom in the back, he expressed satisfaction on observing that the tailors were all sewing by hand and not using the popularized sewing machine, which, despite its speedy stitching, lacked the capacity for the special molding of a fabric's seams and angles that was possible only in the hands of a talented tailor.

Bowing with appreciation, the tailor Cristiani had assured Mr. Castiglia that his shop would never succumb to the graceless mechanized invention, even though sewing machines were now widely used by some leading tailors in Europe and also in America. With the mention of America, Mr. Castiglia smiled and said that he had once visited the New Land, and added that he had several relatives who had settled there. (Among them was a young cousin, Francesco Castiglia, who in future years, beginning in the era of Prohibition, would achieve great notoriety and wealth under the name Frank Costello.)

In the weeks that followed, after Vincenzo Castiglia had placed a down payment on the suit, which had been promised for the day before Easter, and had left in a carriage driven by a rifle-bearing coachman, Cristiani devoted much attention to satisfying the *mafioso*'s specifications, and he was finally proud of the sartorial results—until, on that Saturday, he discovered under a paper pattern spread out on the table Mr. Castiglia's new pants with the inch-long slash across the left knee.

Screaming with anguish and fury, Cristiani soon obtained a confession from an apprentice who admitted to cutting discarded pieces of cloth on the edges of the pattern under which the trousers had been found. Cristiani stood silently, shaking for several minutes, surrounded by his equally concerned and speechless associates. Cristiani could, of course, run and hide in the hills, as had been his first inclination; or he could return the money to the *mafioso* after explaining what had happened, and then offer up the guilty apprentice as a sacrificial lamb to be dealt with appropriately. In this instance, however, there were special inhibiting circumstances. The culpable apprentice was the young nephew of Cristiani's wife, Maria. His wife had been born Maria Talese. She was the only sister of Cristiani's best friend, Gaetano Talese, then working in America. And Gaetano's seven-year-old son, the apprentice Joseph Talese—who would become my father—was now crying convulsively.

As Cristiani sought to comfort his remorseful nephew, his mind kept searching for some plausible solution. The trousers were obviously ruined beyond repair. There was no way, in the few hours remaining before Mr. Castiglia's visit, to make a second pair of trousers even if they had matching material in stock. Nor was there any way to obscure perfectly the cut in the fabric even with a marvelous job of mending.

While his fellow tailors kept insisting that the wisest move was to close the shop and leave a note for Mr. Castiglia pleading illness, or some other excuse that might delay a confrontation, Cristiani firmly reminded them that nothing could absolve him from his failure to deliver the *mafioso*'s suit on time and that it was mandatory to find a solution now, at once.

As the noon bell rang from the church in the main square, and as all the other stores in Maida began to close for the midday siesta, Cristiani grimly announced: "There will be no siesta for any of us today. This is not the time for food and rest—it is the time for sacrifice and meditation. So I want all of you to stay where you are, and think of something that may save us from disaster. . . ."

He was interrupted by some grumbling from the other tailors, who resented missing their lunch and afternoon nap; but Cristiani overruled them with a raised hand and immediately dispatched one of his apprentices to tell the tailors' wives not to expect the return of their husbands until sundown. Then he instructed the other apprentices, including my father, to pull the draperies across the windows and to lock the shop's front and back doors. And then, for the next few minutes, Cristiani's entire staff of a dozen men and boys, as if participating in a wake, quietly congregated within the walls of the darkened shop.

My father sat in one corner, still stunned by the magnitude of his misdeed. Near him sat other apprentices, irritated at my father but nonetheless obedient to their master's order that they remain in confinement. In the center of the workroom, seated among his tailors, was Francesco Cristiani, a small, wiry man with a tiny moustache, holding his head in his hands and looking up every few seconds to glance again at the trousers that lay before him, as if to remind himself that the knee slash was *real* and would not simply disappear with the next blink of an eye.

Several minutes later, with a snap of his fingers, Cristiani rose to his feet. Although he was barely five feet, six inches tall, his erect carriage, fine styling, and panache lent substance to his presence. There was also a gleam in his eyes now as he looked around the room.

"I think I have thought of something," he announced slowly, pausing to let the suspense build until he had everyone's total attention.

"What is it?" asked his most senior tailor.

"What I can do," Cristiani continued, "is make a cut across the *right* knee that will exactly match the damaged left knee, and . . ."

"Are you crazy?" interrupted the older tailor.

"Let me finish, you imbecile!" Cristiani shouted, pounding his small fist on the table; ". . . and then I can sew up both cuts of the trousers with decorative seams that will match exactly, and later I will explain to Mr. Castiglia that he is the first man in this part of Italy to be wearing trousers designed in the newest fashion, the knee-seamed fashion—the latest rage of Paris, or London, or Vienna, or . . ."

As his voice trailed off, the others listened with astonishment.

"But *maestro*," one of the younger tailors said, in a cautious tone of respect, "won't Mr. Castiglia notice, after you introduce this 'new fashion,' that we tailors ourselves are not wearing trousers that follow this fashion?"

Cristiani raised his eyebrows slightly.

"A good point," he conceded, as a pessimistic mood returned to the room. And then again his eyes flashed and he said: "But we *will* follow the fashion! We will make cuts in *our* knees and then sew them up with seams similar to Mr. Castiglia's." Before the men could protest, he quickly added: "But we will *not* be cutting up our own trousers. We'll use those trousers we keep in the widows' closet!"

Immediately everyone turned toward the locked door of a closet in the rear of the workroom, within which were hung dozens of suits last worn by men now dead—suits that bereaving widows, not wishing to be reminded of their departed spouses, had passed on to Cristiani in the hope that he would give the clothing away to passing strangers who might wear them in distant villages and towns.

Now Cristiani was planning to revive the trousers of the dead with his slashed-knee fashion; and while his fellow tailors were initially appalled by the idea, they were soon swayed by the exuberance with which he flung open the closet door, pulled several pairs of trousers off the suit hangers, and tossed them to his tailors, urging a quick try-on. He himself was already standing in his white cotton underwear and black garters, searching for a pair of trousers that might accommodate his slight stature; and when he succeeded, he slipped them on, climbed up on the table, and stood momentarily like a proud model in front of his men. "See," he said, pointing to the length and width, "a perfect fit."

As the other tailors began to pick and choose from the wide selection of clothing discarded by the widows, Cristiani was now down from the table, off with the trousers, and, holding a scissors in his hand, carefully beginning to cut across the right kneecap of the *mafioso*'s pants, duplicating the already damaged left knee. Then he applied similar incisions to the knees of the trousers he had chosen to wear himself.

"Now, pay close attention," he called out to his men as he sat on a stool in his underwear, with the two pairs of trousers spread before him. With a flourish of his silk-threaded needle, he applied the first stitch to the dead man's trousers, piercing the lower edge of the torn knee with an inner stitch that he adroitly looped to the upper edge—a bold, circular motion that he repeated several times until he had securely reunited the center of the knee with a small, round embroidered wreathlike design half the size of a dime.

Then he proceeded to sew, on the right side of the wreath, a half-inch seam that was slightly tapered and tilted upward at the end; and, after reproducing this seam on the left side of the wreath, he had created a minuscule image of a distant bird with spread wings, flying directly toward the viewer, a bird that most resembled a peregrine falcon. Cristiani thus originated a trouser style with wing-tipped knees.

"Well, what do you think?" he asked his men who surrounded him, indicating by his offhanded manner that he did not really care what they thought. As they shrugged their shoulders and murmured in the background, he peremptorily continued: "All right now, quickly, cut the knees of those trousers you'll be wearing, and stitch them with the embroidered design you've just seen." Expecting no opposition, and receiving none, Cristiani lowered his head to concentrate entirely on his own task: to finish the second knee of the trousers he would wear and then to begin, meticulously, the job on Mr. Castiglia's trousers.

In the latter's case, not only did Cristiani plan to embroider a winged design with silk thread that matched exactly the shade of the thread used on the buttonholes of the jacket of Mr. Castiglia's suit, but he also would insert a section of silk lining within the front part of the trousers, extending from the thighs to the shins, that would protect Mr. Castiglia's knees from the scratchy feel of the embroidered inner stitching, and would also diminish the friction against the knee seams when Mr. Castiglia was out promenading at the *passeggiata*.

For the next two hours, everyone worked in feverish silence. As Cristiani and the other tailors affixed the winged design on the knees of all the trousers, the apprentices helped with the minor alterations, sewing on buttons, ironing cuffs, and attending to other details that would make the dead men's trousers as presentable as possible on the bodies of the tailors. Francesco Cristiani, of course, allowed none but himself to handle the *mafioso*'s garments; and as the church bells rang, signaling the end of the siesta, Cristiani scrutinized with admiration the stitching that he had done, and he privately thanked his namesake in heaven, Saint Francis of Paola, to whom he had been praying throughout this ordeal, for his inspired guidance with the needle.

Now there was the sound of activity in the square: the jingles of horse-drawn wagons, the cries of food vendors, the voices of shoppers passing back and forth along the cobblestone road in front of Cristiani's doorstep. The window draperies of the shop had just been opened, and my father and another apprentice were posted beyond the door with instructions to call in with words of warning as soon as they caught a glimpse of Mr. Castiglia's carriage.

Inside, the tailors stood in a row behind Cristiani, famished and fatigued, and hardly comfortable in their dead men's trousers with wingtipped knees; but their anxiety and fear concerning Mr. Castiglia's forthcoming reaction to his Easter suit dominated their emotions. Cristiani, on the other hand, seemed unusually calm. In addition to his newly acquired brown trousers, the cuffs of which touched his buttoned shoes with cloth tops, he wore a lapeled gray waistcoat over a striped shirt with a rounded white collar adorned by a burgundy cravat and pearl stickpin. In his hand, on a wooden hanger, he held Mr. Castiglia's three-piece gray herringbone suit, which, moments before, he had softly brushed and pressed for the final time. The suit was still warm.

At twenty minutes after four, my father came running through the doorway, and, in a high voice that could not betray his panic, he announced: *"Sta arrivando!"*—He's coming. Moments later a black carriage, drawn by two horses, clangorously drew to a halt in front of the shop. After the rifle-toting coachman hopped off to open the door and extend his hand up toward his passenger, the portly dark figure of Vincenzo Castiglia descended the two steps to the sidewalk, followed by a lean man in a wide-brimmed hat, long cloak, and studded boots.

Mr. Castiglia removed his gray fedora and with a handkerchief wiped the road dust from his brow. He entered the shop, where Cristiani hastened forward to greet him and, holding the new suit high on its hanger, proclaimed: "Your wonderful Easter costume awaits you!" Mr. Castiglia shook hands and examined the suit without comment; then, after politely refusing Cristiani's offer of a drop of wine, he directed his bodyguard to help him remove his jacket so that he could immediately try on his Easter apparel.

Cristiani and the other tailors stood quietly nearby, watching the holstered pistol strapped to Castiglia's chest sway with his movements as he extended his arms and received over his shoulders the gray lapeled waistcoat, followed by the broad-shouldered jacket. Inhaling as he buttoned up his waistcoat and jacket, Mr. Castiglia turned toward the three-sectioned mirror next to the fitting room; and after inspecting and admiring the reflection of himself from every angle, and seeing as well the unblinking eyes of a half-dozen tailors, and then turning toward his bodyguard, who nodded approvingly, Mr. Castiglia commented in a commanding voice: *"Perfetto!"*

"Mille grazie," responded Cristiani, bowing slightly as he carefully removed the trousers from the hanger and handed them to Mr. Castiglia. Excusing himself, Mr. Castiglia walked into the fitting room. He closed the door. A few of the tailors began to pace around the showroom, but Cristiani stood near the fitting room, whistling softly to himself. The bodyguard, still wearing his cloak and hat, sat comfortably in a chair, his legs crossed, smoking a thin cigar. The apprentices gathered in the back room, out of sight, except for my nervous father, who remained in the showroom busily arranging and rearranging stacks of material on a counter, while keeping an eye focused on the fitting room.

For more than a minute not a word was spoken. The only sounds heard were made by Mr. Castiglia as he changed his trousers. First there was the thump of his shoes dropping to the floor. Then the faint whishing rustle of trouser legs being stepped into. Seconds later, a loud bump against the wooden partition as Mr. Castiglia presumably lost his balance while standing on one leg. After a sigh, a cough, and the creaking sound of shoe leather—more silence. But then, suddenly, a deep voice from behind the door bellowed: *"Maestro!"* Then louder: *"MAESTRO!"*

The door bolted open, revealing the glowering face and crouched figure of Mr. Castiglia, his fingers pointing downward toward his bent knees and the winged design on the trousers. Waddling toward Cristiani, he yelled: *"Maestro—che avete fatto qui?"*—What have you done here?

The bodyguard jumped, scowling at Cristiani. My father closed his eyes. The tailors stepped back. But Francesco Cristiani stood straight and still, remaining impassive even when the bodyguard's hand moved inside his cloak.

"What have you done?" Mr. Castiglia repeated, still squatting on bent knees, as if suffering from locked joints. Cristiani watched him silently for a second or two; but finally, in the authoritarian tone of a teacher chiding a student, Cristiani responded: "Oh, how disappointed I am in you! How sad and insulted am I by your failure to appreciate the honor I was trying to bestow upon you, because I thought you deserved it—but sadly, I was wrong. . . ."

Before the confused Vincenzo Castiglia could open his mouth, Cristiani continued: "You demanded to know what I had done with your trousers—not realizing that what I had done was introduce you to the modern world, which is where I thought you belonged. When you first entered this shop for a fitting last month, you seemed so different from the backward people of this region. So sophisticated. So individualistic. You had traveled to America, you said, had seen the New World, and I assumed that you were in touch with the contemporary spirit of freedom— but I greatly misjudged you. . . . New clothes, alas, do not remake the man within. . . ."

Carried away by his own grandiloquence, Cristiani turned toward his senior tailor, who stood closest to him, and he impulsively repeated an old southern Italian proverb that he regretted uttering immediately after the words had slipped out of his mouth.

"Lavar la testa all'asino è acqua persa," Cristiani intoned: Washing a donkey's head is a waste of water.

Stunned silence swept through the entire shop. My father cringed behind the counter. Cristiani's tailors, horrified by his provocation, gasped

and trembled as they saw Mr. Castiglia's face redden, his eyes narrow—
and no one would have been surprised if the next sound were the explosion of a gun. Indeed, Cristiani himself lowered his head and seemed
resigned to this fate—but strangely, having now gone too far to turn back,
Cristiani recklessly repeated his words: *"Lavar la testa . . ."*—Washing a
donkey's head is a waste of water.

Mr. Castiglia did not respond. He sputtered, he bit his lips, but he
said not a word. Perhaps, having never before experienced such brazenness from anyone, particularly not from a tiny tailor, Mr. Castiglia was too
wonderstruck to act. Even his bodyguard now seemed paralyzed, with his
hand still inside his cloak. After a few more seconds of silence, the eyes in
Cristiani's lowered head moved tentatively upward, and he saw Mr. Castiglia standing with his shoulders slouched, his head hanging slightly, and
a glazed and remorseful look in his eyes. He then looked at Cristiani and
winced. Finally, he spoke.

"My late mother would use that expression when I made her angry,"
Mr. Castiglia confided softly. After a pause, he added, "She died when I
was very young."

"Oh, I am so sorry," Cristiani said, as the tension subsided in the
room. "I do hope, however, that you will accept my word that we *did* try
to make you a beautiful suit for Easter. I was just so disappointed that
your trousers, which are designed in the latest fashion, did not appeal to
you."

Looking down once again at the knees, Mr. Castiglia asked: *"This* is
the latest fashion?"

"Yes, indeed," Cristiani reassured him.

"Where?"

"In the great capitals of the world."

"But not here?"

"Not yet," Cristiani said. "You are the first among the men of this
region."

"But why does the latest fashion in this region have to begin with
me?" Mr. Castiglia asked, in a voice that now seemed uncertain.

"Oh, no, it has not really begun with you," Cristiani quickly corrected him. "We tailors have *already* adopted this fashion." And holding up
one of his trouser knees, he said: "See for yourself."

Mr. Castiglia looked down to examine Cristiani's knees; and then, as
he turned to survey the entire room, he saw the other tailors, one after another, each lift a leg and, nodding, point to the now familiar wings of the
infinitesimal bird.

"I see," Mr. Castiglia said softly. "And I see that I also owe you my apologies, *maestro*," he went on. "Sometimes it takes a while for a man to appreciate what is fashionable."

Then, after shaking Cristiani's hand and settling the financial account—but seemingly not wanting to linger a moment longer in this place where his uncertainty had been exposed—Mr. Castiglia summoned his obedient and speechless bodyguard and handed him his old suit. Wearing his new suit, and tipping his hat, Mr. Castiglia headed toward his carriage through the door that had been pulled wide open by my father.

10.

As Mr. Castiglia's carriage rumbled down the gravel road and finally disappeared behind the clouds of dust that rose along the verdant slopes of the olive-clustered hillside, the jubilant tailors started to remove the dead men's trousers and reclaim their own clothing—but Cristiani quickly stopped them with an upraised hand. "Stay dressed as you are! You heard me tell Mr. Castiglia that we have adopted this new fashion, and so now we must continue to follow it, at least for a week. We must be sure that if he returns to town, he will find us as he left us."

Despite much demurring, Cristiani imposed his will, as usual, and so for the next several days the tailors wore the wing-kneed trousers, which the apprentices regularly sponged and pressed; and my father, who was then not yet eight years of age, worked in the front of the shop, near the large window, so that he might keep an eye on the street and alert everyone should he observe the return of Mr. Castiglia's carriage.

Young Joseph Talese eagerly accepted this chore as part of his atonement, and he was very relieved that his uncle had retained him as an apprentice; for had Cristiani dismissed him, Joseph might have been forced to spend his nonschool hours toiling on the family farm—a place that, having worked there during the autumn harvest, he loathed with intensity. He hated its sounds and smells, its grunting, snorting animals, its horseflies incessantly buzzing around the dung-strewn stables and stalls.

On dry days, the farm roads were suffocatingly dusty. When it rained, they were ankle-deep in mud. During the harvest, when Joseph and the other students were excused from school so that they could help the farmers, they had to work in the fields among dozens of crude and bizarre-looking itinerant workers who came down from their hillside caves each morning to barter their labor for sackloads of olives and grapes, which they would later convert into cooking oil and heavy, intoxicating wine.

Joseph was repelled by the mere sight of these men from the caves. They were very dark and their skin was craggy; they rarely wore shoes or shirts, but rather worked in filthy, loose-fitting trousers held up by thick leather belts, from which hung small sheathed daggers; and on their heads were conical felt hats that had been out of style since the Middle Ages. Whenever they opened their mouths they showed several teeth missing; and when they communicated with one another, they did so with much hand gesturing and with rasping, guttural sounds understood by no one outside their group.

There were usually a number of women among them, a few of whom were larger and taller than the men—Amazonian figures with broad shoulders, round strong-boned faces, and thick dark hair that they braided high on their heads and covered with handkerchiefs. Leaning over in the fields to gather olives and grapes, they often allowed their breasts to fall out of their blouses; and since the lower halves of their long skirts were pulled up and tied at their waists with pieces of rope, the smooth naked flesh of their thighs was exposed to whoever wished to look. Joseph had never before seen a woman's thighs and breasts, and whenever he was sent to the fields he blushed with embarrassment even on observing this expanse of flesh from afar; and yet he was fascinated.

One day, with a bold sense of daring, he moved quietly through the cornstalks toward a partly naked woman who was working in the nearby fields under a row of olive trees. She was tall, with long muscular arms and large hands that vigorously shook the lower limbs of the trees to release the olives. When the olives had fallen onto the white sheets that she had laid along the ground, she bent over to gather them into sacks—exposing her dark-nippled breasts that protruded beyond the unbuttoned part of her white sackcloth blouse. She was working alone, there was no one near her; and as she shook the branches and filled one sack after another, Joseph could hear her heavy breathing above the sound of the flies and the rustling of the dry leaves in the hot autumn breeze that swept through the sprawling farmland.

Suddenly, she turned and glanced in Joseph's direction. He was about fifty feet away from her, standing within the thick cluster of cornstalks that rose above his head, a cover that he had assumed provided ideal camouflage. As she looked to the left, and then to the right, he could see that she was a sturdy woman of indeterminate age with a rawboned but pleasant face that was roasted brown by the sun and contrasted with her white breasts. Hanging between them was a small wooden crucifix attached to a string around her neck.

Still not spotting Joseph, she held up a hand to shield her eyes from the sun, and then stepped back a few paces, deeper into the shade of the olive tree. She gazed more intently into the cornfields. From the way she continuously looked back to where he was standing, Joseph knew that he had been caught. And yet she did nothing. She just stood there studying him silently, her blouse still unbuttoned. There was no anger in her face. Her expression was impassive. It was as if she was neither shocked nor surprised to discover a young voyeur lurking within the corn.

Too confused to move, Joseph felt a feverish perspiration trickling from his forehead and over his body, clinging to his coarse cotton gray shirt and pants, and dampening his feet, which stood unsteadily within the rag-stuffed oversized boots he had borrowed from his older brother. He tried to say something, but could not. He continued to look at her, though now more obliquely; and she, in her mysterious way, went on looking at him while also wiping her hands slowly with the small towel that dangled from the rope around the waist of her long skirt.

As Joseph continued to stare, the woman smiled at him. It was a wide smile, really a grin, which revealed two missing front teeth. Then she raised a hand indolently in front of her face, pointing toward him, and began motioning with her index finger for him to come closer. Joseph did not budge. But a moment later she was walking in his direction, and he panicked.

Suddenly energized, as if snapping out of a trance, he spun around and fled, thrashing through the sagging leaves of the stalks that flailed his face, and twice he stumbled in his loose-fitting boots while scampering along the narrow path between the rows of corn. He ran through the orange groves, through the cabbage fields, across the cow pasture, past the bewildered faces of dozens of observing farm laborers. Finally, out of breath, he paused in front of a large stone barn where his older brother, Sebastian, was stacking hay with a pitchfork.

Joseph had no intention of telling Sebastian anything about the woman. Sebastian was habitually mocking him, making fun of him; and Joseph knew that if he dared describe the woman to his brother, he would later relay the information in a distorted way to their mother and make everything seem lurid. Sebastian was their mother's favorite child, and whatever he told her she seemed willing and eager to believe. During the two-year absence of their father in America, Sebastian had asserted himself as the masculine head of the family, and he had an almost unchallenged authority over Joseph and the two younger children. Their mother had tacitly encouraged this, welcoming Sebastian's assistance in running the household, his filial devotion when she was lonely or depressed, and, of course, his financial contributions from his job on their grandfather's farm.

Although Sebastian was twelve, his tall and hefty stature allowed him to convince strangers that he was at least two or three years older; and Joseph risked having his ears boxed crimson if he ever challenged Sebastian's presumed right to exaggerate his age. Joseph tried not to challenge his older brother on any issue. He obeyed Sebastian when it was necessary; he avoided Sebastian when it was possible. And now, having escaped the woman in the olive fields, Joseph was trying to avoid Sebastian in the barnyard by stepping quickly behind a wagon loaded with hay and slipping into the nearby woodlands.

"Hey, where are *you* going?" Sebastian yelled from behind a haystack, just as Joseph thought that he had disappeared from view.

"I'm late for school," Joseph called back, not stopping.

"There's no school today, you little fool!"

Sebastian ran after Joseph with his pitchfork. Joseph stopped, eyes focused on the ground.

"And from the looks of you," Sebastian continued, now standing over his brother, "you've just done something terrible."

"I have not," Joseph protested.

"Then how come you're sweating like a pig, and looking like you've just seen a ghost?"

Joseph said nothing. Sebastian jammed his pitchfork into the dirt in front of Joseph's feet. Then he grabbed hold of Joseph's arms from behind and locked them across his back.

"Where have you been?" Sebastian demanded.

"In the olive fields," Joseph replied, grimacing.

"Who with?"

Joseph remained silent.

"Who with?" Sebastian repeated, pulling Joseph's arms up higher and twisting them so tightly up toward his neck that he soon could no longer stand the pain.

"There was a woman down there!" he blurted out.

Sebastian reduced the pressure. But when Joseph did not continue talking, Sebastian again tightened his grip.

"The woman had her blouse unbuttoned!" Joseph cried out finally. "I could see her breasts, and she called me over to her."

Howling with laughter and disbelief, Sebastian softened his grip.

"No woman wants a skinny runt like you! And you wouldn't know an unclothed woman if you saw one."

As Joseph complained about spasms in his back and arms, Sebastian stopped taunting him but did not release him. He held him tightly, laughed, and pressed his face down close to Joseph's neck and asked, in a sniggering manner: "Would you *really* like to see what a woman looks like with her clothes off?"

Joseph did not answer.

"You can come to the main barn with me today during the siesta," Sebastian continued. "There's a ladder in the back that reaches the roof, and from there you can look down and see some of the cave women and men in the hay. You want to know what they do together in the hay?"

"No," Joseph shouted, trying to cover his ears with his hands, and still unable to free himself.

"They do the same thing you've seen the animals do," Sebastian said, pulling him tighter.

Joseph said nothing. Closing his eyes, he remained motionless, now resigned to the pinned position. He felt disgust and humiliation. Sebastian's breath was upon his neck. Except for the chirping of the birds in the trees, and the distant mooing of cows, he heard no other sounds on the farm. He was controlled by Sebastian. Yet he was determined not to cry. He anticipated more harassment, but now Sebastian almost seemed to be getting weary or bored. His head rested on Joseph's back for a few moments, and then he suddenly released him. Joseph slumped forward, his arms falling heavily and numbly to his sides. He crouched with his head between his knees and began to rub his arms. Sebastian came around and stood in front of him. Joseph saw Sebastian's dusty boots but he did not look up.

"I'm sorry," he heard Sebastian say. Sebastian handed him a handkerchief, as if Joseph were crying, but Joseph swatted it away. It fell to the ground. Joseph straightened up and turned away from Sebastian. Across the field he saw a horse-drawn wagon filled with workers, dust rising from the wheels. It was about time for the siesta. Ignoring Sebastian, though aware of his unmoving shadow slanted beside him, he walked quickly toward the woodland path that led uphill to the road back to the village, still feeling pain and numbness in his arms. At this moment, he hated his brother. He hated him, and he also pitied him. Sebastian was stuck on the farm.

While Sebastian had resented their grandfather's forcing him onto the farm, he had also disliked going to school. In contrast to Joseph, Sebastian had been unable to keep up with the daily lessons in the classroom. He could barely read and write. He was also a troublemaker. After several complaints from the teachers, he permanently dropped out of school; and that was when their seventy-three-year-old grandfather, Domenico Talese, the patriarch of the family in Maida, had seized the opportunity to place Sebastian on the farm full-time.

Although fifty other Talese relatives and friends were already employed on the farm, Domenico often complained that they were mostly *pigri,* lazy, and *meschini,* good-for-nothing, and also too old and brittle-boned for the laborious work. The younger, more energetic men of the village had been lured away by the fantasy of democracy in America, Domenico often observed sourly, neglecting to mention that among the pioneering fantasists was his firstborn son, Gaetano, the forty-year-old father of Sebastian and Joseph, who had first fled to America as an adventurous bachelor of sixteen, back in 1888, after a quarrel with Domenico. According to what Joseph had been told by his mother (who had married his father during one of his visits home, but had steadfastly refused to accompany him back to America), the early quarrel between Gaetano and Domenico had arisen from Gaetano's resistance to his father's determination to subjugate *him* to farm life. And now Domenico was trying to do the same thing to Gaetano's oldest son, Sebastian—while seeking to pacify Sebastian with the promise that if he obeyed his grandfather and remained close enough to absorb his wisdom, he would someday become the sole inheritor of his grandfather's estate—which included not only the farm, but also Domenico's wheat mill, his aqueduct, his money-lending business (*if* Sebastian learned to emulate his shrewdness, Domenico emphasized to his grandson), and also the row of stone hillside houses that Domenico owned and the extended Talese family occupied as tenants.

Sebastian sometimes boasted quietly to Joseph about their grandfather's promise to make him rich, but Joseph was never envious of Sebastian—so long as Joseph could go on with his schooling, could continue his apprenticeship among the smartly dressed people in Cristiani's tailor shop, and could remain forever free of full-time service to the farm that would become Sebastian's ill fortune to own. Joseph could imagine nothing worse than being Sebastian—having to rise each day at five to the wake-up call of the whip being lashed by their grandfather against the outer walls of their house; and then mounting a mule and joining the slow-moving procession of farm workers down through the shadowy woodlands into the valley, in the dark light of a fading moon; and finally, fatigued after a day's work in the hot fields, returning home at dusk with his face scorched by the sun, his arms stung by mosquitoes, his boots and clothes grimy and malodorous.

Seeing Sebastian come home made Joseph sad, even made him feel guilty. But his compassion shifted to alarm whenever Sebastian suggested, as he often did in spiteful moments, that this grim existence might also represent Joseph's future; for Joseph feared that this could be true. There was no one to prevent it. Joseph's father, away in America, was a stranger he could not rely upon. And Joseph's mother believed that there was nothing odious about farm labor, having herself been reared on a farm; indeed, Marian Talese considered farming a more practical livelihood than working as an unpaid apprentice in a tailor shop that made fine clothes for clients who, in this ever-worsening economy of southern Italy, might be unable to afford them. At this time she also had, in addition to Joseph, two younger children to worry about—a son of five and a daughter of three—and her husband's irregularly arriving checks from America (where he was sometimes laid off) made her especially appreciative of the coins and comestibles that Sebastian earned on the farm from his affluent but hardly generous grandfather.

While Grandfather Domenico fancied himself an extremely just and religious man, even Joseph knew that he did not believe in charity. Domenico believed in bone-wrenching labor and long hours of sweat—a belief he had impressed upon the tired body and embittered soul of Sebastian, who, as time went on, was beginning to complain to his mother about the unjust conditions of his life.

One evening, as Joseph sat at a small table doing his homework in the second-floor bedroom he shared with Sebastian, he overheard his brother downstairs pleading with their mother: "Why am I the only one around here who has to wake up with the chickens and ride a mule with those old men to the stinking farm?" Hearing her sympathize with Sebastian, Joseph became very nervous; and the next morning, without being asked, he got up with Sebastian at five a.m. to the sounds of their grandfather's whip, and thus began a new policy of Joseph's trying to appease Sebastian, to disarm him with a kindness that might reduce his resentfulness, to bow and cater to him in the manner that Francesco Cristiani often used on the most difficult customers in the store.

It soon became a routine: Joseph would greet Sebastian with a polite good morning, then hop out of bed and bring in Sebastian's work clothes that their mother had washed, then dried over the fireplace the night before; while Sebastian dressed, Joseph would return with a cup of coffee from the pot their mother had just brewed in the kitchen. As Sebastian sipped the coffee, Joseph would go out to the courtyard to gather more wood for the fire, wearing over his nightclothes an old sheepskin coat their father had left behind. From across the courtyard Joseph could hear the animals stirring in the stables, and the hoofbeats of his grandfather on horseback galloping back and forth along the cobblestone road on the interior side of the long wall, occasionally cracking the whip against the houses to remind everyone inside that a workday was about to begin.

After carrying the wood inside, Joseph would return upstairs with a metal tray filled with charcoal that he carefully placed, one piece at a time, in the brazier that burned on the bedroom floor near the washstand that Sebastian was using. Not wanting to draw Sebastian's attention unnecessarily to the different lives they were now living, Joseph kept his schoolbooks under the bed, and the Cristiani-made clothes that he wore each day to the store and to school hanging behind the closed doors of the armoire.

When Sebastian had finished washing and dressing—usually in a sweater his mother had knit for him and the oversized secondhand workmen's attire his grandfather had provided—Joseph followed him down to the kitchen, where their mother would have packed Sebastian's lunch box with slices of sausage and cheese, peppers and figs, and half a loaf of dark brown bread. Their mother was a lively, small-boned woman in her thirties with graying dark hair that she pulled back into a bun; draped over her shoulders was a heavy wool shawl that hung almost to the hem of her long maroon skirt. Until recently, Joseph had thought that his mother was pretty. But lately her lean face had become quite drawn, almost pinched, and bereft of spirit; and except when conversing with Sebastian, she had little to say, seeming adrift in private concerns. A letter from their father had arrived a week before, but she had refused to let Joseph read it—which was just as well, for Sebastian had been in the room at the time, and Joseph knew from experience how sullen Sebastian became whenever Joseph reached for the mail from America and knowledgeably perused what they both knew was beyond Sebastian's capacity to understand.

Each morning, after he picked up his lunch box and kissed his mother good-bye, Sebastian would head for the door, and Joseph would follow him. In the weeks of Joseph's placating new routine, neither Sebastian nor their mother had shown any signs of gratitude; but Joseph repressed any disappointment when, pulling the sheepskin coat more tightly around his nightclothes, he proceeded across the chilly courtyard toward the stable, where he would help Sebastian load the donkey carts with jugs of mountain water that the workers drank instead of the possibly malarial waters of the lowlands.

There were usually at least a dozen men inside the stable bridling the horses, while others were outside along the fence packing the wagons, murmuring among themselves. A few of them would wave toward Sebastian as they noticed him lifting the water jugs, but they never seemed to be aware of the smaller figure of Joseph on the other side of the donkey cart. The men wore bulky sweaters over their rumpled trousers, and peaked caps or wide-brimmed felt hats that were faded and sweat-stained from endless hours in the sizzling sun. The outer soles of the men's boots displayed small iron spikes that were intended to lend traction on the slanting, often slippery gravel roads that curved down from the village to the valley. But even on the flat ground around the stable, the men walked tentatively and slowly, as if suffering from arthritis or some other physical restriction.

Although they all lived somewhere within the row of houses owned by Domenico and were related to him intimately or distantly—being his sons, his uncles, his cousins, the offspring of these or their in-laws— Joseph did not feel particularly close to any of these men, and he often had trouble identifying them by name. One individual whom he did recognize instantly was his grandfather's distant cousin Pepe, a shy and spindly gray-haired man with a ruddy pockmarked face and skin that was scaly, almost reptilian—the result, Joseph's grandfather had explained, of Pepe's parents' having sinned many years before against the moral laws of the Church. They had fallen in love, and concealed the fact that they were first cousins as they stood before the priest marrying them in a distant church near Naples; and subsequently, after returning to Maida, they produced an ugly, blemished child they called Pepe.

Pepe was now in his fifties, his parents were dead, and the young women of the village always kept their distance when they saw him walking through the town, although he was never forward or impolite to anyone. During the day his only companions were the farm workers. At night, he was alone at the end of Domenico's property, in a shack behind the last of the row houses, next to a poultry coop.

Another man Joseph recognized was the rotund and genial Vito Bevivino, the only worker in the group who was energetic and zestful—which was perhaps why Domenico maintained him as the farm's foreman even though he was eighty years old. He was a widower who had been married to one of Domenico's sisters; and now he was Domenico's closest friend, maybe Domenico's *only* close friend, among the kinfolk he employed. It was Vito's traditional duty to emasculate two of Domenico's choice pigs each year so that the animals would be sufficiently tender and tasty for the Easter feast that was held in Domenico's house for the entire clan, including Pepe; and it was Vito's duty each morning to organize the procession of family workers and animals for the seven-mile trek down to Domenico's farm in the valley.

Vito's position as foreman would be taken over by Sebastian after Vito's death—or so Sebastian had recently confided to Joseph; but insofar as Joseph could see in the stable, much life remained in Vito as he pushed and cajoled the others into moving faster. And as was known throughout the village, Vito's father, Antonio Bevivino, had lived to be more than a hundred—despite the tiny fragments of metal and rock that were buried somewhere in his misshapen head.

Antonio Bevivino had been a cavalryman with the French army during the early 1800s, when thousands of Italians were recruited by the Napoleonic Empire, which controlled almost all of Italy. In 1812, Antonio invaded Russia with the units led by Joachim Murat, and it was in Russia that he sustained a strange cranial injury. He claimed that chips from a ricocheting cannonball (fired by his own rearguard artillery) had grazed his skull; and, after surgery, Antonio was left with a hollow spot in the center of his head, an almost fist-sized indentation that suggested the crater of a volcano. Still, he lived on through the 1880s, and Domenico Talese as a younger man often saw him during his final years, the old veteran sitting in the square and smiling at passersby while doffing his tasseled conical hat—and revealing, within the hole in his head, a fresh piece of fruit or vegetable, most often a squash.

Antonio's tasseled hat, which proved to be even more durable than Antonio himself, was later appropriated by his son, who wore it in the stable as he called each morning to the men: *"Andiamo!"*—Let's go! and *"Presto!"*—Hurry up! Then the seven horse-drawn wagons carrying the men and farm tools, and three donkey carts containing food and water, would pull away from the stable and head toward the tall iron gate. Joseph would remain behind, waving good-bye to Sebastian. His brother usually looked back, nodding without expression, seated in the back of the rear cart.

Up ahead, Domenico would be waiting, sitting on a white stallion, on the cobblestone road beyond the gate. He usually wore a dark cape and a wide-brimmed gray hat, white riding breeches, and black boots with silver spurs. Domenico would watch until the caravan had almost reached him, counting the workers, noting who was absent and would thus be penalized with the loss of two days' earnings.

Then, with the tap of his whip across the flank of his horse, Domenico would gallop to the front of the line and proceed at a prancing pace to lead his group downhill toward the valley, through the heavy mist which rose each morning. Soon the sound of hoofbeats and wagon wheels would become muted; silence would return to the village, a silence unbroken until the clanging bells of a church signaled the start of the six a.m. Mass.

Domenico would be attending this Mass, young Joseph knew, since this was part of his grandfather's well-known daily routine. Domenico accompanied his men each morning only to the crossroads at the bottom of the hill; there, entrusting to his tassel-hatted foreman the responsibility of escorting the group to the farm site five miles beyond, he would salute with his whip and turn his horse around toward a bridle path in the bushes that offered a shortcut back to Maida. After tying his horse to a hitching post along the side of the church, Domenico would pass through the arched entranceway into the candlelit interior, and then into an oakwood curtained booth where he knelt for confession. Ever since his days as a youthful seminarian in Naples, Domenico had been a daily communicant; and on those many occasions when he had taken Joseph to Mass—during the harvest or on Sundays, when Joseph was not at Cristiani's or in school—Joseph would sit in a crowded pew watching his white-haired grandfather at the altar rail, his head held back as he received the host from the priest; and then his grandfather would stand with his hands clasped and walk swiftly down the aisle toward Joseph with his eyes closed, a blind man guided by inner light, a figure of such intense religiosity that Joseph felt both uncomfortable and oddly proud.

His grandfather seemed different from everyone else in town. He seemed more ascetic, more commanding; very stylish in an old-fashioned way, and never with mud on his boots—he was not a man of the common earth. He neither smoked nor drank liquor, not even wine. Except for an occasional piece of fish, and perhaps a taste of pork or lamb at Christmas or Easter, his diet was that of a vegetarian, following the custom of Saint Francis of Paola. He was the only member of the family who was an avid reader, mostly of texts on theology and history, interests first cultivated at the seminary. But he also read the Naples newspapers every day, and even periodicals from Rome and Milan whenever they appeared for sale at the rail terminal. He spoke not the dialect of the region, but a more formalized Italian, soft-tongued but distinctly enunciated, and he often expressed himself in proverbs.

"They who have more, want more," he commented one morning with a mildly sardonic smile, after hearing it announced at Mass that the region's two most noble families, both relatively affluent, had approved the betrothal of a teenaged son to an adolescent heiress who was years away from nubility; and yet Domenico respected these families for arranging the marriage in advance, and saw the consolidation of wealth through marriage as a confirmation of the pragmatic wisdom that usually produced wealth in the first place.

"If you took all the assets of the people in this area, and divided these assets equally among all of the citizens," Domenico once postulated to Joseph, "you would find that, in no time at all, the people who had been rich would be rich again. And the people who had been poor would again be poor."

Not only did he have little faith in the individual initiative of the common people of his village, but he refused to be impressed with those returning emigrants who, while briefly revisiting the village, and swaggering through the square wearing American-made suits, boasted of their good lives in the New Land and condemned the customs and traditions of the ancient civilization that had survived the vagaries of southern Italy for more than two thousand years. When Joseph had read his grandfather a recent letter from Gaetano in America, a letter in which his father praised the New Land as a paradise of opportunity and equality, Domenico listened quietly for a few moments, but appeared to be annoyed by the letter's contents. Domenico had never entirely come to terms with his son's decision to remain in America. Gaetano was an unpredictable commuter who revisited Maida every few years, who impregnated his wife— and returned to America before the christening—and left his father with much of the responsibility for the young family's welfare. If America was so abundant in opportunity, Domenico could well wonder, why was Gaetano not making more money? How come Gaetano, who claimed to be working for a multimillionaire outside Philadelphia—a pharmaceutical tycoon who was building a model industrial town with the profits from packaged miracles—was not lining his own pockets with gold and enriching his family as well?

As for the reference in Gaetano's letter to "equality," Domenico *did* think it appropriate to enlighten his young grandson Joseph. "Equality," he told Joseph, "is an illusion. Men were *not* created equal. There is no equality in the human condition, and there never will be. If God wanted equality he would have created it—but he did not, and you have only to look at your hand to find an example." At which point Domenico held up his right hand in front of Joseph's startled eyes and continued: "Look at these five fingers and note how no two of them are alike. The thumb is stubby and strong. The index finger is long and bony. The middle finger is even longer and more prominent than the index finger, and it is also longer than the fourth finger, the ring finger. And next there is the little finger, which of all the fingers is the most easily bent. It is weaker and shorter, and it will *always* be weaker and shorter throughout your lifetime. And yet," Domenico went on, "even though these fingers are all different in size and strength, they work well together as a whole—which was as God intended. If all the fingers were the same size, the same strength, the hand would not function. But they were all made differently, and this is the same throughout all of nature—things are not equal, never were meant to be equal."

Too confounded to reply, Joseph merely listened respectfully, as he always did when his grandfather spoke. His grandfather was like a philosopher to him, an antiquated deductive dogmatist who disregarded most of the views of the younger men of the village, and who also held in disfavor a few of Joseph's teachers whom he considered to be too liberal with the students and too far removed from the traditional values of the Church. Joseph's school had been run by the Church in the years prior to the 1860 revolution, an armed invasion of southern Italy led by the antipapist agitator General Giuseppe Garibaldi. In the prerevolutionary years, when a student was disobedient in class, he was forced to kneel at a distance from the other students during the daily prayers and to wear around his neck, on the end of a rope, a signboard on which was printed a description of his errant conduct.

But the current principal of the school discontinued the practice of signboards, kneeling, chanting and praying; and he brought into the school system young teachers who had been trained in Catanzaro, Cosenza, and the even more distant city of Naples, and were eager to develop a more modern society along the Socialist lines that had been envisioned by Garibaldi and other nineteenth-century Italian revolutionaries. Although

Joseph's teachers said nothing disrespectful about the Church, there were no longer any priests on the faculty, and the students were assigned books to read that portrayed Garibaldi as a hero and the revolution as perhaps the most auspicious event in Italian history. Instigated and financed largely by northern Italian aristocrats and a consortium of bourgeois radicals and youthful adventurers, the revolution finally absorbed the agricultural south into the more industrial north while reducing the temporal power of the Pope and confiscating vast amounts of Church land and property—such property as the old monastery that had been converted into Joseph's school. But despite his grandfather's grievances, Joseph privately liked his school and its teachers, a jovial group of young men who arrived for class each day wearing high-collared capes and colorful cravats, and who habitually smiled when they talked. They were perhaps the only people in the village who smiled a lot. The men and women Joseph knew among his kinfolk and their friends were invariably grim and solemn, if not as severe as his grandfather. Even the crowds he saw every day in the streets and the square conveyed the impression that they were preoccupied with problems or contemplating grave issues.

Why the teachers so often smiled bewildered Joseph, but he could not doubt the positive results that their friendliness and alacrity had on him as a student. In his first four years at school, he received the top academic medal in his class. In his fifth year—taking courses in mathematics, grammar, science, and history—he continued to earn the highest marks in his class on his quarter-term report card. This distinction would have meant more to Joseph had it impressed his grandfather, whose approval he so fervently desired. But after Joseph had brought home the report card, earning an embrace even from his mother, his grandfather merely glanced at it and nodded nonchalantly.

Domenico, as Joseph would later understand, was opposed to bestowing praise on individuals who were young and impressionable. Young people would profit more from the criticism of their experienced elders, he believed, than from receiving possibly head-swelling awards from liberal-minded teachers. The ancient proverb of the south—"Never educate your children beyond yourself"—still held meaning for Domenico, and he regarded patriarchal criticism as an antidote to youthful conceit. As a consequence, hardly a week passed without Joseph's receiving carping comments from his grandfather about his tendencies, however slight, toward smugness or complaisance, vanity or pride, effrontery or unaccountability. The quibbling ranged from Joseph's insufficient sharpening of the axe used for cutting firewood to Joseph's slouched posture in church to Joseph's mispronunciation of a somewhat ostentatious word that he had recently encountered while scanning one of the books in his grandfather's library. The criticism was accompanied by threats of punishment when Joseph once strayed beyond the village walls on a Friday afternoon (a day of bad luck); and placed a loaf of bread upside down in a basket (also bad luck); and uttered a scatological word that he had overheard Sebastian using. And on those occasions when Joseph was sincerely contrite about his wrongdoings, such as the mishap to Mr. Castiglia's trousers, Domenico usually exploited the situation to make him feel worse.

His grandfather had somehow become aware of the misdeed even before Joseph had returned home from Cristiani's late in the day on that horrid Holy Saturday. Domenico had been standing alone on the path that led to his row of houses, wearing as usual his cape and wide-brimmed hat; and after Joseph had greeted him and tried to continue on his way past him, Domenico gestured with his hand. Joseph stopped and waited.

"An apprentice should know his job," Domenico began, in a stern and solemn voice, "and should never defy the rules that wiser men have made. And yet you have defied those rules. And you have disappointed me very much. You, for whom I had high expectations, have shown signs of recklessness, stupidity, and, worse, insubordination. . . ."

As Domenico paused for a second, Joseph began to tremble. He feared that the next words out of his grandfather's mouth would spell out the punishment he most dreaded—banishment to the farm with Sebastian. Before Domenico could continue, Joseph looked up and interrupted. "Grandfather," he pleaded, "it was a *mistake!* It was the first serious mistake I ever made! I was *not* insubordinate. I just did not see that the trousers were hidden under the cloth I was cutting. It was my first mistake after doing many good things that you've never given me credit for." Speaking louder now, though aware that he had never before been so direct toward his grandfather, Joseph added, despairingly, "I can *never* please you! Nothing I ever do is good enough in your eyes. You are always strict with me, harsh with me." Sobbing now, Joseph said, "You just don't love me. . . ."

His grandfather remained silent. He waited several minutes until Joseph had stopped crying. And when Domenico did speak, it was in a voice that was quite unfamiliar.

"I do love you," he said, in the most sympathetic tone Joseph had ever heard. "But you are not yet old enough to understand this love. You confuse criticism with a lack of love. But the opposite is true. People who criticize you *care* about you. They want to see you improve. People who do *not* care about you hold no high expectations for you. They accept you as you are. They allow you to relax. They make you feel contented.

"People who do *not* love you," he concluded, "make you laugh. People who love you make you cry."

11.

THROUGH THE SPRING, the summer, and the autumn of 1911, young Joseph Talese continued his apprenticeship at Cristiani's tailor shop, taking his position each day in the front of the store behind the large window, where, while sewing on buttons and basting seams, he watched the many pedestrians and horse-drawn vehicles in the street, occasionally wondering if the dreaded Mr. Castiglia and his equally fearsome bodyguard would ever return.

While the tailors in the back room ceased wearing the wing-kneed trousers every day, having convinced Cristiani that they were wearing them out, Joseph was warned not to interpret this change in policy as an indication of laxity. "Mr. Castiglia may return at any moment," he was reminded by Cristiani. "You must remain vigilant. You are posted in the front room to warn us in the back as soon as you see him. You must keep one eye on the street even as you sew, which is a little trick that you can easily learn. I myself learned it when I was your age. My beloved father had once infuriated the late baron of Palizzi, who swore he would return to our shop with his sword when he learned that we had burned one of the sleeves of his tailcoat he had left to be altered, after a small fire had broken out in the workroom because of an exploding gas lamp. But I should not bother you with such details now. You have enough to worry about. You must worry about Mr. Castiglia. And your task is even more difficult now with Christmas upon us, and our streets more crowded than usual with shoppers and visitors. So you must search the streets with more care—and let out a loud yell the *instant* you see Mr. Castiglia approaching our door."

Joseph nodded, knowing he would have no trouble identifying Mr. Castiglia or the bodyguard if they did reenter the town. The remembrance of the Holy Saturday incident, though now many months past, was starkly vivid in Joseph's mind; and since that dreadful day he had often been awakened in the middle of the night by visions of the corpulent Mr. Castiglia smashing through the shop's front door with guns blasting and blood splattering, retaliating against the tailors who had so ignominiously deceived him. And as Joseph walked home after work he found himself studying certain faces and figures in the street, particularly those men with broad shoulders, thick necks, and large bellies; and there were moments when he would suddenly stop and hide in the shadow of a building, or lurk behind another pedestrian, as he saw in the distance a pudgy profile or a bulging stomach that reminded him of Mr. Castiglia. Pausing to catch his breath, Joseph would then move closer, slowly and guardedly weaving his way through the crowd—his heart pounding, his anxiety increasing, not knowing what he would do *if* the man he was stalking was in fact the gimlet-eyed gangster whom Cristiani had turned into a fool. But none of these individuals, on closer inspection, happened to be Mr. Castiglia—for which Joseph was most grateful; but he still continued to remain on the lookout, week after week, in accord with his master's mandate.

Indeed, Joseph was becoming an obsessive observer of the people in the village, if not an outright snoop. He became intimately acquainted with their way of walking, their most common gestures, their style in dress, the extent of their wardrobe, the tone of their voices, the topics of their conversations, the gossip they were circulating. For the first time in his life Joseph became aware that most of the villagers were creatures of habit. They seemed to retrace their steps every time they took a stroll; they entered church each time from the same side of the staircase; they invariably sat at the same table at the sidewalk café.

Early each morning, through Cristiani's window, Joseph watched the stout and brooding poet, Don Ciccio Parisi, shopping at the tent-covered market in the town square, selecting his fruit and vegetables as carefully as he presumably chose words; and also shopping in the market were many women in voluminous black shawls that reached to the ground, some with veils covering the lower part of their faces, a vestige of Arab influence, and children wearing small pieces of rock salt tied around the neck, amulets against the "evil eye."

Climbing the slanted cobblestone steps overlooking the square was a firm-footed tall woman with her neck held high and her shoulders arched back; she walked with remarkable grace while balancing on her head a yard-long wooden plank stacked with shawls that she would try to sell to the people she met along the way. As they approached her she paused and curtsied, giving them a better look at the merchandise. After they had passed it by, shaking their heads, the woman straightened up and continued to climb the steps in her nimble fashion, moving toward her next prospective customer, and the one after that, with a patience that matched her poise.

Hurrying down the steps toward the market each morning, minutes after the church bells had signaled the completion of the Mass, would be the impish Padre Panella. A year before, with his most demure and devout parishioner, he had produced a child—or so Joseph had overheard a gossipy tailor allege in Cristiani's back room.

Then there was the almost daily appearance of a six-piece band, loudly playing marching music in the market square while the king's uniformed recruiters tried to enlist men to fight in Italy's war against the Turks in Libya. Rarely did any volunteers step forward. Later in the morning the town's teenaged bully, Pietro Mancuso, would gallop through the square in a wagon laden with barrels of olive oil, snapping a long whip which had often stung Joseph and other students on the back when they wandered along the road too unguardedly after school. Also passing through town almost every day were men wearing white flat-topped caps and belted embroidered green tunics and black boots—they were visitors from Vena, a neighboring village occupied by hundreds of unassimilated Albanians whose ancestors had come to Italy centuries before to escape their Moslem persecutors in the Balkans. These Albanian descendants who lived near Maida adhered to their ancestral language and style in dress, and they worshipped in a Greek Orthodox church, where the priests, unlike their Roman brethren on the Maida side of the mountain, were free to marry.

Among the other strollers Joseph observed daily from Cristiani's window was the town chemist, Dr. Fabiani, whose apothecary was known as an after-hours gathering place for Maida's Socialists and other anti-monarchists; the wood sculptor Carmine Longo, who carved everything from guitars to church altars; and the town's most recent widow, Maria Palermo, who walked slowly through the square wearing a black mantilla and ankle-length black dress while holding on to the arm of her similarly dressed spinster sister, Lena Rotella.

Lena, as most people knew, lived behind the Norman wall in a large building that sheltered children born out of wedlock. There were sometimes as many as a half-dozen infants in that building awaiting adoption. The illegitimate children were usually brought to the rear of the building late at night, being carried in blankets to a ground-floor window that was never locked. Inside the window, on a round table, was a wicker basket large enough to hold a child. The basket was always placed on the edge of the table next to the window. Midway across the table, suspended from the ceiling, was a black curtain that obscured the entire room beyond. After the window had been opened and the child was placed in the basket, the round table was spun on its pedestal, and the child was brought through the curtains into the arms of Lena Rotella or one of the women who helped her operate the orphanage and raise funds for its mainte-nance. The curtain was the women's way of bringing some privacy to the act of parting with a child.

Joseph once knew a boy in school who, though not illegitimately born, had been reared in Lena's orphanage. The boy was two years older than Joseph, and he was difficult to understand because of his stuttering. During his infancy, the boy's mother had carried him in her arms one af-ternoon high up the mountain road toward the town of Tiriolo, where his father was employed as a tree-cutter and had just been seriously injured in a fall. Since the wife had no other means of transportation when she heard the news, and since the weather in Maida was very mild, she thought she could accomplish the journey on foot in three or four hours. But after she had walked for more than six hours, climbing higher and higher without reaching the peak where Tiriolo was situated, a snowstorm swept over the mountainside; and in the sudden inclemency and darkness of the late afternoon she found herself in the woods, lost and frantic. With her child in her arms, and no one around to assist her, she rested against a tree. The temperature began to drop rapidly. During the night it was below freez-ing. She took off her clothes and wrapped them around her child. That night she froze to death. But the boy was discovered by hunters the next morning and was rescued. The child's father, permanently injured by his fall, placed the boy in Lena's orphanage for a number of years—until, at ten years of age, he left Maida and joined his crippled father in Tiriolo, where the father—then working as a sedentary watchman for a timber company—had found him a job as a logger's helper.

Another frequent sight observed from Cristiani's shop window was the striding, elegant figure of the town's most handsome aristocrat, Tor-quato Ciriaco, heading toward Muscatelli's bar, where he would be served an espresso with a drop of grappa in a delicate white cup. Don Torquato was a gray-haired bachelor in his middle thirties who always wore derbies and silk-lined capes (made at Cristiani's) and carried a silver-handled cane. But as the second son in a family that still adhered to the primogenitary practices of the past, Don Torquato would inherit none of his parents' wealth during the lifetime of his older brother; and therefore, like most southern Italian gentlemen in his situation, Don Torquato had a mistress instead of a wife. She was a buxom servant girl who lived with her widowed father in a carriage house behind the Norman wall, not far from Lena Rotella's orphanage. At least twice a week Don Torquato visited her there, but he always returned later at night to his family's palazzo near the square.

The palazzo was a dark granite structure with the Ciriaco coat of arms carved in marble over an arched entranceway; and it had immense front windows that were usually opened wide in mild weather, exuding classical music that young Joseph always paused to listen to in the evening on his way home. One evening Joseph heard what he later learned was the excellent flute of Don Torquato himself playing the overture to Verdi's *Joan of Arc.* Joseph would remember the exquisiteness of that moment for the rest of his life.

Sometimes the music of an orchestra and the chatter of many people could be heard coming from the palazzo; and although the common women of the village never danced with men—the Church discouraged dancing as erotically arousing—it was rumored that the elite couples of Maida occasionally met in the Ciriaco ballroom and, with haughty decorum, would indulge in the waltz. It was said that after the couples had arrived the women would sit among themselves, while the musicians at the end of the empty dance floor played waltzes with patience and anticipation. Eventually, from across the room where the men had assembled, a gentleman would separate himself from the others and approach the circle of women from the rear; and, after singling out the woman of his choice, and leaning over her shoulder, he would whisper into her ear. Instead of turning to reply, she remained seated while lifting her hand mirror to her face, to glance at the reflection of the man who stood behind her—in accord with the ritualistic coyness that virtuous women of the region were expected to exhibit toward the opposite sex. But then, with a gloved hand slowly extended, she nodded her assent to be escorted onto the floor. While moving to the music, however, she held her body rigidly at a scrupulous distance from her partner's, and she made every effort never to look directly into his eyes. One by one, each man would do the same as the first until the dance floor was crowded with stately, stiff-backed couples.

Higher in the hills of Maida, next to a ruined abbey—but still within sight of Cristiani's tailor shop—stood an abandoned watchtower that the Normans had built a thousand years before, to alert the town to seafront infiltrations by the Arabs; and also in the upper hills was the local cemetery, which Joseph visited each Sunday afternoon with his paternal grandparents, to place fresh flowers on the gravestones of Domenico's forebears. Surrounding the burial grounds were tall cypress trees through which the wind whipped and made sounds that often unsettled the mourners, eerie sounds believed to be the wailings of entombed spirits. While the gravestones of poor people were not much larger than dress boxes, the town's property owners, such as Joseph's grandfather Domenico, had mausoleums sizable enough to hold six or eight coffins; and old feudal families such as the Ciriacos, the Fabianis, the Faraos, the Romeos, and the Vitales had grand mausoleums with façades embellished by classical Roman columns and statuary—miniature villas containing private chapels with altars and towering candles and carved wooden pews and sufficient space along the side walls to accommodate dozens of coffins. Affixed to the recently placed coffins were oval framed photographs of the deceased, together with messages inscribed in stone from the dead to the living. *Non torno, vi aspetto*—I will not come back, I will wait for you. *L'alba di ogni giorno ti porti il mio saluto*—May the dawn of every day bring you my greeting.

On the lower cliff, opposite the iron-gated entrance to the cemetery, was a grazing area for sheep and goats; and from the window of the shop Joseph had a distant view of the shepherd Guardacielo leading a flock of sheep down toward a stream and rows of olive trees. In the late months of 1911, when wool was trading even lower than cheese made from sheep's milk, the primary asset of sheep was their fertilization of the olive groves. And yet the sheep were always the first among the animals to be blessed by the bishop at the annual procession of livestock through the square on the second Sunday of March; and the shepherds still valued their sheep sufficiently to bring shotguns as well as watchdogs into the hills to protect the grazing flocks from the attacks of mountain wolves.

Joseph had noticed once that Guardacielo's watchdogs wore around their necks heavy leather collars studded with long, sharply pointed steel spikes. After describing what he had seen to Mr. Cristiani, the latter nodded knowingly and said: "Those collars save the dogs' necks from the teeth of pouncing wolves. When I was your age, the dogs did not wear collars, and those wolves would sneak down from the mountains and bite the dogs' necks—the wolves were twice as fast and ferocious as the dogs in those days—and then they'd run off with the sheep before the very eyes of the helpless shepherds, who were not yet carrying guns for protection. Hundreds of hungry wolves live high in the mountains all around us," Cristiani continued, "and in very cold weather, when the upper forestland is covered with ice, the wolves have a difficult time foraging for squirrels, rabbits, and other things they eat. The wolves then move down the mountain to the warmer areas, down closer to where we live. All it takes is a day or two of heavy snow and ice along the peaks to send the wolves our way. So if we get that kind of weather," Mr. Cristiani concluded, with an oblique smile, "don't be surprised when you open your door and find yourself staring at a wolf."

If it was Mr. Cristiani's intention to frighten Joseph (and it may have *been* his intention, for in this time and place older men believed that a frightened child was a more responsible and obedient child), then Cristiani's intention was fulfilled. Joseph began to worry constantly about the wolves, and one winter afternoon, while kneeling next to his grandfather in the cemetery, in front of the family mausoleum, he could have sworn that he saw a blurred outline of a gray wolf leaping through an open space between two gravestones in the rear of the burial grounds.

Later that night, after Joseph had gone to bed, he was awakened by the echoes of wolves howling down from the mountains. In this part of Italy some mountain peaks are more than five thousand feet above the sea, and the nocturnal sounds of wolves in the higher altitudes carry for many miles down through the hillside villages and valleys; and anyone born within the rocky southern interior of Italy, where each village is an echo chamber of sounds near and far, soon accepts the nighttime howling of wolves as naturally as the morning crowing of roosters. Still, on this particular night, it seemed to Joseph that the wolves sounded nearer than usual to the village. But his brother Sebastian, who lay in bed next to him snoring, was clearly unconcerned. So Joseph said a prayer, and eventually went back to sleep.

Four days later, shortly before seven a.m. on the second Thursday in December, clouds of frosty mist drifted up from the valley as Joseph hastened down the foggy cobblestone road toward the square and Cristiani's tailor shop. Under his arm, in a cloth bag, he carried his schoolbooks and lunch. After two hours at Cristiani's, he would spend the rest of the morning and part of the afternoon in school, which was a five-minute walk from the shop; then he would return to Cristiani's and remain there until seven-thirty or eight. This was his daily routine. His only physical exercise each day was walking. And as he walked to work on this morning, shivering under his thick wool overcoat, he noticed that the cone-peaked Mount Contessa that hovered in the distance beyond the hilltop cemetery was covered with snow. A few days before, the mountaintop had been a brown triangle speckled with sunlit yellowish trees, and the warm air of the sirocco had swept through the valley, blown across the Mediterranean from North Africa. Today there were harsh winds from the north, and the sky that had been clear for weeks was overcast and getting darker. Joseph was unsettled by this change in weather.

It was also unsettling to the tailors in Cristiani's back room, or so it seemed to Joseph as he sat listening in the front, sewing with his legs crossed on the window bench and watching people pacing back and forth outside, their capes and skirts fluttering in the wind. One tailor complained that he had discovered his vegetable garden frozen this morning, and he said he feared for the farmers' crops if the temperature continued to drop. Another tailor added that the small waterfall near his hillside house had been fringed with icicles as he passed it earlier in the morning. A third man said that he had never before seen Mount Contessa so densely packed with snow. Cristiani, who usually did most of the talking in the back room, was strangely silent.

Shortly after eight-thirty, Joseph paused in his sewing and sentry duty and prepared to leave for school. Usually he was replaced by one of the other young apprentices, all of whom were three or four years older than he was, and had dropped out of school; but on this occasion he was surprised to discover that his substitute was Mr. Cristiani's seventeen-year-old son, Antonio, who considered himself a full-fledged tailor. Dapper and diminutive like his father, and nearly as opinionated, Antonio Cristiani had already made several waistcoats and pairs of trousers for the general public, and he believed himself fully qualified to make an entire suit. But every once in a while, to puncture his inflated sense of self-importance, his father would assign Antonio to one of the tasks ordinarily performed by apprentices. The most boring and aggravating of these tasks was Joseph's—it deprived an individual of the camaraderie of the back room and isolated him for hours behind the front window, where he was expected to fasten buttons with one eye while keeping the other eye fastened upon the street.

On an earlier occasion when Antonio had been ordered to replace Joseph, an occasion that was viewed by the other tailors as Antonio's rightful punishment for criticizing the shoulder line of a suit his father had just completed for the marquis of Botricello, Antonio had sulked behind the window the entire time Joseph was at school, sewing buttons with his head down and paying absolutely no attention to what was going on outside.

Now, again demoted to the duncelike duty that only Joseph did not consider degrading, Antonio huffily arrived in the front room, red-faced, biting his lower lip, apparently still smarting from the unpleasant father-son exchange that Joseph had overheard moments before, which had been accentuated by the sound of a tabletop being pummeled by a metallic object, possibly the elder Cristiani's heaviest pair of scissors.

As Antonio slumped in a chair next to Joseph, he shook his head and said, "I hate this place." He spoke in a tone not quite loud enough to be overheard in the back room. "Those old men back there, including my father, have nothing more to teach me," he went on, lighting a cigarette. After a long puff, he added, matter-of-factly: "I belong in Paris."

Antonio liked making grandiose statements and boasting to his younger cousin—Joseph being the only person in the shop who listened attentively and seemed to agree with everything Antonio said. Joseph had in truth always admired Antonio's brashness and confidence, and he was beholden to him for many past kindnesses. It had been Antonio who had begun to teach Joseph the rudiments of tailoring a year before, and who lately had been instructing him in the techniques of cutting and sewing buttonholes for jackets and inserting piping along the edges of lapels. Antonio had been very sympathetic to Joseph after the problem with the *mafioso's* trousers, telling Joseph that this mistake could have been made by anyone in the shop, including the boss himself; and Antonio reassured Joseph that his job was secure and that he need not worry about being exiled to the farm. Antonio was sensitive to Joseph's insecurity, and he frequently walked the boy home after work and discussed the latter's difficulties with Sebastian and their grandfather Domenico; and he comforted Joseph with admiring recollections about Joseph's father, Gaetano—the cherished older brother of Antonio's mother, Maria, and a romantic figure to Antonio as well. Antonio described him as a wandering idealist, a man too curious about life to find contentment along the provincial hillside of Maida.

Antonio had seen a lot more of Joseph's father than had Joseph himself. In recent years, as Joseph was growing up, his father's visits back to Italy were inexplicably less frequent than before. During his father's most recent visit, in early 1909, two and a half years before, Joseph had been bedridden much of the time with diphtheria and had only a hazy sense of his father's presence. When it came time for his father to leave the village, it had been the elder Cristiani and Antonio who had accompanied him on the train to Naples, and then seen him off at the pier where Gaetano took a steamer back to America—wearing as a going-away gift a new overcoat made by Francesco Cristiani.

It was Antonio, however, who made all of Joseph's clothing, practicing his craft by designing smallish jackets, trousers, and coats, and then cutting the material from leftover rolls of fabric that were insufficient for man-sized fittings. Antonio occasionally cut down to Joseph's dimensions, and then remodeled, part of the wardrobe that he himself had worn when he was younger. The heavy wool overcoat Joseph wore to work this morning, and was about to put on again to go to school, had once been worn by Antonio. He had designed it after seeing a fashion illustration in one of the magazines from Milan and Turin that he bought at the local rail terminal and kept hidden at home. The elder Cristiani did not approve of these magazines, Antonio had told Joseph not long before, without explaining why. But Joseph did know that Antonio's strong opinions on fashion had once nearly led to his arrest by the police.

According to Joseph's mother, who remembered the incident well, it occurred six years before, in 1905, when Antonio was not yet twelve. The King of Italy, Victor Emmanuel III, was then passing through Maida as part of an official visit to the southern provinces. The king arrived in a black Fiat touring car, the first automobile that anyone in Maida had ever seen, and the crowds of people along the road were more interested in the car than in its royal passenger—kings rarely being treasured objects in Italy. The previous king, Umberto I, had been assassinated a few years before; and the present king, surrounded by mounted guards, sat rigidly in the backseat waving a hand limply through the closed windows of the coach.

Suddenly there was a loud bang. The guards grabbed their weapons, the royal vehicle stopped, tilting to one side, and the king scrambled out the door onto the roadway. There were sighs from the crowd, whinnying from the horses. But soon, as the cause of the disturbance became known, order and tranquillity were restored. A front wheel had been broken loose by a rock.

While the chauffeur and another retainer proceeded to fix the wheel, the king paced impatiently along the side of the car behind his guards. Among the spectators were Marian Talese, accompanied by her six-year-old son, Sebastian, and her nephew Antonio, who managed to slip close enough to the cordon of guards to see how the king was dressed. Unimpressed with what he saw, Antonio later that day, after the royal entourage had moved on, took a pen and did a series of fashion sketches that he thought could inspire an ideal wardrobe for the king. Without a word to anyone, Antonio mailed the sketches the next day to the royal residence in Rome.

A week later, three members of the regional constabulary arrived at Cristiani's shop with the sketches, which had been intercepted by a postal inspector. The constables declared that the sketches were demeaning to the king's dignity, and, assuming they had been done by Antonio's father, they threatened to incarcerate him.

Professing his innocence, Francesco Cristiani immediately recognized the handiwork and signature of the real culprit, who was then out of the shop on an errand. Cristiani remained silent for a moment, thinking fast. Then he looked humbly into his accusers' eyes and explained that the drawings had been scrawled by his harmless young son, who was mentally retarded. There had always existed extraordinary sympathy in Italy for the parents of mentally retarded children, and the constables seemed moved by Cristiani's explanation. When he guaranteed that the youth would never again be left unguarded to repeat such offenses, the constables accepted the promise with a stern warning and left the shop.

Upon returning, Antonio was greeted by his father's paddle—a slab of oakwood designed primarily to be inserted inside the sleeves of jackets and coats to avoid unwanted creases during ironing and pressing. After it had been warmly applied to Antonio's buttocks, his outraged father accused him of arrogance and impudence, stupidity and blatant irresponsibility. And in the years since this episode, if the elder Cristiani had vastly altered his opinion of his son, it was not evident to Joseph on this particular morning as he stood next to the cigarette-smoking Antonio at the front window.

"I belong in Paris," Antonio repeated, "and I've already made a move in that direction." As Joseph waited for him to continue, Antonio paused to reach into the inner pocket of his jacket, which had pointed lapels and a boutonniere, and he pulled out a folded parchment brochure decorated with the silhouette of a man wearing a top hat and tails. He handed the brochure to Joseph. Under the silhouette was the man's name—Count Boniface de Castellane. And at the bottom of the brochure, in ornate lettering, were the name and the address of a renowned French tailoring school—*École Ladaveze, 6, place des Victoires.*

"I've mailed in my application," Antonio told Joseph, almost in a whisper. "If they accept me, I'm leaving. Immediately! And I don't care what anybody around here says or thinks."

Joseph did not speak. But all at once he felt himself isolated with familiar feelings of despair. The prospect of being abandoned by his debonair cousin, whose closeness had begun to fulfill Joseph's need for a confidant and a trusting friend, so frightened him now that he could only hand back the brochure to Antonio and turn away.

Joseph put on his overcoat and took his cloth bag, and headed for the door. He heard Antonio's voice behind him. He ignored it. The voice became more commanding, and he felt a hand on his shoulder. Turning, Joseph looked into Antonio's intense dark eyes and small chiseled face. Despite their difference in age, and the worldly image that Antonio had all but usurped from his magazines, Antonio was only a bit taller and larger than he was.

"Joseph," Antonio said with a smile, "you'll be coming to Paris with me."

Joseph could not react. It seemed too unbelievable, too absurd.

"Yes, *yes!*" Antonio insisted, holding Joseph's shoulder more tightly. "I'll go to Paris, find a place to live, and then I'll send for you."

Joseph still did not speak. He looked down, avoiding Antonio's eyes. He heard the muted voices of the older men in the back, talking casually among themselves. If he did not hurry he would be late for school. But as he thought about what Antonio had just said, the heavy feeling in his heart was becoming lighter.

"You'll come to Paris only on one condition, however," Antonio went on, quite businesslike now. "You must not tell anyone of my plans. Do you understand?"

Joseph nodded.

Antonio was not satisfied with the response.

"Joseph," Antonio demanded, *"do you promise?"*

Joseph was suddenly excited by the idea of running away to Paris. He would be living with Antonio.

"Yes, Antonio," Joseph said, finally. "I promise."

12.

OUTSIDE IN THE street, as Joseph walked to school, he saw people bustling around the fruit stands and grocery stores, and he heard the sounds of quickening hoofbeats, rattling wagon wheels, and the jingling bell-strung reins in the hands of impatient coachmen. The dry air of the sirocco had been dissipated by the misty currents from the north, nippy winds that flapped the edges of the awnings upraised above the stores. A waiter at a sidewalk café, his white apron swirling around his waist, was pulling tables and chairs inside the door and shoving them close to the bar. There were no customers idling there now.

Looking up, Joseph noticed that the clouds were now more closely clustered and lower than before, and the snowy peak of Mount Contessa was no longer visible behind the cemetery. He did see in the near distance, standing prominently in the elevated piazza overlooking the square, the dark rectangular building that was his school. It was nearly nine o'clock. Roll call was scheduled to begin within minutes. But Joseph was concerned neither about tardiness nor about the weather. He had been invited to Paris. What mattered now was protecting Antonio's secret.

How his cousin would execute the plan was beyond Joseph's imagination. While it was true that young men were regularly leaving the village unannounced, their departures were nearly all underwritten by the steamship companies and the factory bosses in America. Antonio would be going to Paris on his own. And so would Joseph. Where was the money coming from? How could Joseph slip away without the knowledge of his mother, his grandfather Domenico, and Sebastian? Joseph had great confidence in Antonio's resourcefulness. But as Joseph continued across the square into the wind, holding his books and lunch in his bag tightly against his coat, he considered what would happen if he did leave.

Running away from home was not a casual undertaking. The constables would undoubtedly be summoned. He recalled hearing about the beating Antonio had received after the constables had come to the tailor shop carrying those fashion sketches for the king. Joseph could also foresee a furious response from his grandfather Domenico. What would his father in America think after he learned that Joseph had fled to Paris? Was it so different from what his father had himself done when he was younger? Yes, it was different, Joseph thought; his father had left at sixteen. Joseph had only recently turned eight. And at that age he was already engaged in a conspiracy with Antonio, an involvement that was making Joseph more nervous the more he thought about it.

Halfway across the square Joseph thought he felt the cobblestones vibrating under his feet. He looked around to see if other people in the square felt it. It was a tiny tremor, like an earthquake, but no one else seemed to notice anything different. His stomach lurched and he felt dizzy. Joseph had already lived through two earthquakes. He had been three years old during the first one, and six during the second. On both occasions most of the villagers had moved down to the valley to avoid the danger of flying rocks, some of which had already tumbled into the town from the higher hills and from building walls made unstable by the quake. The whole Talese clan, under the direction of Domenico, had lived under tents on the farm for a few days during the last one, and Joseph himself had vague recollections of torchlit evenings and throngs of people who took turns reciting the Rosary throughout the entire night. Joseph believed he had seen his father during the second earthquake, but his mother insisted that his father had been in America then, as he had been during the first earthquake. Joseph nevertheless recalled being face to face with his tall, dark-eyed father at some point during this time when he feared for his life, and it was then that his father had arrived to comfort him—and to give him a gift that Joseph would carry with him always as a memento. It was an envelope, tucked into the inside pocket of his overcoat on this very morning.

It was a green American dollar bill. He remembered his father appearing unexpectedly at night, a sloe-eyed, smiling man with an angular face and a moustache, wearing a pearl tie pin and a derby, looking every bit as handsome as his photograph on the wall of their home, holding the bill outstretched in the tips of his fingers. After folding the money inward, while still holding its ends, he abruptly stretched it out again, producing a resonant *pop*. "Listen to the snap of that paper!" his father had exclaimed, moving the dollar bill in and out like a little accordion. "Listen to the sound of a strong dollar that's made of firm fiber!" Then he took an Italian lira note from his pocket, held it in front of Joseph's face, and began to snap *it* back and forth in a similar fashion—except the note soon snapped in half. "Here in Italy we make the finest silk in the world," his father had said, letting the torn lira note flutter to the floor. "But we still don't know how to make strong money." Then he handed the dollar to Joseph. "Keep this," he said, "and one day spend it in America. You will buy something wonderful."

When he arrived at school, Joseph climbed the high marble steps and passed through the arched entranceway. The school had once been a monastery. The corridor was wide and dark, and the walls so thick that Joseph could no longer hear the blustery wind, the hoofbeats, and the harness bells. At the far end of the corridor, dimly visible in the candlelight of two black metal chandeliers, Joseph saw the assembly hall, in which dozens of students were lining up according to grade, waiting for the principal to begin the roll call. There were almost sixty students registered in the seven grades. All of them were boys, ranging in age from four to fifteen. The girls of the village attended a different school, located on the other side of the square, in the wing of a building that was once a convent.

As he went to take his place in line, Joseph nodded greetings to a few of his schoolmates. There was Francesco LaScala, an affable boy who worked before school each day in his grandfather's carriage repair shop. There was Giuseppe Paone, a diffident and cross-eyed youth who began the day helping out at his uncle's vegetable stand in the square. And there was Vincenzo Pileggi, a barber's apprentice who appeared at school each morning with a pomaded pompadour and a garnet ring on each pinkie, and who marched in the town band on ceremonial occasions, holding a clarinet that he did not know how to play. Nearly every boy worked at a job before coming to school, and for this reason the roll call commenced at nine o'clock and not earlier. With the arrival of the principal, the students stopped talking. He was a stout and bouncy broad-shouldered man who almost waltzed across the platform, trailed by his flowing maroon cape, and high on his aquiline nose was perched a silver pince-nez. His large azure-colored eyes were penetrating and yet reflected a friendly twinkle, and his lofty forehead rising above his jowly pink face was fringed with thinning reddish hair that failed to cover the center of his balding crown. He was a descendant of an old family of Socialist educators and politicians—one of them the courageous antimonarchist mayor of Maida during the prerevolutionary days, when southern Italy was controlled by Spanish Bourbon kings—and his name was Achille Schettini. But in addressing him, the students used only his Christian name preceded by the Spanish title of courtesy that was preserved in his land. He was Don Achille.

"Good morning, students," he said, smiling down from the platform, holding under his arm the leather-bound registry containing everyone's name and attendance records.

"Good morning, Don Achille," they answered in unison.

"First, let me compliment you on braving the weather and getting to school this morning," he said, surveying with apparent satisfaction the seven rows of boys standing before him. He had recently made impassioned speeches in the square urging parents to help him reduce the high truancy rate, arguing that the better-educated pupils would most likely become the richest immigrants—an argument that had perhaps appealed to many mothers whose semiliterate husbands overseas had often complained of being cheated financially by their more educated countrymen who supervised the Italian work gangs in America.

"And I would also like to thank you students for making greater efforts in your classes this term," he went on. "All the teachers have told me that when the term ends this week, higher marks will be given throughout the school in mathematics and science, grammar, geography, and especially history."

He smiled at the reference to history, for it was he who taught these classes—and he did so with such oratorical gusto, with such a robust recounting of history's heroes and villains in picturesque settings, that Joseph was always sorry when the daily class was over. Joseph virtually escaped from his own life while sitting in Don Achille's class, which was the first on Joseph's morning agenda, and the principal added to the appeal of his course by offering guided tours on certain weekends to students who were interested in seeing some of the many historically significant sites that existed within a day's round-trip wagon ride from the village gate.

Joseph had twice joined the tour in recent months, viewing from his teacher's hay-filled wagon along the coastal roads in the neighboring hills an assortment of ruined Roman walls and Saracen towers, Byzantine domes atop crumbling churches, Norman castles with toppled turrets, and a single Doric column that was all that remained of a once grand Temple of Hera. "Here is where civilization began in Italy," Don Achille had declared during the first tour, climbing down from the front bench of the two-horse wagon and standing at the base of the column with an arm outstretched. Grinning broadly, he added: "This was built six centuries before Christ by my ancient ancestors who sailed here from Greece."

Later, as he stood along the rocky gully of a small river, Don Achille had directed his students' attention to a clump of moss-covered boulders rising above the surface, and he announced in his stentorian voice: "Behold the burial place of the barbarian king Alaric, who sacked Rome in 410 A.D., and who abducted the daughter of the Emperor Theodosius, and who ultimately died of fever here as he was scheming to loot the Sicilians. After his barbarian soldiers forced the local populace to block the natural course of this river, and to build a royal sepulcher on the riverbed to contain the king's body and his booty, the soldiers then massacred all the laborers and hurled them upon the sepulcher before restoring the water to its natural channel." As Joseph stared timorously at the river with his classmates, Don Achille intoned: "Such is typical of the many atrocities that mark Italian history."

Farther along on the tour, after informing the students that they were traveling the same route used in the twelfth century by Richard the Lion-Hearted and his knights when they headed south from Salerno toward the Holy Land and the Third Crusade, Don Achille stopped the wagon in front of a well-preserved but totally abandoned feudal castle. This was one of many castles in southern Italy that was occupied during the thirteenth century by the Emperor Frederick II, a restless king who controlled not only Italy but much of the rest of Europe from his court that moved constantly from place to place. In addition to being the sovereign of a vast army, Don Achille emphasized to the students, King Frederick II had been an individual of artistic sensibilities and boundless intellectual curiosity. He spoke six languages fluently, and filled his court with a worldly representation of philosophers, mathematicians, physicians, astrologers, musicians, painters, and poets. He himself wrote poetry in Italian that was acknowledged in the following century by no less a practitioner than Dante Alighieri; and King Frederick's interest in the dissemination of knowledge facilitated the construction of several Italian centers of learning, including the University of Naples, which he founded in 1224.

"Frederick was the first man of the Renaissance," Don Achille had told his students, who sat around him in a circle on the grass in front of one of the parapets. "The first intellectual awakening of Europe after the Middle Ages occurred not in such northern cities as Florence, but right here in southern Italy, within the walls of such a castle as stands before us today."

The king was born in the Italian town of Jesi, uphill from the Adriatic coastline, in 1194. His Norman mother, Queen Constance—whose forebears had invaded and conquered southern Italy more than a century before—had been traveling with her entourage toward Sicily from Germany, "when suddenly she was forced to delay the journey because of her birth pangs," Don Achille explained, reading from his historical notes that he always brought with him on tours. She had been more than forty years old and childless at the time, and she knew there would be much skepticism in the gossipy courts of Europe about her capacity to have a child at her advanced age. This was an era in which women were frequently mothers at fifteen. And the queen was even more concerned that her sudden childbearing in the remote town be verified by numbers of witnesses and chronicles so that there would be no doubt about her offspring's legitimate rights to inherit her royal domain, and that of his father, the German king Henry VI, whom she would conspire to poison fatally a few years later. So the queen decided to deliver her child in the public marketplace of Jesi, under a large tent, into which she invited all the town's matrons. "They arrived in great numbers," Don Achille continued, "and later they applauded the birth of the future king—who, in the early hours of his existence, was carried outside into the crowded square by his bare-breasted mother, who suckled him within view of hundreds of hushed men and women."

The students were also hushed as they sat listening to the tale, and Joseph was embarrassed as well by the vision of the queen standing bare-breasted in a public square. But without pausing, Don Achille continued to elaborate on the boyhood of the future king, explaining how Frederick grew up in the exotic surroundings of the Palermo court, where the walls were decorated with Norman shields and Oriental tapestries, and how as a young man he wandered through the teeming and dusty streets of the city, where he was attracted to the lute sounds of the Arab quarter, and to the dancing girls with snapping fingers, and to the elderly sages from whom he later learned to speak and read Arabic. Frederick also took long walks through the lush royal park that—once the pride of Moorish sultans, and still a Mediterranean preserve of rare African animals and birds—emitted the pungent aroma of citrus groves and bay trees and evergreen shrubs that sprouted blue-black berries and pink flowers.

In time the future King Frederick became a naturalist, as keen an observer of wildlife as he was an expert young horseman and jouster; and even after he had assumed his imperial responsibilities, and built on the Italian mainland such castles as still existed in southern Italy in 1911, he always journeyed in elaborate caravans that included birds and other animals, Arab dancers, and other reminders of his youth. Indeed, Frederick's movements through the towns and villages of Italy, including Maida, recalled less the equipage and retinue of Europe's most powerful king than the menagerie and grotesqueries of a traveling circus.

"First came the light cavalry on Arabian horses accompanied by Eastern music," Don Achille elaborated sumptuously, referring to his notes, which he seemed to have memorized, "and then came the quick-stepping special breed of camels from Babylon; and then, balanced on poles that weighed on the shoulders of black eunuchs, were the palanquins in which lounged the silken figures of King Frederick's harem. Several paces back, far enough to allow the road dust to settle, came the mounted procession of knights and courtiers, and behind them a jumbled assortment of court musicians and attendants, astrologers, magicians, dwarfs and other jesters. And then, more paces back, riding on a black charger, sitting upright but not rigidly, came the king himself. The crowds of roadside spectators never had trouble identifying Frederick because of the deferential treatment accorded him by all the other horsemen, and yet he called no attention to himself.

"His traveling attire was usually a modest brown belted huntsman's outfit that fit snugly over his lean body; and his most distinguishing features, since he was beardless and rarely wore a hat, were his high forehead and auburn-colored hair and the almost hypnotic way in which he directed his blue eyes toward the objects of his concentration—a hawkish manner as natural to him as it was to the flock of his pampered falcons that followed him in the cavalcade, dozens of them strapped to the gloved wrists of tunic-uniformed pages, the falcons' aerial fury grounded and contained under the leather hoods that King Frederick himself had designed. Walking behind the pages were Arab grooms guiding the horse-drawn wagons that carried cages of lions and lynxes, leopards and cheetahs, rare birds and the high-strung imperial hounds with coats made lustrous from attentive brushing. Then came the king's imported African giraffe, the first such creature ever seen in Europe, followed by the lumbering imperial elephant, on which was seated, in a wooden tower, a mahout and two Arab crossbowmen. . . ."

Joseph was mesmerized by the recital, and when he returned home from the tour he could think of nothing but the king's cavalcade, which passed through his dreams that night and the next. When Don Achille later described to the students Frederick's sudden death of acute dysentery in 1250, a death that was foretold by the king's astrologer, Joseph felt the event in an oddly personal way; and he had a lasting image of the majestic procession that had carried the king's body through southern Italy in a purple porphyry coffin into the cathedral in Palermo, where it was dressed and buried in a gold-embroidered linen garment and a red robe decorated by brocaded imperial eagles and clasped by emerald adornments.

Within two generations of King Frederick's death, Don Achille had told the students, the realm would follow him into extinction; the king's sons were either undermined from within their own forces or were overwhelmed by elements invading Italy—and the fate of the king's grandson Conradin was tragic in the extreme. Conradin was only sixteen when he tried to rally an army to regain the crown, and Joseph and his classmates identified with the struggling young prince as he battled against the superior legions led by Charles d'Anjou, a French nobleman and papal favorite who had been invited into Italy by the Pope to destroy the last legitimate male link to the often sacrilegious Frederick.

"Prince Conradin was a courageous youth but an inexperienced and naive military commander," Don Achille explained. "And one day as Conradin and his aides were resting at their secret headquarters—the prince was actually then engaged in a game of chess—their whereabouts were betrayed, and the French attacked, and soon Conradin was dragged off with his aides to face Charles d'Anjou, who had already gained control of Naples. Conradin and his friends were immediately tried and convicted of being enemies of the Holy Church and traitors to the ruling crown, and they were sentenced to die publicly in Naples next to the Church of the Carmelite Friars. Conradin protested to Charles d'Anjou that his friends were guiltless, and he begged that their lives be spared. But this appeal was dismissed. Conradin then asked that he be allowed to die first, so that he would not have to witness the execution of his friends. This request was also rejected.

"And so, days later," Don Achille read somberly to his qualmish but attentive audience, "Conradin and his friends climbed the steps to the platform in the shadows of the church, where a large crowd of spectators had gathered. And there, one by one, Conradin's friends were beheaded—and as each head fell, Conradin stopped to pick it up and kiss it. Finally, Conradin stepped forward to bend his own head toward the blade. But before he did so, he tossed his gloves in the air, out toward the gasping crowd—a farewell gesture from the last survivor of King Frederick's dynasty in Italy."

13.

THE SEVEN ROWS of students stood silently in the assembly hall, as Don Achille held the leather-bound registry in his hands and, peering through his pince-nez, began to call the roll in alphabetical order.

"Amendola?" he cried out in his deep baritone.

"*Presente,*" responded the squeaky-voiced Vito Amendola, in the second row.

"Barone?"

"*Presente,*" replied Nicola Barone, a taller youth of more mellow modulation.

"Cartolano?"

"*Presente,*" said Franco Cartolano, the hefty son of a butcher, and a classmate of Joseph's.

"D'Amico?"

"Presente."
"Gentile?"
"Presente."
"Giardino?"
"Presente."
"Giglio?"
Silence.

"Giglio?" Don Achille repeated, looking up and squinting over his pince-nez. Many students turned immediately toward Joseph's row, for Gino Giglio should have been there. Gino's father was a construction worker in America, and Gino lived with his widowed grandfather, his mother, and her three younger children.

"Giglio has already been absent twice this week," Don Achille said, seeming more disappointed than irritated. "He is probably ill," the principal concluded, in a sympathetic tone. But then, as if not entirely convinced, Don Achille asked, "Has anyone seen Giglio around town in the last day or two?"

There was murmuring within the rows of students. But no one came forward to answer directly. Joseph kept his eyes downward. Earlier this morning, on his way to Cristiani's, Joseph had seen Gino in his grandfather's blacksmith shop. Gino had been energetically banging a hammer on an anvil, with a cigarette dangling from his lips. Many young boys openly smoked cigarettes, which were banned in school, once they decided to drop out and work full-time. Joseph's brother Sebastian smoked. So did the first-born sons in most other families Joseph was acquainted with, especially those in which the father was laboring overseas and the mother was struggling economically in the village with several dependent children. Such a woman was inclined to favor a supportive son who worked full-time to one who, in advancing his education, neglected his family. School attendance beyond the third or fourth year was considered an unaffordable luxury by a majority of poorer families; and despite the spirited lobbying of such dedicated educators as Don Achille, the politicians in the national government had so far failed to repeal the antiquated education act of 1877 that made school attendance compulsory only until the age of ten.

"Giordano?" Don Achille resumed the roll call, after pausing to make a note in his registry.

"Presente."
"Greco?"
"Presente."

It took Don Achille about twenty minutes to complete the roll call. This chore could have been accomplished more rapidly had he divided it among the teachers, to be done before the start of their classroom sessions; but he seemed to relish the opportunity to appear in front of everyone in the assembly hall, exercising his prerogative as a principal who enjoyed large audiences and being the center of attention. He also liked the fact that his campaign against truancy was getting positive results. Smiling, he announced after the roll call that only six of the school's fifty-seven registered students were absent today, and that the absentee rate had dropped this month to a record-low ten percent.

After descending from the platform, Don Achille strode into the corridor with his right hand extended, and paused momentarily while his history students lined up behind him; then they followed him through the wide corridor toward the room where he conducted his class. Similarly, the students in the other grades were summoned by their teachers—Don Bartolomeo and Don Fabrizio, Don Carmelo and Don Enrico, Don Nicola and two faculty assistants who taught reading and writing to the younger students. Soon all the students had been escorted through the corridor into various classrooms, passing along the way two holy-water fonts that had been dry for decades and a large wall plaque that had been hung long before in honor of the ascetic priest, Giovanni Cervadoro, who had converted this seventeenth-century monastery into Maida's first school in 1820.

As Don Achille closed the classroom door, Joseph and his nine classmates sat in the wooden desks that faced the rostrum and, behind it, on an easel the oil painting of General Giuseppe Garibaldi. The painting, which was six feet by four feet and swayed slightly on the spindly legs of the easel, had been on display for more than a month, ever since Don Achille had begun lecturing on Garibaldi. It showed the bearded and plume-hatted general on horseback leading a battalion of red-shirted musketeers. Behind the portrait, the word "Risorgimento" was printed in large chalk letters across the blackboard. *Risorgimento* referred to the nineteenth-century revolution that Garibaldi had boldly personified, and which ultimately led to the unification of Italy in 1861. Now in Joseph's class, as in schools throughout Italy during 1911—in accord with the wishes of the education minister in Rome—the Risorgimento was advocated as a subject for intense study, in the hope of cultivating a stronger nationalistic awareness among the young. This was, after all, the fiftieth anniversary of the unification. It was the Jubilee year in the life of a relatively new nation that had slowly evolved following centuries of chaos and decay after the fall of the Roman Empire. And Don Achille, whose passion for his subject required no encouragement from the education minister, had exceeded himself this year in communicating to his class the colorful, almost operatic saga that constituted Italian history and lent itself so readily to his penchant for melodrama.

"Ready the horses, students, for our final ride with Garibaldi," Don Achille began the morning session. "We shall gallop behind him through the hills and valleys of the south as he fights his way into the capital of Naples. We sense signs of melancholy in his mood, for the war is suddenly coming to an end. Up ahead, surrounded by royal guards, the king awaits his greeting. This is the king whom Garibaldi has fought for, but at this moment Garibaldi has doubts about his decision. Is this king worthy? Will this king be an improvement over the king Garibaldi has just driven off the Naples throne? . . . Oh, Garibaldi was a wise man," Don Achille exclaimed softly. "Look into those sad and knowing eyes, and ponder that wisdom."

All the students looked up from their desks at the bearded, brooding portrait of Garibaldi, his saber on his shoulder. His eyes, which earlier had seemed confident, did indeed seem sad.

The portrait of Garibaldi was a worthless work of art. It was amateur in the extreme. But it served Don Achille's purpose. Convinced that students would relate better to history if they had a visual sense of the historical figures—what they looked like, how they dressed—Don Achille a year before had commissioned an earnest, if untalented, local artist (who happened to be his uncle) to paint portraits of certain kings, warriors, statesmen, and other bygone luminaries whom Don Achille planned to feature in his Jubilee year history of Italy, which would date back to the time of the ancient Greeks and Romans.

When Joseph and his fellow students had attended their first class in the autumn of 1911, they were surprised to discover, hanging across the front wall of the classroom above the blackboard, three garish oil paintings that related to the Greco-Roman period. One showed the muscle-bound Greek warrior Milo, swinging a mace and leading his foot soldiers against the retreating cavalry of the hedonistic colony of Sybaris, which he destroyed in 510 B.C. Another painting depicted the renowned Roman orator Cicero, reclining with his eyes closed in a steam bath on an estate southwest of Maida, in Vibo Valentia, which the Romans built in 192 B.C. and the Arabs toppled ten centuries later. Also on the wall was a picture of the bowed figure of Hannibal, the loser in a drawn-out battle against the

Romans, exiling himself from Italy on a small ship crowded with injured and downcast Carthaginians.

"These paintings, and others that you shall see here in the weeks ahead, represent the diversity of the people who once lived among us and played a role in our history," Don Achille had then explained, as the students looked back and forth at the paintings without comment. "I also hope that these paintings will help you distinguish between the many leading characters who took turns trying to rule us. Because we live in the narrowest part of Italy, with little more than twenty miles of rocky land existing between our nation's eastern and western shorelines, we have been regularly crisscrossed and double-crossed by seafaring invaders and so-called liberators from every part of the world. And thus we have tended to establish our homes as our fortresses, and to survive as best we could against the intruders at our gates. And yet we have also profited at times from the presence of these outsiders. They have enlarged our sense of the outside world. They have enriched our culture. They have made us more adaptable to change. 'Change' is a key word in our history—change for the better, change for the worse—as you will see from the changing pictures on our walls throughout this course."

Joseph's mood had also changed regularly as he sat through Don Achille's classes during the early weeks of autumn, listening to his teacher relate history through the re-creation of dramatic events involving the protagonists. While Joseph enjoyed the stories told about the reign of his favorite emperor, Frederick II, he had nightmares after Don Achille had described the beheading of Frederick's grandson Conradin. Even Don Achille himself seemed to be affected at times by the persuasiveness of his oratory, turning around one day in class to point an accusing finger up at the portrait of the fifteenth-century Spanish monarch Ferdinand the Catholic—who financed Columbus's expeditions to the New World— and declaring: "Oh, you tyrant! You master of the Inquisition! Not only did you allow ten thousand people to be tortured in Spain, but you sent your conquistadors to our shores in southern Italy, and what cruelty they brought us under the banner of their religion!"

Don Achille's face had remained red as he turned back to the class, and it took him a few seconds to gain his composure. "Excuse me, class, for speaking so disrespectfully to the king," Don Achille then explained with apparent embarrassment to his students, who had been startled by his outburst, "but you must realize that the Spanish invasion of Italy has left a deep and lasting impression. Even now, centuries later, you can see the traces of the old Spanish influence in our architecture, which is similar to that in Spanish towns. And you can see it in the mantillas our women wear to Mass, and in the strictures of our religion, and even in the fact that I, as a principal of an Italian school, bear the title of 'Don.'

"You must never forget," he went on, "that our ancestors in this part of Italy lived for the better part of three and a half centuries under rulers who were linked to the Spanish crown. Except for the brief rule of Austrian royalty in the early 1700s, and the even briefer reign by Napoleon Bonaparte's relatives in Naples in the early 1800s, southern Italy was governed by viceroys who were members of the noblest families in Spain, most of whom had come to Naples after service in Rome as Spanish ambassadors to the Pope. So cruel were these Spanish authorities that even our word *spagnarsi,* meaning 'to be afraid,' refers to the Spaniards. When we are afraid we say, '*Io mi spagno.*' When we say, 'Do not be afraid,' it is: '*Non ti spagnare.*' But if we used these phrases in Rome, or Florence, or Milan, or other northern Italian cities that were never under Spanish rule, we would not be understood."

Dedicated as Don Achille was to enlightening his students about the Hispanicization of southern Italy, Joseph found this part of the course a bit boring and confusing at times (too many successors to the Neapolitan throne were similarly named Ferdinand or Francis); but when Don Achille's lectures focused on the challenges to the Spanish Bourbon leadership, especially those challenges fomented by the red-shirted volunteer army led by the fearless *Gesù guerriero* named Garibaldi, Joseph suddenly was riveted while his teacher's stirring words seemed to reverberate within the wooden frame of Garibaldi's portrait, enlivening its face and figure, and transferring Joseph back to another time and place far more exciting than anything he could imagine in present-day Maida. Indeed, for five successive weeks, from November through mid-December, Joseph hurried to class each morning to the fancied sounds of reveille being blown by a red-shirted bugler; and even on *this* particular morning, when Joseph came to school enraptured by the possibility of escaping to Paris with Antonio, he nonetheless knew he would be saddened to leave Don Achille's school. And particularly saddened to no longer hear the daily episodes of the great Garibaldi, for, as Don Achille said, the war against the Spanish Bourbons was coming to a close; King Francis II had just sailed out of the Bay of Naples, abandoning the palace to Garibaldi and his Redshirts, who would in turn relinquish it to a newly arrived king from northern Italy, Victor Emmanuel II—doing something that Joseph, had *he* been in Garibaldi's position, would never have done. Why should Garibaldi step aside for Victor Emmanuel II? It had been Garibaldi and the Redshirts who had driven the Spanish Bourbons out of Italy, and to these victors belonged the prize of the palace and the right to rule. Who could have stood before the Italian people more majestically than Garibaldi? From Don Achille's description, Italy had never produced a greater hero; and disappointed as Joseph was that his teacher's lectures on Garibaldi were coming to an end, he knew that he would carry forever within him the story of this hero that each morning Don Achille had re-created so realistically, beginning at the beginning, when Garibaldi was no older than any student in the classroom.

Don Achille's Story of Garibaldi

Our hero was born on July 4, 1807, in a house on the seashore of Nice—which, alas, had once been part of Italy . . . and like most of you in this classroom, he spent much of his early youth in frivolous pursuits, sometimes happily, and sometimes in tears. In his memoir he admits to us: "I was fonder of play than of study." His mother was very pious. She insisted that he be tutored by monks, but their strictness exasperated him. His father, a sailor, was often away from home, leaving young Garibaldi free to wander with other boys and to experience things that many of us might have experienced ourselves: "One day I picked up a grasshopper, and brought it into the house. The leg of the poor insect got broken in my hands, causing me such distress that I shut myself in my room and wept for hours. . . . Another time I accompanied a cousin on a shooting expedition, and we came upon a poor woman who was washing clothes along the water of a ditch. How it happened I do not know, but she fell head-foremost into the water, and was in danger of drowning. I jumped in after her, and succeeded in pulling her out. In after-years, I have never shrunk from helping any fellow creature in danger, even at the risk of my own life. . . ."

At the age of sixteen, our hero goes to sea as a cabin boy with his father . . . and he remains a seaman for the next ten years of his life. In 1833, when he is twenty-six, we find him working as a crewman on a large cargo boat headed toward Constantinople . . . a boat that is also carrying a dozen red-robed, long-haired men who have just been banished from their native France as undesirable citizens. He introduced himself to these men, who called themselves Saint-Simonians. They were part of an organization that had been founded in the period of the French Revolution, and they hoped to create a society that provided equal rights for women, welfare for the poor, and greater personal freedom for everyone. Garibaldi spent much time in their company during the twenty-three-day voyage to Constantinople. The Saint-Simonians were polite, well educated, and excellent traveling companions. Although Garibaldi at this time of his life was feeling alienated from his religion and his homeland, he resisted the temptation of joining the Saint-Simonians. But he was forever influenced by their idealistic outlook, and by a book that they had given him that expressed their credo. The book would be near his bedside nearly fifty years later at the time of his death.

It was not long after meeting this group that Garibaldi encountered a young Italian who was interesting but also very discontented; his name was Giuseppe Mazzini, and he had just formed an organization called Giovine Italia [Young Italy], which aimed to overthrow all the foreign factions that controlled various sections of Italy. Mazzini wanted to transform Italy into one independent nation.

Our part of Italy, as you know, was then still under the control of the Spanish Bourbon monarchy that ruled from the palace in Naples. The land north of Naples belonged to the Pope, and the papal territories extended throughout the city of Rome and up the eastern side of Italy to within thirty miles of Venice. Venice and its environs in northeastern Italy were ruled by the royal Hapsburg family of Austria; and the Austrians also prevailed over much of Italy's northwest, which included Milan. West of Milan was the Piedmont region, governed by the Piedmontese king in the capital city of Turin, where most of the ruling figures spoke French. The royal family of Piedmont also governed the former Republic of Genoa. South and east of Genoa were the small duchies of Parma, Modena, and Lucca, and the Grand Duchy of Tuscany, which included Florence. Most of Tuscany and the smaller duchies were also under the political influence, if not the outright military rule, of the Austrian Hapsburgs, who, because they were Catholic and archly conservative, had the blessing of the Pope.

Since the Pope also enjoyed the loyalty of the Spanish Bourbons in our part of Italy, the only region of questionable fidelity to the political interests of the Pope was the domain of the Piedmontese, particularly the port city of Genoa, which was the hometown of the young radical Mazzini and the headquarters of many of his antipapist, anti-Austrian agitators. While the Mazzini organization's bomb-tossing and sniping at the Austrian garrisons that were spread across northern Italy were publicly disavowed by the royal family of Piedmont, its king privately approved of much of its activities because they cast doubts on any illusion that the Austrians were welcome in northern Italy. The Mazzinian anarchic tactics continued even at the times when Mazzini and his new colleague Garibaldi and other young underground leaders were temporarily driven out of Italy, which often was the case between the 1830s and the 1860s.

During these years, Giuseppe Mazzini, a brooding, high-strung intellectual who clothed his small body in black garments and appeared to be in a perpetual state of mourning—and who, as a lifelong bachelor and antisocial idealist, rarely let human contact influence his singular viewpoint and radical solutions—lived at various times in France, Switzerland, and England. From these countries he would occasionally sneak back into Italy to organize a raid and then would slip out again before the Austrian troops, or the Piedmontese police, could capture and punish him. Austria's foreign minister, Prince Klemens von Metternich, labeled Mazzini the "most dangerous man in Europe."

Garibaldi was also a frequent fugitive during these years. After joining the Piedmontese royal navy in 1834, he began to recruit sailors for the revolutionary cause, and soon he became involved in a scheme to steal a ship in Genoa for the use of the insurrectionists. But the plan was discovered in advance, and Garibaldi was captured and sentenced to death. Shortly before the appointed time of his execution, he escaped and went to France, where he lived under assumed names for the next two years. The cautious life he was forced to live made him feel unimportant to his radical cause, however; so he soon left for South America, where in 1836 he joined other Italian exiles who had allied themselves with Brazilian rebels fighting against the dictatorship of the Brazilian government.

Garibaldi did not return to Italy until 1848, when sudden political upheavals resulted in an amnesty, which led him to join the Piedmontese king in a war against northern Italy's Austrian overlords. The Piedmontese king's army and the radicals were now working together for the first time to establish a free and united Italy; and while the royal Piedmontese troops would be defeated by the Austrians at the gates of Milan in 1848, and again at Novara in 1849, the volunteer units led by Garibaldi and other officers would invade Rome in 1849, and for five months would rule the Papal City as a republic under the political directorship of Mazzini.

Garibaldi was seen as a great hero at this time to most Italians except the peasants, who refused to join his army because their priests told them that if they followed Garibaldi they would be damned to hell. Garibaldi did not need them. He had more volunteers than muskets, and was obliged to arm some of his six thousand followers with lances. And their uniforms were anything but uniform. They were dressed in an ill-fitting assortment of multicolored jackets, tunics, and trousers until they decided to follow Garibaldi's fashion—and the fashion of his inner circle, who had fought under him in South America—of wearing red shirts. While some journalists claimed that the red shirts of the Garibaldini were traceable to his youthful fascination with the scarlet-robed Saint-Simonians, the color choice actually originated years later, while Garibaldi was in Uruguay in 1843, rallying his four hundred Italian Foreign Legionnaires to support the Republic of Uruguay's war with the dictatorial regime of Argentina. Wanting to lend distinction to the appearance of the Italian legion, but unable to obtain the funds for uniforms from the Uruguayan government, Garibaldi one day learned that a warehouse in Montevideo was storing many boxes of red smocklike shirts for export to slaughterhouses in Argentina, to be worn by butchers not wanting the bloodstains to be so obvious. Garibaldi took these shirts for his Legionnaires, and thus began the fashion that would follow him from the battles of South America into Italy.

In addition to red shirts, Garibaldi often wore ponchos that he had brought from South America. He also favored, as did many of his closest cavaliers, a wide-brimmed felt hat decorated with an ostrich plume. But Garibaldi was always distinguished from the other men by his shoulder-length reddish hair and his beard, his dignified manner, and his deep-set brown eyes, whose gaze often mesmerized his followers and made them regard him less as a military commander than as a prophet or messiah.

But his triumph was destined to be brief, for a few months after his march into Rome, the French government dispatched an army that would total forty thousand by June 1849, when it broke through the barricades and advanced into the Papal City. Sitting on his horse and wearing a bloodstained red shirt as his enemy drew nearer, Garibaldi paused and addressed his loyalists in Saint Peter's Square: "This is what I have to offer those who wish to follow me: Hunger, cold, the heat of the sun. No wages, no barracks, no ammunition. Continued skirmishes, forced marches, and bayonet fights." Then, his voice resounding with confidence, he added: "Those of you who love your country and love glory, follow me!"

More than forty-five hundred followed him in formation northward out of Rome, in the twilight of a sweltering day, before the charging French from the opposite direction could complete their rout of Mazzini's Roman Republic—executing along the way many of the trapped resisters, beating back the lines of teenaged boys and other civilians who jeered or cursed them in the streets, cutting down the tricolored flags of the Italian Republic from the balconies of buildings, and gradually paving the way for the return of Pope Pius IX, who had fled south under the protection of the Spanish Bourbons.

But the cautious Pope, not feeling secure as long as Garibaldi roamed free, took nine months to reenter Rome—by which time it did indeed appear that the revolutionary spirit in Italy had completely expired. Although Garibaldi and his group had zigzagged their way through the hills and valleys of the northern provinces, miraculously avoiding capture by the search party of eighty thousand soldiers from France, Naples, Spain, and Austria, the Garibaldini Redshirts were too ill-equipped, exhausted, and famished to regroup and resume the offensive. Along the road many had died of war injuries and infections, and among the fatalities was Garibaldi's wife, Anita, whom he had met in South America, and who died of fever. After her grieving husband had arranged for her burial behind a farmhouse in a remote village in the area of Ravenna, he led what was left of his army into a pine forest to avoid being seen by Austrian cavalry regiments that were fast approaching between two adjacent hills.

Hiding by day, traveling by night, Garibaldi spent the next few weeks being guided by members of the underground toward the western coast of Italy, where a fishing boat awaited him. His army was now divided into many small parties and scattered in many places, each group trying as best they could to find their way home through the thickets and byways, away from the enemy roadblocks. Before they said good-bye to each other, Garibaldi had reassured his troops that the revolution was not over, that they would reunite in the future. But there was nowhere in Italy—or what we now call Italy—where Garibaldi could feel safe. This was why, in 1850, Garibaldi sailed for the United States.

When he arrived in New York City, many political refugees from northern Italy who had escaped imprisonment for their revolutionary activities had preceded him, and many of these men were gathered along the pier to greet their compatriot. Among them was a general who had served earlier with Garibaldi in Rome; another man had been involved with members of the Italian underground group who called themselves Carbonari, and this man—Felice Foresti—had spent years in Austrian prisons, and was now a professor of Italian literature at the esteemed American university called Columbia; and there was also a prosperous Italian businessman in New York, Antonio Meucci, who provided the funds for Italian refugees and who would be Garibaldi's host.

Garibaldi was very tired after the Atlantic crossing, and during his first days in New York he made it clear that he did not want to be feted at great banquets or honored in the streets with the ceremonial parade that had been suggested by the mayor. Despite the glorious headlines that had been devoted to Garibaldi by American newspapers that had covered the Italian revolution, Garibaldi had no heroic sense of himself. The revolution had failed. Italy was still a fractured nation—ruled in the north by the Austrians, in the center by the Pope, and in the south by the Spanish Bourbons. Garibaldi was still sad about his wife's death. He did not know what he would do next, but he was in no mood for celebration.

After a month in the hamlet of Hastings outside New York City, and another month in a guesthouse owned by an Italian in downtown Manhattan, Garibaldi moved to the quieter Staten Island, which was being favored by many Italian settlers because it had the familiar atmosphere of our own agricultural villages; and it offered a seaside view as well. Garibaldi lived in Meucci's home as his guest. But Garibaldi's pride could not long abide being an almost penniless guest, with little more than two red shirts in his valise. Later he gave one to Meucci, who put it in a museum in Staten Island.

Finally, after Garibaldi had grown tired of playing dominoes and lawn bowling along the shoreline mall, he asked Meucci to give him a job. First he worked in Meucci's sausage factory; later in his candle factory. This experience brought no happiness to either man, since Garibaldi was not a good indoor worker. Fortunately for both Meucci and Garibaldi, during the spring of the following year, some Italian friends of the revolution purchased a large ship quite inexpensively in San Francisco. Many ships had been left idle there by skippers looking for gold, which was said to be plentiful on the west coast of America. And so it was proposed that Garibaldi pilot the ship and become temporarily engaged in merchant shipping, which had been the career of his youth. Garibaldi accepted the offer and did this for the next two years, once crossing the Pacific into Canton with a cargo of guano, cruising through Chinese waters aswarm with pirates who had been raiding and trading in the First Opium War.

In 1853, Garibaldi learned that a new government had been formed in the Piedmont area of northern Italy, one that would allow his return to the realm whenever he wished. Immediately he made plans to return. En route to Italy in 1854, Garibaldi visited his revolutionary friend Mazzini in London, and spent long hours listening to Mazzini's political strategy and plans for additional assaults. Before leaving London for Italy, however, Garibaldi decided against working directly with his old radical comrade. Too many of Mazzini's recent uprisings in Italy had been just noise and destruction without results. What Garibaldi thought was needed now was patriotic men within the political and military ranks of the Piedmontese kingdom. Piedmont was still an autonomous kingdom in the mid-1850s. Its king, Victor Emmanuel II—who, since ascending to the throne, had remained distant from the Pope and the reactionary royal houses of Europe—was steadfast in his desire to eliminate somehow Austria's hold over the Italian territories that included Milan, Florence, and Venice. The Piedmontese king's new prime minister, Count Camillo Benso di Cavour, had similar ambitions; and the latter said he wanted to meet Garibaldi. An introduction was arranged between Cavour and Garibaldi in Turin, and from then on Cavour decided to use Garibaldi's popularity to win public support for another war that Cavour wanted to wage against Austria.

To this end, Cavour held secret meetings with Garibaldi's old enemies, the French; and by 1858, Cavour had succeeded in getting France to pledge two hundred thousand troops to Piedmont's effort to win from Austria the lands that included Milan, Florence, and Venice. As a reward, Cavour promised to give to France two areas of Italy that the French valued highly, both of which touched upon the French-Italian border. One part was Savoy. The other part included a Mediterranean seaport city the name of which Cavour kept secret from his new friend Garibaldi throughout the Austrian war of 1859, which Garibaldi would help him to fight and win. This city was Garibaldi's hometown of Nice.

When the infuriated Garibaldi first learned of this, he was tempted to lead his best guerrilla fighters into Nice, to seize the local government, and to deny to his death France's right to receive Cavour's traitorous gift. Having recently reburied his wife's body in Nice, transporting it from the distant village in eastern Italy where she died in 1849, Garibaldi was further offended by Cavour's insensitivity. But friends dissuaded Garibaldi from letting personal feelings interrupt the unfinished business of making Italy into one nation.

After recapturing Milan from the Austrians, together with much of the Florentine region, the combined forces of French and Piedmontese then won a major victory in June 1859 at Solferino, east of Milan, in which twenty-two thousand Austrian soldiers were killed. It was considered a Pyrrhic victory, however, for the French lost twelve thousand and the Piedmontese fifty-five hundred—and many thousands of injured soldiers were left unattended for days on the hot battlefield, their boots stolen by peasants, their cries of pain unheeded because there were too few stretcher-bearers and medics to tend to the wounded. (One Swiss stretcher-bearer who witnessed the shocking scene was named Henri Dunant, and this experience led him years later to found the International Red Cross.)

The French-Austrian armistice in July 1859 temporarily ended the war, and so Garibaldi, in December 1859, resigned his major general's commission and drifted off on his own, planning to resume the armed revolution with volunteer troops who would not be directly answerable to King Victor Emmanuel II or to Prime Minister Cavour, whom Garibaldi would never again trust.

By the spring of 1860, after making speeches asking for rifles and men to revive the stalled revolution, Garibaldi set sail from Quarto, near Genoa, with more than a thousand volunteers, and they headed down the western coast toward Sicily. When they landed and began to unload their weapons and supplies, many of the Sicilian citizens fled in fear; and those who remained viewed Garibaldi's men at best with suspicion. They were confused by the language of the Garibaldini, most of the latter speaking the dialects of the better-educated classes of northern Italy. The peasants of the north, as Italian peasants everywhere, had generally avoided Garibaldi's crusade; as he himself explained it: "That sturdy and hardworking class belongs to the priests, who keep them ignorant."

Garibaldi's men moved eastward the next day into the village of Salemi, where the people were more cooperative: women waved from balconies, and a few casually confident townsmen wearing dark suits and straw hats, who might well have been *mafiosi,* politely warned the revolutionaries that they were marching directly into the firing range of three thousand Bourbon troops who were poised for an attack, eight miles north, in Calatafimi.

Being outnumbered nearly three to one did not discourage Garibaldi, for he had a low opinion of the Bourbon soldier's ability to fight, and great confidence in his own guerrilla tactics that he had first mastered in South America. Garibaldi led the charge toward the town of Calatafimi on horseback, exhibiting the fearless disregard for his own safety that was his style in battle. His bayonet-thrusting musketeers sent the Bourbons into a confused and scattered retreat, killing nearly forty of them and leaving one hundred fifty wounded. Although there were also thirty dead and two hundred wounded among the Garibaldini, the victory at Calatafimi inspired hundreds of Sicilians, then thousands, to follow Garibaldi's triumphant march through the hot and dusty roads into Palermo.

Three months later, Garibaldi had conquered the whole island of Sicily, proclaiming it part of the Kingdom of Piedmont— even though the Piedmontese king, Victor Emmanuel II, and his prime minister, Cavour, had earlier repudiated Garibaldi's invasion. They were even more critical when Garibaldi, in mid-August 1860, transported his troops in small boats from Sicily onto the southern mainland with the intention of toppling the entire Bourbon kingdom that was ruled from Naples; and Garibaldi later intended to carry the war into Rome, and, after defeating the papal forces, secularizing the Holy City and the Papal States and defining papal power as being based less in Italy than in heaven.

By now, the summer of 1860, Garibaldi's fame had spread from Italy throughout Europe and Asia. His conquest of Sicily and his invasion of southern Italy had made headlines in every major newspaper in the world, and books about his adventures were already being translated into many languages. The elder French novelist Alexandre Dumas had joined Garibaldi and was moving with five thousand of his followers up into the hilly southern mainland. Most Protestants in the United States, if not its many Irish Catholic immigrants, were favorably impressed with what they read about Garibaldi. In Protestant England there were fund-raising rallies for Garibaldi's benefit, and his supporters included Florence Nightingale, Charles Dickens, and the second duke of Wellington, son of Britain's victor at Waterloo. Also in London were clothiers who featured the latest in female fashion—red-colored Garibaldi blouses.

By late August 1860, five days after Garibaldi's Redshirts had landed on the tip of southern Italy, they had moved more than sixty miles up the western coast, but they still had about two hundred miles to go before reaching Naples. At this time Garibaldi learned that Cavour was sending royal Piedmontese troops down from the north, hoping that they would get to Naples before Garibaldi, thereby denying him total credit for being the kingmaker of a united Italy. Garibaldi, however, moved quickly and unopposed with help from many citizens in southern Italy who were eager to be on the winning side. In Vibo Valentia, which is about twenty miles southwest of us, there was a local baron who had contributed handsomely to Garibaldi's war chest and had also provided a three-hundred-man posse of farm workers and shepherds, armed with shotguns, axes, and scythes, to thwart eighty Bourbon soldiers who had been trying to block the road leading into Vibo Valentia.

After Garibaldi's Redshirts had stormed through Vibo Valentia, and continued northward through the coastal town of Pizzo, Garibaldi accompanied an advance guard into the Maida valley on August 29, 1860. Arriving at the crossroads, he was greeted by five elderly men who, hats in hand, were standing under a tree next to a large statue of Saint Francis, in the arms of which someone had stuck the tricolored flag of the Italian Republic. The most senior of the delegates, a slightly stooped white-haired gentleman, Signor Farao, stepped forward in front of Garibaldi's horse, and called out: "Hail to you, invincible General. We salute you as the redeemer of Italy."

As Garibaldi stopped his horse and saluted, Signor Farao asked him to come into our town, where the townspeople were waiting to pay their respects. Knowing that his men needed a rest, since they had not paused since leaving Pizzo, Garibaldi turned over his horse to an aide, and sent out word that everyone should dismount and relax in our olive groves. He then joined Signor Farao and greeted the others in the party. Among these were the town's two outspoken Socialists, my forebears, the Schettini brothers. Riding in the lead carriage with Signor Farao, Garibaldi moved uphill and smiled at the farmers and their families, who stood along the road calling out his name and tossing flowers in his path. They also tossed long loaves of bread to Garibaldi's cadre of young Redshirts who trailed the carriages, and who took quick bites from one end of the loaves before sticking the rest through the bayonets of their muskets.

Church bells were ringing as the entourage arrived in the square, where people were gathered together and a band was playing. . . .

Joseph had heard the story of Garibaldi's entrance into Maida many times before, but it had been told in a manner lacking the celebratory quality of Don Achille's version. Joseph had heard it from his grandfather

Domenico, who had described the event frequently and with disgust, and sometimes extreme anger. Domenico had said that when the townspeople were alerted to the fact that Garibaldi's carriage was approaching, the local band quickly began to play the popular new war song, the "Hymn of Garibaldi"—this same band which, until the invasion, used to begin each evening's concert with the "Hymn of the Bourbons." Domenico also said that although the church bells were ringing, there was not a single priest in the square on that day. Domenico himself was in fact more closely identified with the Church than anyone else in Garibaldi's audience.

Domenico, then twenty-two, had recently left the seminary and returned home to run the farm after the sudden death of his parents and older brother. They had been crushed in a rock slide when they were out riding along the southernmost cliff of the town. Domenico had always reminded Joseph that during those days he wore a crucifix around his neck, and the single-strapped sandals of the seminary, and his hair was cut very short in the manner of the Franciscans with whom he had been studying near Naples. What had angered Domenico most of all during Garibaldi's visit was the red-shirted cadres' riding along with the bread impaled on the bayonets.

The sight had sickened him. Bread to him had always been a sacred substance, the staff of life, the symbolic flesh of Christ himself. Domenico had been taught as a child to handle a loaf of bread with special care, as had most other God-fearing people in the south—the tradition, Domenico observed sorrowfully, had obviously not extended to Garibaldi's heathens of the north. The longer he focused on Garibaldi's horsemen, the more horrendous became their effrontery, their profanity in skewering the yeast of the Eucharist with blades that were doubtless stained by the blood of Bourbon soldiers.

Hearing hoofbeats behind him as he stood waiting in the square for Garibaldi to speak, Domenico turned to see a young red-shirted soldier prancing forth, lifting a cup to his lips, and pulling a piece of bread from his upraised bayonet. Without hesitation, Domenico leaped forward, grabbed the bridle, and screamed: "You blasphemous pagan pig! I hope you choke in hell on that bread!"

Just then the band finished playing the "Hymn of Garibaldi," and Domenico's wrathful voice carried throughout the square—where it was heard by hundreds of people, along with the neighing of the soldier's bolting horse, and the cursing of its rider, nearly toppled from the saddle. Everybody in the square, and in the balconies above, turned toward the scene, including Garibaldi. Jumping up from his chair on the platform, Garibaldi called out: "What's the meaning of this? Come to order over there!"

"I was insulted and struck by this man here," the soldier cried out, still struggling to control his nervous, high-kicking horse.

"You have desecrated our bread with your vicious weapon!" Domenico replied, adding with an accusing finger directed toward the guards: "You, and your companions over there, are *savages!*"

With these words the tension in the square seemed to thicken, and a few farmers and shepherds, armed with shotguns, began to shout harsh-sounding words in a dialect that Garibaldi could not understand. Signor Farao rushed to his side, whispering into Garibaldi's right ear. Nodding, Garibaldi then turned back to the crowd and lifted both hands in the air in a gesture of peace.

"Brothers and sisters," he called out, "please remain calm. There has been a slight misunderstanding between two sons of Italy." Turning toward the soldier who had been attacked, Garibaldi continued: "Dellepiane, remove that bread from your bayonet *at once!*" He then repeated his command to the soldiers who had posted themselves behind the platform, and said: "Signor Farao has kindly offered to take our bread to the church and have it blessed."

As the red-shirted soldiers lifted the loaves up from their bayonets, the church bells began to ring again, and, at Signor Farao's suggestion, the musicians picked up their instruments and played once more the "Hymn of Garibaldi." Garibaldi removed his kepi, bowed toward Signor Farao, and then handed it over as a souvenir. Signor Farao accepted it with a smile, held it above his head to be seen by all, and beckoned with his hands for a round of applause. Some applause followed, and, as the guards surrendered their bread on the platform near Signor Farao's feet, the audience relaxed and remained as patient as before to hear, when the band had finished, a few memorable words from the mouth of the renowned visitor.

Domenico, however, had already left the square. . . .

Oh, it was a glorious day—that August afternoon in 1860 when our hero visited our village on his way to unifying the nation. Within a year, the great unifier had brought together the north and the south under the single rule of Victor Emmanuel II. The first capital of the new nation would be Turin, the former capital of Piedmont. In 1865, the capital of Italy would become Florence. And finally, in 1871, against the will of the Pope, it was moved to Rome. Victor Emmanuel II established his court at the Quirinal Palace, which had been the papal residence, and the Pope established his residence within the Vatican.

Now, in this Jubilee year of 1911—fifty years after Garibaldi inspired our unification—Rome is the site of a huge white monument to King Victor Emmanuel II, which I hope you students will someday visit. It overlooks the Piazza Venezia, and it's more than seventy yards in height, and it is adorned by marble columns, mosaics, fountains, winged statues, and, towering above the center staircase, an equestrian figure of the king. The king died in 1878, and his grandson now occupies the throne. Our first prime minister, Count Camillo Cavour, died at fifty in 1861, shortly after the first meeting of our national parliament. Giuseppe Mazzini, the Risorgimento's most radical promoter, died in 1872. And our hero died at seventy-four, in 1882. During the American Civil War, the United States' President Abraham Lincoln had offered Garibaldi a generalship if he would fight in the Union Army, but Garibaldi at that time had too many reservations about leaving Italy to fight abroad.

On the occasion of Garibaldi's death, his obituary appeared in every major newspaper in the world. . . .

14.

THE SKIES HAD darkened and the wind was colder as Joseph left school shortly before two p.m. to return to Cristiani's tailor shop. With his collar turned up, he made his way across the wet cobblestones while holding slung over his shoulder the cloth bag that contained his books and the lunch he had brought from home and intended to eat in the back of the shop. It had rained while he was in class, and pigeons waded through the puddles on the ground. Above the wind Joseph could hear the hammering of two workmen who were building a wooden stage in the center of the Piazza Garibaldi for the Nativity scene. A life-sized statue of the Christ Child in the manger would be placed on the stage later, joining two costumed citizens representing the Madonna and Joseph. Down in front of the stage a half-dozen bagpipers would gather to serenade the crowd with their reedy, high-pitched melodies.

Reaching the edge of the square, Joseph paused to let the shepherd Guardacielo pass with his flock, which had been grazing in the upper hill near the cemetery and was now being led down toward the cliffside barn owned by Domenico. The barn was on the edge of his grandfather's property, behind the shack occupied by Pepe, Domenico's distant cousin with the reptilian skin who lived apart from everyone else. Guardacielo nodded under his hood toward Joseph as he strolled behind the sheep, holding a long stick in one hand and a shotgun in the other. The fleece of the sheep was beige-colored and still wet from the earlier rain or the heavy mist drifting down from the mountain and sweeping across the square.

Trotting next to the sheep were three watchdogs with steel-spiked collars. Joseph remembered Mr. Cristiani saying that when it was freezing in the mountains the wolves often foraged for food in the lower hills; and as they pursued the sheep, they became entangled with the defending dogs. Joseph shuddered as he looked at the sharp points of the collars, realizing that he had not seen them before on the dogs this year.

Nearing the tailor shop, Joseph saw his seventeen-year-old cousin Antonio seated at the window, sewing with his head down. He quickened his pace, anxious to talk more to Antonio about what they had discussed earlier—his cousin's running away to Paris, finding an apartment and job, and then arranging for Joseph to join him there *if* Joseph in the interim could be trusted to keep it all very secret from the rest of the family. Learning about Garibaldi in school had sparked Joseph's interest in travel and adventure; but the enormity of his cousin's plan, and Joseph's responsibility in maintaining its secrecy, had made him quite nervous as he had gone off to school in the morning, minutes after Antonio revealed his scheme. Now Joseph was again apprehensive as he approached Antonio. The beating Antonio had taken from his father after mailing those fashion sketches to King Victor Emmanuel III had alerted Joseph to the possible consequences of doing things without family permission. Still, he did not want to be left behind in Maida if Antonio succeeded in getting to Paris.

Joseph opened the door and waved toward Antonio, and was about to say something about Paris—but his cousin, as if reading his mind, quickly leaned back in his chair and pressed a finger to his lips. Joseph softly closed the door and looked puzzled as Antonio began to frown and seem tense. Joseph then noticed that Antonio's father was standing within earshot, behind a counter to the left of the door, measuring material. The blood rushed to Joseph's face as he realized how close he had come to blurting out something that would have probably tipped off Mr. Cristiani to their secret.

"Ah, there you are, Joseph," Mr. Cristiani said pleasantly, looking up from the counter. "How are you?"

"Fine," Joseph said, weakly.

"How was school?"

"Fine," Joseph replied, swinging his shoulder bag to the floor.

"Joseph," Mr. Cristiani said with concern, "are you all right?"

"Yes," Joseph said. "I was a little tired, but I'll be all right."

"Maybe you shouldn't work this afternoon," Mr. Cristiani said. "Maybe you should go home and get some rest."

"No, I'll be fine," Joseph said, looking at Antonio, who was sewing busily with his head down.

"I'm not sure," Mr. Cristiani said, walking over and placing a hand on Joseph's forehead. "There's some fever here, I think. It would really be better if you went straight home. I'd thought of that earlier, in fact, because a storm is supposed to be on its way. I wouldn't want you walking home in that kind of weather when it's dark. We'll all be working late tonight to catch up with our Christmas orders, and it will be too late then for anyone to walk you home. So leave now, Joseph, while there is still light. And tomorrow, bright and early, you will come back to us well rested, yes?"

Before Joseph could reply, Mr. Cristiani had placed his bag on his shoulder and, with a light pat on the head, escorted him to the door. Antonio looked up from his sewing and waved as Joseph passed. Joseph waved back, concealing his disappointment in not having had a chance to talk about Paris.

The streets were almost empty, the majority of villagers still being at home for their siesta. A few shops had reopened at two o'clock, like Cristiani's, but most would remain closed until three. Joseph was very hungry as he walked through the narrow streets along the damp hills to the east end of the village, where his grandfather's row of houses was located. Joseph had rushed off to school in the morning without breakfast, and his lunch was uneaten in his bag; but he was too cold to stop and eat along the street. He decided to run to keep himself warm, and in less than five minutes he could see the high tottering wall that bordered one side of his grandfather's property, a wall that had often crumbled and been rebuilt after many earthquakes and that now appeared to be held in place by the thick intertwined vines that stretched along its stone surface.

The first in the row of two-story houses that could be seen behind the wall was the one the Cristianis lived in, it being Domenico's wedding gift to his only daughter, Maria, when she married the tailor. As religiously devout as her father, and known to be his favorite child, Maria Cristiani regularly fasted and said novenas, and she often went to church in the afternoons to crawl on her knees as she made the Stations of the Cross.

The house next to the Cristianis' was occupied by the youngest of Domenico's three sons—Vincenzo, an indolent man in his early thirties who worked on the farm and had married a woman Domenico had not approved of, and thus had received no house as a wedding gift. Vincenzo Talese dwelled on his father's property with no more status than a tenant farmer—which was equally true of most other members of Domenico's extended family and circle of acquaintances (numbering sixty-one) who were sheltered in his six other houses and four shacks that dotted the estate.

The house that Joseph lived in with his mother and her three other children was adjacent to his grandfather's, the latter occupying the center position in the row and being somewhat larger than the other buildings. Domenico's house had a stone balcony in the front, overlooking the wall, and a smaller wooden balcony in the back that overlooked the courtyard. Living in the house with Domenico was his sixty-four-year-old wife, Ippolita, an ethereal woman with long braided gray hair who, because of her linkage to the Gagliardi family of Pizzo, was treated deferentially by everyone in the Talese compound, and most particularly by Domenico himself. She was the only individual to whom he was never curt or demanding. Pleased with his wife and the esteem in which she was held even by the aristocrats in the village, Domenico sought all the comfort that a proud man could feel with the knowledge that he had married above his status.

As Joseph climbed the outside staircase and entered the second floor of his house, he saw his grandfather's stable behind the courtyard, and among the returning farm workers whom he thought he recognized was his brother Sebastian, helping unload the wagons. His grandfather, on horseback, was behind them; and beyond the stable was the fenced-in barnyard where Guardacielo was assembling the sheep.

The house was quiet as Joseph entered the dining room, removing his bag and coat. At this hour his mother was usually out with the two younger children, visiting her own parents in the valley. She was always home before nightfall, when they would have a light supper. The table was already set. At one end, as always, was a place setting for his father, although he had not occupied the chair for more than two years. The overturned wineglass and plate and the silverware were there every day, occasionally dusted but not often, awaiting use by the man who might return at any moment, unannounced. The setting was there to remind the children of their father's existence, adding credibility to his photograph on the wall. Joseph had recently wondered if his father would be home for Christmas this year, as he had not been the last two; but today he did not give it more thought.

Suddenly feeling weak, Joseph sat on the bed. He was shivering and cold. There was no wood in the fireplace, no coal in the braziers; but even if there had been he would not have dared strike a match, for he had promised his mother that he would never do that when he was alone. Only Sebastian was allowed to strike the large matches that were kept on the mantels. So, without removing his clothes, Joseph wrapped himself in blankets and lay on the bed, drifting into a sleep from which he did not fully awaken for hours. Even as he heard voices in the house, which he recognized as his mother's and Sebastian's, he remained under the covers, unable to get up or reply to the questions that he faintly heard his mother asking at the side of the bed. He did not want to eat, to talk, to get up—he just lay there as the day turned dark, and his family's voices faded in and out, mixed with a kind of howling in the distance that reminded him of wolves.

His room seemed to float, as his eyelids grew heavier and the weight of the blankets comforted him. Shaken slightly when Sebastian climbed into bed, he lay tranquil again within the familiar fabric of his father's old bathrobe and the scent of burning wood and charcoal. When he heard a hysterical cackling of hens, followed by a strange snorting of pigs, the restless stomping of donkeys and horses in the stables, and the growls of watchdogs, he thought that he was dreaming. Then he heard his mother unhinge the shutters and open a window in her bedroom. Across his warm brow he felt a gust of chilling wind.

Marian Talese had gotten out of bed when she heard the noises rising along the back of the house; as she looked down over the window ledge into the courtyard she saw, in the hazy dim moonlight, crawling over a wooden fence, a bushy-tailed wolf poised to jump into the pen where Domenico kept the lambs.

She screamed, terrifying Joseph and the other children, and alarming as well her relatives in the two flanking buildings; and within moments the entire row was astir with confusion and panic. In bedclothes, everyone leaned out of rear windows, or hastened onto balconies with gaslamps and torches, to stare across the courtyard toward the animal pens and poultry coops. Domenico and his son Vincenzo began to fire their shotguns up into the sky, hoping to scare off the intruder. Soon other screaming female voices joined Marian's, as there appeared in the reflected light two more wolves scaling the stone wall, then moving toward the area where the domestic animals were enclosed. Since the spike-collared watchdogs had been leashed to chains for the night, the wolves went unchallenged, attacking many lambs and fowl that died quickly; others scampered and flapped about the courtyard trying to avoid the clutches of the pursuing wolves and the flying objects that were now being thrown down by the furious, yelling people in the houses. They threw pots, pans, boots, knives, and bottles; and Domenico and his son were now directing their gunfire to the targets—but nothing seemed to distract the wolves' continued mauling of their prey. Four wolves had now been counted in the courtyard, and two others had earlier been seen dragging off the limp carcasses of lambs into the darkness beyond the stables.

Marian, having run from room to room bolting windows, searched futilely for a pistol in her husband's bureau. Then she exerted the full strength of her lean body to shove a china cabinet against the locked door that opened into the second floor from the outside staircase. Finally, clutching a broomstick in one hand, and cradling her crying three-year-old daughter with the other, she stood wide-eyed and ashen behind one of the windows that looked down over the staircase. Although she was within view of dozens of Talese relatives who were now gesturing toward her from their balconies, shouting inaudibly in the din, there was no connection aboveground between their buildings and her own. She was isolated with her four children, feeling, as rarely before, forsaken by her husband in America.

Her son Sebastian tried to remain calm as he sat on the edge of the bed comforting Joseph and the six-year-old Nicola, who had run in from the adjoining room. But Joseph noticed that Sebastian's hands shook as he kneeled to place chunks of coal into the brazier, and Sebastian suddenly blessed himself as a blast heard above the roof destroyed one of the stanchioned streetlights that stood on the other side of the wall in front of Domenico's house.

The explosions and disruptions continued for much of the night, not only on Domenico's property but throughout the village—from the low ground near Lena Rotella's orphanage, to the high ground near the ruined abbey and the cemetery, and into the middle ground of the town square itself. There, watching from the torchlit balconies of the palazzos, many horrified villagers saw two entangled wolves rolling on the cobblestones, using their teeth and claws to fight over the bloody remains of a tiny lamb. Nothing could distract them—until a wagon of armed men, pulled by four horses, arrived to explode fusillades at close range. Only then did the voracious rivals fall away dead from one another and from the lamb's sundered body.

Moments later more wagons appeared, carrying spike-collared watchdogs that were released in the streets to join the attack; and a posse of black-capped equestrians in hunting attire galloped through the square, led by Torquato Ciriaco, who, saddled on a prancing horse, held a pistol in the air and carried a jeweled sword at his side. Following Don Torquato's group, in an open carriage driven by Maida's barrel-chested chief of police, rode the town's newly elected monarchist mayor, accompanied by his spinster daughter, who gestured with her hands up to the crowds to put down their weapons and cease throwing things into the streets—which now were so littered with household objects, rocks, and shattered glass that the horses were forced to trot in an awkward, side-stepping gait.

As the early-morning light exposed the town in sharper focus, seven wolves and several dozens of their prey were found dead in gutters, courtyards, alleys, and in the square. Six of Domenico's lambs had been lost, along with four chickens. No wolf was found dead on his property. One wolf, its gray mangy remains riddled with ruptures, lay bleeding in front of the Farao palazzo. The animal's haunted, undernourished face and body showed the depth of starvation that had driven it down from the mountainside.

It took two days to scrub the streets clean with scalding water, and to burn and bury the carcasses of the wolves and their victims in a ravine beyond the valley. The monsignor led a crowd of onlookers in prayers over the charred bones of the animals, and he gave special thanks to Saint Francis of Paola—whose statue was carried down the hill by eight men, including Domenico—for protecting human life from death, injury, or other mishaps. The mayor also appeared at the site to acknowledge the courage of his fellow citizens, and to comment that Maida—which during its long history had been overrun by an infinite variety of transgressors, although rarely before by representatives of the animal kingdom—had again proved its capacity to endure. As a precaution against the possible lingering presence in the hillside of those wolves that had not been shot, the mayor said, two new constables had just been hired to join the three-man Maida police force. Standing next to the mayor, the police chief nodded his approval. One of the new constables was his cousin.

After the wolf incident, Joseph and his family vacated their house and moved in temporarily with his grandfather next door. Joseph's mother was still fearful of additional attacks, even though, as the cold weather passed beyond the region, there were no new reports of lurking predators. In fact, very warm weather suddenly arrived in Maida just before Christmas—hot moist winds of the sirocco returned from North Africa; and the villagers removed their capes and shawls as they swept up the last of the debris from around their doorsteps and courtyards and decorated their balconies with carved wooden religious figures and festive Christmas bunting wrapped around the railings.

The evening chorus of strolling holiday balladeers carrying guitars, mandolins, flutes and ribboned torchlights was a diverting sight to the entire community, and comforting to Joseph; and on Christmas Eve most of the village children were allowed to stay up to receive their gifts and attend the four a.m. Mass, passing along the way the Nativity scene and the bagpipers in sheepskin clothing playing their music. After Mass everyone gathered in front of the church, exchanged greetings and kisses, and visited not only the homes of friends but those of casual acquaintances as well. It was "open house" throughout the village on this night, and even the aristocrats opened their palazzos to the general public.

On entering the Ciriaco mansion, accompanied by his grandparents, Joseph saw for the first time the interior of the salon and ballroom that had been the locale of the merriment and classical music he had so often heard from the street; and he got his first close glimpse of the entire Ciriaco family in the receiving line, a dozen descendants of eminent but presently shrinking estates and depreciating dowries, dressed in time-worn gowns and tailcoats—and adorned by antique jewels and meaningless medals awarded by the now exiled Bourbon crown—welcoming warmly the effusion of local politicians, bureaucrats, artisans, farmers, and their kinfolk as if they were all cherished cousins. Then the Ciriacos' valet, with an exaggerated bow, directed the long line of visitors toward refectory tables laden with sliced ham and stuffed eggplant, homegrown wine and imported liqueurs, a variety of fruits, cheeses, and cakes, and the crispy fried, sweet, doughnutlike *zeppole* that were a holiday specialty.

Joseph noticed that his grandparents were very relaxed in this setting. And indeed, Domenico's reserved and confident moneylender's manner, fortified no doubt by the fact that a few of the younger Ciriacos (including Torquato) were mildly in his debt, induced a certain pluckiness and perhaps undue familiarity on his part toward his titled hosts; whereas Domenico's wife, the blue-eyed and genteel Ippolita—the progeny of a grandmother's mésalliance long before with a secondary scion of the Gagliardi family of Pizzo—greeted her hosts with modesty and grace, as if assured of her welcome at such receptions as the one the Ciriacos were generously providing, at whatever strain to their solvency, on this bountiful Christmas morning.

Joseph's mother never attended these festivities. By nature shy, and even more so during the prolonged absences of her husband, Marian preferred spending Christmas in the unornamented surroundings of her own parents' house to visiting palazzos in the custody of her overbearing father-in-law. And so, while her favorite son and most frequent escort, Sebastian, helped her bundle the younger children into a carriage that would carry them downhill to the farmhouse of her family, the Rocchinos, she permitted young Joseph to accompany his paternal grandparents to the palazzos, knowing he liked to be with them at such social gatherings, wearing custom-made clothing and listening to accomplished musicians.

Maida was too small to support its own concert hall, but those professional singers and instrumentalists born and trained in the area who returned each Christmas to visit their parents were invited to appear as honored guests at various palazzos. And a kind of competition had developed gradually among palazzo owners, as each was eager to provide the finest music in the town. On this particular night at the Ciriacos' residence there was a retired but still vibrant soprano who had been featured not long before at La Scala opera house in Milan; while at the Vitales' would be heard a Mozart piano recital given by the son of a local music teacher who, as an emerging pianist on tour in northern Italy, had received acclaim as a soloist earlier in the year in Bologna.

At the Farao palazzo, the crowd was introduced to a robust young baritone who had recently made his debut at the San Carlo opera house in Naples, and was now, through the Faraos' open windows, belting arias by Rossini and Donizetti across the square and into the not always appreciative ears of the owners of the Ciriaco and Vitale palazzos.

Along with the music and food, the hosts offered their guests brief sightseeing tours through the spacious houses and verdant courtyards.

Wishing on his first visit to see all that he could, Joseph convinced his grandparents to ascend the grand staircases of three or four mansions before morning and, with countless other visitors, to traipse through the moldering but magnificent rooms with their frescoed walls, coffered ceilings, fading emblazoned tapestry, and ornately carved gilt Baroque furniture designed in Naples two and three centuries before, when that proud capital was the most populated city in Europe next to Paris, and in Italy second only to Rome as a center of patronage for artists.

On the walls of these deteriorating palazzos in Maida, as well as in hundreds of other palazzos in the towns and villages of the fallen kingdom, hung heroic portraits and other reminders of the affluence and style of old Naples: contented faces of the bejeweled seventeenth-century Spanish viceroys and the eighteenth-century Bourbon kings who ruled the realm; stoical faces of Christian martyrs who catered to the zealous Hispanic religiosity of Naples' Catholic court; and other vivid depictions of men and women who personified the good life and the good death in those years prior to the defeat of the kingdom in 1861 by invading soldiers subsidized by northern Italian money and inspired by Garibaldi. The unification of Italy, as Domenico often emphasized to Joseph, did nothing for the south except sink it further into poverty and despair. Naples lost its throne, its autonomy, and its importance as a center of trade and patronage; and its once thriving seaport was now principally active as a point of embarkation for emigrants.

More than a million native-born Italians were already in the United States, with many others in South America, Canada, Australia, and New Zealand. The overwhelming majority of these outflowing Italians were from the disenfranchised Bourbon kingdom of the south—farmers' sons, for the most part, toiling in faraway factories and mines to support themselves and their families; and Domenico could only lament this situation and belatedly resent that so many of his fellow citizens back in 1860 had allowed General Garibaldi to think, on that warm day of his speech in Maida, that their applause was sincere. Domenico was convinced it was not.

And he could see confirmation of his belief all around him on this early Christmas morning, in these palazzos, where—in contrast to the Garibaldi plaque on the Farao palazzo's exterior wall, and the sign bearing the general's name in the public square—the interior walls displayed no heroic portraits or tributes to the conquering general. Inside the palazzos, close to the true sentiments and hearts of the people, were paintings and decorative tapestries that evoked a spirit of nostalgia for the old regime and for the Baroque period in which it flourished.

On the walls of the Ciriaco ballroom was a large oil painting of a procession of courtiers and cavalrymen leading the first Spanish Bourbon ruler of Naples, King Charles, into that city in 1734. And here, too, was a portrait of Charles's son and successor, the devout if slovenly Ferdinand, who was chased into Sicily by the French, where he prayed to Saint Francis while his wife took opium.

In addition to the regal portraits there were many other mementos and relics of the old regime on display in the palazzos of Maida; and as the crowds of Christmas visitors continued the festive tour from mansion to mansion, their hosts seemed to take pleasure in explaining the historical significance of each artifact and heirloom.

At the Vitale palazzo it was pointed out that the enameled gold fan encased in glass atop the piano had once belonged to King Ferdinand's wife, Marie Caroline, who had received it as a gift from her sister, Marie Antoinette. Also in the Vitale palazzo, hanging over a mantelpiece, were British muskets and bayonets that had been used during the 1806 battle of Maida, after which the victorious British commander, General John Stuart, stayed in the mansion as an honored guest.

A noteworthy victim of morbidly operatic years in Italian history was memorialized in the Farao palazzo by a diamond-studded gold snuffbox exhibited in a display case on the wall of an alcove. A member of the Farao family told the Christmas visitors that this snuffbox had been the property of Napoleon's brother-in-law Joachim Murat.

Murat's name was legendary in southern Italy. Although he was part of the secular French regime in Naples that closed down monasteries and banned chaplains from the military, as king he nonetheless held the dramatic interest of his Italian subjects with his theatrical flair in court, his chivalrous valor on the battlefield, and finally the melodramatic circumstances of his death—an event that he himself directed in the courtyard of a castle, downhill from Maida, in the village of Pizzo.

Murat died in 1815. Seven years earlier, in the autumn of 1808, having been placed on the southern Italian throne by Napoleon, Murat was greeted by cheering crowds who were dazzled by the sight of him riding through the triumphal arches of Naples attired in one of his many glittering costumes—a gold-embroidered tunic topped by a scarlet velvet cloak; riding boots of bright yellow leather; a scimitar-shaped sword with a diamond hilt; and a three-cornered hat with ostrich feathers and a diamond buckle. His long dark hair flowed in curling locks, while his otherwise youthfully pallid countenance was solemnized by a whiskered jaw bearing a scar—the sign of an injury from a pistol fired by a Turk during the French invasion of Egypt in 1799.

Murat had been at Napoleon's side in that conflict, as he would be in many conflicts to follow—from the coup d'état by which Bonaparte seized control of the French government, to the disastrous march into Russia that presaged the decline of Napoleon's entire empire. By the late spring of 1815, Murat had been driven out of Italy by forces loyal to the exiled King Ferdinand; and when the elderly Spanish Bourbon monarch returned to Naples from Palermo in June of that year, the Catholic populace accepted him as their ruler by divine right. In all the churches, Te Deums were sung; and when Ferdinand first appeared in the royal box at the San Carlo, the opera house built by his father, Charles, the audience stood cheering for more than half an hour. Ferdinand was very appreciative and moved by their reaction. There were tears in his eyes.

But four months later, in early October 1815, Murat left his hideout in Corsica and sailed south, past Maida toward the adjacent beachfront of Pizzo. He was accompanied by only thirty men in two ships; but—as the great Bonaparte had proved after escaping Elba—remarkable things were possible with a minimum of men. Murat believed that he had the charisma and power to repossess the Italians. He was under the illusion that as a king he had been loved, particularly in this area around Maida and Pizzo, where he had been enthusiastically welcomed whenever he passed through the valley with his cavalry and retinue.

It was nearly noon, on a bright Sunday morning, as Murat climbed out of his boat and walked knee-deep in the water toward the beach and the town of Pizzo. Church bells were ringing. The square was crowded with people going to Mass or taking a leisurely *passeggiata*. It was also market day, and dozens of noisy vendors were touting their wares under tent-covered wagons, and a small band was playing on the steps of the municipal building, over which was flying the recently unfurled Bourbon flag of King Ferdinand.

Crossing through the square, on her way home after attending an early Mass and completing her shopping, was the grandmother of Domenico Talese's wife, Ippolita. Her name was Maria; she had been born in the countryside north of Maida in 1777, the daughter of the caretaker of a ducal estate. Maria had been living in Pizzo with her husband, an enfeebled but active municipal bureaucrat named Vincenzo Gagliardi, one of the unendowed younger sons of the prestigious Gagliardi family, which occupied a palazzo in the nearby clifftop town of Vibo Valentia.

As Murat arrived with his troops at the seafront edge of the square, and momentarily observed the preoccupied gathering of people moving back and forth before him (while his black boots and white nankeen trousers were still dripping with water), Maria was walking in his direction, carrying groceries and flowers, intent on arriving at her small house below the square in time to prepare for the visitors her husband had invited to lunch. With her eyes downcast, as modesty required, she walked right past the former king and his troops without any awareness of their presence, and she had practically disappeared down the stone staircase that led from the square to her house before she abruptly stopped, hearing what resembled the sharp popping sound of a pistol.

Turning, she saw from a distance of perhaps fifty yards two rows of soldiers standing at attention, their muskets held in front of their faces in a vertical line, but their uniforms of differing colors and styles. In front of them, pointing a small smoking pistol in the air, was a sable-clad soldier with a tasseled coat and plumed hat, who announced vigorously and repeatedly to the crowd:

"Viva il nostro re Gioacchino!"—Long live our king, Joachim!

Hundreds of people in the square suddenly turned toward the soldiers, astonished and confused. There was much murmuring and sighing from the crowd as the soldier with the pistol bowed toward the flaunting figure that approached him, a proud man wearing a light blue tailcoat with gold epaulets and a large tricorn hat gleaming with a cockade of gems. Maria recognized him immediately.

In past years she had sometimes stood among the roadside spectators watching Murat lead his cavalcade toward one of his military outposts in the mountains; and once, at a town reception in his honor, held in the public garden across from Palazzo Gagliardi, she had passed through his receiving line and had curtsied before him. But now in the square of Pizzo, on this late Sunday morning, she was inclined to back away with fear as the crowd began to react to Murat with hostile comments, and even obscenities, after he had called out to them: "Do you not recognize me? Do you not recognize your own king?"

"Ferdinand is our king!" one man angrily corrected him, and then picked up a small cobblestone and hurled it high in the air toward the Frenchman. It was an erratic toss, missing Murat by several feet; but suddenly, as the soldiers raised their guns, women screamed, dozens of people fell to the ground in panic, and dozens more turned around and raced from the square—even though Murat, whose quick upraised hand prevented any shooting, was now trying desperately to stop the people from running away.

"Brothers and sisters," he called out to them, "I came in friendship. Please hear what I have come to tell you."

But they continued to run, and were soon joined by others who had been lying on the ground. Maria, watching from her position behind a bush near the steps, saw the square become vacated, except for Murat and his soldiers, now huddled around him. Murat removed his hat and gestured with his hands. Then the soldiers moved in formation, leaving the square and heading uphill toward the road to Vibo Valentia.

Maria climbed unsteadily down the steps and walked along a narrow path until she reached her neighborhood—a row of stone houses filled with disquieted people who, through the partly opened shutters of their windows, could be heard speaking anxiously about the arrival of Murat. Ahead she saw her husband hastening toward her, hobbling with a cane because of his deformed leg, urging that they immediately seek shelter in their house; he had heard there might soon be bloodshed. Armed forces loyal to King Ferdinand were about to ambush Murat's group along the hillside, he said, and the whole area might then be endangered by stray bullets and invading men in wild retreat or pursuit.

Within the hour, as Maria and her husband, together with their one son, Giuseppe, remained in their house behind bolted doors, they heard in the vicinity the repeated explosions of guns; but later in the afternoon, when quiet was restored, a neighbor knocked on the door to announce that Murat had been captured. He had tried to escape along the beach into a boat, the visitor said, but the golden spur on one of his boots became entangled in a fisherman's net that had been left lying in the sand, enabling the charging local militia to capture the former king and drag him to the Pizzo castle, where he was now locked behind bars.

Early the next morning several hundred people, including Maria and Vincenzo Gagliardi and their son, stood outside the castle by the sea, waiting to learn the fate of Murat, hoping to glimpse the former king peeking out from his cell. The news of Murat's capture had already been semaphored to King Ferdinand in Naples; but no reply had yet been received from the Bourbon monarch.

In Pizzo on this day, and during the days that followed, little work was accomplished by the town bureaucrats and artisans, or by the farmers in the area, for they were busy socializing around the castle, debating whether Murat should be hanged, shot, or incarcerated for life.

Although the local militia maintained absolute control over the gates and bars that confined Murat and his followers who had not been killed in Sunday's skirmish, the fifteenth-century castle itself was owned at the time by the duke of Infantado of Madrid. And the duke's steward in Pizzo always had access to the palace. The steward was a humble and kindly man named Francesco Alcalá, a good friend of Maria's husband, and he kept the latter informed on what was transpiring within the castle—and that is how the details of Murat's imprisonment became so well known to Maria and her son, a teenager at the time; and he would subsequently pass the tale along to his daughter, Ippolita, who would in turn describe Murat's demise to *her* grandchild Joseph.

"They kept Murat locked up in the Pizzo castle for five days," Ippolita Talese told Joseph, during a quiet afternoon in her house after Christmas. Living with his grandparents after the wolf attack had provided Joseph with his first opportunity to spend time with his grandmother, and her re-counting of the Murat story was as engrossing as anything he had heard in Don Achille's history class. "When Murat was captured on the beach by the militia and marched off to the castle, a mob of citizens and brig-ands, hundreds of them, attacked him along the way," Ippolita continued. "They gashed his face. They tore at his clothes. They stole his gold epaulets, his spurs, his jewels, and the snuffbox you saw. The militia al-lowed these brutal people to have their way with Murat, and when he was finally carried into the castle he was almost bleeding to death.

"It was my grandfather Vincenzo's friend, Alcalá, the steward, who saved Murat at that time. Alcalá got a doctor to treat the wounds immedi-ately. And it was Alcalá who also saw to it that Murat should have new clothes, for the poor Frenchman's clothes had been torn to shreds by the mob. Three tailors from the area were called in to measure and make Murat his garments, one of these tailors being an ancestor of your men-tor, Cristiani.

"But none of these garments was as fine as Murat was accustomed to wearing. There simply was not enough time to make them properly. The garments had to be delivered in two days, for that was when King Ferdi-nand's military commander, General Nunziante, was to arrive in Pizzo with his staff to interrogate Murat, and Murat had insisted that he had the right to make a dignified appearance for this official occasion. But it made no difference. Murat was found guilty of starting a civil disturbance against King Ferdinand, and he was condemned to death.

"Murat died on the fifth day after his capture," Ippolita told Joseph, her voice conveying a sympathetic tone that her grandmother had perhaps used in retelling the tale decades before; her grandmother Maria was known to have had much compassion for the Frenchman. "On the day of his death he had a shock of his hair cut off and asked one of the officers to enclose it with a letter he had written to his wife, Napoleon's sister, and his children, who were then all living in Trieste. Then Murat took off his watch and gave it to the officer as a gift. But before he parted with the watch he removed from its lid a tiny carnelian on which was carved a portrait of his wife. Murat held this carnelian tightly in the palm of his hand as he followed the soldiers out to the courtyard, where they were preparing to kill him.

"The sergeant of the firing squad offered Murat a chair, but Murat said he wanted to die standing up. The sergeant offered to cover up his eyes with a cloth, but Murat said he wanted to die with his eyes open. 'I do have one request,' Murat then said. 'I have commanded in many battles, and now I would like to give the word of command for the last time.'

"The sergeant granted his wish. Murat then stood against the wall of the castle and called out in a loud voice: 'Soldiers, form line.' Six soldiers drew themselves up to within about ten feet of him. 'Prepare arms—present.' The soldiers pointed their muskets at him. 'Aim at the heart, save the face,' Murat said, with a little smile. And then, after he had held up his hand to look for the final time at the carnelian showing the portrait of his wife, he issued his final command—'Fire!'

"The muskets exploded, and six bullets struck him in the chest. Murat fell to the ground without even a groan."

15.

IPPOLITA TALESE HAD an aura of mystery about her that often puzzled her grandson, a detachment that sometimes made Joseph ill at ease in her presence; and yet he was oddly pleased that she was his grandmother. He was impressed by her. He was impressed by her well-groomed appearance, her delicate face and fair skin, which was remarkably unwrinkled for a woman of her age, and he was impressed with the fact that she changed her dress each evening before supper, or, at the very least, came to the table wearing a beautiful lace collar, and always emitted a slight but pleasant fragrance of perfume.

She held her slim shoulders back when she walked, and sat upright during dinner in one of the high-backed chairs that had cushions and were much more comfortable than the furniture that Joseph was accustomed to at home. His grandmother's dining table was polished and had candelabra; and the cookies she had baked for Christmas were displayed on the sideboard on cut-glass plates with silver rims. She spoke softly but directly, as had been her manner when recounting to Joseph the life of Murat; but she did not talk much about family matters or town gossip, and often she lapsed into long silences at the table, ignoring the conversations around her and seeming to be self-absorbed. She wore a variety of rings and had a nervous habit of turning them around again and again on her fingers, as if they were loose-fitting. There were objets d'art on the shelves of her living room, and mauve-colored fringed draperies along the windows; and on the wall above the fireplace was a gilt-framed painting of a cliffside manor at dusk that Joseph could not identify.

There was much in his grandparents' house that was unfamiliar to Joseph. His previous visits to the house had been rare and brief, and until this occasion, prompted by the attack of the wolves, he had never been an overnight guest. He and Sebastian slept in a rear bedroom on the first floor that, during the days of the Bongiovanni barony, had been the quarters for a servant. Next door was a room where Joseph's mother stayed with the younger children; but after two nights she moved out and took them to her own parents' house in the valley. Joseph could see that his mother was uncomfortable around his paternal grandparents, and after she had overcome her fear that the wolves might return, she proposed spending the Christmas holidays in her girlhood home, and Ippolita made no effort to discourage her.

But Joseph remained with Sebastian, and each day Sebastian accompanied his grandfather's crew to the farm, as usual, while Joseph went to Cristiani's tailor shop. The shop was open only half-days until after New Year's, and so Joseph often found himself alone in the house, or with Ippolita. Overcoming his shyness one afternoon, Joseph asked his grandmother about the painting of the manor that hung above the fireplace, and she identified it as the Gagliardi residence in Vibo Valentia, where she had spent much time during her girlhood. However, the place had greatly declined in recent years, she said, and added with a sigh: "But that is only natural. The Gagliardi family itself is in decline—and that, too, is natural. All families have their ups and downs, and sometimes a family can go from rags to riches, and from riches to rags, in three or four generations—and then the process starts all over again. It all depends on whether any energy is left. In the beginning, a family's energy usually springs from misery. And this misery often produces a family member's drive to escape to a better life; and sometimes he paves the way for other members to follow. So you have a family on the rise, motivated and industrious. And within a generation this industriousness can produce wealth. And with wealth can come status, even nobility. And with nobility comes pride, and often arrogance. Arrogance is usually an element that leads to decline, and in time back to misery. The process continues," she concluded without a tone of regret, and Joseph had no idea if she was referring to the Gagliardis or to families in general.

Most of what he knew about the Gagliardis he had picked up at Cristiani's, the back room being an endless source of information about the region's distinguished families, their scandals and other misfortunes. Mr. Cristiani had once recalled making two suits for Marquis Gagliardi and not being paid; although Joseph never knew how the marquis was related to his grandmother Ippolita, if indeed he was directly related. The Gagliardi family was large, with many branches, extending from Vibo Valentia, southwest of Maida, to the town of Amantea, which was northwest. What Joseph did know from personal observation was that his grandmother had better furniture and more jewelry than anyone else in his family, and that she was the only family member who did not go to church.

Not only did she not go to church, but—and Joseph was equally amazed at this—nobody in the family criticized her for it, or even commented upon it. His grandmother was seemingly accepted by everyone in the family, including her husband, as innately different from the rest of them.

Joseph instinctively did not inquire into the reasons for her absence from church during his stay at his grandparents', but he could not fail to notice—during quick glimpses into their bedroom—that all the religious articles in the room were on his grandfather's side of the bed. These included the missal on his bedside table, the crucifix on his bureau, and the wall niches containing the statuettes of Saint Francis, the Virgin, and other holy figures. On Ippolita's bedside table were secular books, one being the poetry of Ovid; a tapestry was hung across the wall behind her armoire, and on her bureau was an ornamented bronze box with a padlock that Joseph imagined held some of the valuable gems she was said to have inherited.

The subject of Ippolita Talese's gems had been much discussed during the previous summer in Cristiani's back room, after an incident in early July in which Domenico was also involved. According to the tailors—and

Joseph's mother later confirmed the story—Domenico Talese was on his horse heading home after Mass one morning when he was greeted along the road by three brown-robed nuns.

"Good morning, Don Domenico," the nuns said in unison, addressing him in a respectful manner that pleased him; but he was also surprised to hear his name spoken by nuns he did not know. He knew every nun in Maida, and many in nearby convents; so he assumed that these were affiliated with one of the convents on the other side of the mountain and were perhaps on a pilgrimage to Paola—for during this week many traveling monks and nuns were en route to the shrine of Saint Francis to celebrate his feast day and to revisit the grotto where he performed the first of many miracles.

"Good morning, Sisters," he said with a smile, continuing on his way.

"You are a holy man, Don Domenico," one of the nuns called after him. "It is a pity that Donna Ippolita does not follow your example."

Jerking the reins of his horse, Domenico suddenly turned around. He stared at the three nuns standing on the side of the road. He was confused and angry.

"By what right do you judge her?" he shouted. "And how is it that you know her?"

"We do not know her," replied the oldest nun, who stood in the middle. "We just know of her. Her family is well known in this region. But we mean no offense, Don Domenico," the nun continued, softly. "In fact, today we bring you good tidings. Because of your devotion to the Church you will be receiving a heavenly reward. Your wealth, Don Domenico, will soon be multiplied."

He regarded them suspiciously. The three figures stood meekly together, with their heads now bowed. They were tiny, birdlike women who seemed undernourished from excessive fasting. They remained silent and still for several moments.

"So my wealth will be multiplied," Domenico said finally, almost sneeringly. "And from where did you receive such information?"

"It came to us through our prayers," the oldest nun replied, looking up, while the two others kept their heads bowed. "We are sisters from the convent near Serra San Bruno," she explained, referring to a town in the mountains about twenty miles to the south. "We are affiliated with the Carthusian monastery there. The other night, during the seventh day of our novena, your name entered our prayers with the promise of your reward. We were entrusted to inform you, and we have walked many miles to do so."

Domenico had never been to Serra San Bruno, but he had certainly heard of the Carthusians, an ancient contemplative order that predated even the monasticism of Saint Francis. And despite Domenico's skepticism of the nuns, he had never been skeptical of the mysterious methods by which the Creator often communicated with his true believers. If Domenico's reverential life had now earned him the reward of multiplied wealth, then he stood ready to accept it; for next to religion there was nothing that interested him more than multiplied wealth.

"And when do I receive this reward?" he asked in a voice now friendly. He removed his hat in a belated gesture of courtesy.

"Soon," the nun said. "By tomorrow morning, if you wish. All that is necessary is that you pray with us before nightfall. We must complete the five decades of the Rosary. And you must reveal nothing about this reward to anyone except, of course, your faithful wife, Donna Ippolita."

"And where shall we pray?" he asked.

"We can pray at your house," she said. "It will be more private there."

Domenico nodded, and was about to give the nuns the directions. But the oldest one held up her hand.

"We know the way," she said. "We will be there at twilight."

Domenico galloped home to deliver the news to his wife. Ippolita responded to it in a manner that he might have anticipated. She laughed. She found it all quite amusing. Had she not known that he lacked a sense of humor, she might have accused him of concocting the tale by way of boasting of his virtue and suggesting that he was indeed worthy of a God-sent acknowledgment. But she was also a woman of tact and sensitivity. She knew how deeply he believed in God and the probability of miracles; and while one side of her considered him naive, her stronger side loved him for his irrationality and blind faith. She herself, although she avoided priests, was certainly neither a heathen nor an atheist. She even admitted to praying in private at times. Especially during earthquakes. And so when her husband requested as a special favor that she welcome the nuns to their house, and kneel at his side while he joined them in prayer, she dutifully agreed to oblige him.

At twilight they arrived. Domenico was waiting for them behind the wall near the front gate. Their dark veils concealed their faces as they bowed slightly and followed him along the cobblestone path and up the side steps into the living room on the second floor. Domenico could hear from across the courtyard the voices of his returning farm crew, the neighing of the horses, the barking of Guardacielo's dogs. The nuns moved soundlessly behind him, and Domenico was confident that nobody had spotted them as he ushered them into a large room where Ippolita was waiting.

The oldest nun introduced herself to Ippolita as Sister Carmela, but the other two nuns kept their heads bowed and remained silent. Refusing Domenico's offer of something to eat or drink, Sister Carmela quickly surveyed the room. Then she walked down the hall and looked into the main bedroom, and, seeing the statuettes in the wall niches and the crucifix atop Domenico's bureau, she said: "Here is where we should be."

After summoning everyone into the bedroom, she directed that Domenico and Ippolita kneel in the far corner, while she and her companions would kneel together at the foot of the altarlike bureau, which held candles in tiny crimson glass cups.

"You must concentrate completely on each word of our prayers," Sister Carmela told Domenico and Ippolita, "and one thing more—I will need some of your valuable articles so that they may be multiplied to many times their worth." Seeming perplexed, Ippolita glanced toward her husband. Before he responded, Sister Carmela pointed her right hand from under her veil toward the rings on Ippolita's fingers, saying: "Those will be fine, and also your earrings. And some of those gems that I see over there on that other bureau near the jewelry box." Ippolita again looked quizzically at her husband. But he paid no attention as he walked to Ippolita's bureau, fetched all the gems he could gather in his palms, and then handed them over to the nun, who had meanwhile pulled a black silk scarf from out of her habit and formed it into a little bag. Into this bag she placed the gems Domenico had given her, and also the jewelry he then directed his wife to remove from her ears and fingers.

"Thank you," said Sister Carmela, examining each piece before depositing it into the bag. "This jewelry will remain under the silk in front of the crucifix on this bureau for the entire evening. By sunrise, if you do not touch it, and if we have said our prayers properly, the jewels will have expanded to twenty times their size and value. And now, let us all kneel and begin the prayers."

Domenico did as he had been instructed, taking his place in the far corner of the bedroom, kneeling next to Ippolita, while the three nuns knelt facing his bureau and began the Lord's Prayer. Sister Carmela's voice rose above the others', and as she continued to lead the prayers through the first decade into the second, Domenico became aware for the first time of her strange accent, one that he had never before heard in this region or any other.

But then he concentrated on the prayers, as the nun had requested, and soon he closed his eyes and felt himself comfortably adrift in the repetitious familiarity of the Rosary—while his wife, unaccustomed to kneeling, fidgeted in place next to him and kept both eyes open. In front of her she saw the backs of the bent nuns silhouetted in the candlelight, and she heard their blended voices and the slight rattling of their beads as they progressed from prayer to prayer without any indication of fatigue or tedium with the singsong sameness of it all. Ippolita did not join them; and since her husband's eyes were closed she did not move her lips for his benefit. She thought only of how empty her hands felt without her rings, and wondered how much longer she could remain in this painful position on the hard stone floor. She quietly recited poetry to help pass the time, and also began to count the number of her cousins in the Gagliardi family, and had reached close to forty when she suddenly became aware in the reddish light that Sister Carmela's right hand was reaching toward the bureau where the gems were stacked under the silken cloth.

Ippolita held her breath as she noticed that Sister Carmela was placing what resembled an acorn under the cloth while removing a few gems and slipping them into her habit. Ippolita watched this happen again: the nun tucked another acorn under the cloth in exchange for more gems! Finally, as this was about to be repeated once more, while the praying continued unabated, Ippolita screamed: "Thief!"—and she also poked her husband in the ribs with an elbow to arouse him from his prayerful reverie. "The nun is stealing the jewelry!" she exclaimed. Domenico jumped to his feet and lunged forward to grab Sister Carmela by the shoulders, seeing for himself that she held a few gems in her fingers.

"Take your hands off me!" Sister Carmela demanded, as her companions shrieked and tried to get up and run toward the door. Domenico threatened them with his fist, kicked the door closed, and almost in one motion reached for his shotgun that had been hanging behind the door. Pointing the barrel toward the nuns, he said: "Stay kneeling as you were."

While Ippolita ran out to get help from his relatives along the row, Domenico kept the nuns under gunpoint. The two younger nuns resumed praying, while Sister Carmela stared at him icily and spat out harsh-sounding words that he could not understand.

Soon the police arrived, and the nuns were escorted to the local station house. There they were later visited by the monsignor of the parish, who, after interviewing them, told the police: "They are not nuns. They are gypsies. They have stolen their clothing from a convent in Catanzaro, and they have practiced this trick on other devout people."

After spending a night behind bars in the dungeon of the Norman castle, the masquerading nuns, still wearing their habits, were manacled and transported by carriage to be tried before the magistrate in the provincial capital. Domenico and Ippolita were among the crowd of villagers who gathered outside the castle to witness the gypsies' exit. Behind his back, there was much tale-bearing and joking among the villagers at Domenico's expense. It had been his avariciousness that had lured him into the gypsies' ruse, they pointed out. Ippolita herself refused to discuss the episode with anyone. After she had recovered her gems and placed the rings back on her fingers, she resumed her life with Domenico as before, making no further mention of the gypsies and, of course, not questioning his belief in miracles. She had been married to him for nearly forty-three years, and during that lengthy period she had not seen, nor did she expect to see, much change in his nature. She did not expect miracles.

She had met him, ironically, inside a church. It was during a sunless Sunday morning in early March 1867, a day when limited light streamed down upon the parishioners through the windows of the church in Maida. Ippolita sat next to an older female cousin, privately commemorating the first anniversary of her father's death. In the course of two years, the almost twenty-year-old Ippolita, an only child, had lost both her mother and her father. Her mother, Teresa, had died of influenza at the age of thirty-nine. Then her father, Giuseppe Gagliardi, who was thirty years older than her mother, died of a heart ailment that had doubtless been aggravated by the unexpected death of his younger wife and after much anguish over the failure of his banks, small branches of the Banco Nazionale, which had been financially shaken by the 1861 fall of the Bourbon dynasty.

Since the death of her father, Ippolita had been living in Amantea with the cousin who had brought her to church this morning, Michelina Gagliardi. Michelina was thirty-two, and the administrator of a church hospital for the blind, located between Amantea and Maida. But in the spring, Michelina planned to marry an emigrant and move with him to Argentina. Ippolita did not know where she would live after that.

While Ippolita had an inheritance from her parents, her father's quarrel with the patriarch of the Gagliardi family in Vibo Valentia, when Ippolita was thirteen, had prompted her parents to move almost forty miles up the coast to Amantea; and as a result she had lost contact with the main branch of the family. It was that branch that controlled the social and political life of Vibo Valentia. Its patriarch was Marquis Enrico Gagliardi, who was the town mayor, the tax collector, the commissioner of real estate administration and permissions, and the owner of the tuna industry that employed dozens of fishermen and vendors along the waterfront of the neighboring village of Pizzo. The marquis's aristocratic title and the foundation of his wealth stemmed from his grandfather Luigi Gagliardi, a lawyer who during the 1780s had skillfully managed his stepmother's baronial estate and then—solidifying his wealth as he curried favor with its source—had married his stepmother's least beautiful daughter, Beatrice, with whom he had eleven children.

Luigi had lived in a grand palazzo in Vibo Valentia with his family and servants, and had also welcomed into his household his slightly infirm cousin, Vincenzo Gagliardi, a courtly man who would become the grandfather of Ippolita. Vincenzo had been born in 1760, the congenitally crippled son of a brother of Luigi's late father, Domenicantonio; and Domenicantonio had adopted Vincenzo after the latter's immediate family had perished in the earthquake of 1783. Despite his physical handicap, which caused a gimp in his left leg, Vincenzo got around very well with a walking stick, and he traveled by carriage many miles each day as a property appraiser and tax assessor for the Spanish Bourbon crown. Often he was called upon by the local magistrate to arbitrate some of the boundary disputes that, since the earthquake, had provoked years of litigation among the land barons of the region; and because of Vincenzo's fairness and diplomatic manner, he not only negotiated many settlements but also made several friends among the claimants.

One of Vincenzo's friends was the stately wife of Duke Nicola Ruffo. Her ill husband, stricken with an apoplectic fit during the earthquake, was cared for by a young woman who had grown up on the property, the beautiful, dark-haired, blue-eyed daughter of the head caretaker of the Ruffos' estate. Her name was Maria Aversano, and Vincenzo soon fell in love with her. Her father, who had recently died, had lost his entire family—except for then six-year-old Maria—in the 1783 earthquake. She had survived the trauma in the protective arms of the duchess, who treated her as a daughter throughout her girlhood. Maria gradually assumed the duties of caring for the sickly duke.

Maria Aversano was sixteen when she first met Vincenzo Gagliardi, during one of his early visits to the mansion, and they were initially drawn together by the shared experiences of being the survivors of families largely destroyed by the great earthquake. Later, when they acknowledged their love to the duchess and their intention to marry, she helped with the arrangements and held the wedding in the mansion. Before the eighteen-year-old Maria had left the Ruffo estate near Maida for the neighboring highlands of Vibo Valentia with her husband, the duchess gave to the bride—and future grandmother of Ippolita—a wedding gift of valuable gems.

There had been a trend toward greater equality and caring between the social classes in southern Italy during the 1790s; the rigid rules and customs that had long distinguished the nobility from the commoners had begun to erode. Part of this change was the result of the French Revolution, which instilled much fear and uncertainty within the Spanish Bourbon court in Naples. Consequently the king's advisers tried to pacify the people with hints that a liberal constitution was in the offing, and they also suggested that the earlier policies of land reform and ecclesiastical taxation would be revived, despite the threats of those clergymen who had cited the 1783 earthquake as God's reaction to those policies.

But a more democratizing influence on the south than France's bloody revolution had been perhaps the earthquake itself. In a single February day thirty thousand people had died; the homes of rich and poor had been destroyed unprejudicially, and the survivors within all social classes were reminded of their common vulnerability and interdependence. During this time many palazzos were opened to the general public as hospitals and sanatoriums; noblemen were frequently seen serving their ailing servants; and the earthquake left for years thereafter a less restrictive social order. There was increased intermarriage between the classes, and there was less adherence to the tradition that had long limited a family's wealth to the fewest members—the tradition of primogeniture, whereby the eldest son inherited the estates of both parents. This custom had left the siblings of the male heir economically dependent on his goodwill and generosity, or else they had to consider other means of supporting themselves. They might seek careers in the military or the Church; and if they married—many did not, and had children out of wedlock—they might marry into lower-class families that were prospering and seeking upward mobility. However, in instances where a firstborn son and heir apparent had chosen as his bride a woman from the lower classes, a "left-handed" wedding had often been insisted upon by the young nobleman's family—a wedding in which the groom offered only his left hand to his bride as they approached the altar, making it clear to all witnesses that he was willingly forfeiting his rights to the family title and to an exclusive inheritance.

But such ritualistic obeisance to tradition was considered anachronistic in 1795, when Ippolita's future grandparents, Maria and Vincenzo Gagliardi, went to live with Vincenzo's wealthy cousin Luigi; and Luigi's generosity was such that he not only provided the couple with spacious quarters in a wing of his home in Vibo Valentia but also made available to them as a wedding gift a new carriage with two horses.

While Vincenzo continued his career as a tax assessor for the Bourbon crown, and also performed accounting and other administrative services on the side for the entrepreneurial Luigi, Maria volunteered her usefulness around Palazzo Gagliardi. She helped Luigi's wife, Beatrice, supervise the children, compensating for the servants' now tolerated laxity, and she became a companion as well to Baroness Fortunata, Luigi's stepmother, who occupied the largest bedroom suite in the mansion, and who had a hauteur about her that kept Maria on guard. Maria did not want the baroness to perceive her as a servant, or as the daughterly nurse that she had been to the senile Duke Nicola Ruffo. At times Maria feared that this was the role she was destined for, to care for the ailing and elderly nobility; and she wondered if the patriarchal Luigi, whose generosity seemed not entirely devoid of pragmatism, might have welcomed her into his household with this in mind, that she would look after his spindly white-haired patroness and stepmother—indeed, Maria could also wonder if her crippled husband, Vincenzo, had not found comfort in this devotional aspect of her life when he first met her at the Ruffo estate. These were thoughts Maria expressed in a gilt-edged diary the duchess had given her, after the duchess had taught her to read and write; and that book, into which she would later record her memories of Murat, would become part of her legacy to her offspring—offspring that, fortunately for her, arrived early enough in her residency at Palazzo Gagliardi to extricate her from whatever expectations of servitude her benefactors might have cultivated had she long remained a childless woman.

Maria's first and only child was born at Palazzo Gagliardi during the winter of 1796. Maria named him Giuseppe, in memory of her father, the Ruffos' caretaker. During Giuseppe's childhood and early youth, he was reared in the grandeur provided by Luigi. But a decade later—after Napoleon's army in 1806 had avenged its British-imposed defeat at the battle of Maida, driving the Spanish Bourbon king out of Naples onto the British-protected island of Sicily—a certain bickering arose within Palazzo Gagliardi between Vincenzo, a Bourbon loyalist, and his politically accommodating cousin Luigi. Vincenzo soon left the palazzo and resettled his family downhill in the seaside town of Pizzo.

Deprived of his Bourbon-sponsored career as well as the comforts of Luigi's palazzo, Vincenzo lived modestly with Maria and young Giuseppe, ultimately finding work as a minor customs official in the Pizzo marine terminal building—a position supervised during this postwar period of loose French administration by an ex-Bourbon magistrate whom Vincenzo had known during his earlier days as a tax assessor for the now exiled King Ferdinand. Luigi Gagliardi meanwhile contrived introductions to the ruling French faction, and in late 1810 he gained audiences with Napoleon's brother-in-law Joachim Murat, who was much taken by Luigi's brio and buoyantly opportunistic personality, finding it a welcome contrast to the stoicism of most hill-country Italians. But before Luigi could amass huge profits through his cooperation and participation in Murat's many projects for improving living conditions in the southern countryside, Napoleon pulled his brother-in-law out of Italy to help lead the French army into Russia in 1812. This would prove doubly upsetting to Murat. He would fail with Napoleon in battle; and then, on returning to the throne he had been forced to leave for several months untended in Naples, he would find himself among ministers and courtiers who viewed him as an impotent Napoleonic *beau sabreur,* a man whose regal days were numbered and whose future use to them (and to Luigi as well) was negligible. At the same time, Murat's British and Spanish Bourbon enemies in Sicily, as well as on warships floating near Pizzo and Maida, were marking time until his deteriorating kingdom was most vulnerable to an attack and most receptive to the return of King Ferdinand—who, while Murat had been freezing in Russia, was living in sunny exile at his hunting lodge outside Palermo, riding to hounds and submitting to the varied ministrations of his priestly counselors and his dark-eyed mistress.

By 1815, after Murat had led what was left of his loyal cavalry on a vainglorious attempt to unify the entire Italian peninsula, an attempt that succeeded only as pageantry, he slipped out of Italy, vacating the Neapolitan throne. It was soon occupied by Ferdinand, who returned triumphantly from Sicily, and the saga of Murat was now reduced to the final tragic act that would ensue four months later, when he would dramatically reappear on the beach of Pizzo on that fateful Sunday morning in early October.

After Murat's execution, the grateful King Ferdinand ordered that a monument be erected along the shoreline where the last French king of Italy had properly perished. The monarch ordered that the monument be inscribed to read: "Heaven has reserved for the inhabitants of Pizzo the glory of saving our fatherland and Italy from fresh revolutionary calamities." King Ferdinand also decreed that the royal treasury would pay for the restoration of the Pizzo church that Murat's administrators had never gotten around to doing, and he further stated that all the citizens who had resided in Pizzo at the time of Murat's capture would be perpetually exempted from royal taxes, and that they could in the future expect other privileges and special treatment from the Bourbon crown.

Suddenly this small seaside village was the envy of the entire realm; and whenever a resident of Pizzo traveled elsewhere in the kingdom and made known his place of origin, that acknowledgment usually elicited a favorable comment or a reaction that made him feel heroic and blessed. Even Vincenzo, who during the time of Murat's capture had done nothing except to remain steadfastly uninvolved, was now regarded as an influential figure by most people whom he knew in neighboring villages—including his cousin in Vibo Valentia, Luigi Gagliardi. One evening Luigi paid Vincenzo a visit and asked if Vincenzo might intercede in his behalf with the Bourbon authorities should Luigi's past dealings with the French ever be raised as an issue. Vincenzo quietly said that he would do whatever he could if the problem arose—and to his relief, it never did.

Vincenzo and Maria's son—who would become Ippolita's father—was at this time an ambitious young man in his early twenties who had already begun to benefit from the favored treatment extended by King Ferdinand to the residents of Pizzo. Even before this turn of events, Giuseppe Gagliardi had been prepared to take advantage of it; his early education, provided by visiting tutors in the Gagliardi manor in Vibo Valentia, had given him a foundation in learning superior to what had been available to the young people of Pizzo, where the Church-run school offered a most rudimentary curriculum and stressed mainly religious obedience. And with the revitalization of Pizzo's economy due to the king's munificence—the tax concessions, the royal subsidy to new businesses, the king's designation of Pizzo as a port through which the realm funneled part of its olive oil and silk trade with England—Giuseppe had many opportunities for employment that were varied and remunerative.

Tall and slender, amiable and well-spoken (even in French, although it was now impolitic to speak it), Giuseppe followed his interest in mathematics by working first in an accounting office. A year later he moved on to the weights and measures section of the seaport terminal building, where his father was the director of cargo inspection. Two years later, Giuseppe took a job as a clerk to the director of loans at the Pizzo bank, an enterprise recently enriched by the substantial deposits made by the region's land barons who sought to be associated with the king's favorite city.

After nearly three years at the bank, Giuseppe gained a transfer to Naples, where he received wider experience at the main office of the

Banco di Napoli. There he lived in a one-room flat overlooking the bay, in view of Mount Vesuvius. On Sundays he often strolled down to the pier to watch the arrivals and departures of large sailing vessels. He became acquainted with ship owners and captains, and befriended the minister of navigation for the Bourbon crown. One day Giuseppe suggested to the minister that the new twice-weekly mail steamer between Naples and Palermo, which sailed along the western coast of the peninsula, should stop at Pizzo. The minister considered it a worthy request, and with little delay it was arranged.

In 1831, at the age of thirty-five, Giuseppe left Naples to accept a higher position closer to home. He was named a subdirector of banking for the kingdom's southern region, headquartered in Catanzaro, a city of more than twenty thousand residents that was about forty miles northeast of Pizzo via a bumpy and circuitous route that cut through the valley of Maida. In 1832, Giuseppe took that route to return to Pizzo for his father's funeral. Vincenzo Gagliardi had died of heart failure at seventy-two. Giuseppe convinced his mother after the funeral to return with him to Catanzaro. Maria shared his small house there for three years, but she was never happy in Catanzaro. During the summer of 1835, Giuseppe took her back to Pizzo for a visit. A week after their arrival, Maria asked her son to escort her up to Vibo Valentia so that she might see Luigi. Wizened but not feeble at ninety-one, Luigi rose from his tree-shaded chair in the garden as their carriage approached. He greeted Maria and Giuseppe with a vigorous embrace, and he seemed almost as pleased to see their carriage after Maria had reminded him that, forty years before, he had given it to her as a wedding present.

The mansion she had lived in as a new bride had been sold by Luigi; he had moved into an even grander palazzo that stood behind him now, a fifty-room edifice with windows filled with figures and faces of people old and young, most of whom Maria did not recognize. Luigi's wife, Beatrice, and his stepmother, Baroness Fortunata, were now dead. So were five of his eleven children, and twelve of his thirty-one grandchildren. Maria Gagliardi was of course not a blood relative, being related to the family through her late husband; but even before she entered the house to begin the greetings and introductions, she felt more than reunited with the Gagliardis when the old patriarch informed her that a suite in the palazzo would always be available whenever she wished to move in.

With her warm reception in Vibo Valentia she felt less isolated and lonely than she had after Vincenzo's death; and when she told Giuseppe that she preferred not to return with him to Catanzaro, he deferred to her wishes without much discussion. She was clearly happier away from Catanzaro. And in Catanzaro he would not be entirely alone. Giuseppe would continue to see, and now less furtively, the woman his mother had not approved of—his part-time housekeeper and mistress, a widow of almost forty whose husband had died with Murat's army in Russia.

Giuseppe had first hired her four years earlier, shortly after his appointment to the Catanzaro bank, and before his father's death had brought his mother into his home. The housekeeper was a handsome olive-skinned woman who wore white blouses and colorful skirts, suggesting that her mourning days were behind her. There was never any question of marriage—to her, or to anyone else. Cautious in all things, Giuseppe was particularly cautious regarding women. Most young marriageable females in the provinces of southern Italy were ever under the watch of protective male relatives and aspiring suitors, and the back roads of the kingdom were lined with white crosses under which were buried the bodies of unwary men who had looked twice at the wrong woman. Giuseppe was also fortunate in not having in his veins the hot blood of a daring Lothario; he was, except for his occasional dalliances with his housekeeper, as cool and correct in his private as he was in his professional life. He determinedly saw himself as a bachelor for life. Having felt claustrophobic as a child within the lower level of the Gagliardi hierarchy in Vibo Valentia, and as the overly protected single offspring in his parents' house in Pizzo, Giuseppe wished to remain free of additional binding, clinging relationships.

This continued to be his attitude even as he approached his fiftieth birthday and was beginning to find his business routine tedious, and his personal life empty, as there had gradually disappeared from his life every individual who had played any part in it. First, his housekeeper abandoned him one day with the announcement that she had fallen in love with a man whom she refused to name but was leaving to marry. A month later his mother died in her sleep at her home in Pizzo, willing to him her diary and the gems the duchess had given her. Before Giuseppe had returned to Catanzaro from his mother's funeral he learned of the death of Luigi Gagliardi at ninety-seven. Giuseppe went to Vibo Valentia to attend the Requiem Mass and walk in the funeral cortege. More social than solemn, and joined by nearly every nobleman and politician in the deep south, the long procession to the cemetery afforded Giuseppe an opportunity to eavesdrop on the men's unflattering comments about the king and their complaints about the worsening conditions in the provinces. The local economy was depressed, this Giuseppe knew for sure, but the extent of the people's rancor against the present occupant of the throne of Naples was deeper and more emotional than what he had been hearing in Catanzaro. Giuseppe got the feeling that the area of his birth was now almost ripe for insurrection.

Ferdinand II, grandson and namesake of the revered old monarch who had rid the country of Murat, was now the king. Many of the concessions granted by his grandfather had become loosely administered or were ignored entirely by his ministers, including the annual supply of free salt to Pizzo citizens, which many complained they were no longer getting. Salt was much craved by people throughout the realm because the crown had always made it scarce by monopolizing its supply and distribution, thereby gaining large revenues in sales taxes. Citizens had been warned against collecting even small amounts of salt water, on the assumption that they would expose the water to the sun for the purpose of crystallization. Guarding against this, the Bourbon police and coastal patrol had been entrusted to maintain an alert watch along the beaches; and while they had rarely been vigilant in the past, they suddenly became so after the coronation of Ferdinand II. And lately their watch came to include even the beach of the once privileged town of Pizzo.

During the time Giuseppe Gagliardi spent in Pizzo and Vibo Valentia attending the funerals, he refrained from expressing any opinions about the king's administration—not entirely because he was afraid of being overheard and reported, but also because as a banker Giuseppe was appreciative of the efforts the king was currently making to ameliorate the economy through a more aggressive approach in international trade. At the remodeled port of Naples there had been under Ferdinand II an impressive increase in the number of merchant ships afloat and the volume of business conducted—indeed, in the last year the king could boast that his ships had carried to foreign ports two-thirds of the realm's domestic produce. At factories in and around Naples there was record production of such popular export items as gloves, soap, perfumes, coral ornaments, silks, earthenware, hats, and carriages. The king had made Naples the first city in Italy to have a railroad system. After opening the first line from Naples to Portici in 1839, Ferdinand would extend the tracks farther north to Caserta in 1843, and to Capua in 1845—and he hoped to reach Rome in his lifetime, although the Pope remained rigidly opposed to any trains entering the Eternal City or the Papal States. The Pope believed that a train's noise, filth, and monstrous unsightliness would mar the lovely panorama of the countryside and disturb the contemplative mood of those kneeling in the pews of churches.

While Giuseppe had not yet seen a train—he had not been back to Naples since their introduction—he had quickly and unequivocally accepted the Pope's lowly opinion of such conveyances, which was shared by everyone he knew; and he was therefore much surprised to hear a spirited advocacy of the rail system expressed one night by the guest of honor at a dinner party he attended in Catanzaro some time after returning from the funerals. The guest of honor was a petite young woman from Naples who wore a white lace dress and was named Teresa Mazzei.

Giuseppe had been invited to the dinner by a banking colleague in Catanzaro who was married to Teresa's older sister, and it was this sister whom Teresa had come from Naples to visit. When Giuseppe had been introduced to her he was not immediately taken by her physical appeal or charm, although she seemed pretty enough and sufficiently sociable by any standard. It was rather her enthusiasm that appealed to him, her blithe spirit and outgoing manner that would have been considered risqué among country maidens in Italy; but she was clearly a citified woman beyond the measure of country convention, and she was also young enough for her exuberance to be accepted by her older dinner partners as a genuine part of her nature and not merely an attempt to command their attention.

And yet she did command their attention during dinner, and after it as well, by her humorous accounts of current social activities in Naples and by her optimistic assessment of the role the railroad would play in helping Naples to maintain its position as a leading world capital. She described the festive opening of the new terminal building, glowing with stanchioned gaslights that had only recently removed the city's streets from centuries of dim dependence on candles, and she reveled in the fact that the terminal's iron rafters had seemed to reverberate with the voices and instruments of the performers from the San Carlo opera house, assembled near a platform to serenade the passengers, who climbed aboard wearing long dresses and tailcoats. While she admitted that she would not go for a train ride wearing the white dress she had worn on this evening of her sister's dinner, Teresa said that the black soot flying from the locomotive had not been as pervasive as she had expected, and that none of the frightening jolts and sudden turns along the tracks could diminish the thrill of the adventure.

Giuseppe left the dinner that night imagining he would never see Teresa Mazzei again; and had it been left to his personal initiative, he probably never would have. Much as she held his interest, he assumed that she would soon be returning to Naples and to suitors who were far closer to her age than the thirty years that separated the two of them. But a few weeks later her brother-in-law at the bank asked Giuseppe to join Teresa and her sister at a picnic lunch in the country one weekend, adding that they would come by for Giuseppe and would ride out together.

The weather for the outing was bright and balmy, and during the short walk after lunch Giuseppe was able to speak more intimately with Teresa, although he still felt awkward with a woman so young, and his response to her lighthearted commentary and banter was expressed mainly with avuncular bemusement. When she casually mentioned that she was extending her stay in Catanzaro, Giuseppe still did not think it appropriate for him to propose that they meet again, but he was quite pleased when her brother-in-law proposed it for him.

Several subsequent dinners, all proposed by her brother-in-law, made it clear even to the reluctant suitor that *he* was being courted; and while he delicately expressed his concerns to Teresa's brother-in-law, he remained receptive to her presence, even to the point months later of accepting her invitation to come to Naples to meet her parents. After Teresa had welcomed him at the gate of their large stone house on the outskirts of the city, and had escorted him through a corridor into her father's library, Giuseppe saw before him a trim, gray-haired smiling man of exactly his own age whose dark eyes and general physiognomy bore a striking resemblance to his own.

Giuseppe and Teresa were married in 1846; and in the spring of the following year, in a newly acquired house a few miles downhill from Catanzaro in the direction of Maida, there was born a daughter, whom the couple named Ippolita. In the choice of the name Teresa deferred to her husband, who had been uncharacteristically decisive in proposing it, even though it had not been a name in either of their families. It was the name of a woman Giuseppe's late mother had often referred to, who had given her a dowry of gems on her wedding day.

The child Ippolita grew up in a kingdom beset by political chaos and warfare, and in a home of personal tragedy and sadness. When Ippolita was two, in 1849, her mother nearly died of an infection contracted while bearing a stillborn son; and before her recovery Teresa learned that her father in Naples had been imprisoned for treason, and was marked for execution, because of his alleged membership in a Mazzinian underground society that had been plotting against King Ferdinand. Such cliques were now proliferating in the kingdom, encouraged by the fact that the followers of Mazzini and Garibaldi had just invaded and conquered Rome, and killed the papal prime minister and the Pope's personal secretary, having already forced Pius IX to flee southward to the city of Gaeta, in the protective realm of the Spanish Bourbons.

The provincial capital of Catanzaro was disturbed almost daily by public demonstrations and violence, as the police and royalist crowds battled with antimonarchists who circulated leaflets attacking Ferdinand's oppressive regime and advocating a coup d'état. Giuseppe arranged a transfer out of Catanzaro for himself and his family in 1850; he became a director of four small banks along the western coast, one located in Pizzo, and acquired a secluded house with high walls near the sea that he hoped would provide a salubrious atmosphere for his wife's recovery. But Teresa only descended further into despair on learning of her mother's fatal heart attack after the execution of her father. This melancholia would remain with Teresa always, and young Ippolita would never know her mother as the carefree and cheerful woman who had attracted her father in their courting days.

Ippolita's father sometimes took her to Vibo Valentia to visit his relatives in the Gagliardi family. The current patriarch was Luigi's thirty-year-old grandson, Marquis Enrico, who controlled the local grain and fishing industries, served on the town council, and was running for mayor. Like the late Luigi, who had married his stepmother's daughter, Enrico had not ventured far in finding a wife. He had married his niece.

When Ippolita was eight, in 1855, her father gladly accepted Enrico's suggestion that she be tutored along with the other children who were assembled each day in a classroom in a wing of Palazzo Gagliardi, next to the family chapel; and for the next five years, until she was thirteen, she spent more time with the Gagliardis in Vibo Valentia than she did with her own parents in Pizzo. Her father was on the road most of the day, traveling by carriage to the banks under his supervision, and her mother, now a chronic depressive, was under the constant care of a nurse. Sometimes Teresa, still in her thirties, was lucid and even cheerful, but then her voice would trail off into a jumble of inaudible words, or she would remain silent for hours and even days.

Giuseppe now divided his time as valiantly as he could among his disturbed wife, his demure daughter, whom he visited daily, and his banks, which were slowly declining along with the Bourbon regime that was their foundation. The sudden death in 1859 of the cruel but astute Ferdinand II accelerated the demise of the Bourbons, because the crown passed to his twenty-three-year-old son, Francis II, who was incompetent. Tall like his father, and with a long nose and thin lymphatic countenance topped by close-clipped black hair, the young king displayed his superciliousness to his embarrassed court on the very day of his coronation.

King Francis stood on the carpet in front of his throne with such impudence and apathy that, as his subjects lined up to kneel at his feet and kiss his hand, he did not even take the trouble to raise it. It dangled numbly at his side as they reached for it, to bring it forward to their lips; and then it limply fell back in place, like the stuffed arm of a doll. The king did not look at the people who were paying him homage, but rather stared out into the distance toward the back of the room where the line was forming. When an old man tripped and fell as he climbed the carpeted steps to kiss the king's hand, the king made no effort to help him, nor did he express a word of sympathy. He simply continued to gaze into the distance as the old man, with difficulty, moved away and made room for the next person to genuflect.

Giuseppe did not enjoy hearing a recounting of this incident one night at dinner at Palazzo Gagliardi; unlike his front-running kinsman Enrico, who was already in contact with the agents of Garibaldi, Giuseppe remained committed to the Bourbons. The reactionary Bourbon monarchy and its equally reactionary allies within the highest levels of the Church were at least deeply rooted to the traditions of the agricultural south—they and the south were inseparable, in Giuseppe's view; the vast majority of southerners were simple and humble people of few needs and wants, spiritual people who condoned a hard life and even welcomed it as a properly rigorous route to a heavenly reward. The irreligious Garibaldi and the iconoclastic Mazzini, linked as they were to the industrial interests of the north, had little to offer the south—although Giuseppe did concede that the termination of strict Bourbon rule might accrue further gains for the Gagliardis of Vibo Valentia. Despite the family's history of generosity to himself and his forebears, Giuseppe found himself resenting the ease with which southerners like Enrico Gagliardi could shift their allegiances—their loyalties were primarily to power.

After Garibaldi's Redshirts had crossed over from Sicily onto the southern tip of Italy the following summer, 1860, and quickly began to overrun the Bourbon defenses situated to the south of Vibo Valentia, Enrico organized a militia to lend support to Garibaldi's invaders. When the Redshirts entered Vibo Valentia, they were offered the use of Palazzo Gagliardi as their temporary headquarters. After a banquet in Garibaldi's honor, to which the entire household had been invited, including young

Ippolita—her father stayed away—Enrico made a large financial contribution to the Garibaldini, and he received at the same time an official commission to serve as Garibaldi's deputy in running the city until the end of the war.

The political disagreement between Giuseppe and Enrico that preceded the fall of the Bourbons was never resolved; and around the time Enrico began serving as a senator in the new kingdom headed by the Piedmontese monarch, Victor Emmanuel II, Giuseppe took his family out of the area and moved up the coast to the town of Amantea. His banks were insolvent, the days ahead seemed bleak. The entire country was now ruled by northern politicians in Turin, and to that faraway capital now flocked many of the best minds of the south, the educated and industrious elements who were qualified to play roles in the new, centralized government; meanwhile, the shattered pieces of the old Bourbon realm were picked up by the leading southern families and subverted into a neo-feudalistic economy, controlled at the top by patriarchal alliances and retained through intermarriages.

In Naples, still more than twice the size of any city in Italy, there was increased pauperism and crime among its more than four hundred thousand residents. Neapolitan industries, which had been supported by the protectionist policies of the Bourbon crown, were being undermined by the free-trade policies of northern politicians. The tracts of Church lands that had been previously designated for the poor in the countryside were most often co-opted by the entrenched wealthy families, many of whom hired *mafiosi* as their property guards and enforcers.

Giuseppe continued to live quietly in Amantea, supported by his savings and comforted by young Ippolita, while he dedicated himself to the care of his wife. In 1865, Teresa died after an attack of influenza, and a year later, at the age of seventy, Giuseppe was a victim of heart failure. Ippolita went to live nearby with her cousin Michelina, who was now her only close friend. But with Michelina's impending marriage and emigration, Ippolita would be alone, unless she followed Michelina's suggestion and made an application to move with her to Argentina.

The two young women had been discussing this on their way to church in Maida on that cloudy Sunday in 1867, attending what for Ippolita was a private commemoration of the first anniversary of her father's death. After the service, Michelina waited outside the refectory door on the side of the church to pay her respects to the pastor. When the pastor came out he was accompanied by a slim, ascetic-looking man in a dark suit and tie. Ippolita assumed that he was a deacon in the church, or the priest's personal attendant.

She had seen the man during Mass, kneeling alone a few rows ahead of her, engrossed in his missal. In the dimness of the church she had the impression that his head was tonsured, but now in the daylight she could see that his graying reddish hair was in fact cut extremely close to the crown, and that he had a pleasing though serious face with firm skin and a florid complexion. He appeared to be about thirty, and he now stood rather commandingly behind the priest, seeming restless as the priest carried on an animated conversation with Michelina.

Finally, bowing with apologies, the elderly pastor smiled and extended his hand to Ippolita, as Michelina presented her. Then the pastor, again begging forgiveness for the forgetfulness that he cheerfully attributed to age, reached out and gently held the arm of his companion and brought him forward.

"This," the pastor said to the two young women, "is my friend Domenico Talese."

16.

AFTER A COURTSHIP that was in part fostered by Michelina—who encouraged Ippolita's mild flirtatiousness while predicting a bleak future for spinsters in an impoverished south bereft of eligible men—Domenico Talese overcame his seminarial aversion to women by proposing that Ippolita become his wife. They were married in mid-November 1868 in the church where they had met, by the pastor who had introduced them.

The maid of honor was Michelina, who could now contentedly depart for Argentina knowing that her young cousin would not be alone in Italy. The best man was Domenico's brother-in-law and the foreman on his farm, the jovial and partly deaf Vito Bevivino.

Vito's wife was Domenico's older sister, Carolina, a gaunt, graying, intense woman dominated by dark moods and fathomless superstition. She never wore necklaces, bracelets, or earrings that were not inlaid with amulets to protect her from the evil eye; and she never appeared in public wearing anything but black dresses and mourning veils, even when she went to church to marry Vito. On that occasion she explained that she was still haunted by the rock slide two years before that had crushed her parents and older brother; but she was known to have cloaked herself in mourning attire long before that tragic occurrence.

Like her mother before her and like many of her countrymen, Carolina was a conspicuously devout individual whose sense of reason was shaded by ancient Greek sophistry and notions of medieval diabolism; she identified mainly with the gloom in the Gospels, the vengeance of the Creator, and the omnipresence of death. To hear anyone express a personal compliment or interpret an event as a favorable omen would alert her to the possible presence of the invisible *jettatura*. Had she not married Vito Bevivino, who was deaf to her despairing words, she might have found comfort in walking among the flagellants who bloodied the pathways to every southern shrine, or singing in the choruses of professional wailers who were ever in demand in the dark sunset of this fallen kingdom.

Domenico was not unaffected by her elegiac temperament. He had always been emotionally close to his older sister, who had brought him up as a boy during the frequent absences from home of their tubercular mother. His sister had taken him to Mass each morning, and had later recommended him to the monsignor as a youth called to the cloth. She had stalwartly supported him during his doubting days at the seminary, and had calmed his rage against God after the accidental death of their parents and brother. Though eccentric and ethereal, she was equally strong-willed and dependable. Domenico knew that there was no one more dependable and trustworthy in his life than Carolina, his last surviving sibling. His trust in her extended to his belief in the validity of her spiritualism, in the divinity of its essence, for it sprang from a fear that they shared equally, a fear so disturbing and shamefully personal as to seek redress only in heavenly guidance and protection.

Domenico believed with his sister that the two of them might indeed be living under the influence of a curse. It was she who had passed on this foreboding suspicion to him shortly after he had left the seminary after his parents' death. Before that she had for years kept her suspicions to herself, suspicions that had arisen in the form of a rumor she had overheard as a young girl in Maida. Once she had overcome her timidity and approached her father—but he had so vehemently denied the rumor, Carolina later told Domenico, that she had come away concluding that the story was probably true, adding that her father had begged her never to discuss the subject with anyone. But she had nonetheless shared it with

Domenico: the rumor that their late father's father, a man named Pasquale Talese, had been born the son of a priest.

Hoping to find evidence to expunge this hearsay, Domenico devoted much time after leaving the seminary to trying to trace the genealogy of Pasquale through municipal files and the archives of churches in and around Maida. This was difficult and time-consuming because a high percentage of this material had been misplaced or lost in the upheaval of the 1783 earthquake; and after Domenico had spent three months of perusal to no avail, his sister learned from one of the local octogenarians that Pasquale had not even been born in the Maida area, as they had always assumed, but instead northeast of Naples in the countryside near the town of Benevento.

This was in the vicinity of the seminary that Domenico had attended, and the brothers there not only allowed Domenico to return and live among them as their guest but assisted him in getting the cooperation of the record-keepers in various neighboring churches. With such help Domenico was finally able to confirm Pasquale's birth in the outskirts of Benevento, in the spring of 1765, and to learn that the couple listed as his parents had produced three children previously. But there was no way that Domenico could confirm Pasquale's blood ties to his father-of-record, or even determine that the latter had been living at the time of Pasquale's birth, because the date of the older man's death could not be found in any of the church files.

Domenico was also at a loss to explain why it was that after Pasquale had turned seventeen, in 1782, and had married for the first time—not to Domenico's grandmother, who was Pasquale's second wife, but to the young spouse who would die in the 1783 earthquake—he spelled his surname differently from the way it had been spelled on his birth certificate. Was this slightly altered spelling—to "Talese" from "Telese"—the careless mistake of some municipal scrivener who had issued Pasquale's wedding license? Or had it been a deliberate attempt on Pasquale's part to separate himself from the three older Telese children born to his mother? If this last possibility were the case, then it might have been corroborated in Domenico's discovery of an ecclesiastical property deed indicating that in 1788 Pasquale had become the sole inheritor of two parcels of Church-owned farmland from an anonymous benefactor. Was this benefactor the clergyman who had perhaps sired him? There was no individual's name on the deed that Domenico saw, only the seal of the rectorship and the notary; but Domenico was embarrassingly aware of the fact that one of these parcels was located in the Maida valley, and that upon Pasquale's death it had been inherited by his son, Gaetano—whose demise in the rock slide had made Domenico its inheritor. And now this vast and fertile acreage, together with the adjoining land Domenico had bought, constituted the main source of Domenico's wealth.

He spent five months in this region of southern Italy where his paternal grandfather Pasquale had been born and reared; and one day, while riding his horse along a bridle path in the countryside west of Benevento, Domenico saw a small road sign pointing in the direction of a town called Telese. Having never known that such a place existed, Domenico followed a narrow winding route through the thickets and past the stumps of chopped trees until he came to a clearing in which appeared the remnants of an abandoned hamlet. It consisted of a few cracked ancient walls enclosing gardens of wild flowers and high weeds and several eroding stone buildings. This, Domenico assumed, had been the place of origin of his family clan. And while there was nothing in this soundless and wasted place that would date its inhabitation, Domenico did discover, days later, in the archives of a nearby monastery, many historical references to the hamlet of Telese.

Settled in pre-Christian times, it had been partly destroyed by the Romans in 214 B.C. in retaliation for the hospitality its citizens had shown Hannibal; but later the community was colonized by the Romans, and still later it endured the presence of Visigoth, Arab, Norman, and other invaders. In the early 1600s, however, several minor earthquakes produced ground ruptures that created an atmosphere so noxious that for the next two hundred years the place was uninhabitable. Many residents moved to the island of Ischia, off Naples, or to more distant parts of Italy, while others remained in the general vicinity, founding a newer community of Telese several miles west of the old settlement, one that was irrigated by sulfurous waters the people believed to be therapeutic.

Domenico read that the name Telese was derived from the Greek verb *telein,* meaning "to initiate to mysteries"; and he was pleased to learn that many people from that town had become initiated into the mysteries of the Church as priests and monks, among the first being the twelfth-century abbot Alexander of Telese, a medieval scholar and author of four volumes outlining the relationship between the Norman rulers and the papacy. But nothing that Domenico read or heard during his sojourn answered the basic question about his grandfather's paternity, nor did Domenico feel upon his return to Maida any less susceptible to the suspicions of his sister.

Carolina remained strongly predisposed to the notion that they were plagued by a curse, and while there was no certain antidote she urged that they dedicate their lives to prayer and vigilance; and when, after he had fallen in love with Ippolita during the summer of 1868, Domenico informed his sister of their marital plans for the following November, his sister warned that the only safe day for his wedding would be November 18—for that date marked the tenth anniversary of the rock slide. It was mandatory that they express their obeisance to the wrath of the Lord on that day as well as celebrate the sacrament of matrimony, she insisted. Otherwise it would be disrespectful to the departed souls and their maker who had summoned them, and it might also bring bad luck in the future to Domenico's offspring. Domenico and Ippolita were married on November 18, 1868.

When Ippolita first learned that the wedding date had been influenced by Carolina's conjuring, she was bewildered and even frightened, having never before encountered people who were so swayed by the possible effects of ill omens or curses. But then she began to resent that her supposedly joyful day would also commemorate a disaster that had occurred ten years before. Although she was a young woman of twenty-one, she had hardly been a stranger to disasters and death; and yet this family she was marrying into seemed almost to take comfort in the resurrection of gloom. While she did not express her objections to anyone but her husband—and even to him she did not give full vent to her feelings—Ippolita was clearly appalled on her wedding day as she saw black bunting intertwined with the white streamers and flowers on the altar, and observed her tearful sister-in-law dressed entirely in black, and heard the pastor invoke the blessings of the dead parents on the couple about to be joined in the sacrament of matrimony.

Ippolita blamed Carolina entirely for the air of despondency that had been introduced to the setting, excusing her husband as a temporary victim of his vexatious sister, an uncertain man trapped between the loyalties of the past and those of the present, a smiling bridegroom in a white suit who covered his heart with the black ribbons that streamed down from the boutonniere in his lapel. His best man was similarly attired. Ippolita, of course, was dressed completely in white, as was her maid of honor, Michelina. But the two dozen guests—all of them invited by Carolina, and all of them employed on the farmlands and in the mills that she presumed to co-own with her brother—also displayed black ribbons or armbands on their clothing in deference to Carolina's disposition.

When Ippolita said good-bye to Carolina and the other guests after the reception in the courtyard of Domenico's house, a crucifix-walled house that was now hers to share, she vowed that she would henceforth keep her distance from Carolina—difficult as that would be with her sister-in-law living next door. But Ippolita began by not attending Mass with her husband, since Carolina invariably accompanied him; and she also managed to live according to a schedule that ran counter to Carolina's predictable routine: she was out shopping when Carolina was at home; she was at home when Carolina was out shopping; she always slipped in and out of her house through a side door not visible from Carolina's windows; and she pretended to be napping whenever she heard her front door resounding with Carolina's impatient knocking.

If Ippolita was not feeling well she kept it secret; otherwise Carolina would insist on visiting and prescribing her strange herbal remedies—while at the same time exaggerating the extent of Ippolita's illness throughout the neighborhood. Ippolita learned soon after joining the row of houses occupied by her husband's kinfolk and friends that the favorite subject of conversation was illness, maladies of every type—rheumatism, dyspepsia, neuritis, neuralgia, food poisoning, canker sores, tooth decay, heat prostration, frostbite, malnutrition, invalidism, headaches, backaches, heartaches, brain tumors. Not only Carolina, but most of the other neighbors as well, complained constantly and publicly of their each and every pain, as if admitting to good health would jinx them.

Fortunately for Ippolita, her self-cultivated image as a shy young bride permitted her to avoid each afternoon the circle of complaining people, all of them women at this hour, who gathered around Carolina at the fountain in the courtyard to describe and compare their latest insalubrity, real or imagined. But during the summer of 1871, Ippolita's relationship to these women was quickly altered by a new circumstance. She was pregnant. And so noticeably pregnant that everyone was aware of it, and talking about it, and apparently very happy about it. Unfortunately for Ippolita, as a topic of conversation her impending motherhood began to rival even the popularity of ailments.

Ippolita now felt that she had no choice but to yield herself to her neighbors' attention, to give them daily reports on her condition, and sometimes to join them on their shopping excursions, for to do otherwise would seem rude and unresponsive to their expressions of goodwill. She even became receptive to her sister-in-law in ways she had vowed she would never be: she politely welcomed Carolina on her daily visits and accepted with thanks her offerings of herbs and special soups deemed ideal for the health of expectant mothers (the forty-year-old childless Carolina considered herself an authority on motherhood), and also allowed Carolina to make the arrangements for the child's christening, on the condition that there be no black ribbons or bunting, or other symbols of mourning, displayed in the church.

A baby boy was born in the late summer of 1871. Cheerfully ignoring his customary abstemiousness, Domenico shared a barrel of wine with his farm workers and friends. Later, in the church, where the christening was witnessed by a larger and far more festive crowd than had attended Ippolita's wedding, tradition was adhered to and the boy was named after his paternal grandfather—in this case, Gaetano. During the pouring of the holy water over the child's head, and the enunciation of his name, the pastor dutifully honored Ippolita's request to refrain from memorializing the tragic death of the child's namesake.

After Domenico and Ippolita had taken the baby home, and had gradually become engrossed in the involving duties of child care, she realized that her maternal obligations now provided her with the perfect excuse once more to avoid socializing with her neighbors. She was able to feign fatigue when they sought her company, and, since her husband had employed a farmer's daughter to do the shopping, Ippolita could politely refuse their willingness to help with that. Although she felt misanthropic at times, she recognized as rarely before her need for privacy—not only as a guard against her well-meaning neighbors, or out of a desire to become the devotional mother that her own ailing mother was unable to be, but rather because she wanted in each day a prolonged period of solitude that she could selfishly call her own.

During her son's first year she was able to find this time; while her child napped and her husband was out on his business rounds, she could read and embroider, and let her mind wander in ways that had been habitual since her early youth as the introspective only child of an elderly father and a melancholy mother.

But when a second son was born the next year, and a third the year after that, and then a fourth child, this time a daughter, the luxury of quietude ceased to exist for Ippolita—suddenly she was overwhelmed by her duties, exhausted from lack of sleep, unnerved by the complaints of the overworked servant girl, who threatened to return to the farm. It was then that Ippolita's sister-in-law and another woman from the neighborhood knocked on her door one afternoon with flowers and a basket of fruit, and asked if they could be of help. With tears of gratitude, the young mother of four welcomed them into her house.

In time Carolina had become especially fond of Ippolita's dark-eyed infant daughter, Maria. After the child had been weaned, Carolina frequently took her to her own house, where she played with and cared for her; and in the years that followed, Maria began regularly to accompany Carolina and Domenico to church. She followed the motions of the priest with interest and joined in the communal prayers with a fervor that, as Maria approached her teens, suggested to Carolina a possible religious vocation. But Domenico did not want this. Maria was his only daughter and favorite child, and he liked having her close to him. She was obedient and modest without being timid. She also possessed a serene comeliness that Domenico knew was not going unnoticed by the young men who saw her in church.

When she was fifteen, one of these men, twenty-one-year-old Francesco Cristiani, a tailor in the family firm that made Domenico's clothes, privately approached Domenico in the shop one day and acknowledged an aspiration to have Maria for his wife. Domenico had known Francesco since his early youth, had been impressed with his devotion to the Church, and knew that he was hardworking and reliable. Francesco's family had little land, and the tailoring trade was not a lucrative business, but Domenico had never heard of any scandal attached to the Cristiani name, and he admired young Francesco's forthrightness in coming to him directly, rather than relying on an older male relative, as was the custom, to broach the sensitive subject of taking away a daughter. And yet Maria was too young for even a preliminary agreement to be arrived at, Domenico told Francesco, although he promised to discuss the matter again within a year. At that time, Domenico said, he would also meet with Francesco's father and uncles. If all went well at this meeting, Domenico said, he would then invite Francesco and his entire family over to his house for a Sunday luncheon at which young Maria would also be present.

The attention and affection that characterized Domenico's relationship with his daughter did not exist in the case of his sons. The two younger boys, Giuseppe and Vincenzo, were good-natured but lethargic, inattentive in school and greatly spoiled at home by their adoring mother and the neighborhood women who fussed over them, indulged them, and never made any demands upon them. Slow to walk as babies, and unadventuresome as young men, Giuseppe and Vincenzo grew up to become barely competent as the employees of their father, who sullenly supported them but extended to them little responsibility or respect.

Domenico's oldest son presented a different problem. Lively and intelligent, Gaetano was initially perceived by his father as a worthy successor, until he began to reveal during his early adolescence a streak of stubbornness and independence. As a baby Gaetano had quickly learned to walk, and it seemed to his mother that he was precociously disposed to leaving home. She saw him change from a contented child accustomed to receiving her undivided attention, to a restless and roving child once his younger siblings had been added to the household. Whether he had been unable to adjust to the more crowded circumstances, or simply was incapable of sharing her affections, his mother did not know; she knew only that if she did not keep an eye on him, he would soon disappear from her sight.

Gaetano loathed the farm, and constantly escaped his father's efforts to keep him there. He seemed not content to remain in the village, either, preferring to wander off by himself to the edge of a cliff overlooking the sea and to stare for hours at the passing steamships. There were now many trains running along the shorelines of southern Italy, and one night during the early autumn of 1887, after Gaetano had turned sixteen, he followed two older companions through the open panel of a train stock car and rode all the way into Naples.

The police were summoned, notifications were circulated throughout the regional precincts; but his whereabouts were not traced. Gaetano's traveling companions, both natives of another village, had been sought by the police earlier that year to answer for their role in political riots that occurred the previous spring in the provincial capital of Catanzaro. In the south there were now constant protests against the rule and policies of the new centralized government. One large group of dissenters was led by radical Catholic laymen who opposed the reduction of the Pope's temporal power by the politicians who had already dislodged him from the Quirinal Palace and were now running the nation from the once saintly city of Rome. A second group of dissenters was against the Pope *and* the government—they were, in fact, internationalists who were inspired by such leaders as the late Mikhail Bakunin, the Russian anarchist and pamphleteer, who had admirers in cities throughout Europe, including such southern Italian cities as Naples, Palermo, Cosenza, and Catanzaro. The two men with whom Gaetano had jumped on the train were revolutionary Socialists and adherents of Bakunin; and when Gaetano's father learned of this, he felt great embarrassment and humiliation in the presence of his fellow churchmen and villagers.

When Gaetano returned home in November, with an unsatisfactory explanation and little contrition about his absence, he received a thrashing from Domenico and was tied up in a barn for two days, subsisting on water and stale bread. Gaetano's mother and the rest of the family were upset by this punishment, although they were not critical of Domenico for imposing it; but Gaetano himself accepted it uncomplainingly, as if he were a martyr strengthened by some noble cause that transcended pain and suffering.

What this noble cause might be was unknown to Domenico, but from the political jargon that came out of Gaetano's mouth in subsequent weeks during their sometimes heated discussions, Domenico guessed that his son had been smitten by revolutionary Socialism, which was currently spreading in popularity throughout the land. A few Socialist proselytizers had recently visited Maida making speeches, and Domenico was familiar with their slogans and rhetoric, although he preferred to believe that their appeal to his impressionable young son was sparked more by his youthful impetuosity and personal rebelliousness than by any reasoned conviction. For this was indeed a period of youthful bravado in southern Italian history—the bright promise of General Garibaldi's revolution had drifted with the dust of the Redshirts' horses; and the political and economic decline of the autonomous southern kingdom was accompanied by the decline in the power that the fathers had over their sons. Even a devoted son would not follow a father forever along a path that led only to continuing poverty and subjugation. In Gaetano's case, however, his estrangement from his father was attuned not to the economy but rather to the personal nature of their relationship, an imprecisely expressed but deeply felt divisiveness that would only harden unless there were some compromises and a deeper understanding on both sides.

Hoping to improve the situation, for he still regarded Gaetano as his most capable heir, Domenico tried to see Gaetano as his prodigal son, and in a rare display of affection and forgiveness months after Gaetano had returned home, he embraced his oldest son one day and offered to step aside and let him exercise authority over the daily operation of the farmlands and mills. But Gaetano responded, as tactfully as he could, that he was not interested. He would soon be leaving for America, he said. He had spoken to an agent in Naples who was recruiting workers for employment in Philadelphia; and he had been promised that his travel costs would be advanced in the spring. When his reasoning failed to convince his son to change his mind, Domenico's rage, which until now had been kept tightly under control, suddenly erupted. He vowed that if Gaetano went, he would never speak to him again, nor would he ever wish to see him.

In the spring of 1888, Gaetano left for America. He was not yet seventeen. He took a mail boat from Pizzo to Naples, signed the documents that the agent presented to him, and with forty other young men began the twenty-day crossing that would take him eventually to Philadelphia. He said good-bye to his mother and his siblings, but not to his father. Domenico had remained behind the closed door of his bedroom, ignoring Ippolita's pleas that he wish his son a safe voyage.

Gaetano stayed away from home for the next six years. During that time he wrote often to his mother, describing his work and what he had seen in the New Land. He said he was being trained as a stonemason and artisan. He sent a photograph of himself posing in front of City Hall in Philadelphia, wearing a suit that Francesco Cristiani had made for him, and a second photograph showed him in work clothes, standing with other men in front of a fountain they were building in the Philadelphia suburbs for the renowned asbestos manufacturer Dr. Richard V. Mattison, who was their primary employer and had sponsored their trans-Atlantic crossing. Gaetano also occasionally sent from Wanamaker's new store in Philadelphia small gifts for his mother, his brothers, and his sister; and in 1892 he sent a wedding present to Maria on the occasion of her marriage to the tailor Francesco Cristiani.

Maria had half expected that Gaetano would return to Italy for the wedding, for he had been informed that in the years since his departure his father's attitude toward him had greatly mellowed, partly because of the appeals and persuasive reasoning of Ippolita and, until her death earlier in 1892, of Domenico's sister, Carolina. But Maria learned from her husband that more than discord with Domenico was keeping Gaetano in America. Gaetano feared that if he returned he might be arrested for questioning about certain radical Socialists in Naples he was known to have befriended, especially those who had helped him obtain a berth on the overcrowded ship that carried him to America.

The conservative authoritarian government in Rome was not opposed to the fact that each year many thousands of Italians were leaving for America (it actually welcomed the exodus because it reduced the nation's economic burden, particularly in the overpopulated unindustrial south, where most of the departing passengers had come from); but the government *was* opposed to the network of Socialists and anarchists who had somehow gained enough influence within the Naples seaport—conspiring no doubt with Mafia-connected dockworkers and crewmen—that they managed to obtain cabin space for their political associates and their friends on ships where no space was listed as available.

The network also concealed the identity while at sea of political fugitives and other individuals in trouble with the law, and when necessary it could supply falsified traveling documents and employment papers. In addition to booking the passage of the American-bound migratory workers they had recruited (using funds advanced to them by American employers eager for cheap labor), members of the network sometimes loaned money to the workers that their partners abroad later collected with interest. Most American bosses, speaking no Italian, entrusted to them the workers' salaries and relied on them to distribute it fairly.

In Gaetano's case, the network not only provided him with a berth on a steamship and an American job that would enable him to reimburse his travel costs, but also arranged for his lodging in a boardinghouse owned by an Italian immigrant. The house was near Gaetano's first job site in the outskirts of Philadelphia. The owner of the boardinghouse, who spoke English, was named Carmine Lobianco, and he was a cousin of two of the men who had helped Gaetano sail out of Naples; Lobianco was friendly with most of the other men who operated out of offices in the terminal building along the Bay of Naples. Like his cousins, Lobianco was a radical Socialist. A few of the others were anarchists.

In 1892, the year of Maria's wedding in Maida, Lobianco's cousins and their associates gradually began to disappear from their seaport jobs as bureaucrats, clerks, and other covering positions, because the Italian government was now embarking on a new campaign to harass and curb the livelihood of the troublemaking Socialists and anarchists. It was not the covert dealings in the migrant-worker travel market that stirred the government nearly so much as the labor strikes and raucous demonstrations that Socialist and anarchist leaders were fomenting throughout Italy—most frequently in such separatist cities as Naples and Palermo—against the miserable social conditions, the stagnant economy, and the nation's imperialistic foreign policy in East Africa (Eritrea, Somaliland) that was summoning young Italian men into the army and increasing the already high rate of taxation. Even though the agitators had failed to politicize sufficiently the southern peasants to lure them away from their ties to the Church, it was not for a lack of trying. The government issued harsh prison sentences to those political antagonists whom it was able to capture and convict, and persistently pursued those others who remained in hiding in Italy rather than seek asylum in the United States—as Lobianco's cousins did, moving into his already crowded boardinghouse near the asbestos factory site in Ambler, Pennsylvania, seventeen miles north of Philadelphia. While Gaetano had never played an active role in subversive activity in Italy or the United States, his acquaintanceship with many Italians who did, and who remained his friends, was enough to keep him away from Maida and his sister's wedding.

17.

THE GRANDEUR AND opportunity of America was personified to Gaetano each day by the decorous appearance at the job site of his sponsor and boss, Dr. Richard V. Mattison, a tall, bewhiskered, nonpracticing Philadelphia physician who had elevated himself from humble origins as a barefoot farm boy in nearby Bucks County to make a fortune manufacturing pharmaceutical concoctions that reputedly cured myriad physical ailments and disorders as well as certain maladies of the spirit. Of him it was said by a longtime medical associate: "Dr. Mattison was not always right, but he was never in doubt."

A scholarship student at the Philadelphia College of Pharmacy and the University of Pennsylvania Medical School, Dr. Mattison in 1873 opened a modest laboratory along the city's waterfront, and, financed by a wealthy young partner who had been his classmate at pharmacy college, he experimented with various compounds and elixirs that before the end of the decade would be blended and contained within thousands of small, varicolored baroque bottles and sold as over-the-counter cures in apothecaries around the nation and in such foreign cities as London, Paris, Lucerne, and Rome.

Dr. Mattison's Bromo Caffeine—advertised as a palliative for the frayed nerves of "the neurasthenic woman or the congestive or anaemic headaches of the fin de siecle man"—was the most famous of his curatives; but nearly as popular was his Alkalithia for rheumatism, and his Cafetonique for dyspepsia.

Shortly after his thirtieth birthday, in 1881, while he was in his laboratory testing one of his remedies that contained milk of magnesia, it was reported that he accidentally spilled some of the solution on a hot pipe, where he soon noticed that it clung steadfastly to the metal—alerting him to the insulating properties within magnesium carbonate and prompting his subsequent experiments with magnesia, asbestos, and other substances to create eventually insulation cloth that could be wrapped around steam pipes in homes to reduce fuel costs greatly.

This departure from his preoccupation with pharmaceutical preparations gradually led Dr. Mattison to an entirely new career, one in which he would manufacture not only insulation materials but also a brand of fabric and millboard that was fireproof and could be used in construction materials to increase the safety of private homes, workshops, and schools. As a result of his desire to specialize in fireproof products, Dr. Mattison became increasingly dependent on the use of asbestos, an unburnable, often whitish substance found in the crystallized veins of certain rock formations of volcanic origin in many parts of Africa, as well as in Canada, Russia, China, Australia, and Italy. In its most valuable condition, asbestos is a silky, unctuous, thread-thin fiber two or three inches in length, with the tensile strength of steel wire and flexible enough to be spun with cotton or flax to form yarn that is resistant to heat and repellent to fire. Asbestos fibers that are too short for spinning can be ground up and mixed with cement to be made into incombustible roof shingles, wallboards, and floor tiles.

In ancient times, asbestos was commonly referred to as "the magic mineral." The Emperor Charlemagne was known to have enjoyed duping his visitors occasionally by tossing his asbestos tablecloth into a fire and then pulling it out, unburnt by the flames; and medieval conjurers wearing hooded robes made of cotton blended with asbestos were able guilefully to exhibit their flame-thwarting talents before astonished crowds of naive spectators. In the pre-Christian era the Greeks and Romans covered the bodies of their dead leaders with asbestos shrouds during cremation ceremonies. But the widespread use of this always rare and costly mineral was not possible until the discovery of huge deposits of it in Quebec during the 1870s.

First British industrialists became its major consumers, then such Americans as Henry Ward Johns (whose company was the forerunner of Johns-Manville); but no less active, beginning in the early 1880s, was Dr. Mattison, who, as he continued to experiment with asbestos in his laboratory, became almost obsessed with the mineral's wondrous and profitable possibilities. And he also saw himself as one day heading a giant firm that mass-produced asbestos items on a national or even international scale—fireproof asbestos curtains for theaters, asbestos uniforms for firemen, asbestos linings for kitchen ovens and factory kilns, asbestos gloves for foundry workers and bakers, asbestos conveyer belts to bear smoldering objects, asbestos toasters and iron holders, asbestos knobs on radiator valves, asbestos awnings over the porches of summer homes.

But before he could venture into the business so grandly, he first had to build a manufacturing plant equal in size to his ambitions—meaning that he had to vacate his modest quarters in Philadelphia and relocate somewhere in the expansive Pennsylvania countryside. His multimillionaire partner, Henry G. Keasbey, a mild-mannered individual who considered Dr. Mattison a genius and rarely took issue with him, accompanied him on weekend carriage rides outside the city to explore stretches of farmland that might be quickly adaptable for industrial development. Wearing dark suits and bowlers, and carrying walking sticks as they stepped in and out of the cow dung in weedy pastures, the two men represented an odd sight to the dairy workers, blacksmiths, and wheelwrights who stood quietly observing from the sides of dirt roads that had not been widened since William Penn himself had claimed the territory in the 1680s for his fellow English Quaker immigrants, at the expense of the eased-out Indians.

At six feet, four inches, with broad shoulders, narrow hips, and such disproportionately long, thin legs that he seemed to be walking on stilts, the sternly spectacled Dr. Mattison towered over the five-foot-seven-inch Mr. Keasbey, who had a round ruddy face and muttonchop whiskers and nodded affirmatively at nearly everything he heard the talkative doctor say. Bystanders could have justifiably assumed that Dr. Mattison, and not Mr. Keasbey, was the scion of a powerful family of Anglo-Americans who had been social leaders and philanthropists for generations, and who decorated their grand residences in Morris County, New Jersey, with mounted moose heads over the mantels, and burnished medieval-style breastplates flanking the staircases beneath staffs of jousting banners and suspended battle-axes. In deference to Keasbey's wealth, and with the understanding that he would continue to underwrite his aspirations, Dr. Mattison placed Keasbey's name in the primary position on their joint enterprise. It was called Keasbey & Mattison Company.

On one of their weekend excursions into the countryside in 1882, the partners came upon a 408-acre spread of land that had been called Wissahickon by the Indians but was now a declining village of obsolete gristmills and small farms, called Ambler. The most newsworthy happening in Ambler history had been a long-ago train wreck, in 1856, a year after the Pennsylvania Railroad had ceremoniously introduced trains to this part of the state. The first rescuer to arrive at the disaster was a tiny Quaker woman named Mary Ambler, the widowed mother of nine, who came in a buggy packed with her petticoats and bedsheets, which she would soon tear into bandages after pulling as many bodies as she could from the flames. Twelve years later, months after Mary Ambler's death in 1868, some of the passengers she rescued attended a dedication ceremony in which the railroad company renamed its Wissahickon station in honor of Mary Ambler. In 1869 the village of Wissahickon also changed its name to Ambler.

When Dr. Mattison and Mr. Keasbey first visited Ambler in 1882, it had a decreasing population of fewer than three hundred, and several large plots of land and vacated mills for sale at low prices in the vicinity of the railroad tracks. The railroad that had been heralded as an economic stimulant to the village had become instead its financial nemesis. Farmers who had once lined the roads into Ambler with their horsecarts filled with grain to be ground by Ambler's millers could now more conveniently load their unground grain onto freight trains and send it directly to large urban food distributors that provided their own grinding service. Since milling had long been the sole industry in Ambler—in the mid-1800s the town had seven gristmills, a sawmill, and a silk and fulling mill—the influence of the railroad was profound. By 1880 the mills, which in some cases had existed for two hundred years, and which during the Revolutionary War had supplied food, clothing, and firewood to General George Washington's nearby military encampments, were either bankrupt or operating unprofitably. Ambler's antiquated sawmill was similarly affected by the changing conditions, and the silk and fulling mill—which had once kept dozens of looms busy with wool weavers making fringed shawls for women around the nation—was additionally victimized during the 1870s, when the fringed shawl gradually went out of fashion. Large quantities of these unsold garments were stored for years by one of the owners of the mill, a wool and silk importer in New York City named Eberhard Flues; and after his death in 1896 his surviving partners donated some of the shawls, still in good condition, to Admiral Robert E. Peary when the latter announced plans for his first expedition to the North Pole.

But when Dr. Mattison rode past the abandoned grounds of Ambler's once popular county fair, having earlier seen the defunct mills and other examples of a village in decline, he did not pause to reflect on his decision to make this his home and the locale of his ambitious enterprise. On the contrary, he was pleased by Ambler's weakened condition—it was now malleable for his remaking. Its economy was stagnant, but its strong and abundant streams of pure spring water that had once powered the mills would flow ideally through his chemicals, mixing more predictably with his concoctions than had the waters of Philadelphia's polluted river. The railroad could swiftly and regularly carry tons of asbestos into Ambler from the big mines in Quebec. The limestone in Ambler's surrounding hills could be quarried to form factories along the tracks, convenient for the receipt of raw materials and the delivery of finished products. Dr. Mattison and his partner could pave the wide dirt road that cut through the center of town, perpendicular to the tracks, and they could also brighten all the village routes and walkways with electric streetlamps. They could loan money to the village businessmen for the renovation and repainting of the weatherworn buildings in the vicinity of the train station—the general store, the barbershop, the carriage repair shop, the rooming house, and the corner apothecary that (Dr. Mattison was pleased to observe) was well stocked with bottles of Bromo Caffeine.

Dr. Mattison and his partner would surely need more than one architect to design all the new buildings that were planned—not only the factories but also the domestic residences for the workers, the foremen, the top executives and chemists who would be employed by Keasbey & Mattison. These dwellings would not be the common clapboard bungalows or shantytown rows that characterized most company towns in the United States; they would instead be thick-walled, enduring structures of stone bedecked with the special features and ornamentation that appealed to the doctor's aesthetic sensibilities. Dr. Mattison had always been enamored of Gothic architecture. During the previous summer he had become more enraptured by it than ever as he toured western Germany and looked upon the conical turrets, finials, and dormer windows of Rhineland mansions, which reawakened in him a responsiveness that he had first felt as a young boy while staring at the Hänsel and Gretel illustrations in a book that his teacher had passed among the students in the one-room Bucks County schoolhouse. He had often dreamed after that of living in a turreted mansion, and he freely revealed that fantasy to his fellow students in a paper he read in English class. And now in Ambler two decades later, as he was about to transform an agricultural community into an industrial mecca—following his own route from farm boy to magnate—his youthful dreams were taking a realistic shape, thanks to his deep thinking and to Mr. Keasbey's deep pockets.

This was an era of unlimited possibilities across America. Industrialists of vision and determination were converting raw materials and raw energy into gold and were living like kings—residing in mansions, and even castles, while ruling over masses of people and vast factories with an audaciousness, and at times a gallantry, that was unprecedented in American history. Dr. Mattison had read about some of these men—J. P. Morgan and Andrew Carnegie, George Pullman, John D. Rockefeller, Andrew Mellon, the late Cornelius Vanderbilt. And new men were on the horizon—William Randolph Hearst, Henry Ford, and dozens more. Fortunes had been made, and would continue to be made, in an astonishing variety of ways; and now Dr. Mattison saw his chance, in this age of steam, through insulating the nation's pipes and boilers, from its household basements to its battleships, and through fireproofing thousands of its private and public buildings with his Ambler-made shingles and siding encrusted with the asbestos fibers that the ancients believed were magic.

As for the workers who would first build Dr. Mattison's Gothic town, and then be employed in the factories that would manufacture his products, he had already arranged for the arrival of a trainload of men from southern Italy. He had advanced the cost of their Atlantic crossing through a New York steamship company that docked at Naples, and he had been assisted in recruiting these workers by an Italian immigrant in Philadelphia who had earlier been a custodian and general factotum in Dr. Mattison's pharmaceutical laboratory. The man's name was Carmine Lobianco. He had arrived in Philadelphia from Naples in the mid-1870s, initially as a construction worker on a riverfront road-building project that extended past the Keasbey-Mattison property on Front Street. During Dr. Mattison's early-morning strolls, which constituted his only exercise, he had often paused to watch the Italian workers, to listen to their strange language, and, although they tended to be short and more wiry than muscular, to admire how robustly they swung their sledgehammers and pickaxes, and hurled the heavy chains around the boulders and beams that were then hoisted high in the air by the cables of a steel crane powered by a team of sweating horses. Dr. Mattison observed this activity with keen interest while wondering about these dark-skinned exotic workmen, their origins, their motivations, their dreams of the future. He was a man of incorrigible curiosity—this characteristic traceable in part to his intrinsically laboratorial nature, his training as a dissector and an experimenter, and in part to his intemperate personal nosiness. He could not walk down a street without staring at people, analyzing their faces and body movements, even eavesdropping whenever possible. His propensity for prying would bring him severe pain during his final year in Philadelphia, 1882, when—while peeking into the windows of a competitive pharmaceutical factory one night in an attempt to learn why its employees were working so late—his large, two-hundred-twenty-pound body fell through a trap door on the sidewalk and his jaw was fractured in three places. His jaw would never be reset properly; and for the rest of his life he would have to avoid eating heavy meat, such as steak, and the lower part of his face would display the scars of his misadventure—and this was why, at the age of thirty-one, Dr. Mattison began to grow a beard.

But he was an unscarred, beardless man of twenty-nine when he first caught sight of the Italian road gang during his morning constitutionals; and he was particularly drawn to a spirited, snub-nosed crane operator wearing a helmetlike hat and lashing the horses with a long whip, while calling persistently down to his dust-covered colleagues swinging their axes—evoking for Dr. Mattison the image of a Roman chariot driver engaged in a heated skirmish. As the doctor stepped forward on the dirt road to get a closer look, he felt an empathy with this vigorous man in the crane, this high-riding ruffian seated determinedly above the obscurity of pick-and-shovel enterprise; and at the first opportune moment, after the men had paused to share a bucket of water, the doctor approached the man and doffed his bowler.

"Good morning," he said, "I am Dr. Mattison."

"Good morning," the crane operator replied, in surprisingly good English and with a lively smile. "I am Carmine Lobianco. And I am at your service."

Dr. Mattison reached inside his jacket for the small prescription pad on which he never wrote prescriptions, scribbled down his name and address, tore off the page, and handed it to the crane operator. Two months later, when the road project was completed and the Italians were laid off, Lobianco appeared at Dr. Mattison's office in search of a job. The only position available was that of a janitor. Lobianco accepted it with alacrity.

But in his eagerness to become more useful he was soon doing other work as well. He stood on the assembly line with the laboratory technicians filling the unending procession of bottles with Dr. Mattison's various cures. Twice a week he delivered carefully packed boxloads of these by wagon to apothecaries throughout the city, as well as to the train depot for distribution around the nation and overseas. On weekends, after Dr. Mattison and Keasbey had decided to expand their business in the countryside and leave Philadelphia—soon after Dr. Mattison had fallen through the trap door—Lobianco drove their carriage as they scouted locations; and he was with them during their first visit to Ambler. When they began to make inquiries for architects to design the new factories and Gothic community, Lobianco was given permission to bring in his Italian workers from Philadelphia to begin unearthing stone from the quarry and digging ditches for water pipes; and when Dr. Mattison said that many more laborers were needed, in addition to some highly skilled stone artisans, Lobianco announced that he knew just where to find them. The best stone artisans in the world, Lobianco said, came from the mountains of southern Italy, near his home village, where centuries of building and rebuilding villas and monasteries amid rock slides and earthquakes had provided such men with abundant opportunities to practice their craft. Lobianco also told Dr. Mattison that he had cousins and friends employed in and around the Naples seaport who could quickly recruit excellent artisans and hardworking laborers at reasonable rates if the doctor would advance payment for their passage. Lobianco did not tell Dr. Mattison that his cousins and friends were revolutionary Socialists and anarchists wanted by the Italian police. He assumed that what mattered most to Dr. Mattison was getting the job done quickly and well. And what mattered most to Lobianco was getting his share of the proceeds that the steamship company kicked back to recruiters, as well as the considerable profits to be earned from the incoming Italian workers for his efforts as their *padrone.*

Lobianco had long aspired to become a *padrone,* which was a somewhat exalted title given to those opportunistic Italian immigrants who functioned as ethnic middlemen during the first years of the mass movement of Italian workers into America. The *padrone* was enriched both by the American employer, to whom he delivered cheap labor, and by the laborers themselves, who surrendered to him a percentage of their salaries. In addition to providing jobs and shelter, the *padrone* in the beginning was the guiding influence, if not the outright enforcer, of all that the newcomer did during almost every hour of every day into the night. Lacking a family or friends in America, and not speaking the language, the average worker was totally dependent on his *padrone.* Since at least half of the workers were illiterate even in their own language, the *padrone* handled all their postal correspondence between Italy and America. Having never before been away from home, these workers were now involved for the first time with composing letters, including love letters, which were not only written but sometimes embellished by *padroni* with florid prose styles. Much of the exaggerated operatic longing expressed in some of these letters was more indicative of the *padrone*'s amorous fantasies, or his devil-may-care roguishness, than of what actually existed within the heart of the worker. In their helpless state of dependence on *padroni* many workers remained nonetheless aware that a single sentence of overstated affection in a letter to a village maiden might be interpreted by her—and also by her family, who were never remiss in learning the content of such letters—as a vow of eternal love, and an irrevocable proposal of marriage.

But marriage was far from the minds of most of these pioneer Italian workers, who could as yet ill afford the expense of bringing over a bride. And most of these workers themselves did not intend to stay forever in America. More than fifty percent of this first wave of workers were not settlers but sojourners, birds of passage, young bachelors who intended to toil hard for two or three years, and also sow some wild oats while sweating for American dollars in ditches and tunnels, and then to return to Italy—richer, wiser, and no longer dependent on the *padrone.*

But for those Italian laborers who did settle down in America, or who returned home temporarily and then came back with a bride (the groom in some instances ensnared by the effusions of his ghostwriter), the *padrone* continued to play a significant role; and by the early 1880s, when Lobianco began as a *padrone* under the aegis of Keasbey & Mattison Company, several *padroni* were already prominent and powerful in New York City and Philadelphia, in New Haven, Syracuse, Utica, and in other eastern industrial cities and towns where large numbers of Italians had been assembled. Thus long before there were Mafia "godfathers" coining money in America—this did not commence until the 1920s, when gangsters from Sicily and southern Italy began to thrive in the bootlegging trade inspired by Prohibition—there was a syndicate of *padroni* who were prospering legally, if at times exploitatively, as business agents and personal advisers to their usually less astute, less educated countrymen.

Perhaps the most eminent *padrone* in the United States at this time lived in New York City, which had the largest collection of Italian immigrants in the nation. His name was Luigi Fugazy; he was a diminutive man with a professorial air who dwelled in baronial style in a large house on Bleecker Street in the Little Italy section of Manhattan's Greenwich Village. Born into a well-to-do northern Italian family in Piedmont, where his father was a teacher, Luigi Fugazy served as an officer in the Piedmontese royal army during the Risorgimento and briefly had been assigned to a unit commanded by Garibaldi. After sailing to New York in 1869 with a knowledge of English and a substantial inheritance from his father—whose surname, Fugazzi, Luigi later changed to Fugazy, justifying it as a gesture toward assimilation—he promptly increased his net worth by becoming a travel agent for a steamship company, a labor negotiator for Italian employees, and also the owner of a neighborhood bank and a service company that issued loans, provided translators and letter-writers, and notarized immigrants' mortgages, licenses, wills, and other documents. Luigi Fugazy also founded several Italian fraternal organizations, social clubs, and mutual aid societies.

A second New York *padrone,* while not as prominent as Fugazy, was nonetheless very influential because he used part of his earnings as an Italian neighborhood banker and landlord to found the nation's largest Italian-language newspaper, *Il Progresso Italo-Americano.* His name was Carlo Barsotti; and, like Fugazy, he had been reared in privileged circumstances in northern Italy. Barsotti had been born and reared in Pisa. The activity for which he would become most identified in the United States, which he achieved through his newspaper's editorial campaign, would be the inauguration of the commemoration of Columbus Day, beginning in 1892—the four-hundredth anniversary of the discovery of America. Funds were raised for the erection of a statue to Columbus in New York, and this was also done in several other cities that had large gatherings of Italians and persuasive *padroni* who could influence them.

In New Haven such a man was Paolo Russo, a grocer, banker, and attorney (the first Italian-American graduate of Yale Law School, in 1893); in Syracuse, the leading *padrone* was Thomas Marnell (born Marinelli in Naples), who began as a railroad laborer and became a banker; and in Philadelphia, the most prominent *padrone* was a mortician named Charles C. Baldi, a virtuoso consoler of mourning families who also presided over a coal business, a travel agency, a real estate brokerage, and the Italian-language newspaper *L'Opinione.*

The *padroni* who guided the Italian workers in the less industrial sections of the country—in the rural South, the Central Plains, and along the Rockies toward the Pacific—were less wealthy than their eastern counterparts partly because most of the immigrants, being predominantly southern Italian escapees from the farmlands of their fathers, resisted settling in the isolated hinterlands of America. They had seen enough of isolation in their own country, and they not only lacked the money to invest in farm equipment and land, but also were unprepared, linguistically and temperamentally, to venture out into the wide open spaces that had already been homesteaded largely by Irish, Germans, and Swedes, and, of course, by native-born American frontiersmen and gunslingers who had little fondness for foreigners in general. The Italians preferred the protective insularity of ghettos, where their dialect could be understood, where they could buy imported Italian sausage and olive oil at the corner grocery store owned by their *padrone.* And when the imports from Italy included women, they began to nurture their families in towering crowded tenements that in a strange way evoked the mountain village atmosphere that had surrounded them from birth. The fact that few trees lined these city streets was considered a blessing by the women—who, accustomed as they were to the age-old daily habit of sitting at their windows in Italy for hours and spying down on their neighbors, would have become frustrated in America if their view of street life was obscured by leaves casting dark shadows.

And to these city-dwelling Italians there came always enough tales of horror and woe about life in the provinces to convince them that they were better off where they were. One such story concerned a gang of workers who had been escorted by their *padrone* into the Deep South to pick cotton on a Mississippi plantation: When they visited the town they were treated as miserably as the blacks, and sometimes confronted along the roads at night by men with burning crosses. The small Italian restaurant that had been opened near the plantation by the *padrone* was destroyed after an Italian cook served a black man. Another tale involved Italians who organized an agricultural commune in Arkansas, enduring not only droughts and tornadoes, but also the attacks of nativists baiting them as "dagos." The Italians who had been sent into the midwestern wilderness to labor for the Chicago & North Western Railway had been unable to find housing throughout the winter. When they sought shelter and warmth within the haystacks of cattle cars in the railyards, they were awakened by holdup men who stole whatever money the Italians had saved from their nine-dollar-a-week salaries. Many Italians who had been recruited to work in the copper mines of Colorado during a work stoppage were nearly clubbed to death by mobs of laid-off unionists who cursed them as strikebreakers. In Louisiana, after a New Orleans police chief had been killed while investigating reports of extortion and violence among rival gangs of Italian dockworkers, eleven Italians were arrested on charges of murder—but none was found guilty. Outraged by what was regarded as excessive courtroom leniency, a citizens' group of vigilantes raided the New Orleans prison, captured the Italians who had stood trial, and lynched every one of them.

But such atrocities that made headlines in the American press, and also in the newspapers back in Italy—bringing satisfaction to some Italian landowners burdened by the labor shortage caused by emigration—represented only a partial and often distorted picture of Italian immigrant life as it was being experienced outside the ghettos and mill towns of the Northeast at the turn of the century. Equally relevant, if insufficiently dramatic to warrant circulation through journalism or ghetto gossip, was the slowly evolving yet persevering assimilation of the Italians who generally coexisted peacefully with non-Italians throughout the South, the Midwest, and the Far West, and whose next generation often grew up speaking English with a Dixie drawl or a Texas twang, and learned to recite the Pledge of Allegiance in such places as the fraternal hall of the Italian Society of Victor Emmanuel III in Waukesha, Wisconsin.

The Ogden, Utah, native son of an Italian father and a Mormon mother would become a leading American essayist, Bernard De Voto. At Fort Huachuca, Arizona, growing up among soldiers, Indians, and bronco riders, was the adolescent son of an Italian-born U.S. Army bandmaster and a Jewish mother from Trieste; he would one day be elected mayor of New York—Fiorello La Guardia. There was a cowboy born in Texas of an Italian father and an Irish mother who would write best-selling westerns under the name Charles A. Siringo; and an Italian immigrant who ran a small hotel in San Jose, California, had a son, Amadeo Pietro Giannini, who would one day found the Bank of Italy in San Francisco, which would later become the Bank of America, one of the largest private banks in the world.

It is true, the Italians who put down roots west of the Mississippi constituted barely twenty percent of all the Italians who entered the United States before, and slightly after, the turn of the century. But this twenty percent probably arrived at "feeling American" far sooner than did the eighty percent who lived more sheltered lives in industrial towns and ethnic neighborhoods east of the Mississippi, and who continued to rely on a *padrone* as their primary liaison with the American mainstream. In California, where Italians were quick in gaining social acceptance and material success, there were hardly any *padroni*.

It was also true, however, that the Italians who moved into California were predominantly of northern Italian stock; and being the beneficiaries of a higher level of education than the southerners, and from less impoverished circumstances, they came better equipped to function in America on their own. Less than twelve percent of the northern arrivals were illiterate, as compared with more than fifty percent of the southerners. While southerners had been held back for centuries by the oppressive, anti-intellectual traditions of the Spanish Bourbon crown and the Catholic Church, the northerners' heritage had been more worldly, if no less spiritual, as they interacted, and intermarried, through the ages with diverse groups of Europeans who dwelled along or near Italy's northern borders—the French, the Swiss, the Germans, the Austrians: citizens of foreign nations with which Italian authorities had often quarreled, but with whose language and customs many Italian people were at least familiar, and whose religious differences, when such existed, were tolerated in ways that would have been unacceptable to a Bourbon bishop in Naples.

The northern Italian heroes who sparked the Risorgimento—King Victor Emmanuel II, Count Cavour, Mazzini, and Garibaldi—all were lapsed Catholics; and while there was never evidence to indicate that northern Italians were less God-fearing than southern Italians, the northern Italian immigrants in America (unlike their southern compatriots) were not so readily perceived by America's Protestant majority as peons of the Pope and dregs of the earth.

Their physical appearance alone helped northern Italian immigrants blend in better than southerners. Their body structure and skin tone were closer to that of the angular, ruddy Anglo-Nordic European Protestant colonists, pioneers, and arrivistes who most frequently represented, in physique and physiognomy, the American prototype. Northern Italians tended to be taller and less swarthy than most southerners, often having light-colored hair and eyes and, according to the writer William Dean Howells, United States consul at Venice during the 1860s, a "lightness of temper." Not only were northerners more formally educated than southerners, and more inclined to master the English language, but they were as a rule more outgoing personally, less guarded around strangers, more entrepreneurial. They were also fortunate in having a significant number of their northern countrymen arriving in the bustling San Francisco Bay area almost simultaneously with most of the native-born settlers, at the time of the 1849 gold rush, when the tenor and tempo of the region were characterized by a mobile, not yet socially stratified, materialist group of individuals with whom the Italians proved to be quite compatible. Among the early prospering Italians of this period was Domenico Ghirardelli, who traveled through California's mining towns peddling chocolates and harder candy, *caramelle*. Out of his energies would emerge a sweets and syrups factory that would flourish in San Francisco long after his death.

A contemporary of Ghirardelli's, and among the first of many Italians to prosper as a vintner of California wines, was Andrea Sbarbaro, a Genoese banker who founded ItalianSwiss Colony in California's Sonoma Valley. In the waters of San Francisco Bay and beyond, competing with the Chinese fishermen sailing their junks, were immigrant Italian fishermen, mostly from Genoa. But later, in the 1880s, as the Genoese began to advance themselves to more remunerative livelihoods along the shore and in the town, many sold their deep-water feluccas and small crab boats and nets to the most recently arrived Italian fishermen, several of them Sicilian. Among the Sicilians to arrive at the turn of the century was a fisherman born in Isola delle Femmine, an islet off Palermo, where his forebears had earned their living on the sea for generations. His name was

DiMaggio. In America he would have five sons, the two oldest of whom would become fishermen. The three younger sons lacked the discipline and temperament for sea life, and as small boys they would often wander away from Fisherman's Wharf and stroll toward the sandlots, swinging broken oars that they pretended were baseball bats.

Not only in northern California but in the Los Angeles and San Diego areas as well, Italian immigrants would in time contribute significantly to the state's economic development, some as vintners, others as large-scale vegetable and fruit growers. Almost everything that could be grown in Italy could be grown in the fertile soil and mild climate of California, which of all the American states most resembled the peninsula of Italy. The transported Italians who capitalized most on the California climate were, to be sure, those immigrants born in Italy's more industrial north, men who eschewed the other side of the country, with its smoky factory towns and ghettos, for a better place in the sun. Ironically, the Italian southerners, who had been toppled by northern invaders during the Risorgimento, in America found themselves still in an inferior position to their northern countrymen—and still ruled by opportunistic men from the north, their *padroni*.

With few exceptions, the *padroni* who governed the lives of Italian manual laborers in America were natives of northern Italy. An exception was the protégé of Dr. Mattison in Philadelphia. Carmine Lobianco's canniness had been cultivated during his youth along the scheming waterfront of Naples, and, as a provider of laborers for Keasbey & Mattison Company of Ambler, he soon attained the prosperity that had been his primary ambition.

But by the mid-1880s there began to appear much negative publicity about *padroni* in the big-city American newspapers, and there were hints that United States immigration authorities were recommending legislation that would ban many practices of *padroni* that were deemed exploitative and devious. Many *padroni* were accused of dishonest dealings with the American employers who advanced the immigrants' passage fares to the *padroni:* the latter would exaggerate the actual cost that the steamship company charged to bring laborers from Italy to the United States (pocketing the difference), and then record the higher passage figure on the list of debts that the laborers were later obliged to repay out of their wages.

On payday, some unfortunate workers discovered that they were penniless after they had reimbursed their *padrone* what he claimed was owed for lodging, food, transportation to and from the job site; such personal services as letter-writing, translating, and notarization; and the interest rates charged on personal loans. Some workers unable to repay the loans were forced to forfeit their small plots of farmland in Italy that the *padrone* had held as collateral. The loss of such land caused deep bitterness among the workers in America and their kinfolk in Italy; and the resultant protests against these and similar situations brought the whole *padrone* system under scrutiny by American lawmakers and the press in the mid-1880s, and tarnished the image of many *padroni* who had long and justifiably enjoyed reputations for being gentlemen of humanity and integrity. Such a gentleman, however, was not Carmine Lobianco.

In the latter part of 1888, Lobianco had gradually drifted into voluntary semi-retirement. With the intensified campaigns waged by American immigration authorities Lobianco became haunted by thoughts of imprisonment. He was now wealthier than he knew he had any right to be; and while this did not plague his conscience—he had achieved affluence, after all, in a manner not dissimilar from that of the barons of his native land, and of such American *prominenti* as his patron, the eminent mixer of potions and a fellow profiteer in the market of cheap labor—Lobianco now wished to devote more time to his diversified business interests. From his profits after six years as a *padrone,* Lobianco owned in the Italian district of South Philadelphia two red-brick rental properties, a neighborhood bank, a travel agency, and a grocery store. He also owned two rambling boardinghouses in the outskirts of Ambler, where work was proceeding on Dr. Mattison's Gothic community and asbestos-manufacturing center. Supervising the boardinghouse was Carmine Lobianco's wife, the sister of an anarchist from Naples who, like him, had been slipped into the country illegally.

Living in the boardinghouses, and sleeping on cornhusk mattresses, four bunks to a room, were many Keasbey & Mattison laborers. At dawn each morning they were led by Lobianco's foreman up the dirt road into the stone quarry to dynamite and haul more rock uphill, to continue building the more than four hundred residences and factory structures that would make up the industrial community in Ambler.

During his years as a *padrone,* Lobianco had been responsible for shuttling more than five hundred men between Naples and Ambler. But in this period of adverse publicity, the countless responsibilities of that position—greeting the arriving boatloads of workers, escorting them onto trains, lodging and feeding them, tending to their varied needs and requirements, serving as their daily guardian and social consort, and all the other thankless tasks—were no longer worth the aggravation and money to Lobianco. He would subcontract most of the customary chores to his cousins and friends from Naples, while he moved back to Philadelphia to spend more time in less demanding circumstances.

The last boatload of workers for which he was directly responsible arrived in late April 1888. On board were forty-three men, all of them bachelors. All of them had jobs awaiting them with Keasbey & Mattison Company, either in the quarry or as apprentices to the stonemasons and artisans who had already completed dozens of Gothic buildings that Dr. Mattison himself had redesigned after expressing displeasure with the original plans submitted by his architects.

The forty-three newcomers did not have written contracts with Lobianco specifying the terms of employment—this practice had been banned by American immigration authorities under pressure from the unions; but Lobianco had been assured by his recruiter colleagues in Naples that each and every man had pledged to remain in the United States, under the guidance of the *padrone,* for no less than two years.

One of the workers who had agreed to these terms was Gaetano Talese.

18.

THE EXPLOSIONS IN the quarry roused the birds in the trees, stirred the animals grazing in nearby meadows, and one day blew off part of the left arm of a demolition worker who had climbed too slowly out of an opening in the rocks where he had moments before ignited the fuse on a keg of dynamite. Six months after the accident, when Gaetano Talese arrived in Ambler in the spring of 1888 to begin his job, he saw the victim working behind the grocery counter of the Keasbey & Mattison company store, wearing an artificial arm with a metal hook. Dr. Mattison did not believe in prolonged idleness.

Each morning, six days a week, Gaetano was sent with eighty other Italians into the quarry, where the rocky interior of the earth was hauled up daily after being detonated by kegs of dynamite and gunpowder, and by the shells of a Civil War cannon fired by an Irishman named Michael Herlihy. A gaunt, pugnacious ex-soldier who had fought for the North under Philadelphia's renowned commander General George ("Little

Mac") McClellan, Michael Herlihy was now in charge of rock-blasting for Dr. Mattison.

Herlihy appeared each morning at the quarry on horseback wearing a black kepi, overalls with brass-buckled suspenders, boots, and a pearl-handled pistol hanging from his waist. There he was joined by his five-man demolition team, who arrived in wagons from the arsenal carrying the cannon and kegs of explosives. Heavy packs of dynamite were placed in the drilled openings of the quarry where the rock was to be pulverized for Ambler's new roads, while the less potent gunpowder was used to crack loose larger chunks of rock for the walls and foundations of Dr. Mattison's buildings. When it was necessary to split these larger chunks for easier hauling by the Italians, Herlihy took aim from behind the cannon, fired a ball at a distance of about ninety feet, and usually broke the rock into two or three parts.

The oval quarry, which resembled an ancient amphitheater, was more than a hundred feet deep, and three times as wide; its interior walls were rimmed with jagged, rocky tiers smoothed into a corkscrew path wide enough to accommodate the two lanes of traffic coming and going at all hours of the workday. Crews of Italians gathered along the tiers with their horse-drawn cranes and cables, waiting for Herlihy's demolition team to finish their job before moving down the winding trail to begin hoisting the rubble of rocks in wagons and hauling it away toward the building sites.

No Italian was on Herlihy's demolition team. He could not entrust such precise and perilous chores to the limited competence of the Italians, he had said in essence to Dr. Mattison, insisting that he be aided only by the men he could understand and trust. Herlihy's team consisted of two other Irish veterans of the American Civil War and three sturdy blond Swedes who had once worked in a gristmill. The sixth member of his team, the slow-footed Dutchman named Faust who had been the victim of the earlier accident and who now worked in the company store, had not been replaced.

In the evenings the explosives and cannon were transported through the woods and stored in a stone barn that Herlihy had converted into his arsenal. There he also kept his hunting rifles and a still for making corn whiskey. The barn was off-limits to everyone except Herlihy's men and the hook-armed Faust, who had long been his closest friend and most frequent drinking companion. Lobianco had often warned the Italians never to walk within fifty yards of the barn, saying that if Herlihy considered them trespassers he might toss a stick of dynamite at them, or fire at them with a gun.

But one day during Gaetano's third month on the job, Lobianco assigned one of his anarchist friends, a man named Nicola Bosio, to lead the young workers to the quarry. Lobianco was beginning to phase himself out as a *padrone* and was spending more time in Philadelphia; and he believed that Bosio, who had been running the boardinghouse where Gaetano and many of the other newly arrived workers were staying, was a man he could rely upon to maintain discipline and settle any quarrels within the group. Nicola Bosio was also his brother-in-law, as Bosio's serene and fair-skinned sister was Lobianco's wife. But there was no physical resemblance between brother and sister; Bosio was an intense, dark-complected man with owlish eyes and a slight facial tic. Two years of being hunted by the Naples police had merely confirmed his antisocial sense of himself, and during his five months in America he had lived quietly within the boardinghouse, where he earned his keep as the cook and custodian and at night added to his earnings by beating the tenants at cards. He was a shrewd cardplayer. No matter what he held in his hands, his eyebrows arched in apparent satisfaction and even his tic seemed to be held in check.

After constant urging by Lobianco, Bosio finally agreed to cease living in habitual seclusion in the boardinghouse and to venture outdoors to see something of the American countryside; and his first step in this direction, although he had yet to learn a word of English, was to serve as the substitute *padrone,* and rise at dawn to the piercing sound of Dr. Mattison's watchtower whistle and accompany Gaetano and the other workmen to the quarry.

At thirty years of age, Bosio was more than a decade older than some of the new recruits; and as Bosio assumed a commanding posture at the head of the line, Gaetano and the others fell in step behind him, saying nothing during the first week when he took the wrong path through the woods on four out of six mornings and added at least ten minutes to the one-mile hike.

During the day, as Herlihy's men bombarded the western wall, Bosio stood observing from the upper tier with Gaetano and the others, although he lent them no assistance when it came time to hoist the rocks onto the wagons. Being an anarchist who advocated the overthrow of the ruling order did not imply his interest in joining the ranks of workers who got their hands dirty on the job. In his temporary position as *padrone,* which he soon began to relish, Bosio left the manual labor to his minions; and when the steam whistle signaled that the day's work was done, he nodded silently and knowingly at his men and led them back toward the boardinghouse, one evening choosing a path that soon brought them dangerously close to Herlihy's barn.

Some of his men hesitated, drifting back but saying nothing, while Gaetano and the others marched behind the nonchalant Bosio, who was whistling an aria from *Così Fan Tutte* and paying no heed to the craggy-featured man who suddenly emerged from behind a tree holding a long-barreled pistol.

"Hey, dago!" Herlihy yelled. "Get yourself and these other dagos out of here fast, or I'll shoot you all dead!"

Bosio, understanding not a word, whirled around. Seeing the gun, his dark eyes began to twitch, widened, then narrowed brutishly. The square shoulders of his squat figure, clad in a white shirt buttoned at the neck, tensed, and his forehead was moist beneath the peak of his black cap. He dug his heels firmly into the ground and placed his hands on his hips. Behind him, Gaetano and the other young men, stunned that they would be facing a gun so soon after their arrival in America, frantically whispered to Bosio in Italian that they should flee at once. But Bosio cursed them, ordered them to stand fast, while he stared menacingly over the barrel of the gun into Herlihy's face, hard into his eyes. Bosio's twitching stopped, his whole countenance became composed, and his persistent stare challenged the gunman.

Herlihy's pistol clicked. Bosio did not move. Herlihy spat at Bosio, again threatened and cursed him, but the immutable Bosio only looked unblinkingly into Herlihy's eyes. One minute passed, then another. Herlihy kept his finger on the trigger, but he did not shoot, and soon his gaze drifted away from the seemingly crazed Italian in front of him to Gaetano and the others gathered behind Bosio. Expressions of concern spread along their faces, but they, too, were refusing to move and were saying nothing. After a few more moments of tense silence, Herlihy let out an exasperated sigh. "Dumb fucking dagos," he said aloud to himself, shaking his head.

The silence continued. Finally Herlihy lowered his gun and turned around, avoiding further eye contact with Bosio. Herlihy entered the barn and slammed the door behind him. The tic came back to Bosio's cheek, but his eyes softened as he faced his men. Repressing a smile, Bosio then led Gaetano and the others back toward the boardinghouse.

Being a member of a group Herlihy disliked sufficiently to keep them off his demolition team was very agreeable to Gaetano, for whom the deafening job—to say nothing of the back-breaking task of hauling rocks—hardly represented what he had in mind when he had left home for America. What he wanted was something creative—such as an apprenticeship to one of the skilled artisans Dr. Mattison had brought over from Italy to carve the finials and other stone ornaments that would adorn his residence and the nearby Gothic mansions scheduled to rise along Ambler's most exclusive street, Lindenwold Terrace.

On a late-summer day more than a year after his arrival, during a thunderstorm and continuing rain that interrupted all work in the quarry, Gaetano left his friends in the boardinghouse and followed the path that led to the railroad terminal, across from which was the Keasbey & Mattison headquarters. It was a temporary building, a rambling frame structure surrounded by many shacks and tented enclosures scattered along the grounds where a huge stone foundation was already in place for the company's four-story office and emporium. Had it not been raining, the area would have been busy with carpenters, stonemasons, and loading crews; but the only people on duty now were those who could do their work indoors.

Gaetano finally found the room where the architects and engineers were gathered, and, after wiping the mud and leaves from his shoes and removing his rain cloak and cap, he approached a portly, bearded, white-moustached Italian who appeared to hold some position of authority. The man was speaking Italian in an almost magisterial tone to two younger men, both of whom sat on tall stools next to a drawing board on which were large sketches of conical turrets and finials that Gaetano assumed would grace the buildings of Ambler in the near future.

"Excuse me," Gaetano said to the older man, who turned away from the other two, "could you tell me how I might apply to become an apprentice to the artisans who will be making the beautiful buildings for Dr. Mattison?"

The man turned toward Gaetano and with a bemused smile asked, "How do you *know* that they will be beautiful when they are not yet even begun?"

"Sir, it is the opinion of my *padrone,* Signor Lobianco, and he is a very wise man. He told me that the artisans brought from Italy are the finest in all of Europe."

"Signor Lobianco *is* wise," the man said, nodding cordially and stroking his Vandyke beard. "They are indeed the best in all of Europe. And I am their master."

Respectfully silent, since he could think of nothing appropriate to say, Gaetano then became self-conscious as the older man, taking a step back, began in a casual but obvious way to study him from head to toe. Gaetano felt his feet cold and damp within his soggy socks, and the wet soles of his high-buttoned Italian shoes, and he was aware that his Cristiani-made trousers, which he had put on in place of his work pants before coming here, were more than an inch too short in the cuffs—he had grown taller since leaving Italy. At the boardinghouse he had also changed to his one clean shirt, although he had no idea what importance might be attached to this by the man who was now scrutinizing him. Did not the artisans and their apprentices don coarse attire while working outdoors, and become as soiled and sweaty as the people who worked in the quarry? But the master artisan whose eyes were now on him did appear to be a man of a certain vanity: he wore a pearl stickpin through the blue tie knotted within the hard rounded collar of his white shirt; and extending a bit below the waist of his brown trousers, and across his slight paunch, was a gray waistcoat with a watch chain looped through it. In one pocket of the waistcoat were several pencils, each with a small metal cap on the point to prevent the lead from smudging the material.

"And what is your name?" he said finally, and pleasantly enough.

"Gaetano Talese."

The man seemed suddenly curious.

"Are you any relation to my old friend Domenico Talese?"

"You mean the Domenico Talese of *Maida*?"

"Yes," the man said. "We were once in the seminary together."

Gaetano paused before going on, feeling uneasy about the conversation. It was possible that the man was aware of Gaetano's difficulties with his father and his abrupt departure from home. But chancing that there was only a remote possibility that the man could know about any of this, Gaetano decided to give the impression that he was on the best of terms with his father.

"I am his first son," Gaetano announced, with feigned pride.

"Bravo," said the man. "Your father was a most religious man, much more than myself. I left the seminary when I was about your age. After that, the closest I came to God was as a stone craftsman working sometimes on ecclesiastical buildings.

"My surname, by the way, is Maniscalco, and as it happens, we do need additional apprentices around here. Let me speak with your Signor Lobianco and see if we cannot arrange your working with us."

Mr. Maniscalco shook his hand, and in a loud voice he announced: "Gaetano, this may be your lucky day!"

To this, Gaetano could only nod and say, "Yes."

It was also his eighteenth birthday.

During the next three years as one of Mr. Maniscalco's apprentices, and in subsequent years when he functioned as a full-fledged artisan with an apprentice of his own, Gaetano dwelled in a world of corbeled arches and crenellated molding, of steeply peaked Gothic rooftops transected by Baroque curvilinear gables and shadowed by spindly finials of Saracenic influence. Domineering as Dr. Mattison was in so many ways, he was remarkably lenient toward Maniscalco's crew, allowing them to impose their own creative impulses upon the architectural concepts that strictly adhered to Gothic principles.

While these deviations offended the senior architects from Philadelphia and New York who had originally been commissioned, and who later ceased to work for Dr. Mattison when their protests went unheeded, the doctor himself clearly approved of the eclectic embellishments that the Italians molded and mounted, chiseled and carved into the tops and sides of the large, widely spaced rows of stone buildings. As more and more buildings went up, more and more liberties were taken by the Italians, who, perhaps unintentionally but unmistakably, were reproducing what many of them had seen as younger men growing up in the villages and towns of their native land—a land built by conquerors who were in turn conquered but who invariably left behind with their dust some remnant of their architecture; and it was the random re-creation of these varied architectural styles that was apparent in the workmanship of the rooftops and façades, the dormers, the buttresses, the pilasters, the portals, and the balustrades of Ambler's new buildings at the turn of the century.

When Gaetano stood on a scaffold with his pointed hammers and chisels, refining the carving that spanned the main arch of a porte cochère, he was guided less by the architect's Gothic drawing than by what he remembered as a boy playing around the arch of the Norman wall that spanned the entrance into Maida. Others systematically diluted through the recollections of their villages the architect's Gothic purity by introducing elements of the Baroque or Ionian, Romanesque or Byzantine; and the fact Dr. Mattison liked what he saw was all that mattered. His partner,

Henry Keasbey, went into semi-retirement on turning forty-two, in 1892; he moved to the south of France with his wife, whose health had rapidly and inexplicably deteriorated not long after she had joined her husband in the colonial house he had rented in Ambler while awaiting the completion of their mansion. With Mr. Keasbey departed from the asbestos-manufacturing center that he largely owned—and from which he would continue to receive profits that were due him as its major stockholder—Dr. Mattison was free not only to decide how the community would look, and how the asbestos business would be run, but also to govern unofficially the political and economic affairs of the increasing number of citizens who had moved into the area in the wake of the land boom that had been unceasing ever since the Philadelphia company had relocated to the village.

In 1888, six years after the partners had built their first factory along Ambler's railroad tracks (the factories were of a utilitarian design and were completed years before the residences), Ambler's population had quadrupled and the village had incorporated itself into a borough, selecting civil officials as its administrators—but administrators nonetheless dependent upon the goodwill and support of Dr. Mattison, who now presided over the borough's bank, and its water, gas, and electric companies.

When the doctor decided to raise the rates he charged the borough for providing the electricity for its shops, its private residences, and its streetlamps, he was at first challenged by the burgess and other politicians, many of whom declared that the doctor could not be as arbitrary with them as with his company's employees and construction crews. The doctor responded by turning off all the switches that were connected to the borough's electrical circuits. That night, the streets were dark, and they remained so for several evenings—except when the doctor was traveling about in his carriage, and had left instructions that the streetlights should be put on. Dr. Mattison did not make himself available to debate this issue with the borough officials; as far as he was concerned, there was nothing to debate. He owned the power system, and he determined the cost of its use. Having no option, the borough soon agreed to his rate increase.

Dr. Mattison arrived at his second-floor offices each workday no later than seven a.m., which was when he expected his hundreds of employees and construction crews to be busy on the job. It was he who had ordered that the whistle atop the main factory begin sounding at five forty-five a.m., rasping persistently and loudly enough to rouse the most drowsy of the workmen in the distant boardinghouses and shacks, and the factory employees, foremen, and executives now residing in the newly completed houses up the hill. Hundreds of other employees for whom housing was not yet available arrived from the outlying areas each morning by train or wagon, being spared the grating sound that offended almost everyone who heard it—particularly the borough citizens who did not work for the company but who nonetheless were awakened, as Dr. Mattison thought everyone should be, at five forty-five a.m. When Dr. Mattison's secretary arrived one morning at a few minutes after seven, because of a train delay, and cheerfully commented, "Well, better late than never," he looked up from his desk and snapped, "Better never late!"

While Dr. Mattison had a subtle sense of humor, it was rarely evident in the office; nor did he smile often. But there was much that brought him quiet pleasure as he studied the monthly and annual progress reports of his diversified company. The Keasbey & Mattison pharmaceutical division, which had followed him to Ambler and continued to supply apothecaries throughout the nation and overseas, was earning millions in annual profits—and, after the turn of the century, it was even surpassed by the firm's asbestos division. The national demand for asbestos products had increased to such a point that in 1906 the doctor had to buy a one-hundred-twenty-acre asbestos mine in Quebec to obtain enough of the mineral to meet the requirements of the factories in Ambler.

The variety of fireproof and heat-condensing items manufactured in Ambler included a large percentage of the insulation material used within railroad locomotives and steam-powered plants around the nation; thousands of nonflammable curtains hanging in numerous American homes, auditoriums, and theaters (including the world's largest stage curtain, at the Hippodrome in New York); and the doctor's popular brand of asbestos brake lining for America's growing number of faster automobiles, which quickly burned out the leather lining used in the first cars that had top speeds of twelve or fifteen miles per hour.

But the largest profits were coming from Keasbey & Mattison's asbestos-cement roof shingles. After experimental examples of this mixture had been used in making shingles for the roofs of the first fifty buildings in the Gothic community—in time, all four hundred buildings would have such roofs—Dr. Mattison mailed out advertisements throughout the construction industry heralding his product as the most durable and safest roof covering in the entire land. Asbestos-cement shingles were lighter than slate shingles and yet virtually indestructible when compared with the easily breakable slate; they were also obviously safer than combustible wood shingles, as well as longer lasting. He reported that his chemists and construction engineers, conducting experiments throughout the nation, discovered that asbestos shingles were ideal in places such as Texas and Oklahoma because, unlike slate, they would not break during hailstorms, and in frigid areas such as Michigan and Minnesota, where the snow would not stick to the shingles' highly polished surface. They were equally desirable along coastal areas, he claimed, where they never required painting and where fog, rain, and frequent dampness would actually improve their appearance and add strength to their texture.

Whether all this was true or not, the doctor proved to be as adept at selling shingles as he had been with his internationally popular Bromo Caffeine: fifteen million shingles were shipped out of Ambler during the first year that his shingle factory was fully operational, and they soon were on the roofs of houses, schools, churches, and other buildings across the country: on the Pabst brewery in Milwaukee; on the dairy barns of William Rockefeller's farmlands in New York State; on the stables of the Miller Brothers' ranch in Oklahoma; and on the residence of the celebrated Egyptologist Theodore M. Davis in Rhode Island.

By the early 1900s, Dr. Richard V. Mattison was perhaps the most listened-to physician in the country who did not practice medicine—which did not mean that he wished the public to forget that he held an M.D. degree. The reminder accompanied his name on all his mail circulars, his newspaper advertising, his business cards; and it was affixed behind the initials ("R.V.M., M.D.") imprinted on his silver cuff links, on the gold cover of his watch, above the pockets of certain shirts, on the side doors of his carriage, and later on the large red electric automobile that he had specially designed with a high glass enclosure and an asbestos-cloth roof.

Tall as he was, Dr. Mattison could sit in the back wearing a top hat without touching the car's velvet ceiling; and as he was driven between the office and his mansion, he would often tip his hat to the workers he saw along the roadside or up on the scaffolding, and they would remove their caps and wave back. In warm weather, when the glass top was removed, he would call out to them, "Good day, gentlemen," and they would reply, sometimes in the only English they knew, "Good day, Dr. Mattison." Among the socially elite of Philadelphia, to which the doctor now tangentially belonged, as a boxholder at the opera and a devotee of horticulture, he was seen as a somewhat eccentric representative of the Gay Nineties, a bit pompous but too successful to ignore; to the Italians in Ambler, he was an awesome figure out of an earlier age—an age that Gaetano Talese and the others understood, even if they had gladly left it behind in the old country. They did not judge him with the harshness of most non-Italians in Ambler; and to the young Gaetano, who never failed to nod his greetings toward his white-bearded boss in the red car, Dr. Mattison represented America. He was big, bold, aloof, and successful.

Gaetano was also aware of his human side—how he had personally attended to one of the apprentices who had broken a leg in a fall from a scaffold, and had escorted the youth by train to a Philadelphia hospital; how he had paid the expenses back to Italy for another young man who wanted to spend time with his mother after the death of his father; and how the doctor himself had tearfully and publicly mourned the death of his own daughter—who died of typhoid fever at the age of four, and in whose memory the doctor had built, across from his seventy-two-acre private estate, a Gothic Episcopal church, which was consecrated in 1901.

Dr. Mattison had initially hired an architect named Samuel Franklin to design the gray stone church on a three-acre plot, but the doctor was impossible to please. Nothing seemed good enough for his daughter now dead. Finally he released the architect and redesigned the entire structure himself, making it larger and more ornate. He specified that high pointed turrets should jut out along the lower ridges of the red terra-cotta tile roof, which was topped by a one-hundred-foot tower that would reflect the glow of several small hidden rooftop spotlights—which would burn with more intensity whenever the organist in the church pressed his feet upon the pedals. Electrical wiring connected the roof lights and the organist's pedals. The three-chamber Haskell organ with sixteen-foot pipes was in turn powered by water pressure pumped up from the church floor through a four-inch-thick pipe that was fed by the water system of the doctor's mansion a half-mile away. The church's main altar was carved from a single piece of marble; the sanctuary was encircled by five opalescent windows depicting scenes from the Bible; and the high-domed roof, inlaid with carved oak, was complemented by elaborately carved columns and beams extending the length of the church. All the woodwork was done by carvers and carpenters working under the doctor's new foreman, a crusty Pennsylvanian named Leidy Heckler, while the stonework continued to be done by Maniscalco's Italians.

Each day, wagonloads of rock would arrive from the quarry, and Gaetano would wave from his scaffold in the cloisters down to some of the laborers in Bosio's gang, grateful that he was no longer among them. Gaetano did notice, however, midway through the construction, that several black men now worked in the quarry. He knew from the talk in the boardinghouse that there was beginning to be a shortage of Italians because Carmine Lobianco had stopped bringing in new men from Naples, preferring to concentrate on his business interests in Philadelphia. Gaetano had never seen a black man before, and he had yet to speak to one, but one evening he had paused along the road to listen to the black workers singing as they pushed into town, on a huge, flat eight-wheeled wagon, a white clapboard church that had stood ten miles away, where the men had been laying railroad tracks. About thirty black men now lived in shacks on the south side of Ambler, a section that Dr. Mattison had designated for them; and before bringing their wives and children into the area they were relocating their old Baptist church, to be placed atop a wooden foundation in Ambler built by Leidy Heckler's carpenters.

As Gaetano would in time clearly see, Dr. Mattison believed in racial segregation and in establishing a kind of caste system within his residential community. He had selected certain areas of Ambler where housing could be built for black and Italian families—two groups that he saw as having potentially a stable place in his community as employees of Keasbey & Mattison's asbestos factories after the construction work had been completed. While he would not permit blacks and Italians to rent houses on the same blocks, both groups would inhabit the residential area closest to the factories and on the opposite side of the tracks from where the doctor's other employees and their families would reside. Cordial as Dr. Mattison was to the Italian construction crews, he would not accept them as neighbors should they accept factory jobs and bring up families in Ambler. Nor would the doctor accept most of his other non-Italian white employees as his close neighbors. Everyone who settled in Ambler would be socially stratified; status would be identified by the size of home each employee was permitted to rent, and by its distance from the community's main residence. This residence, of course, was Dr. Mattison's turreted mansion, majestically situated at the top of a hill and protected behind stone walls patrolled day and night by guards and watchdogs.

Near the bottom of the hill, yet sufficiently elevated to overlook the flatlands across the tracks that had been designated for the blacks and the Italians, would live the most common non-Italian factory workers, dwelling within rows of sturdy but smallish stone residences that had a minimum of ornamentation and no space between them. On the higher streets in the direction of Mattison's estate was the residential area for the Keasbey & Mattison foremen and managers. Here stood rows of sizable two-story houses separated by enough space for small lawns on the sides, and with more ornamentation than on the workers' houses but noticeably less (no finials, no turrets) than on the spacious three-story houses set aside for higher management employees and within view of the church that memorialized the doctor's daughter.

Across the road to the right of the church, along Lindenwold Terrace, which extended outside the westerly wall of Dr. Mattison's private domain—a domain in which he would soon have his towering Gothic residence remodeled to resemble a castle—were the eight mansions upon which Maniscalco's men had been permitted to be their most creative, and which the doctor planned to rent only to top executives, senior chemists, and other individuals he happened to favor. The rent charged for these mansions, as well as for the plainer residences downhill, was perhaps half of what would have been charged for similar-sized residences elsewhere in the far countryside of Philadelphia.

By charging low rents the doctor increased his subordinates' dependence while at the same time making them willing to receive salaries below the prevailing pay scales of other towns and cities.

The homes in Mattison's community received their water, heating fuel, and electricity from the utility companies he owned; and if employees failed to keep up with their rents and utility fees, or did not repay loans from his bank, they would soon discover that portions of their weekly salaries were withheld and applied toward their restitution. While the doctor seemed businesslike in the extreme in his relationship to his subordinates, he had one custom that, on the surface, appeared to contradict this.

From the first days of his community, he always made available to the residents, free of charge, wagonloads of flowers and small plants that had been grown in his gardens and greenhouses. At the end of each week his wagon drivers would place wooden boxes of plants, and bundles of flowers wrapped in newspaper, along the curbs of the gently sloping streets down to, and beyond, the railroad tracks. Sometimes Dr. Mattison himself could be seen watching from his red car as the people hastened out of their homes to help themselves to the assorted samples of his horticulture. If he was waiting for some sign of gratitude, he did not reveal it. He merely sat in the back of the car, behind his uniformed Swedish driver, watching from a distance beyond acknowledgment as the men and women carried away the flowers and plants, which, unknown to them, had already been on display in vases and porcelain pots within his forty-room mansion and were now only a few days away from withering and dying.

19.

GAETANO TALESE'S FIRST visit home to Italy in more than six years was made memorable a week after his arrival, when, while standing one evening beneath the balcony of a young woman with whom he was having a prolonged and lightly flirtatious conversation, he was grabbed and choked from behind by a man who, before stabbing him with a knife, whispered: "You have no right to speak to this woman."

As Gaetano fought the man off, then felt the blood flowing from his right temple, the assailant disappeared into the shadows between two buildings, never to be taken into custody. The woman later swore to the police that she could not identify the attacker; nor could she suggest the name of any man in whom she might have encouraged such impassioned possessiveness. But at that time it was not unusual for a woman in Maida not to know that a particular man had laid private claim to her, since such a man felt compelled to inform only his close male acquaintances, whose noninterference he sought and required while he watched her window at night, and frequently followed her during the day, learning all that he could about her until he was ready to reveal his ardor and marital intentions to her family.

This ancient rite of remote courtship, which still existed at the turn of the century in southern Italy, was seen as both natural and proper: the woman was secretly desired and pursued; her family was later informed and consulted; and finally the nuptial terms were agreed upon by mature representatives of both parties—devoid of the ambiguous utterances, the furtive liaisons, and the fickle dalliances of a young couple in love. A stable society was founded on pragmatic matchmaking.

But recently, the return of many native sons visiting from the New World who presumed the right to speak to any woman who caught their fancy was causing agitation among the population. While most people publicly expressed regret at what had happened to Gaetano, in private many believed he had gotten what he deserved.

Other offenses by returnees had gone unpublished. Several naive maidens, swayed by the men's exaggerated tales of their wealth and accomplishments overseas, and believing their promises would deliver them from the poverty and stagnation of the village, later found themselves pregnant and abandoned by their persuasive lovers, who returned alone across the sea. Even when a young man was honorable, and wanted to marry his *innamorata* in Italy, he was sometimes rebuffed by her parents, who feared that if she joined him overseas they would never again see her. For the first time in local history it seemed that the closeness of the large Italian family could be weakened and fractured by its transoceanic extension.

Therefore these visits home by workers from abroad were viewed apprehensively by many elders, who saw the migrants not as returning sons but as young men on the prowl, soldiers of the economy who were here today and then gone forever as men with a personal role in the village's future. Their American experiences had desensitized them to local customs, made them another in the long line of invaders. And during the *passeggiata* they were conspicuous in their foreign-made clothes, pridefully striding arm in arm with their more modest relatives, often failing to tip their hats to the passing priests or to members of the aristocracy, as if *they* were now the new aristocrats.

Financially generous as many of them undoubtedly were to their relatives in Maida, and thus an asset to the local economy, they nonetheless by their very existence prompted questions about the worth and courage of those hometown bachelors who had shunned the opportunity of enriching themselves overseas. The choice of local men to remain at home would not have become an issue had so many local women not become attracted to the travelers, and to the idea that a woman's life might be improved by taking chances and deviating from the path chosen by her elders. Even if she remained at home, the typical village maiden was no longer contented with what she had—her horizons had been widened, options were in the offing; the hometown boulevardiers, walking in circles, now lacked the mystery of the men visiting from abroad.

Gaetano was unaware of the tension between the young women and men of his village during his first days home, prior to the stabbing incident. He had, in fact, been gratified by the friendly greetings of everyone he met, and particularly by the loving reception of his family at the Maida train station, a group that included his mother; his married sister, Maria, and her husband, Francesco Cristiani (holding their infant son, Antonio); and even his father, in his mid-fifties, his reddish hair now turning white. Domenico embraced him tightly within his cape, misty-eyed and strangely sentimental; and later, during a private moment, his father admitted that he had prayed for Gaetano's safe return during each and every day of his absence. While Gaetano was moved on hearing this, he hoped that his father was not counting on his resettling in Maida and fulfilling some function in the family enterprises. Gaetano intended to return to the United States within a few months, when the milder spring weather melted the frozen mortar and permitted the resumption of stonework outdoors on a full-time basis. He liked his job—and also the three-month hiatus each winter that had permitted him to board trains in Philadelphia and wander about the country.

During the previous winter, that of 1893–1894, he had spent six weeks in New Orleans. The winter before, he had gone by train to California, then traveled by stagecoach from Santa Ana to the Mexican border. Having learned to speak and read English, Gaetano was a knowing and communicative traveler; and despite the expense of such trips (and having to pay off almost three hundred dollars in gambling debts to Bosio), he still had a few hundred dollars left in a safety deposit box in Philadelphia after he had advanced the payment for his passage back to Italy. Had he been more frugal he could have saved five times that amount. But Gaetano spent money nearly as fast as he made it, living for the day, unconcerned about tomorrow. During his fourth year in America, before turning twenty-one, he vacated Lobianco's boardinghouse for a small, expensive apartment in Philadelphia, which he shared with a fellow worker of his own age, Carlo Donato, who commuted with him each workday to Ambler. Donato came from a village just south of Maida called Jacurso. Each evening after returning to Philadelphia, and all day on Sundays, Donato earned extra money working as a waiter in an Italian restaurant, where Gaetano went to eat.

Gaetano had no idea what he would do after Dr. Mattison's Gothic community was completed. He had been told by his mentor, Mr. Maniscalco, who was almost as casual and unconcerned about making plans as Gaetano, that there would always be plenty of work for stone artisans in the eastern area of the United States. Maniscalco had predicted that the current building boom in the region would last for decades, and Gaetano had readily agreed. He had noticed several busy construction sites from his train window during his excursions—signs of a prospering economy in a growing nation to which he would soon apply for citizenship, a young country that differed greatly from what he saw when he returned to Italy in late 1894.

Disembarking from the steamship in Naples for a three-day stopover before boarding the train to Maida, Gaetano observed that little had changed in the city since he had been there in 1888. It seemed as boisterous, dirty, and overcrowded as ever. Nothing new was being built; nothing old was being renovated. Beggars were everywhere. Herds of goats clopped through the teeming streets among the carriage drivers and pedestrians, and between tight rows of beige stone houses that fanned out from the harbor up toward Mount Vesuvius. Herdsmen sometimes escorted goats *into* the ground-floor apartments of customers wanting milk, and even up the steps to top-floor apartments, leaving behind a trail of animal droppings that no one seemed to mind.

On the Piazza del Plebiscito was the royal palace, its throne long vacant; and behind the equestrian statues of two Bourbon kings was the Church of Saint Francis of Paola, its dome eroding and parts of its columns cracking and chipped. Within the arcade of the church, and within other sheltered spaces throughout the city, stood itinerant cooks, their pots steaming with macaroni, fish, and sausages; and mingling around them were vendors hawking a variety of items—gloves, hats, rosary beads, trays of cigar ends (retrieved from gutters), stolen jewelry, and ornaments made of lava. As usual, the citizenry kept an eye on the volcano as a guide to forecasting the weather. On the day of Gaetano's arrival, the crater was concealed behind a thick layer of clouds, and the wind was coming from the south, indicating wet weather was due. By noon, the city was drenched in rain.

The newspaper headlines were no less grim than they had been six years before. Italy was still engaged in colonial wars in East Africa. Gaetano had seen several Italian soldiers in the streets of Naples, a few wearing bandages and walking with the aid of canes. The government in Rome had kept up its campaign against the anarchists and radical Socialists. Nearly all of the radicals Gaetano had known in Naples were now in the United States, lamenting from afar Italy's decision to disband the Socialist Party and to institute strict new laws against anarchists. But not even the most ardent of antianarchist legislators in Rome believed that the life of King Umberto I, son of the Risorgimento king, Victor Emmanuel II, would ever be endangered by an anarchist assassin.

After three days in Naples, Gaetano checked out of his hotel, took a carriage to the east end of the city, and boarded a southbound train to Maida, having sent a telegram to his parents the previous night, announcing his presence in Italy and his scheduled time of arrival in the village. It was a tedious journey: the train stopped at almost every town along the route, allowing passengers to use the toilets in the stations (there were none on the train), and some second-class travelers in the rear car to walk the baby goats and lambs they had brought on board. Gaetano sat alone in one of the first-class smoking compartments, which were in the front of the train behind the compartments reserved for women.

On this day the train had left Naples with no women aboard, and only five men in addition to Gaetano in the front section. Unlike the gregarious young travelers with whom he had drunk wine and sung songs while crossing the ocean, his rail companions were middle-aged seignorial figures in dark suits and hats who exchanged few words even when standing together in the aisle. Each sat alone within a glass-paneled enclosure, surrounded by empty seats, reading a newspaper or a book, smoking a cigarette or small cigar, and occasionally glancing out at the passing countryside with a facial expression that was pensive, even sad. Gaetano thought they might be Neapolitan landowners en route to survey the fallow fields of their plantations, anticipating the dismal financial reports they would soon be receiving from their foremen in the deep south.

The land did indeed seem barren, no matter where Gaetano looked out from the train as it slowly chugged and choked its way through the black smoke of its locomotive, following tracks that at times skimmed along the edge of the Tyrrhenian Sea, then swerved inland and climbed high on viaduct bridges into promontory tunnels, rumbling and swaying in the darkness for several moments before emerging again in the daylight and down again toward the bleak coastline. Only rarely did Gaetano see a fishing boat in the sea. Even the once ubiquitous scavenger birds seemed to have disappeared. But the mountains inland, to Gaetano's left, never disappeared—they remained framed within the rows of windows during the entire trip, dominating the skyline with their snowcapped peaks, fir-forested hills, remains of ruined castles and ancient watchtowers, and cliffside villages that were invariably lopsided. Gaetano knew that many of these villages had been struck by earthquakes decades before, centuries before; but only now, with the perspective that a long absence from home can bring to a returning native, could he contemplate with fresh clarity this mutilated and precipitous land, and acknowledge the adaptability required of those who chose to remain here.

As the train pulled slowly in and out of stations and brought him closer and closer to Maida, Gaetano saw gathered along the platforms many people he thought he had seen before; but he could recognize none of them. Most of those in the waiting crowds were young men of his own age, often accompanied by older men and women who stood next to luggage and sometimes dabbed their eyes with handkerchiefs. The young men did not board Gaetano's train. They were waiting on the opposite side of the platform for trains heading north toward Naples. From the quantity and size of their luggage Gaetano guessed that the young men were going away for a long time, perhaps via a steamship to America, and that the older folks were relatives and friends who had come to say good-bye.

At the station in Amantea, about an hour upcoast from Maida, Gaetano saw a young couple who gave the impression of being newly married. The woman was very pretty and looked barely twenty, and she carried a bouquet of flowers tied with a long white ribbon that trailed against her maroon skirt and brown fringed shawl. She stood in the center of the platform, opposite Gaetano's window, and as he leaned forward and studied her under the stanchioned light she seemed to be in a mood of much gaiety and anticipation. Her cheeks were flushed, her eyes were bright; and while she appeared attentive to what was being said between her boutonniered young companion and the elders who stood next to him, she also glanced down the tracks constantly in the direction from which the train would come.

Gaetano was affected by her spirit, and he imagined himself one day marrying such a woman and embarking on a new adventure. He had never had a close relationship with a woman of his age during his earlier years in Maida, or since he had been away. Despite his travels in America, and the widening circle of people he had befriended since taking the apartment in Philadelphia, he had met few eligible women. America was open-armed, but its daughters were invariably off-limits. There was the social barrier that existed between non-Italian women and such workers as himself, as well as the fact that practically all the young Italian women he was aware of in America were already married or engaged. He had therefore been very pleased and receptive when his roommate, Carlo Donato, had suggested that Gaetano look up a certain cousin of his who lived with her family in the valley of Maida. Donato described her as being very attractive but a bit stubborn, and said that her name was Marian Rocchino. Donato also composed a letter of introduction and gave it to Gaetano to deliver to her home—which Gaetano did five days after he had arrived in Maida.

Having borrowed one of his father's horses, but without informing him of the purpose, Gaetano followed Carlo Donato's directions to the Rocchino farm three miles downhill, only to discover that no one was home, and learn from a neighbor that Marian's parents were away for a few days in the provincial capital of Catanzaro, but that she and her youngest brother were staying at the home of family friends in the village, down the road from the Talese family compound.

It was siesta time when Gaetano located the house, and so without knocking he left the letter with a note of his own, saying that if Marian was agreeable to meeting him he would be standing in front of the balcony of her friends' house at seven o'clock that evening.

When he returned and saw her waiting for him, he at first thought he was again seeing the young woman from the train station in Amantea.

Gaetano was in bed for several days from the knife wound, feverish, dizzy, and scarred. Ippolita cried when her son was carried home by the police, but after the doctor had reassured her of his complete recovery, she devoted herself to his daily care, changing the bandages as the doctor had instructed. His father did not visit his bedroom after the first day. Domenico regarded the situation as scandalous and could not help wondering whether Gaetano, or the woman he had been talking to, had not somehow provoked the violence that had transpired.

Domenico knew the Rocchino family slightly, and understood them to be simple but honorable people, although he knew nothing of Marian. He had spoken to her father, who was more remorseful than angry, acknowledging that the incident might impede his daughter's chances of marrying anyone in the village. But Marian seemed concerned only with Gaetano's recovery. Against her parents' advice, she insisted on visiting him every day. She was as her cousin in Philadelphia had described her to Gaetano—stubborn but very attractive. Gaetano liked her more each time he saw her.

When his bandages had been removed and he was feeling better, he began to take walks with Marian in public. This was in February 1895, some weeks after the stabbing, and nearly everyone in the square nodded and smiled as the young couple passed. Their budding romance was obvious to all in Maida, and Gaetano was very pleased and proud as he escorted his petite twenty-year-old *innamorata* home each day before twilight, his three-inch scar plainly visible to all since he had decided not to wear his customary wide-brimmed fedora—partly to avoid scraping the hat's inner edge against his wound, and partly to flaunt the wound in defiance of his attacker. While he hoped there would never be another confrontation, there was a new boldness, an intensity and watchfulness, about Gaetano. When he found himself face to face with other young men on the road, and properly returned their acknowledgments, he made it a point to look directly and probingly into their eyes. He also carried a heavy malacca walking stick, which, if necessary, he intended to use as a weapon.

At the end of the month, Gaetano proposed marriage to Marian. She was at first reluctant, suggesting that they should wait until they had known one another longer. But his enthusiasm and romanticism about marriage were persuasive; and soon it was she, more than he, who was pressing their families to complete their prenuptial discussions, which involved everything from the dowry to the church date. It was now a foregone conclusion on her part that the marriage itself was inevitable, and was not a subject for debate by the families of either party.

Of all the relatives, Gaetano's father was, surprisingly, the most positive about the union. Domenico saw the marriage as perhaps a solution to the mysterious waywardness of his oldest son; and so he demonstrated uncommon warmth toward his future daughter-in-law and ingratiated himself as well with her parents and brothers. He also promised as one of his wedding gifts to the couple the deed to the two-story house located next to his own. Privately he hoped that Gaetano would show his gratitude by withdrawing from America and assume, at long last, a modicum of filial responsibility.

At this time Domenico had no idea, nor should he have had one, given Gaetano's persistent vagueness, that his son was committed to living in America. Unbeknownst to anyone in the family, Gaetano had received a wire at the post office from Mr. Maniscalco extending his time in Italy, because of the circumstances of his injury, but he expected Gaetano back on the job no later than the end of July. Gaetano had also received a letter from Marian's cousin Carlo Donato, with the pleasant news that he had accepted a high-paying foreman's position with a construction company in Delaware, and as a result he would be leaving the Philadelphia apartment entirely to Gaetano for the foreseeable future. Without consulting Marian, Gaetano determined that this would be their future home. He booked their passage on a ship that would get them from Naples to the United States within the time limit that Maniscalco had imposed; and in so doing, Gaetano spent most of what was left of his savings on the sea voyage that he saw as their honeymoon.

Two days after the wedding, held in early July 1895 in the Maida church where his own parents had been married, Gaetano informed his wife of the travel plans. She responded in a tearful manner that in no way diluted her decisiveness that she was not going. She argued that, in accepting Domenico's wedding gift of a house, her husband had allowed her to assume this would be their home; much as she loved him, she reminded him, she was acutely hydrophobic and could never travel anywhere by sea. She also recounted certain sad tales she had heard about the living conditions of immigrants' wives in America, and nothing Gaetano could say or do in the days ahead could dissuade her. He finally understood what her cousin in Philadelphia had meant when he said that Marian had a mind of her own.

She was fundamentally a woman of the provinces, a woman who would always be wed more to her village than to a husband who was abroad. And so after three more days of futile effort, Gaetano angrily left Maida without her, sailing from Naples on choppy waters under an ashen sky. Wearing a new suit that had been a wedding present, and his favorite fedora over his now healed wound, and holding on to the brass rail within a glass-enclosed stateroom of the second deck, Gaetano stared at the waves and watched his native land recede in the distance. As far as he was concerned, the marriage was over.

For five months, the couple did not communicate. Then one Saturday evening after Gaetano had returned to the Philadelphia apartment from Ambler, a messenger arrived to say that an important letter from Italy awaited him at the home of a Philadelphia mortician named Francesco Donato, a distant relative of Carlo, his former roommate. Gaetano knew of the mortician but had never met him, and from the worrisome look on the young messenger's face, he assumed that the letter would inform him of the grave illness or death of a member of the family. Gaetano had never given anyone in Maida his new address in Philadelphia, and he thanked the messenger for the efforts taken in locating him. Then, after donning a dark suit and following the messenger's directions to the funeral parlor on the other side of South Philadelphia's Italian section, Gaetano found himself standing on the white marble floor of a reception room, surrounded by flowers and empty open caskets, shaking hands with Mr. Donato, a portly, balding man wearing a black suit and a white carnation, and large diamond rings on both pinkies. There was a jovial expression on his round face.

"I have good news," Mr. Donato said. "Soon you will become a father."

He handed the letter in the opened envelope to Gaetano and smiled while Gaetano read it, anticipating a joyful reaction. But Gaetano's long face and somber dark eyes remained unchanged. Then he put his wife's letter back into the envelope and, remaining silent, handed it to Mr. Donato, who frowned with disappointment. It then occurred to Mr. Donato that perhaps Gaetano was unable to read; and so he asked softly, "Would you like me to read it to you?"

"But I have just read it," Gaetano said, looking at him curiously.

"Well, then," Mr. Donato continued, after a pause, "when will you be returning to Italy for the birth and the christening?" Mr. Donato was a travel agent as well as a mortician, earning almost as much from the first business as the second.

"I have no plans for returning," Gaetano said, in a manner that Mr. Donato found odd and irritating. Having taken the trouble to locate him, Mr. Donato now saw no guaranteed reward in the sale of a steamship ticket. "But when I do get my plans in order," Gaetano went on, more sociably, "may I contact you?"

"Yes, thank you," Mr. Donato said with a smile. And when Gaetano offered to reimburse him for the expense involving the letter, Mr. Donato waved his right hand in the air in a grand gesture of dismissal.

He was confident that Gaetano would soon return to buy his ticket.

Three years passed before Gaetano returned to Maida. But during this lengthy separation, aided by the exchange of several warm letters and Gaetano's generous financial support of both mother and child, a marital rapprochement was established that was perhaps more harmonious than if the couple had tried living together in the same country—as they never would during nearly twenty years of marriage and the birth of seven children.

Gaetano did what he liked to do best—he worked with stone, and traveled extensively, sometimes to Italy, sometimes around the United States—while his steadfast wife, joining the ranks of the white widows, remained firmly in the home of her choice, in the familiarity of her village, where she had more than enough income for her children and herself, and an unusual yet romantic relationship with an enigmatic husband whom she never knew well enough to find predictable. She idealized him when he was away and quarreled with him when he was home (which was rarely more than a few months every two or three years)—just long enough to guarantee that, after he had gone back to America, he would receive a letter saying that she was again pregnant.

While Gaetano always promised to return to Italy in time for the birth and christening of a new baby, he invariably failed to do so, and his offended wife soon found ways to retaliate. No longer following the village tradition of naming infant boys in honor of their father's kinfolk (Marian had done this once in naming her first son Domenico; he would contract a fatal case of meningitis, and she would similarly name her last son Domenico), she proceeded in the absence of her husband to supply her other sons with names from her own family. Her second son, born in 1899, she named Sebastian in honor of her father, with whom she was exceedingly close and whom she visited almost every day at his farm. More than three years later, after her unpredictable husband had again failed to be on hand for the birth of the third son, Marian named the child Francis, after her father's younger brother—a decision that so insulted the Talese family that many of them absented themselves from the child's baptismal ceremony. One member, however, who did appear in church was Gaetano's devout and superstitious sister, Maria, who begged Marian to rename the child, hinting that her obstinance could invoke the wrath of God; but neither the entreaties of her sister-in-law nor those of the parish priest who had married her persuaded Marian to change the new child's name. When she finally did agree in 1904 to rechristen the boy Francis Joseph, it was at the urging of her father, who implored her to do so as a loving favor to him. But two years after the birth of Francis Joseph (whom the Talese family would address only by his middle name, the same as that of one of Gaetano's younger brothers), Gaetano would again disregard his promise to be with his wife when the next child was born. This would occur on December 6, 1905, and there would be twin boys, one of whom died at birth. The twin who died Marian named after her husband's second younger brother, Vincenzo; the one who survived she named Nicola, in honor of the saint whose feast day coincided with the birthdate.

When Marian bore her sixth child, a daughter, in 1908, Gaetano was ill with pneumonia in America, and was forgiven for his failure to be present for the birth and christening. But he sailed home unaccountably during the winter of 1908–1909, arriving with presents for the entire family and especially for his first and only daughter, Ippolita, named, of course, after his mother. He remained away from the United States for the next five months, not returning until the spring of 1909. But much of his time in Italy was spent outside Maida. Often he was said to be receiving medical treatments at a respiratory infirmary in Naples. At other times he was known to be in Rome, and as far north as Bologna, for reasons unexplained. He was restless, and often unhappy, while he was in Maida, and twice he was involved in unpleasant scenes in the town square.

Early on a spring evening, as Gaetano was playing cards for small stakes in the back of Pileggi's butcher shop in the square, his father appeared unexpectedly and asked that Gaetano return home with him. Gaetano, who was now thirty-seven, looked up from his cards and frowned at his white-haired father. As Gaetano looked down to reconsider his cards with seeming concentration, Domenico took hold of the tablecloth and jerked it, sending several cards and glasses of wine to the floor. Without apologizing to the other men at the table, Domenico turned and walked out, ignoring the puzzled protests of the cardplayers. Caught in a silent struggle of indecision, Gaetano stared around the room without expression for a few moments; then he stood up and followed his father home, seething with anger.

Several days later, during the Sunday-afternoon *passeggiata,* as Gaetano, in suit, white starched collar, sprucely knotted polka-dotted cravat, and homburg, walked arm in arm with a male friend, he was aware of a group of elderly men looking at him and speaking in what he sensed were hostile tones. They were gathered on wooden chairs around a table outside the café, and as he circled toward them with his friend a voice was raised toward him contemptuously: "Who do you think you are? You're not a gentleman."

Taking a few steps forward, Gaetano recognized a wizened and slightly intoxicated member of the Bongiovanni family, who years earlier had forfeited much of their baronial estate in an enforced sale to Gaetano's father. Enraged, Gaetano charged toward the man, but his friend held him back. A few men in the café, mumbling words in Bongiovanni's behalf, got up from their chairs, while other passersby stopped to watch. As Gaetano turned away from Bongiovanni, he knew that he was no longer in the right place. He had to return to America.

He often quarreled with his wife during this visit home, and young Joseph, eavesdropping one day from his room upstairs, heard his father denouncing his mother for her failure to accompany him overseas. His father also threatened to break up the family in the not too distant future: Sebastian, he declared, could remain in Maida with the younger children, but Joseph would be headed for America. Joseph's father had already revealed this to him in private. He had come into Joseph's room the night before and, while reminiscing fondly on his travels through the New Land, had said: "I'm sorry I can't bring you with me this trip, you're still too young. But when I come back the next time, I promise I'll take you."

A week later, as his father began to pack his large suitcase for the voyage on the weekend to follow, Joseph helped him, with a sense of excitement and involvement—he was only one trip away from a big journey of his own. Meanwhile he had also received permission from his mother to go with his father on the train to Naples, joining his uncle Francesco Cristiani and his older cousin Antonio to see his father off on the ship.

But on the morning of the departure Joseph woke up ailing with what was feared as a recurrence of his earlier bout with diphtheria, and so the others left without him. Throughout the day and the week that followed, Joseph seemed ill more from disappointment in missing the trip to Naples than from any actual relapse. Antonio, when he returned from Naples, had reassured Joseph that everything would turn out as planned, that his father would be back to fulfill his promise within a year, or perhaps even a few months.

Antonio became closer than ever to Joseph during this period, while Joseph's relationship to his mother became oddly distant. It was as if she had already given him up as a hostage in her marital agreement with her husband; she had her favorite son, Sebastian, as her main source of comfort and support, and, sustained as well by her tight links to the Rocchinos, who helped raise her youngest children, she was absorbed in the warmth of her own family.

When the entire year of 1910 passed without Joseph's father returning, and as his relationship with his brother Sebastian became more strained, Joseph's dependence on his cousin increased—and continued to increase as *another* year came and went without any sign of Gaetano. Joseph had been especially disappointed by his father's failure to come home in time for the Christmas season of 1911, for this was when the wolves attacked the village, and Joseph had felt more vulnerable in the aftermath of that incident—and more eager to leave home—than he had even during two earlier earthquakes. He was also greatly affected during this winter by the changing attitude of Antonio, now seventeen. His cousin's remoteness did not come from any diminished affection for Joseph, but rather from his realization that he could no longer stand working in his father's tailor shop. "I belong in Paris," he had boasted to Joseph that memorable morning in the shop.

20.

ANTONIO HAD CHOSEN to leave Maida during the Christmas holidays, when the trains were crowded with travelers, because he thought he would have the best chance of being inconspicuous as he made his escape. He carried two large suitcases packed with clothes he had designed, which he intended to sell along the way, supplementing the savings he had sewn into the lining of his jacket and stuffed into the money belt tied around his waist inside his trousers. Antonio felt fat but rich.

His entrance into France had been accomplished without deviating from the plan he had plotted long in advance, in which Joseph had been his sole confidant. Antonio had gone directly from the Naples train station to one of the waterfront bistros where, he had been told, arrangements could be made to smuggle passengers onto ships sailing to every part of the world. Arriving at the bistro at midday, when there were no customers at the tables and the bartender was slumped on a stool with his head resting against a wall, Antonio had gone directly to the cashier and said: "I would like to go to Marseilles, but I have no papers."

As Antonio later described in one of his many highly descriptive letters to his cousin that kept alive in young Joseph a spirit of adventure and an impatience to leave home, the cashier was a thin mulatto woman with a red handkerchief tied around her head and a sea captain's cape draped over her shoulders, and, astonishingly, she was puffing on a cigarette. Antonio had never before seen a woman smoking. Such bold habits in women were beyond Joseph's imagination. Blowing smoke in Antonio's direction, she studied him momentarily and then yelled across the room to the big, snoring, scraggly-bearded bartender: "Bruno, this man wants to go to Marseilles, and he has no papers." The bartender slowly lifted up his head, opened one eye, and yawned. "Does he have fifty francs?" he finally asked. When Antonio answered that he did, the bartender said: "Come back at ten o'clock tonight, and pack enough cheese and salami for a two-day trip." Then the bartender again rested his head against the wall and seemed to go immediately back to sleep.

That night, after Antonio had paid the francs to the cashier, she introduced him to a sailor waiting to escort him on foot to the waterfront, and then by wagon to a dockside warehouse. There Antonio saw a dozen shabbily dressed men carrying sackcloth bags and small suitcases. Two sailors stood near the warehouse door, sliding it open and closed after each new arrival. Those waiting did not seem to know each other, and there was very little conversation. Shortly after eleven o'clock, Bruno arrived, wearing the same cape that the cashier had worn earlier in the bistro. With a wave of his right hand, Bruno directed everyone to follow him.

After passing through a small door in the rear of the warehouse, then out onto a pier, Antonio could see the silhouette of a large steamship in the moonlight. Nearing the ship, he read the lettering that identified it as Austrian. He heard dance music coming from the upper deck, and sounds of laughter and clinking glasses. But all notions of a pleasurable cruise began to fade as Antonio and the others followed Bruno to the stern of the vessel, where a rope ladder dangled from the deck. Bruno said good-bye. A sailor helped Antonio with his luggage up onto the deck, then resumed leading the travelers down through a narrow interior staircase and several hatchways until they had arrived in a dimly lit dormitory, forty by forty feet, in the bowels of the ship. Bolted to the floor along the walls were steel cots and on them, Antonio would soon discover, mattresses stuffed with straw.

Throughout the night, the next day, and the night that followed, Antonio and the other passengers were confined there. They had access to buckets of water that the sailors had provided, and to whatever food they had brought along with them. Everyone slept fully clothed. Antonio remained awake throughout the first night because of the snoring that surrounded him, and the discomfort of his money belt bloated with coins. An early-morning storm caused the vessel to tilt and lurch so convulsively that some people were tossed to the floor. Antonio climbed down from his cot, held on to the metal leg that seemed the most securely bolted, and prayed that he would get to Paris.

Though polite to the other passengers, Antonio communicated with them as little as possible. He felt embarrassingly well dressed around his disheveled fellow travelers, and he was wary of nearly all of them. He had the feeling that many were vagabonds, military deserters, thieves, or worse. He saw that a few carried sheathed knives on their belts beneath their jackets or capes. One man had a holstered pistol strapped high to one side of his chest. He was fierce-looking, with a hooked nose, a square jaw pointed with a Vandyke, and slit eyes under beetle brows, and he covered his oily head with a battered shako from which all the military insignia and plumage had been removed. A few hours after the storm, he sidled over to Antonio's cot and asked in a strange accent, almost accusingly: "What did you do?" The man's assumption that he had committed a crime from which he was now fleeing concerned Antonio far less than the possibility that, if he denied being a criminal, he might offend his visitor by appearing to be morally superior. Not knowing how to reply, Antonio placed a hand on his stomach and bent his head down between his legs, as if he were suddenly seasick and on the verge of vomiting, and finally the man got up from the edge of the cot and walked away.

The only individual Antonio felt comfortable with was a shy, pimply, ruddy-haired youth, a year or two his junior, who wore a faded blue jacket on the breast pocket of which was embroidered the name of the Orti Brothers Hotel. The young man was a night porter at the hotel, near the docks at Marseilles, who had gone to Naples to visit his ailing mother. She had run away years before from his French father, a violent alcoholic. The young porter told Antonio that if he wished to save money, he could stay at the hotel at no charge. He had a room there that he did not use at night, for he was required to be on duty in the lobby from midnight until six-thirty, while the concierge slept. Antonio was grateful, and immediately accepted the offer. He had given no thought to staying in Marseilles, but now he had a chance to get his clothes pressed as well as to catch up on his sleep before going to the railroad station to check the schedule of trains going to Paris and the cost of the ticket.

Although he was laden with money, he was not exactly sure of his financial worth. Before leaving Maida he had calculated that he had saved from his earnings about four hundred lire; he was carrying also much foreign currency and some antiquated Italian money—gold and silver coins, as well as bank notes—that dated back to the eras of southern Italy's now defunct conquerors. Antonio had collected this old and foreign money, along with some contemporary Italian currency, from the pockets of dead men's clothing that bereaving widows and kin had brought into his father's tailor shop to be sold or given away to traveling strangers.

The mourners usually delivered the clothes to Francesco Cristiani's counter wrapped in blankets, not wanting to touch or see again the sad and familiar sight of the departed men's garments; and these people were by and large too overwrought or superstitious about death in general to dip into the pockets of wardrobes that the deceased had left behind—unlike Antonio. Always on the alert for the arrival of doleful-looking people carrying blankets, he was quick to greet them, and, if they had clothing for the widows' closet in the back of the store, he would assure them that the clothes would be treated with the utmost respect and would be passed on to the most worthy of wearers. And then, as he hung the clothes in the widows' closet, unseen by his father and the other tailors (although Joseph was in on the secret), he would riffle through the pockets and discover not only new and old lire and francs, but also—usually from the pockets of migrant workers and the traveling wealthy—coins and bank notes from the Americas and various parts of Western and Eastern Europe, not excluding the Papal States, the Duchy of Lucca, the Republic of San Marino, Monaco, Romania, and Serbia.

But while this might have made Antonio the envy of numismatists, it did not necessarily represent exchangeable currency after he had begun his journey toward Paris in December 1911. This was why he particularly welcomed the idea of being a nonpaying guest at the Orti Brothers Hotel, to which he and his porter friend went directly by hired carriage after disembarking from the Austrian steamer in Marseilles. True to his word, his new friend did have access to free lodging at the hotel, but to Antonio's immediate disappointment these accommodations were not much superior to those on the ship. Unfurnished except for a cot and a small table, the room was located off the service entrance in the rear of the ground floor, next to a large stable for the horses and carriages of the guests. Still, despite the smell and neighing of the horses, Antonio slept soundly for the first time in several days, rising reluctantly at six-thirty when his friend returned to take over the bed.

During the morning and afternoon, after a pleasant introduction to French coffee and *pâtisserie* at a café in the train station—where he had gone not only to book a reservation but also to try to sell one of the three suits that he carried under his arm—he sold two suits to transient Italian businessmen, for a total of forty francs. This was more than enough to buy a ticket on the sleeper that left for Paris the following evening.

Antonio spent most of the next day wandering around Marseilles observing how the pedestrians were dressed, examining the merchandise in store windows, and trying to understand the French words printed on street signs and in the headlines of newspapers that people in the cafés held in front of their faces. He returned to the hotel later in the afternoon to say good-bye to his friend, but the concierge told him that the porter had taken the night off and gone to visit his father in the countryside. After the concierge had unlocked the door to the porter's room, Antonio left a note of thanks on the table and took his suitcases, which he had packed earlier. He did not notice that the suitcases were unusually light, and did not open them until he was on the train. It was then that he discovered that his two extra pairs of shoes were missing, along with one of his suits. He regretted losing the shoes more than the suit, which he had remodeled but which had been made by his father. As the train rattled through the night he could not believe the porter had stolen them.

At nine a.m. the train slowed up along the right bank of the Seine and pulled into Paris's Gare de Lyon, with its glass arcade and its roof tower encasing a grand four-sided clock. Antonio hurried off the train with his bags, resisting an offer of help from a porter, and followed the crowd along the platform, through a great hall, and then out the front door. There he paused, inhaled deeply, and filled his lungs with the Paris air.

Downhill in the distance he could see spread before him, under the subdued sunlight of early winter and behind the morning mist, endless rows of brownish-green trees and gaily colored awnings along a wide, white boulevard; and there were also rows of ornate buildings, taller than any he had seen before, crowned by flat-topped curved roofing that, he later learned, was the architectural specialty of a man named Mansart. What he saw was like a magnificent painting in a museum; and when a cheerful carriage driver wearing a top hat and a pale blue frock coat appeared before him and offered him a ride in his open carriage, Antonio's most lasting impression of Paris was complete.

Antonio removed from his coat pocket the letter of acceptance from the Paris cutting school, the École Ladaveze, which he had received two weeks before at the post office in Maida. He showed it to the driver, pointing to the address on the letterhead as his destination. Noting that the letter had been sent to Italy, the driver began speaking to Antonio in fairly fluent Italian; he said he had first heard the language years before, when he had served with Italian mercenaries affiliated with the French Foreign Legion in North Africa. When Antonio explained that he had chosen Paris as his new home, the driver became even more friendly; and as the carriage headed downhill along the Rue de Lyon, and then turned left on the Rue Saint-Antoine toward the Rue de Rivoli, the driver pointed out certain distinguished buildings and landmarks—the July Column in the Place de la Bastille, the Hôtel de Ville, the Louvre Museum. When the carriage turned right and headed toward the Place des Victoires, where the cutting school was located, the driver pointed his riding crop toward the equestrian statue of Louis XIV, explaining that this statue had replaced an earlier one of the king that had been destroyed by a mob during the Revolution. The driver's casual shrug accompanying his comment left little doubt that his sympathies were with the mob.

Antonio sat on the second bench, saying nothing but listening attentively, leaning forward to within a few inches of the driver's neck. As the horses clopped steadily along the boulevard, the happy young tailor from Maida found it necessary to remind himself, again and again, that he was not dreaming. He really *was* in Paris.

The driver stopped in front of No. 6 Place des Victoires, a stately building that Antonio thought worthy of an embassy. The driver brought Antonio's bags through the door into the foyer and then announced in French to the École Ladaveze receptionist at the top of the staircase that a new student from Italy had just arrived. Antonio expected to be charged more than the two francs the driver requested for the ride, but this was all he would accept; and then, doffing his top hat, the driver was gone. Moments later, Antonio saw a slim, balding man, dressed in a tailcoat, coming down the staircase toward him with the agility of a dancer.

"Welcome to Paris," the man said in Italian, introducing himself as Monsieur Melhomme, one of the directors. With more fluency than the carriage driver, Monsieur Melhomme explained that he had learned the language growing up in Tunisia, the son of an Italian mother. He took one of Antonio's bags and escorted him out to a small hotel in the neighborhood, where Antonio registered, and then to a nearby café for an early lunch. The waiter automatically placed a basket of bread on the table, which surprised Antonio; at the restaurants he had been to in Italy, bread had to be requested and its cost was added to the bill. Antonio was also impressed by the fact that Monsieur Melhomme ordered for one price a three-course meal that included dessert and coffee, and that was half as expensive as these items would have cost individually in Naples. After consuming a full plate of sardines with oil, croquettes made with beef, fried potatoes, and steamed tomatoes, followed by fruit and a lightly liqueured coffee, Antonio concluded that life in Paris was less costly than in Italy. It was an impression that lasted only through the end of lunch.

When he returned to the hotel he found tucked under the door of his small room the weekly bill, which had to be paid in advance. He went immediately to the school to deposit his registration fee of one hundred francs and to show what money he had left to Monsieur Melhomme. The director confirmed that Antonio's net worth would soon be zero. Most of his remaining cash was of dubious value, being too old for contemporary use and not old enough to redeem its listed worth from collectors of rare and ancient currency. So Antonio reluctantly wired his father in Maida, begging his forgiveness, and requested a loan.

21.

JOSEPH WAS IN the tailor shop when the postman delivered the message in an envelope. It had been five days since Antonio's departure. The elder Cristiani had initially been furious when his son failed to appear for work; he had slammed a heavy pair of scissors down on the table, and characterized Antonio as spoiled and irresponsible. But when Antonio remained away that night, the next day, and the night that followed, Francesco Cristiani conceded the possibility that his son had been hurt in an unreported accident. He left the running of the shop to the other tailors while he joined his grieving wife and the rest of the family at a special midday Mass dedicated to Antonio's safe return.

In the afternoon Francesco Cristiani traveled to the provincial capital of Catanzaro to be with the police chief who was directing the search, and who would be the first to receive whatever information was forthcoming from the precincts that had been alerted throughout the region. At night, Cristiani returned to participate in the novena at the church in Maida, which Joseph also attended with his mother, his brother Sebastian, and his grandparents Domenico and Ippolita.

Although Joseph at first could not believe that any harm had come to his cousin, and certainly did not want to go back on his promise, by the third day he felt intense pressure to betray his pledge to Antonio. Surrounded by mournful and tearful relatives who would be greatly relieved to know that Antonio had merely run away, Joseph finally decided that evening to go to his grandfather's house and tell him all he knew. But just as he was walking across the courtyard, he heard the voice of Sebastian, who had been sitting on the steps smoking a cigarette. He had regarded Joseph with a certain suspicion ever since Antonio had left, or so it had seemed to Joseph; but now Sebastian accused him outright: "You *know* where he is, but you're just not telling." "I know nothing!" Joseph shouted back, so loudly that he feared he might be overheard by others in the compound. Then he returned quickly to his room, where he decided he must continually guard the secret of the young man who was more his brother than Sebastian.

But the arrival of the postman on the fifth day increased the anxiety of everyone in Cristiani's tailor shop. Francesco Cristiani had stopped in at the store just a few moments before, and was in the back room when the postman asked Joseph to summon him. A signature was needed. Joseph could not tell from the look on the postman's face whether he was aware of the contents of the message. When Mr. Cristiani came in to receive the envelope he was extremely tense, saying nothing to the postman as he unsealed the envelope and began to read. The other tailors had come in from the workroom and stood behind him. Joseph watched as tears appeared in his uncle's eyes. Then he looked up and announced with relief, and even a certain pride: "Antonio is alive and well, and has gone all the way to Paris!" As the tailors cheered, and Joseph felt lightened of his burden, Cristiani rushed out of the shop to tell his wife and the others. Later that evening there was a feast at Domenico's house, and by the following morning Cristiani was at the post office to arrange that a money order of more than four hundred lire be sent as quickly as possible to Paris. Along with it, he enclosed a message to his son: "Sew with love."

Letters from Antonio arrived with regularity in the subsequent months, and his father read them aloud to everyone in the shop, including the customers. Antonio's experiences became a public event, like a serialized novel that everybody in the village was eagerly following; and hardly a day passed without a customer's stopping by to ask: "Anything new from Paris?" The town's most sophisticated aristocrat, Torquato Ciriaco, while being measured for a new suit, told Mr. Cristiani that in the two-thousand-year history of Maida, Antonio was probably the first native villager ever to enter the famed French city. This seemed very significant to Mr. Cristiani, and he bowed with appreciation toward Don Torquato.

Joseph also received letters, and in one of them Antonio said that he was keeping a diary and recording much of what he saw and heard in his neighborhood and the city at large. In a letter dated February 5, 1912, Antonio wrote that all of Paris was talking about a French tailor who had designed an aviator's parachute and had tested it by jumping from an upper level of the Eiffel Tower. The parachute failed to open, and the tailor was killed.

A month later, Antonio wrote that the tuxedo he had made for himself before leaving Maida was coming in very handy; he and a half-dozen other students at the École Ladaveze who owned evening attire had been invited by the *chef de claque* of the Opéra (a friend of Monsieur Melhomme's) to be nonpaying occupants of the orchestra seats at operas, concerts, and all theatrical events—so long as they came formally dressed and applauded the stage performers with unrelenting enthusiasm. Paris had been experiencing an acute decline in attendance by opera buffs and theatergoers, Antonio said, adding that some people blamed it on the competition of the cinematograph, while others faulted the inferior offerings of the producers. In any case, Antonio said that he and his fellow tailors were busy most evenings clapping their hands energetically and yelling "Bravo, bravo!"

Even before Antonio had taken his midterm examination he was suggesting to Joseph that he was the best student at the École Ladaveze. More than one hundred students—two-thirds of them from Paris or the French provinces; the rest almost entirely from leading cities in northern Europe and South America—were enrolled in junior- and senior-level courses in cutting and fitting. Although most students were five to ten years older than the seventeen-year-old Antonio, and were more experienced by virtue of their previous full-time employment in tailor shops, the rarely modest Antonio saw himself as the master of even the advanced students when it came to designing and cutting suits, sewing, shaping, and molding the fabric to fit perfectly on the wooden mannequins and also on the bodies of the live models who were often hired for the classes.

Antonio complained in one letter that a majority of his classmates, despite their previous experience, still ignored the proper technique in precisely fitting the newly made suits to the bodies of the models for whom the garments had previously been designed and cut. Although the students took their tape measures to the models and rechecked the measurements and analyzed the fit while the models posed in a standing position, they did not insist that the models walk around the room, sit in a chair, assume a squatting posture. "The tailor must notice how the new suit behaves during these movements," Antonio reminded Joseph. "He might then discover that he must make further adjustments to guarantee that a man's suit and his body move together in perfect harmony."

Joseph could only admire his cousin's exacting standards and his lack of timidity. He would never forget the story of how Antonio, as a boy of eleven, had dared even to improve the sartorial appearance of King Victor Emmanuel III. And yet Joseph sometimes worried, after receiving Antonio's opinionated accounts from Paris, that his cousin might inadvertently be antagonizing people, as he often antagonized his father during his tailoring days in Maida. In fact, there was a teacher at the École Ladaveze whom Antonio had already offended, as he admitted in his letters. The teacher was named Loubert. Apparently taking exception to what he perceived to be Antonio's know-it-all attitude, Monsieur Loubert often referred to him in class not by his name but as "our smart little Italian." When the other students failed to give the correct answer to a question, Monsieur Loubert would sometimes turn toward the dapper five-foot-five-inch Antonio, sitting erectly in the front row, and say, "Now let's see how our smart little Italian might respond to this question."

During one of the classroom sessions devoted to the cutting and fitting of formal wear—a session at which the hired model had failed to appear—Monsieur Loubert announced: "Since our smart little Italian has little to learn about the proper wearing of evening clothes, being a favorite of the *chef de claque*, we will ask him today to serve as our model."

Antonio was embarrassed and offended. But, as he later wrote to Joseph, "I quickly decided that I would not give this teacher the satisfaction of seeing me upset, so I stood up in front of the class, removed my jacket, shirt, and tie, and began to accept the topcoat, the white vest, and the frilly white shirt that he handed me. But as I was putting on the shirt I heard some snickering and also noticed that some people in the class, including Monsieur Loubert, were looking at me in a curious way. Suddenly I realized that the undershirt I was wearing had been made by my mother, who as you may know is not a good seamstress, and the shirt is badly sewn and fits badly. It is made of the heavy wool our farmers wear; and it has a little button to enclose the opening at the neck. I brought it to Paris to have something from my mother, and now these bastards in class were making fun of it—and making fun of me, too, for I have so often been outspoken in class about things that are not well sewn and do not hang right. My blood was boiling, but I tried not to show it. They thought that they had something on me, but they didn't have a thing. I put on the white vest over the frilly shirt, and then the topcoat, and remained as silent as the models always do during the measurements and discussions. After the class, I quickly dressed in my own clothes and waited to see if the teacher or the others would say anything about the undershirt. But they didn't dare. Monsieur Loubert was actually very polite. As I left the room he addressed me by name, and sincerely thanked me for modeling."

In June, Antonio completed the six-month course with top honors, and was appointed to be one of the two students who would represent the school in competition with a dozen other cutting schools in the citywide young tailor's contest sponsored annually by the Society of Master Tailors of Paris. The candidates were to assemble on a Sunday morning in late June in the ballroom of a large hotel and, after measuring a model for a suit, to prepare the pattern, cut the material (all of it donated for the occasion by the major woolen firms of Paris), and to baste it on the model by late afternoon in preparation for the first fitting. At this time the committee judges would examine the basting, the cutting, and the general craftsmanship; the winners of the first and second prizes would be announced at a banquet to be held in the hotel on the following Sunday evening. Antonio had heard that the winners received handsome trophies, gold for first place and silver for second. Among the four hundred to attend the banquet were most of the leading members of the French male fashion industry, together with the candidates, their families, and the directors of the school.

Antonio believed he had performed well in the contest, and when he attended the banquet a week later with his classmate and Monsieur Melhomme, he sat anxiously through the meal and the speeches awaiting the announcement of the winners of the gold and silver trophies. Finally the president of the society was introduced to present the awards, and to Antonio's disappointment the first prize was won by a student from Toulon who had attended one of the other cutting schools. But as the applause subsided, Antonio heard his name mentioned as the second-prize winner, and suddenly Monsieur Melhomme was shaking his hand and leading him up to the rostrum. After the first-prize winner had received his trophy and made a short speech of appreciation, Antonio was congratulated by the president, but he could see that there was no trophy awaiting him: instead he received a commemorative scroll. After he had expressed his thanks in French, he returned carrying his scroll to the table. Later, when he had a private moment with Monsieur Melhomme, he asked if it was not true that in previous years silver trophies had been given to the runners-up; and Monsieur Melhomme replied: "Yes, but it is unfortunate in your case—the society gives trophies only to the winners who are citizens of France." Expressing his dissatisfaction in a letter to Joseph, Antonio concluded: "They boast a great deal in this country about égalité, but in reality there is no such thing."

At this time Antonio was living in the Latin Quarter. He had moved out of the costly little hotel on Rue du Bouloi two months earlier to join a new young friend from Rome, a custom shoemaker named Lauri, in a spacious apartment where Antonio's share of the rent was only ten francs per month. At a flea market he had purchased a bed and a few other pieces of furniture for a total of twenty-five francs, and this price included the loan of a wagon so that he and Lauri could push the furniture across town to the apartment on the Place du Panthéon. Antonio was still receiving financial help from his father, and also bolts of material with which to extend his wardrobe; but now with his diploma from the École Ladaveze, and his newspaper clippings of the awards ceremony, he was confident that he would soon find a good job and become independent.

He made a list of nearly forty tailor shops within walking distance of his apartment, and spent most of July going from one to another, always wearing a freshly pressed suit, a boater, and one of the three pairs of two-toned wing-tipped shoes that Lauri had made for him. He kept a news clipping about the banquet folded in an inside pocket of his jacket, and tucked under his arm was an expensive umbrella he had bought at the Du Louvre department store. There had been frequent summer showers since he had begun job hunting.

After he had gone through the list, and had returned to some shops three or four times in order to meet the owners who had been away earlier, he received only two offers—part-time work in one rather dilapidated shop, and full-time work in another, at unacceptably meager pay. Several proprietors in the better shops suggested that he come back and reapply in the middle of autumn, for the summer of 1912 had been a poor season, and things would get no better until the weather was cooler.

There was one shop on his list that Antonio had avoided. Despite his usual high opinion of himself, even he felt that he as yet lacked the experience, and perhaps even the confidence, to offer his services to an elegant shop that already had fifty employees, and six master tailors who enjoyed the finest reputations in all of Paris. It was called Damien, and was located on the Rue Royale, down the street from Maxim's restaurant. Antonio had often stood near the front door, but each time he had resisted going in. Instead he had drifted over to the display windows, where he gazed admiringly upon the various wooden mannequins garbed in the latest of frenchified Edwardian fashion recommended for wear to the opera, to the office, and to country houses on weekends: black silk-lined capes and gibuses, chesterfields and homburgs, invernesses and bowlers, equestrian caps and light-toned hunting coats with red lining and ornamental gold buttons; single-breasted belted tweed jackets with matching waistcoats and narrow-cut trousers with center creases (obligatory since the recent popularization of the pants press); white and yellow silk scarves flung casually over the broad shoulders and pointed lapels of double-breasted gray herringbone suits suggested as informal evening wear in the cooler nights to come.

From the sidewalk Antonio also observed the arrival by carriage of many of Damien's customers, nattily dressed men who often issued instructions to their departing drivers in foreign languages, frequently Russian, and then proceeded into the shop to be greeted along the counters by a receiving line of bowing clerks, and then by the circle of master tailors assembled near the mirrored fitting rooms, and finally by a genial round-faced man with reddish hair who was usually seated at an antique desk in the rear of the shop, and who wore a gray cutaway and striped trousers and smoked cigarettes that extended out of a gold holder. Antonio's attention was drawn to this man every time he looked through the windows, and from his proprietary air, and the deference accorded him by the employees, Antonio deduced that he was the owner and renowned cutter, Monsieur Damien himself, about whom the faculty at the École Ladaveze had often spoken with veneration.

One day as Antonio watched Monsieur Damien rise from his chair to shake hands with a customer, he became aware of something that he had failed to notice earlier. Monsieur Damien was very short. He was certainly no taller than Antonio. The more Antonio looked at him the more approachable he seemed. Antonio was then seized by an impulse to walk right in and ask him for a job.

But first he headed in the opposite direction, toward the nearby Church of the Madeleine, at the end of the Rue Royale. Unlike his mother and his grandfather Domenico, Antonio was not exceptionally religious. The only times he had previously entered this church, before purchasing his umbrella, had been to avoid getting wet during showers. But now, after climbing the steep row of stone steps and passing through the colonnade of Corinthian columns, he fell to his knees within the imposing and darkly magnificent sanctuary that Napoleon had dedicated to his army. Antonio crossed himself and prayed to Saint Francis that he might be inspired to make a favorable impression upon Monsieur Damien. He then hastened out of the church back onto the Rue Royale, and soon he had pushed through the front door of Damien's and was marching up the center aisle, ignoring the foppish young clerks who stood in his path offering their assistance. He did not stop until he had reached the back of the shop and stood over Monsieur Damien, who sat quietly at his desk exuding a fragrant scent of cologne and the acrid smell of his burning Turkish cigarette.

Slowly looking up, Monsieur Damien removed his cigarette, pushed aside the papers he had been reading, and, rising to his feet, smiled at this diminutive well-tailored visitor whose suit size he recognized as identical to his own.

"I am from a tailoring family in Italy," Antonio began, in a voice unhurried and confident, "and I came to Paris to attend the École Ladaveze . . ."

"Ah, yes," Monsieur Damien interrupted amiably, "I recall seeing you recently at the banquet when you went up to receive your award."

"I am honored that you were there," Antonio said, feeling his fortunes rising, and, wasting no time, he added: "I would be honored even more if you would hire me as an assistant to one of your master tailors. I want to work at Damien's."

The proprietor studied him momentarily, regarding him with a certain ambivalence.

"But why would you wish to work at Damien's?" the owner inquired finally, in a tone of false modesty that was well known to his longtime employees.

"Damien's has the finest tailors in Paris," Antonio replied. "Here I will learn from the best."

Monsieur Damien let his glance stray briefly to the shoulder line of Antonio's suit, which, he noted approvingly, fit snugly to the neck.

"Well," he said, still seeming somewhat ambivalent about hiring Antonio, "if we could use you here, when would you be available to start?"

"At once," Antonio said.

"Oh, very well," the owner then said, with a soft sigh, "we shall give you a one month's trial, beginning tomorrow morning." Antonio was filled with excitement and satisfaction. But Monsieur Damien went on to say, with a decisiveness he had not shown earlier: "During this trial period, of course, you will receive no salary."

Antonio said nothing. He was deeply disappointed, even a bit insulted, and his first inclination was to reject the proposal. He had thought the interview had gone well; and while he had not expected high pay, he certainly had expected *some* financial compensation for his efforts. But being unsalaried would prolong his dependence upon his father, whose support he could not count on indefinitely. Antonio's only option would be to return to one of the lesser shops he had visited earlier and accept a low-paying job on a part-time or full-time basis. In such places, of course, he would not have the opportunity to learn what he might at Damien's. Returning to Italy, which his father would have undoubtedly welcomed, was out of the question.

Antonio was aware that Monsieur Damien was waiting for his response, and was perhaps becoming impatient. A clerk had just approached the desk and was about to whisper something into Monsieur Damien's ear. Antonio hesitated no longer.

"I'll be here in the morning," Antonio declared, forcing a smile. "And thank you very much."

"We shall await your arrival tomorrow with pleasure," Monsieur Damien answered cordially, as he turned toward his clerk and at the same time waved good-bye to Antonio with his burning cigarette in its gold holder.

During the weeks that followed, Antonio remained financially solvent by eating irregularly and lightly—restricting himself at lunchtime, for example, to a single cup of heavily sugared coffee bought at the bar of a nearby

café—and by taking in extra mending and alteration jobs from a secondary tailor shop, completing the work at night in his apartment and delivering it early in the morning on his way to Damien's.

His role at Damien's was that of roving apprentice to several tailors,
both master and subordinate, and he performed many of the same chores
that had been assigned to him in Maida—making buttonholes, basting
and sewing seams, turning, tacking, and ironing trouser cuffs. But in Paris
he worked with more energy and enthusiasm, particularly during the
lunch period, when he was most often alone in the large workroom. In a
letter to Joseph at this time he wrote: "One sure way to impress your superiors is to work hard when they're not there. While the owner, the tailors, and even the apprentices and clerks are out enjoying long lunches, I
return to the shop after my cup of coffee, and do huge amounts of work
that my superiors notice when they return. I have become known as a
man who does not need to be supervised or pushed to get work done.
Some apprentices have grown to hate me. But the other tailors respect
me. They give good reports about me to Monsieur Damien. Last Friday,
which was the end of the trial period, he came to me and said: 'We do not
really need you. But I'm going to keep you.' "

Antonio received a modest salary of seventy-five francs a month. But
by November 1912, he was a junior tailor with a fifty-franc raise, and he
was singled out by Monsieur Damien to assist him while he cut the patterns for the clothing of certain important customers whose wardrobes
commanded the owner's personal attention. Among such clients were
three wealthy, vain Russian princes; a stout Bavarian banker who insisted
that his jackets be made without buttons; a querulous literary critic and
legal adviser to the French tribunal, Léon Blum, who would one day become the nation's first Socialist premier; the celebrated French aviator
Louis Blériot, who in 1909 had crossed the English Channel from Calais
to Dover in the record time of thirty-seven minutes; and Baron Edmond
de Rothschild, whose ever-fluctuating weight prompted him to return his
new suits regularly for alterations. All of the baron's suits came back displaying on their lapels the rosette of the Legion of Honor, and when Antonio was alone in the workroom at lunchtime, he would often stand
proudly in front of a mirror wearing one of the baron's jackets, imagining
that he had just been installed in the Legion of Honor.

One afternoon Antonio found himself standing next to the baron
himself, holding a silver tray filled with the pins that Monsieur Damien
was using while in the process of reducing the size of the dinner jacket the

baron was wearing, and Antonio heard Rothschild boast to Monsieur Damien that he now had seven thousand sheep on his country estate. Just then one of the Russian princes arrived and said: "On my country estate I have seven thousand *shepherds*."

The most challenging client for Monsieur Damien to fit properly was France's flying hero Blériot, who had been injured often in plane accidents and had a disproportionate figure. His hips were conspicuously off-center, and one of his legs was a few inches shorter than the other, requiring that one of his shoes be constructed with an elevated heel. Still, he was a fastidious dresser; and, favoring pin-striped suits, he ordered several at a time—all of which Monsieur Damien designed and tailored in slightly tilted ways that allowed the material to hang most compensatorily and flatteringly on the slanted body of the aviator and achieve an illusion of sartorial symmetry.

At times Antonio accompanied Monsieur Damien in his carriage to the private fittings in the homes or apartments of these leading clients; and early one evening, in a grand suite of the Hôtel Crillon, where an archduke from Hungary was being fitted, Antonio could hear someone playing the piano magnificently in an adjoining room. "The music consisted almost entirely of southern Italian love songs and the arias that we have grown up listening to," Antonio wrote to Joseph. "The door was slightly open, and as I stood helping Monsieur Damien with the archduke I felt carried away by the sadness and beauty of the music. Then it stopped, and a lovely woman with blond hair appeared in the doorway, wearing a long gown and a sparkling necklace. She apologized to the archduke because she did not realize we were there. The archduke introduced her as his wife to Monsieur Damien, who complimented her on her playing. She thanked him and said that she had studied only as a young girl at a conservatory in Naples, and that the music of Italy was the only music she had deep feelings for. Later, before we finished the fittings, she returned to play again, and as I left the hotel that night I had tears in my eyes. It is the first time since I've been here that I've felt a little bit homesick."

Working day and night during the fall into the early winter of 1912, Antonio had no time to attend the opera, concerts, or the other cultural entertainment that had been provided by the *chef de claque;* and when he had some free time he usually lacked the funds and energy to go out at night, denying himself as well the Folies-Bergère even though it enticed him every time he passed its glittering archway. During the Christmas holidays of 1912, however, when Damien's and other shops were closed for a few days, he did accompany his roommate one night to a dance hall called Magic City.

"Shortly after we arrived and had gotten ourselves a drink at the crowded bar," Antonio wrote to Joseph, "my friend Lauri spotted two young women who were alone at a table. They seemed to be smiling in our direction. Lauri went over and introduced himself, and then waved me over to join them. They both were friendly and seemed to be wealthy. They wore fur coats and had on good jewelry. Lauri and I thought that we had gotten lucky and had fallen in with a pair of rich women. But when we asked them to dance and they had taken off their gloves, the skin of their hands was hard and rough. They were working girls, servants who had borrowed the fur coats and jewelry from their mistresses to wear to Magic City on this night during the Christmas holidays. The girls were actually as poor as we were. Paris is filled with masqueraders."

Still, there was nothing about Paris that Antonio did not find wondrous and stimulating, and in the letters that he continued to write Joseph throughout 1913 he constantly reminded him that he, too, had a future in Paris if he wanted to consider it over America. Within a year or two, Joseph could enroll at the École Ladaveze, Antonio said, and subsequently get a job at Damien's. Antonio had recently received a number of salary increases and added responsibilities, and now had sufficient funds to pay for Joseph's travel expenses to Paris. But he urged that Joseph apply soon for a visa so that he could cross the border legally and avoid dealing with the smugglers in Naples. There was a room reserved for Joseph in Paris, Antonio wrote in late 1913; Lauri had decided to return to Rome, and Antonio would occupy the apartment alone until Joseph's much-anticipated arrival.

Shortly after the Christmas holidays, in January 1914, Antonio received a short letter from Joseph thanking him but saying that his father had finally returned to Maida. Joseph said that Gaetano was ill, however, and made no reference to when he might be returning to America. Midway through the summer of 1914, Antonio's letters to his father and to Joseph began to reflect changes in the atmosphere of the city, changes that seemed to occur within a very short time, and Antonio confessed that he was becoming confused and concerned. In one letter to his father, he described the festivities surrounding the annual Bastille Day celebration—all-night dancing in the streets, a balloon pilots' competition in the Tuileries Gardens followed by a homing-pigeon race involving five thousand birds; but in the next letter to his father, Antonio told of hearing police whistles and bomb explosions in the streets, and of hostile demonstrations by Serbian and other Slavic students outside the Austro-Hungarian embassy on the Rue de Varenne.

Antonio had read in the Paris newspapers weeks before that the heir to the Austro-Hungarian throne, Archduke Francis Ferdinand, together with his wife, had been murdered by a young Serbian radical in Sarajevo; but it had seemed to Antonio that this remote incident, involving hostilities only between Austria and Serbia, did not interest the people of Paris for more than a few days. But in late July 1914, a full month after the murder, political demonstrations began to proliferate throughout Paris, and in Damien's shop many of the customers said they were taking their money out of their banks and leaving the city. On July 28, after Serbia had rejected an Austrian ultimatum that would have terminated Serbia's status as an independent country, Austria declared war. Russia mobilized on behalf of Serbia; Germany, supporting Austria, delivered an ultimatum not only to Russia but also to France, demanding French neutrality in the event of a German-Russian war. Failing to get this from the French, Germany declared war on France on August 3.

"You must return to Italy immediately," Monsieur Damien told Antonio, stopping him as he appeared for work after lunch on the day of the announcement. "My carriage is waiting to take you to your apartment, but you must hurry. It has just been announced that all foreigners must leave Paris without delay." He embraced Antonio and slipped an envelope into his pocket, then guided his disbelieving young employee out to his carriage and ordered the driver to take him first to his apartment for his luggage and then to the Gare de Lyon.

The streets were crowded with people rushing in all directions, and Antonio heard people singing the "Marseillaise" and shouting *"Vive la France!"* and *"Vive la Russie!"* At his apartment, Antonio packed one suitcase and left everything else where it was. His landlord, in saying goodbye, promised that the apartment would be retained for him until his return. Antonio locked his door and ran out without making his bed. (His bed would remain unmade for the next five years.)

At the Gare de Lyon, Antonio stood for ten hours with several hundred people on a long, slow-moving line, unsure of his destination. No rifle bullets or cannons had yet been fired upon the French nation, and he remained hopeful that a last-minute solution by world leaders could bring the belligerent governments to the peace table.

Italy had declared its neutrality in this conflict, but most of the Italians Antonio overheard talking in the crowd favored the French, British, and Russians over the Germans and Austrians. Nearly everyone was especially hostile toward the latter. Austria was Italy's hereditary enemy. Italian unity had been achieved only after three wars with Austria, and many believed that another war with Austria was necessary to complete the goals of the Risorgimento, to wrest from the hated Hapsburg kingdom certain Italian-speaking seaports and alpine villages to the north and east of Venice. Antonio voiced no opinion in these discussions, which were conducted largely by older men who were natives of northern Italy. He merely listened and inched his way up in the line. When he finally got to the ticket window he impulsively gave his destination as Turin. Of all the major cities of northern Italy, Turin was the closest to the border of the French nation that he was reluctant to leave.

He rode all night in a noisy and crowded train, standing most of the way. By midmorning he had arrived in Turin. After checking into a small hotel near the railroad terminal, he wired his family in Maida that he had departed safely from Paris. Then he went out to a square and stood among the throngs of bystanders waiting for the latest bulletins to be posted on the billboards, and for freshly printed editions of newspapers to be delivered by cyclists to the kiosks in front of the terminal. Many speeches were being made, by both antimilitarists and interventionists, and there was loud cheering and booing as some people began singing the "Internationale." Police carrying rifles and clubs separated the demonstrators who were shouting and swearing at one another. When demonstrators began to throw fruit and even bottles at the speakers, the police fired shots in the air and restored order. Antonio stood among the crowds watching quietly at the bar of an outdoor café, remaining as far as possible from those making speeches and throwing things.

He spent all of August in Turin, still believing there was a chance that the mobilizing nations were bluffing one another and might yet back away from plunging Europe into a massive and bloody showdown. But each day the headlines announced the escalation of threats and the hostile declarations of increasing numbers of nations. As the German army marched into Belgium, presumably headed toward Paris, Britain joined France in the war on Germany. Montenegro and Serbia declared war on Germany. Days later, as troops from Britain crossed the English Channel to ally themselves with France, both nations declared war on Austria. In late August, Japan declared war on Germany and Austria, and Austria declared war on Belgium. The Germans by this time had entered Brussels. The German warships *Breslau* and *Goeben,* allowed to pass through the

Dardanelles by the friendly Turks, would soon be in a position to bombard Russian coastal cities. Russia would later declare war on Turkey, as would France and Britain. In the first weeks of September, the German army, having advanced through Belgium, became militarily engaged with the French in what would be the first battle of the Marne. Antonio conceded that he had no choice but to make his way back to Maida.

With newspapers tucked under his arm, he went to his hotel to pay his bill and pack his belongings. There the concierge handed him a telegram. It was from his father:

"Come home quickly. Uncle Gaetano is dead."

22.

YOUNG JOSEPH TALESE did not understand his father's death any more than he had understood his father's life. His father had died suddenly and inexplicably, in the bedroom of his home in Maida, in the middle of a sunny afternoon, on the first day of September 1914.

Joseph had been out of the house at the time, working at Cristiani's tailor shop, to which he had gone directly from school. He had been happy all day, reveling in his father's rare presence in Maida. Gaetano had been away in Naples for more than a month and had returned unexpectedly the night before. When Francesco Cristiani had abruptly decided to close the shop early, shortly before five p.m., for reasons unexplained, Joseph hastened home with the hope of having some time alone with his father before the evening meal. But once he had run through the square and down the curved road toward the family compound, and had climbed the staircase on the side of his house and entered the living room, he knew immediately that something was wrong.

The room was crowded with people, some of whom he did not know, and others, including his mother's Rocchino relatives, whom he knew slightly but had never seen in the house before. They sat in small groups within the bare walls shaking their heads and looking at the ceramic floor. Whatever was being said was softly spoken. Joseph's grandmother Ippolita stood by herself facing a window that overlooked the cliff and the distant shoreline. Her usually braided white hair seemed longer, and its wispy ends were visible in the light streaming through the window. Hearing the door close, his grandmother turned toward Joseph, but she did not seem to recognize him. One of his mother's aunts reached out to him and smiled encouragingly. He ignored her and hurried toward his parents' bedroom, confused, looking for his mother.

When he entered the doorway, Joseph saw a priest standing at the foot of his parents' bed, his arm consolingly around the slim shoulders of Joseph's aunt Maria. Joseph looked toward her for some explanation, but she remained quiet and still, her face shadowed within her black mantilla. Sitting at the near side of the bed, staring across it, was his mother, wearing the same pretty maroon dress and yellow shawl she had worn that morning at breakfast. She had cheerfully prepared breakfast for Joseph alone, after his brother Sebastian had left for the farm. Gaetano had still been in bed, exhausted after the long train ride from Naples. The suitcase he had brought with him was still downstairs, locked where he had left it in a corner of the carriage shed, on top of the big wooden trunk he always carried to America and back.

Joseph's mother had been in a pleasant mood for days prior to his father's return from Naples, spiritedly reminding Joseph and the other children of their father's impending arrival while she implored them to be tidy. She filled the house with fresh flowers, and polished and repolished the silverware at the head of the table where Gaetano had last sat weeks before, coughing and wheezing, his face thinner and paler than it was in the framed photograph on Marian's bureau.

Now as Joseph stood next to the bed and touched his mother's shoulder, Marian turned around to face him; he noticed that she held a handkerchief over part of her face and that a reddish welt rose puffily on her right temple. Her yellow shawl had fallen from her shoulders, and as she continued to look at him she tightened her lips. Trembling, Joseph turned away from her and looked at the bulky white covers of the bed; the figure stretched out underneath seemed huge. Then Joseph felt his grandfather Domenico's hand on his arm, gently but firmly pulling him away; and after guiding him out of the bedroom into a corner of the crowded living room, his grandfather said in a kindly voice: "Joseph, your father is dead."

Not that afternoon but much later, years later, Joseph would hear from one of his mother's sisters that his father had not come directly home to Maida after his final overseas crossing in the summer of 1913; he had gone instead to a hospital near Naples, where he received the first in a series of new medical treatments that would be repeated during subsequent visits in the final months of his life. On the afternoon of his death he had been seized by a delirious fit, and had angrily swung out his hand and hit Marian.

Joseph also learned that his father's last years in America had been unhappy ones. A financial recession had interrupted America's building boom despite optimistic forecasts, and Gaetano had been irregularly employed. He had also gotten himself into debt through gambling, and in order to meet his expenses and support his family in Italy, he had begun working a double shift in the Keasbey & Mattison asbestos factory. Soon he had difficulty breathing; his ailment, first diagnosed as a mild case of bronchopneumonia, had continued to worsen.

Marian was not aware of the extent of her husband's illness after he returned from America in 1913. On the afternoon of his death, as was her custom, she was paying a visit to her father's farmhouse with her three youngest children. When Gaetano woke up in the early afternoon, feverish and shaking, he began to call to his wife. When she did not come, he began to call louder, berating her for being away. A neighbor who was passing in front of the wall of the compound, and who paused to listen, thought she was hearing a domestic quarrel and continued on her way. Later in the afternoon, when Marian returned home, she found her husband gasping for breath, the pillows and blankets tossed out on the stone floor while he twisted and turned on the damp sheets in a cold sweat. As Marian tried to comfort him, he became even more uncontrollably irrational, blaming her for not being with him; and then one wildly flailing arm struck her, causing the welt on her temple. Within moments he had become unconscious, and then suddenly he was dead.

Marian did not attend the funeral. Whether it was to conceal the welt, or whether it was her own resentment at his striking her, Joseph would never know. Although his mother did begin to wear black in the house, and a long black veil to the memorial services that his grandfather Domenico arranged to have said in church every Sunday evening for many weeks after the funeral, Joseph never saw his mother shed a tear, or carry flowers to the cemetery, or complain of missing his father. Many of her late husband's relatives were bewildered and offended by her behavior, and even blamed her for being absent during the final hours of his life. This information was passed on to Joseph years after the funeral by his mother's younger sister, his aunt Concetta Rocchino, who also told him about his father's gambling problems in America. While Concetta did not intend to demean the memory of Joseph's father, she was eager to defend her sister against the criticism that she assumed was widely circulated on the Talese side of the family.

Concetta insisted to Joseph that his mother mourned his father in her own private way, and was very uncomfortable with the public display of grief that had been carried out by Domenico and his dutiful daughter, Maria. This pair of religious zealots, Concetta suggested to Joseph, tried with their use of church bells and burning incense to endow the deceased with a spiritual essence that Gaetano during his lifetime neither had nor wanted. In an attempt to prolong the memory of this wandering man whose family did not know him sufficiently to have much memory of him, Domenico and Maria had also hired professional mourners to wail each night at the grave site and to sprinkle dirt each Friday night with the *fiori da morti,* crushed geranium leaves; and at the weekly Sunday services in church, which even Gaetano's nonbelieving mother Ippolita felt compelled to attend, Domenico and Maria led the family clan through endless litanies and even recited death chants composed during the Dark Ages. Father and daughter both fasted every weekend in the autumn of 1914 and on into the following year, and they kept the interior of their homes glowing dimly with burning candles instead of gaslamps, and decked the outside of their doorways and windows with black bunting and ribbons that remained there until, years later, faded and worn, they were carried away by the wind.

Concetta reminded Joseph that at the funeral his aunt Maria had become Gaetano's self-appointed "widow" after Marian had failed to attend. Maria had accompanied the priests behind the casket, had not combed her hair in several days, conforming to ancient custom, and had not allowed cooking in her home for many weeks. Relatives and friends had brought food during this time to the Cristiani household as well as to Joseph's mother, Concetta recounted, adding that these kind gestures had not gone unnoticed by village gossips and that the awareness of much unpleasant talk exacerbated the awkward situation between Joseph's mother and Maria. It was difficult for Marian to represent herself in public on the day of the funeral as a bereaving wife, Concetta said, particularly while she still bore the sting of her husband's hostile farewell. It was no wonder, Concetta concluded, that Marian soon began to avoid Sunday church services in favor of spending weekends with her three youngest children at her family's farmhouse in the valley. There she was surrounded by relatives and friends who ignored the time-honored practices of mourning and allowed her to retain some of the independence she had become accustomed to during her nearly twenty years as a white widow.

What Joseph most remembered of his mother's first days of true widowhood was that, despite being withdrawn and virtually speechless, she was extremely active and efficient around the house, accomplishing tasks during September—which had begun with her husband's death—that she usually delayed doing each year until October or November. She preserved great amounts of food in jars for the winter; mended and altered the younger children's winter clothing; took stock of the leftover supply of logs and charcoal and dispatched Sebastian to get what was needed for the frosty weather ahead. She also purchased a new set of wheels for the carriage, anticipating the additional use she would be making of it: one month after the funeral she began dividing her time almost equally between her marital home in town and her girlhood home in the valley.

It was her oldest son's responsibility to drive her and the younger children back and forth at prearranged times, usually during the midday siesta, when Sebastian could spare an hour or two from his job as the junior foreman on Domenico's farm. It was also Sebastian's duty to look after the village house during his mother's absence. Sebastian Talese, a strapping boy of fifteen, more than four years older than Joseph, was now the nominal head of the family.

Soon Sebastian was occupying his father's chair at the dinner table, and becoming more active in disciplining the younger children. He would have tried disciplining Joseph, too, but within a week of Gaetano's death Joseph had more or less moved out of the house, thanks to the efforts of Antonio, who had returned to Maida and convinced Marian that since Joseph was attending school and working in the tailor shop each day, his daily routine would be best maintained if he ate and slept at the Cristianis', and went back and forth with them each morning and night between the town square and the family compound. Joseph would be only three doors away from his mother's home in the compound, and would be within easy reach whenever she wanted him under her own roof.

Disregarding her strained relations with Maria Cristiani, Joseph's mother complied; it was as if she were honoring her husband's wishes expressed in the previous year, his desire to break up the family and take Joseph with him to America. Now that this was impossible, Marian seemed to be doing the next best thing—releasing Joseph to the care of her late husband's sister, and allowing the boy to begin living a more separate life. She had already sensed increased independence in his nature and foresaw much conflict in the near future between Joseph and Sebastian—and recurring scenes of the sort she had witnessed two nights after the funeral.

The younger children were in bed at the time, and her older sons had been helping her—polishing the floors, beating the rugs outside with willow swatters, and carrying a heavy chest that had been filled with her husband's things down to the carriage shed, to be stored in a corner near his padlocked steamer trunk and the unpacked suitcase he had carried home from Naples.

"I think we should take your father's clothes from the suitcase and trunk and deliver them to Cristiani's shop," she had said. Sebastian immediately reached for the keys that were hung on a nail and proceeded to look for the one that would open the trunk.

"Put those keys away," said Joseph in a quiet voice that surprised his mother but that Sebastian seemed not to hear.

"Put those keys away!" Joseph said again, louder. "I don't want you to touch those clothes!"

"Joseph!" his mother said. "What are you saying?"

"I don't want those clothes given away," Joseph repeated. "I want to keep them."

It was a strange thing to say. Nobody in Maida ever kept the clothes of a deceased family member. It was considered unseemly, morbid, surely an inducement for bad luck.

"Why don't you go upstairs?" Sebastian demanded, still not looking at his younger brother, but having now opened the trunk for his mother's inspection. Without replying, Joseph turned around and ran up the staircase. A few minutes later he came down, brandishing in his right hand a heavy poker he had taken from the kitchen fireplace, and quickly he headed toward the crouched figure of Sebastian who was pulling clothes from his father's trunk. Sebastian fell back as he saw Joseph coming toward him, and he watched as Joseph stood over him, waving the rod menacingly in front of his face.

"Stop, Joseph!" their mother protested. *"Stop!"*

"I said I didn't want these clothes touched," Joseph said, looking down at his brother. "Now give me those keys you're holding, and get away from those clothes." Sebastian dropped the keys on the floor and slid backward, never taking his eyes off the poker. "And now *you* go upstairs," Joseph ordered. Sebastian looked at his mother momentarily, then back at Joseph, bewildered by the crazed manner his younger brother had suddenly manifested. Then he got to his feet and walked upstairs.

"Joseph," his mother said quietly, walking toward him. "What is the matter with you?"

Joseph stood silently for a few moments, lowering the poker, and then said: "I don't want the clothes to go to Cristiani's. I don't want them to be given away for other people to wear. I want to keep them."

Without waiting for her response, he put his father's suits, both summer and winter ones, back into the trunk and lowered the lid. He also refastened the suitcase that Sebastian had opened.

He locked the trunk and the suitcase, and then placed the keys in his pocket.

23.

DURING LATE 1914 the funereal atmosphere of the Talese household seemed to permeate the entire village, oppressing the population each day with premonitions of disaster and death. The *passeggiata* was now more like a cortege, a procession of slow-moving men lamenting the fact that their draft-age sons had received notices stating that they would be summoned soon for military service. Although the government leaders in Rome still proclaimed their neutrality in the war in Europe, in which untold numbers had already been killed, there was little doubt that in the near future Italy would be involved in the bloodshed.

The Fiat automobile company in Turin was producing military vehicles as fast as possible, and the Ansaldo shipbuilding and armaments firm near Genoa had doubled its labor force and would recruit an extra eight hundred women to meet the needs of its assembly line. Small factories throughout the peninsula had hired mechanics, blacksmiths, carpenters, and other artisans to forge and fabricate various military products and spare parts; and vast amounts of cotton and wool had been requisitioned to make tents, blankets, and uniforms for the Italian military contingent of nearly nine hundred thousand men. Among the hundreds of clothing manufacturers and tailor shops that were approached by military authorities to make uniforms for the soldiers was Francesco Cristiani's shop in Maida.

Joseph had been alone in the front of the shop on the day that two officers from the quartermaster corps in Catanzaro had paid a visit. It was a late afternoon near the end of October, nearly eight weeks after Gaetano's funeral. Joseph's cousin Antonio, who had worked irregularly after returning from Paris, was not in the shop. He had been feverish and depressed ever since receiving his draft notice earlier in the week.

"Is the proprietor available to speak with us?" the older and larger of

the two officers asked in a polite voice, while the younger man, an emaciated, almost weasel-like individual with a long nose and thick glasses,
squinted around the room at the stacks of material piled on the shelves.
Both men wore gray-green uniforms with stars on the collars and insignia
above the peaks of their hats that Joseph could not identify. The larger
man wore boots and carried a holstered pistol on his belt, while the other,
who was unarmed, wore puttees and carried a leather briefcase under his
arm.

As Joseph turned to go back to the workroom to get Mr. Cristiani, he
saw him coming forward, frowning. Joseph also caught a glimpse of the
other tailors in the back room, gathered behind a table, whispering among
themselves. They had observed the entrance of the officers, and seemed
even more upset than Mr. Cristiani.

"Good afternoon, I am Captain Barone," the larger man called out as
Cristiani came closer; and then, gesturing airily with a hand toward his
bespectacled companion, he added, "And this is my adjutant, Lieutenant
Faro."

Cristiani quickly shook hands with both men, told them his name,
but said nothing more. He had only recently resumed shaving after weeks
of ignoring his whiskers in accord with the custom of mourning, and in
the past week he had become aggrieved once again by the arrival of his
son's draft notice. Twice during the previous evening he had awakened in
terror after dreaming of Antonio's death in distant trenches and swamps;
and the very sight of these two military men standing before him in their
gangrene-colored uniforms made him both nauseated and caustic.

"We bring you greetings from the quartermaster general himself,"
Captain Barone went on blithely, oblivious to Cristiani's mood. "He is
quite familiar with the high standards of your workmanship, and it has
been suggested that you and your fellow tailors might be able to produce
fifty uniforms for the Forty-eighth Infantry Battalion, now being assembled in Catanzaro, by the end of this year. Do you think you can do this?"

Before Cristiani could reply, Lieutenant Faro had removed from his
briefcase a cardboard brochure from which folded out a tailor's pattern for
the uniform, and on which was pasted a tiny swatch of the gray-green material to be used; he waited for Cristiani to take the brochure and examine
it. But the tailor, letting the brochure remain in the lieutenant's outstretched hand, turned toward Captain Barone and slowly shook his head.

"I am sorry," he said, "but I lack the manpower to fill this order. And
besides, I may soon lose a few of my tailors to the draft, including my very
best tailor, who has been trained in Paris. He is to be called any day now."

Captain Barone nodded and remained silent for a moment. Then he raised an eyebrow and gave Cristiani a little wink.

"Perhaps something can be arranged," the captain said, with a knowing smile. "Making uniforms for the army is essential to the war effort, is it not?"

Cristiani, catching the drift of his thinking, felt a surge of excitement rising within him, but he remained silent.

"Yes," the captain went on, "it is possible, it just might *be* possible that a deferment could be arranged."

Cristiani was unable to restrain himself, and his grim facial features, characteristically so since the death of Gaetano, burst into an expression of relief fast approaching elation.

"Yes, a *deferment*," Cristiani said, and then he repeated the word in a faraway, almost spiritual manner; Joseph, standing in a corner behind the officers, could see the young tailors in the back reacting favorably to the sound.

Meanwhile, the transformed Cristiani had snatched the brochure out of the hands of Lieutenant Faro, and was now studying the pattern of the uniform with an interest that had been totally nonexistent moments before.

"It is really a *simple* design," Cristiani conceded aloud, shifting his glance back and forth between the pattern of the military trousers and that of the jacket. "And I see that there are no epaulets or belt loops on the jacket, which should save us much time. . . ."

"Yes," Captain Barone eagerly interjected, "and it will not be necessary to put cuffs on the trousers, or even to baste them at the bottom, for they will be covered by puttees, or tucked into the soldiers' boots. . . ."

As Cristiani continued to peruse the patterns, Captain Barone went on talking, explaining proudly that while the fabric was drab-looking, it had been proven scientifically that the gray-green color was almost invisible in outdoor combat conditions. Lieutenant Faro, who had until now remained silent, said that boxloads of the material would be on Cristiani's doorstep in the morning.

After the officers had left, Cristiani told Joseph to locate Antonio, to convey the encouraging news, and to urge him to return to the shop at once. Joseph hastened out the door, very excited, and took a shortcut to the Talese compound that avoided the square but required him to sneak through the courtyards and vegetable patches of some private estates, and thereby risk the wrath of their proprietors and their watchdogs. But nothing mattered more to Joseph now than cheering up Antonio, reviving the spirit of his cousin who—until depressed by the draft notice—had been a stalwart source of strength and hope in the aftermath of Gaetano's death. Antonio had taken many long walks with Joseph, reassuring him that they would soon be in Paris together, that the war in northern Europe would soon end, and that in any case the Italian people had nothing to fear, thanks to their government's strict neutrality. Unlike France, Italy had not been invaded, Antonio had reasoned, and Italy had nothing to gain in the war; so why should it become involved?

But then, overnight, everything changed. The Italian government, while insisting it was still neutral, nonetheless announced its plan to mobilize even though there had not been the slightest hint that the Austrians or the Germans intended to invade Italy. All bachelors of draft age were contacted by the police and told not to leave their area without reporting first to the local precinct. The only bachelors exempted in Maida were the village idiots, the incurably crippled, and the police chief's son, who had just been appointed to the force.

Emigration was immediately terminated, and Italian citizens in the United States who were eligible for the draft were called back to Italy. Two of Joseph's maternal uncles, who worked at the Keasbey & Mattison asbestos plant in Ambler, were notified to take the next ship home, all expenses to be paid by the Italian government. The names of Maida's first round of draftees, a total of fourteen men, were printed in large letters on a billboard in front of the municipal building. On seeing it for the first time, many mothers screamed and fainted, or, crossing themselves, fell to their knees. The billboard was viewed as a death warrant. Heading the list, which was in alphabetical order, was "Cristiani, Antonio."

Now Joseph, bearing promising news for Antonio, made his way through the brambles and thorns and ran up the dirt road toward the compound. But after entering the Cristiani home he saw no sign of Antonio or anyone else. The bedroom that Joseph shared with Antonio, who was gone before Joseph had risen for work that morning, was exactly as Joseph had left it. The two cots were made up in his earnest if inept fashion, and the small ashen chunks of charcoal in the brazier had not been added to since he himself had placed them there and ignited them. The wood in the kitchen fireplace was now all cinders, although there was still the slight smell of the incense his aunt Maria usually burned in the house during the midday Angelus.

Joseph looked out the window and saw no one in the courtyard behind the row of houses. His mother had been away the entire week with her parents; and his brother Sebastian had not yet returned from the farm with the other workers. But along the upper road, beyond the wall, Joseph could see his grandfather Domenico riding downhill, his black hat and cape silhouetted against the fading sunlight and his white stallion. Joseph went down and waited along the road to greet him and ask if he had seen Antonio. "I have just left him," Domenico said. "He's at the rally in the square, wasting his time listening to the Socialists."

After thanking his grandfather, Joseph quickly turned and ran toward the square.

Antonio had spent the morning and most of the afternoon walking alone in the mountains. He had risen at dawn with his mother, had escorted her to Mass, but had not gone into the church. He was uncomfortable at the sight of all the black-shawled women passing beneath the torchlit arcade into the church, mourning in advance the departure and possible demise of their loved ones. After leaving his mother at the door, he continued up the rocky road that he had not climbed in years, and made his way in the nebulous light to the peak of Mount Contessa just as the noonday sun had reached its height; here he had a panoramic view of the entire landscape.

To the west he could see the rocky, indented Tyrrhenian coast, its beachfront promontories topped by two watchtowers, its azure waters drifting out to the misty dark bulk of the isle of Stromboli. To the east was the Ionian Sea, which extended to Greece, its Italian shoreline eroded and abandoned, left to the legends of Ulysses.

For Antonio, the past week had been the strangest in his life. It had begun with his seeing his name at the municipal building, together with the names of thirteen of his contemporaries whom he thought he had left behind forever; but now they were all suddenly reunited in a disquieting bond of apprehension. He who had never wanted to return to Maida now did not want to leave it. Nobody he knew wanted to join the army. He suspected that very few people in his village or in the entire south felt that they were part of the Italian nation. The unification of Italy a half-century before had been forced upon the south by the north, by the promoters of the Risorgimento, and since then the ruling government of Italy—gathered first in Turin, then in Florence, and finally in Rome—had brought to the south nothing but worsening poverty and the necessity of emigration. It had driven out the Bourbons, deglorified the capital city of Naples, and replaced it with nothing. Domenico said this often, and now Antonio more or less agreed with his grandfather's view that the south had become more isolated than ever, and that today it owed the north nothing. And so why should the south now yield young men from its villages and emigrant ships to support the wartime profit-making ambitions of northern industrialists and their irredentist friends in parliament who wanted a deeper penetration into the Austrian Alps, and more seafront territory to the east of Venice, and more farmland to its north? How would this help solve the problems of the south? If Austria were threatening to reclaim Venice, which it had lost to Italy in 1866, then Antonio could understand the present mobilization, and would undoubtedly support it. But as things stood now, he was more patriotically inclined toward the government of France than the government of Italy, for France had been provoked and forced to defend itself against the German invaders. He could only hope that the French would prevail, for it was in France that he saw his future.

Antonio spent the entire morning in the mountains, eating nothing, seeing no one; then early in the afternoon he began his walk back, and arrived in Maida after the siesta, just as a crowd was gathering in the Piazza Garibaldi to hear speakers from the Socialist Party. They had not yet taken their positions in front of the fountain, but Antonio, recognizing two of the speakers from the rallies of the previous days, assumed that he would be hearing more of what he had already heard, and what hardly anyone in the village disagreed with.

Its Catholicism aside, Maida's population had become increasingly sympathetic to Socialism largely because of the threat of war. The Socialists had been tireless in their support of continuing neutrality. Each day orators from the local party or from outside the village could be heard reiterating their position that Italy should stay out of the war, that Italy had already invested too much blood and money in recent years on its colonial adventurism in Libya. Antonio had already heard this theme expressed in Turin two months before, when he had left Paris; but there he had also heard speakers attacking the Socialists, urging intervention behind France, Britain, and Russia, and soliciting funds for Italian volunteers eager to go at once to northern Europe to battle the Germans and Austrians. Among the Italian volunteers now fighting alongside the French were two of Garibaldi's grandsons and many other young red-shirted Italian interventionists. But Antonio saw no red-shirted Garibaldini among the crowd in Maida on this day. As he stood at the bar of a café waiting for something to eat, he noticed that there was only one policeman in this crowd of perhaps four hundred people. In Turin, many policemen were needed to separate the arguing factions; here, no confrontations were anticipated, because the people were by and large like-minded, and even some Catholic clergymen had come out to hear the Socialists. Antonio counted four priests, three monks, and the monsignor with his rector. While perhaps adverse to Socialism in general, the clergymen agreed with its antiwar stance, which was in accord with the position of the Pope. The last thing the Pope wanted was for Italy to be fighting the Catholic nation of Austria. The Austrians, it was often said, were more devout than the Italians.

As the first speaker began, Antonio left the café and moved closer to the fountain. Along the edge of the square he saw his grandfather Domenico turning his horse around and leaving. Antonio was glad his grandfather had not noticed him and come over, for he had heard enough of Domenico's haranguing at dinner the night before. It had become Domenico's habit, since Joseph was living at the Cristianis', to dine at least twice a week with the family. Domenico was against the war, the government, *and* the Socialists. He was among the last adherents of Bourbonism, a period piece from the Baroque. Antonio moved through the crowd toward a few of his fellow draftees who had waved him in their direction. Among them were the sons of a court clerk, a carriage maker, a cobbler, and a miller. There were a number of other draftees standing nearby who were farmers' sons from the valley.

Much cheering followed the lengthy introduction of the first speaker, a stocky bald man who was the party boss in Cosenza; he began the program by attacking a disgraced Socialist in Milan, Benito Mussolini. Antonio had never heard of Mussolini until his name began making headlines in recent days. Mussolini had been the editor of the Socialist newspaper *Avanti!* and had written many articles advocating neutrality, but then, without warning to his staff or the leaders of his party, he confessed in print that he had heretofore been unwise and ill informed, and he urged that Italy get behind the British and French and enter the war at once. So vehemently did the Socialists around the nation react that Mussolini resigned his editorship and severed his connections with the party. "Mussolini is the slimiest of snakes," cried the speaker in Maida, as the crowd roared its approval. "He sold out his principles to the northern industrialists who are his true friends, and we now hear that they are giving him money so that he can publish another newspaper to spread their warmongering propaganda!"

After this man had concluded his diatribe and been replaced by a speaker who was similarly critical of Mussolini and interventionism, Joseph entered the square and soon located Antonio among his companions. One of them had an arm around Antonio's shoulder, and both were cheering on the speaker. Joseph stood unnoticed next to his cousin for several minutes. When Antonio saw him and smiled, Joseph was tempted to tell him about the officers' visit, but he decided not to while Antonio was surrounded by his friends. He tried instead to concentrate on what the speaker was saying. He was a white-haired man who waved his hands in the air and repeatedly yelled out "Salandra, Salandra"; and each time he did the crowd booed and hissed in support of his denunciation of this "Salandra." Although Antonio leaned close to Joseph and explained that Antonio Salandra, Italy's prime minister, was suspected of trying to nudge the country into the war, it made little sense to Joseph: the crowd also hissed and booed whenever the speaker mentioned Gabriele D'Annunzio, whom Antonio identified as a poet, neglecting to mention he was also an outspoken interventionist.

The speeches continued until almost twilight, impressing Joseph mainly for the enthusiasm they engendered in those around him. The talk and excitement about the war this week had, if nothing else, drawn his attention away from himself. He was not so preoccupied with his father's death, or the fact that he would not be going to America, or maybe not even to Paris. Joseph's concerns now were centered on Antonio. When the rally ended, and some of Antonio's friends suggested that he accompany them to a café, Joseph pulled him aside and told him that his father was waiting for him at the shop and had something important to tell him. Joseph would not say what it was, only that it was necessary to go to the shop at once.

Antonio's father was in the back room working when they arrived. The other tailors had left, and all the shops on the street had locked their doors. Joseph waited in the front room while Antonio joined his father in the back. For the next five minutes Joseph could hear his uncle speaking rapidly but quietly, doing all the talking except for a concurring word now and then from Antonio. When the two of them had finished and closed the lights, the elder Cristiani patted Joseph on the shoulder and led him outside to the street.

Antonio came slowly behind, inserted the keys to lock the door, nodded toward Joseph, but said nothing. If he was in the least elated by the possibility that he would be avoiding the army, he seemed determined to repress it. But even Joseph knew that it was considered bad luck in the village to anticipate happiness.

———

On the following morning, when Joseph was awakened by Antonio, he saw that his cousin was already dressed and was leaving for work early.

Later, when Joseph arrived at the shop, he saw that the gray-green cloth had arrived from Catanzaro as promised, and was being unloaded from a truck by two soldiers under the supervision of Lieutenant Faro. After the soldiers had left, the tailors began at once the process of producing uniforms for the Forty-eighth Infantry Battalion. Three sewing machines had been provided by the army to speed up the work. Twenty uniforms were to be completed by the end of November, and the remaining thirty by the end of December.

Throughout the final days of October and into early November, Antonio and his father cut all the fabric and basted the suit sections together, leaving to three other tailors and the older apprentices the final sewing with the machines, which produced results, if not prideful tailoring. Joseph, the youngest apprentice, attached all the buttons to the jackets and trouser fronts, and sewed the sweat pads onto the lower part of the armholes, and the piping around the bottom of the jacket cuffs. Everyone worked long hours throughout the week, and on Sunday afternoons into the early evening. Francesco Cristiani had strung up some faded velvet draperies at the workroom doorway, wanting to conceal from his customers as best he could the extent of his cooperation with the military. While he knew there was no way such a thing could be kept secret in a small place like Maida, especially as the fabric for the uniforms had been delivered by the army in full view of everyone in the street, he still saw no reason to expose his workroom to the daily scrutiny of customers strolling around the front room of his shop. Were he to be asked by anyone about his military contract, he would confirm it but add that he had been given little choice. The military was part of the government, after all. Even the town's most ardent Socialists should understand his predicament. Nonetheless, he was surprised and relieved that as his employees continued to labor each day at the long tables covered with gray-green material, none of his customers expressed any curiosity about the sounds of sewing machines and the muffled voices that could be heard coming from behind the draperies.

As each uniform was finished it was hung in a beige cloth bag in the widows' closet, next to dozens of civilian suits, capes, and coats, and several pairs of trousers with wing-tipped knees. The closet was really an L-shaped room spacious enough to be put to uses other than storage; but Cristiani could never imagine what these uses might be, besides as an occasional hiding place from customers he wished to avoid—such as the *mafioso* he had duped years before, the gullible but potentially life-threatening Mr. Castiglia.

When the first twenty uniforms had been completed on schedule, Lieutenant Faro returned in a truck driven by a sergeant from the Forty-eighth Infantry Battalion. All work stopped as Cristiani held back the draperies to admit the lieutenant, while the sergeant remained in the front room to keep an eye on the truck.

"Lieutenant Faro has come to inspect the first batch of uniforms before taking them to Catanzaro," Cristiani explained to his tailors, while the lieutenant, his briefcase under his arm, bowed stiffly. Then he followed Cristiani into the widows' closet and for the next half-hour checked to see that the uniforms met military specifications; with a tape measure he verified that five of the twenty uniforms were cut small, as requested, while the other fifteen were large. The army reasoned that it would be better for the quartermaster corps to issue the troops uniforms that were too large rather than too small.

"Very well," the lieutenant said finally, after inspecting the last of the uniforms, "all of these are ready to go." He removed from his briefcase a bulky envelope and handed it to Cristiani, who thanked him without opening it and placed it on a shelf in the closet. He assumed it contained the agreed-upon sum to cover the labor costs, plus a modest profit.

"By the way," Cristiani said with some hesitation, before they had left the widows' closet, "have you anything to tell me about what Captain Barone mentioned when he was here?"

Lieutenant Faro regarded him with a blank stare of confusion.

"The *deferments*," Cristiani whispered intently, "the *deferments* for my tailors—and especially for my best tailor, who happens to be my son, Antonio. Don't you remember that Captain Barone said that this might be arranged?"

"Ah, yes," the lieutenant said, after a pause. "I believe he is working on it. I shall remind him when I see him." Then he walked into the workroom, bowed again to the tailors, and, parting the draperies, notified the sergeant to begin loading the truck. Antonio and the others worked busily with their heads down as the husky sergeant made four trips back and forth. Meanwhile Francesco Cristiani walked the lieutenant to the door and, before saying good-bye, thanked him for his offer to consult with Captain Barone about the deferments.

"I shall remind him," the lieutenant repeated, "but keep up the pace.

Finish those other uniforms as fast as you can. Maybe you can finish in three weeks instead of four. What do you think?"

"I will try," Cristiani said.

"Try hard," the lieutenant said, "and it may make a fine impression on Captain Barone."

After the truck had pulled away, Cristiani returned to the workroom and reported what he had been told. One tailor, Cerruti, appeared to be upset that his deferment had not yet been confirmed, but Antonio seemed to take the news without reacting.

"There is nothing we can do but work and wait," he said. "Let's finish this contract as fast as we can, and hope for the best."

Cristiani agreed that they had little choice, and for the next three weeks, the tailors worked at an accelerated pace and also subcontracted the job of lining the jackets to a few village seamstresses Cristiani knew in the neighboring village of Jacurso. By the third week of December, a week ahead of schedule, the thirty uniforms had been finished and were hung in the widows' closet, awaiting inspection. Word of this reached Lieutenant Faro in a message that Cristiani sent to Catanzaro via a carriage driver, and within a few days the army truck reappeared in Maida carrying not only the lieutenant but also Captain Barone.

Jovial as usual, the captain strolled into the workroom and complimented the tailors for the work they had done the previous month. Then, accompanied by his adjutant and Cristiani, he entered the widows' closet to begin the inspection; but he did not remain as long as the lieutenant had on the earlier occasion.

"Bravo," he said as he reappeared before the tailors, while Lieutenant Faro summoned a sergeant and another soldier to begin loading the truck. "You have once again performed impressively under pressure. The quartermaster corps joins me, I know, in my salute to all of you." After a snappy salute he sallied past the draperies, and was out the door when Cristiani caught up with him.

"Captain Barone!" he called urgently, "what about the deferments?"

"Oh," the captain paused, "forgive me." He reached into his pocket, removed a tiny notebook and began to flip through the pages. "Here it is," he said finally, and began to read what he had written. "As for your tailor Cerruti, who is thirty, his deferment was granted. As for the twenty-year-old Antonio Cristiani, he will have to report to the Pepe Barracks in Catanzaro this weekend. He is assigned to the Forty-eighth Infantry Battalion."

As Cristiani stood at the curb, stunned, Antonio came out of the shop and joined him.

"I am sorry, young man," Captain Barone said, "but I did all that I could."

Antonio put his arm around his father, and the two stood silently for several minutes as the soldiers finished packing the truck and started up the engine. Little did Antonio know during the past several weeks that he had been making his own uniform.

24.

DURING THE WINTER and into the spring of 1915, Private Antonio Cristiani underwent basic training at the Pepe Barracks in Catanzaro, where he learned to load and fire a cannon, to maneuver on his belly without permitting dirt to jam his rifle, and, while clutching a pair of steel clippers in his soft tailor's hands, to cut barbed wire. Twice a month he was allowed to return home for the weekend; but on a Friday afternoon in late May, as he was about to hitch a ride on a Maida-bound coach, a military policeman intercepted him at the depot and told him to return to the barracks at once. All traveling soldiers stationed in Catanzaro, as well as in dozens of other military posts around the nation, were being ordered to their units. Italy was about to declare war on Austria.

Two days later there was a farewell parade through the main thoroughfare of Catanzaro, and Antonio's entire family came to see him march with eleven hundred other troops toward the rail terminal and the northbound trains that would carry them to the edge of the Austrian border. His mother and father watched in tears, and the rest of the kinfolk—which included everyone from his grandparents to Joseph—were equally solemn as they blended in with the throngs of black-clad spectators who lined the parade route, unreceptive to the lively music of the brass bands and indifferent before the politicians who stood making patriotic speeches from the main balcony in the Piazza dell'Immacolata.

Among the speakers was a royal emissary from Rome, a top-hatted man wearing a morning coat crossed by a tricolored sash; and as the troops stood at parade rest with their rifles and bayonets, and after the bugles had summoned the attention of the multitudes of spectators gathered on all sides, the emissary said in a stentorian voice: "Sons of Italy, for the conquest of national independence your fathers have fought on three occasions. Now this nation must again bear arms to complete what was left undone. This goal represents, in the words of our king, 'your good fortune and your glory. . . .'" There was little applause as the emissary quoted further from the king's prepared text; and Antonio, perspiring in the sun and trying to blow the flies away from his face, hoped that the king's generals would function more smoothly on the battlefield than had the king's entourage when he visited Maida a decade before. Antonio recalled seeing the stranded Victor Emmanuel III on that occasion, strolling impatiently along a dusty road behind his guards, while his chauffeur and other retainers kneeled at the fender of his broken-down Fiat touring car.

Now Victor Emmanuel III was in Rome dreaming of victory; and Private Antonio Cristiani, who had recently turned twenty-one, was listening to speeches with eleven hundred other conscripts, sweating through his winter uniform fashioned for fighting in the Austrian Alps, feeling weighed down by his weaponry and bulky knapsack.

In his knapsack, in addition to his personal articles, were a metal tool for digging trenches, white cans of nearly indigestible food, his rain gear, a blanket, and an extra uniform made of the same gray-green woolen fabric as the one he was wearing.

Soon after his uniforms had been issued to him by the supply sergeant, Antonio had covertly begun to rip them apart, a little at a time, and gradually to refit them to the measurements of his body. He had brought a tailoring kit with him to Catanzaro; and in the early evenings when his fellow soldiers were at the canteen, or playing cards in the sergeant's room in the rear of the barracks, he would resume his alterations, replacing the machine stitching with his own handiwork and inserting extra padding in the shoulders to lessen the pain he felt from the weight of his knapsack and rifle during even short marches.

When resewing the lining of one of the jackets, Antonio recognized the crude stitching of the seamstresses his father had employed in Jacurso; and he could also identify the tailor Cerruti's slanted, left-handed interlooping style of sewing on the waistband of the trousers of the same uniform. Antonio's other uniform, which, he could tell, had not been made in his father's shop, had been entirely machine-stitched with seam lines that wavered unevenly, indicating that whoever had been assigned to use the machine had been a novice, an uncertain first-timer more concerned about puncturing his thumbs than sewing straight lines.

From his place in the ranks, surrounded on all sides by taller men,

Antonio doubted that he was within view of his family in the crowd. He was in the middle of the eighth row. His company commander believed that the unit would create a more formidable impression during parades if the taller soldiers marched on the outside and the shorter ones were kept inside, out of sight. But Antonio had already said good-bye to his family earlier in the morning, after Mass. They had gone together at seven to the cathedral, where, after confession, they had lined the altar rail for Communion. It was the first time Antonio had received the sacrament in six years.

After the final speech had been completed, there was an explosive salute from the town's ceremonial cannon, followed by marching music, and the parade continued past the stately buildings and palm trees along the Corso Mazzini to the train station. At the head of the parade were senior officers on horseback, flanked by orderlies carrying banners and lances; then came the region's uncharacteristically sharp-stepping Bersagliere corps with their flat-brimmed, rakish hats decorated with drooping black feathers; and next the cavalry regiments with their sabers raised in the sun, the artillery with their horse-drawn howitzers, and finally the battalions of common infantry conscripts, many of them out of step, Antonio among them, doubting the worthiness of their mission and fearing what lay ahead.

In the late afternoon on this day, May 24, 1915, on the train that carried him and the rest of the troops northward up the coast, Antonio wrote in his diary—a diary he had begun keeping in Paris: *Ventiquattro maggio—a sad day in the history of the South . . . Salandra had his way, and now we are being taken to the Austrian mountains to kill or be killed. . . . We are as helpless as the pigs we slaughter on our farms. . . .*

As the train traveled northward, it made many stops; it took nearly an entire week to get to the front. The ten-car locomotive moved up along the Tyrrhenian Sea past Paola, Naples, and Rome before pausing and puffing for half a day at Civitavecchia because of a jam-up of troop trains along the tracks ahead. Then, with blasts of steam, the train resumed the journey at full speed, continuing past Grosseto, Livorno, and Pisa. All along the route Antonio saw the Italian countryside littered with thousands and thousands of white cans that had been tossed out the windows by troops in the trains that had preceded his own; and from his train, too, he saw his fellow passengers taking up the sport, cocking their arms and hurling their food cans—some empty, some half eaten, some unopened—out the windows as far as they could. It was either a game of tossing for distance or a final fling before every soldierly movement would be strictly regulated. In any case, the farther north the train traveled, getting closer and closer to the battle zone, the more wildly and densely covered with white cans were the grassy slopes on both sides of the tracks.

All of Antonio's friends from Maida had been assigned to other companies, and the only soldier in the car who came from his area was a robust, large-eared farm boy named Muffo whose father owned land in the valley next to the Rocchinos'. Muffo had seen Antonio sewing in the barracks one night in Catanzaro, and since he was too fat for his jackets he approached Antonio for help. Antonio accommodated him by removing and repositioning the buttons for a freer fit, and Muffo had been very appreciative; from then on during the entire trip, though Antonio would have preferred not talking, Muffo was sitting next to him, or following him around the car, or sleeping near him on the floor at night. Muffo snored louder than anyone else in the car.

After three days and nights along the coastal route, the train curved inland into Lombardy, parting the gentle fields of maize, the pastures and meadows. It wove through modest towns and pastoral villages approached through sentinels of poplar trees, and finally stopped at Milan, allowing four high-ranking officers and two dark-suited civilians wearing homburgs and carrying briefcases to board one of the first-class cars in the front. Meanwhile, members of the military police quickly lined up along the platform to prevent any troops in the rear cars from getting off; but vendors were permitted to run alongside the train selling things through the windows—sweets, cigarettes, baskets of fruit, chunks of cheese and sausage, long loaves of bread, and small bottles of wine. Although the vendors were not supposed to sell newspapers to the soldiers, whose commanders wished to shield them from any antiwar sentiments that might appear in the columns, Antonio managed to bribe one vendor into going to a kiosk and purchasing an assortment of journals and then delivering them to him, folded within the paper wrapping of a long loaf of bread, just as the train was pulling away. Antonio was not overly concerned that he would be caught reading. Though part of the military, he felt quite detached from those who presumed to regulate his life. It was not his war, after all; and besides, the commanders were all riding in the first-class section.

It began to drizzle as the train left the outskirts of Milan, and then to thunder and rain heavily upon the leaky roof of Antonio's car as the locomotive churned eastward along the Lombard plains for another lengthy, grinding ride along the rails. Drinking two bottles of wine with his bread and cheese, Antonio read through the newspapers as Muffo leaned over his shoulder, seemingly interested; but Antonio believed that Muffo, despite his having somehow met the army's entrance requirements, was practically illiterate.

From what Antonio could deduce from the editorials and the reports of correspondents attached to the French and Russian armies, the war was not going well for Italy's allies. The French, British, and Belgians on the western front had been mostly on the defensive since the war had begun more than nine months before, months of Italian neutrality. Now the Germans held a large slice of northern France. The Austro-German forces facing the Russians on the eastern front also appeared to be getting the better of it. And the Austrians in the Balkans were no longer being challenged by the unaccountably quiescent Serbian army.

What Italy hoped to gain by entering the war would be at the expense of Austria (Italy had not yet declared war on Germany); Italy claimed as geographically Italian the land northeast of Venice approaching the Julian Alps, which Antonio believed was where he was headed, as well as some territory on the opposite side of the Adriatic Sea, which included the port city of Trieste. Italy also wanted a large chunk of the eastern Alps that Austria controlled—namely the Dolomite region up to the Brenner Pass, below Innsbruck, and the Trentino region southwest of the Dolomites. While a substantial percentage of the population in this area spoke German and was partial to Austrian rule, Italian patriots nonetheless argued that it was more Italian than anything else, and had been since Roman times, even though it had been regularly invaded and occupied by barbarians from the north—by Alaric and his Visigoths, by Attila and his Huns, and by numerous others whom many Italians now associated with the Austro-Hungarian regiments controlling the area. Whether it was worthwhile for Italy to go to war in the hopes of repossessing this region of mountain ranges and deep-cut canyons was a question Antonio had not been able to answer when it had been raised during his final furlough in Maida by his father's favorite customer, the aristocratic Torquato Ciriaco. Don Torquato, who had once traveled through the alpine country on his way home from a holiday in Zurich, said it consisted mostly of infertile soil and huge, useless rocks. But in Paris, Monsieur Damien, who before the war had taken a vacation trip into the Dolomites and Trentino and down through Lake Garda, had described the region's natural beauty and salubrity, its Tyrolean country inns, mineral water spas, and majestic cliff-side hotels. Monsieur Damien remembered balmy summer evenings on white terraces with wealthy and elegant sojourners from every part of Europe and America, dancing to Viennese waltzes, drinking French champagne, dining on Italian cuisine; and he recalled a delightful ride in a paddle steamer on Lake Garda.

The tracks over which Antonio now rode would soon take him past the southern edge of that same lake, as he knew from consulting the map he carried folded in his pocket. The train had been moving east since leaving Milan. It had paused overnight at a railhead somewhere west of Brescia, where it attached to itself two stock cars loaded with timber, rolls of barbed wire, heavy gun barrels covered with canvas, and replenishments of canned rations that were passed through the cars (amid the groans of troops). In the morning the train returned to the main tracks, and before noon it was slowly edging along a hillside toward the southern rim of the lake. Looking out the window to his left, Antonio was amazed at the calmness of the water, with barely a ripple rising to mar what appeared to be a gigantic mirror. The southern basin of the lake was in Italian territory; but its northern end, which was more than thirty miles away, and skirted the cliffs of Trentino, was controlled by the Austrians. The train moved very slowly past the lake, as if the engineer had become cautious. But Antonio saw no sign of movement in the surrounding hills, and not even a bird flew over the water. It was a scene of total abandonment and tranquillity, the sun brightening the surface and leaving soft shadows behind the tall trees in the hills and the groves with their empty picnic benches. *The paddle steamer that carried Monsieur Damien is probably being stored for the duration of the war,* Antonio wrote in his diary, *and maybe the hostelries that he mentioned are deeper in the lake region, where the Austrians are. I see a dark outline far to the north that might be a range of mountains. Maybe the Austrians are up there somewhere, sitting on terraces with their boots on tables, drinking champagne. . . . Soon we should be past Venice, heading north into the mountains. Maybe tomorrow, or the next day, we will meet the Austrians up there. . . .*

In the middle of the afternoon, after bypassing Venice and heading northeast through marshlands and hillside towns that appeared uninhabited, the train finally stopped at an unmarked station along the foothills of a cavernous mountain. The sun that had shone over Lake Garda was now hidden, and it was beginning to rain. Two military policemen who had been riding in one of the front cars jumped onto the platform and began to blow their whistles; then a sergeant major appeared with a megaphone and ordered the troops to step out hastily and line up for inspection. Hopping off behind the others and taking a position in the ranks, Antonio could hear the thundering echo of big guns exploding in the distance. The explosions were perhaps twenty miles away, yet Antonio thought that he could feel along the oakwood platform under his feet a tingling sensation not unlike the earthquake tremors that sometimes rattled the cobblestones of Maida.

Standing at attention, holding his rifle in front of his face in the now steady rain, he looked past the barrel at the terminal building adjacent to the tracks, a barnlike structure of recent date, flanked by supply depots that had tents overhead and resembled some of the vendors' stalls in his village square. Stacked under these tents, however, were dozens of ten-gallon cans filled with motor fuel, engine parts and tires, pontoons for floating bridges, and thousands of rations in the white cans with which he had become nauseatedly familiar. After the sergeant major and two young lieutenants had marched past him without looking at his rifle or scrutinizing his knapsack to see if it contained all that was required, Antonio relaxed at parade rest for nearly a half-hour, until the inspection team had gone the entire length and width of the five rows of troops that extended along the platform. Then, at the bark of the sergeant's voice, the troops raised their rifles to their stomachs, turned to the right, and marched as directed away from the platform and across a rain-sodden field into huge rectangular tents set off by stakes and ropes. Inside the tents were several long tables. At one table, on which were spread piles of gas masks, each soldier was told to take one and insert it inside the steel helmet strapped on the outside of his knapsack. At another table, on which were caldrons of steaming soup and stacks of paper-covered beef sandwiches, the troops were told to take out their steel cups and help themselves to the soup, and to tuck a single sandwich, unopened, into their knapsack. The sandwich would be eaten later, the sergeant major emphasized, *after* permission had been granted.

Antonio finished his soup as he moved through the line, and then he and the others were hustled out of the tent back into the rain by a sergeant who waved his arms and pointed toward a long line of green canvas-roofed trucks parked in puddles of mud so deep that all their tires looked flat. The troops lined up in single file to hop into the back of the vehicles, and as Antonio ran, keeping his rifle dry under his trench coat, he saw a drenched officer standing next to the fender of the first truck, screaming obscenities up at the driver, who could not get the motor started. The driver of the second truck was immediately appointed to lead the convoy, while the troops huddled under the canvas of the first truck were ordered out into the rain, along with their humiliated driver, to direct traffic around their battery-drained vehicle.

Antonio climbed into the fifth truck and found a place on the back bench between the soggy wool coats of two soldiers sitting on the edge of their seats, their bulky knapsacks taking up most of the space behind them. Just as the driver was about to close the truck's rear gate, Muffo came splashing through the mud and jumped in, and landed on Antonio's feet. Seconds later the motor started and the wheels turned forward, skidding now and then until finding traction on a macadam road that led up into the mountain, in the direction of the sounds of the thundering guns.

As Antonio watched the train station getting smaller and the long line of mud-splattered trucks following his own up the curved road at the base of the mountain, he thought of writing something in his diary, but he was too squeezed in to reach into his knapsack for his book. None of the soldiers spoke. They either stared into space, wincing when the guns boomed louder than before, or, like Muffo on the floor in front of him, they closed their eyes and appeared to be sleeping. On the other side of Muffo, however, was a young soldier who was busy with a pencil, writing or sketching on a piece of cardboard that he held on his lap and partly concealed within the folds of his unbuttoned coat. He had a pale, chubby, innocent-looking, almost cherubic, face; he was beardless and appeared too young for conscription, maybe no older than fifteen. His peaked cap was pushed back on his head, revealing his schoolboy bangs, and he somehow gave the impression of being effeminate. He had not been in Antonio's barracks at Catanzaro and must have boarded the train at one of the stops along the northern route, perhaps in Milan or during the layover near Brescia. He reminded Antonio of a youth he had known in the Paris claque, an opera buff and homosexual who was apprenticed to one of the city's leading milliners. Antonio had not been aware of homosexuals when growing up in Maida, but in Paris he had met a few of them. A fellow student at the École Ladaveze had alerted him to a homosexual on the faculty. As Antonio kept watching the soldier, the young man looked up and smiled at him, and then turned the cardboard around to show what he had been doing. Across the top he had drawn a line of soldiers holding their rifles in a firing position, and under that, in block lettering, were the words of Gabriele D'Annunzio, the poet and advocate of intervention: "May every blow find its mark, every citizen be a warrior, every warrior a hero." Antonio had heard that quoted by one of the speakers at the farewell parade in Catanzaro. The young soldier continued to exhibit the cardboard, as if waiting for some sign of approval. Antonio coolly looked away.

It was now nearly five p.m., according to Antonio's not always reliable watch, an American-made confirmation gift from his late uncle Gaetano that he was required to wind at least twice daily. He was not sure what day it was. It was perhaps the last day of May, or the first day of June, or maybe the second or third. The newspapers he had read on the train had been slightly outdated. Having drifted through sleepless days and nights since leaving Catanzaro, he had no precise sense of time. He knew only that he was living through a long day in the spring of 1915, a day made miserable by the driving rain, and that it was the year in which Italy had entered the war, and that his truck was zigzagging higher and higher. The mountains here were twice as high as those in his part of southern Italy. Some of the ranges in upper Italy and lower Austria had peaks between eight thousand and twelve thousand feet high—the latter being comparable to a dozen Eiffel Towers standing on top of one another. This war would be fought along the summits of Europe, and Antonio began to feel dizzy as his truck continued its climb and the guns became louder; and he *knew* he was approaching the danger zone, because the outer edge of the cliffside road was now camouflaged with ten-foot-high wire fencing interwoven with thick reeds and grass matting. This was designed to protect Italian motorized movements from detection by Austrian observers who were possibly positioned with telescopes on the snowcapped peaks across the canyon. The camouflaging extended over the top of the roadway as well, dangling down so close to the truck's roof that some of the grass flew into the air as the vehicle passed. The grassy tunnels, which darkened the roadway and forced drivers to slow down, had recently been strung across by Italian military engineers working at night with no light except for that of the moon. The engineers managed to complete their task without being spotted by Austrian observers; and so far, since the first Italian trucks had begun transporting troops along this route a week or ten days before, none had been targeted by the enemy. The flimflammery of the camouflagers had been masterful.

Still, Antonio was relieved when the convoy detoured off the tunneled road, where he believed his luck was being pushed to the limit, and turned sharply through a crevasse in the mountain onto a dirt road lined on both sides by bushes and trees threaded with barbed wire. The trucks moved slowly for nearly half a mile, passing along the way a waterfall and rock stream in which Antonio saw some Italian soldiers bathing and doing their laundry. He realized it had finally stopped raining. At the end of the road the trucks were waved through an opened gate by two sentries with carbines. After the trucks had stopped, several sergeants and corporals appeared behind the vehicles and ordered everyone to get out and line up for inspection.

As Antonio jumped out and looked around, he saw that he was under an immense overhanging rock; he was standing on rocky flatland surrounded on all sides by mountain walls that rose hundreds of feet and tapered toward one another at the top. The edges of the walls were jagged, and through an opening in the top was a view of the cloudy sky. The flatland on which he stood was as spacious as the town square in Maida, and along its fringes near the walls were dozens of tents and wooden shacks surrounded by soldiers, some of whom stood next to mule carts and small trucks loading and unloading supplies and equipment.

Hundreds of troops seemed to be encamped in this hollow hideaway that surely was within easy artillery range, if not yet within telescopic sight and knowledge, of Austria's alpine teams of observers and gunners. Indeed, Antonio suspected that some of the shells he now heard exploding in the far mountainside and valley were actually sailing over the apex of this rather cozy concavity. And yet, as he stood at attention while the sergeant major and a lieutenant made their way along the line inspecting each soldier's identity papers, he could not help being amazed by the nonchalance exhibited by many of the officers and enlisted men he saw moving around across the way, in the vicinity of a large shack with an Italian flag on top that he assumed was the base headquarters.

Strolling arm in arm out of the shack were two officers, who conversed as if they were enjoying a *passeggiata*. Next to the shack Antonio caught a glimpse of a few soldiers standing casually in line at the counter of a wheeled field kitchen, which was parked next to a wheeled post office, to which other soldiers carried parcels and letters for mailing. He also saw a wheeled blacksmith shop, its smithy working lustily with a steel hammer, seemingly unconcerned about the loud clanging sounds he was sending up through the interior, assuming no doubt that the echo of this noise would be muted by the louder sounds coming above from the artillery. Next to the medical aid station and a row of latrines were two large steaming wooden tubs in which a half-dozen soldiers were bathing themselves.

The new arrivals could take a bath, the sergeant major informed them after they had been counted and their documents verified; but first he led them to their barracks, which were located in the woods and were reached by walking a few hundred feet past a wide opening in the shelter, the same opening through which the trucks had come in earlier. The trucks had just been turned around and were headed up the dirt road, presumably on their way back through the grass-mat tunnels toward the train station to get more troops.

The barracks to which Antonio was assigned with Muffo was the second in a row of six, all of them painted the same gray-green color as the soldiers' uniforms. Otherwise there was no camouflaging except that provided by nature, the deciduous trees in early bloom adding to the cover already offered by cypresses and pines. In the near distance Antonio saw the wooden gate through which they had entered, with its barbed-wire fence, and two steel-helmeted sentries carrying carbines. In the barracks, Antonio, Muffo, and the others were told to select a cot, to change into dry clothes, and, after going to the tubs and the field kitchen if they wished, to return and rest.

"It may be your final siesta until the war is over," the sergeant said, grinning. Then he added: "Tonight, after midnight, all of you will be going out on patrol." The room became silent, and Antonio no longer had any illusions that he had found a safe haven in the shadows of the war.

He spent the last part of the day walking around, too anxious to sleep, not hungry enough to eat. He filled his cup with coffee at the field kitchen, then sat nearby on a tree stump, while Muffo and the others helped themselves to soup and macaroni and sat eating at one of the long tables. By wandering about and overhearing conversations of officers as well as soldiers, Antonio got a sense of where he was and what military role the troops stationed here would be expected to play.

He was on a crest of a mountain some miles west of the Isonzo River, which flowed from the Austrian-controlled Julian Alps in the north down to the Austrian-controlled Gulf of Trieste in the south. The Austrians also commanded the mountains to the east of the Isonzo, but the Italians were planning to infiltrate the river area at night and mass troops there, and, after crossing the river on pontoon bridges, to fight their way up into the mountains and drive out the Austrians. The reconnaissance team Antonio would join on this night was an advance unit in the big campaign.

Antonio was rejoined by Muffo and the two sat talking, when a lieutenant called to them: "You men look like you need something to do." Before they could reply, he ordered them to follow him. Soon they were back in the woods, not far from their barracks, approaching a stable and a barn. Two cavalrymen were brushing their horses near the stable, and in the barn were several mules attached to two-wheeled carts containing hay. There were soldiers nearby with pitchforks and smaller tools bent over bales of hay, hacking the hay into smaller sections and then picking it up in their hands and examining it before loading it into the carts.

"They're checking to see if there are any tiny steel prongs in the hay," the lieutenant explained to Antonio and Muffo, adding that word had come down from the commanding general's office that some of the hay purchased by the Italian army from its allies—hay that had come from the United States—contained prongs that had been inserted possibly by German and Austrian sympathizers in the United States wanting to kill the horses and mules of the Allies. Prongs had been discovered in the hay delivered to other Allied theaters, the lieutenant said; consequently all Italian commands were taking precautions before feeding their animals. The hay in this barn had to be inspected before nightfall, the lieutenant went on, and therefore he wanted Antonio and Muffo to lend a hand to the task. The corporal in charge of the detail handed them two pitchforks, and the lieutenant thanked them and left.

Antonio and Muffo worked next to the other soldiers for nearly two hours, until it was too dark to continue; but during this time not a single prong was discovered by anyone, nor had any been found earlier in the day. Still, the activity had taken Antonio's mind off the possibly precarious night that awaited him; and when the corporal had given them permission to leave, Antonio and Muffo wandered over to the tubs and took a hot bath before returning to the barracks.

By now it was completely dark, and Antonio saw some soldiers already asleep in their cots, while others sat in their underwear rearranging their knapsacks and cleaning their rifles. Antonio again saw the young soldier he had noticed on the truck, the one who had been drawing a sketch of riflemen in action with the quotation from D'Annunzio; but the soldier did not smile at him now. He actually gave Antonio a scowling look; and when Antonio stared back at him, he turned away but began to click the bolt of his rifle back and forth as fast and as loudly as he could. Although Antonio was not afraid of him, he knew he would keep his distance from him in the field. He was weird, Antonio decided. Any soldier who went off to war drawing pictures of soldiers shooting guns was weird.

Antonio removed his clothes and got into his cot, glancing at Muffo, who was already asleep. Antonio reached into his knapsack for his diary and made a few notes, listing the date as June 5 with a question mark. *I must be careful of this crazy young man, this patriot, or whatever,* Antonio wrote. *Maybe he's a spy for the army. I'd heard that the army has spies among the troops, people who keep their ears open and report to the superiors everything they hear. . . .* Antonio began to write about how he had spent the evening in the barn looking for prongs; but then a sergeant came into the barracks and extinguished all the lights.

It seemed but a few minutes before Antonio was awakened by an order to get out of his cot. The troops had ten minutes to assemble outside, a sergeant announced, with their bayonets on their rifles. There were latrines outside the barracks, and also buckets of water and caldrons of coffee. After folding his blanket into his knapsack, getting dressed and helping himself to the coffee, Antonio joined the others in a lantern-lit clearing in the woods and followed the motion of a sergeant's arm toward a major who stood near a group of Bersaglieri and some members of the spirited Alpino corps, who wore jaunty pointed gray-green hats adorned with an eagle's feather.

These two fighting branches represented a prideful minority within the uniformed ranks of young Italian manhood. They seemed to relish military life and Spartan discipline. They not only marched in step but did so on the double. In a land that adored saints and heroic individualists, but had yet to achieve a collective appreciation of itself as a nation, and certainly not as a militaristic nation, Bersaglieri and Alpini were no doubt anomalies, but they presented themselves with a boldness that demanded respect. And they got this respect even from such reluctant warriors as Antonio, who on this night was comforted by their presence, and who, after learning that he would reconnoiter among them, felt honored. His job, and the job of the other infantrymen, was to march behind these elite troops and protect their rear and flanks while they moved ahead, setting the pace, undaunted and daring as they encroached upon the enemy.

Directing this reconnaissance contingent was Major Riccardo Reina, a stout, broad-shouldered veteran of the Libyan campaign. Major Reina had divided the contingent into three groups; and, as he explained after the sergeants had brought order to the ranks, each group would travel through the woods along a different path down to the river, where they would establish three bridgeheads before daybreak and begin to mark the way for the large-scale offensive that would follow. Major Reina himself would lead one group. The other groups would be headed by two captains whom he introduced, both of them Bersaglieri. Members of the Alpini would be integrated into the three groups; they were trained in the preferred methods of advancement on steep acclivities, and were also qualified to assist the accompanying engineer corpsmen in erecting wire-rope tramways for conveying supplies and ammunition up the sides of mountains and across chasms. The engineers would be responsible for selecting the best places along the river for the pontoon bridges; division headquarters would be informed about these locations by telegraph, and the bridge-building cadres in the vanguard of the attack would use these locations. Each of the three reconnaissance groups was assigned a dozen infantrymen whose main role was to provide protection in the event the group was discovered and pursued along the way by Austrian ground forces. Antonio and Muffo were assigned to Major Reina's group, which, including engineers, the Bersaglieri and Alpini, totaled twenty-six men. The cherub, Antonio was pleased to note, had been assigned to another group.

After what seemed to Antonio an endless delay, Major Reina and his first sergeant formed their group into two lines and moved out. Without being told, the Bersagliere riflemen—whose very name reflected their reputation as sharpshooters—moved to the head of the line behind Major Reina and his sergeant. Antonio and the other infantrymen composed the middle and rear, intermingled with the engineers and Alpini. Although Antonio had gone on night maneuvers as part of his training in Catanzaro, this first real wartime excursion made him nervous, and as he marched beyond the light of the lanterns he suddenly could see nothing at all. Reaching forward he caught on to the strap of the knapsack of the soldier marching in front of him. For several moments he moved ahead, following the footsteps and rhythm of those before him, gradually becoming aware of the breath of someone behind him grazing his neck, someone who now lightly held on to *his* knapsack. As their eyes slowly adjusted to the darkness, each man let go of the knapsack in front of him and walked naturally behind the leaders along a narrow leafy path through the mountain forest.

The major and the Bersaglieri could occasionally be heard talking softly among themselves, but those in the middle and rear said nothing. Antonio was marching abreast of a moustachioed, hawk-nosed man named Conti, a cabinetmaker from Reggio Calabria who had spent nearly two years as a road worker in Massachusetts under a *padrone*. Antonio had chatted with him briefly during the train ride up the coast, and Conti had appeared then to be a frolicsome, devil-may-care sort of man. He told jokes to the troops standing in the aisle, played in every card game that was formed on the floor, and led in the singing of risqué songs. Conti had also hurled more than his share of cans out along the tracks. But now, during the march, Antonio was aware that Conti carried rosary beads around the butt of his rifle, and that his lips were moving soundlessly.

Marching ahead of Antonio was a big farm boy named Branca, who was born in the southern countryside near the town of Filadelfia, near Maida. Branca carried in his knapsack a sawed-off ox horn, which he had used on the farm to calm his pigs. An inspecting officer had considered confiscating it as the troops boarded the train at Catanzaro, but had relented when Branca argued that it was a good-luck charm and would help him survive the war. Marching next to the hefty Branca was Muffo, who was stockier and a bit taller, and whose jug ears were silhouetted in the moonlight. Both men moved as calmly as if they were escorting a docile herd of cattle through a lush and idyllic meadowland.

The Austrian gunners had been silent since nightfall, but Antonio assumed that they would resume their random bombardments in the morning. He was surprised that he was neither tired nor hungry after his group had marched through its first hour, and then through its second, third, and fourth. During the rest periods, when the troops were allowed to sit along the roadside and sip water from their canteens—but not to eat, smoke, or speak—he remained standing, sustained by nervous energy, too restless to relax. The deeper into the woods they went, the more clearly he could see in the darkness, and the more acute his senses. Above the light rustle of the wind and the soft steps of the soldiers, he heard the sounds of distant crickets and owls, and the scampering of small scavengers through the leafage and brushwood. He assumed there were wolves in these parts, but did not dwell on that thought.

Shortly before dawn, his group arrived along the foothills of the mountain. Here the trees were shorter, the ground moister; and, as they entered the clearing, Antonio caught a glimpse of the river curving below, less than a half-mile away. Major Reina now led the troops in a flanking movement parallel to the river toward a ridge that stood about two hundred yards above the river's western bank and offered concealment from the mountains on the other side. Here they would settle until the major ordered their next move.

As Antonio and the others lowered their knapsacks to the ground behind the ridge, the sergeant passed among them whispering that all of them must begin digging their foxholes at once. Antonio pointed his entrenching tool into the ground and began to shovel as quickly and deeply as he could. But it did not take him long to realize that he was lagging behind everyone else. He felt pains in his arms and his back; his shoulders and hands lacked the strength and whatever finesse was necessary to cut a man-sized hole into the earth as readily as those around him. After a while the other soldiers began to sink from sight, and eventually only the tops of their steel helmets showed above the ground. Frantic and sweating heavily, aware that dawn was emerging and that he would soon be exposed in the daylight, Antonio continued to shovel; but despite his best efforts his hole was only waist-high. It was as if the others had cut through soft sand while he was confronting hard rock. Too proud to seek help, and too exhausted to continue, he tried to burrow into his undersized hole as best he could, crouching down with his knees and elbows bent, and his chin squeezed into his chest; but his bowed back remained conspicuously humped above the hole. Uncomfortable as he was, he remained fixed in this position for several moments, then squirmed slightly as he felt something crawling up his back.

Fearing that it might be a rodent or other alpine animal, and hoping it would go away, he tried not to move; but as the crawling sensation gave way to a harder tap on his shoulders, he slowly turned and looked up. There in the dim light he saw the hulking figure of Muffo leaning over him, motioning for him to get out of the hole. Antonio did so and Muffo crawled into it, and, after a number of powerful pokes with his shovel, the hole became large enough to contain Antonio's entire body. Antonio grabbed his knapsack and slid down. Before he could express his thanks, Muffo had moved back into his own underground retreat.

The troops stood in the dirt, breathing as softly as they could. The sun rose rapidly on the horizon, and with it came the heat, which in time began to bake the men's heavy, damp wool uniforms. Antonio shifted in his foxhole as he felt the sweat on his skin drying beneath his clothes, making him itch and imagine that bugs had penetrated his carefully stitched seams. The day's heat burned on, but still no order was given; and as time blurred imperceptibly, Antonio drifted between sleep and reveries, bomb sounds and mosquito buzzing, while alternately and unconsciously charting the slow arc of the sun as in late afternoon it slid behind the trees. Relieved by the cooling twilight, he reached into his knapsack for his diary. *At any moment,* he wrote, *I think some Austrian in the mountain with a telescope will spot our boot tracks around the ridge, and order that the ridge be blown up. But all morning and afternoon the guns have been firing away from our location. I can't see the mountain across the river because of the ridge. I can see behind me the mountain we came down last night. Some trees at the top of this mountain are on fire from the explosions. Throughout the day I have slapped at mosquitoes and crushed bugs crawling up from the dirt. They feast on the shit in this hole and the crumbs of rations I drop. This afternoon in my knapsack I found the beef sandwich that they gave us when we got off the train. The bread was moldy and the meat was green around the edges. I ate what wasn't green and threw the rest down the hole to the bugs. . . .*

When there were pauses in the explosions, Antonio could hear snoring from some of the foxholes, and an occasional sigh or cough, and the tapping of the little telegraph machine that Major Reina's orderly had carried in a canvas bag through the night. Antonio thought that Major Reina was exchanging messages with the other reconnaissance groups along the river, and with the headquarters of the chief of staff, General Count Luigi Cadorna, far in the rear. Cadorna's father had been a general during the Risorgimento and had led an army against the Pope in 1870, to take over Rome as the national capital. The younger Cadorna, while a successful leader in Italy's recent colonial wars in Africa, had never been spoken of admiringly by any of the veterans Antonio had overheard during the months he had been stationed at Catanzaro. General Count Cadorna was seen as a lofty aristocrat and disciplinarian who was well versed in military history and strategy, but who cared little about the morale of the rank and file and had yet to prove himself as a great commander in any major battle. Now he had close to a million men under his authority in the Italian army—half of whom at this moment were stationed along a four-hundred-mile front that extended from the northwestern corner of Italy, bordering Switzerland, to the northeastern mountains, below Austria, and that included this ridge on the western edge of the Isonzo River, which Antonio's unit was planning to cross.

As the sky darkened and the moon came out, most of the men along the ridge were fast asleep; but then, at about two a.m., a sergeant knocked against Antonio's helmet and told him to wake up. All around him he saw the others climbing out of their holes and shaking the blankets in which they had enclosed themselves against the bugs and dank dirt. The night was still, as the gunners had maintained their usual nocturnal silence, and Antonio slowly realized he had experienced vaguely pleasant dreams while standing up, leaning his head on a small pillow he had made of surplus cotton socks he had taken from a supply room in Catanzaro.

After acknowledging Muffo and Branca, and sipping water from his canteen and daubing some of it on his face, Antonio fell in line with the others and followed Major Reina down a path below the ridge toward the river. Everyone moved cautiously. The intense quiet exceeded the vigilance of the previous evening's march; now not a sound was uttered by anyone. Major Reina led the way with a drawn pistol, surrounded by his elite corpsmen and his sergeant with their rifles and carbines extended; and then came the others with bayonets attached to their rifles, protecting the flanks and the rear. Antonio kept looking to the left and the right as he marched next to Conti, while the two soldiers behind them marched backward. The trepidation that Antonio now felt was prompted not only by the possibility of confronting the Austrians but also by the fact that he would be required to cross the river. He was a product of his family's, and his village's, tradition of hydrophobia. Like nearly everyone he grew up with, Antonio could not swim.

But as the group approached a clearing to the riverbank, Antonio was surprised to see that hundreds of soldiers had already arrived there. Wherever they had come from, they were now busily floating and linking pontoon sections across the narrower parts of the river; and Antonio saw further that one bridge was already operational. Crossing it were riflemen and soldiers escorting horses and mules, with some of the mules pulling two-wheeled carts containing guns and cannons.

Inexplicably, the Austrians who presumably were stationed high in the mountains seemed unaware of the Italians gathered around the river. The Austrian artillerymen surely must have heard the noise echoing from the crossing animals and men, Antonio thought. Either the Austrians up there were deaf, he decided, or they were in the process of moving to lower levels on the mountainside, where their big barrels would soon catch the Italians crowding on the bridges in a crossfire.

Major Reina thrust his pistoled hand in the air and motioned for his troops to follow him on the double toward the one completed bridge. Soon Antonio had wobbled his way over a dozen pontoons, resisting the temptation to grab on to the knapsack of Branca running in front, and finally he landed ankle-deep in mud on the other side. Slogging behind the others up to the dry land where the major stood waiting, Antonio had barely caught his breath when he again saw the major's signal to move forward. This time they climbed along a rocky path, sending small stones tumbling behind them, until they reached a dirt trail that led through the lower woodlands above a ridge into a thick forest. Antonio felt that he was in the same place he had been the night before, except now his group was not alone; it was preceded and followed by other small units on this same trail, as well as units to the left and right who were climbing along parallel trails. He had no idea where they were going; he merely kept pace with Branca, Muffo, and Conti until they were ordered to stop momentarily while the major's telegraph operator wired some information to the other advancing units or to the commanders in the rear. Then they were moving again, higher up the fir-forested mountainside, and *still* there were no bombardments from the enemy perched on the highest peaks.

At daybreak, shortly before six, when Austria's long-range guns commenced their activity, the gunners continued as previously to shell far to the west, lofting their explosives high over the heads of Antonio's group and the other units gradually making their way up under the barrels of the

Austrian artillerymen. Antonio sensed that he was indeed part of a surprise attack, that the Austrians did not yet know of the Italian presence in the thick cover of trees beneath their noses. Antonio also believed, however, that it was just a matter of time before they would come face to face with the enemy.

Less than an hour later, after proceeding cautiously up through the woods, Antonio's group came upon a small village in a clearing close to the edge of a cliff. It was a charming village with a dozen white stone chalets along a curved cobblestone street, and on the corner was an inn with red shutters and a rooftop porch that had a flagpole without a flag. On the other side of the street was a row of small shops, a few stables and barns, and, at the far end, behind a campanile, a stream that fell a few hundred feet from an upper cliff into a granite basin before spilling over the mountainside. While the shops were padlocked, some of the doors and windows of the houses and the inn, and the gates to the barn, were open, and goats and other animals wandered wherever they wished. There were no villagers in sight.

Crouched close to the ground, Major Reina and his Bersaglieri, joined by elite troops from two other reconnaissance patrols, surrounded the village; after tossing hand grenades into the doorways of some of the buildings, and even into one of the windows of the inn, hoping to drive out any snipers who might be posted inside, the Italians charged through the doors with their rifles extended, ready to shoot. But there was no one to shoot at.

All the buildings had been evacuated. It was evident, however, that they had been lived in until quite recently. In the kitchens the troops found fresh fruit and vegetables, and leftovers that had been cooked during the previous night or even this morning; and some of the cinders in the fireplaces were still warm. Despite the damage and disarray caused by the grenades, most of the rooms retained signs of their proprietor's up-to-date care and orderliness. The floors had been swept, the beds had been made, the kettles scrubbed, the firewood neatly stacked. It was as if the inhabitants of these remote villages, unaware of the war, had been expecting houseguests, perhaps the tourists or other lodgers who normally rented rooms while on mountain-climbing or hunting expeditions.

Except for helping themselves to the food, and capturing pigs to be roasted later at their camp in the woods, the Italian soldiers adhered to the military policy against pilferage; there was little of monetary value to be found, anyway. There were nonetheless so many personal items and articles left behind—family photographs, letters, eyeglasses, medicines, keys—that there was little doubt about the villagers' hasty departure.

As Antonio toured one house he saw on a bureau a framed photograph of a handsome soldier wearing an Austrian uniform, with an arm tightly around a young blond woman who was kissing him on the lips. The couple had posed in front of the house that Antonio now stood in, but in the photograph there was snow on the ground, and icicles hanging from the roof eaves—uncommon sights to Antonio—and he imagined that the soldier had been here during a furlough last Christmas, perhaps visiting from the Russian front, where the Austrians were then heavily engaged, or from a unit stationed atop this very mountain. As Antonio indulged his curiosity by opening the drawers and looking in the armoires, he saw only the young woman's clothing and shoes; there was nothing anywhere in the house that belonged to a man. The couple who had appeared so intimate in the photograph were not married, Antonio concluded, and because of the war they might never be.

In another house, while browsing through a bookshelf, Antonio noticed an Italian history book written by an Austrian professor, in Italian; he leafed through it and saw negative references to the Risorgimento, to Garibaldi, and to other men who had been portrayed as heroes by Antonio's teachers. Intrigued by this alternative view of history, Antonio was tempted to tuck the book into his knapsack and keep it for later reading; but he decided he had better approach Major Reina outside and get permission to confiscate it.

The major, who was standing in the sun talking with the Bersaglieri, gave a perfunctory look at the volume Antonio held before him, and told him he could have it. Major Reina was in a very agreeable mood. He had just wired his superiors that he had taken over the Austrian village without any opposition whatsoever, and he had reason to believe that the enemy troops atop the mountain might have fled behind the civilians. The Austrian guns had been strangely silent along the peaks ever since the Italians had swarmed into the village. Perhaps they had lacked sufficient manpower up there, or had run out of ammunition. In any case Major Reina thought it was a perfect time to move boldly to the top; and after discussing his strategy with the Bersagliere officers, the major told his sergeant to assemble the troops so that he could make his announcement.

The Italian troops at this time were still ambling around the village, enjoying the novelty of moving unguardedly in the daylight and basking in whatever glory accompanied an unchallenged triumph. Many soldiers were gathered near the spring, splashing water on their faces, rinsing their shirts, and some were even jumping naked into the shallow water for a bath or a short swim. Muffo and Branca were wallowing in the water, and Antonio, after slipping his book into a compartment of his knapsack, wandered over to join them. It was not quite noon, the sun was burning brightly over the snowcapped mountains, and the sergeant had not yet blown his whistle.

Slipping off his knapsack and unbuttoning his shirt, Antonio watched his naked friends for a moment, enjoying the sight of the fun they were having as the water cascaded over their laughing faces and flailing arms; and since the water was only waist-deep, Antonio confidently prepared for what would be another affront to his hydrophobia. But as he was about to climb over a granite ledge into the basin, the water suddenly stopped coming down; a barricade of timber had been laid. Antonio and the others looked up, squinting in the sun. There, at the top of the cliff, a few hundred feet above their heads, was a row of helmeted enemy soldiers with guns, their view now unimpeded.

Then the bullets and grenades rained down, and explosions blasted through the water, setting off flying rocks and clouds of smoke streaked with yellow flame. As the Italians hurled themselves screaming out of the basin, tumbled to the ground, and raced for cover toward the forest, Antonio ran behind them—but not before he had seen Muffo and Branca disappear into the basin, their bodies riddled with bullets, darkening the color of the water that trickled over the mountainside.

25.

T HE SURPRISE ATTACK that killed Muffo, Branca, and two other soldiers in Antonio's unit and injured half a dozen more was one of many setbacks suffered by Italian reconnaissance patrols in the early summer of 1915; and things only worsened in the weeks and months ahead, as the big battles began—battles characterized by the attempts of thousands of mountain-climbing Italians to scale the strategic peaks and topple the enemy perched along the jagged and crusty four-hundred-mile front. But it soon became apparent that more Italians were being shot down than were charging up, and the casualty figures at the end of the year shocked the nation. More than 62,000 Italian soldiers were dead, 170,000 were injured, and Italy had nothing to show for it except mortification and grief. The Austrians still controlled the dominant cliffs, and there was no reason to believe that this situation would change.

This is not what Italians had expected when the country entered the war in May 1915. At that time Italy's involvement was seen as a limited adventure, not unlike the recent campaign in Libya, with much to gain and little to lose. It was believed that Austria, already at war with Serbia in the Balkans and with Russia on its eastern front, would offer scant resistance along its southern borders to the encroaching Italians. Italian strategists, however, had underrated the Austrian army's strength and tenacity; and now after the unanticipated bloodshed there were angry debates in the Italian parliament, protests in towns and villages, and calls for the resignation of the Italian commander, General Count Cadorna.

But General Cadorna refused to blame himself or his staff entirely for the depressing turn of events. It had been the politicians, not he, who had drawn Italy into this war; and the war he had inherited had forced his inexperienced young troops into uphill battles whenever they ventured into enemy territory, while the inadequate supply of Italian weaponry and ammunition lent an added edge to the better-equipped Austrians. Italy's industrial capacity, even at maximum efficiency, was no match for Austria allied with Germany (Italy had no coal, and before the war had relied extensively on Germany for hardware and machinery); and contributing to the low morale of Italian fighting men, General Cadorna believed, was the antiwar propaganda of the nation's Socialists and other unpatriotic citizens who were spreading dissension and doubt.

Among the general's doubters, however, were several of his own senior officers and veteran soldiers. They often saw him as a pawn of the other Allied commanders, a man who had needlessly sacrificed troops in risky assaults against the Austrians in response to the wishes of his high-ranking colleagues. But the French and British had also suffered heavy losses on the western front, as had the Russians on the eastern front; and the last thing these nations wanted, especially since their Serbian allies had seemingly gone into hibernation in the Balkans, was an unaggressive Italian army taking the pressure off the enemy along the southern border of Austria. Still, with nearly a quarter of a million Italians out of action in 1915 without achieving a single important object, General Cadorna's wisdom as a leader was certainly open to question; and many Italian soldiers were also disturbed by persistent rumors of unfair conscription policies on the home front that permitted able-bodied young men, primarily from privileged families, to avoid the draft by getting jobs in the much-needed munitions industries. These men were denounced at the front as *imboscati*—shirkers.

As the war continued to go badly in 1916, and as resentment grew against the increasing numbers of *imboscati,* many troops refused to fight, feigning mental illness or various ailments that excused them from front-line duty; and some soldiers even shot themselves in the legs to avoid what they saw as the ceaseless and almost callous annihilation of the underprivileged. While Antonio remained at the front during this time, rejoining the Forty-eighth Infantry Battalion after his shattered reconnaissance team had been disbanded—he was among the lucky few to escape the attack without injury—he did share the sentiments of the most disgruntled foot soldiers. Like him, a majority of these malcontents were conscripts from the rural areas of the south; and it seemed to them—and published reports later confirmed their suspicions—that the southern boys were being disproportionately victimized by the war because, lacking the influence to gain a fair share of the deferments or rearguard assignments, they were the most exposed to battle. The young men from the north, on the other hand, on the average better educated and more literate than southerners, were viewed by their commanders (who were predominantly northern-born) as more qualified for clerical jobs and other rearline military assignments. And since Italy's industrial enterprises, insufficient as they proved to be in the early part of the war, were located mostly in the north, the jobs there and the deferments went more often to northern men.

Thus the Italian army was divided as the nation itself was divided. The unification of Italy more than a half-century before had failed to unite the south with the north; and southerners like Antonio felt no more assimilated nationally in 1916 than had his grandfather Domenico in 1861 after the Risorgimento and the fall of the Bourbons.

In Antonio's letters home, and in his diary, he expressed his complaints and those of his fellow soldiers. He told of seeing many *imboscati* during his brief furloughs in northern cities, men strolling merrily through the streets and sitting contentedly in the cafés. These "vital" workers, he commented sourly, earned five times more than the troops risking life and limb at the front. Worse, he pointed out, Italy's war industry was producing much defective equipment. Shells failed to explode. Small amounts of mud could jam a rifle. The grenade launchers quickly overheated, and sometimes blew up the soldiers who were doing the loading and firing.

Heavy rains made swamps of what limited flatland existed between the mountains, and the Italian cavalry was virtually useless as a fighting force. Antonio described proud equestrian officers, their boots and riding breeches submerged in mud, holding on to the tails of their horses while crossing the swamps; and he repeated an often quoted line used by one senior officer to describe the Italian infantry: "Pieces of walking mud." This phrase, which appeared in Italian newspapers, had offended General Cadorna, and he criticized the officer who had said it. But although General Cadorna raised barriers against the press and instituted censorship over the soldiers' mail, he was unable to halt the increasing number of demonstrations against the war by the unhappy families of servicemen.

While Antonio saw the war from the vantage point of a southerner—in his view, everything above Naples was north—there were also under-privileged families in northern and central Italy with relatives in the army who fought side by side with southerners and endured every hardship with a similar sense of weariness and wrath. There were citizens' antiwar protests in Mantua, Florence, and other northern and central cities. Protests in the south, however, seemed more frequent and more passionate. Southern leftist leaders could point to the war as yet another example of the south's being sucked dry by the north. It was the old class struggle—the powerful profiting at the expense of the powerless; the urban bour-geoisie being favored over the rural poor. Government administrators were more efficient with their pension and private assistance programs in the cities than in the countryside; but their efficiency noticeably im-proved in the rural areas when it came to forcing the sale of livestock, and requisitioning timber, and drafting farm workers to meet the needs of the war. Widowed women with young children were often left to operate large farms by themselves, with unfortunate results. There was a marked increase in soldiers' mutinies in such outposts as Catanzaro; and in such villages as Maida, there were nightly rallies against the war, and ultimately a riot in which young Joseph participated.

It erupted on a Sunday evening in the early spring of 1916. Although the riot was led by Socialist leaders who were not residents of the village, it was widely supported by the local people, and among the most actively involved were pre-draft-age teenagers from Maida who had been re-cruited into the Young Socialists club. Joseph, who was not yet thirteen, had been brought into the group by a politically engaged older cousin of his mother's who had been drawn back by the draft from a job in America with Keasbey & Mattison Company. Neither Joseph's mother nor his grandfather Domenico contradicted his leftist politicization; even local churchmen, who during the previous year had preached in favor of national obedience, now voiced no objections to the Socialists' war policies. Five of Maida's native sons had already died at the front—five of the original thirteen who had been called up with Antonio—and three others had been seriously wounded. And the Talese household's opposition to the war was additionally influenced by the fact that Joseph's brother Sebastian, who had recently turned seventeen, had received his notification to report at once to Catanzaro for military training.

Both his mother and his grandfather had visited the municipal building to protest to the recruitment office, and his uncle Francesco Cristiani had traveled to Catanzaro to appeal to the review board at the army base, emphasizing that Sebastian was needed on the farm and was the main support of his widowed mother, who had four younger dependent children. But the army desperately needed troops, and no exception was made for Sebastian.

A week after the conscription of Sebastian and a dozen of his Maida contemporaries, a particularly rancorous nocturnal rally was held in the square, drawing a large crowd carrying torches and also some shotguns. When one speaker suggested that everyone march on the municipal building and burn the town records, which the military consulted for conscription purposes, loud cheers greeted the proposal, and soon more than three hundred individuals paraded through the narrow streets toward the dark stone structure some blocks from the square, singing, shouting slogans, and blasting out overhead lamps along the way. Oddly, there were no police posted to block their path, nor had there been any on patrol in the square. Joseph, following the example of other marchers, picked up stones along the road and hurled them up at the streetlights, and later also toward the windows of the municipal building, where again there were no guards—even though the precinct house was a few doors away, lights glowing within but the officers on duty seemingly deaf to the hue and cry of the crowd. It was obvious that *nobody* in town wanted to prevent the upheaval, and that the dissenters represented every level of local society. There was the principal Don Achille; the butcher Nicholas Pileggi; the stonemason Nicola Muscatelli (recently returned from America); the chemist Dr. Fabiani; the aristocrat Don Torquato; and also Padre Panella (the child he had supposedly fathered was now rumored to be in the care of a neighboring nunnery). There was the poet Ciccio Parisi; Lena Rotella, who ran the orphanage; the spinster Nina Bevivino, grandniece of the late, lamented Antonio Bevivino (who got a hole in his head while fighting under Murat on the Russian front in 1812); and the shepherd Guardacielo, accompanied by his dog wearing a collar studded with steel spikes. There were Joseph's uncle Francesco Cristiani; Joseph's maternal grandfather, Sebastian Rocchino (Joseph's paternal grandfather and the women of the Talese family were attending the nightly Mass); and Joseph's fellow Young Socialists: fourteen-year-old Nicholas Pileggi, one of the butcher's sons; fifteen-year-old Francesco LaScala, who worked after school in his grandfather's carriage repair shop; sixteen-year-old Gino Giglio, the blacksmith's grandson and a recent school dropout, who grimly awaited his draft call; and sixteen-year-old Giuseppe Paone, a student and vegetable vendor who, despite being cross-eyed, feared that he would be acceptable to the Italian army.

All these and more gathered unchallenged around the municipal building, continuing to sing and chant while the leaders broke down the door, then smashed open the filing cabinets containing the birth records, and soon set everything ablaze. By the time the police and firemen had finally appeared, striving as best they could to look surprised and disturbed, the interior of the building was a furnace of black smoke and extinguished data, and the crowd had suddenly vanished. Three of the area's best-known Socialists were arrested for questioning the next day; insufficient evidence as well as insufficient interest resulted in their early release. Military inspectors from Catanzaro arrived in Maida swearing vengeance, but there was little they could do except search out duplicate birth records from the provincial clerk's office, or from the bishopric, and issue statements demanding that civilian subversives be punished in the manner that the army was now using for disloyal soldiers.

No less than 167 soldiers were executed for committing mutiny and other acts of insubordination in 1916. This was a hundred-man increase over the number shot for similar offenses in 1915. Appalled by the ongoing violations of patriotic duty, General Cadorna endorsed the execution of 359 soldiers in 1917, but he still did not get the results he desired. The army of 1917 was no better than the army of 1916.

There were many Italian soldiers who fought heroically, but their valor was likely due less to discipline or patriotism than to what had always motivated men in danger—the will to survive. All combative nations forced their young men to bear arms, to confront one another and live or die on the battlefield; and some lived, some died, and some ran. The determining factor had little to do with national propaganda or love of country, and much to do with good eyesight, fast triggers, and trench loyalty. The men who fought hard did so to save themselves and their buddies. The number of miles gained in battle was almost incidental, though usually gratifying. But for every mile gained by the Italians, their route being primarily uphill and perilous, thousands were killed or maimed, and those who survived rarely understood why they were fighting, except to survive. The ground gained was mostly rocky and infertile. Italy already had enough mountains without seizing more from Austria. If Italian soldiers could have imagined that they often risked their lives for territory that in future decades would be most suitable for ski resorts, their patriotic zeal, such as it was, would have diminished further.

Still, in 1916 and 1917, Italian soldiers were ordered uphill, again and again; and those who disobeyed were often executed, and those who obeyed were often cut down by enemy howitzers or machine guns, or by rock slides caused by bombardments, or by avalanches of snow that buried and froze them until spring—when their corpses would be discovered along the melting mountainsides, stiffened in the same positions and attitudes that they had assumed as they perished.

Soldiers advancing across mountain streams often stepped on bodies of men who had drowned there weeks and months before; and when food and ammunition were sent by cable car to units fighting on the peaks, the perforated containers of the *teleferica* would usually return carrying dead or wounded soldiers, their blood reddening the ropes, their bodies swaying in the sky and inviting additional target practice from Austrian riflemen crouched along the cliffs.

Unrestricted German submarine warfare sank many Allied ships transporting supplies desperately needed by the Italian nation; and the bread riots of Italian women on the home front, no less than an Austrian assault north of Lombardy and continued political bickering in Rome, caused the frustrated Antonio Salandra to resign as prime minister and brought renewed cries for the ouster of Cadorna.

But the Italian army's ability to drive out the Austrians in the north, and also to move eastward and capture the fortress city of Gorizia, temporarily saved the career of the general, even though he continued to subject his units to massive losses. More than 90,000 Italians were killed and wounded in the campaign north of Lombardy—a casualty figure forty percent higher than that of the Austrians. The taking of Gorizia, east of the Isonzo River, resulted in 48,000 Italian deaths and injuries, more than double the total for the Austrians. One Italian injured at Gorizia was Antonio Cristiani.

Antonio was knocked unconscious by the explosions around the trench in which he and his fellow infantrymen were gathered, about to join an uphill charge. His friend Conti, with whom he had served in the reconnaissance patrol, was killed in this barrage of machine-gun fire, mortars and heavy artillery. Bleeding from internal injuries caused by shattered rocks and bits of shrapnel, Antonio was carried by two soldiers into a medical station in a cave, and was then transported downhill via *teleferica* to a wagon crowded with fallen troops bound for the base hospital. There he slowly recovered from his wounds and the concussion, high fevers, and, later, pneumonia; during several weeks of convalescence, in which he regularly drifted in and out of consciousness, he saw dozens of soldiers dying around him, soldiers who prior to death received an ersatz form of extreme unction from crucifix-bearing medics in dark suits impersonating priests.

There were never enough clergymen in the battle zones to administer the last rites to those with fatal injuries, and during much of the war the Vatican seemed tentative about the secular role it should play with the two belligerent Catholic nations. If Pope Benedict XV was privately partial to the Austrians, as many Catholics on both sides suggested, it was perhaps understandable, given the contrast between the Hapsburg crown's history of homage to the Church and the seizure of the Papal States by the Italian leaders of the Risorgimento—led by the Pope-baiting Garibaldi. Even the passage of nearly fifty years had failed to heal the rift between the Italian government and the Vatican. The papacy had yet to recognize officially the nation of Italy.

By the late summer of 1917, however, as more and more Catholic soldiers on both sides continued to die, to the detriment of the Church's international solidarity as well as its numerical strength, Benedict XV finally did speak out against the war and volunteered to mediate a peace based "not on violence but on reason." But Italy would declare war on Germany, which Austria had summoned for assistance after the Italian capture of Gorizia; and the Germans in 1917 were in no mood to stop a war they thought they could win. While the United States had recently joined the Allies, the Germans believed that the Anglo-French forces on the western front would collapse before the American presence in Europe could save them—the British, for example, had suffered nearly six hundred thousand casualties in the Passchendaele offensive; for every yard of ground gained, fifty-six British soldiers were killed or wounded—and on the eastern front the Russian army was stalled by combat fatigue and undermined by the armistice-seeking Bolsheviks, who were rising to political power in the wake of the czar's abdication. If the Pope's peace initiative, made public in August 1917, had any influence on the war, it was probably to the disadvantage of General Cadorna, for it provided Italian men who had no stomach for battle with an added excuse for laying down their arms. This was particularly true among soldiers from the south and Sicily, where the influence of the Church was strongest, and where even heretics and agnostics now might attribute their desertion or draft-dodging to a belated spark of religiosity.

So the Italian army's sick list became longer in the war zones, while the number of mutineers and deserters increased at the front and at training bases around the nation (in Sicily alone there were twenty thousand military insurrectionists); and there was little General Cadorna could do except continue his policy of executions, which he did, and make life so miserable for the ambulatory but allegedly ill rearline troops that they soon would welcome the front as an escape from the excruciating labor and demeaning drudgery that he summarily ordered upon them.

Since Antonio was legitimately incapacitated and hospitalized during this period, he was not subjected to such attention; and as a consequence, in October 1917 he avoided the possibility of being sent to Caporetto. In this he was fortunate. For the battle of Caporetto would prove to be Italy's most horrible and humiliating experience of the entire war.

It began early in the morning on October 24, a day of thick mist and heavy rain that on the mountaintops was turning to snow. The town of Caporetto was situated along the upper part of the Isonzo River, far north of where the Italian and Austrian armies had conducted most of their mountain and waterside warfare in the previous twenty-nine months. General Cadorna had not been expecting a big attack in the vicinity of Caporetto, believing that the narrowness of the land between the mountains, and the difficulty in crossing the river, which in those parts flows in a deep gorge, would make a powerful widespread thrust by the enemy impractical and unlikely. So he left it minimally defended, and the Italian troops he posted there were generally exhausted and undermotivated. Many had seen considerable combat in the past and had not received furloughs in nearly a year.

A number of soldiers in these units were Socialists, it was later rumored, a few of whom had actually sneaked over into the enemy camp and fraternized with Austrian Socialists; and such men were said to have spread subversive propaganda within their ranks to escalate disobedience and sabotage the war effort. The Italian troops were reminded that their nation had been the aggressor against Austria; unlike France and Belgium, Italy had not been invaded, and yet in 1915 it had violated the northern borders and initiated hostilities against the Austrians.

In any case, the war had now gone on too long; on this point most soldiers could agree. Many Italians had actually thought the war would end four or five weeks before, in mid-September 1917, as their officers had optimistically predicted, after General Cadorna's attacking forces had captured the Bansizza Plateau, south of Caporetto along the Isonzo. But this triumph of dubious significance, which was also the *eleventh* extensive clash between the two armies in the area since the war began, brought peace no closer and cost the Italians 40,000 dead and 108,000 wounded. The futility of their efforts in the Bansizza campaign had a demoralizing effect on the surviving Italian troops in the autumn of 1917, and doubtless was a factor in the lack of esprit de corps that characterized their performance against the retaliating Austrians and their German allies at Caporetto.

On the eve of the attack, on the high ridges that the Austrians controlled miles below the peaks of the Julian Alps northeast of the Isonzo, the Germans made the final preparations for the launching of 894 projectiles containing poison gas, a mixture of phosgene and chlorine that they intended to lob upon the Italian contingents controlling Caporetto. For weeks the Germans had been slipping down quietly into this area from the highlands behind them, and at the time of the attack six German divisions had joined seven Austrian divisions to form the new Fourteenth German Army, under the command of Germany's General Otto von Below, who had been transferred from the western front.

The Italian failure to detect this buildup was due to its insufficient air reconnaissance as well as to the adroit precautions of the enemy; and the fact that the attack itself caught the Italians completely by surprise can be attributed to the heavy mist that prevailed on the morning of October 24. The Italians could not see what was coming until it was too late to respond to it effectively; and they were not only outnumbered but ill equipped to combat the gas brigades who exploded shells all around them. Hundreds of Italians died within seconds. Thousands of others retreated in panic, struggling for breath while trapped between the river and high slopes of the mountain that prevented the gas from dissipating. Even those Italians wearing gas masks did not survive. Either the respirators malfunctioned, or other aspects of the design proved to be vulnerable to the lethal compound spread by the Germans. Although chemical warfare had been used on the western front by the Anglo-French forces as well as the Germans, this was Italy's first experience with it in battle, and countless Italians died in a state of delirious bewilderment.

General von Below's army meanwhile penetrated Caporetto, not only overwhelming the Italian frontline with gas, machine guns, and artillery, but routing the second line as well, and thus nullifying the Italians' capacity to counterattack and also to communicate, since the telephone system was totally destroyed. The commanding officer whom General Cadorna had placed in charge of the area had left his post four days before the assault because of illness, but the single fact of his absence or presence mattered little against the combination of factors that thwarted the Italians. They were largely beaten from the start. The men were tired and apathetic, underarmed and underfed—the latter conditions exacerbated by the Germans' submarine success against Allied shipping into Italy.

Spearheading the Caporetto invasion were blitzkrieg specialists, elite German troops recently trained in ground tactics that were novel in their ferocity, and that would prove equally effective against Italy's allies the next year on the western front near Saint-Quentin. The front-running Germans at Caporetto had been selected for their speed, stamina, and steadfastness. They would race boldly ahead and create havoc with their blasting guns while their opponents were still swooning and choking from the gas. Supporting the German advance guard were heavy rear guns that fulminated deafeningly, but at short range and for limited lengths of time; the artillerymen wished to shatter the defenders without unduly destroying the terrain and scorching the atmosphere and the surroundings through which the fleet German frontline would soon be passing. Speed and surprise, not heavy and continuous bombardment, were favored in this strategy. The main mission of the forging units was to move ahead unhesitatingly and to penetrate deeply, to level whatever opposition stood in front of them, but *not* to widen the attack, or to mop up those staggered defenders who might be lingering along the sidelines, or to engage the Italian soldiers who might be shooting down from the nearby hills. This would be the responsibility of the masses of regular Austro-German infantry who were moving quickly behind, providing the knockout punch to the wider surface that had been cut through the middle by their predecessors.

As a result of these tactics many Italian soldiers stationed in the hills suddenly saw the enemy in front *and* behind, and their ability to defend themselves depended on the amount of ammunition they had with them in the highlands. Since they were cut off from added sources of supply, and frequently cut off as well from telephone contact with their superiors, they were left in perplexed isolation and chaos. This had been the fate of several Alpino units who, before the seizure of Caporetto, believed they could dominate the area from their higher vantage point. But with the startling appearance of the German vanguard pouncing through the misty morning, followed by the regular infantry advancing behind clouds of flying bullets and floating poison, the marooned Alpini found themselves desperately on the defensive. They fought as long and as courageously as they could. After their ammunition ran out, they hurled rocks down upon the Austro-German soldiers who were climbing up to eliminate them. Finally the Italians were reduced to fighting with knives and rifle butts. Such deterrents against their heavily armed pursuers, however, were futile. The Alpini died almost to a man.

Those Italians who did not die on the hills or on the plateau from bullets, shell blasts, or gas—and who did not abandon their units, or join them in the orderly retreat that General Cadorna was compelled to command—usually surrendered to the enemy quickly and compliantly, happy to be alive. Territory that had taken the Italians two years to conquer, including the town of Gorizia, was lost within hours as the breakthrough at Caporetto soon destabilized the entire Italian front. General Cadorna could not push up reserve troops from the rear because the narrow roads between the mountains ahead were jammed with retreating troops and pack animals, trucks and ambulances. The frantic and uncontrollable scene would be re-created by Ernest Hemingway in his novel *A Farewell to Arms.* Von Below's army overran the Italian military headquarters at Udine, west of the Isonzo, five days after the invaders' initial drive. King Victor Emmanuel III had often traveled from his villa outside Udine to visit the Italian front in happier days, early in the war—"the King pass[es] in his motor car . . . his face and little long necked body and gray beard like a goat's chin tuft," wrote Hemingway—but he was long gone from the ancient city as the Austro-Germans arrived on October 29, having crossed the path that had been used some fourteen centuries before by Attila and his Hun warriors on their way to burn and plunder Aquileia and other Roman cities on the Venetian plains. In fact, many injured but uncaptured Italians later claimed that as von Below's ferocious troops crushed through their line, they were shouting loudly and in unison: *"Roma! Roma! Roma!"*

By the end of the month, the German vanguard had gotten twenty miles past Udine and driven Cadorna's defenders back to the Tagliamento River. Nearly 40,000 Italians had already been killed or wounded, and 250,000 had been taken prisoner. One young German lieutenant leading an attacking unit had himself captured 8,000 Italians in a single day, while his unit suffered less than a dozen casualties in the whole campaign. His name was Erwin Rommel. The fleeing Italians left twenty-five hundred artillery pieces in place, and tons of food and clothing supplies. Much of what had not been sunk earlier by German submarines now fell into the hands of the German foot soldiers entering abandoned depots. In Rome, angry politicians in parliament demanded and accepted the resignation of the man who the year before had replaced Salandra as prime minister—Paolo Boselli, whom one colleague described as heading "the ministry of weakness simulating strength." Boselli was replaced by the minister of the interior, Vittorio Emanuele Orlando, who had been christened in honor of the current king's grandfather, the crown head of the Risorgimento. Trying to bring unity and revive discipline in a nation stunned by defeat and despair, King Victor Emmanuel III urged in a public statement: "Citizens and soldiers, be a single army. All cowardice is treachery, all discord is treachery." The poet Gabriele D'Annunzio, and the Milan newspaper editor he so profoundly influenced, Benito Mussolini, expressed similar sentiments. Mussolini, Socialist turned interventionist, had served in the army until February 1917—when, while operating a faulty grenade thrower during a training exercise, he killed five of his fellow soldiers and was hospitalized with forty fragments. Released from the army, he resumed editing *Il Popolo d'Italia;* and with the continued failings at the front after the fall of Caporetto, he increased his denunciation of the quality of the army's leaders and the disloyalty fomented at home by his former companions the Socialists. What Italy needed, in his private view, was not a squabbling, impotent parliament but rather a single powerful figure, a dictator who could militarize the nation and restore pride to the Italian people.

But no pride would be evident through the first week of November, fourteen days after the beginning of the blitzkrieg. The war news continued to be disastrous. Of Italy's original army of sixty-five divisions, only thirty-three were now militarily functional. Although the French would send six divisions to the Italian front in reaction to Caporetto, and the British five, nobody knew exactly what to do with these troops when they finally arrived. There was no organized plan of cooperation among the Italian, French, and British officers in the field, and as a result the incoming troops were not integrated into Italy's frontline resistance.

Seeing the inadequacies of his army in correlation with his ever-declining opinion of the Italian officer corps, General Cadorna continued to downgrade or dismiss his commissioned subordinates. He would evict no fewer than 217 generals and 255 colonels in the course of the war. But on November 7—the day the Kerensky government fell to Lenin's Bolsheviks in Russia—General Cadorna himself was dismissed by the new prime minister. Cadorna was replaced by General Armando Diaz, who had been born in Naples and was respected as both a military leader and a man who could communicate with the common soldier. But the war situation was gloomier than ever. The battered Italian army had been driven back more than seventy-five miles since the assault on Caporetto. It was now lined up behind the Piave River, with General Otto von Below's forces charging forth from the other side. The attackers were now less than twenty miles from Venice.

But as one military historian, paraphrasing Samuel Johnson, wrote: "Nothing concentrates the mind like the imminent prospect of being hanged." The Italian army and its nation, which had for weeks been disgraced by inept officers and men, and by a disgruntled but insufficiently supportive citizenry, and which now seemed on the verge of surrender, suddenly established the Piave River as the locale of a dramatic turnabout, a point from which Italy would retreat no further.

26.

RELEASED FROM THE hospital in early December 1917, Antonio Cristiani hitched a ride to Milan and walked through the crowded corridor of the main railroad terminal toward a southbound train that would bring him home in time for Christmas. It would be his first visit back to Maida in more than two and a half years. He had tried to inform his family that he was coming, but he doubted they had received his wire. There were few enough telegraph offices in the south, and all were currently overburdened with the handling of top-priority messages of the sort he was thankful the government was not sending in his behalf.

Yet reminders of death and tragedy were everywhere around him now as he continued along the stone floor under a high ceiling amid the sounds of whistles and hissing steam. Caskets were stacked at loading ramps. Groups of tearful civilians dressed in black lingered along the platforms. Hundreds of bandaged soldiers, many moving with the aid of canes, crutches, or wheelchairs, proceeded slowly within the lines of passengers headed toward dozens of trains bound for every part of Italy.

Carrying a small duffel bag, Antonio climbed the steel steps and entered a car in which all the seats were taken and some people were standing in the aisle. Except for two nuns and a half-dozen elderly people dressed entirely in black, the car was totally occupied by young soldiers in gray-green uniforms. Several windows were open, but there was a pervasive smell of disinfectant, medicine, and sweaty woolen fabric. The bandages wrapped around some soldiers' heads were slightly bloodstained. Many pairs of crutches lay horizontally along the overhead baggage racks on both sides of the car. As each newly arrived soldier entered, he was met with discreet glances that appraised his condition. If he seemed too disabled to stand or balance himself on an armrest in the aisle, a seated soldier who was less infirm would rise and offer to exchange places. Even the elderly women and nuns tried to yield seats to ailing servicemen. Except in the cases of the severely injured, the women were politely refused. Never was a crowded railcar more abundant with courtesy and concern.

Antonio made his way slowly up the aisle and stood in the rear next to a metal door that, as the train began to move, resounded with a loose chain banging against it from the outside. Near him stood three other apparently healthy servicemen. One was an airman, the others artillerymen. After greeting one another briefly, they stood in awkward silence for several moments as the train pulled out of the station and daylight streamed in to make more obvious than before the extent of the injuries suffered by many of the passengers. Half of the legs stretched out in the aisle bore casts or metal braces secured with leather straps. At least a third of the seated servicemen had cloth bands knotted around their necks to support the slings that held their damaged or partially amputated arms. There were a few groans now and then from soldiers in pain, and Antonio was reminded of his time in the hospital. He thought of Muffo, Branca, and Conti. The engineer moved the train very slowly, as if stalling for time until the soldiers' tender flesh could become adjusted to the motion.

The airman standing with Antonio suddenly became quite talkative. He was a stocky round-faced man in his mid-twenties with a trim moustache and a cap that was too small for his head. He announced he was from Avellino, near Naples. He had served in the air force for two years and was part of the ground crew, not a flier. He said that he could fly planes very well, but that his instructors, all of them from Genoa, had given him failing grades whenever he took the pilot's examination. In his voice there was little doubt that he had failed because he was not from Genoa. He had most recently been stationed at an air base near Udine that had been shelled and captured by Austro-German troops after the breakthrough at Caporetto. During the past summer, he said, he had helped fuel the squadron that Gabriele D'Annunzio had led to bomb the Austrian port of Pola in the Adriatic. The Austrians had placed a price of twenty thousand crowns upon the poet's head, the airman said, but he added that they would never catch him alive. As the airman continued to talk about D'Annunzio's heroics and the war in general, Antonio and the two artillerymen mostly listened. One of the latter, who held on to his companion's arm whenever the train took a sharp turn, listened intently while staring fixedly into space. Antonio soon realized that the man was blind.

The slow-moving ten-car train stopped at every station, and at each station one or two servicemen hobbled off. By the time the train arrived in Livorno, along the Tyrrhenian Sea, there were enough empty spaces in Antonio's car for him and the other standees to sit down. Antonio sat next to a skinny eighteen-year-old who had lost his right leg below the knee during the big battle *before* Caporetto, the one on the Bansizza Plateau, when General Cadorna had been in command. The young soldier, who was returning home to his village just north of Naples, said that half the people in his unit had been killed by Austrian artillery, and that he had survived probably because the stray horse of a dead cavalry officer had fallen on him during an explosion—crushing his right leg, but protecting the rest of his body from the destructive impact of the shell.

After a night in which many passengers remained awake to the sounds of one another's nightmares and physical suffering, the train pulled jerkily to a stop at yet another station. The sign bearing the name of the station was so weatherworn that Antonio could not read the lettering. In the middle of the platform, several feet from the track, stood three military policemen and hundreds of civilians of all ages, two-thirds of them women, straining against ropes trying to get a closer view of the troops seated in the train. Since the train had left Milan, every station had been jammed with people who apparently had received word that a spouse, son, or other relative would be returning home from the front during the day or night. Never knowing precisely on which train the persons expected would be traveling, the crowd waited with rising anticipation and hope as each train came and went. Every town's station house was now the site of around-the-clock vigils, a place where people congregated for hours, noisily or in silence, until some among them yelled that they heard a whistle in the distance, or saw the smoke of a locomotive rising above a hill. Then all the others would hurry out to the platform, their heads all facing northward, their eyes transfixed upon the narrowing gauge of the tracks as they wondered if the train they had yet to see was the one they were waiting for.

People had been known to become uncontrollable in such gatherings.

Newspapers had recently reported that the mothers of two returning servicemen, overly eager to greet the train they assumed was carrying their sons safely home, tripped while running along the platform and died after hitting the tracks.

As a result of such incidents, the crowds were now cordoned off at all stations and overseen by the military police and local authorities. But Antonio could see that the police were having difficulty with this crowd. It was a dark, rainy morning, and after the train had stood idle for several minutes and no soldier had gotten off, many people began to push against the ropes and to direct their anguished cries toward the open windows of the train, calling out the names of the men they were waiting for. *"Giuseppe Nardi! Giuseppe Nardi!"* screamed one middle-aged woman, her sodden cloak hanging heavily over her gaunt features, while a younger woman next to her called out louder still: *"Andrea De Marco, Andrea De Marco!"* Two teenaged boys brandished their fists at the military policeman who had given them a hard push backward with his club after they had climbed under the ropes; an elderly woman at the end of the line, after calling out someone's name, fell to the ground in a faint.

None of the soldiers in Antonio's car said anything to those held behind the ropes. The people were detained at a distance too remote for conversing, and most of the soldiers were now asleep or were too incapacitated and weary to speak after a harrowing and painful night. With a sound of the whistle and a pump of steam, the train began to move away from the station. Antonio could see the people's shoulders slacken, and he sensed their deepening disappointment. Many of them had undoubtedly been waiting all night and had seen too many trains come and go without bringing home any men from this town. But Antonio was also aware that the train had not brought home any caskets.

It did deliver caskets to eight of the next twenty towns it stopped at that day, and the farther south the train went, the more caskets it released. Soldiers, too, left the train at most stops, but whatever joy Antonio saw in the reunions along the platform was overshadowed by the forlorn figures who stood near the undertakers' wagons waiting to claim the bodies. As the names were read aloud by the two quartermaster sergeants who accompanied the caskets in the freight car, Antonio saw wailing women collapsing to the ground, and men cursing while looking scornfully at the sky. He saw priests trying to console the mourners, and flicking holy water upon the caskets, and waving in the air brass containers smoldering with incense. He saw mule carts filled with flowers in the background, and young women draped in black silk veils carrying children not yet old enough to walk. But Antonio could watch very little of this. It made him too self-conscious about being alive.

Having survived battles that killed his friends, and having now spent hours riding with soldiers disabled for life, he was haunted constantly by the question: Why them, and not me? To what do I owe my life, my limbs? He had begun to put these thoughts in his diary, but he had resisted. Such thoughts were better not written, he decided. Even *thinking* them might bring him bad luck. And yet it had been impossible to avoid them ever since he had seen Muffo, Branca, and the others cut down in front of him during the ambush. Unconsciously he now often behaved in ways that reflected what he wished to repress. He had slowed the pace of his walk, had even affected a slight limp, after he had entered the Milan terminal and crossed the corridor surrounded by soldiers who relied on canes and crutches, wheelchairs and stretchers. He had looked straight ahead in the railcar as he moved up the aisle past the seated victims, searching for a place to stand in the rear, behind the backs of his unfortunate comrades. When there finally were empty seats on the train after many hours of riding, Antonio had been the last of the standees to claim one. What was he resisting? What was he ashamed of? Never during his time in the army, including this trip on the train, had anyone encouraged these feelings. Never once had he detected in the facial expressions of injured soldiers, or overheard in their comments, anything that should give him reason to suspect that he was envied or resented.

On the contrary, and especially since Caporetto, the mere act of wearing his uniform in public had brought him signs of respect and cordiality from every soldier and civilian he met along the streets or elsewhere in Italian-occupied towns behind the frontlines. The truck driver who had gone miles out of his way to take Antonio into Milan; the waiter at the café near the terminal who would not let Antonio pay for breakfast; the middle-aged men and women waiting to board the train who insisted that Antonio move to the head of the line—all these people, and others, were showing respect for the Italian uniform, and deference to the men wearing it, making no distinction between soldiers who had been badly wounded and those who appeared to be perfectly healthy. Respect is what a soldier deserved and appreciated—not sympathy. Antonio knew this. He knew it rationally. But within him stirred ancient warnings against ever *appearing* to be better off than his neighbor, ever taking comfort in his sense of well-being, ever assuming that what was good about his life would last for very long. He had been reared among pessimists, mystics, people shaped by earthquakes, plagues, and other calamities beyond their control. Nothing was a sure thing in his village, nothing could be counted on. Maida was a warm, bright place in the mountains where nobody truly saw the sun. People wore black there when they had nothing to mourn. They mourned in advance. In that place the most casual of compliments could be construed as a curse.

Antonio remembered as a boy of five or six playing along the road near his house one afternoon when a stranger who was strolling through the village paused nearby to rest. He was a white-bearded, emaciated man in his seventies, wearing a sackcloth tunic and sandals, and he carried a walking stick and had a leather bag slung over his left shoulder. He had a kindly face, and, after settling himself under a tree, he called Antonio over and asked him to find water for the empty bottle he held. After Antonio returned with it filled from a nearby fountain, and the stranger had drunk from it sparingly, he looked around and asked Antonio the name of the town, and the distance between it and the next village to the north, and a few other questions about the area. Antonio spoke freely and politely, prompting the man to compliment him on his manners and to ask what he hoped to do with his life when he became older. Antonio had given it no thought; but imagining what would please his religious mother and her father, Domenico, he replied that he wished to become a priest.

"You seem to be a very nice boy," the man said. "You would make a fine priest. And even if you do not, I see many wonderful things happening to you in the years ahead."

Soon the man was on his way, and later at home Antonio told his mother about the man's favorable prediction. Immediately alarmed, Maria speculated that this stranger may have been trying to place a hex on his future. She hastened to consult with *her* father across the courtyard; then she returned and told Antonio that he *must* pursue the man at once, look directly into his eyes, and declare that he had given him false information. If the man asked further questions, she warned, Antonio should say nothing more and come directly home.

Confused but obedient, Antonio ran out the door and up the road the old man had been following. But there was no sign of him anywhere. Antonio passed the outer boundaries of Maida, and continued northward a few miles more in the direction of the next town, Nicastro. Losing hope of ever finding him, since none of the people he questioned along the route reported having seen him, Antonio turned and headed back to Maida. He wanted to get home before dark. Along the way he met his concerned parents and grandfather, who feared he had gotten lost. Reassured that he was all right, they then revealed their disappointment on learning that Antonio had not made contact with the old man. His mother and grandfather seemed to be particularly upset, although they did not scold him or verbalize their disappointment. They merely talked quietly between themselves on the way home, staying a few paces behind Antonio and his father, who had his arm around Antonio's shoulder and said comforting things while keeping him distant from what was being discussed behind them—Maria's voice rising now and then to reveal her concern over the consequences, the possible consequences, of what had happened. And what *had* happened? Antonio did not know. And he never would know, exactly, since nobody in his family could or would adequately explain it. All that he understood was that something had been visited upon him, something that was pleasing in sound but possibly evil in intent. Because he had been unable to confront the man and take back what he had said, an ill omen was now adrift, a prognosis that (though positive) could bring negative results even if it fulfilled itself. It could bring, at best, pride and conceit; at worst, the envy of others, their contempt, perhaps their vengeance. It could have disadvantageous results, in any case. And yet it was part of Antonio's psychic burden, part of his boyhood inheritance from Maida that he had carried with him to France, and that he had lived with for almost three years in the most enlightened and sophisticated city in Europe. Now, back from the battlefield, he was returning home with this burden, limping with it along a platform at the Naples train station, several feet from where a group of people fell screaming to the ground as caskets were unloaded from the train.

Antonio sat at a back table in a café within the noisy rotunda of the Naples terminal, with a view of the station's clock hanging high on the stone wall. His own train was currently sidetracked, not only to allow time for the removal of the many caskets but also to permit mechanics to service the malfunctioning locomotive. Moments before the train had pulled into Naples, the chief engineer had entered the car to announce apologetically that there would be a two-hour delay due to slight compression problems with the engine. Antonio had been delighted with the announcement. He could finally get off the train for a while. There was a telegraph office in the Naples terminal, from which he could send another message to Maida. There was also the café, where in the past he had eaten well and where the bar held a vast assortment of wines and whiskeys, the latter traditionally stocked for British travelers. Since leaving Milan, he had eaten only what the vendors sold through the train windows, and very little of that.

Having already sent his telegram, Antonio sipped a glass of wine while waiting for his pasta and watched the crowds passing before him. He paid particular attention to the groups of young soldiers heading toward the tracks and presumably to the front. Though lively, they lacked some of the spirit and spunkiness of the troops he had accompanied before along this path. He remembered his first ride on the troop train—the cardplaying and gambling on the floor, the singing and joking in the aisles, the tossing of white ration cans out the windows along the rolling green countryside of Lombardy in late spring. Almost all his companions then had believed they were off to a war that would be short and victorious. The young men he saw today had no such illusions, and he doubted there would be any signs of gaiety as they traveled north.

From the newspapers he had bought near the telegraph office he learned that the Italians continued to hold the line along the western banks of the Piave River, and that the Italian Ninth Corps had been particularly effective in driving back one ill-conceived assault by the enemy. General von Below's forces had pushed ahead so rapidly since breaking through at Caporetto that they had gotten too far ahead of their supply system. Now as von Below's attacking units assembled along the east side of the river, they lacked the bridging material and other equipment necessary to fight their way across the water and overwhelm the well-positioned and reinforced Italians. Snow was also falling heavily throughout the mountains and valleys, making supply movement doubly difficult, and it was generally assumed by the Allied commanders that there would be no further blitz attacks until early spring.

By that time, Antonio would surely be back in action, but most likely in a different theater of operations. On being released from the hospital he had received a new set of orders: After his Christmas leave in Maida he would report to Turin and join Italian units preparing to be transferred to France. In an exchange program being tested by the Allied commanders, some Italian divisions would join the Anglo-French divisions on the western front and some Anglo-French divisions would be intermingled with General Diaz's army in northern Lombardy and along the Piave River. This program was largely the result of the Allied commanders' conclusion that they had up to now been functioning too independently, that there was a need for a more assimilated effort under a single mind who would establish a unity of command and reduce much of the inefficiency that had characterized their methods in battle. It had been emphasized, for example, that after eleven British and French divisions had arrived to assist the Italians in the post-Caporetto campaign, none of the

Allied generals could agree on how or where they should be deployed. Now, under the new plan, such a decision would be entrusted to the new commander in chief of the combined Allied armies, France's Marshal Ferdinand Foch.

While the Americans, under General John J. Pershing, would not subordinate themselves to Foch, they would of course cooperate with the French marshal; and what Foch's elevation meant at the very least was that all the Allies would now be communicating more in the French language. Within General Diaz's staff it was soon discovered that many Italian officers who claimed to be fluent in French could not be understood by Frenchmen; and as a result there were solicitations for more civilian interpreters and translators, and for Italian military personnel with a true mastery of the French tongue.

One day during Antonio's last week in the hospital, he overheard an inspecting colonel asking one of the doctors if he knew of anyone who spoke perfect French. Without waiting for the doctor's reply, Antonio piped up from his sickbed: *"Oui, mon colonel!"* Thus Antonio was appointed as an interpreter and courier between Italian and French officers on the western front. He had still to be assigned to an Italian infantry unit, but it was expected he would be detached often to accompany some of Diaz's field officers to staff meetings with their French colleagues. It was hinted that Antonio, already a corporal, would soon become a sergeant, although his Christmas furlough to Maida had been reduced from three weeks to two.

When he heard an announcement through a megaphone that his train was ready to continue its journey, Antonio finished his coffee and left the café for the exit on the opposite side of the hall. As he made his way through the crowd, he saw more fresh-faced recruits, walking hunched forward as they carried their knapsacks, rifles, and gas masks, which, Antonio hoped, were improved over those issued at Caporetto. In addition to the elderly civilians and the many injured servicemen traveling through the station, Antonio noticed that large numbers of Naples's street beggars and derelicts, more popularly known as *lazzaroni,* had been pressed into employment as station porters, sweepers, pushers of postal wagons, and even maintenance crewmen along the tracks.

The *lazzaroni,* whose name derived from that of the Biblical beggar Lazarus (Lazzaro in Italian), for centuries had fended for themselves in the open air and shadowed covers of the city; but every once in a while, particularly during national emergencies, they were summoned from their hand-to-mouth existence to serve the needs of the state. When the army of the French Revolution had entered Naples in 1799, thousands of them were recruited to help defend the city; and in alliance with the Bourbon troops and Cardinal Fabrizio Ruffo's vigilantes, they rebuffed the invaders. Now with the labor shortage brought on by World War I, the *lazzaroni,* decrepit and undernourished as most of them were, performed tasks around the terminal and at other places in the city; and as Antonio watched some of them assisting ailing soldiers with luggage, it was often impossible for him to tell who was the more incapacitated.

It was nearly twilight as the train moved south past the Neapolitan hills, and Antonio got his final view of Vesuvius, its vapors flowing west through a slight drizzle. Farther down the coast he saw desolate beaches, rows of overturned fishing boats, and clusters of palm trees, the first he had seen in two and a half years. His railcar was half occupied, or so he guessed from the volume of snoring, coughing, and sighing he heard coming from the seats where most soldiers had spread themselves. The younger one-legged infantryman with whom Antonio had sat during much of the trip had gotten off somewhere south of Rome. So had the airman who had fueled D'Annunzio's squadron, and the blind artillery-man and his companion. Antonio was not sure whether he had been rid-ing for two days, or three, or even longer. After countless stops, and after drifting in and out of sleep, he had lost his sense of time. But now that the train continued down the coast along the familiar route he had so often taken when returning home from fabric-buying trips to Naples with his father, Antonio began to sleep deeply, as he had always done as a boy; and when he woke up, it was morning, and the train was approaching the val-ley of Maida.

He stood up and reached for his duffel bag in the overhead rack. He wanted to be among the first off the train. He did not want to be on the platform and perhaps witness the arrival of local men in boxes. It was pos-sible that caskets deposited at this coastal stop, Santa Eufemia, would not contain Maida men, for the station was used not only by the residents of Maida but also by people from neighboring hill towns and coastal com-munities. Still, Maida was the largest village in the area, and chances were good that if caskets were due here they would be carrying someone from his village; he did not want to risk seeing the agonized faces of the parents or spouses who were here to claim the bodies of young men he had proba-bly grown up with.

So he jumped off the train even before it had stopped completely; and, pulling his cap down low over his eyes, he walked quickly across the platform away from where the roped-off crowd was standing. He did glance in their direction briefly, curious to see if any member of his family was trying to get his attention. But no one was waving toward him, nor did anyone even appear to be aware of him walking toward the station. Everyone was engrossed in watching the quartermaster sergeants exiting from the freight car that was trimmed with black bunting and had the tricolored flag of Italy flying on its roof. Antonio's telegram home apparently had not been received, but he was not disappointed. Now he would not be detained as he headed directly toward the line of coachmen waiting with their horses.

Tossing his bag up to the back bench, Antonio told the driver to take the hill road to Maida; and he was about to board the carriage when he felt someone holding on to the back of his jacket. He turned and saw a woman in a black veil weeping and softly calling his name, and repeating it several times as if in disbelief. As she reached forward and embraced him, Antonio recognized his mother. They held one another silently for several moments until Antonio, feeling self-conscious, and aware that the coachman was waiting and that people in the crowd were watching them, firmly guided his mother up into the coach.

They rode for many minutes without speaking. Maria had pulled the veil back from her face, which seemed luminous with her smile, and Antonio felt her hand tighten around his arm. In reply to his question, she said his telegrams had not been received. During the night, she said, she had had a premonition that he would return home in the morning, and that was why she had been at the station. Francesco and the rest of the family were not aware she had come.

As the coachman continued toward Maida, Maria asked that they take a different route, one that would lead them off the main road to a back road in the woodlands. The coachman objected, saying that the road she suggested was not much wider than a bridle path, and that his coach would become entangled in bushes and tree branches. But she was insistent. She had often traveled by coach through the woodlands, she said, and turning to her son she explained she had a vow to fulfill along this route, one that she had made during her prayers begging for his safe return. Now it was essential that she be taken to this place to do as she had promised.

At Antonio's urging, the coachman complied, and for the next half-hour they traveled through a narrow path surrounded by trees, which finally widened and led to a small dark-stoned chapel Antonio had never seen before, or known existed. It was built along the path that Saint Francis of Paola had walked when he had visited Maida centuries before, Antonio's mother explained, and she asked the coachman to stop so that she could briefly visit the chapel. Antonio said he would accompany her, but she shook her head saying she must go in alone. He helped her down and watched her walk into the chapel. He and the coachman waited for five minutes, and then ten. It was a cool December morning and the night's frost was still on the trees. They stood waiting next to the horse for another five minutes, when Antonio, more concerned than impatient, decided to join his mother.

When he opened the wooden door, he saw ahead of him an altar aglow with candles, and a row of benches in which no one was sitting, and paintings on the walls of figures he could not identify. He looked around the room but saw no sign of his mother. She was neither kneeling at the altar nor sitting in the pews.

He walked slowly down the aisle, then suddenly stopped. There, on the floor, Antonio saw a dark figure—his mother prostrating herself, crawling slowly forward with her veil tied back and her tongue licking the stones.

Horrified, he watched her. He waited for a few moments, then could watch no longer. Against her protests, he pulled her to her feet and, with his arm firmly around her shoulders, forced her out of this place where the faithful still made primitive bargains with God.

27.

AFTER FOUR DAYS in Maida, Antonio was ready to return to the front. In the field of battle he at least had been diverted by his duties, had been preoccupied with staying alive, and had learned to remain emotionally detached from much of the death and destruction he had witnessed. But in the familiarity of his hometown, where he had too much time and too little to do, and where everything he saw had a personal meaning, he found himself tormented by the surrounding sadness; he felt the pain of everyone's wounds, and sensed in particular the bitterness and hopelessness in the hearts of those amputees he had known when they possessed all their limbs and when they could dream, as he had, of one day discovering a better life far from this backward and pessimistic place.

Now not only had the war maimed and disfigured them, and left some demented from poison gas, but it had deprived them of the likelihood of ever leaving the village. Only able-bodied workmen were wanted overseas. And those casualties who had already worked abroad, and been told they could reclaim their jobs after the war, were now doubly disheartened. Having seen the future, they were now dropped back into the past, to whatever degree there still *was* a viable past in such moribund places as Maida.

The economy was bankrupt. Most of the shops were closed. The lack of farm labor had limited the planting and the care of livestock, and the people generally subsisted on what they grew in their own gardens or what they obtained through bartering with neighbors. Dozens of children had dropped out of school because half the faculty had quit to work in munitions factories farther north. The town was dark at night, the lamps overhead not having been repaired after the riot in 1916. During the day, one-legged men on crutches leaned and elbowed themselves forward along the stone walls of buildings as they made their way cautiously up and down the curved and lopsided cobblestone streets. Several families shared their homes with black-veiled young mothers and fatherless children. For the first time in decades, Maida was without white widows.

There was practically a moratorium on Christmas in 1917. The bagpipers were not in the square, there were no open-house feasts and concerts in the palazzos. The usually festive Midnight Mass was more like a requiem, and this melancholy atmosphere hung over Antonio's household throughout his furlough. Much as everyone tried to rejoice in his presence, the telegram that his grandfather Domenico had received from the War Ministry two hours before Antonio's arrival in Maida weighed heavily on everyone. Sebastian Talese had been belatedly identified as one of the casualties at Caporetto.

Sebastian was now barely alive at a hospital in Bologna. He had been gassed, and badly injured by an exploding shell. The family was not permitted to visit the hospital. Information that Francesco Cristiani had gotten from an army doctor he knew in Catanzaro indicated that Sebastian was suffering from slight brain damage and physical enfeeblements that would inhibit his ever resuming a normal life.

Joseph's mother was in shock. Her oldest and favorite son would never return as she remembered him. When Marian's parents heard the news they came to take her to live with them in the valley, as they had after her husband's death three years before. Her three youngest children accompanied her. Fourteen-year-old Joseph was looked after, as usual, by his grandparents Domenico and Ippolita, by his aunt Maria and uncle Francesco Cristiani, and temporarily by Antonio himself.

"The war will soon be over," Antonio told his cousin many times during Christmas week, when Joseph seemed to be overwrought with anxiety and confusion, "and then you and I will be living together in Paris."

Joseph listened, as he always did when Antonio spoke, but he did not appear convinced. The years since the death of Joseph's father had been filled mainly with false hopes. Joseph no longer worked at the tailor shop, which Antonio's father had recently been forced to close because of lack of business. Customers had neither the money nor the occasions for new clothes these days.

During Joseph's free hours from school he helped out on his grandfather's farm. If Sebastian's physical condition proved as bad as the prognosis of the doctor in Catanzaro, then he would never resume his foremanship on the farm, and Joseph saw himself as being pressured by Domenico, now nearly eighty, to take over the responsibility. But Joseph vowed that he would not allow this to happen.

"I'll run away, like you did," Joseph said on the eve of Antonio's departure for Turin.

"You won't have to," Antonio replied. "I'll come and get you. As soon as the war ends, I'll come here, help you pack, and then we'll travel together to France. I'll probably be sent to France before the end of January, and I'm sure I'll be able to slip into Paris before long, and then I'll begin making the arrangements."

Antonio was indeed in France before the end of January 1918, but he was far from Paris. He was stationed 135 miles east of the French capital in the fortress city of Verdun, on the Meuse River, sixty miles from the German border. The Germans had attacked Verdun two years before, in February 1916, initiating a ten-month battle that would be the longest of the war. The French suffered 348,000 casualties, 20,000 more than the Germans, but they defended Verdun so stalwartly that the Germans finally withdrew and reinforced their aggressions elsewhere.

In 1918, however, reconnaissance reports indicated that the Germans planned a new offensive in this area; and the French officers whom Antonio had come to know at Verdun, and with whom he attended staff meetings while interpreting for the newly arrived Italian commanders, regarded the future with such pessimism that Antonio was reminded of his fellow villagers in Maida. But perhaps the French gloom was unavoidable. The war had persisted for more than three years in France, had killed off a large percentage of its young male population, and still the nation could not rid itself of the German invaders. There were now, in fact, more Germans than ever garrisoned in France and Belgium, threatening to smash through the fatigued Allied defenders at several points and capture Paris as well as drive the British guarding northwestern France back into the English Channel.

The collapse of Russia the year before had allowed the Germans to transfer to the western front many troops who had fought on the eastern front, and thus obtain a numerical advantage there. This prompted the French to recall four of the six divisions, and the British two of the five, that had been loaned to Italy after the Caporetto setback in 1917. If this decision at first did not please the Italians, it did at least flatteringly attest to General Diaz's own sense of himself as an obstinate commander who could hold the line south of the Alps in 1918 with his fifty Italian divisions (plus three British, two French, and one Czechoslovak) against sixty Austro-Hungarian divisions that were not as well positioned or well armed as Diaz's forces. The British also transferred men into France from detachments in the Middle East, where Field Marshal Edmund Allenby had been harassing the Turks with increasing vigor, aided by Colonel T. E. Lawrence, better known as Lawrence of Arabia. And the Italians, too, now that their line seemed secure and their munitions industry productive, were called upon to contribute men of their own to the western front. General Diaz complied in January 1918 by releasing the advanced elements of a promised fifty-thousand-man contingent (Antonio had been among the first trainload, accompanying ranks that included eighty other soldiers who spoke French well enough to serve as officers' interpreters), and he promised to send an even larger number of Italians before the middle of the year.

All of Diaz's men, organized into fighting units and ready for battle, would become affiliated with larger Allied units and serve under French generals entrusted to defending Verdun, or the Argonne Forest, or the Marne River near Paris, among other vital points, or under those British generals who were in charge north of Paris near Amiens and the Somme River, and on up to the tip of Flanders edging the English Channel. The Italians would thus be bivouacked in dozens of camps in the proximity of French, British, and Belgian troops, as well as troops from French and British colonies and other Allied nations—there were Tunisian, Senegalese, Sudanese, Annamese, Australians, Canadians, Portuguese, Moroccans, and many others. Encamped around the provincial city of Chaumont, far southeast of Paris near the headstreams of the Marne, were the first Americans, including segregated, all-black divisions, such as the 369th Regiment, the "Harlem Hellfighters."

This influx of Allied troops into France at this moment, however, would not offset Germany's numerical advantage. Nor was it merely the enemy's larger number of troops and guns that made the Allies pessimistic about the outcome. The Germans also had their men in locations that offered the best opportunities for attack, as had been true from the first days of the war—which was why the Allies had been constantly on the defensive. And when the Allies *had* risked taking the offensive, as the British had in the summer of 1916 at the battle of the Somme, the high cost in lives had been shocking.

Of the first sixty thousand British troops to charge out of their trenches on the first day of that attack, almost every one was killed by German machine-gunners and artillerymen who zeroed in from key vantage points; and as the British casualty figures climbed in the months ahead, the British commanders—hoping to compensate for their losses by staging a dramatic turnabout—prematurely introduced to the Germans a new weapon that had not yet been manufactured in sufficient numbers, or tested enough in combat, to affect the situation decisively.

This large, heavy weapon had been designed and produced with such haste and secrecy in England that, even as several examples were placed under canvas coverings and loaded onto freight trains to be shipped to the front, the British military had overlooked giving them a name—although the conspicuously draped objects could hardly escape the notice of anyone who might see the trains moving through the countryside. Finally, in an attempt to allay people's curiosity and still guard the secrecy of the weapon from enemy spies, the military spread the word that these were actually "water carriers" en route to British soldiers in the Sinai Desert— and thus the weapon came to be called a "tank."

The tank did indeed surprise the first German soldiers who saw it in action at the Somme, watching with wonderment and alarm as dozens of the monstrous oval steel vehicles with exploding cannons rolled toward them on caterpillar tracks that scaled bunkers and cut through barbed wire, grinding onward as bullets ricocheted off their thick armor. In one case, three hundred petrified Germans surrendered to a single tank. But soon the German commanders were able to maneuver their units out of the path of the clumsy, slow-moving craft (top speed: not quite four miles per hour), a number of which also broke down because of mechanical failure or the unskilled handling by inexperienced crewmen.

And so the battle of the Somme, like nearly all other confrontations in this war, settled down to be a struggle between men in the mud, infantrymen versus infantrymen—a test of individual will, nerve, and hostility generated for the purpose, as one historian phrased it, of "mutual destruction." The British gained territory of little strategic value around the river, while more than 400,000 of its men were killed, injured, or taken prisoner. The French units who fought alongside the British suffered more than 200,000 losses, while the German number was estimated at 600,000.

Still, their losses in 1916 at the Somme and also at Verdun did not affect the Germans' fighting morale in the year ahead, especially as troops from the eastern front began to bolster the western ranks; and when Antonio arrived in France in 1918, the Germans seemed to dominate not only on land, but on the sea and in the air as well. German pilots were now penetrating the Allied aerial defenses, and on January 30, 1918, they bombed Paris, killing forty-five civilians and injuring one hundred. German submarines were sinking Allied military supplies and causing acute food shortages on the British home front, where there was already much anguish and political unrest about the rising death tolls and the necessity of sending more troops to the Continent—while at the same time the government in London recognized the need to retain an adequate number of troops at home to deal with a possible Irish rebellion.

There was bickering between French and British government officials over how much frontline territory each nation was committed to defending, and in what amount and where troops should be deployed. Britain's senior military officers naturally were most interested in protecting those vital areas of the northwest, from Picardy through Flanders, that backed into the English Channel, which was the source of their soldiers' supplies—and which might, in desperation, provide their routes of escape. French officers, while dismissing none of the importance that the British attached to defending the Channel, were nonetheless most concerned about defending the roads leading into their capital city.

From the French military interpreters with whom Antonio associated at Verdun—most of them university-educated enlisted men who gossiped like tailors in a workroom—he learned that there were also disagreements between French and American commanders. While there were four United States divisions now training in France, and many more on the way, General Pershing did not consider any of them ready for combat yet; and when a division *was* ready, he did not want it, or any portion of it, to fight under French or British leadership. Pershing was perhaps worried that America's late arrivals to the war might be subjected to the most dangerous duty if they were placed under French or British command, but in public he acknowledged nothing of the sort. From his headquarters at

Chaumont he explained simply that he wanted each American division to fight as a unit, to remain under its appointed officers, and not to be separated into smaller sections and sent out to be used at the discretion of other officers.

In March, Allied reconnaissance reports and other sources (including recently captured POWs who had been induced into talking) indicated more than ever the probability of a major German attack before the end of the month. In anticipation of this, new groups of Diaz's promised Italian soldiers (whose officers were instructed to serve loyally under French and German superiors) were rushed into France from Turin. Many trainloads traveled through Lyon and Dijon northward to Verdun, while many others turned westward south of Verdun toward Paris, or headed northwest toward Picardy and Flanders.

At Verdun, Antonio, who technically was assigned to an Italian fighting unit elsewhere within the French Fifth Army, was kept on full-time duty as an interpreter for the Italian officers of the incoming troops, the first three thousand of whom were greeted at the rail depot outside the town by a French military band that played the "Hymn of Garibaldi" and by villagers who handed out bottles of local wine and monk-made cognac that they were eager to bestow on friendly forces rather than risk leaving behind for the Germans. The Italians were then taken by truck to Bois de la Ville, just south of Verdun, where on the following day they would begin relieving French infantry units who had not had a furlough in more than a year, and who now, with the rumors of a new German attack, wasted no time in vacating the area.

The French soldiers who remained were extremely cordial to the Italians, and each morning at Bois de la Ville trucks delivered fresh bread and pastry, cheese, meat, coffee, and cigarettes. The troops from both countries became better acquainted after a few weeks of trench duty; they began to understand a bit of each other's language, and many engaged in card games during their off-duty hours—the Italians playing for money, the French playing for the Italians' boots, which were better made than the French ones: more durable, less porous, of softer leather, more comfortable during long marches. The Italians who lost at cards either exchanged their boots with the Frenchmen or procured extra pairs in appropriate sizes from Italian supply sergeants, who cooperated if adequately compensated in lire or francs. The superiority of Italian bootmakers, which in future decades would be acknowledged worldwide, was recognized early by French soldiers.

Daily at midmorning, Antonio rode in a staff car with an Italian major and captain from Bois de la Ville to the Verdun headquarters of an elderly and stout French colonel who had been lured out of retirement by the war, and whose father (shown in a small sepia photograph on the colonel's desk) had been a veteran of the Franco-Prussian War in 1870. Father and son had the same type of moustache, a walrus with the ends twisted up into points. While the Italians tended to be clean-shaven, most of the French officers grew moustaches, a high percentage of them styled in imitation of Marshal Foch's, which was a bushier walrus than the Verdun colonel's, and not so pointed on the ends. Officers serving prolonged duty on freezing days outdoors usually had tiny icicles dangling from their moustaches.

The colonel's office was located far underground, and was reached by a wooden staircase that descended nearly forty feet below a line of trenches. It was a spacious office, about thirty by thirty feet, with a twelve-foot-high timber ceiling and a boarded floor; enclosed within mud-plaster walls, it was brightened by electric light, and it was furnished with antiques and other pieces that soldiers had picked from out of the rubble of private homes and public buildings shelled during the last battle in the area, two years before. The colonel's desk was a refectory table from a monastery; and his high-backed wooden armchair, which was missing one arm, retained part of the brass plate of a noble family's escutcheon. In front of the colonel's desk were four mismatched rustic chairs for his guests, and in one corner of the room was a sturdy chest-high table with shelves that held bottles of liqueur below and a gramophone above. Hanging from the wall behind the desk were maps of the eastern sectors of France within a hundred-fifty-mile radius of Verdun, with different-colored pins in the maps marking the locale of Allied and German strongholds. On the colonel's desk, in addition to the photograph of his father, his wife, and his daughter, and a postcard-sized flag of the French Republic, were stacks of cablegrams, military documents, a silver bowl filled with pipes, and two black telephones.

Accustomed as Antonio was to the small, putrid, rat-infested trenches and dugouts of the Italian front, he could marvel at the colonel's agreeable and generous use of space so deeply burrowed in the dirt—space that not only accommodated the colonel's office, but extended on both sides of it to several other rooms reached by a network of tunnels. There was a weapons room, a clothing-supply room, a laundry room with caldrons and a fireplace for boiling water. There was a kitchen with pots and pans hanging on the walls, and a bathroom with toilets. There were rooms with cots, complete with blankets, sheets, and pillows—these were bedrooms for the duty officers who worked around the clock overseeing the twelve hundred riflemen and machine-gunners who took turns manning the trenches above, which were reached by ladders.

The trenches were also commodious, many of them split-level. On the upper level, standing on timber platforms supported by vertical beams, were gunmen on the alert, leaning behind sandbags, presumably facing the direction of the unseen enemy. Relaxing below them were off-duty soldiers, sitting on boxes or barrels around wooden-crate tables playing cards or talking, or curled up in their sleeping bags along the front edge of the wall between the beams and the extended ladders leading up to the platforms. Here and there, cut into the stone-pitted walls, were recesses for wood-burning stoves and nooks for storing food, medical supplies, rain gear, blankets, barrels of water, and boxes of mosquito netting. There was something all-seasonal, almost permanent, about these trenches and the colonel's subterranean development below. The French forces had been stymied for so long at Verdun that they apparently had decided to make the best of it and domesticate the dirt, as if this hollowness might well represent their final resting place. The old fortress a mile away was no longer a source of protection. It had been obsolete since the end of the Franco-Prussian War, and now it was abandoned altogether as a conspicuous and vulnerable target for heavy enemy artillery. *So the French now wait for the Germans in this big excavation, and in many other excavations like this one all across the defense lines of Verdun,* Antonio wrote in his diary. *I'm always amazed when I walk down all those steps and see the colonel and his staff directing the war from within that maze of rooms and tunnels. But I guess it's not surprising that a place like this would be built in the nation that built the Paris Métro.*

28.

EARLY IN MARCH 1918, Antonio was sent with a French and an Italian captain twenty miles west of Verdun into the Argonne Forest to expedite the arrival of the latest trainload of Italians. Nearly two thousand infantrymen would join six thousand French reservists at a camouflaged base near a point where the enemy was soon expected to advance. This was outside the forest along a road that led west into the cathedral city of Reims. It was in the Argonne that two of Garibaldi's grandsons, Bruno and Costante, had been killed while serving with a legion of red-shirted Italian volunteers supporting France before Italy entered the war. Now in 1918, as the Italian infantrymen lined up in a clearing for the first day's inspection, the French major in command welcomed them in a speech that paid homage to the two young men, and also to General Garibaldi as symbolic of the strengthened Franco-Italian alliance.

While Antonio stood nearby to do the interpreting, the major urged the assembled Italians to enhance this relationship further in the battles ahead; then he asked for a moment of silence in memory of the Italians who had already died in the war. At the close of the ceremony, a French band played the "Hymn of Garibaldi." Antonio had never heard it played in all his years in southern Italy, but now on the French front he had heard it twice already. Garibaldi was clearly something of a hero in this country, most likely for supporting France on the battlefield in 1870 during its war lost to Prussia. Victor Hugo had in fact remarked, with more admiration than accuracy, that Garibaldi was the only general in the French army not defeated in that war.

After a week in the Argonne Forest, Antonio and another Italian sergeant named Graziani were assigned to an important courier mission in Paris; the senior Italian military attaché there had a new set of directives to be circulated to the various Italian units in the field, and Antonio and Graziani were ordered to take a train to Paris's Gare de l'Est to receive the documents that pertained to the Italians in the Verdun area, and then to deliver them to the Italian commanding officer at Bois de la Ville.

Although this would be a fast trip, Antonio was nonetheless excited at the prospect of returning to Paris, where he had not been since his abrupt departure in August 1914. And his nostalgia became focused in a specific way when, while waiting at the motor pool, he saw a long row of brightly colored Paris buses parked in the woods. These buses had apparently been used during the recent emergency to accelerate the transfer of extra French troops into the Argonne, much as Paris taxicabs had been a means of rushing reinforcements toward the Marne River to help repel the first German attack of the war. But now these neglected buses, unsuited to render further military service within the forest's rocky and often roadless terrain, were waiting out the war under the trees, and they created for

Antonio an odd but gladdening remembrance of Paris in peacetime—especially when he noticed above the windshield of one bus a sign bearing the letters "AB."

He used to take an AB bus each morning to work. He would board it before eight at the Place de la Contrescarpe, near his Latin Quarter apartment, cross the Seine, and then get off and walk to the Rue Royale and Damien's tailor shop. As Antonio continued to stare at the bus in the woods he imagined it moving along festive boulevards, past familiar buildings and landmarks, past cafés with soapy wet sidewalks and aproned men pushing brooms, past top-hatted carriage drivers and businessmen in motorcars and people walking dogs, past couples holding hands and strolling through a spring morning scented with the fragrance of flower shops, bakeries, blossoming gardens and parks, past schoolchildren standing on corners waiting to cross the street, past white-gloved gendarmes who, with upraised hands and waving arms, orchestrated the movement and flow of each new day. Antonio was so absorbed in his reverie that it took a weighty tap on the shoulder from Graziani to turn him around and alert him to the fact that their driver, in a mud-splattered camouflaged truck, was waiting to take them to the rail depot.

They rode the train through the night, which was the safest time to be traveling by rail now that German bomber pilots were playing a greater role in the war; and at daybreak their train pulled into the Gare de l'Est. It was a dark and drizzling Saturday in mid-March. Even before the train had stopped completely, three military policemen had hopped aboard to locate the courier sergeants, to examine their credentials, and then to escort them to a restaurant near the main hall of the terminal, where a representative of the Italian military attaché awaited them for breakfast.

The representative was a young blue-eyed lieutenant who spoke Italian with a Florentine accent. After a peremptory greeting from his chair, and a snap of his fingers toward a waiter, the lieutenant told the sergeants to sit down and order something to eat without delay, for he had very little time to spend with them.

The waiter took the breakfast order, and the lieutenant lit a cigarette without offering one to the sergeants; he stared at them momentarily through the rising smoke, and gradually his attention drifted toward Graziani. The sergeant was a big, jowly, broad-shouldered man who towered over Antonio; in civilian life he had worked as a stevedore in his hometown of Brindisi, a seaport on the Adriatic along the heel of the Italian boot. On the outer sides of Graziani's wrists, partially visible below the cuffs of his undersized jacket and trench coat, were tattooed a pair of mermaids, one of whom was exposed nearly to the level of her breasts. The lieutenant edged forward, as if to get a closer look, but then, with a slight flaring of his nostrils, he leaned back in his chair. Graziani reeked of garlic.

During the previous day, before joining Antonio at the motor pool, Graziani had been treated to extra helpings of lamb stew, afloat with garlic cloves, by a mess sergeant he knew. Antonio had been subjected to Graziani's garlicky stench through the entire night on the train, smelling it even through the visored cap that he wore over his face in an unsuccessful attempt to sleep through the spicy draft of Graziani's snoring.

"Now then," the lieutenant said, leaning back farther to reach under the table for his briefcase, "the parcel I'm about to give you men *must* be on the desk of the commandant at Bois de la Ville before noon tomorrow, is that understood?" As the sergeants nodded, the lieutenant removed from his briefcase a thin, wax-sealed cardboard box, similar in size to a box a customer might carry out of a store after purchasing a pair of gloves or a wallet. Undecided on who should carry it, the lieutenant looked first at the big smelly stevedore, then at the perky slim-shouldered tailor, then back to the stevedore.

"Here," the lieutenant said to Graziani, "guard this with your life."

Graziani put it at once into an inner pocket of his trench coat, next to his holstered pistol. The lieutenant then gave them a document to sign, making them equally responsible for the safekeeping and delivery of the parcel.

"You both will spend the entire day in this building," the lieutenant continued. "And you will be out of here on the first train leaving after dark." He took the document they had signed, examined their signatures, and tucked it back into the briefcase. "Under no circumstances," the lieutenant went on, "will either of you leave the building, even briefly. There will be no sightseeing in Paris today." Saying this, he looked pointedly at Antonio, as if reading his mind.

Conceited, very sure of himself, Antonio later wrote of the lieutenant in his diary. *A typical Florentine.* Before Antonio reached for his cigarettes, he was careful to ask the lieutenant if it was permissible for him to smoke, even though the lieutenant had just lit up another of his own. The lieutenant signaled his approval with a careless wave of his hand and, turning toward the passing waiter, called out to complain about the delay in their breakfast. The waiter soon appeared with coffee, rolls, and three cheese omelets. It was the lieutenant who had ordered the omelets—the sergeants had asked only for coffee—but in his earlier haste with the waiter the lieutenant had mistakenly ordered eggs all around, and the sergeants had preferred not to correct him. Now as the lieutenant took his fork to his omelet, Graziani did likewise—but Antonio, who was allergic to eggs, slowly doubled his omelet over on his plate with his fork and began to pack it down, making it look smaller.

As the others ate quietly, Antonio sipped his coffee, picked at a roll, smoked, and looked around the restaurant. The other tables were occupied mostly by moustachioed French officers wearing horizon-blue uniforms. In the doorway stood a trio of Italian military policemen, dressed in gray-green uniforms with Carabiniere emblems on their sleeves. Pistols hung from their waists, billy clubs were in hand, their feet were shod in highly polished, highly negotiable boots.

Beyond the door of the restaurant Antonio could see crowds of people making their way to the exit, and he fervently wished he were among them. Just a fifteen-minute walk down the Champs-Élysées would satisfy his craving for civility after his lengthy military tour with the likes of Graziani and this insolent lieutenant. Antonio had not expected this courier mission to be a pleasure trip, but he also had not expected to be trapped in the terminal all day with Graziani.

When the lieutenant had finished eating, and looked across the table with nothing to say, Antonio broke the silence by asking about the wartime morale of the Parisians and living conditions in the capital. For some reason, perhaps because he had just had a flashing fantasy of himself riding to work on an AB bus, he posed his questions in French. But it was also possible, as he himself later conceded in his diary, that he had switched to French in an unconscious, though deeply felt, desire to prick the pride of this inflated lieutenant—who, if he spoke French at all, which Antonio doubted, would surely speak it badly. In any case, Antonio would have the pleasurable option of watching this Florentine expose his ignorance of the language.

As it turned out, the lieutenant spoke French perfectly. He shifted into it automatically, and in this language he was even more disagreeable than he had been in Italian.

"My God, Sergeant, are you so unaware of what's going on in Paris?" he exclaimed, with the convincing inflections of a petulant Frenchman. "There's panic in the streets, bombing raids almost every day! Just two days ago, one hundred civilians were killed, and many more injured! Which is why I've ordered you to remain in the terminal all day, and to go directly to the shelter on the lower level if you hear the air-raid siren. I want you both to stay alive *at least* until you've delivered my parcel to Bois de la Ville."

Antonio and Graziani remained silent as the agitated lieutenant, looking at his watch, stood and announced that he was late for his next appointment. With a nod, but without saying good-bye, he turned from the table. Antonio watched him nod again as he passed the military policemen near the door. Antonio suspected, rightly, that the lieutenant had stuck Graziani and him with the breakfast check.

It was a long and tedious day in the terminal. Everywhere the sergeants went, policemen followed. When they took a seat on a bench, policemen sat on a bench opposite them, talking quietly among themselves, looking idly around the big hall, but never letting the sergeants out of their sight. Antonio felt sure that if he or Graziani should initiate a conversation with anyone in the station, it would arouse the suspicions of their guardians and the latter would somehow intrude. So Antonio spent the hours browsing through the French journals and magazines he had purchased at the newsstand. Graziani was next to him, sometimes glancing over his shoulder at the headlines and pictures, and occasionally making inane comments, but mostly sitting silently with his thick arms and fishtailed wrists folded across his chest, feeling his gun and the parcel he guarded. Graziani now smelled not only of garlic, but also of the ellipses of raw onion that had covered his omelet.

Having heard the lieutenant's somber description of wartime Paris, which Antonio accepted with the understanding that Italians usually liked to make things sound worse than they really were, he was pleased to get from the newspapers a sense that the French people were undaunted by the war, that Paris was still the city of light and revelry. While the newspapers did admit that bombs had been landing, and in one instance had come close to hitting a crowded theater, it was pointed out that the audience had refused to leave, choosing to remain in their seats and sing along with the orchestra that played the "Marseillaise." Flipping through the pages of one newspaper, Antonio noticed among the advertisements of department stores, retail shops, and ladies' boutiques an ad placed by Damien's chief competitor, Kriegck & Company, a men's shop located at No. 23 Rue Royale. The management at Kriegck was announcing that the firm's tailoring talents were now expanding into military attire, and offered the finest fabric and cut in French, British, and American officers' uniforms. Antonio could not imagine that this would please Monsieur Damien.

As Antonio sat reading on the bench, and sometimes got up to stroll around with his escort in tow, he saw many American officers and enlisted men arriving at the terminal, along with the military personnel of other Allied nations. Some lined up at the information booth, or along the platform, or at the Red Cross canteen at the far end of the hall, where snacks and nonalcoholic beverages were offered free of charge. The Americans were as a rule taller and bigger than the other servicemen, and had larger ears. Antonio had yet to meet an American. He had met a few English customers at Damien's, but never an American, and he understood hardly a word of English. Still, he was curious to hear Americans speak, and he was about to wander over toward the Red Cross canteen, when suddenly he heard thunderous sounds—and Graziani jumped up from the bench yelling, "Bombs! Bombs!"

The military policemen leaped across the aisle and grabbed both sergeants by the arms, just as the sirens sounded, and hundreds of people began to run in all directions. There was another explosion, heavier than before. Blowing their whistles, waving their billy clubs in the air, the policemen elbowed their way through the thick crowds, and soon they had led Antonio and Graziani down the steps into the presumably safer area below. Dozens of civilians and servicemen were already gathered in the lower lobby, shouting in different languages, facing one another in confusion, staring up at the ceiling as if expecting it to come crashing down at any moment. Finally a station attendant with a megaphone announced that the enemy planes had passed. Soon the sirens subsided, and most people in the crowd of two thousand proceeded up the ramps and staircases toward the main hall.

Antonio and Graziani, however, were detained below by two of the three policemen. The third had gone up to telephone the attaché's office. He returned an hour later, at three-thirty, to say there had been no changes in the sergeants' plans; they would leave as scheduled on the first of the eastbound trains. It was not expected that the planes would return, since the enemy was not known to stage two raids during a single day. The Germans should also be satisfied with the havoc they had caused already on this day. They had hit a munitions and grenade factory at Le Courneuve, in the northern sector of Paris, the policeman said; but the full circumstances of the attack would not be known to Antonio and Graziani until later in the week, after they had delivered the parcel to Bois de la Ville and had returned to trench duty at Verdun.

The explosions, which had been heard forty miles from the factory, and which had destroyed hundreds of doors and windows, roofs and telegraph poles within a one-mile radius of the target area, had killed or wounded more than six hundred people.

Although the Allied commanders were not yet aware of it, the destruction of the munitions factory, early on that Saturday afternoon, March 14, was the opening salvo of the Kaiser's big spring offensive aimed at winning the war during the late summer of 1918.

Now equipped with long-range guns that could fire projectiles more than seventy miles, the Germans pounded Paris at will; and a massive German breakthrough northeast of Paris later in March forced the Allies to transfer troops from all parts of the country to block the roads, rail lines, and river crossings leading toward the French capital. No longer could the United States' commander in chief in France, General Pershing, insist in good conscience that his divisions fight as a unit only under American supervision. As thousands of newly arrived Americans began their training in France, thousands of combat-ready Americans were released by Pershing to be used as Marshal Foch saw fit. Soon Americans were serving under British generals in Picardy and Flanders, and under French generals along the Marne River near Paris, and seventy miles northeast near Reims, and farther east in the Argonne Forest and at Verdun, where Antonio was stationed.

During this time at Verdun, Antonio became acquainted with several Americans, one of them a French-speaking infantry captain from Niagara Falls, New York, who, after touring the elaborate underground retreat of the French colonel, hailed it as a *"bon secteur."* But he didn't stay long, Antonio wrote in his diary in early May 1918. *He and the U.S. Second Division were pulled out of Verdun one night and rushed toward Gisors, thirty-five miles northwest of Paris. The Germans are expected to attack there very soon. Every day we hear rumors of a new German attack.*

By mid-June, Antonio himself was transferred out of Verdun, temporarily relieved from his headquarters role as an interpreter and reassigned once more to an Italian fighting unit linked to the French Fifth Army. *Ever since I went on that courier mission with Graziani, I suspected that my pleasant job as an interpreter would soon come to an end,* Antonio wrote. *Whenever I think things are going well I know bad things are ahead of me. Graziani was sent out with an infantry battalion two days after he'd delivered that little parcel to General Albricci's adjutant. Then a week later General Albricci and his entire staff left here for Reims to be under the French command of Gouraud. That was a month ago. Lots of other Italian officers and men were shifted recently near Épernay. Lots of shifting going on. Convoys of trucks packed with troops leave Verdun and head east, toward Paris, or they veer off into the Argonne Forest, where I'm headed. . . .*

A month later he wrote: *I'm still in the forest, and it gets hotter by the hour. My unit is an infantry brigade in zone 115 assigned to road-building jobs at night, and fortifying the defenses during the day. The Germans are to the north and east of us, blasting the roads that our convoys use, and every night we're out there patching things up in the moonlight. Yesterday our trucks brought in a few thousand American infantrymen, and the hot July weather doesn't agree with them—they're still outfitted in heavy woolen uniforms with choker collars, and as they march past us we can see them sweating right through the heavy material. They wave at us but few of them smile. They must envy the lighter uniforms we and the French wear. They probably didn't think they'd be called into action until the winter. . . .*

More than a million Americans were serving in France by midsummer of 1918, and their battered allies were soon resuscitated by the transfusion of fresh blood; indeed, before the end of July—partly because of the errors of the German high command, and partly because of the American presence—there was a definite shift in the momentum of the war. The serious mistake made by the German commanders was in procrastinating after their spring breakthrough, and then pushing ahead in places that overextended their fighting forces beyond their supply and counterdefensive capabilities. Meanwhile the Allies—the French, British, Italian, Belgians, Canadians, Australians, and others—began to fight with more vigor and more conviction that they could win. This uplift in morale did not go unnoticed by the German officers in the field, but it was perhaps articulated best by the German chancellor, Count Georg von Hertling, who noted after the armistice: "At the beginning of July 1918, I was convinced, I confess, that [by] the first of September our adversaries would send us peace proposals. . . . We expected grave events in Paris for the end of July. That was on the 15th [of July]. On the 18th, even the most optimistic among us understood that all was lost. The history of the world was played out in three days."

During these days, Marshal Foch changed to an offensive strategy. At last he had enough manpower to act more aggressively, and he also benefitted from the deterioration of German morale. In early July a number of German POWs who had been captured very recently, and who were very weary of the long war and wanted it to end at any cost, revealed the location where, on July 15, at precisely twelve ten a.m., more than sixteen hundred German batteries would attack French troops in the Champagne region east of Paris. As a result, the French were able to key in on the enemy stations and obliterate them before the Germans could begin their bombardments; the French shelled German gunners, munitions supplies, communications systems, and the German storm troopers standing ready for the scheduled dawn raid.

In addition to the declining German spirit, it was apparent to the Allies that the prisoners they were now taking were much younger than those captured in previous months; the German army—whose years of aggression on two fronts had killed off a high percentage of its most committed soldiers—was now forced to fill its ranks with servicemen who were unwilling or unworthy to serve its objectives. And before summer's end in 1918, the Allies had won back nearly all the land they had lost in the spring.

Most German units were now outnumbered, outgunned, and often adrift in fields and forests searching for food and shelter while being pursued on all sides by men of hostile nations. A Moroccan division, flanked by American regiments, attacked the Germans south of Reims. A Scottish division joined American and French forces east of Paris to help thwart a last-ditch German attempt at counterattacking along the southern bank of the Marne. And Italian units from Verdun who had been shifted in late summer from the Argonne to the Marne also fought effectively against the Germans. Antonio was among the Italians dispatched here, and his assignment—to help coordinate the delivery of munitions to rows of machine-gunners positioned along the river—afforded him a view of enemy transport boats, each carrying twenty soldiers, being riddled and capsized. The German soldiers who survived the flying bullets swam through the water, along with several horses that had jumped from punctured pontoon bridges now sinking under the weight of German motor vehicles and other equipment. With the German opposition nullified, the Allies continued their drive to the northeast, led by advanced guards of Americans who crossed the Marne on footbridges kept afloat by large empty gasoline tins.

The journey from the Marne across France toward the German border would be costly for the Allies—the United States alone would suffer forty thousand fatalities; but the autumn shadows were much darker on the German side of the battle lines. Their renowned Hindenburg defense, near the French–Belgian border, was broken through by contingents of British, French, and Australians during the first week of October. The German chief of staff, General Erich Ludendorff, was soon dismissed by the Kaiser—while he himself contemplated abdication and escape to neutral Holland. Germany's ally Bulgaria had collapsed at the end of September 1918; and by the end of October, the Turks would also quit fighting in the Near East. Another ally, Austria, persisted throughout October in the war south of the Alps, but was fighting now against optimistic Allied divisions commanded by Italy's General Diaz.

Diaz initiated a counteroffensive against the Austrians along the Piave River on October 24—the first anniversary of the Italian collapse at Caporetto. Now the situation was reversed—the Austrians were driven back inexorably and swiftly at the battle of Vittorio Veneto, and by November it was all over. This month would mark the collapse of the Austrian army and bring to a close the rulership of the ancient Hapsburg kingdom. A clause in the armistice terms gave the Allies the right to use the Austrian railroads, and as a consequence the Germans could now be invaded from Austrian soil.

General Diaz was a national hero, but the triumph was shared as well by foreign Allied soldiers who had accompanied Diaz's men throughout the months of retreat that preceded the glorious retaliation. Among the many Americans who had identified themselves with the Italian struggle was an Italo-American airman who had participated in raids on Austrian installations and who would be awarded a Flying Cross by the Italian king, Victor Emmanuel III. The airman had also served as an intermediary between Diaz in Italy and General Pershing in France during the final year of the war. He ended the war with the rank of major, and had been a freshman member of Congress before his enlistment, but he would be remembered best for his achievements later in life as the mayor of New York City—this was Fiorello H. La Guardia.

29.

WORLD WAR I ended on November 11, 1918, but Antonio Cristiani—and many thousands of other able-bodied Allied soldiers—were kept on active duty for an additional year or more to help remove the debris and the body parts that had been strewn throughout Europe during the four and a quarter years of turmoil that had brought death to ten million people.

In January and February 1919, Antonio worked with a Franco-Italian road gang clearing barbed wire and mines from the southern bank of the

Marne River; in March and April he served as a supply sergeant in a field hospital at Bar-le-Duc, near Verdun; and in May he was assigned to Paris as a French interpreter for an Italian colonel who was part of General Diaz's military group attending the peace conference.

Although the commanders of the victorious armies were now taking a backseat to the statesmen representing Britain, France, Italy, the United States, and the other Allied nations, the officers were consulted regularly by their civilian leaders in an effort to clarify the many disputes that arose at the victors' bargaining table. The shooting had stopped, but the Allied negotiators were now fighting among themselves over the spoils, and Italy was in the middle of the bickering. Italy's prime minister, Vittorio Emanuele Orlando, had walked out of the conference, and remained away for two weeks. He was displeased with President Woodrow Wilson of the United States, who wanted to withhold from Italy (and yield to the newly created nation of Yugoslavia) much of the territory held by the Austrians before the war that the French and British had secretly promised Italy in 1915 as an incentive to join the Allies. The Italian nation, having sacrificed the lives of more than 530,000 soldiers, was in no mood for bargaining; and many of its citizens were indeed pleased when Gabriele D'Annunzio, aided by thousands of invading insurgents, had gained control of some of these lands by force.

With this issue unresolved, the peace conference confronted other disturbances—such as the arguments between the French and British prime ministers over Belgian claims to Dutch territory, and the ways and means of extracting Germany's reparations payments. At one point in a debate, the British prime minister, David Lloyd George, grabbed the collar of his French colleague, Georges Clemenceau, and demanded an apology for the allegedly false and insulting statements uttered by the Frenchman. President Wilson stepped between them to halt further physical abuse, but Clemenceau refused to apologize; he suggested instead that Lloyd George might seek satisfaction "with either pistols or swords."

Antonio was pleased to be back in Paris that spring and summer as a linguistic aide to the Italian colonel, particularly because it allowed him the chance to begin negotiating for his own return to civilian life. When he arrived one day at Damien's tailor shop, Antonio's former employer embraced him warmly and offered him a large raise if he came back to work after his discharge; Monsieur Damien also made available at low rent an apartment on the sixth floor of the building he owned that housed his shop on the Rue Royale. After Damien's suggestion that Antonio lease it immediately, even though he was required to remain billeted near the site of the peace conference, Antonio borrowed Damien's driver to help with the moving, and in a few hours he had cleared out of his old apartment in the Latin Quarter—where he had to collect only a single suitcase containing two suits and a tuxedo, and to gather up the musty blankets, pillows, and sheets from the bed that he had not made in five years.

His new apartment, although it consisted of only one room with an alcove, would be large enough to include Joseph, at least temporarily; and there were other apartments on the sixth floor that Antonio thought he might obtain in the future. One was currently used for storing the firm's old business records and furniture. Another was leased to an Algerian woman who had not been seen in several months, even though her rent arrived regularly through the mail. Another apartment was occupied by the building's superintendent, an elderly, heavy-drinking Basque.

Antonio's apartment, in the front of the building, had two windows that offered a fine view of the skyline and the street below. The forthcoming Bastille Day parade would pass along this route; it would be a huge spectacle, a triumphant procession of Allied marching bands from every part of the world, and Antonio planned to watch it from one of his windows. But on the morning of July 14, when he got to the sixth floor and entered his apartment, he saw a dozen strangers leaning out of his windows. The superintendent, who was also in the room, smiled sheepishly. Then he reached into his pocket, walked over to Antonio, and handed him some francs, claiming that this was half the amount the people had paid for their viewing space. Antonio accepted the sum without thanks, and sat out the parade on the staircase.

Antonio and Joseph exchanged several letters during the summer and autumn of 1919; and in January 1920—by which time Antonio was discharged and back at Damien's—Joseph wrote saying that he had received permission from his mother and grandfather to join Antonio in Paris later in the spring. Postwar life in Maida continued to be bad, Joseph wrote; the town was still operating largely on the barter system, and many customers in Cristiani's tailor shop, recently reopened, were paying for new clothes with bushels of flour, heads of cattle, and other tradable commodities. The family farm was operating, but with Sebastian bedridden and Grandfather Domenico, almost eighty-two, less active, half its acreage was untilled, and laborers were scarce even in this time of vast unemployment.

Many of the returning veterans who were physically able to work seemed unwilling to do so. They spent their hours playing cards in the café, or in the back of Pileggi's butcher shop; barely subsisting on their wartime savings and small pensions, they cursed the government that had promised so much but was doing so little to improve the peacetime economy in the south. There were antigovernment demonstrations in Maida and elsewhere during the winter of 1920, all of them led by disillusioned veterans. But the most ambitious of these men, instead of demonstrating, were packing their bags and leaving the country. They were en route to promised positions as high-paid laborers in North and South America and in Australia.

Two of Joseph's uncles, the older of the four Rocchino brothers, left the village in late February 1920 to take up the factory jobs being held open for them at the Keasbey & Mattison asbestos plant in Pennsylvania. Joseph had accompanied his mother and other relatives to see the two men off. It was a bitterly cold morning, but the Rocchino brothers wore the same lightweight American linen suits and boaters they had worn back to Maida in answer to the call of conscription. Now, waving good-bye from the windows of their slow-moving Naples-bound train, they looked like two carefree tourists off on a grand adventure. Joseph, sixteen years old, watched from the platform, wishing he were with them.

Three months later, however, Joseph made his own exit. His mother came to the station with him, along with his grandparents, his younger siblings, and other relatives from both sides of the family. Domenico and Ippolita stood arm in arm a few feet back from the others on the platform; they were more reserved and better dressed than Joseph's outgoing Rocchino grandparents, his sheepskin-jacketed uncle on his mother's side, and her two gold-toothed, black-veiled widowed cousins. Joseph's aunt Maria had stayed home to look after Sebastian. Joseph had gone earlier in the day to the bedside of his brother, but Sebastian had merely whispered unintelligible words and did not seem to understand that Joseph was saying good-bye. Joseph's youngest brother, six-year-old Domenico, had been crying, disappointed that he would not be traveling on the train; and now on the platform he sat sullenly on Joseph's suitcase, his right hand firmly holding on to the handle. The old suitcase had belonged to their father, and jagged strips of American steamboat stickers still clung to its sides. Behind the suitcase stood Joseph's eleven-year-old sister, Ippolita, and fourteen-year-old brother, Nicola, looking at Joseph but saying nothing.

"You won't forget about us, will you?" Joseph's mother asked.

Joseph shook his head. He felt awkward with all eyes upon him, and he could barely wait to board the train. He was wearing the new brown overcoat and matching cap that his uncle Francesco had made for him, and delivered in the morning on his way to the shop. Tied around Joseph's waist, inside his trousers, was a money bag containing the American dollar bill his father had given him, plus five hundred dollars in lire loaned to him by the Rocchino uncles who had departed for America. They had told Joseph he could live with them in Ambler if things did not work out in Paris. He had been happy to hear this, for the bombing of Paris about which the elder Cristiani had spoken so often as he worried about Antonio had made the city lose some of its appeal; as a result Joseph was now more receptive to his father's affection for America. But Marian was expecting her son to return to Maida within a matter of months. This train ride to Paris was intended only as a summer visit in which Joseph would decide whether or not he liked Paris well enough to want to live there.

"You'll be home before your birthday?" his mother asked, more as a reminder than a question, for this had already been decided. On October 6, his seventeenth birthday, his grandfather Domenico was having a Mass said in his honor and would give him a party. The age of seventeen marked his arrival into manhood. Only then would he be free to decide his own destiny.

"Yes," Joseph replied, not looking into his mother's eyes. Antonio had said that the important thing was to get *out* of Maida; once you were out, there was little that anyone could do about it. Joseph had prayed regularly to Saint Francis, seeking guidance and wisdom; but at this moment on the platform—as the train stood waiting, and the porter pulled the suitcase out from little Domenico's grip and swung it up onto the steel steps of the car—Joseph was consumed with conflicting emotions.

The train traveled overnight up the coast, and by the next morning it had passed Rome and was rolling toward Tuscany. Joseph had spent his hours quietly in the compartment, alternately sleeping and reading through a French phrase book and a French dictionary that Antonio had sent him. But after the stop in Rome, the train became crowded, and Joseph shifted on the velvet bench closer to the window to accommodate the two nuns and the elderly white-haired gentleman who sat down on his right. Now across from Joseph were two young women in black dresses and lace mantillas, and a portly bespectacled man wearing a black suit, a black tie, and a black bowler, with a black ribbon sewn across the left sleeve of his jacket. The man took the young women's valises and placed them on the overhead rack. Then he removed his bowler and fanned himself with it a few times before sitting down between the women, the hat in his lap. His fingers drummed impatiently along the brim until the train began to move. He said something to the young woman on his right, then to the one on his left. The first was about Joseph's age, the other a few years older. Both were pretty in a serene and delicate way, and the man's familiarity toward them made Joseph think that he was their father; from the way they were dressed Joseph guessed that the three were either going to or coming from a funeral.

Joseph went back to his French book, but every so often he gazed out toward the shimmering sea outside, and up at the mountains and hillside towns overlooking the train to the east. Diverting as the scenery was, it did not look all that different from what he remembered of earlier train rides between Naples and Maida with his uncle Francesco; and Joseph had to remind himself constantly that he was now passing through unexplored territory—he had *indeed* left home, and he was traveling up the Tyrrhenian shoreline into northern Italy, and would soon reach Turin and cross the French border en route to an entirely new life. Having never before ridden in a plush compartment, he was grateful to his grandfather Domenico, to whom the stationmaster in Maida was in debt, for procuring this window seat in the first-class section.

As the journey continued, however, Joseph began to feel uneasy. The man seated between the young women kept looking at him. It was not a critical look, as if Joseph were guilty of some mild indiscretion; but neither did the man's attention suggest the amiable curiosity that a paternal figure might bestow upon a studious-looking young traveler cradling a French dictionary. The man obviously was troubled by some aspect of Joseph's appearance; and after he exchanged a few words with his female companions, they too studied Joseph with expressions that, though passive, were concentrated.

Joseph shifted in his seat behind his book. Twice he looked up, and both times the women averted his glance. But the man continued to stare. He seemed to be looking at Joseph and *through* Joseph. It occurred to Joseph that the man might be blind. But Joseph recalled that he had lifted the women's luggage effortlessly to the rack after they had entered the compartment.

The train was now passing through a tunnel, and the compartment lights were flicking on and off. A hollow echo permeated the car, and the sounds of the wheels rolling over the tracks rose a full octave. Beams of twilight sun flashed again through the windows as the train sped out of the tunnel, and the man looked down at his feet. But in the flickering light of the next tunnel, Joseph again saw the man staring at him, as if Joseph were projecting some sort of aura.

The nuns on Joseph's right seemed oblivious to all of this. They continued to talk between themselves as they had since boarding the train. The elderly gentleman, his head bent to one side against the corner cushion near the door, was fast asleep.

When the train stopped at Genoa, the nuns stood up and one of them nudged the old man. He quickly got up, took the nuns' valises, opened the door, and led them out. Joseph also stood, intending to wander the train in search of a seat in another compartment. If he found one, he would return for his suitcase. He was tired of being the object of this mysterious attention. But as he headed out, he felt a hand holding on to his arm; and the man asked in a gentle voice, while extending in front of him an empty cut-glass pitcher: "Excuse me, please, but would you mind getting us some water?"

Joseph stopped and looked directly at the man for the first time. He was certain he had never seen this person before. The man's face was round and kindly, with a crown of receding light brown hair, and a broad chin tipped by a grayish-red goatee. His steel-rimmed glasses fit tightly on his bony nose, and his pale-colored eyes were quite bloodshot. The two young women adjusted their mantillas and edged forward on their seats but made no attempt to rise. The older of the two studied Joseph momentarily and did not turn away as he looked at her; she in fact bowed her head slightly and smiled after he took the pitcher and said he would get the water.

He stepped down into the evening air and filled the pitcher at one of the fountains along the platform. The air was very chilly and damp, smelling slightly of the sea. After the departing passengers had disappeared, the platform became quiet except for the hissing of the locomotive and the chatter of a few newly arrived passengers who were going on to Turin or possibly onward across the French border. The smile of the young woman had been heartening, but Joseph's earlier uneasiness now returned as he heard the conductor's final whistle and he climbed back into the car. Holding the handle of the pitcher carefully, he waited as two passengers in front of him dragged their hefty luggage into their compartments, and then he continued until he arrived at his own. The man stood in the aisle, near the door.

"You are very kind," he said. He took the pitcher and handed it directly in through the door to one of the women, and then shut the door. Joseph stood in front of him for a moment expecting him to reopen it, but instead the man blocked the doorway and leaned closer to Joseph.

"I wish to apologize," he said, almost in a whisper. "I know we've probably made you uncomfortable, the way we've been watching you. But I'm afraid we cannot help ourselves. You see, you could be the identical twin of my only son. You not only look like him, but you hold yourself and move like him." Joseph stood speechless in the aisle, then lowered his eyes as the man added: "My son is dead."

"I'm sorry," Joseph said.

"Yes," the man went on, "he died during the war. On the last day of the war. He might have been the last Italian killed in the war. He was only seventeen. He had been at the front for less than a month."

The train started with a jolt, and the man lost his balance and bumped against one of the aisle windows, grabbing on to Joseph's arm for support. Even when he regained his balance, he continued to hold on to Joseph, although his grip was now very gentle as the train smoothly picked up speed.

"We're returning to our home in Turin, my daughters and I," he explained. "We're coming from Rome. There was a memorial service there, and we received the personal condolences of the king and members of parliament. We felt very honored. But," he added, his eyes moistening, "there are still times when I do not think I want to go on facing life. . . ."

Joseph nodded but could think of nothing to say. He wished the man would let go of his arm and permit him to leave the aisle and return to the compartment, although he was not really sure he wanted to. He would be boxed in there with this man's sadness. Here in the aisle, other passengers might stroll through, restless passengers unable to sleep and wanting to talk—potential company. But no one was afoot now as the train moved steadily northwest, leaving the last lights of Genoa fading in the evening fog.

"Where is your destination?" the man asked. Joseph told him, but volunteered that he might later sail on to America.

"And what of your family?"

Joseph's natural caution regarding strangers did not inhibit him, for despite his earlier discomfort at being scrutinized, he now understood the reason, morbid as it might be. This man seemed to be a sincere individual, rather than a prying one; and as the trip progressed, and as Joseph remained standing close to the man even after he had removed his hand from Joseph's arm, he replied to the man's ongoing questions with increasing candor and trust. Joseph spoke of his family in Maida; Sebastian's illness; the postwar poverty in the village; and the fact that he must soon assume the main responsibility for the support of his mother and kin, since his father was no longer alive.

"I'm sorry about your father," the man said, but in his voice there was now a certain piquancy and enthusiasm. He stopped questioning Joseph and began to talk about himself. He said that he owned a large manufacturing firm in Turin, one that he had inherited from his father and that his son was to have inherited from him. His daughters, university students, lived with him on the family estate and would continue to oversee it, he hoped, because their mother—his wife of twenty-five years—had died of tuberculosis three years before. As the man talked on, Joseph could see in the train window a reflection of the daughters enclosed behind the glass, their pale skin draped in black mantillas, their figures so close together on the seat that they almost appeared to be a split image of a single person. Joseph did not hear the question as it was asked, and so the man repeated it.

"Would you like to come with us to Turin?"

Joseph looked puzzled.

"I would like to show you our city," the man explained, with a reassuring smile. "I would like to give you a tour of my plant, and have you stay in our home, and let you see how we live. Turin is a beautiful city, and I assume you've never been there. You might find it so much to your liking that you'll never want to leave."

"But," Joseph interrupted, tentatively, "I'm being met by someone at the station in Paris."

"Don't worry," the man said, "I'll see that the railroad informs them of your change in plans, and later today we shall wire a fuller explanation and even try to reach them by telephone. And should you wish to resume your journey to Paris after seeing Turin, I will, of course, make the arrangements. . . ."

Joseph looked into the man's face. The expression there seemed kindly and reasonable. Joseph understood the situation: He was being sought out to serve briefly, or perhaps continually, as this man's substitute son. What still bewildered Joseph was whether this proposition represented a temptation or a blessing. To succeed as the substitute son of this wealthy man certainly meant opportunities beyond any that could be guaranteed elsewhere, and in an instant Joseph could imagine his grandfather Domenico, and even his mother, approving of this detour as a good omen. Joseph would remain in Italy. He would become the minion of a *gran signore,* with his financial future perhaps assured.

But as the man awaited a reply, Joseph began to shake his head, and then, in a strong voice that he hardly recognized as his own, he said: "I'm sorry, but my heart is set on going to America."

"You may be making a grave mistake," the man said, not concealing his disappointment. "I do think you should give it more thought."

As Joseph stood in the aisle, facing the darkness beyond the tracks, he again felt the man's hand on his arm. The train was swaying along a curved route as it entered the outskirts of Turin.

"Let me at least give you my card," the man finally said. He removed his hand and reached for his wallet, then offered a white card to Joseph. "If you become disappointed in Paris, or change your mind about America, I trust that you will contact me."

"Yes," Joseph said, accepting the card, "I will."

The man then turned toward the compartment and opened the door. His daughters had already stood and were reaching for their valises. Joseph stepped forward to help, but the man politely refused.

"The luggage is very light," he said, "and our driver will be meeting us at the platform."

The train had now come to a complete stop at the Turin station. The two young women bowed as they passed Joseph in the aisle, and the man shook his hand and wished him well. After they had left, Joseph returned to the compartment, which was now empty. He sat for a few moments, then stood again and watched from the aisle window as a tall man wearing livery and a gray peaked cap took the luggage and led the man and his two daughters away.

The rest of the trip was quiet and uneventful; Joseph slept most of the way. When the train pulled into Paris's Gare de Lyon the next day, Joseph spotted Antonio waiting for him along the platform. Before getting off, Joseph took the man's card, crumpled it, and left it on the floor of the compartment.

30.

THE PARIS THAT Gustave Flaubert had praised for its "amorous effluvium and intellectual emanations" was not the Paris that Antonio introduced to Joseph in the spring of 1920. The Paris that Joseph saw was scented by the perfume of strolling prostitutes, was overcrowded with war refugees and White Russians, and was debunked by poets and painters representing an avant-garde movement called Dadaism.

The Dadaists believed that nothing from the past was worth preserving—the Great War, and the psychic syndrome that fostered it, had poisoned everything; and as a symbol of the new movement's rejection of traditional standards in art, the artist Marcel Duchamp in 1919 produced a print of Leonardo's Mona Lisa wearing a moustache and goatee.

As if validating the Dadaists' view of a world gone amok, the president of France was discovered early one morning in 1920 (two days after Joseph's arrival in Paris) wandering barefoot through the countryside in his pajamas, having fallen out of the sleeping car of his train during the night; and this same individual—Paul Deschanel—would later be observed leaving an outdoor political gathering to embrace a tree, and still later to walk fully clothed into a lake. By summer's end, France's manic-depressive president had been replaced and institutionalized.

If the aftereffects of the war were more pronounced in France than elsewhere, it was also true that France experienced more death and destruction than any other nation. One million four hundred thousand of its soldiers were killed—17.6 percent of its army, as compared with Austria's 17.1 percent, Germany's 15.1 percent, and Britain's 13 percent. Of France's three million injured soldiers, more than a third would be permanently disabled.

"When the war finally ended, it was necessary for both sides to maintain, indeed to inflate, the myth of sacrifice so that the whole affair would not be seen for what it was: a meaningless waste of millions of lives," wrote the art critic Robert Hughes, more than half a century later. "Logically, if the flower of youth had been cut down in Flanders, the survivors were not the flower: The dead were superior to the traumatized living. In this way, the virtual destruction of a generation further increased the distance between the old and the young, between the official and the unofficial. One result of this was a hatred, among certain artists, of all forms of authority, all traditional modes. But the main result was a longing for a clean slate. If Verdun represented the climax of the patriotic, nationalist, law-abiding culture of the fathers, then the sons would be pacifists and internationalists. Some of them . . . wanted to create literal Utopias of reason and social justice, created (not merely *expressed*) by architecture and art. Others were less ambitious; they simply wanted to get out of the madness."

The predominant impression that Joseph had during his seven-month stay in Paris was that it was a city of old men and young women; and what surprised him, initially, was how many of these young women seemed to know his cousin Antonio. From the afternoon he had been escorted out of the rail terminal, and during the subsequent perambulations of the city, women approached Antonio in a familiar way and spoke words in French that seemed to make him blush. But he waved the women away and refused to interpret the words for Joseph.

Although Antonio was only twenty-six, Joseph now saw him as a much older man, a patriarchal figure rather than the cousin and confidant he had been in Maida. At Damien's, where Antonio had arranged for his apprenticeship, Joseph was impressed with his cousin's self-assurance in the presence of Monsieur Damien and the other veteran craftsmen, as well as the distinguished clientele who came in to be shown the bolts of now unrationed fabric from which would be cut looser, more leisurely postwar fashions. The clients included aristocratic émigrés from Lenin's Russia; members of the Rothschild family and other leading bankers; and some of the important Allied ministers who were continuing to oversee the peace conference at Versailles.

During the previous summer the Allied ministers had issued harsh terms to the delegates of the defeated Germans, Austrians, and Bulgarians; and during the spring and summer of 1920 the ministers were behaving similarly toward the Hungarians and Turks. But when many of these same ministers entered Damien's hall of mirrors to select their autumn wardrobes, the most decisive individual on the premises seemed to be Antonio. It was he who told them what to wear, and how to wear it. *They* had carved up Europe; *he* would cut their clothes.

The source of this decisiveness continued to amaze Joseph, for even the experience of the war years and achieving the rank of sergeant could not fully account for Antonio's commanding personality and persuasiveness. But as the summer progressed, and Joseph continued to observe his cousin at work, during their tours of the city, and in the privacy of their apartment, he began to recognize in Antonio's nature some of the qualities of their grandfather Domenico. Both men presumed to know what was best for those around them; and both conveyed, no matter where they were, a proprietary air—which in Antonio's case was all the more impressive since he owned no property.

To watch Antonio greeting clients each day in the wide and crowded corridors of the shop—his prematurely graying dark hair slicked back with brilliantine; his lapel flower one of two that daily adorned his buttonhole; the elevated heels of his two-toned shoes under his longish trouser cuffs lifting him to the Napoleonic height of five feet, six inches—was to see a man who had traveled far from Maida, and was possibly en route to becoming the next director of the firm and heir apparent of the owning family; and Monsieur Damien hardly discouraged that impression by inviting Antonio home frequently on weekends to dine with his wife and daughters.

But Antonio's ambitions went beyond this. As he himself confided to Joseph, he wanted a business of his own, wished to see *his* name emblazoned above the portal and scrawled in gold lettering across the front windows. As much as Monsieur Damien paid him, Antonio considered himself underpaid, and his view was reinforced during the late summer when he was offered a contract at higher pay from a competing firm, Larsen's. While pondering the offer, Antonio proclaimed to Joseph that he could probably gain a similar contract from the even more prestigious establishment of Kriegck & Company. Even under Antonio's present arrangement at Damien's, it was no secret that he was devoting some of his energies elsewhere; on three evenings a week, after Damien's had closed its doors, Antonio supervised tailoring classes at a trade school not far from the École Ladaveze. Several of the students were unemployed Eastern Europeans who had entered Paris as war refugees; others were disabled French veterans wishing to learn a craft in which ambulatory limitations were of little importance. Joseph served as one of Antonio's classroom assistants; the position earned him some welcome francs (he was unsalaried at Damien's) but also meant that three nights a week he went to bed hungry.

Since Damien's closed at eight and the school (which was fifteen minutes away by bus) began at eight-fifteen and ended at midnight, there was insufficient time for Joseph and Antonio to eat *and* rise at dawn on the following day, which was required because Antonio had been entrusted by Monsieur Damien with a key to the shop so he could receive the fabric deliveries, which were usually at six-thirty. But on nonschool evenings, Antonio saw to it that Joseph was treated to a full, if inexpensive, meal. Antonio of course selected the restaurants and did all the ordering.

Italian restaurants were avoided in favor of French bistros and cafés during Joseph's first two months in Paris; Antonio insisted that the patronage of such places would hasten Joseph's familiarity with the local language and the customs of Parisians. But despite Antonio's diligent correcting of Joseph's faulty pronunciation, and Joseph's continued study of French language books, he lacked Antonio's facility with French; or perhaps he lacked Antonio's sincere desire to master it. Instinctively, if not yet declaratively, Joseph knew that he would not remain long in Paris. It was clear that Antonio belonged there, that he had found the place that suited his temperament, his style, his craving for excitement. But for

Joseph, the French capital was merely a way station to America. Until he became seventeen in early October, Joseph was of course resigned to his status as Antonio's ward, a role that at least saved him from being sent back to Maida. But with Antonio so protective and controlling, albeit necessarily, given Joseph's dependence in Paris, Joseph soon felt trapped and claustrophobic in ways he had not even felt in Maida.

When Sebastian had gone off to war, Joseph had become accustomed to having a bedroom to himself; and while this changed with Sebastian's return, the latter's incapacities negated the manner in which he had formerly tried to give orders as Joseph's older brother. Their grandfather Domenico, who suddenly seemed older and withdrawn after Sebastian's tragedy, also declined as a guiding force in the household during Joseph's final year at home. But now in Paris, probably the world's most liberal and libertine city—one that seemed to absorb the sounds of the noisy Bolsheviks in the boulevards advocating insurrection, and overlook the lesbian bars and bordellos that lined the side streets—Joseph found himself confined with his commanding cousin five flights above the tailor shop to which he was apprenticed without pay, while getting a minimum of sleep each night on a small cot in a one-room apartment that was triple-locked to keep out the prying, alcoholic Basque superintendent.

Antonio had fortified the security after catching the superintendent on three occasions trying to pick the lock—while the superintendent feebly justified himself each time with claims that he had smelled smoke and thought a fire might be smoldering within. Whatever misgivings Antonio did not have about the superintendent, he had for the other tenant on the sixth floor—the soft-stepping, taciturn Algerian woman who, wearing dark glasses, came and went along the squeaky staircase at odd hours, and rarely remained overnight in her apartment more than twice a month. Antonio believed, without a shred of evidence, that she was an espionage agent involved in schemes to overthrow the French government. More plausibly he felt ill disposed toward her because, contrary to his hopes, she did not become a dead martyr to her cause and leave her apartment vacant for him to take over and make available to Joseph.

Although neither of them complained about it, by midsummer both Antonio and Joseph were feeling cramped in the close quarters of the apartment, three-fourths of which was tacitly monopolized by Antonio, while the corner alcove was Joseph's dominion. A six-foot-high freestanding mahogany-framed mirror, borrowed from Damien's storage room, sectioned off Joseph's corner from the rest of the room. Behind the mirror was his cot. His suitcase, laid flat on the floor and draped with a piece of damask material, served as an end table, while his wardrobe hung heavily from a clothes tree that had two pegs missing, causing the pole to tilt against the wall.

Antonio's many suits and coats filled the armoire that stood at the far end of the apartment, between the two front windows. To the left of the armoire was a bed with a brass headboard that he had bought at a flea market and had transferred from his old apartment in the Latin Quarter. Next to the washstand (the toilet was in the hall) was a five-drawer bureau whose top displayed Antonio's many brushes and combs, pomades, colognes, mouth rinses, and other bottled toiletries, all lined up as evenly as a row of soldiers awaiting inspection. His extra pairs of shoes were aligned precisely on the floor of his armoire. Antonio carefully made his bed each day instantly upon getting up.

In contrast to Antonio's orderliness, a spirit of disorder and abstract grotesquerie was expressed on the walls of the apartment, within the frames of oil paintings he had bought cheaply from sidewalk artists along the Seine. Some of these paintings were in the Cubist style that had been fashionable before the war; others showed signs of what in later years would be called Surrealism; still others were nondescript blotches of garish paint that might have been tossed onto the canvas from buckets. There was one painting, however, that was unabstractly erotic. It was a painting of a buxom naked woman standing in a bathtub fondling her breasts.

Joseph could not look at it without feeling embarrassed, although he never commented on it to Antonio. Still, its position above Antonio's bed made him wonder if his cousin was truly as prudish as he made every effort to appear in the streets when he brusquely rejected the appeals of prostitutes and the male peddlers of risqué French postcards. And the fact that nearly the entire wall was devoted to modern art, with not a holy picture or tiny crucifix in sight, added to Joseph's wonderment about his cousin. The ungodliness of the war had perhaps induced some skepticism, and its brutality seemed to linger in Antonio's dreams. Joseph had been privy to some of these nightmares, being awakened by the sounds of Antonio banging a hand against the headboard and screaming what sounded like military commands, or battle orders, or panicked words of warning. Often two particular names were mentioned, and they were the most urgently repeated: "Muffo! Branca! . . . Muffo! Branca! . . ." In the middle of one hot night Joseph awoke to find Antonio sleepwalking, moving slowly in circles in his underwear, then heading toward a window that was wide open. Joseph ran and grabbed him by the shoulders. Antonio swung around and swore angrily at Joseph, as he had never done before. After calming down, Antonio explained that he had not been sleep-walking, but had become agitated in the oppressive heat and was going to the window for cooler air. In the morning, as they dressed quickly for work, neither mentioned the incident.

Later that afternoon, after Antonio had gone off with Monsieur Damien to visit a client in a hotel, Joseph slipped away from the shop and followed the directions he had plotted on his pocket map of Paris to the Italian embassy. He hoped to apply for a visa to America without telling Antonio. Uncertain of Antonio's reaction, and not even sure whether he could get a visa application, since he was not yet seventeen and also lacked the required documents from an overseas sponsor, he thought it best to inquire in private before risking a family quarrel over a possibility that might not yet be possible. In this reasoning Joseph was guided as well by the example Antonio had set in running away from Maida. Act first, explain later.

Wearing a straw hat and a beige flannel suit from whose jacket Antonio had removed most of the lining to make it lighter and cooler, Joseph proceeded through the late-afternoon heat along a tree-lined boulevard with a novel sense of independence and nervousness. This was his first walk through Paris unaccompanied by Antonio. The avenue was crowded with strolling couples, many of the women smoking cigarettes, their hair cut short like boys'. Their escorts were frequently gray-haired officers with polished boots and rows of chest ribbons, or ministerial-looking men with top hats and walking sticks, who seemed comfortably cool despite their starched collars and weighty dark suits. Joseph heard a variety of languages being spoken around him, and now and then a voice he thought American, although he could not be sure. He had been told that Paris was now filled with American tourists, lured by the dollar's climb from seven francs a year before to now nearly twenty—attracting bargain hunters from abroad to all areas of French trade except prostitution. That industry had lost a high percentage of its clientele since the repatriation of the millions of soldiers who had frequented the city's brothels during furloughs from the front and layovers. "These prostitutes are now desperate for money," Antonio had recently explained to Joseph, justifying the gruff manner in which he had kept his distance from one persistent woman in the street. "If they don't get their money in one way, they'll try another—with the help of the knives they carry in their garter belts," he added, knowingly. "Or with the help of their pimps, who are always close by in the shadows."

Avoiding the shadows, Joseph continued along the outer edge of the sidewalks toward the Italian embassy, moving at a brisk pace and veering away from all female standees while trying to remain close to male pedestrians in military uniforms, these being the men he could most safely assume were not pimps. Joseph's personal safety was of secondary concern to him; more important was the fact that he carried around his waist, inside his trousers, the resources he hoped would buy his passage to America—the money bag containing the five hundred dollars in lire that his Rocchino uncles, now in Ambler, had loaned him. Joseph wore this belt everywhere, even at night in bed. While it added to the sense of confinement that he had felt in so many ways since arriving in Paris, he saw no alternative. The streets were swarming with potential thieves, according to his cousin, and even the superintendent of his residence had a predilection for picking the tenants' locks.

Seeing the tricolored flag of Italy flying behind the stone-walled embassy building, Joseph hastened toward the plume-hatted Carabiniere who stood guarding the gate. The officer, who wore a silver sword and a black-holstered pistol at the waist of his blue uniform, lifted a white-gloved hand toward his peaked cap in casual salute. After Joseph requested permission to visit the travel consul's office, and had shown his passport, he was given directions and waved through the gate with a wink from the officer, a wink that the officer repeated to the two pretty young women who had exited the building and were heading toward the street.

After passing through the main foyer, where there was a wall portrait of King Victor Emmanuel III, Joseph climbed two flights of steps and entered a long room with a high, intricately carved ceiling; the room was crowded with people standing in two lines waiting to be interviewed by two dark-suited men, one white-haired, the other balding, who occupied large desks stacked with papers and books. The people in line were very quiet, and throughout the room the questioning by the two men was audible, rising above the less audible replies of the applicants at the desks.

The white-haired man spoke Italian with an accent that was unfamiliar to Joseph, who assumed it was characteristic of some region in northern Italy. The voice of the balding official, however, was intoned with southern traces that Joseph recognized at once; and despite his recent efforts to distance himself from his roots—from his family, from his village, and today also from Antonio—he was immediately drawn back to what was familiar. He joined the line leading to the southerner's desk, even though this was the longer one. There were about fifty people here, compared with fewer than forty in the other. Nearly everyone in both lines was much older than Joseph, ranging in age from at least forty to seventy, maybe even beyond, and while they were presentably attired, Joseph knew from his perusal of tailoring magazines and his exposure to style at Damien's that these people were dressed predominantly in a way that was quite old-fashioned, predating the war by years.

The men's trousers were narrow and cuffless, tapering at the ankles; their jackets tended to be a bit long, tight-fitting in the waist, and curved out along the sides like riding coats. Many wore spats on their narrow pointed shoes, and collars with bow ties, and had beards with side whiskers. The women favored long full skirts of bright summer shades that in many cases were faded, starched blouses with unusually high collars, brimmed straw hats or felt bonnets; and several women also carried furled parasols underarm. They could have walked out of the large fin-de-siècle poster of a Paris street scene that Joseph had recently paused to look at with Antonio in front of a department store window. But Joseph reminded himself that these people in the embassy were not French but Italians, or relatives of Italians, or possibly Franco-Italian émigrés from rural areas along the border who had moved here during the war to escape the Austrians. They were among the oldest survivors of the Great War, and now they were getting travel information so that they might begin life anew in some faraway place. The gray-haired couple standing in front of Joseph were holding hands. The man's left hand and the woman's right were clasped within the folds of her long skirt, causing a slight wavering of the material as they loosened their interlocked wrists and intertwined their fingers.

The woman's silvery hair, braided back in a bun, was topped by a wide-brimmed straw hat with a rose tucked into the side band. Tall and broad-shouldered, she faced the front without whispering a word to her companion; but occasionally her shoulders rose, crinkling the back of her starched linen blouse. The man was heavyset and had thick gray hair parted in the middle. Sewn across the left sleeve of his black jacket was a thin mourning band of matching color; it blended in so well with the jacket that it was barely noticeable. In his hand not enclasped with the woman's he held a Panama hat that looked newly bought. The smooth, palmlike texture of the white crown cast a sheen in the window light, and the hat's wide brim seemed as thin and sharp as a knife. Having never before seen an elderly couple holding hands, Joseph did not know what to make of it; but their warmth for one another was nonetheless comforting, making him feel more hopeful and less estranged than he had felt on entering the room.

The line moved slowly forward, advancing a few paces every five or

ten minutes. Joseph was concerned that Antonio would have by now returned to the shop, and would be alarmed at not finding him there. It was
already four in the afternoon. Listening to the people up ahead, Joseph
was aware that most of them had requested guidance in getting to South
America and Canada. The cities most mentioned were Buenos Aires and
Montreal. Ships headed in those directions left twice weekly, and the
counselors, for a fee, volunteered to expedite the procurement of visas
from the Paris-based representatives of the countries the applicants wished
to enter.

Since none of the applicants had so far expressed interest in visiting
the United States, Joseph wondered if American ports were still closed
to foreigners, as they had been during the war; his Rocchino uncles, after
all, had somehow managed to get in recently aboard a ship sailing from
Naples. Perhaps only ships sailing from France were limiting civilian
travel into the United States. The idea of trying to book passage from
Naples was discouraging to Joseph, for if he returned to southern Italy he
would feel obligated to visit his mother and the others in Maida, and they
would surely try to make him change his mind about America.

By four-thirty, Joseph had almost reached the travel counselor's desk.
The gray-haired couple, who had stopped holding hands when they moved
up to be next in line, were now standing at the desk explaining that they
wished to embark on a journey to Australia within the next three to five
weeks. They said they were Protestant missionaries from Piedmont, and
were being reassigned to a mission in Melbourne. Joseph had never known
any Protestants before, as they were almost nonexistent in his area of the
south, but he was aware that some Italians, including a cousin of his late
father's, had settled in Australia.

The room was now nearly empty. The last of the people in the other
line had just left, and the white-haired counselor was counting the money
he had collected for promising to expedite the securing of visas and making the passengers' travel arrangements. The balding counselor at the
desk in front of Joseph was thumbing through large books and quoting to
a couple the various train and boat schedules that might be used in getting
to Australia.

Nearly fifteen minutes passed before they made their decisions, deposited their down payment, and, with prolonged expressions of gratitude, finally turned to leave. The woman almost brushed against Joseph
as she whirled around in her long skirt and adjusted her hat, and for a moment he had a view of her face, which was angular and handsome, and

unadorned by rouge. Her companion, an individual of sturdy but refined features, acknowledged Joseph with a nod and a smile before escorting the woman away.

"Passport, please," the counselor called out.

Joseph stopped watching the couple and quickly stepped forward with his passport. The man examined it for a second, then raised an eyebrow.

"Ah, I see you're from Maida," he said, now in an agreeable tone.

"Yes," Joseph replied.

"Well, I was born near Maida. I'm from Cosenza. You have been to Cosenza?"

"No, but I know where it is," Joseph said. "It's a provincial capital." Joseph was glad that he knew this. It seemed to impress the counselor, who went on to say, "Well, I not only know where Maida is, but I have *been* there. It's a pretty little town on a hill. There's a castle in the center. It was many years ago that I was there, but I remember the visit. It was Eastertime. I went with my uncle to a tailor shop in Maida. He was having a suit made for Easter." He paused before adding: "He had some disagreement with the tailor there."

Joseph began to tremble. He remembered how he had accidentally cut the trouser knee of the new suit that his uncle Francesco had made for the *mafioso* from Cosenza, Vincenzo Castiglia. Joseph's heart was pounding heavily, and he felt dizzy. The counselor noticed his unsteadiness.

"Young man, are you all right?" he asked.

"Yes," Joseph said, "I think I'm just a little nervous."

"Nervous about what?" the man asked. There was curiosity as well as concern in his voice. Looking up from his desk, squinting, he carefully studied Joseph's face. Joseph lowered his eyes. There was silence in the room for a few seconds.

"I'm worried about drowning," Joseph lied, although he had often imagined this in his nightmares. "I've never been on a ship before."

The man settled back in his chair. His inquiring frown softened and he smiled broadly, revealing two gold molars.

"Have no fear, young man," he said. "Our ships are very safe. And by the way, where do you want to go?"

"Can you get me to the United States?" Joseph asked, tentatively.

"Maybe," the man said. He reached through a stack of papers on his desk, found the one he was looking for, and read it briefly to himself.

"The English have just taken over some German ships, and they'll be using them for civilians," he said. "The route will include New York. The ships will begin leaving next month, from Cherbourg. You know where Cherbourg is, don't you?"

Joseph hesitated.

"Cherbourg is in northern France," the man went on. "It's a simple train ride from here. And I think I can arrange everything, including your passage and the visa." He took a visa application form out of his desk and handed it to Joseph with a fountain pen.

"Here, fill this out," he said, "and I'll also need your application fee. Do you have forty francs, or fifty lire?"

Joseph did not reach for his money bag filled with lire, for he kept this secret from everyone except Antonio. Instead he removed from his jacket an envelope that held the francs he had saved from his nighttime job as Antonio's classroom assistant. He believed he had barely enough to cover the cost of the fee. But in his eagerness to pay the man—Joseph was overjoyed that there had been no questions about age or sponsorship—he dropped the old and brittle envelope on the counselor's desk, where it split open to reveal not only the francs, but also the cherished dollar that Joseph had been given years before by his father.

"American money!" the counselor cheerfully announced, snatching it in his fingers; and before Joseph could protest, the man had tucked it, and a fistful of francs, into his pocket.

"This will cover it," he declared with a finality that discouraged further discussion. "And *quickly,* fill out the form," he added. "We're about to close the office."

Joseph cheerlessly complied, then watched as the counselor examined his form and placed it in a desk drawer. The other counselor, who had been waiting at his desk, now joined his colleague and helped carry the many books and pamphlets from the desktop to the open drawer of a nearby filing cabinet.

"You should return here in about three weeks," the counselor told Joseph. "By then we may have a report on our progress."

Joseph nodded good-bye, left the building, passed through the gate, and received another casual salute from the Carabiniere.

The boulevard was now more crowded than before, the cafés were filled, and the sidewalks were entirely in shadows. It was shortly after six. As Joseph walked on, he wondered what he would say to Antonio, and he was still saddened by the loss of the souvenir from his father. But there was also a certain spring in his step, a vague sense of accomplishment he was aware of. In the course of the afternoon he believed that he had moved closer to his final destination. And he also remembered that on the day he had been given the dollar, his father had told him that he should spend it one day on something wonderful. Joseph could think of nothing more appropriate than a visa to America.

31.

FORTUNATELY FOR JOSEPH, his cousin was not there when he returned to Damien's at close to seven that evening. But later, before he and Antonio were about to go out to dinner, Joseph could no longer conceal what he had done. So he told Antonio of his visit to the embassy, and his hope of leaving France as soon as possible. Much to his relief, Antonio was not angry; on the contrary, he seemed pleased. "Tonight let's eat at a café I know on the Left Bank where the Americans go," he announced. "And later we can go listen to American Negro musicians play this new kind of music. It's called jazz."

Many years later, long after Joseph had established himself in the United States and all but forgotten his seven-month sojourn in France, he would realize from reading the reminiscences of famous journalists and novelists that he had resided in Paris during the postwar influx of many creative and influential young people from Europe and the United States. Pablo Picasso, James Joyce, and Gertrude Stein had already settled there. Ernest Hemingway and other writers and artists would soon join them, along with university graduates and affluent exiles and other travelers along what the writer Malcolm Cowley would call the "longest gangplank in the world."

Many black American soldiers who had served in Europe were discharged in Paris, and they chose to remain with their French wives rather than accept repatriation on American troop ships that required their traveling alone. Couples could live cheaply and eat well in France if they had American money. The dollar would be worth fifty francs by the mid-twenties. While the sale of liquor was now outlawed in the United States, it flowed freely in Parisian cafés and jazz clubs. Sylvia Beach opened Shakespeare and Company, which was as much a meeting place for English-speaking residents as it was a lending library and book shop. The young composer Aaron Copland attended a new school for American musicians at the Fontainebleau palace southeast of Paris. The already prominent French designer Gabrielle ("Coco") Chanel, mourning her lover killed in an auto accident, would soon influence world fashion with her little black dress.

But if Joseph saw any of these achieving individuals during his time in Paris, he was never aware of it. While he was impressed by the innovations that surrounded him—the city's underground trains and electric lighting, its many telephones and elevators, its buses and taxis, and the installation of cable wire to initiate radio broadcasts from the Eiffel Tower—he would remember France in 1920 mostly from the vantage point of the small apartment with Antonio and his job at Damien's. And on a cold and blustery day in mid-December, after traveling by train to Cherbourg, he embraced Antonio on the pier and climbed the gangplank onto a huge German-made British ship bound for New York.

He had already written his family in Maida about his departure, and had also written his two uncles in America, requesting that they meet him at Ellis Island. In his pocket he carried his passport and visa. Antonio had accompanied him to the Italian embassy, and had gotten on well with the travel counselor. Indulging the man's fondness for reminiscing, Antonio was able to learn that his *mafioso* uncle was no longer alive.

"He passed away last year in Chicago," the counselor sadly acknowledged.

"Oh, I'm sorry to hear that," Antonio had replied. "May God rest his soul."

Joseph then followed Antonio's example in lowering his head in front of the counselor and assuming a demeanor of sympathy.

It took eight days to reach the United States. The ship encountered storms most of the way, and Joseph was so petrified and nauseated that he remembered little of the journey except the horror of being on board. He spent most of the time in his cabin, holding on to an iron bar above his bed as the ship pitched and churned choppily through the night, and then proceeded each day through heaving waters and under dark clouds and rain.

Despite his reliance on Saint Francis, to whom he prayed constantly, his dreams of drowning had been more persuasive than the conscious force of his faith. Indeed, on the fifth morning of the trip he was convinced that the ship was sinking, that he was seconds away from death; and in a state of despair he fell out of bed screaming and tumbled to his knees, and beseeched the saint to save him.

The ship seemed immobile. Its engines were silent. He heard the sounds of bubbles popping softly outside the porthole. For the first time since his departure from Maida Joseph felt shame in his decision to leave, which he now admitted was most likely forever. While it was true that his family's economic problems could be alleviated only by money earned elsewhere, he saw himself as a deserter, a fugitive from family ties, an escapist from the hard times at home. He waited in his cabin, kneeling on the floor with his head pressed down on the cot, acknowledging that perhaps he deserved to die. He had forsaken his family, his widowed mother and ailing brother in his quest for self-betterment, a life in a land of opportunities and wealth.

The ship sailed quietly into New York Harbor after dawn on December 23, 1920, a morning so foggy that Joseph could not see the Statue of Liberty. The waters were calm, however, and he remained with the crowd on the upper deck, wearing his best suit under his overcoat, and also the gloves, scarf, and cap that Antonio had presented to him as a going-away gift at Cherbourg.

Despite his clothes he was extremely cold, and he huddled close to the people standing three deep along the rail. Many of the women, and even a few men, wore full-length fur coats. Joseph had never before seen men in fur, nor had he ever seen men drinking from flasks, as several were now doing. Some of the young women, their bobbed heads covered with turbans or small-brimmed hats, also drank from the silver containers that the men passed around. What most surprised him was the carefree manner in which the women put to their lips what seconds before had touched the lips of several men. Joseph was indeed entering the New World.

He began to feel better among the friendly and boisterous passengers on deck, a crowd that was gleeful and easily amused. They laughed when one older man's homburg blew off his balding head and sailed into the sea, prompting him to shrug gallantly and smile. They applauded when one of the scavenger birds circling overhead caught in its beak a piece of bread that a passenger had tossed into the air. There was even more applause as the sun streamed through the clouds and the skyline of lower Manhattan came vaguely into view. At first glance Joseph thought he was sailing toward a cluster of cornstalks, dense and golden in the misty morning light. The land was fertile, overplanted, growing before his eyes. Everyone on deck was now concentrated upon it, as if seeing it for the first time, although Joseph was fairly sure that most of these passengers were Americans. He had heard a few older couples on deck speaking

French, but the great majority spoke English in the unaffected and slightly blunt way of those people he had seen in the Left Bank cafés and jazz clubs. He might have seen a few of these passengers before in Paris; he was quite sure of having seen the tall black-haired man who stood near him now, wearing a voluminous raccoon coat, facing the sea with his long shaggy-sleeved arms draped over the shoulders of the petite women in fur-trimmed leather coats and spike-heeled shoes with dark stockings. In Maida the sight of a man standing with his arms embracing two women simultaneously would have invited trouble from at least one aspiring or jealous suitor, but no one on deck appeared to be concerned, certainly not the women snuggled merrily within his grasp. One of them sipped from a silver flask. The other gazed through a pair of binoculars and pointed enthusiastically toward something that delighted her on shore.

The ship was now within a few thousand yards of a row of piers, its bow cutting through chunks of ice, driftwood, and debris. Barges and small steamers were moving slowly up ahead, along the edge of the river-front, and so was a red-and-white ferryboat trailed by low-flying birds feeding on what was churned up behind the ferry's stern. Beyond the shorefront, visible between the anchorages and a few seaport shacks, was a roadway being crossed by motor vehicles and horse-drawn wagons; and rising in the background were massive buildings of stone and steel. Some of them looked nearly as tall as the Eiffel Tower, but so much bulkier and weightier it was a wonder they did not sink through the thin layer of the ground and disappear under the sea.

With its horn sounding, the boat edged into the slip, and Joseph could see gangs of stevedores standing on the pier below, and many people waiting on the deck of the anchorage. He had been told earlier that he could pass through customs and immigration here in Manhattan, together with the other cabin-class and first-class passengers; but since he had asked his uncles to meet him at Ellis Island, he had to board a ferry with the third-class passengers.

The ferryboat was waiting at the pier near where the big ship had set anchor. Blue-uniformed immigration authorities were assembled to direct the passengers. Instructions were called out in different languages, and after forming lines the passengers were taken aboard. These were people Joseph had not seen during the crossing; they were plainly dressed, in heavy wool coats and long scarves and with blankets wrapped around their shoulders. A few women carried babies; the men carried wooden boxes or leather valises or cloth bags in their ungloved hands. Some of the men were not much older than Joseph; these men were not accompanied by women. They were sturdily built and ruddy-complected for the most part, and seemed clannish in the way they stood apart from the others as the ferry pushed off noisily through the pilings and headed back out to sea.

Joseph sat on a rear bench behind rows of couples and children, listening while they communicated loudly in French and in languages that he could not identify but thought might be Scandinavian or Slavic. He heard no Italian spoken, and not even English. There was none of the friendliness and frivolity that had existed earlier on the deck of the ocean liner, but mercifully the ferry took only fifteen minutes to cross the waters and approach an odd, almost arabesque red château with four domed towers and a big spike sticking up through each.

Uniformed officials speaking a variety of languages waited at the pier, and then escorted the arrivals, with all their trappings, into the four-domed building. Here, on Ellis Island, the immigrants would spend most of the day, standing on lines waiting to be interrogated by agents and physically examined by doctors. Joseph stood with the others, quite anxious as representatives of the United States Public Health Service took turns scrutinizing his eyes for signs of trachoma, his hair for lice, his neck, arms, and hands for sores, tumors, moles, or other possible indications of insalubriousness. Medical machines probed him for evidence of tuberculosis, heart deficiency, nervous disorders. Joseph had heard that newcomers sometimes failed these examinations, and were turned away back to the boats—deported from America, separated from fellow-traveling kinsmen. But on this day, Joseph and the other ferry passengers moved unchallenged from one medical station to the next; no one had the back of his coat chalked with white letters signifying possible ailments that required further examinations and possible deportation, his travel costs to be absorbed by the shipping company that had booked his passage.

Joseph was eventually escorted by an interpreter toward a row of desks. The same interpreter, a slightly stooped man in his forties, with a moustache and steel-rimmed glasses, who had introduced himself as Professor Carlino, helped Joseph through the medical stations. He said he had come to America as a two-year-old from Naples. He now taught engineering at a city university, and he worked on weekends and holidays as one of the Italian interpreters on the island. "You could not have arrived at a better time," he told Joseph. "Tomorrow's Christmas Eve, and the staff here wants to leave early this afternoon to complete their shopping, including the deportation officers. Only the extreme cases should be detained, the terminally ill and any Bolsheviks carrying arms."

"Who paid your ship's fare?" an official asked Joseph, not looking up but flipping through papers on his desk, where he noted that Joseph had traveled cabin class.

"I did, sir," Joseph responded in Italian, then listened to the translation by Professor Carlino. The benign-looking interpreter stood behind the chairs of the two uniformed interrogators, a hopeful tutor supporting his pupil. The interrogators were both gray-haired and stout, but one appeared much older than the other. Both had gold insignia on their lapels bearing the letters "U.S."

"What is your occupation?" the younger official asked.

"I am a tailor," Joseph replied.

The officials looked at how Joseph was dressed, and neither showed signs of disapproval. His white shirt was clean, he wore a bow tie, and he had polished his shoes before leaving the boat in the morning. He carried his topcoat over one arm, his cap in hand, and wore the new suit that he had left hanging over the portal in his cabin, where it not only masked the sight of the moving sea but also avoided becoming wrinkled in his suitcase or in the cabin's dank cubbyhole closet.

"So tailors can achieve prosperity even at your age," the older official remarked with a smile, while the other added: "And I assume you have a job waiting for you in this country?"

"Yes, sir," Joseph said forthrightly, hiding his uneasiness about the fabrication. Antonio had told him that in front of immigration officials it was wiser to be very positive than very truthful.

"And where will you work?" the same official asked.

"In Philadelphia."

"Ah, yes," he said, "it seems that every Italian tailor who passes through here is heading for Philadelphia."

"Can you read and write?" the older man asked.

"Yes, sir."

"Have you ever been in prison?"

"*No,* sir."

"How much money are you carrying?"

Hearing the translation, Joseph looked with concern toward the professor. Professor Carlino had witnessed the rejection of even some well-dressed people because they were discovered to be destitute, but the financial question was unexpected for someone who had traveled cabin class. Now the professor himself had no reason *not* to wonder if this young man, traveling alone, carried at least the required minimum of ten dollars in foreign coins or currency that most inspectors demanded prior to validating an applicant's entry into the United States.

"I have a hundred forty dollars in lire," Joseph said, and the professor, who seemed quite pleased, was about to relay the figure to the officials, when Joseph interrupted to explain that it was hidden in a money bag strapped around his waist inside his trousers. He added that it was locked, and that opening it would necessitate his lowering his pants practically to his thighs, for the lock was affixed to a lower part of the bag.

"I hope I won't have to show them the money," Joseph said, aware of the fact that he was standing within view of hundreds of people; there were very few walls and partitions in this great hall of Ellis Island— symbolic of an open society perhaps, but potentially embarrassing to an individual who might be asked to lower his pants. In fact the great hall was now jammed, as several ferries had unloaded passengers since Joseph's midmorning arrival. Worse, a disproportionate number of these were female.

"Do not concern yourself," the professor reassured Joseph, while at the same time he nodded toward the inspector, who had turned around to express impatience at the delay in the translation. As Joseph stood waiting, he heard the interpreter using the word "dollars" and saw the younger official, with a raised eyebrow, saying something that made the professor frown. After more discussion, the professor shook his head, lowered his eyes, and announced softly:

"Joseph, they insist on seeing your money."

Joseph blushed. He looked pleadingly at the officials. The older one was looking at his wristwatch, the younger one tapping a pencil on the desk. The professor, looking pale, was staring absently around the room. Joseph wondered if the professor had made it clear to them that the money was hidden inside his pants, and that to retrieve it here would be undignified.

But the officials were waiting, and Joseph knew that he had no choice, so he bent down and placed his topcoat and cap on the floor in front of him. He unbuttoned the jacket of his suit, trying not to imagine the people who might be watching him, especially the young woman he had noticed standing in line nearby, her flaxen braids dangling behind her bonnet.

He unhitched his trouser belt. One of the officials coughed, but said nothing as Joseph placed two fingers behind his bow tie and pulled out the chain that hung around his neck; on it were his Saint Francis medal and the silver key to his money bag. Discreetly he unbuttoned the top three buttons of his fly front and tried to untie the money bag around his waist. But the knot was too tight—it was now necessary to undo a fourth button and reach down to try to unlock the money bag with the key.

The officials now suddenly seemed confused and aghast, and the older man turned around to the interpreter and asked: "What the *hell* is he doing?"

The professor had apparently not explained how complicated it would be to fulfill their request; or perhaps he had underestimated the difficulty Joseph might have in reaching into the internal pocket.

"This isn't burlesque," the official went on huffily to the professor, who stood speechless and flustered behind the chairs. "Tell him to button up. We'll take his word that he has the money."

After the professor had communicated the message, and Joseph had rearranged himself, the professor instructed him to express his gratitude in English.

"Thank you very much," Joseph said, picking up his coat and cap from the floor and following the professor out of the area.

"You're welcome," the older official said, "and welcome to America."

Joseph walked into a large reception room that was noisy and crowded with people waiting to greet their newly arrived relatives and friends. He looked around, moving from group to group, but saw no sign of his uncles. After searching for almost a half-hour, he became worried. The professor, who fortunately had stayed with him, suggested that they go to the Western Union counter; and there, among stacks of yellow envelopes, the clerk discovered one addressed to Joseph.

The professor translated:

"SORRY YOUR UNCLES CANNOT COME. ENTRAIN TO PHILADEL-PHIA, THIRTIETH STREET STATION. CALL ARRIVAL TIME NUMBER BELOW. WILL MEET YOU. YOUR FATHER'S GOOD FRIEND. CARLO DONATO."

Joseph had never heard of Donato, and did not know how to get on the train. But the professor said: "Come, I owe you a favor for all that embarrassment. I'll see that you get there. We can buy the ticket here, and the terminal is just across the water in New Jersey, where we'll go together by launch."

After the professor had helped Joseph convert his lire into dollars at the exchange office—Joseph had visited a washroom beforehand, and discreetly laid claim to his funds—a card bearing the number 6 was pinned to the side of his cap by a transportation guide helping to process passengers after they had purchased their rail tickets. The numbered card would remind the train conductor that Joseph's destination was Philadelphia.

Carrying his suitcase and escorting Joseph to the track of the Philadelphia-bound express, the professor reminded him: "Stay on until it no longer moves and everybody is off. That'll be Thirtieth Street Station, the final stop. Mr. Donato will find you. I'll phone him to tell him when you're scheduled to arrive. Good luck. And Merry Christmas."

32.

IT WAS AFTER seven p.m. as the train headed across the swamplands of northern New Jersey toward the Pennsylvania border, and Joseph saw nothing through the window except his own reflection and that of an elderly fur-coated woman who sat next to him on the aisle reading a book. Several people were standing, a few carrying brightly wrapped packages. The railcar was not so well appointed and clean as the one he had ridden several months earlier through Italy and France, but he was more excited now than he had been when en route to Paris; Philadelphia had been his father's favorite city, and Joseph sensed within himself for the first time some of his father's spirit of adventure and independence.

After several stops, the train moved through a tunnel, then slowed down as it rolled into a steel-girdered enclosure, yellowishly lit by hanging lamps; then it came to a halt. The passengers stood and gathered their belongings from the overhead racks, and Joseph followed the others out of the car and up a long ramp that led to the marble floor of a huge hall that seemed to be larger, and certainly more festive, than the one on Ellis Island. A chorus of women dressed in blue capes and bonnets sang Christmas carols near the information booth, accompanied by uniformed men playing trumpets and trombones. Someone dressed as Santa Claus was ringing a bell and soliciting donations next to a thirty-foot-high Christmas tree in the center of the rotunda, and everywhere Joseph looked he saw people greeting each other with embraces and handshakes. Behind him he heard a voice asking somewhat tentatively, in Italian, "You are Gaetano's son?" Turning, Joseph saw a tall gray-haired man examining him with much curiosity. He wore a black homburg and a black overcoat with a white carnation in the lapel. Before Joseph could reply, the man said: "But of course you are." He stepped forward, introduced himself as Carlo Donato, and kissed Joseph on both cheeks.

"I'm sorry there was no one to meet you at Ellis Island," Mr. Donato said. "Your letter arrived only a few days ago, and your uncles could not get away from their jobs in Ambler today. Tomorrow the plant is closed, and they'll come and bring you back with them. But tonight you are *my* guest." He took the suitcase out of Joseph's hand. "And many people are waiting to greet you. Come, we must get a taxi while we can."

He escorted Joseph outside toward a taxi stand under the porte co-chère of the building. A driver waved to them and opened a door, but just as Joseph was about to step in he was delayed momentarily by Donato's hand on his shoulder. Donato then unpinned the number 6 tag from Joseph's cap, crumpled it, and tossed it into a curbside trashcan. "Now nobody will notice that you're not an American," he announced, smiling as he waved Joseph into the backseat of the vehicle.

It was a thirty-minute ride through the traffic downtown to the Italian area of South Philadelphia. Along the way, in addition to pointing out a few unlit landmarks and statues that Joseph had difficulty seeing through the smudgy side windows of the cab, Donato spoke about his old-time friendship with Joseph's father.

"We shared a little apartment before your father got married," he said. "He didn't want to live among the Italians, he wanted to live close to the train station we just left, because he was always on the go. He made many trips back and forth to Italy, as you know, and before one of these trips I sent along a letter that arranged for him to meet a cousin of mine, Marian Rocchino. That's how she became your mother." Joseph thought that Donato would probably inquire about his mother's health and welfare, or about Sebastian's condition, but he did not, and Joseph was relieved and pleased as Mr. Donato went on about his father. "We'd first met as stone-masons on a big job in Ambler, and we lived in a boardinghouse there for a while. When the job ended we moved here to an apartment I'll show you someday. I know the old couple who now live in it. Your father liked working with stone, but I hated it. He liked moving from job to job, and not staying very long in one place. I liked regularity. He traveled all the time, as I said, and once, I remember, he went out to California or Mexico. I don't know what for. Me, I've never been farther away from Philadelphia than Delaware since I came here off the boat, back in 1888. I was a foreman on a job in Delaware when your father got married in Maida, and then he came back alone to Philadelphia, and stayed in the apartment by himself. . . ." Donato paused. Something seemed to be troubling him, and he remained silent for a few moments, squinting as he tried to see through the rain-streaked windows. Then he said something in English to the driver.

With the windshield wipers on, Joseph had a clearer view of the street. The driver had just circled around a tall granite building that had flags in front, and across the street he saw a large store whose display windows blazed with light, and a theater marquee nearby with an illustration of a woman painted on the signboard. It was after eleven p.m.; motor vehicles and horse carriages were moving everywhere, and the sidewalks were filled with pedestrians. This was obviously an important avenue—not wide and elegant like most boulevards in Paris, but zestful in the way of the streets in the center of Naples.

"Finally I quit working outdoors and found something easier to do," Donato went on in Italian, as the cabbie took a right turn and soon entered a narrow street that was lined on both sides by brick houses with white stone steps, all looking exactly the same. "I became an embalmer's assistant. I started this about twenty years ago, a few blocks from here. We're in the Italian area now, and these people never move. They live here and die here. They are thrifty all their lives and then spend fortunes on funerals. I should know. I have my own funeral business now. I also have relatives in the business."

The taxi stopped in front of the white steps of one of the row houses. It had a Christmas wreath on the door, a bit larger than the wreaths on the houses flanking it. The driver placed the suitcase on the sidewalk, and as Donato was paying the fare Joseph became aware that people were looking in his direction from behind the drawn draperies of the upper- and parlor-floor windows on both sides of the street. As the cab pulled away, the door of the house nearest to him opened and a group of men and women came rushing down the steps toward him, all speaking at once as they took turns kissing him on both cheeks and welcoming him to America. Donato introduced them. Everyone was surnamed Donato.

Other people awaited Joseph inside, relatives and friends of the Donatos and also natives of Maida. As they embraced him, a few claimed distant kinships with both sides of his family in Italy. The parlor seemed too small to contain everyone. Some people were backed into one corner against the branches of the Christmas tree. Others stood perilously close to the mantel, on which were spread ceramic figurines and a gold-trimmed glazed white vase filled with ceramic roses. The blue velvet sofa and matching chairs, in which no one was sitting, had white linen doilies on the backs and armrests. The only person in the room who was close to Joseph's age was a niece of Carlo Donato's named Carmela, a friendly, somewhat plump young woman with braided dark hair and large sparkling eyes. Carmela's kiss of salutation had lasted a bit longer than customary and was planted rather close to Joseph's lips—prompting a frown and shake of the head from the dignified-looking man standing behind her. Joseph assumed he was her father.

Behind the parlor, and separated from it by sliding doors, was the dining room. The doors were partly open and Joseph noticed an oak table with chairs around it and a crystal bowl in the center. There were no place settings, however, for dinner would be served in the more spacious quarters downstairs, where Joseph was soon led by Mr. Donato—after he had been taken to the top floor to put away his things and see the bathroom, of which his host was unreservedly proud. He heralded it as the first indoor bathroom on the block.

Three tables of slightly varying heights were pushed together and covered with tablecloths, and thus fifteen people were accommodated for dinner in the converted basement, although not everyone ate. A white-haired man from across the street, complaining of dyspepsia, limited himself to drinking anisette. Two other neighbors, a white-haired couple who had introduced themselves as distant cousins of Joseph's grandfather Domenico, explained politely that they had already eaten (it was now past midnight), but they helped themselves freely to the sugary fried *zeppole* and other dulcified holiday specialties. What they did not finish they handed to the two toddlers in high chairs, who either finished it or dropped it on the floor.

"How's your grandmother Ippolita getting along?" asked one middle-aged woman who wore a black dress and tiny gold earrings, as she placed a carafe of red wine on the table.

"She's very well," Joseph replied.

"But she's had problems with bursitis all year," added another woman, who explained that she had spoken to someone who had arrived recently from Maida. "She's had to see Dr. Mancini in Jacurso."

"Domenico is not much better," Carlo Donato said from one end of the table. "I hear he can't get out of the house."

Joseph had known none of this. Nor was he sure he wanted to. Fortunately, the food began to arrive, and the conversation lightened with celebrations of the aroma.

The cooking was done on a large coal-burning stove, and before the food was served, the plates were kept warm atop a stone ledge in front of the fireplace. Hanging above the mantel, in addition to the crucifix and picture of Saint Francis, were framed photographs of Carlo and his late wife. Joseph had not realized until midway through dinner that Carlo was a widower, and that the jovial gray-haired woman wearing a maroon silk dress and circular earrings, who was acting as hostess, was Carlo's spinster sister. The other women helping out were younger and dark-haired, perhaps in their mid-thirties or early forties, but very matronly in manner and solemnly attired in dark brown or black dresses, with their hair pulled back in a bun at the nape of the neck. Two of them were married to younger cousins of Carlo's, who wore carnations on the lapels of their gray suits; like Carlo, they were undertakers. There was also a tailor at the table named Raphael Donato, who wore a handsome light brown worsted suit and a red cravat with a stickpin below the rounded collar of his white shirt. Carlo had explained privately to Joseph upstairs that Raphael was a ladies' tailor with the large local firm of Strawbridge & Clothier, and that perhaps he would help Joseph find a job. Joseph hoped this would happen, but during dinner he found Raphael very aloof and uncommunicative. Joseph sat directly across from him, on Carlo's right, but Raphael avoided making eye contact. It was Raphael who had frowned earlier on witnessing Carmela's warm greeting; Joseph by this time was sure Raphael was her father.

Carmela had been too preoccupied during dinner to pay further attention to Joseph; she carried dishes back and forth, stoked the fire, and tended to the toddlers—the children of her oldest sister, who was elsewhere this evening with her husband. At one-thirty, when her sister and brother-in-law had still not returned, Carmela took the sleeping children upstairs. Joseph himself was exhausted, having been up since dawn; but he knew he could not politely leave the table. Presumably he was the reason everyone was here, although the conversation now largely excluded him, and was centered around people and matters that he could not readily follow. The man on Joseph's right, a chef in a neighborhood restaurant, was complaining about the inability of Italian-born waiters to get jobs in the restaurants of the city's leading hotels. One of the younger morticians blamed the waiters themselves for this, saying that they spoke broken English and shunned the union organizers. Carlo denounced the union as anti-Italian, but his cousin reminded him of the role many Italians had played as strikebreakers since coming to America. Joseph wished he could find a way to ingratiate himself with Raphael and perhaps receive an offer of help toward his own employment; but Raphael remained as before, listening with detachment, saying very little, and ignoring Joseph.

The last of the fettuccine, the sole, and most of the vegetables had now been consumed; and the women were removing the plates and bringing to the table bowls of fruit, trays of pastry, and more wine. Carmela had returned from upstairs and was now carrying a bowl filled with several pieces of *finocchio,* fennel, to the table. She placed it in front of her father Raphael, ignoring the stern look he was giving her. Her long shiny hair, which had been pulled back in a braid, was now hanging loosely around her shoulders and down the back of her white blouse. Her tan wool skirt fit snugly around her hips, and she moved with a hint of boldness that was uncommon in young Italian women. Joseph guessed that she had been born and brought up in the United States.

After pouring herself a cup of coffee from the pot on the table, Carmela took a seat by herself at the far end, where before she had sat next to the children's high chairs. The women who had been seated near her were now toweling dishes and scrubbing pots in the kitchen, which was separated by a screen from the dining area. Joseph had smelled Carmela's fragrance as she passed behind him; and after keeping his attention on the men momentarily, he slowly turned toward her. She was lifting the cup to her lips, and her lively eyes above the rim seemed to be searching him out. They looked at one another for only a second, but in that second she smiled lightly and winked.

Joseph turned immediately back to the men gathered on his side of the table, relieved that none of them had seemed to notice. Carlo and one of the other morticians were arguing, cracking open two chestnuts simultaneously in their palms as they talked, while the other men drank wine and interrupted frequently. Except for Raphael, all the men had loosened their neckties and had their jackets hanging on the back of their chairs. Raphael sipped his wine and reached for a knob of fennel; he peeled away a stalk and bit into it daintily as he nodded in agreement with something Carlo had said.

Joseph again shifted his attention back to Carmela. She placed the coffee cup back on the saucer and returned his glance. Once more, she winked. Pleased, he did not look away; and he was about to smile at her, when suddenly he noticed her expression turn fearful and saw her raising her hands as if to protect her face. Something flew through the air and hit

Carmela squarely on the forehead, driving her backward. It was a knob of fennel, shaped like a hand grenade, and after it hit her it landed on the coffee cup, breaking it, and rolled to the floor. There was absolute silence. The women appeared from behind the screen. The men who had been arguing sat rigidly with their hands in the air, their mouths open. Raphael sat behind the bowl of fennel, his face red, his temples throbbing, his eyes looking at the floor. Carmela, touching her forehead, glared across the table at him.

"Oh, my poor child," Carlo's sister cried out, heading in from the kitchen, but Carmela waved her back.

"Let me be," she insisted, and the older woman stepped back. Carlo, forcing a smile, tried to make light of the incident, but the others remained silent. Hardly anyone knew what had happened; they sensed only that it was a private matter between Raphael and Carmela, one in which they should not intrude. Soon Carlo and the man with whom he had been arguing continued their discussion in a softer tone. Another man filled up Raphael's empty wineglass. The women resumed their activities in the kitchen. Joseph left the table and approached Carmela.

"Are you all right?" he asked.

She nodded, but there were tears in her eyes.

Joseph picked up the piece of fennel and placed it on the table. With his napkin, he gathered the broken pieces of the cup and placed them in the saucer. The cup had been practically empty and there were only a few coffee stains on the tablecloth.

Joseph turned when he heard footsteps behind him. A young couple entered the room, apologizing for being so late—they had remained long at a party—and begging forgiveness from everyone in the room. Carlo and his sister came forward to greet them, other people waved and stood up, and Carmela also rose and soon introduced Joseph to her sister and brother-in-law. The latter wore a tuxedo, and Carmela's sister, who wore a long dress with sequins and had her hair bobbed in the style of the American women Joseph had seen on the boat, explained that they had been to a wedding in New Jersey. Carmela's sister was skinny, mousy-haired; as far as Joseph could see, she bore absolutely no resemblance to Carmela.

Joseph remained for a few minutes, but could barely keep his eyes open. He offered a word of explanation to Carlo, who summoned everyone's attention in a final toast to the young Talese's arrival in America; to which Joseph expressed his thanks before waving good night and going upstairs to bed.

—

Joseph slept soundly on the cot that had been placed in the small room in the rear of the third floor; and he might have slept through the day had not Carlo, fully dressed and smelling of cologne, awakened him with word that his uncles were waiting for him downstairs. The Rocchino brothers had been there for more than an hour, Carlo explained, and were eager to catch the noon train back to Ambler.

Joseph dressed hurriedly, strapped up his suitcase, and drank the coffee that Carlo had brought up to him. No one except Carlo was in the living room when Joseph came down—the others were asleep—and his uncles were waiting for him out on the sidewalk, next to the open door of a cab. He remembered seeing them off at the Maida train station earlier in the year, when they were leaving for America. Like most of the Rocchinos, they were not tall, and Joseph straightened with pride as he recalled he had always been told he physically resembled his father's side of the family. He was not sure which uncle was Anthony and which was Gregory, for on those infrequent occasions when he had seen them, he had never seen them separately. He still considered it remarkable that his mother's brothers, to whom he had never been close, had become his benefactors with their five-hundred-dollar loan and were now escorting him toward his first American home.

Embracing him, they seemed genuinely glad to see him, although he immediately saw them as changed somewhat from the blithesome travelers he had watched leaving Maida; in less than a year, they had become noticeably older, and slower in the way they moved. Although they were presentable enough in appearance, there was a dustiness about their dark eyebrows and rather delicate pastel features—they were fair-complected, unlike his mother—and the overcoat worn by one of them was threadbare around the elbows and cuffs. They certainly were no match for the cologne-scented, precisely pressed mortician who had just wished him well at the curb; but as the cab headed toward the rail terminal, Joseph sat contentedly between his uncles, eagerly anticipating the start of his new life in America.

The train station was less grand and festive than the one he had entered the night before; this was the Reading Terminal in the center of the city, on Market Street, a hub for commuters and other short-distance passengers bound for such company towns as Ambler. On the way through the outskirts of the city Joseph imagined his father commuting on this same train, perhaps in this very car, during the days Carlo Donato had referred to; but when he asked his uncles to tell him more about his father, assuming they had learned things from his mother, both men apologized for knowing very little. "Unfortunately, he passed away before we arrived in America," one of them said. "And when he was in Italy on the last trip before the war, he was in a hospital near Naples most of the time, trying to cure that chest sickness, and your mother never liked to talk about it."

The train passed over a bridge, dirt-colored water with a few barges and small steamships floating below; and then it rolled through farm country, with cows, horses, and other animals grazing on fading green pastures covered here and there with patches of snow. There were no high peaks here reminiscent of Italy, but one uncle said that not far from Ambler was a mountain area that produced much of the nation's coal.

His uncles were not very talkative, despite Joseph's efforts to start a conversation; he hoped something they said would reveal who was Anthony and who Gregory. Joseph thought they were probably tired; they looked tired, and they rode on in silence. As the train slowed to a stop alongside a small wood-framed building with a sign bearing the familiar name "Ambler," one of his uncles reached up for Joseph's suitcase. The aisle of the car was crowded with people getting off, and as Joseph waited he leaned toward the window and watched a majestic black automobile, longer than any he had ever imagined, pulling in against the edge of the platform.

Following his uncles down the steps of the railcar, Joseph saw a very tall white-haired man stepping out of the rear door of the limousine that was held open by a uniformed driver. The man wore a black homburg and a black suit, and a gold chain dangled in front of his vest; but what Joseph noticed more, in addition to his impressive height, was that the gentleman was carrying in his hands a pair of men's black shoes.

Joseph's uncles stopped when they spotted the man, as if they were mindful about keeping their distance. They waited as he strode across the platform and then paused at a shoeshine shack where a small man wearing a heavy sweater over his apron accepted the shoes with a little bow.

"Who's that?" Joseph asked his uncles, watching as the gentleman turned around and walked back toward the chauffeur, who again held open the door.

"That man owns this town, and everyone in it," one of the uncles said. "That's Dr. Mattison, and he lives like a king."

"Well, he carried his own shoes to the shoemaker," Joseph said, as the big car began to pull away. "In Italy, no rich man would be seen doing that. He would have a servant do it. This is really a different country."

His uncles said nothing.

33.

D R. RICHARD V. MATTISON approached his seventieth year with the same sense of direction and drive that a half-century earlier had carried him from his father's farm in rural Pennsylvania to the top of a multimillion-dollar industry and the ownership of a private domain in Ambler that made him worthy of the nickname the American press had recently given him—"the Asbestos King."

Although his firm still supplied drugstores around the country with the over-the-counter cures he had developed for headaches and rheumatism before the turn of the century, the six-foot-four-inch pharmacist and physician was now dispensing antidotes and precautionaries primarily for the betterment of buildings, utilities, and machines. Each week miles of his asbestos-treated adhesive tape and sheathing—fireproof, leakproof, erosion-resistant, fuel-saving—rolled off his Ambler assembly lines to be delivered nationwide and worldwide to industries that would wrap or fit the textile around the pipes, joints, and valves of its boiler rooms, reservoir chambers, and various other sources of supply and power. In the early postwar years there were few newly built factories, public buildings, or apartment houses in urban America that did not contain asbestos in some form within their structures—as insulation material within the walls, or as an incombustible agent within the floor tiles, or as the primary substance of the outer siding and roof shingles. During the war Dr. Mattison's firm—along with such competitors as Johns-Manville—were especially active in fulfilling defense contracts placed by American military officials who requisitioned asbestos wrapping tape for steamships, asbestos brake pads and clutch facings for military vehicles, and asbestos strap linings to fit within soldiers' steel helmets. As a patriot, Dr. Mattison was honored to fill the orders. As a capitalist, he was pleased with the profits.

Now he had branch offices in New York and Chicago, Boston and Buffalo, Detroit and Minneapolis, and a dozen other American cities; and he lived with his wife and a multitude of servants in a multiturreted castle on a hill fronted by more than seventy acres of lawn. The lawn was graced with sunken gardens, a pond with a tiny stone bridge and a gazebo, and several fountains bearing statues of mythological creatures that spouted water out of assorted orifices whenever the doctor passed through the main gate in his high-roofed, asbestos-peppered gray Packard limousine. At least twice daily, as the doctor was driven to and from the fortresslike company headquarters a mile west of the castle, the female servants on the lawn would curtsy, the gardeners and other male laborers would doff their caps, and an armed guard at the gatehouse would salute with one hand while holding back a barking mastiff with the other.

The doctor's chauffeur was a fastidious, rigid-spined Swede named John Frederickson, who, when driving, appeared from the road to be standing up. Nearly as tall as the doctor, though considerably less bulky, Frederickson wore spit-polished cavalry boots, white gloves, and usually a beige choke-collared uniform with a peaked cap of matching color; and he took almost perverse pride in never stopping his car during duty hours to go to the bathroom, even when driving his employer on long trips to such branch offices as the ones in Pittsburgh, Cleveland, or Providence—and he remained dutifully behind the wheel also while the car was parked at a station waiting to be refilled with gas. In warmer months, when Dr. Mattison was often in Europe on business, Frederickson would drive Mrs. Mattison and selected female servants to and from the Mattisons' summer home in Newport, Rhode Island; the journey usually exceeded twelve hours, during which time the ladies frequently requested rest stops. After helping them out of the car, Frederickson would wait patiently behind the wheel. In the not too distant future, Frederickson would die prematurely of a pelvic disorder.

The maintenance of the doctor's limousine and the other motor vehicles in his garage, the feeding of his horses, the oiling of his workmen's wagon wheels, the upkeep of the lawns and gardens surrounding the castle, as well as the roads and the cattle, all were under the regulation of the doctor's superintendent and chamberlain, an old Civil War veteran of the Union Army named William J. Devine. Craggy-featured and battle-scarred, slight but sinewy, Devine confronted almost everyone with an attitude connoting either aloofness or abrasiveness. The one exception to this was the doctor, whom he both feared and adored. Devine had never requested a day off during his two decades of employment by Dr. Mattison. Nor did the doctor ever suggest that he take one.

Although he had authority over nearly one hundred workers on the castle grounds, in the castle itself, and on the rear grounds—the latter consisting of three hundred forty acres of farmland, forestland, a reservoir, and two lakes used for fishing, boating, and skating in winter—the employees' assignments were so vastly spread, and thus mostly performed beyond Devine's purview, and so often subjected to last-minute changes fomented by the doctor's countermands that in the resulting confusion the doctor himself sometimes ended up doing menial tasks—such as delivering his shoes to the cobbler's shack near the rail terminal.

Also promoting confusion was the fact that a high percentage of Devine's work force (a force favored by the doctor primarily because it represented cheap labor) consisted of Italians who could not understand English, but who convincingly pretended to Devine that they could. They reacted to all of his demands with amiable nods and other illusory manifestations of compliance that not a few of their ancestors had perfected to an art during centuries of subjugation to feudal and other foreign rulers in southern Italy. During the spring of 1919 Devine was given permission by the doctor to hire a university-educated Italian who was fluent in English to serve as a combination interpreter-paymaster; but this man soon ran off with the sack containing the employees' weekly pay, and the doctor refused to replace him.

Dr. Mattison was never eager in his private life or his business life to take on extra intermediaries to function between himself and his hired help. He rarely kept more than four vice-presidents to help him direct his two-thousand-employee asbestos business in Ambler (two of the vice-presidents were his sons); and while he thought that having a superintendent like Devine around the castle was necessary, he believed that providing Devine with subalterns was not. Adding subalterns could turn the estate into a spawning ground for lower-management drones—or, just as bad, supply Devine with scapegoats whenever the doctor wished to point an accusing finger. And so as far as the estate was concerned, the doctor believed that Devine represented enough management; and even though Devine was *not* enough, he knew enough not to argue with the doctor.

Devine was dependent on Dr. Mattison not only for his job but also for the shelter and sustenance that Devine in turn shared with six members of his family, all living with him in a three-story, twelve-room, rent-free stone building located downhill behind the castle, nestled within thick shrubbery and surrounded by tall oak and maple trees that kept the house out of sight from the vantage point of the castle's front lawn. In addition to Devine there was his crippled wife, Francine, a victim of a congenital bone disease that had worsened through the years; their thirty-five-year-old adopted daughter, Hannah; Hannah's husband, Charles Hibschman, a quiet man who had once aspired to be a country schoolteacher but who now kept Devine's books; and the couple's three school-age sons (one of whom would succeed Frederickson's successor as the doctor's driver).

Behind Devine's house, and also obscured by abundant bushes and forestland, were smaller stone dwellings occupied by some of Devine's factotums and their kinfolk. Among the innumerable duty assignments— many of which changed with the weather as well as the doctor's impulses—were the upkeep of the boathouse and the two lakes (the larger one measuring six acres); the care and operation of the farm (on which were two thousand chickens, fifteen cows, eight riding horses, four plow horses, three pigs); and the filtering and conservation of water in the tank house, an eight-story structure whose four top floors were occupied by huge water drums that serviced the estate, and whose four lower floors were divided into apartments for workers and their dependents, on whom drops of water occasionally fell.

Devine's underlings were also called upon seasonally to chalk the lines of the doctor's lawn tennis court (he had a big serve, erratic ground strokes); prune and water the plants and flowers in the greenhouse; pack with hay in the icehouse each winter large frozen chunks of lake water for summertime use in the kitchen's iceboxes; remove from the edges of the lawn's roadway each autumn dozens of portable palm trees, potted in large containers on steel rollers, for sheltering until spring; perform as glaziers, plumbers, wheelwrights, blacksmiths, or at other endeavors for which their jack-of-all-trades-master-of-none abilities might be put to use. If the doctor suspected they had free time, they might be temporarily shifted across town to work in one of the plant's assembly lines, or to help the stonemasons and carpenters in the new housing project that was under way in 1921 to fulfill the housing needs of the increased number of asbestos workers the doctor's growing business was expected to require by late 1922.

An architect named John Bothwell was brought in to work under Devine on the plans, and he set up his drawing board in a shed next to Devine's house. One night, after Bothwell had left for the day, Dr. Mattison strolled over to inspect the sketches for the new residences; he borrowed a pencil from Devine and drew over each rooftop an adornment shaped exactly like a pawn from a chess set (the doctor excelled at the game). On the following morning, after Devine had shown Bothwell the doctor's handiwork, the architect became enraged and threatened to quit. "It won't make any difference to the doctor if you quit or not," Devine told him, explaining that the doctor considered architects as replaceable as grass cutters. Bothwell, who needed work, thought better of it; and when the stone row of houses began to go up the next year, each asbestos rooftop supported the knob of the pawn.

These houses were constructed along Church Street, just southwest of Trinity Episcopal Memorial Church, which the doctor had redesigned in 1891 after firing the Philadelphia architectural firm that had thought too highly of its original sketches and quarreled with him over his suggestions for change. Consecrated in 1901, the Gothic edifice had been dedicated in memory of the doctor's only daughter, Esther Victoria Mattison, who had died suddenly in 1887 at the age of four, of typhoid fever. The mother of the child, the first Mrs. Mattison—Esther Dafter Mattison, whom the doctor had married in 1874—had died unexpectedly in 1919 at the summer home in Newport, where she had gone to escape an allergic ailment so acute that her only relief in Ambler had come when sitting, wearing a fur coat, in the icehouse. Nine months after her death the doctor married her close friend Mary Cottrell Seger, a divorcée from Princeton, New Jersey, who was ten years younger and considerably less dowdy. But shortly after the wedding, which was held in Trinity Memorial Church in April 1920, the second Mrs. Mattison was injured in an auto accident while being driven through Fairmount Park in Philadelphia with the doctor. Although Frederickson had seemed somewhat fidgety behind the wheel before the accident, as the doctor later told his older son, the doctor in no way held Frederickson responsible for the collision; another car, out of control, had rammed the limousine on the side where Mrs. Mattison had been sitting, and, while the doctor's injuries healed, she was unconscious for three days and suffered broken bones that would immobilize her for nearly two years.

During this time she never left the castle, spending most of her days on the top floor in a wheelchair, surveying the world beyond the curved windows of the turrets through the high-powered binoculars that the doctor had brought back to her from a business trip in Germany. Through the lenses she could see faraway things with astonishing clarity, intimate and sometimes shocking things that at first she thought she had no business seeing—but later, becoming more accustomed to being *Mrs.* Mattison, she concluded that it *was* her business, that all within view fell under her concern as the proprietress of the castle, and as the marital partner of the man to whom all owed allegiance and respect.

Her husband's cofounding partner, Henry G. Keasbey, had long ceased to be a factor in Ambler. The born-rich, chubby, muttonchopped Keasbey, whose photograph she had seen on the harpsichord downstairs with an arm around her husband after they had started Keasbey & Mattison, had left Ambler in the early 1890s with *his* ailing wife for southern France; the Keasbeys had not revisited Ambler since. Deferring to Dr. Mattison in all financial matters, Keasbey's only contact with his partner now came in the form of occasional greeting cards from the Riviera, and rare acknowledgments of thanks for the large sums he received semi-annually as an equal shareholder—and, a *year* after the doctor had taken a second wife, a note of condolence on the loss of the first.

During the last year Dr. Mattison had also been out of touch with his two married sons, even though they continued to reside in Ambler—in large homes well within the range of Mrs. Mattison's binocularity. But neither of them had visited the castle since the doctor's remarriage, not even after the auto accident (for which Mrs. Mattison was acutely grateful; she disliked having to entertain guests even when she was healthy); and although both men continued to be named on the company stationery as vice-presidents, it was no secret in the town, where there were few secrets indeed, that the doctor now gave them practically nothing to do. One could hardly blame him. Both were notoriously incompetent and irresponsible. The doctor's first son, forty-year-old Richard Jr., was an alcoholic. He obtained his liquor through bootleggers in Philadelphia, or through Italians on the other side of the tracks, and he had provoked altercations with the shopkeepers who requested payments on his unpaid bills, and he was invariably rude to the employees in the plant. Richard Jr. lived a half-mile north of the castle's north gate, with his second wife, Georgette, a Philadelphia socialite, on a seventy-acre estate that had been the doctor's gift after Richard Jr. had complied in divorcing the actress he had met and married in London—a "floozie," the doctor had called her, an opportunist who had boasted of being the grandniece of Dickens's illustrator. The doctor investigated this claim and discovered it to be untrue. "Not that it would have mattered," the doctor later explained to his second wife.

The doctor's second son, whom he had named Royal, was now twenty-seven, and lived in one of the Gothic mansions just outside the castle gates on Lindenwold Terrace with his wife, Florence, and six-year-old son, Royal Jr., who would be the couple's only child and the doctor's only grandchild. Of the doctor's two sons, Richard had had by far the more difficult life—not only during his adult years (in which he had been pressured into following his father's professional path, after matriculation at his father's alma maters; his thesis at the Philadelphia College of Pharmacy was entitled "Asbestos"), but during his boyhood as well, growing up while his parents were mourning the death of their four-year-old daughter, which had occurred during Richard's eighth year and had been memorialized constantly thereafter, as the doctor practically beatified her.

But Royal, thirteen years younger than Richard, was reared in less mournful times, and grew up to be as spoiled and undisciplined as he was tall and handsome. Unlike his stocky and resentful brother, Royal was not pressed into attending the college of pharmacy, where the doctor was a trustee; and when Royal decided to drop out of the University of Pennsylvania after his sophomore year with the intention of getting married, his parents not only failed to dissuade him but immediately celebrated his decision. His bride-to-be was the lovely, genteel daughter of a minister who preached during summers in Newport, and on her maternal side she hailed from an old Philadelphia family that had enjoyed personal and professional ties to the great statesman and scientist Benjamin Franklin.

The wedding gift to Royal and Florence from his parents in 1914 had been a twenty-three-room mansion on Lindenwold Terrace, complete with a gardener and maid billed to the doctor's castle account. But now, while Florence Mattison was devoted to raising young Royal, whom she would forever call "Bubbles" and would unreservedly adore as her only child—spoiling him no less than his father had been spoiled, and prompting by her indulgence the walkout of so many nurses and maids that finally she could employ none at all—her husband was involved in a sexual affair with a married woman who lived across from Trinity Memorial Church and whose husband commuted each workday to the Philadelphia branch office of Keasbey & Mattison.

From her turreted vantage point, with the aid of her binoculars, the doctor's crippled wife could watch her tall and deceitful stepson paying noonday visits to his lady friend, parking his Packard convertible tactlessly at the curb in front of the modestly substantial stone residence near a corner on Highland Avenue; and an hour or so later, Mrs. Mattison would focus upon his departure, watching as he stepped back into his car and readjusted his tie in front of the dashboard mirror, the door to the house having been slowly closed a moment before with a soft wave of the hand from his bathrobed paramour.

If Mrs. Mattison did not keep the doctor abreast of such details, it was because she suspected he was already aware of his son's dalliance and was responding to it in his own way; or, if he was not aware, that he deserved to be shielded from such unpleasantries: he had experienced enough sadness and disappointment within his immediate family. The doctor's only other close living relative, an older brother named Asher, whom Mrs.

Mattison had never met, and probably never would, was also a source of discomfort to her husband. The brothers had not had much contact since their early upbringing on the farm, and this was not surprising given the vastly different circumstances of their adulthood; but at least they had been on cordial terms. Now this was no longer true. Mrs. Mattison had not heard this directly from the doctor during their marriage (the doctor had not even told her that he *had* a brother); instead she had learned of it years earlier, when the doctor had still been married to Esther, who was also the present Mrs. Mattison's closest confidante—and the source of most of what she knew about the doctor's rarely discussed humble origins.

Richard and his brother, Asher, who was four years older, were the only children born to a Quaker farmer and carpenter in Pennsylvania named Joseph Mattison and his wife, the former Mahala Vanzeelust—whose Dutch surname the doctor would always account for with his middle initial on his stationery and business cards, on the doors of his cars and carriages, on his gold cuff links, the brass plate of his church pew, and other surfaces on which he wished to reflect his identity fully. His mother had been born in 1819 on a farm in central New Jersey along the Delaware River, where her ancestors from the Netherlands had settled during the previous century; and although Mahala's insistent and overbearing manner as a married woman gave neighbors the impression that she was more astute and better educated than her kindly husband, the fact remained that she went through life without ever knowing how to read or write.

When Mahala married Joseph Mattison in 1846, at a Quaker ceremony held in the county seat of Flemington, New Jersey, it was he who had to sign her name next to his own on the marital document. Then he packed her few personal belongings into the back of his buggy, waved good-bye to her dry-eyed kinfolk, and transported her over a wobbly wooden bridge to the Pennsylvania side of the Delaware River, onto the eighty-two-acre Mattison family farm. It was bordered along the east by the river and was three miles north of the community of New Hope, in Bucks County's Solebury Township. The farmland was of superior quality, being of alluvial soil in the eastern half and limestone soil in the western half, but the boundaries of the family property had shrunk more than tenfold since one of Joseph Mattison's ancestors had arrived on a Quaker ship from England in the autumn of 1682, to claim the thousand-acre tract he had purchased from the English Quaker leader William Penn, who was then in the process of founding the colony of Pennsylvania. Mattison's pioneering ancestor, related to him through the female branch, was a yeoman named George Pownall. Accompanied by his wife and five children (the oldest his thirteen-year-old son, Reuben; the youngest of the four daughters three-year-old Abigail), George Pownall braved the Atlantic for three stormy weeks on a vessel aptly named *Friends' Adventure,* before sailing into the calmer currents of the Delaware River and leasing two wagons along the shore to carry his family and possessions uphill onto their newly bought and patented piece of America.

Thirty days later, while the Pownalls and their hired laborers were hastening to complete the construction and furbishing of the shanties and sheds that would shelter them temporarily through the winter, a tree fell on the head of George Pownall and killed him instantly. But after eleven days of mourning, the Pownall family spirit was brightened by the birth of a sixth child and second son to the widow Elinor, and she named him in memory of her deceased husband.

George Pownall, Jr., was born on November 11, 1682, on the northern section of the property that he would never leave during his long lifetime; and in 1707, in his twenty-fifth year, after being deeded this portion of the property by his siblings, who had settled to the south or had dispersed to more distant places, he married a neighboring farmer's daughter named Hannah Hutchinson. From this union would come four children; then twenty grandchildren; then more great-grandchildren than old George Pownall could shake a stick at, although he often waved one threateningly in an effort to keep them from running wild over his productively planted, and now cooperatively owned, five hundred acres of property. One of the more frisky and attractive of his great-granddaughters, Mary Pownall, as a budding teenager in 1805 would meet a young wandering farmer and tinker who was robust and hearty, and who told charming tales even taller than himself—and he was six-feet-two in his bare feet, which was his constant condition since he failed to own a pair of shoes. His first name was Richard; his surname was presently spelled "Mattison," but it was really Mathieson, he explained, adding that his ancestral line was linked to the Mathieson feudal clan that still dwelled on the Isle of Lewis in the Outer Hebrides, off the western coast of Scotland, and was in possession of 650,000 acres. On this island resided his kinsman Sir Kenneth Mathieson, at Andross Castle, with 400,000 acres; and also Lady Mathieson, who occupied Stornaway Castle at Loch Alsh; and the family also owned other large tracts in the county of Ross and Cromarty in Scotland, he said. But what most impressed Mary Pownall about this barefoot prince named Mattison or Mathieson were not his high-flown claims or his engaging voice with its Scottish burr, but rather that he was a big handsome hunk of manhood who stood in pleasant contrast to her short, stout male relatives and the similarly shaped prospective Quaker suitors who were their friends. So Mary Pownall took whatever initiative was necessary to get Richard Mattison to marry her, which he willingly did on January 1, 1807; and they would have ten children—one of whom, Joseph Mattison, born in 1813, would marry Mahala Vanzeelust in 1846 and have two sons: Asher Mattison, born on Christmas Eve in 1847; and, on November 17, 1851, Richard Vanzeelust Mattison, the future doctor.

The brothers grew up in a two-story white framed colonial house that had been built more than a century before and had been little improved since. It had a high peaked roof with a brick chimney, two small shuttered windows on each side of the second floor, an equal number of larger windows on the lower floor, and a white door with a wooden knob and no lock on the porch that stood four steps above the ground. A white wooden banister and widely spaced vertical columns extended the length of the porch, which was six feet deep, and arranged haphazardly along the deck were a half-dozen rocking chairs. The chairs appeared to be as old as the house, and possibly had been rocked back and forth millions of times by five preceding generations of Pownalls. When the former Mahala Vanzeelust arrived here in 1846 as Joseph Mattison's bride, the seven-room house was occupied by two of her husband's orphaned nieces and his spinster sister, Martha Mattison.

Martha Mattison was two years older than thirty-three-year-old Joseph; his delay in marrying Mahala, and Martha's not marrying at all, were partly attributable to the devoted care they both gave to their ailing mother, Mary Pownall Mattison, whose once vigorous health immediately declined following the birth of her ninth and tenth children. Mary died a year before Joseph's marriage to Mahala, and six years after she had buried her tall, hyperbolic husband Richard, the scion of Scottish feudal nobility—who died, rather appropriately, of an advanced case of the scrofulous illness known as the king's evil.

When the newly married Mahala, following repeated breakdowns of her husband's buggy, arrived after midnight at the Mattison farmhouse, she found her spinster sister-in-law Martha ensconced in the largest bedroom, with no intention of relinquishing it to the bridal couple. Mahala sulked for days but accepted it as her first and last concession to the status quo among her in-laws. From then on—as she joined her husband in the smaller bedroom he had used as a bachelor, which was next door to the bedroom occupied by his noisy and nosy nieces—Mahala Vanzeelust

Mattison exerted her will over everyone in sight: she turned the nieces into scrubwomen, got her sister-in-law to do all the cooking and mending, and harangued her husband until he and a few male relatives rebuilt the buggy, repainted the house, and replaced the broken boards on the porch and front steps. As her two sons were growing up—Asher and Richard slept on hay-stuffed mattresses in the attic—neither knew a day of leisure, although her effect on her sons was radically different. Her prodding of Asher seemed to make him more primitive—hardworking, yes, but little motivated in the manner he went about working; he attacked outdoor chores with tools from the Stone Age, or no tools at all. He dug dirt with his hands, he hammered nails with a chunk of rock, he fished in the creek with his fingers, always catching more than anyone could eat. He never in his entire life would don a pair of socks, and he invariably wandered around outdoors without shoes, developing calluses thick as any leather. But Asher Mattison was not quite as tall as the late barefoot pretender who had been his paternal grandfather. He did not reach five feet, ten inches, and in later life his frame seemed to revert to the stout, slope-shouldered shape of the earnest Pownalls.

It was his younger brother, Richard, who inherited the height of his forebears, and even added to it; but everything else behind Richard's appearance and achievements in later years remained largely a mystery. What was the source of his scholastic brilliance, his mercenary zeal, his unswerving optimism, his scientific inventiveness, his conquering spirit? No less interesting was the origin of his passion for opera and poetry (he claimed he could recite every line written by Byron, trying to keep in practice often to the tedium of his sons); to say nothing of the fact that while in medical school he taught himself not only to read and write German, but to speak a refined *Hochdeutsch* so naturally, and without grammatical errors or dialectal detractions, that it astonished his aristocratic doctor friends at Cologne University even more than his regaling them (while sailing past the cliff of Lorelei on the Rhine) with Heinrich Heine's lyrical lines to the nymph: *Ich weiss nicht, was soll es bedeuten, / Dass ich so traurig bin.*

Dr. Mattison's first wife, Esther (the daughter of a retired British career officer whom the doctor met at her home in Cranbury, New Jersey, through an introduction by his college classmate and colleague from Morristown, Henry G. Keasbey), was one of the rare individuals who could perceive the great length of his upward spiral, since he permitted her to accompany him during his infrequent visits back to where he had been born and reared. The most memorable, if not the first such occasion in Bucks County, was on February 12, 1885 (a date she noted well in her diary), for this marked his brother's elevation to domesticity: At the age of thirty-seven, Asher was finally getting married. And while the groom did not wear socks for the occasion (although no one could tell, for he wore one of the doctor's old suits, which was long in the cuff), Asher did appear at the Friends' ceremony in Solebury Township wearing, in addition to a borrowed bow tie and shirt, a new pair of shoes. Asher's bride was a neighboring farm lady named Hulda Pearson, who was close to his own age, and who would bear no children; but she was tidy and cheerful, and self-possessed, too, in the way she entertained the guests as a folk dance soloist after the ceremony, and accepted the applause with gratitude but hardly a semblance of modesty. She seemed to agree that she was good.

At this time the doctor and Esther had been married about ten years; the Keasbey & Mattison plant in Ambler was beginning to prosper; and the couple had just moved into the multitowered Victorian mansion that the doctor had not yet thought of reconstructing into a Gothic castle. The doctor had recently marked his thirty-third birthday, but because of his size and stalwart manner, his walrus moustache and thick peppery-colored beard (which he had begun growing a few years before to hide the jaw scars incurred during his nighttime tumble down a trap door while snooping around a pharmaceutical competitor's plant in Philadelphia), he appeared to be much older than he was, and certainly more patriarchal than the multitude of elders in the room, including especially the small-ish, wizened Pownall-related octogenarians who were gathered in one corner standing with the aid of their canes. Also there was the doctor's seventy-two-year-old father, Joseph, who had boasted to Esther before the ceremony that he was wearing the same shiny black suit he had worn some forty years before, when he had journeyed to Flemington to marry Mahala, and he was almost right when he claimed that the old suit still fit him perfectly. There was a sense of merriment about Joseph Mattison that seemed totally absent in his son Asher, who, posing with the bride in a semblance of a receiving line, seemed as cheerful as a man doomed to the gallows. Asher's sixty-six-year-old mother looked only slightly less grim. Mahala was stocky and square-jawed, with a crown of closely cropped black hair hanging down as straight and thick as the bristles of a paintbrush, and the only sign of emotion she communicated during the entire outing, as far as Esther could see, was a slight tightening of her lips when Asher's bride did her folk dance. This was apparently unseemly behavior for a Quaker, even though Hulda was not a practicing Quaker.

Nor was the doctor, having become an active Episcopalian even before meeting Esther. But he seemed quite comfortable among the Friends at the community center in Bucks County, moving easily among all the wedding guests as he made polite inquiries about their personal welfare and the economic conditions of their properties; and finally, when he heard the sounds of hoofbeats and bells coming from the path in front of the building, he invited everyone to join him outside for the presentation of his gift to Asher and his new bride. It was an elegant English carriage trimmed with floral wreaths and pulled by four high-stepping caparisoned horses. After a short speech, in which he wished the couple the best in health and happiness, the doctor insisted on serving as their coachman as they sat in the vehicle and were driven down the path to the main road and back again, while the other guests stood watching and applauding from the lawn. Esther had never before seen her husband holding the reins behind a team of horses, and she was again impressed by how comfortable he seemed in this rural setting. Nearby she noticed her mother-in-law watching her; Mahala said nothing but nonetheless made her feel like a tourist from a faraway place who had strayed in to watch some quaint rustic sideshow.

The wedding guest whom Esther liked most was her husband's spinster aunt, Martha Mattison, who was now seventy-four and *still* occupied the largest bedroom in the old house she shared with Mahala and Joseph. Martha was high-strung and verbose, and a malicious gossip especially in matters regarding Mahala; but unlike Mahala, she could read and write— a fact that Martha was not wont to keep secret—and she also possessed in her bedroom a stack of illustrated Gothic fairy tales and poetry books that she said she used to read to young Richard when he was growing up. Esther saw some of these books when they stopped briefly at the doctor's boyhood home after the wedding; while the doctor toured the farmland with his parents and his two children, Esther spent time alone with Martha and sensed that she had undoubtedly been part of the reason why young Richard had developed along different lines from Asher.

Martha Mattison had apparently been a second mother to Richard, his literate mother who not only read to him but encouraged him in believing that he had a destiny to fulfill in places far from the farm. Martha was the oldest daughter of that big barefoot fantasist, Richard Mattison or Mathieson, who, while he might have been eight-tenths malarkey, had nonetheless stimulated her imagination to a degree that captivated young Richard, who would later try to transform family myths into reality. On some of his grade school books, which his aunt Martha had kept, Esther could see his boyhood drawings of castles in the margins of the pages, and his listing of his classmates' names with noble titles, and the ostentatious Gothic lettering he used in printing on the back of one book the name of the former farm boy who was then serving as president of the United States, Abraham Lincoln. Some of the family folklore that Martha recalled hearing from her father was familiar to Esther—who had heard her husband, the doctor, essentially repeat it in bedtime stories to *their* son, Richard Jr.—tales of a noble family who lived in a castle by a great lake in Scotland called Loch Alsh, which as Esther realized was what the doctor had named the deepest lake on their estate in Ambler.

On their way home from the wedding, the doctor pointed out to Esther the small stone building where he had first attended school. It was two miles from the farm and was now surrounded by weeds. He told her that Asher had attended the same school but had dropped out after two years. The doctor remained there to complete the six-year course, leading his class academically, as he always would at the country high school. His aunt Martha had mentioned the special interest that a certain teacher had taken in him, and, with some financial help from an affluent Quaker pharmacist in the town of New Hope, the teacher had facilitated Richard's entry into the Philadelphia College of Pharmacy in 1872, where there were Quakers on the faculty and the board of trustees. Richard graduated from there with top honors, as he subsequently did as a medical student at the University of Pennsylvania. Befriending his classmate, the wealthy Keasbey, had been essential to launching their pharmaceutical firm; but it was Dr. Mattison who had made the business successful.

The doctor was an energetic entrepreneur as well as an exploring scientist. He was a doer as much as a dreamer. He was, in Esther's opinion, most likely a genius. And in believing this, she found it unnecessary to understand rationally every aspect of his ascendancy from rusticity to majestic pretensions. If that was how the doctor wished to live in this free country, then he had earned the prerogative to do so. Her role was not to regulate him, as her soldierly English father had tried to regulate her, all but forbidding her courtship with the then dirt-poor pharmacy student; her role as his wife was to encourage him, as his aunt Martha had done. And so Esther did not take issue with the doctor when their marital life in later years became excessively sumptuous and unreal. She did not question him when he ordered a castlelike façade to cover the surface of their mansion; or when he insisted on naming their second son Royal; or when he spent a fortune in Munich to have three castle gates designed and forged by some of the costliest artisans in Europe. The walls around his estate also were made higher at this time, for the doctor complained of needing more privacy. His business empire was growing, there were more demands on his time, and every day people were arriving unannounced at the castle seeking alms, or loans, or dispensation from their debts. He was not only the chief operating officer of the asbestos firm but also the landlord of four hundred domiciles, the sole provider of all their coal, water, and steam; he was the director of the First National Bank of Ambler, the president of the Philadelphia Drug Exchange, and a board member of several companies around the nation and overseas. There were times when he simply did not want to see *anybody,* and his orders were strictly enforced by the guards posted behind the gates with their sidearms and mastiffs.

Late on a summer Sunday afternoon, while the doctor and Mrs. Mattison were having tea on the veranda with two important Canadian mining officials and their wives, Mrs. Mattison heard the dogs barking in the distance more persistently than usual, and minutes later she overheard the conversation of a guard in the pantry reporting to the butler that there was an angry man at the gates who stubbornly refused to leave until he had met face to face with Dr. Mattison.

"It's a barefoot fellow with some woman in a dirty old carriage," Mrs. Mattison overheard the guard telling the butler. "And this fellow claims he's the doctor's brother!"

The superintendent, Devine, was then in a remote part of the estate, overseeing the repairs being done on the drainage system at Loch Alsh, which had overflowed during a rainstorm; and an inexperienced guard, who was filling in this weekend, had taken the liberty of coming directly to the castle rather than taking the trouble to track down Devine. It had been many years since Mrs. Mattison had seen Asher and Hulda; decades had passed since their wedding, and Mrs. Mattison had revisited the farm only to attend funerals—the first for the doctor's father; the next for his mother; and finally for his maiden aunt Martha, who died peacefully in her sleep in the largest bedroom in the farmhouse. During these brief visits the doctor had seemed less cordial to Asher than before, possibly because the latter was planting unproductively and was neglecting the upkeep of the property, including the once elegant carriage that had been the couple's wedding gift. Esther had discovered that Asher had sawed off the roof to make it into an open vehicle, and he seemed to be using it more for hauling dirt and wood than for the purpose for which it was designed and constructed.

Now as the butler stepped out onto the veranda, carrying a silver tray with a note that was intended for her eyes only, Mrs. Mattison looked across the table toward her husband. Although he continued conversing with their guests, she could tell he was distracted. He, too, had overheard the guard. She was sure of it from the ashen tone that had just come into his face, and from the panic she saw in his eyes during the single second she had gotten his attention; and his wishes regarding this situation seemed very clear to her.

"The doctor and I do not wish to be disturbed by *anyone*," Mrs. Mattison said to the butler standing at her side, and she waved away the note without reading it. The doctor paused in his conversation, nodded, then redirected his attention to the guests.

"The individual is *quite* insistent," the butler added, before turning to leave.

"Well," Mrs. Mattison said, as politely as she could, "tell the guard to be even *more* insistent."

Asher and Hulda Mattison were soon confronted by four guards and their dogs; and although Asher's profanity could be heard high above the barking, he finally did back the coach out onto the main road and become resigned to the fact that he would not be paying the doctor a Sunday visit. Hulda, in her quiet way, was more enraged than her husband. She had just purchased a red taffeta cape for the occasion, and midway during their journey back to the farm another rainstorm descended upon the region. The dye in Hulda's new cape soon drained out of the fabric, covering her dress and her arms with red splotches and streaks.

When she returned home, she hung it to dry, but it was forever ruined. Still, she kept the cape throughout the rest of her life (she would die in 1935), and hung it above the mantel, a red flag that would always remind her of the day when she had been turned away by the doctor, a man to whom she would never speak again, or allow to reenter the home in which he had been born.

34.

THE DOCTOR'S SECOND wife, the crippled Mary Mattison, who since her auto accident viewed the entire world primarily through binoculars, had never been aware of seeing any Italians in her entire life until she married the doctor in 1920 and moved from Princeton to Ambler; now, however, she saw almost nothing *but* Italians every time she looked down from her turret window, and often she wished she could change the scenery.

In her isolation as the mistress of the castle, and captive in her wheelchair as her husband moved freely through the town, Mary Mattison watched the Italians digging ditches and laying pipe around the malfunctioning front fountain; they seemed to her grimier than the dirt they wallowed in, and they apparently thought nothing of urinating in broad daylight. The Italian gardeners, though better paid than the common laborers, appeared no more trustworthy. With infuriated amazement, Mrs. Mattison would see them pretend to be devotedly clipping hedges around the service entrance *just* as the delivery truck arrived, loaded with household supplies; and as the unsuspecting driver was knocking on the kitchen door waiting for the butler or the cook to unlock it, the Italians would swiftly move in under the canvas covering of the vehicle and take everything they could, concealing it in their shirts or in their large refuse sacks. There was nothing they would not steal: bottles of seltzer, rolls of toilet paper, cans of floor wax, boxes of dressmaker's pins, candles, flypaper, and the doctor's favorite foamy bath oil from Cologne even though none of these Italians owned a bathtub—or so she assumed from the looks of them.

Irked as she was, Mrs. Mattison was slow in complaining to the superintendent or to the police about these offenses, but not out of any compassion for the lowly Italians. Nor was she trying to preserve the domestic tranquillity she knew the doctor wanted and deserved once he returned from a busy day at the office (this was also why she had avoided mentioning the liaisons of his son Royal with the woman on Highland Avenue). No, Mary Mattison's delay in this situation was entirely self-centered and explainable with one word: fear. She feared that harm would come to her if she informed against the Italians. She was virtually surrounded by Italians, and she suspected that if she induced the police or the superintendent to take action against the gardeners, her role as informant would leak out sooner or later and she would be vulnerable to their vendettas. She may not have known any Italians before coming to Ambler, but she certainly knew about Italian vendettas. Newspapers had long been writing about the grudge crimes of Italian gangmen in Chicago, New York City, Philadelphia, and elsewhere; and there was no reason to assume that there were not some gang members in Ambler, a few vicious schemers who would contrive to deal with her in any number of subtle and sinister ways.

One day she read that humble Italian-born laborers in America were also capable of committing great atrocities: A factory worker named Sacco and a fish peddler named Vanzetti had been arrested on charges of shooting the paymaster in a shoe factory in New England and running off with fifteen thousand dollars. While both claimed to be innocent men who had come to America to earn a decent living, they were identified as anarchists. It was no wonder the United States government was now limiting the number of newcomers to Ellis Island, especially those from places in southern Europe like Italy. But it was already too late to halt their flow into Ambler.

More than half of the Keasbey & Mattison factory employees, the construction workers, and the castle crew under William Devine were Italian by birth or heritage. Fortunately for Mary Mattison, her husband did not permit any Italians to live on the castle grounds, or to rent homes near Trinity Memorial Church or elsewhere close to the Mattisons' private estate. The row of spired and turreted mansions on Lindenwold Terrace, beyond the north gate of the castle, was occupied by people whom the doctor himself had screened and accepted as desirable neighbors. Originally these mansions were intended for his top executives (before he decided he did not want any); and so now the residences were the domiciles of his son Royal and his family, and certain socially prominent Pennsylvanians who did not work for the doctor but who attended his Episcopal church, or who offered compatible company and useful connections.

Southwest of the castle's front gate, beyond the Bethlehem Turnpike, which edged past the lawn of Trinity Memorial Church, were rows of three-story stone houses with spires and finials, which were rented out to native-born American white-collar workers and plant superintendents of Keasbey & Mattison (including the commuting sales representative of whose wife Royal Mattison was fond); and farther downhill were rows of less decorative dwellings for foremen and favored workers, who might be of Quaker background, or with roots in Germany, England, Ireland, or Scandinavia.

Still farther downhill, along the other side of the railroad tracks, close to the factories, were the simple stone row houses and frame buildings occupied by the Italians. Dr. Mattison had named one of the streets there in honor of General Garibaldi, thinking it would instill some ethnic pride in the Italian quarter; but soon the street sign had been pulled down, and Devine heard from a workman that some of the Italians were less than worshipful of Garibaldi. What the Italians *did* worship, as Mrs. Mattison could see through her powerful lenses, was the statue of the brown-robed monk that they carried around their neighborhood on their shoulders on feast days and other holidays, when they would also pin dollar bills on the long ribbons attached to the figure; and often they dressed their children in brown-hooded robes with rope belts in imitation of the saint. Not Mrs. Mattison alone, but the majority of non-Italian Ambler residents, thought that the display of a holy statue festooned with money was in poor taste and quite primitive; and she was not surprised to learn that the Italians were not encouraged by the town's Irish Catholics to attend Mass at Saint Anthony's—which was why the Italians had built Saint Joseph's, a short walk from where they lived.

On Sundays, the one day the plant was closed, Mrs. Mattison would sometimes watch the Italian women going to Mass with their children, while the men strolled in an open field near the church, arm in arm, walking in circles. Rising in the background behind the tracks were the high-peaked factory buildings with their smokestacks, and a white cliff composed of asbestos waste. She had no idea how many Italians resided in this area, for she had heard that a goodly number had entered the United States illegally and borrowed the work cards of registered Italian employees to clock time on the night shift, later sharing the proceeds with their countrymen. But on Sundays it did not matter to her how many Italians were assembled in Ambler, for they were all at a safe distance. On Mondays, however, the five forty-five a.m. steam whistle alerted them for work; and at daybreak, as the dogs barked, she knew that the gardeners and other laborers had arrived at the castle.

Devine was always at the service gate with the guards to meet them, to count them and check their identity papers before allowing them to proceed back to the barns where their tools and overalls were kept. He would then drive around the estate in one of the doctor's locomobiles to check on what the other workmen were doing, and by seven-fifty sharp he would be in the pantry to inform the butler that the doctor's limousine was waiting to take him to the office. Mrs. Mattison and the doctor had completed breakfast in the dining room by this time, and, as a parting ges- ture of affection, the doctor himself would carry her in his arms up the staircase to her studio in the turret—where, until the doctor's return for lunch, she would spend the morning reading, writing letters, crocheting, and observing the activities and foibles of God's creatures below.

Only the squirrels—graceful and quick, always alert, never lazy—met with her constant approval. She could watch them for hours and *did,* fo- cusing in on them through her glasses as they climbed up and down trees, and scampered across the lawn and around the fountains in tireless pursuit of whatever morsels of nourishment sustained their energy; although there were hundreds of them, of different colors and sizes, she never once saw them fighting among themselves, or disturbing the doctor's flower beds, or rummaging through the trashcans in the backyard like the pilfering Italian gardeners. One day she had caught the gardeners pulling out some of the doctor's discarded clothing, including his long johns and the stained top hat that he used to wear to the opera and that, at her urging, he had finally replaced; the old hat had a frayed brim and its crown was coming loose, and she was glad to see it go—except *now* it was back again, on the head of a little Italian gardener! With the hat down over his ears, he was strutting around the yard to the amusement of his friends—and to such resentment on her part that she came very close to contacting Devine. What most offended her was the gardener's increasing brazenness the longer he wore the hat. No doubt encouraged by the roars of approval he was getting, he suddenly had the temerity to try to imitate Dr. Mattison! He pushed the hat up on his head and tilted it to one side, as the doctor had worn it, and he moved with exaggeratedly long strides, his hands clasped behind his back, as the doctor did while walking. This rude little Italian was mimicking the very man who was saving him from poverty!

So angry that her hands shook, Mary Mattison picked up the phone on her desk, but she had difficulty dialing Devine's number, even though it consisted of only two digits. And then when she did dial it, and had heard the phone ring once, she suddenly hung up. She was frustrated and confused. What good could come of reporting this to Devine? What could he do except scold the Italian, and then reclaim the top hat and the long johns and whatever else they stole, and then what could he do with it? Burn it? Burn it with the leaves that were piled high in the backyard and were torched twice weekly by these very same Italians? Who could be sure they wouldn't let the fire get out of control?

Removing her hand from the phone that rested next to her binoculars, Mary wondered, not for the first time, whether it was in anyone's best interest for her to be seeing so much. Was it her duty to spy for her husband, to serve as his second pair of eyes so that he, or his superintendent, could deal with the indiscretions that transpired in his absence? If, on the other hand, he did not rely on her for added vigilance, why then did he give her the binoculars?

Mary Mattison's main pleasure nonetheless remained watching the squirrels, which became her favorite, though distant, companions through the summer of 1920, when she was unable to be in Newport. She could identify many of them individually by their stripes and varying patches of color, by the length of their bodies, the shape of their tails and ears. Many had long, beautiful ears. But there was one reddish squirrel that had a uniquely high tuft of hair on the tip of each ear. Nearly all had eyes like tiny bright round buttons, but a few had eyes that were almond-shaped and more deeply set. Some had extremely bushy tails; some tails were more black than gray, or were chestnut red, or a blend of all three. Some squirrels were striped along the bottom of their bodies, while others were uniform in color. Their claws varied in shape; they ran in different ways; one squirrel had a permanently injured left front foot but seemed as swift as the others, covering three feet per second at full speed—which was attained whenever a stone landed nearby, hurled by some heartless Italian. Some squirrels lived entirely in the trees, others spent all their time on the ground, and on hot summer days Mary observed a number of baby squirrels with their mothers cooling off at the base of a fountain, just within reach of the soft spray.

Two hawks flew over the castle one afternoon, and Mary nervously watched them circling over the lawn, high above the trees—and as she focused on a branch where two of her favorite squirrels had been resting, she noticed the animals flatten out their bodies along the horizontal extension of wood. Within seconds, as she continued to watch, the squirrels seemed to blend in with the branch so completely that she could no longer clearly see them. The hawks soon flew away.

With the arrival of autumn, Mary had given names to many of the squirrels, and, although she was at first reluctant to admit it to her husband, she knew she wanted to be more of a factor in their lives. This was odd coming from a woman who before her accident had not had the slightest interest in wildlife; nor had she been attached to pets as a girl. She loathed the doctor's watchdogs, although she never said so, and during her brief healthy period as Mrs. Mattison she never once ventured back to see the farm animals. Nevertheless, she now loved squirrels. She admired the sense of responsibility they took in storing food away for the winter, and their nurturing manner with their young, and the fact that they did no damage to the estate's property. Eager to contribute to their welfare in the harsh months ahead, she asked the doctor at breakfast one morning if he would order the construction of a community of houses for squirrels, sturdy little domiciles that would offer greater protection against the icy rain and snow of winter.

The doctor thought it was a grand idea. At once he consulted with Devine, who in turn brought in Bothwell, the architect, who drew a sketch of a squirrel house that the doctor, of course, later changed. Knowing no reason why squirrels might not share his fondness for Gothic architecture, the doctor added spirals and finials to Bothwell's functional concepts; and by mid-January 1921, with snow predicted for one weekend, fifty houses were completed, each three feet high, two feet wide, four feet deep; at least half of them were two-storied, all had floors covered with leaves and twigs, and in the corners were piled nuts and grain. All the houses were painted a brown-toned green that blended in with the estate's landscaping and tree branches. No fewer than twenty Italians contributed to their construction under Devine's guidance; they followed him around to put each house in a spot specified on a map Mrs. Mattison had given him.

Mrs. Mattison watched through her binoculars as each house was placed in a certain fringe area of the lawn that she knew to be favored habitually by a number of squirrels she had in mind; and she had been equally precise in pointing out what branches of what trees should serve as the locations for the higher dwellings. She wished she could have been personally in command of this project, for when Devine was not paying strict attention, the Italians did things their own way; they dug a foundation for a house not in the spot that *she* had chosen but rather in one that *they* preferred, where, she assumed, the dirt was softer. And they were equally careless in the trees, nailing the houses to the most convenient branches rather than to the higher ones, where she knew her more altitudinal pets would feel more at home. Often she watched screaming as the workers deviated from her map, but none knew of her anger—nor, she hoped, was any of them aware that she was spying on them.

At least Devine fulfilled his pledge to complete the task before the arrival of the snow, and this was no simple matter—for, on the final day, a clumsy Italian fell from a ladder and broke his arm and a few ribs, provoking a work stoppage for more than an hour as he lay writhing in the dirt, his face in anguish, kicking his feet at those who tried to help him. Finally they were able to carry him away, but before he disappeared from view, he lifted his head up from the stretcher and, with his one good arm pointed toward the tree house, extended his outer fingers in a jabbing motion—an ugly gesture that Mrs. Mattison could only assume was representative of some primitive curse, for it prompted the other workmen to step back from the tree and cross themselves.

That night at dinner, having not yet been told of the accident, the doctor delivered a pleasant toast at dinner calling for a winter of warmth and happiness for Mary and her squirrels; and during the period of freezing weather that followed, from late January through February and March, the doctor regularly inquired about the welfare of the squirrels, in a manner that was usually jestful but never lacking sincere interest. "Well, Madam Ambassador," he might ask his wife after dinner, as they both sat sipping sherry by the fireplace, "what news from our friends in the trees and in our glacial greensward?"

Her replies were always cheerful, if never accurate. For, much to her great disappointment, none of the squirrels, insofar as she could tell, had yet entered the threshold of a single house, either on land or in a tree. During snowstorms she preferred to believe that some of them were surely inside somewhere, taking advantage of their shelters; but she could see nothing through the snow, and her view was guided by her desire. On clear days, however, although she watched hopefully for hours, she could see that the houses were as empty as if there were a kind of quarantine. She thought perhaps it had been a mistake in having the houses painted. The color might have repelled the squirrels; or, being the wise creatures they were, they might have known that the green-brown-painted houses were too easily seen by hawks. Or maybe the squirrels did not like the *smell* of the paint, which perhaps exuded a poisonous odor. At least Devine, if not the Italians, might have considered this before issuing the paint order.

But she said nothing about this to Devine, taking whatever comfort she could in the fact that the squirrels survived the winter in their own way, homeless by choice, healthy as ever; they were among the few self-sufficient and independent-minded creatures in Mattison's Ambler. This observation, of course, she kept from the doctor, to whom she continued to convey cheerful observations of their compatibility within the "little castles" he had created. To tell him otherwise would no doubt disappoint him. All his effort for naught. He would not want to hear of it. And she would never tell him.

35.

AMBLER WAS DEFINITELY not what Joseph had imagined when he had dreamed of coming to America. This was very clear to him after his first winter in Dr. Mattison's industrial community, a winter in which he inhaled the foul air dominating the sky and became temporarily resigned to his lowly status in this place that was not at all what it had seemed when he first stepped off the train. The nine hundred Italian workers of Keasbey & Mattison were forced to live with their families within the shadows of the factories and the funneled flow of pollutants. The Italians occupied five narrow streets that sloped down from the rail tracks in parallel rows, each street lined with small stone dwellings, clapboard bungalows, and boardinghouses, one of the latter belonging to Joseph's uncles Anthony and Gregory. The only other people who lived on that side of the tracks were the hundred black employees who resided in shacks to the south and west of the Italian quarter.

On the east side of the tracks, along wider avenues that led uphill toward Trinity Memorial Church and the castle, were the more spacious stone residences of the eight hundred other employees, the native-born white Americans or white immigrants from Europe. These people worked next to the Italians and blacks on the assembly lines, and might mingle with them socially in the factory yards during the five-minute rest periods; but when the whistles signaled the end of the shift, the released workers would drift off in two groups, each heading home in an opposite direction from the tracks.

Few Italians seemed to mind this. Most of them, including Joseph's uncles, did not come to Ambler seeking social acceptance and stability; they came to earn money and save it, and then either to repatriate to Italy or to move on to one of the congenial "Little Italys" that now existed in most major American cities. Whatever unflattering observations might be made in Ambler, no one could doubt that it was an ideal place for saving money. The work was steady, there was little to do but work, and the cost of living was half of what it would be if the workers were employed and residing in Philadelphia or towns closer to the city. Except for the daily newspaper, which was two cents everywhere, prices in Ambler were lower than elsewhere: a loaf of bread sold for eight cents; a pound of beef for sixteen; the town's highest rentals, the mansions on Lindenwold Terrace, were less than seventy dollars per month. This meant that people tended not to move, be they mansion-dwellers or black asbestos laborers paying six dollars a month for a shack; and it also meant that Dr. Mattison, who charged low rates for coal, water, and firewood, was able to reinforce his employees' dependence upon him while at the same time keeping their salaries lower than those in other industrial communities. Ambler's workers were aware of this, but it was not their primary concern, for most of them thought that after they had saved sufficient sums they would find a better life elsewhere. Years later many of these same workers, while still planning to move, would die in Ambler.

Joseph's uncles paid twelve dollars a month for their three-story, eleven-room boardinghouse; and since they had six boarders each contributing four dollars a month for the use of three bedrooms—three night-shift workers slept during the day in beds that during the night were slept in by day-shift workers—the Rocchino brothers were operating at a profit. They were able to put away large portions of their factory salaries of approximately twenty-five dollars a week, exclusive of the overtime pay that was usually available when they had the energy for extra hours of labor.

One of the uncles, Anthony, had his young wife and child living with him; and soon another factory worker, not a relative but a native of Maida, was joined by his wife, who was an excellent cook. On Sundays she would prepare a meal for everyone in the house. During the rest of the week, however, the single men got their own meals, each storing a bag of food in the icebox marked with his initials. For a dollar a month, the women provided the men with once-a-week laundry service. In the winter afternoons of his first months in Ambler, Joseph would watch the eerie spectacle of men's laundered pants dancing from the clothesline in the backyard—frozen stiff.

Joseph slept rent-free in a relatively spacious private room in the rear of the house on the ground floor, behind the kitchen. After stringing up a maroon curtain that concealed his cot, he used the room as his first American-based tailor shop. He placed a sign on the lawn announcing that alterations and repairs were done in the rear, with instructions to knock on the back door. Joseph's uncles helped him construct a worktable against one wall, and gave him a secondhand sewing machine and a coal-heated iron, and enough needles and thread to inaugurate what they naively assumed would become a thriving enterprise.

But Joseph's highest weekly income during the business's first six months would be fourteen dollars, and he achieved this only once. Most weeks he earned less than ten dollars from the neighborhood Italians who brought in trousers, suits, or dresses to be altered or repaired, and who usually haggled over his prices—which, by Paris standards, he knew to be very modest. As time went on, his descending prices became modest by *Ambler* standards—but still, there were days and even weeks when not a single customer would come to his door. Joseph became depressed and lived with increasing anxiety; unable to send as much money as he had hoped back to his mother in Maida, he also knew that at this rate it would be years before he had repaid the five-hundred-dollar debt to his uncles. Although they often made it clear that they did not need the money, their generosity only partly lessened his sense of responsibility and failure.

Joseph tried to show his gratitude in various ways. He served as the baby-sitter for his uncle's infant daughter when the child's mother was out shopping or visiting. He voluntarily applied his sewing abilities in replacing the torn and timeworn window curtains throughout the house with fabric he had bought on sale at the company store, near the front gate of the plant. He of course did all the pressing and mending of clothes for the entire household free of charge. This gesture required little time, however, for his fellow residents—and indeed the residents throughout the Italian neighborhood—seemingly cared far less about personal appearances in Ambler than they had when they lived in Italy.

Joseph noticed this soon after his arrival in Ambler. As he stood one afternoon in front of the house awaiting his uncles' return from the factory, he spotted them in the near distance strolling down the dirt road with other Italian workmen, all of them wearing overalls and carrying lunch boxes; and he remembered how impressed he had been by the sight of these same two uncles in Maida as he watched them in the early-evening *passeggiata,* both wearing white shirts and ties, and carnations in the lapels of their double-breasted suits, their feet in two-toned shoes, and their wide-brimmed fedoras sportively tilted to one side—they surely must have been the envy of those Maida men too timid to venture overseas, and they clearly were the recipients of demure smiles from the ladies on the flowered balconies, to whom emigrants were pioneers. And yet here in Ambler, although his uncles were prospering by the measure of any man in Maida, they returned home with sagging shoulders, their faces covered with layers of white asbestos dust. Had it not been for their familiar stride, Joseph would hardly have recognized them.

It was of course unreasonable to make comparisons between how they looked after a hard day's work in a factory and how they had looked during a jaunty outing in the town square of Maida. Still, during the Sunday *passeggiata* in Ambler, while the women were at Mass, Joseph had observed that there was a total absence of the well-dressed males who abounded in the squares of southern Italy, those strutting poseurs eager to project an impressive *bella figura*. Here in Ambler they walked humbly, and in dreary attire—dark peaked caps, shirts without cravats, rumpled trousers, unshined shoes, coarse woolen sweaters usually black in color—worn not in mourning but rather to blend in with the soot-filled sky that darkened more deeply as each of a dozen Philadelphia & Reading Railroad locomotives came and went between dawn and dusk in the Ambler station. Here in Ambler's Italian quarter there were no clean cobblestone walkways, no flowered balconies basking in a soft twilight sun, no green-leaved vegetable gardens untinted by black specks of coal and the white dust of asbestos. Here people were awakened not by the crowing of cocks but by the rasping whistle from the factory; and yet these were the sounds by which Ambler's people prospered. For Joseph, however, the whistles were signals that he must move on. Ambler was no place for a tailor.

But first he must learn English; and although the southern Italian dialects still prevailed in the neighborhood, it was Dr. Mattison's intention that all newcomers be English-speaking as soon as possible, and he provided language instruction free of charge to workers who would attend classes at the Italian church on Wednesday and Sunday nights. Joseph registered under his uncles' surname, and during one of these sessions in early 1922 the instructor introduced a special visitor to the class, Dr. Mattison's superintendent, William Devine. With the instructor serving as interpreter, Devine announced that part-time jobs in construction work were now available to individuals wishing to earn extra money during their off-hours from the factory. The new row of residences going up on Church Street demanded more unskilled laborers at once, Mr. Devine said, energetic men who could help haul timber beams to the carpenters and push wheelbarrows filled with stones to the masons; and for such jobs, the starting pay was fifty cents per hour. Anyone interested was to appear for an interview on the following day, between noon and one o'clock, at the north gate of the castle.

As Mr. Devine waved good-bye, leaving application forms on the instructor's desk, Joseph quickly calculated that by devoting only four hours daily to such activities he could add twelve dollars to his weekly income *and* complete whatever tailoring jobs came his way. He believed he could arrange for one of the women to be at home to answer his door when he was away; and when he returned to the boardinghouse that evening, both women unhesitatingly agreed to cooperate. His uncles, however, argued against his doing hard labor. He was too slightly built for such work, they said, and he was foolish to risk his health in order to make payments on a loan that, as they had often said earlier, they were in no hurry to collect.

Joseph again thanked them, but emphasized that it was the urgent needs of his mother that now compelled him. He told them that in her most recent letter she admitted to being burdened with debts she was too proud to acknowledge to anyone but him—debts resulting largely from the mounting medical costs of the bedridden Sebastian. Not wanting him to be confined to a distant military hospital, she was caring for Sebastian permanently at home, along with Joseph's three younger siblings; but the expense of the doctor's visits and the medicines prescribed was more than she could continue to afford. Now Joseph insisted to Anthony and Gregory that it was his responsibility, and his alone as the nominal head of his family, to contribute every dollar possible during this difficult period. And in a lighter vein, he reassured his uncles that a few hours of arduous work and daily sweat outdoors would, instead of diminishing his health, probably enhance it.

On the following day, after his uncles had rearranged their factory hours with friends so that they could accompany him to the interview, Joseph was escorted across the railroad tracks and guided northward along tree-lined streets and uphill past rows of gradually more embellished stone houses that would eventually extend to the boulevard running parallel to the walls of Dr. Mattison's estate. Joseph had on two previous occasions been given a tour of this area, in a milk wagon owned by a man who lived next door to the Rocchinos; both tours had been on Sundays when the avenues had been crowded with carriages and motorcars filled primarily with people on leisurely excursions, and along the sidewalks Joseph had seen processions of well-dressed couples—many homburg-hatted men, nearly all the women wearing crocheted white gloves—either going to or coming from Trinity Memorial Church.

But on this Monday, shortly before noon, there was hardly a vehicle moving anywhere in the streets; and the sidewalks were so empty that all Joseph heard clearly were the unfamiliar sounds of his uncles' heavy leather-heeled boots on the pavement—sounds ordinarily muted on the dirt roads of the Italian quarter. Occasionally he became aware that they were being watched from the windows of some of the houses. And it made Joseph feel like a trespasser.

He imagined that his uncles were uneasy too, for they were walking more quickly than they normally did, and staring straight ahead as if to avoid making eye contact with what they assumed would be unfriendly faces if anyone did appear. Joseph wished that his uncles had dressed with a bit more care on this day. Not long before, he had taken from their closets, and had sponged and pressed, the double-breasted suits he had seen them wear only in Maida; but still he could not bring himself to drop hints to these kindly men, his mother's brothers, about how they should dress. Today they were in their usual off-duty outdoor attire—gray peaked caps, heavy dark sweaters and creaseless woolen trousers, and shirts without ties, buttoned to the tops of their necks. Joseph on the other hand had refused to lower his sartorial standards even *if* he was about to apply for work as a lowly laborer. His uncles had seemed surprised earlier in the morning when they saw him dressed, as was his custom, in suit, vest, and tie; and his uncle Gregory, who was closer to Joseph's size than his stouter uncle Anthony, wondered aloud if Joseph might want to try on an extra pair of his overalls and one of his work shirts.

"I'm not hired *yet,*" Joseph replied, with a smile.

"You may never get hired if you go dressed like that," his uncle Gregory responded, also in good humor.

"We'll see. Maybe they'll ask me to work in the castle."

Joseph was immediately sorry he had said that. But Gregory only shrugged, and Anthony also did not appear to interpret the remark as a criticism of them. Joseph was relieved.

The three of them continued uphill, passing homes larger and more widely spaced than before. A Packard convertible drove swiftly past them, cutting near to the curb before screeching to a halt at an intersection. Then it turned sharply to the right.

"There goes Dr. Mattison's son," Anthony said, shaking his head slowly, but intoning a paternal tolerance that most workingmen reserve for their bosses' sons—a tolerance their own sons rarely know. Anthony and his brother watched as the vehicle picked up speed along an adjacent street, then slammed to a stop in front of one of the houses.

"And there goes Dr. Mattison's son to warm up the bed with his *puttana,*" added Gregory.

"Is *that* any way to talk?" Anthony asked angrily, stopping and turning toward Gregory. Joseph also stopped, confused and surprised. He had never before seen his uncle Anthony so suddenly overbearing. Joseph was reminded of how Sebastian used to talk to *him.* Not knowing his uncles' ages, Joseph decided that Anthony was older. But Gregory remained indifferent to Anthony's ill temper, and ignored his question.

"Is it any business of *yours* how Dr. Mattison's son lives his life?" Anthony went on, demanding a reply.

"No," Gregory responded sharply, "not if such a faithful husband as *you* doesn't think so."

Anthony's face quickly became red. Joseph had no idea what Gregory had been referring to, but he saw Anthony take a step toward his brother. Joseph immediately rushed in between them.

"Please," he said, "I don't want to be late."

Anthony, breathing heavily, looked startled at Joseph, as if he had completely forgotten that his nephew was there. "Yes," he then agreed, "you shouldn't be late."

"We're less than ten minutes away," Gregory said calmly. "We'll get there."

"So let's get going, then," Anthony said, not looking at Gregory, but trying to match his brother's composure while taking charge.

Anthony led the way, but Gregory was soon beside him, keeping pace although Anthony was moving even faster than earlier. Joseph struggled to keep up. They walked on in silence, their arguing now behind them, but it appeared to Joseph that the heels of his uncles' boots were hitting the sidewalk with unnecessary force.

Joseph could see the tower of Trinity Memorial Church rising above the distant treetops. He knew that the castle was located a short distance behind the church on the far side of the boulevard. He heard some harsh, strange noises coming from the corner house they were now approaching. As they reached it, he saw a parrot perched on a pole suspended from ropes that were attached to the ceiling of a stone-walled porch. The pet had green, yellow, and red feathers, a thick hooked bill, and a long pointed tail. Its claws were strapped to the pole. Joseph had seen a parrot once; it belonged to a priest in Maida, and it chanted in Latin. But this parrot was twice as large, and it became agitated as they passed, flapping its wings, straining against the claw straps, and thrusting its head in their direction as it called out: "*Dago, dago, dago, dago, dago!*"

Joseph's uncles stopped and stared at the bird. It remained silent for a second. But as they were about to continue on their way, the bird repeated the words as clearly and boldly as before: "*Dago, dago, dago, dago, dago!*"

Anthony's face was red once more, and, brandishing a fist toward the parrot, he shouted: "Shut your dirty mouth, you stupid ugly animal, or I'll come up there and break your neck!"

"*Dago, dago, dago, dago, dago!*"

Anthony left the sidewalk and ran toward the porch steps, but his brother grabbed him from behind, urging him to remain calm; in the tussling, however, both men tripped and fell on the muddy brown grass of the lawn.

"I'm going to kill that fucking thing!" Anthony yelled, flat on his stomach, while Gregory—immediately assisted by Joseph—prevented him from getting up and rushing onto the porch. Although Joseph was as bewildered by this latest flare-up as he had been by the earlier one—he had never heard the word "dago" before, and would not know it as an insult to Italians until Gregory explained it that night—he realized that many people were now frowning down upon them from the windows of the neighboring buildings. The third-floor window directly above them had just opened, and a round-faced woman with red hair thrust out a rolling pin and screamed down: "Get away from here, you brutes, or I'll get the police!"

"C'mon, Uncle Anthony," Joseph pleaded, leaning low into his uncle's muddy ear, "we must get away from here."

Anthony nodded. No longer resisting Gregory's grasp, he got to his feet. Joseph wiped the dirt from Anthony's face with a handkerchief, and Gregory with his free hand brushed some of the mud from his brother's clothing. Having landed *on* his brother, Gregory was largely unsoiled and dry. Next door another window opened, and an elderly man poked his head out and began to shout; but his frail voice could not be understood. Anthony looked at him, and then at the woman waving the rolling pin in the air, but he said nothing as he turned toward the sidewalk with his brother and nephew beside him. The parrot, equally silent, watched them as they departed. They did not look back at the parrot. Five minutes later, outside the north gate of the castle, they heard Dr. Mattison's growling dogs.

Joseph took his application form out of the pocket of his jacket and held it up to be seen by the armed guard who stood on the other side of the bars with a snarling mastiff on a leash. A second guard, who was dogless, came forward to inspect the document, and after opening the gate he pointed Joseph and his uncles in the direction of the gazebo. Joseph recognized Mr. Devine standing behind the gazebo, talking to a circle of workmen. Turning, Joseph quickly glanced at the towers of the castle rising in the fog, and he noticed that the estate's grass was green, not brown as it was on the lawns of the homes they had passed. One of the men who had been standing with Mr. Devine was now coming forward to greet Joseph and his uncles, and Gregory waved as he recognized him. He was a large gray-haired man wearing overalls and a black sweater, and as he got closer Gregory whispered to Joseph: "This is Nicola Muscatelli from Maida. He's worked as a foreman on many road gangs in America, and if he's on this job with Mr. Devine, you might be in luck."

Joseph recognized the name as being that of the family who owned the bar in Maida's town square, and he remembered his grandfather Domenico speaking fondly of the Muscatellis, although claiming they owed him a bit of money.

"Greetings, my friends," Muscatelli said, speaking in Italian as he embraced Gregory and Anthony, "but don't tell me you're looking for a little outdoor work?"

"Not us, but our nephew here is," Gregory said, introducing Joseph. Muscatelli looked wonderingly at the way Joseph was dressed, at the slenderness of his shoulders, and then he looked back at Gregory and Anthony with a smile, as if they were indulging in a friendly joke.

"Don't worry," Anthony spoke up, "he's a good worker. And he has clothes at home. And he'll be on time."

"He's thin," Muscatelli said.

"His suit makes him look thin," Gregory said. "He's got lots of energy. I give you my word."

As Joseph stood listening uncomfortably, looking out at the group of heavy-shouldered older men who were gathered around Devine at the gazebo, Muscatelli reexamined Joseph.

"Who's the boy's father?" he asked Gregory.

"My father is dead," Joseph himself answered. "He was Gaetano Talese."

Muscatelli's face softened. Saying nothing, he continued to look at Joseph with an intensity that only added to his discomfort. Then there were tears in Muscatelli's eyes.

"He was my friend," he said finally. "We worked together many years ago in Delaware." There was silence as Muscatelli wiped his eyes. "A wonderful man," he added. And then he asked: "When can you begin?"

"This afternoon," Joseph said.

"How about tomorrow morning," Muscatelli said, "at six o'clock? Your uncles will show you where we'll be working."

Joseph thanked him, as did his uncles.

"You're welcome," Muscatelli said to Joseph before turning back to Devine and the other men. "And don't show up wearing that suit."

36.

O N THE FOLLOWING day, and throughout the winter of 1922, Joseph served as a part-time employee with Nicola Muscatelli's gang of Italian laborers. He pushed wheelbarrows filled with rocks, drove a horse wagon loaded with timber, and, as the gang's junior member, was responsible for supplying and refilling the men's buckets of drinking water. Although Muscatelli privately favored him, the foreman was careful not to show it until Joseph had gained acceptance from the others. Very quickly, however, Muscatelli minimized Joseph's involvement with hard labor and shifted him to logistical chores. Joseph was told to examine the daily delivery of building material at the job site, and to verify that it was what Muscatelli had ordered and in the amount listed on the billing. If the men's hand tools had become broken or lost, or if the heavy machinery malfunctioned, Joseph was dispatched to arrange for replacements and repairs. Soon, and without expressed disagreement from the men, Joseph was functioning as Muscatelli's record-keeper and construction assistant. Whenever Muscatelli was summoned to report to Mr. Devine's office a mile away at the estate, Joseph drove him there in the wagon. One morning as Joseph stood waiting next to the horses near the castle's north gate, he noticed glimmerings of light coming from one of the turret's upper windows. When he realized it was caused by the sun reflecting off the upraised binoculars held by a woman staring down at him, Joseph took a step forward for a better look. The woman at the window quickly vanished.

Years later, long after Joseph had established himself elsewhere as a tailor and clothier, he would remember much of the strangeness he had felt during this period of life in Dr. Mattison's domain—the sheer irony of his having left his village in the crumbled medieval kingdom of southern Italy for a town in Pennsylvania run by a man who behaved in ways like a medieval king.

But during the fifteen months that Joseph lived in his uncles' boardinghouse—from Christmastime 1920 until his departure in the spring of 1922—he concentrated less on Ambler as an idiosyncratic place in the "New World" and more on Ambler as a source of economic enrichment, particularly after he had been promoted to Muscatelli's assistant. Although Joseph continued to work only part-time in construction—he arrived six days a week at six in the morning, and returned home after one in the afternoon to whatever clothing jobs awaited him in his bedroom tailor shop—Muscatelli saw to it that Joseph's earnings were between twenty-five and thirty dollars a week. Equally gratifying to Joseph, although initially quite mystifying, was that as soon as he began earning good money from Muscatelli, his tailoring business increased almost beyond his capacity to keep up with it. Joseph recalled the maxim of his uncle Francesco Cristiani in Maida: "You'll always have more customers than you need when you need them least." But Joseph later concluded that the main factor in his rising popularity as a tailor during early 1922 was that a significant number of Ambler Italians had put on weight.

Every customer who approached him at this time requested that he enlarge the width of their trousers or skirts, suits or coats. Joseph remembered the people of Maida as characteristically lean, if not actually underfed. Maida was part of the undercultivated, overpopulated south; it was occupied by highlanders and coastline settlers who favored seafood, rice, beans, and pasta with limited amounts of sauce. Joseph knew his grandfather Domenico and others in Maida to be slender vegetarians; and none of the patrons of Cristiani's tailor shop could be described as obese except for the late *mafioso* Vincenzo Castiglia.

But the Maida natives in Ambler were undoubtedly being thickened by what Joseph could only assume was their greater assimilation of the heavier American diet: more beef, less seafood; more milk, butter, bacon, and eggs than had been available in Italy; soft and heavily larded white American bread instead of the brown whole wheat loaves baked daily by Joseph's mother and most other women in Maida. Here in Ambler the Italians cooked more with butter and less with olive oil, as Joseph had noticed during Sunday-dinner preparations at the boardinghouse. While Italian olive oil and other old-country staples could be purchased in South Philadelphia's Little Italy, or even locally at Palermo's small grocery shop, such imported items were more expensive than American-made substitutes. Clearly, many Italians in Ambler cared more about saving a few pennies than gaining a few pounds.

Joseph noticed that his uncles seemed heavier than they had been in Maida, and he wondered if they had shunned their suits because they could no longer fit into them. This certainly was true of the local Italian priest, who had visited Joseph one day and confessed to having gained more than twenty pounds in six months. Addicted to American pies and ice cream, the priest was now too fat for his suits and his cassocks. Joseph volunteered to enlarge his entire wardrobe free of charge, but the priest insisted that Joseph be paid. He eventually paid him a total of sixteen dollars in cash, plus a largesse in plenary indulgences.

From his earnings as a tailor, and the payments from Muscatelli, Joseph was averaging close to forty-five dollars a week. He was increasing the sums sent to Maida, and he was finally able to convince his uncles to allow him to start reducing his debt to them. The winter of 1922 was quite satisfying to Joseph, even though he was often physically exhausted. Sometimes he would sew through the night by candlelight, almost semiconsciously following the silver needle as it wormed its way in and out of the fabric; then, at five forty-five, he would be startled by the first sounds of a factory whistle. After quickly splashing water on his face at the basin, and jumping into his tailored overalls that his uncles had outgrown long before, Joseph would arrive at the construction site at six, ready for work outdoors.

But it was not only his fatiguing schedule that would influence his decision to leave Ambler and his high earnings there. One morning not long after Muscatelli had made him his assistant, Joseph noticed on a list of new workers hired by Devine a surname the same as his own—another Talese was in Ambler, although Joseph had never met this person in Maida, or been aware of his existence. When Joseph mentioned this to his uncles later that night, both Anthony and Gregory solemnly advised him to keep his distance from this other Talese.

"There was bad blood many years ago between this fellow's grand-father and your own grandfather Domenico," Anthony explained. "This other grandfather was either a brother, a half brother, or a cousin to Domenico, and when he died your grandfather swindled some property from this man's heirs, or at least he tried to. This man in Ambler today is one of those heirs. He also has other relatives in Ambler. So," Anthony went on, "I think you should be careful."

Not knowing exactly what being "careful" meant as far as proceeding with his daily life, and receiving no further advice from either uncle, Joseph merely stored away the information and categorized it as yet an-other potential encumbrance that had followed him from the Old World to this peculiar place in Pennsylvania. Meanwhile he worked through the late winter in close proximity to Muscatelli, making no effort to meet his Talese kinsman; and the latter never stepped forward and made himself known to Joseph.

Around this time Joseph did meet and befriend a young Philadelphia tailor whose father and uncle were asbestos workers in Ambler, and who had been introduced to him by the grateful local priest whose clothing Joseph had altered. The tailor was a few years older than Joseph, and had worked in Naples prior to finding employment in Philadelphia. Recently he had been laid off in Philadelphia because of a cutback at the department store where he worked, and for this reason he was living temporarily with his father in Ambler. But the tailor, who commuted to Philadelphia each day in search of a new job, was optimistic about finding one, and he promised that when he did, he would use his contacts to get Joseph hired as a full-time tailor as well. Joseph was very appreciative and hopeful that this could be done; and after his friend had been hired by Pincus Brothers, a Philadelphia clothing firm, he visited Joseph to tell him the good news and also reassure him that he would soon find him a position.

"But first I'd like you to do me a small favor," the tailor said. Joseph replied that he would be happy to comply in any way he could.

"I'd like to be introduced to your niece," the man told Joseph.

"Niece?" Joseph asked. "I have no niece."

"Well, I'd heard from the priest that you're related to that pretty young girl who lives two doors away, in that other boardinghouse."

"Oh, she's not my niece," Joseph said. "She's the daughter of my uncle Anthony's wife's sister. Her name is Angela. But I hardly know her."

"I hear she visits your place all the time, and helps your aunt with the laundry. . . ."

"Yes," said Joseph, "but Angela's very shy and very religious."

"I am, too," the older tailor insisted. "The priest will vouch for me. I just want you to arrange for me to meet her someplace. I'd just like to talk to her for a few minutes in private, and try to get to know her a little."

While Joseph did not feel entirely comfortable about this request, he had no reason to doubt the honorable intentions of his new friend, nor was he unappreciative of his friend's promised efforts in his own behalf. He also knew that Angela, who was perhaps not yet seventeen and had come to Ambler from Maida a year before, lived a very sheltered life under the constant scrutiny of her parents and kinfolk in this Italian habitat, and he knew that his friend could never talk privately to Angela unless he, Joseph, took steps to become the intermediary.

"All I can do is try," Joseph told his friend.

"You won't regret it," his friend said with a smile and a handshake as he left the boardinghouse.

One afternoon days later, when Joseph noticed Angela hanging clothes on the line and knew that his aunt and the other woman were out on errands, he put aside his sewing and approached her.

"Angela, please forgive me," he began softly, as she turned and faced him with a look of timid suspicion, her outstretched hands still holding the wooden pins that pinched a soggy pair of men's white underdrawers to the line. "But I have a friend who would like to meet you."

Angela's dark eyes looked downward, and her furrowed brow now forced her heavy eyebrows together above her nose, and she began to blush.

"Angela, don't worry," Joseph went on in a tone that sounded uncon-

vincing even to him, for he was totally lacking in experience as an inter-
nuncio in romantic matters, and he was also upset by the discomfort he
seemed to be causing her. "Angela," he pressed on anyway, "he only wants
to meet you, to say a few words. . . . Perhaps you can tell me when you're
going to confession, and I can tell him, and he can meet you outside the
church. . . ."

Angela now began to tremble, her outstretched hands on the pins
shaking as if the clothesline were electrically charged. She was a martyr
suffering in silence, and Joseph could only back away and say repeatedly,
"Angela, I'm sorry, I'm sorry. Please forgive me. Please forget what I said,
Angela. . . ."

Not only did Angela not forget, but, seeing her mother passing along
the road with an armload of groceries, Angela ran tearfully toward her and
reported Joseph's request in such a way that her mother suddenly saw
him as an evil broker wishing to prostitute her daughter's virtue. As Angela's mother shrieked on the sidewalk, Joseph ran back to his bedroom,
locked the door behind him, and pulled down the shades.

But ten minutes later, he heard his uncle Anthony's wife, Caroline
Rocchino, pounding on the door, reproaching him for his insults to her
sister's daughter. Joseph, refusing to respond, began to pack his suitcase.

It was time for him to leave Ambler. He was ready to move on from
this place with its castle, its enduring grudges, and its imported traditions
of village virtue.

When his uncles returned from the factory that evening, their faces
covered as usual with the white dust that they tracked home every night,
Joseph said: "I've dishonored your house. I am sorry. I must go away."

They both tried to convince him to change his mind, saying that it
was all a misunderstanding; but Caroline remained cool to him, as did the
other woman in the house, and later that night, as Joseph sat sewing alone
in his room, he could hear a boisterous argument coming from the porch
of the boardinghouse two doors away. He recognized his uncles' voices,
and that of Angela's father, and he again heard the shrieks of her mother,
while imagining as well the blushing presence of the desired but diffident
Angela.

He buried his head in the heap of clothing that he had been entrusted
to expand in size, and fell asleep at the table, a threaded needle dangling
above the tops of his shoes. At five forty-five he was aroused by the factory whistle, but for the first time he felt physically unfit to report for
work. He had chest pains. He could not breathe normally. Nevertheless

he forced himself up, dressed as quickly as he could, and ran out the back door and across the tracks toward the construction site. Embarrassed that he was ten minutes late, he apologized to Muscatelli. The foreman turned around, studied him, and said: "Joseph, you don't look good. You look like all the blood's been drained out of you."

"I'll be all right," Joseph said; but by midmorning he was so dizzy he thought he would faint, and Muscatelli insisted on driving him to the home of one of the factory's night workers who had served with the Italian medical corps on the Austrian front during the war. The former medic had returned home from work shortly before their arrival, and his heavy snoring could be heard from the second story as Muscatelli rapped on the door. His knock brought forth an angry wife who opened the door only a few inches and yelled: "He's asleep!"

"Wake him up!" Muscatelli yelled back.

The snoring stopped, and the awakened man upstairs began to swear. Muscatelli took this as an invitation to barge into the house, and, with one arm helping the wobbly Joseph up the steps, he entered the bedroom.

"This is an emergency!" he announced to the startled medic, a small man with a long nose who had been sleeping with a towel over his head to keep out the daylight. "Take this boy's pulse. See what's wrong with him."

Lifting his head from the pillow, the former medic obediently reached out to hold Joseph's right wrist. Joseph stood quietly at the edge of the bed for a few moments.

"This boy's got no pulse," he said finally, looking wonderingly at Muscatelli.

"Get him some water, then," Muscatelli said. "Let him lie down, keep him warm. I'll go to his house for some clean clothes, and then I'll be back to take him to a doctor I know in Philadelphia."

Joseph's uncles were at work when Muscatelli arrived at the boardinghouse, but Caroline Rocchino was there to lead Muscatelli to Joseph's room; and she was not noticeably remorseful when Muscatelli, carrying away the suitcase that Joseph had packed earlier, told her that the ailing young man might not be back for a while.

After Joseph had changed his clothes at the onetime medic's house, he entrained for Philadelphia with Muscatelli and was taken to the South Philadelphia home of a physician who had been a boyhood friend of Muscatelli's in Maida. Dr. Fabiani greeted the foreman with warm kisses and excused himself from the patients who sat in the alcove awaiting his care. The white-coated, effusive physician insisted that Muscatelli and Joseph follow him to his private den in the rear, where they could have fresh coffee and a piece of his wife's just baked cake.

"My dear friend," Muscatelli politely interrupted, "this boy here is very sick."

"Oh?" the doctor asked nonchalantly, as if wondering whether that was reason enough to delay tasting the cake. "Well," he said finally, leading Joseph into a tiny examining room off the hall, "let's step in here for a second and have a look."

Joseph had removed his shirt, and the doctor listened to his breathing through the stethoscope, but his manner was no less ingratiating than when he had proposed tasting the cake.

"There's nothing really wrong with this boy," he announced cheerfully. "All he needs is a little fresh air." Then, turning toward Muscatelli, the doctor asked: "Do you remember our little friend in Maida whose father was the shepherd?"

"Guardacielo?" Muscatelli asked.

"*Yes,* Guardacielo," the doctor repeated. "Well, our little friend Guardacielo has become a big man in Atlantic City. He owns a hotel down there. It's the first hotel you come to after you get off the train. And I think it will do this boy good to go down there. A few days by the sea, his lungs will be clear, he'll be good as new."

Dr. Fabiani took his prescription pad and wrote Joseph a note of introduction to Guardacielo, then handed it to him along with an envelope containing pills for his wheezing. Three hours later, after Muscatelli had taken Joseph to the Philadelphia terminal and bought him a rail ticket to Atlantic City, Joseph was traveling alone through the swamplands of southern New Jersey, feeling better already. He was tired, but no longer dizzy. The sooty air floating through the railcar was a marked improvement over Ambler's polluted sky. The car was nearly empty; it was mid-April, hardly yet the season for sunbathers. In the overhead rack was Joseph's suitcase, containing most of his personal possessions, including nearly seventy-five dollars in savings, half of which he had planned to mail to his mother at the end of the month.

After stepping down onto the platform at the Atlantic City station, Joseph followed the doctor's directions to Guardacielo's Seaside Hotel, a five-story red-brick onetime tenement building that Joseph later learned was a mile away from the nearest beach. The hotel was in the center of town, in a honky-tonk area with jazz clubs and black women strutting along the sidewalk, and a taxi stand where the drivers leaned against the fenders of their parked vehicles, smoking cigarettes and soliciting business for the speakeasies less than two blocks away.

Entering a small terrazzo-floored lobby with a large painting of the Bay of Naples hanging on one wall next to a grandfather clock—it was now nearly ten p.m.—Joseph at first believed the room was unattended. But then he noticed a young man wearing a porter's cap asleep in a wicker chair behind the waist-high front desk. Not without some perverse pleasure, Joseph banged the domed bell on the desk to arouse him from his slumber. The young man jumped up, eliciting apologies. He was no more than Joseph's age, and had a sad long face with pimples, and sparse wisps of hair around his jaw and cheeks that suggested his premature desire for a beard.

"I'm looking for Signor Guardacielo," Joseph said.

"Oh, I'm sorry," the porter said, "but he's visiting his relatives in Italy."

Joseph could picture him prancing in the *passeggiata*.

"Well, I was told to come here for a room," Joseph said.

"Someone suggested us?" the porter asked, almost in disbelief.

"Yes, a Dr. Fabiani in Philadelphia."

"Oh, that's my uncle," the porter said.

"Well," Joseph said, resting his heavy suitcase on the floor, "do you *have* a room, a very *quiet* room?"

"The quietest rooms are on the fifth floor, and you can have your pick," the porter said. "Nobody's up there."

As Joseph wrote his name in the registry, the porter locked the front door, reversed a cardboard sign on the knob stating that he would return soon, and, after taking the suitcase, led the way up a squeaky staircase to the top floor.

"This room I'll show you first is the nicest and largest," the clerk said, opening the door with some difficulty. The room light was so dim that Joseph could barely see the big bed in front of him, or the large window behind it with red damask draperies that seemed to match the coverlet on the bed.

"This will be fine," Joseph said.

"Can I bring you something to eat or drink?" the porter asked. "I can get something from the jazz club next door and be back in a minute."

"No, thank you," Joseph said. After the five-story climb he wanted only to lie down. When the porter had gone, Joseph unpacked his suitcase, hung up his clothes, opened the window slightly, hoping to reduce the room's musty smell, and got into bed. From the street he heard the jingling of trolley bells, the cabmen's catcalls at the promenading women, and the blaring of the musicians at the club next door. Even after closing the window he could not avoid the noise, although he lay still for a long time with pillows pressed over his face in an attempt to muffle the sounds. Finally he got up, dressed, and returned to the lobby, where it was doubly noisy, but where only after repeated poundings on the bell could he awaken the porter.

"I can't *stand* it here!" Joseph complained, as the porter jumped up from his chair. "I can't sleep in all this racket! Dr. Fabiani sent me here for peace and quiet, and . . ."

"He sent you *here* for that?" the porter asked, rubbing his eyes, and speaking in the same incredulous tone he had used earlier when Joseph had told him that this hotel had been recommended. "Well, I'm sorry," the porter went on. "My uncle made a mistake. There is no peace and quiet here. For that you have to go somewhere else. You have to go to a place like Ocean City."

Joseph shook his head slowly. What he wanted least now was more advice. But finally he asked, softly, "Where is that?"

"It's near here," he said. "You just get on one of those trolleys outside, and stay on till it stops. The last stop is Ocean City. It's a place with lots of Protestant ministers and clams."

Joseph had never met a Protestant minister, had never seen a clam, but early in the morning, after the porter had helped him get his ticket, Joseph was on a trolley heading southward along the Atlantic Coast, rolling along weed-strewn rusty tracks between a desert of white sand and swampy ponds so still that not even a bubble rippled on the surface. He remained on the trolley for more than an hour, looking out through the morning fog at the fishing boats and ocean waves that usually were on his left, but sometimes were behind him as the trolley veered inland through thickets and pine trees, passing small farmhouses and barns where people wearing overalls waved at the conductor. In a red peaked cap, he sat on a high metal stool behind an angular steering apparatus that he never seemed to steer; the trolley appeared to guide itself independently over the curving tracks, and soundlessly, too, except for some slight electrical sputterings when the little wheels rubbed against the rooftop wiring. Joseph sat near the back of the car. Up ahead were three other passengers, white-haired men wearing homburgs and overcoats, seated separately, reading newspapers.

The trolley now left the pineland and was dipping toward a rickety timber bridge no wider than the trolley tracks that extended for two miles across the bay, supported by hundreds of vertical poles that rose up crookedly from the marshland and the choppy waters. Joseph closed his eyes and prayed as he glimpsed the trolley gliding over the tracks suspended thirty feet above the water, and he kept his eyes closed for ten minutes as he heard the high-pitched clicking hollowness and smelled the boggy breezes of the bay rising up through the car.

"Asbury Avenue," he heard the conductor call out, and when Joseph opened his eyes he saw that the trolley had passed beyond the bay, and noticed the American flags flying from the porches of white bayfront houses and from the masts of the taller ships anchored along the docks. Moving smoothly across the island, the trolley soon stopped at an intersection of a wide paved street. It was lined with shops and had a bank on the corner. This was the island's business district, as Joseph would later learn, named in honor of a Methodist missionary, Francis Asbury.

"Wesley Avenue," the conductor said next, and Joseph soon saw the town's principal residential block, named for the founder of Methodism. It was a tree-lined street with large Victorian residences, so white, so different from the dark Gothic mansions of Dr. Mattison's Ambler. Joseph, staring out the window, failed to notice that the three other passengers had just left the car; and not knowing what to ask the driver in English to find out whether he, too, should get off, Joseph sat with uncertainty as the trolley continued across town. It now moved past blocks where most of the homes had boarded-up windows, where no motor vehicles or pedestrians could be seen on the streets, and where the neighborhood's single traffic light was covered with a canvas hood.

"Boardwalk, final stop," the conductor called up. The trolley came to a halt in front of the silhouette of an elevated wooden promenade with silvery railings etched across an open sky. Joseph heard the conductor pulling down on a lever and saw him turn around to announce: "This car will start back to Atlantic City in ten minutes."

Joseph nodded, as if he understood. The conductor stepped down and stood in front of the trolley, smoking a cigarette he had lit before leaving the car. Joseph reached for his suitcase and exited from the side door. Briefly he glanced down the tracks in the direction of the midtown streets he had passed. He could see a few motorcars and tiny figures walking in the distance. Then he stepped onto the sand-covered sidewalk and headed in the opposite direction, toward the sounds of the sea. Holding on to the cold iron railing with one hand, and his suitcase with the other, he made his way up the ramp to a deserted boardwalk that seemed to stretch endlessly above the sand and surf, without a soul in sight, without any living creatures except the sea gulls circling overhead.

The nearness of the sea, which had always intimidated him, somehow now did not. He was soothed by the steady sounds of the breaking waves, was refreshed by the misty spray that shot up through the boards as the ocean smashed against the pilings below. For some reason he felt he had finally arrived at a place where he wanted to be.

37.

THE ITALY THAT Joseph had left behind was about to succumb to the rhetorical flair and Fascist political policies of a strong-willed Milan newspaper publisher and onetime schoolmaster, Benito Mussolini. At thirty-nine Mussolini was stocky and prematurely balding, and bothered by acute stomach pains that he mollified only slightly by bloating himself daily with glasses of milk. He rarely complained of his ailment, however, and in public he presented himself as a man of vigorous health and inner contentment, of intellectual acuity and statesmanlike vision. He was a tennis player, a jogger, and a steeplechase rider. He spoke German and French, and could recite poetry in five languages. Though merely five feet, six inches, he seemed much taller because of his erect posture, his broad shoulders and massive chest, and the fact that when speaking behind a lectern he stood on a box. His dark penetrating eyes, jutting jaw, and stern brow projected a sense of fearlessness that often prompted people to compare him to a Roman warrior—a comparison that pleased him, for he did indeed see himself as historically linked to the ancient era of Italian grandeur. It was a grandeur he intended to restore.

"History is nothing but a succession of dominant elites," he once said, paraphrasing an Italian sociology professor whose lectures he had audited in Switzerland in 1904 during his wandering days as a student and social activist. Now, in 1922, having supported himself in the intervening years mainly as a dissatisfied schoolmaster and an even more dissatisfied editorial writer, Mussolini was ready to stage a political coup and elevate himself into the ranks of dominant elites. He was convinced that now more than ever Italy was in need of a dissatisfied man like himself.

Chaos and political corruption prevailed throughout the nation. Strikes and lockouts, arson and riots interrupted industrial production in urban areas; and in the countryside, thousands of tenant farmers refused to harvest their proprietors' shares until the government abided by its land-reform promises made years earlier, when it had rallied farm workers' support during the dark days of World War I. But the large landholders, backed by their powerful friends in government, stalled corrective legislation while concurrently accusing the reformists of being Bolsheviks determined to turn Catholic Italy into a state of godless Communism.

Such an eventuality seemed likely to devout Catholics among the bourgeoisie and the working classes, elements already alarmed by the sight of their streets and squares constantly invaded by a procession of sullen men waving red flags and advocating insurrection. The Vatican was also concerned, and, hoping to overcome leftist candidates at the ballot box, priests for the first time in a half-century did not discourage parishioners from voting—although the Pope continued officially to ignore the political existence of Italy's parliament and its king. The quarrel between the Italian government and the papacy dated back to the mid-nineteenth-century Risorgimento, when such excommunicants as Victor Emmanuel II, grandfather of the present monarch, while unifying Italy, occupied Rome and the Vatican territories, and confiscated vast ecclesiastical landholdings throughout Rome and up through northeastern Italy almost to Venice.

But in the early 1920s, the Church could channel its political influence through a newly created Catholic party, which was a forerunner of the Christian Democratic Party. Supporting the party's anti-Communist position, though in a manner deplored by the Church, were groups of right-wing agitators and military veterans' associations. They tossed rocks and grenades at the red-flagged demonstrators and fired bullets into factories taken over by striking workers. Many right-wing attackers were on the payroll of factory owners, and they received weapons and ammunition from their friends in the police departments and from troops still on active duty. Loyal soldiers and veterans shared a particular grievance against the strikers and militant pacifists, who were assumed to have been shirkers or deserters in the army, and most likely to have participated in the civilian antiwar protests that saw many soldiers, returning to the home front with injuries, being spat upon and even assaulted by unpatriotic local mobs and alien Reds.

Amid such civil discord, transportation and other public services were unreliable in most of the nation. Trolleys regularly broke down. Train schedules were meaningless. The mail was delivered infrequently, if at all. Everywhere there were reports of increased theft, unsolved murders. The pessimism among peasants was such that charity workers noted in their dialect a conspicuous absence of the future tense. And yet in the overpopulated south, where there were spreading signs of famine, the government raised taxes to help underwrite industrial modernization in the north. The government also sought funds to defray its wartime debts to its allies as well as to absorb the continuing costs of its virtually worthless colonial expansionism before World War I in the deserts of Libya.

In such villages as Maida, which had been on the barter system for years—and where such property owners as eighty-four-year-old Domenico Talese operated their farms exclusively for the welfare of relatives and friends, most of whom worked gratis in the soil for the privilege of eating—there was no money in circulation except that sent from emigrants working abroad. More and more young southern men dreamed of sailing to America, including Joseph's younger brother Nicola, who was sixteen; but the restrictive 1921 immigration policy in the United States reduced by eighty percent the number of incoming Italians. There were already close to four million Italians in the country, far more than most native-born Americans desired. In opinion polls reflecting native-born American preferences in new neighbors, Italians ranked near the bottom. They were seen as clannish, uncouth, instinctively criminal. The most publicized immigrants in the United States during the early 1920s were Nicola Sacco and Bartolomeo Vanzetti, who had been found guilty of robbery and murder in a jury trial of disputed justice in New England—and branded, to a greater or less degree, as anarchists; they were now in prison, awaiting execution. The American prohibition law that was imposed upon the nation primarily by white Anglo-Saxon Protestant zealots of sobriety—a law that went into effect in 1920 and was not repealed until 1933—lent credibility to the image of typically wine-drinking Italians, who were by nature lawless; and the American press, by making anti-heroes of such bootlegging gangsters as Alfonso ("Scarface") Capone, heightened the notoriety attached to many people with Italian names.

In an effort to become less identifiably Italian, increasing numbers of Italians in the United States changed their names legally, or conducted their businesses under aliases. A blue-eyed Sicilian bantamweight prize-fighter who settled in New Jersey and fought in the American ring under the name Marty O'Brien thought that having an Irish name would make him more employable with the many Irish-American promoters and more popular with the fans. But the only lasting popularity that came his way was through his son, who in later years readily found employment *without* changing the family name. The name was Sinatra.

Although there were nearly one million Italians in New York City in 1922, they were not a significant voting bloc. Either they were not registered to vote, or as noncitizens they were unqualified to do so. There was not one New York district leader with an Italian name among local Democrats and Republicans. When Fiorello La Guardia, frustrated by the powerlessness he felt as a junior legislator in the House of Representatives, entered the Republican primary of the New York mayoral race of 1921, he failed to carry a single borough. (It would be 1933 before he was elected mayor.) Until 1922, the public high schools of New York banned the teaching of the Italian language. The school system offered no courses in Italian history or culture. An educator named Leonard Covello, who grew up in an Italian ghetto in East Harlem and attended Columbia University, lamented that the process toward Americanization for Italian youths began "by learning to be ashamed of our parents."

The Italian government in Rome occasionally registered complaints against anti-Italianism in the United States, as well as the country's continuing limitation on immigrants arriving from southern Europe; but the parliament in Rome had no influence in America. The parliament in Rome barely had influence in Italy. The only bold voice in the government belonged to the Milan newspaper publisher, Benito Mussolini, who in 1921 was elected—along with thirty-four other Fascist candidates—to parliament, where the largest number of deputy seats was held by 122 Socialists, followed by 107 members of the Catholic party.

Mussolini's main strength, however, was not in the political arena in Rome, but in his connection to northern Italian industrialists and merchants who were weary of strikes and leftist solicitation and were willing to subsidize the gangs of strikebreakers and leg-breakers who had rallied to his call for a military-style response to civilian disorder and affronts to patriotism. Mussolini's newspaper, *Il Popolo d'Italia,* had empathized with the veterans who had returned home from the trenches only to find hollow lives open to them. In Mussolini's private meetings with many veterans, his stirring articulation of their grievances soon earned him their gratitude, and eventually their recognition of him as their spokesman and the mastermind they referred to as *"il Duce."* They saluted him, as he preferred, with their right hands above their heads in the manner of the ancient Romans. His calling them "Fascists" was also of Roman origin: *fascio* came from the Latin word for "bundle"; and specific to Mussolini's purpose, it referred to the bundle of sticks tightly bound to an axe that had been the emblem of the Roman magistrates' authority.

Mussolini's battle-experienced henchmen and their companions, among them student dropouts and restless vagabonds who had been found unfit for military service, adopted the fashion of an Italian wartime unit that had worn black shirts, and they organized themselves into several brutish, mournful-looking brigades throughout the nation—an appropriately dark version of the red-shirted Garibaldini in this bleak period of Italian history. More than half a million Italians had died in World War I, and the government in Rome felt far from compensated; much of the foreign territory it had been promised by the Anglo-French alliance in 1915 as an inducement to enter the conflict as an ally had been disputed at the Paris peace table by President Wilson of the United States, the late entrant to the war. Wilson believed that natives of the contested territories had legitimate rights of their own in determining their national affiliation. Italy's warrior poet Gabriele D'Annunzio became outraged, and in an article in Mussolini's newspaper he fulminated against the "mutilated" settlement being offered to Italy for its part in winning the war. American bankers simultaneously issued economic threats against Italy because of the nation's tardiness in repaying its war debts, while Italy often waited in vain with its European wartime allies for defeated Germany to abide by its schedule of reparations payments to *them*. But even if Italy had been a nation of less insolvency and more jobs, many of its returning veterans would have been unable to hold such jobs, being too maimed or mentally disturbed, like Sebastian Talese, or otherwise unqualified; a high percentage of them had been rushed to the front as teenagers with no occupational skills for civilian life.

Now, however, through Mussolini's militia, some of these men of sound body, if not always sound mind, could find work where the prerequisite skill was the ability to intimidate. When a nationwide strike was proposed by Socialist organizers in the summer of 1922 to protest the government's laxity in curtailing the callous tactics of "reactionary forces," Mussolini's underlings threatened reprisals; and before the strike could achieve its ends, members of the militia, together with many like-minded citizens and students, seized control of several utility centers and manned the operation of streetcars, trains, mail delivery, and other public services. Although they performed with limited efficiency, their gesture was appreciated by great numbers of average citizens, and it tended to convince many vacillating Italians that Fascism offered the best hope for restoring enterprise and order to Italy.

In late October 1922, Mussolini was the honored guest at a Fascist rally in Naples. There he spoke before a parade attended by thousands of his supporters, many wearing black shirts, others in business suits or plain workmen's attire. He also addressed a smaller gathering within the Bourbon-built San Carlo opera house, before a set for *Madama Butterfly;* here he stood facing rows of glittering boxes occupied by dignitaries who the previous year had mourned the death of their hometown hero, Enrico Caruso. Mussolini received bravos and Roman salutes from the crowds wherever he spoke as he announced his plans for economic improvements and firm leadership. He envisioned a Fascist state that would continue to respect the existence of a royal dynasty but would expect little monarchic opposition. He was confident that this arrangement would be acceptable to the king in Rome. Victor Emmanuel III was a diffident sovereign, perhaps influenced by the fact that the life of his father, Umberto I, had been terminated in 1900 by the bullets of an anarchist.

But if the king or his supporters in parliament attempted to thwart the rise of Fascism, their opposition would be overpowered—this was made clear by Mussolini in his talks to the people in Naples. "I'll tell you with the solemnity that the moment calls for: Either the government will be given to us, or we shall take it, descending upon Rome. It is now a question of days, perhaps of hours. . . ." To this the crowd chanted its approval: "To Rome! To Rome!"

Before leaving Naples on October 24, 1922, Mussolini composed a proclamation, which he dated October 27. It began:

> Fascists! Italians!
>
> The hour of the decisive battle has come. Four years ago at this time the national army unleashed the supreme offensive that led to victory; today, the army of Blackshirts seizes again the mutilated victory and, pointing desperately toward Rome, restores it to the glory of the Capital. . . .
>
> The Army, supreme reserve and safeguard of the nation, must not participate in this struggle. Fascism states again its highest admiration for the Army. . . . Neither does Fascism march against the police, but against a political class of half-wits and idiots that in four long years has not been able to give a true government to our nation.

Among Mussolini's principal advisers at this time were retired military men, patrician landholders, and fellow journalists. (A Fascist in 1919 had been the conductor Arturo Toscanini, who was a candidate for parliament that year—when all the Fascists, including Mussolini, had been defeated in a Socialist landslide. Soon, emerging political and personal differences between Toscanini and Mussolini prompted the former to leave the party and become in time an ardent anti-Fascist, and eventually an exile in the United States. Within Mussolini's circle there was room for only one maestro.)

Despite Mussolini's highly publicized life—a life much analyzed in print by his friends, his enemies, and even himself in personal essays and an autobiography—he remained a perplexing figure. Once a committed Socialist, now a committed Fascist, he was perhaps not so much a man of the left or the right as he was a man of accommodation and opportunism. In a sense it might be argued that he was typically Italian, the creation of a vulnerable peninsula that endured intrinsically, along with its changing tides, its visiting visionaries and invaders, its endless welcoming ceremonies and shifting loyalties. Garibaldi once expressed his wrath toward his Italian contemporaries by calling them a "generation of hermaphrodites"; and he also cited the "jealousy and the bickering which is unfortunately a quality" of the Italian temperament. "We Italians have suffered enough from being able to see too many sides at once," complained a character in Peter Nichols's historical novel on Cardinal Fabrizio Ruffo; and if this was indeed an Italian dilemma, then Mussolini's solution was in offering Italy a singular vision, his vision. In later years, however, after he had accomplished his coup and when he believed he had imposed his will upon the nation, he would say that governing the Italians "is not hard—it is merely useless."

But in 1922, a week before his coup, he was eager for the opportunity to remedy the ills of the Italian nation. He had no intention of turning Italy into a republic; nor would the Blackshirts re-create in the piazzas of the Italian capital the bloody spectacle of the French Revolution or the punitive purges of the Bolsheviks in Russia. And yet how could the king's loyalists trust Mussolini when, insofar as anyone could deduce from his chroniclers, his life had been marked by intrigues and duplicity? It had been suggested that he was a split personality, smitten by conflicts that were traceable to the divisiveness of his upbringing within his native village of Dovia, in the countryside of the town of Predappio, in the Romagna region far northeast of Rome. His mother, Rosa, had been a demanding schoolmistress and pious Catholic; his father, Alessandro, an atheist blacksmith who liked revolutionary politics and strong wine better than he liked working hard over his anvil to contribute to the financial needs of his wife and three children. Alessandro's political beliefs were an amalgam of anarchism, Marxism, and the anticlericalism of Mazzini and Garibaldi. When his first child was born, on July 29, 1883, he named him Benito, in honor of the revolutionary liberator of Mexico, Benito Juárez.

During his early adolescence, when forced to attend Mass, Benito at times seemed hypnotized by the burning candles and the glittering garments of the priest, but he invariably became restless in the pews, and often fainted after smelling the incense. Once when his mother ordered him to await her outside the church, he climbed to the top of the nearest tree and, as the parishioners filed out, pelted them with acorns and stones.

When Benito was nine, having completed with much disruption the only two grades taught in his mother's elementary school, he would crawl back into her classroom and pinch the legs of the younger students. The Mussolinis' living quarters were then located within the school building, next to the classroom, and Benito seemed to resent the attention his mother was giving the other children. She had wondered at times if he might be mentally unbalanced—as she had previously feared during the prolonged silences of his early childhood. When he began to express himself in words and sentences, however, they frequently came forth in torrents of anger and threats, which during his tenth year were accompanied by hostile acts: bloody fights with other young boys in the town; vandalism, or at least charges of it, levied against him by local merchants and street vendors that brought warnings from the police already familiar with his surname, since in the past they had often arrested his insurrectionist father. His mother wanted Benito out of town. When her husband was not in jail, the boy followed him around and assisted in subversive underground activities. Alessandro agreed with his wife that his left-wing radicalism would subject their son to excessive scrutiny from the law; and so he did not object when Rosa registered Benito in a boarding school twenty miles from home, a religious institution under the tutelage of Salesian friars. Troublesome as he was, young Benito was very bright. He was an omnivorous reader. His writing showed imagination and an impressive vocabulary. When not ill tempered, he spoke articulately and with a sense of reason that was convincing. His mother was sure he could become a teacher.

At the Salesian school the students were required to rise at dawn and to attend Mass; to supplement their hours of study with spiritual exercises and meditation; and to remain silent during meals. They dined at three tables, the composition of each determined by the amount of money the students' parents or guardians had paid toward their enrollment. The students whose tuition had been fully paid sat at the first table, where the food served was the finest and in the largest quantity. Those at the second table were fed by lower standards, while those seated at the third table were discriminated against even more noticeably. Benito Mussolini, at the third table, resented the more privileged pupils, and he shared as never before his father's contempt for the Church.

During his second year, he led his tablemates in protests against the food, and he would not appear at daily Mass unless the monks dragged him there bodily, as they always did. After being hit during class by a teacher's ruler, Benito retaliated by hurling an ink pot at his disciplinarian. Often he got into fights with his classmates; after he stabbed one with his penknife, he was expelled.

A year later, in 1895, his mother entered him in another boarding school, in the town of Forlimpopoli, which was closer to home, and not under the direction of clergymen. Here church attendance was voluntary; the food was better, and all the students received the same servings. Benito would attend classes here for the next six years, maintaining passing grades in all his studies. He was most interested in history, particularly the era of the Romans and, second, the Risorgimento. He also was drawn to music, playing the trombone in the school band and later taking up the violin. He could quote long passages from Dante, but he was no less engrossed in contemporary fiction and in the Marxist tracts recommended by his father, who visited him frequently and drove him home by wagon for school holidays. Much as Benito preferred the school at Forlimpopoli to that of the Salesian friars, he still had clashes with the faculty and his fellow students. Twice he was suspended—the first time for impertinence, the second for knifing a student—but the school's administrators permitted him to return; and during his last year he was selected to address the entire school at a program dedicated to the composer Giuseppe Verdi, who had died days before, on January 27, 1901. Benito turned it into a political occasion, associating Verdi not so much with his operas *Il Trovatore* and *La Traviata* as with his conscience as an idealist and social reformer, and the fact that he had been a member of parliament during the Risorgimento. The speech by the seventeen-year-old Benito would be praised the next day in the Socialists' leading newspaper, *Avanti!* This would be the first mention of "the comrade student Mussolini" in the press. Almost twelve years later, in late 1912, twenty-nine-year-old Benito Mussolini would become that newspaper's editorial director and a leading voice in the Italian Socialist Party.

Between these two events, Mussolini traveled often, wandering through Switzerland and France, Austria and Germany; but he would never escape the conflicting forces that linked him to his mother, the educator, and his father, the agitator. His first job after graduating in 1901 was as a substitute teacher in an elementary school in Gualtieri, northwest of his home. But he was hostile toward his disobedient pupils and directed threats at them which they repeated to their parents, and his position was soon in jeopardy—and was terminated altogether before the summer of 1902 with disclosures of his heavy drinking, gambling, and carousing with the wife of a local soldier on active duty.

Mussolini himself was now approaching the age of required military service; and this among other unpleasant circumstances surrounding his life in Gualtieri—not the least being the querulousness of his unpaid landlord, and the pressures from those demanding he redeem his gambling debts—influenced his decision to leave Italy for Switzerland. Waiting at the train station in Chiasso, on the Italian–Swiss border, he read a newspaper account of his father's imprisonment for disrupting recent elections in Predappio. Benito was tempted to return home, but after communicating with his mother, he was convinced to proceed to Switzerland. Only by his remaining far from his father did she believe Benito could avoid becoming his cellmate.

Shortly after arriving in Lausanne, Benito was nonetheless arrested for vagrancy by police who discovered him sleeping outdoors under the Grand Pont. He moved on to Bern, where he finally found employment with a gang of Italian stoneworkers and ended up in jail for ten days after helping to organize a strike. Migrant Italian laborers had for years been welcomed in Switzerland so long as they toiled uncomplainingly for low wages and constructed railway tunnels through mountains, and paved roads and sidewalks, and functioned as janitors and porters in the hotel and tourist trades, and performed other tasks that the Swiss preferred not to do—and that Mussolini preferred not to do, either. Mussolini loathed subservient labor. He found contentment only as a labor organizer and battler against the workers' bosses. And this is what consumed much of his time during his first tour of Europe, between 1902 and 1904; under the auspices of the Socialist radicals whom he sought out in every city he visited, he served as a junior ringleader of protest rallies, a distributor of revolutionary leaflets, and a maker of so many speeches that in his latter-day reminiscences he would call himself a "walking gramophone."

When there were no Socialist causes to which he could attach himself, and no "peoples' kitchen" to satisfy his hunger between speeches, he *was* forced to accept jobs he considered demeaning—hauling stones at four dollars a week in helping to build a chocolate factory; serving as an errand boy for a grocer and as a line worker in a plant producing agricultural machinery. In Paris, speaking an exotic, Italianized French, he even represented himself as a fortune-teller. But he rarely continued with any scheme or endeavor for more than a few days—except when it came to writing for radical newspapers, which was what he most enjoyed doing. He pursued the editors of Socialist weeklies and dailies wherever he traveled, and charged no fees for his impassioned prose; his pieces would appear in the proletarian press circulated throughout the leading cities of Europe as well as in such American cities as New York and Philadelphia. In these periodicals he lashed out at the industrialists and the upper classes of Europe, and all the kings still enthroned. "Their mentality is barely sufficient to sign decrees," he wrote about ruling royalty, in the newspaper *Il Proletario,* published in the United States, in 1903. "Their military career, the education they usually receive from Jesuits, the stupid court etiquette, in the long run crush their brains and deprive them of their thinking power." In another article he referred to priests as "black microbes," and in a pamphlet he wrote: "Religion in science is an absurdity, in practice an immorality, in men a disease." He described the army as "a criminal organization designed to protect capitalism and bourgeois society"—while the army at the same time described him as a "deserter," a man subject to immediate arrest should he reappear on Italian soil.

But late in 1904, after the Italian king had celebrated the birth of his first son by offering amnesty to deserters willing to fulfill their military duty, twenty-one-year-old Benito Mussolini expeditiously put aside his contempt for monarchism and returned to Italy, volunteering his services to the Bersaglieri and being sent to Verona. The military authorities had access to a police dossier branding Mussolini an "impulsive and violent" young man, and he was watched carefully during his time in the service. His behavior, however, was surprisingly exemplary. While he left the army in September 1906 with the same rank of private that he had received on entering in January 1905, he never complained aloud or in his writing about his military experience; on the contrary, he complimented the army for introducing him to the pleasures of physical exercise and for channeling his energies toward the formation of a more orderly life that he would later try to impose upon all Italians.

In February 1905, while he was in the army, his mother died at age forty-six. Benito was shaken by her death, unable to speak at the funeral. After his discharge from the army, he returned to teaching. In November 1906 he accepted a position at an Italian elementary school in the town of

Tolmezzo near the Austrian border. In March 1908 he took a job at a private school at Oneglia, on the Italian Riviera. But his overbearing classroom manners and his extracurricular leftist journalism invited criticism from many quarters, and during the summer of 1908, while he was visiting his father, his career as an educator was suddenly sidetracked by an eight-month prison sentence.

His father for once was not personally involved in the latest violent strike by farm workers against the landholders and their tenant managers; the elder Mussolini was in fact suffering from the first symptoms of the paralysis that would end his life within two years. But Benito represented him characteristically by leading the strikers against their employers, upending and damaging the proprietors' threshing machines and injuring several bystanders. He was arrested for "revolutionary expression," and was sent to the same prison that in the past had confined both his father and his grandfather.

Although Benito's imprisonment would be greatly curtailed (his case was soon appealed, and the verdict overturned), he was in prison long enough to appreciate a number of visits from a young woman named Rachele Guidi. He had first known Rachele as a child in his mother's classroom. Now nearly seventeen, Rachele was living with her widowed mother, Nina, who was a combination mistress, nurse, and bartending companion to the ailing Alessandro Mussolini. Shortly after the death of Benito's mother, Alessandro sold the smithy in Predappio and relinquished the family's living quarters in the school building to the schoolmistress who had succeeded his late wife, and moved with his younger children to the nearby town of Forlì, where he opened a tavern that catered to politicized workers and their organizers. Young Rachele and her mother helped out at the tavern, tending bar and serving food at the tables; after Benito had come to visit his father in the summer of 1908, it took little time for the young couple to become lovers.

Like Benito's late mother, and like nearly every other woman whom Benito would get close to during his young manhood and early middle years—an eclectic consortium of women that included the Russian-born Socialist traveler Angelica Balabanoff, who helped him learn German; the anarchist Leda Rafanelli, who would convert to Islam and later embarrass him with her memoir; an affluent Jewess from Milan, Margherita Sarfatti, who would become the art critic at *Avanti!* and follow him into Fascism, only to lose favor with him during the Hitler-induced Italian Prussianization period of the 1930s; and an Austro-Italian shopkeeper from Trent, Ida Dalser, with whom Benito would have an illegitimate son—Rachele Guidi was not a physical beauty, nor would her role in his life be anything more than fragmentary.

Shy, practical, kindly, and very loyal, with almost platinum-colored hair braided in a matronly manner, she represented a maternal figure to Benito well before she would produce the first of their five children. In 1909, after they had begun living together, he left for a job with a Socialist weekly in a town near the Austrian border, where he would at the same time improve his German by translating some of the philosophical works of Arthur Schopenhauer and Immanuel Kant. He never wrote to Rachele during his seven months' absence. But she took him back uncomplainingly. In 1911, after he had been convicted of staging a riotous protest in the streets of their town against Italy's colonial war against the Turks in Libya, Rachele visited him faithfully each day at the local jail, carrying in her arms their infant daughter. The child would be four years old before Benito would marry Rachele in a civil ceremony. And it would take ten more years, and the birth of two more children, before he would marry her in a religious ceremony.

The coup by which Benito Mussolini took over the government of Italy was completed on the morning of October 30, 1922, when—wearing a black shirt, black trousers, and white spats—he strode into the royal palace in Rome, shook hands with the timid king, and said, "Your Majesty, will you forgive my attire? I come from the battlefields."

He had actually come from the train station, having arrived in Rome on a sleeper from Milan. Such an admission, however, would not have been dramatic enough; more to Mussolini's liking would have been galloping into Rome on a black charger after having crossed the Rubicon. But it would have been highly inappropriate on this occasion, for Rome had surrendered without opposition—meaning that Mussolini's men were also deprived of the triumphant procession that would have appealed to his operatic sensibilities and those of most Italian citizens. This omission had to be rectified. As Mussolini himself had previously stated, the Italian people respected only those conquerors who arrived with much fuss and fanfare. So on the day *after* the government and the king's army had yielded to his leadership, Mussolini staged an invasion that might appease the theatrical needs of the national character.

While boasting earlier that 400,000 fully equipped Fascist marauders awaited his beck and call, the most Mussolini could produce for this pseudo-event was a somewhat bedraggled contingent of fewer than 30,000 who had been rained upon for hours while forming crooked ranks in the outskirts of the city, and who in many cases marched through Rome entirely unarmed. But the demonstration was sizable and churlish enough to induce the respectful fear that Mussolini sought, especially after some of his more evil-tempered Blackshirts began to ransack and burn Socialist bookstalls along the sidewalks, and to force foreign embassies to fly Italian flags, and, as they had before, to pour castor oil down the throats of those spectators overheard making unwelcoming comments (the elixir was now commonly called "Fascist medicine").

So self-involved was Mussolini during this slow-moving spectacle through the city that he paid it only perfunctory attention as he stood near the window of his hotel suite, in a state of excitement provided mainly by his dowdy mistress who had no view of the parade. The sexual prowess of Mussolini was a subject he did not discourage his propagandists from circulating, so long as it was kept at a discreet distance from Rachele, who had remained at home with the children in Milan—which is where he would encourage them to remain for *years* until it became politically advantageous for him to move them to Rome and appear with them in public as befitting a proper Catholic family man. But trysts would always remain a part of his agenda, although never so time-consuming as to compromise his prompt attendance to the affairs of the state. Punctuality was a Fascist virtue.

Fascist photographers printed the pictures Mussolini had ordered taken of the "invasion" in order to lend credibility to his version of what had transpired. According to Fascist accounts released to the international press, on October 31, 1922, there had been a massive attack on the Italian capital by black-shirted legions who, amid much opposition and bloodshed, overcame the defenses of the unpopular government to win the hearts of grateful citizens—citizens who implored their new conquerors to make Rome again worthy of the caesars. Since Mussolini had earlier seen to the destruction of the opposition Italian press, there was no strong editorial voice to refute his version, and thus his so-called March on Rome became a heroic event in the annals of Italy. He also ordered that the Italian calendar should disregard all previous events, starting with the birth of Christ, and begin with October 1922 as the first month of *anno primo*.

At thirty-nine, Benito Mussolini became the youngest premier in the nation's history. He achieved this not because he was truly powerful but because he had convinced the king and the parliamentarians that he was, and therefore he *was*. Whether he was an egomaniacal buffoon, as some politicians privately believed, or a ruthless, demented tyrant, as others thought, he was effective in establishing doubt and fear in those who differed with him, a feat made all the more attainable since his opposition now consisted mainly of men who were weak, worried, and willing to accept any leader if it was hinted that they might continue their employment in the government. For a while Mussolini had duped them into thinking that he would welcome diverse opinions and coalitions, just as he had earlier manipulated the king into believing that to oppose Fascism was to invite a bloody left-wing revolution that would topple the monarchy.

Most of the nation's business leaders saw in Mussolini's appointment the enhancement of their own interests—an auspicious future with more tax concessions, fewer strikes, smaller state bureaucracies, less zeal directed toward the breakup of large estates; a possible termination of rent controls, a reduction in unemployment relief, and fewer annoying inquiries concerning surplus war profits and tax evasion. That Mussolini lacked experience as a government leader was also interpreted by many businessmen as an asset, for in recent years the most experienced leaders had committed the greatest blunders. And the Mussolini who in 1919 was condemning priests and advocating the confiscation of ecclesiastical property would be announcing through his controlled press in the mid-1920s that he was a "profoundly religious man" eager to enforce religious instruction in schools and universities, and to increase state subsidies to priests and bishops. He called for the ban of obscene books and periodicals, and would also make it illegal to swear in public. The sale and distribution of contraceptives would be not only a sin against the Church but a crime against the state. And while Mussolini's regime in 1924 would become the first Western government after Britain to recognize Soviet Russia, Mussolini was soon expressing aloud his fear of world Communism in the hope of ingratiating himself further with Pope Pius XI—who, as a papal nuncio earlier in Poland, had been stunned by the Bolshevik siege of Warsaw, and who now as the Vicar of Christ wished to eradicate world Communism, Socialism, and other godless manifestations of liberalism and secularism.

Mussolini stood ready to indulge him—to convert Italy through Fascism into a state of prudery and repression. Not only did contemporary depictions of nudity and other pornographic expression come under severe Fascist review, but an Italian neo-Victorianism also looked disapprovingly upon nightclub entertainment and the "Negro dances" made popular in America, and upon any Italian woman who appeared in the streets wearing high heels, short skirts, or cosmetics, or who ventured onto beaches in anything but the most demure of bathing attire. Since Mussolini did not smoke, and since his ulcers discouraged him from drinking anything stronger than milk, he was a natural spokesman against cigarette and alcohol consumption; and since he was an adherent of horsemanship, jogging, and tennis, he recommended sports activities as a healthy outlet for Fascist men and women—until the Vatican differed with him on the question of women's participation. "If a woman's hand must be lifted," said a Vatican spokesman, "we hope and pray it may be lifted only in prayer or for acts of beneficence." Mussolini's further silence on the subject was interpreted as his concession to papal wisdom, and his diplomacy was to lead in 1929 to the Lateran Treaty in which the Church and the Italian government would officially recognize one another for the first time since the Risorgimento. The treaty created the autonomous State of Vatican City; affirmed Catholicism as the national religion; validated religious teaching in intermediate-level schools; and recognized religious marriage as binding under civil law.

Although the State of Vatican City was little more than one hundred acres—consisting primarily of the Vatican Palace, the Basilica of Saint Peter, and the piazza in front of it—the Church was compensated for the loss of ecclesiastical property confiscated during the Risorgimento with a financial settlement approaching two billion lire—after which an apparently satisfied Pope announced that for the treaty to have been completed "a man was needed like the one that Providence has placed in our path."

That the Duce was now acclaimed by Catholics worldwide was a miraculous achievement for this onetime Socialist priest-baiter whose anticlerical writings in the past included a tawdry novel entitled *The Cardinal's Mistress*. Mussolini had written it two decades before, while serving a prison term for left-wing insurrectionism; and while the book had not been published in Italy, it had been translated and sold in foreign editions, including an English-language edition distributed in the United States. But after the signing of the Lateran Treaty, Mussolini's popularity in America was even shared by the nation's leading cardinals (he was praised by William O'Connell of Boston and Patrick Hayes of New York), and his already established shift toward capitalism had won his regime goodwill from American business and political leaders.

Mussolini began inviting to Rome thousands of Italian-born business and professional men who had become successful in foreign cities. Their visits were marked by many ceremonies and grand tours that allowed Mussolini ample opportunities to congratulate both his guests and himself for achievements in the name of free enterprise; and he also used these occasions to promote closer bonds, through Fascism, among influential Italians at home and abroad.

Among the invitees to Rome in July 1928 was a group of Italian-born entrepreneurs and artisans from France, ranging in occupation from contractors to jewelry designers, from engineers to restaurateurs. The members of the 102-man delegation had been encouraged to bring their wives, in keeping with Mussolini's recent pro-family attitude. His own wife, Rachele, was not with him to greet those from France because she was pregnant with their fifth child (the year before, at thirty-five, she had produced their fourth child), but her image as an ideal Fascist wife was so well publicized that her presence was not required; Mussolini tirelessly boasted of her virtues to all but his mistresses (even in the privacy of their bedroom Rachele now addressed him as Duce). There were ninety-eight wives with the group from France; the four single men were widowers wearing mourning bands.

After boarding a special train in Paris, the group was taken first to Turin for a banquet in their honor given by the city's leaders, and they were further celebrated with a parade on the following day at which bands played both the "Marseillaise" and the Fascist anthem "Giovinezza." The group then continued south into Rome, where, after another orchestrated ceremony at the rail terminal, the guests were taken to luxury suites in the Grand Hotel and briefed before proceeding on to Palazzo Venezia for their first meeting with Mussolini.

"The Duce respects people who speak directly and to the point," one of Mussolini's protocol ministers explained to the group leader in the lobby, as everyone gathered to board buses for the palazzo. "We received your countrymen from South America the other day, and their spokesman was so nervous and intimidated in the Duce's presence that little was gained from the meeting. These meetings are for learning about our brothers working in other countries. We want to know them better, want them to know us better. The Duce does not want a lot of courtesy and flattery from his visitors—he wants facts and figures."

"I understand perfectly," said the French group's leader, who would be called upon to speak at Palazzo Venezia. "So let's load the buses and move on without delay."

Mussolini awaited them at his office in the palazzo, an imposing brick edifice that was built four centuries before, in the style of the early Renaissance with some stones from the Colosseum. Near the palazzo, and the neighboring white monument to Victor Emmanuel II and Italian unity, stood the Forum of Trajan and the Tower of Nero. Mussolini's office, on the second floor, was approximately sixty-six feet long and forty-three feet wide, and on one wall was an ancient map of the world—which was why the office was referred to as the Sala del Mappamondo. A double row of windows looked down upon the square below, and the tall center window opened onto a balcony from which Mussolini liked to make speeches. He was seated at his desk in the far corner of the room as the delegation arrived, and with a smile he quickly rose to greet them.

He wore a gray double-breasted silk suit—he was two years away from adopting military uniform as standard dress—and his hair was shaved off in preference to allowing his receding hairline to make further inroads across his crown. Escorting the group was a Fascist minister named Giuseppe Bottai, a onetime journalist. After saluting Mussolini, who briefly welcomed the group in the name of Fascism and the king, Bottai nodded in the direction of the group's leader, summoning him forward to say a few words.

The latter wore a gabardine suit with a striped white vest, and pointed tan shoes with spats, and carried a pearl-handled walking stick. Short as he was, barely five feet, six inches, he was nonetheless an imposing figure even in the exalted company of the dictator of Italy; and he looked directly into Mussolini's eyes as he began, in a firm voice: *"Duce, cifre volete . . . eccole"*—Duce, figures you want . . . here they are. Rapidly, he went on:

> "There are a total of 2,348 members of our group in France, a group broken up into fifteen specialized categories specific to our various trades and professions, and today we in this room proudly represent all of them with the same pride that in France we bring to our work as energetic and progressive Italians. To the people of France we uphold Italy's highest standards in craft and service, in innovation and reliability. We can be seen each day in any of three hundred ninety French towns and cities—from Marseilles in the south to Calais in the north. We are most numerous, of course, in the capital of Paris, where each of us thinks of himself as an unofficial Italian ambassador of goodwill, as an exemplar of . . ."

Unhesitatingly he continued, barely pausing to take a breath, and Mussolini listened with raised eyebrows, seemingly impressed with the perkiness of his visitor. Then Mussolini turned questioningly toward his minister Bottai, who stood next to him.

"He's a tailor from Paris," Bottai whispered. "He has won many awards there. His name is Cristiani. Antonio Cristiani . . ."

38.

ANTONIO CRISTIANI WAS a happily married man of thirty-four, was thriving financially, was a frequenter of fine restaurants—and was no less hungry for success now in 1928 than he had been when he had first come to Paris as a seventeen-year-old runaway from Maida in 1911, arriving at the Gare de Lyon on a misty day that he would remember with lasting clarity.

But his impressionistic early days in Paris were eventually replaced by indistinguishable weeks and months of hard work and little time for enjoyment of the city—and then by the war. And then Joseph had come and gone.

It had been nearly eight years since Antonio had seen Joseph. His cousin had spent most of those years living alone on a small island off the shore of New Jersey. His letters indicated he was struggling as a tailor. Antonio would have welcomed his return immediately. Although he already employed half a dozen tailors, he needed another one. His business was expanding.

Antonio's new shop was on the fashionable Rue de la Paix, near the Place de l'Opéra. The director of the Opéra was a client and friend, and Antonio was often invited to sit in the management's box overlooking the center aisle—where nearly two decades before, as a young member of the claque, hiding his poverty under a tuxedo, Antonio used to applaud every soloist generously and without discrimination. But the applause was now coming *his* way in the form of praise from customers who patronized his shop, and from French charitable and military societies which during the postwar years became appreciative of his civic-mindedness.

He had helped raise money for the welfare of elderly citizens displaced during the war. He had worked toward the establishment of more trade schools for disabled veterans who were potentially employable as tailors or other craftsmen. He was commended for founding a Paris-based association of former Italian servicemen currently living and working in the French nation that had once been part of their combat zone. In the postwar years, as these Italian veterans cosponsored benefits with French veterans and joined them at memorial ceremonies, they revived feelings of camaraderie that had existed between the two nations during the Great War.

In his role as an intermediary between leading French citizens and the resident Italians, Antonio had maintained connections with most of his French wartime acquaintances, some of whom had remained in the military and were now senior officers, while others had returned to civilian life to pursue careers in the government. One morning in 1928 he was visited by a friend from the French Foreign Ministry who cheerfully reported having overheard that Antonio would soon be made a chevalier in the Legion of Honor. Antonio was delighted. But weeks later his friend returned in a somber mood to say that the nomination might be overturned. Some members on the selection committee apparently resented the fact that Antonio, having first come to Paris in 1911, had never applied for French citizenship.

"But that's not fair," Antonio said. "The Legion of Honor is often given to citizens of other nations. And besides, when you and I were in battalions fighting side by side at Verdun, and later along the Marne, nobody in France was complaining about my Italian citizenship. And even more to the point: If I revoked my Italian citizenship, I'd be a bad Italian. Would a bad Italian make a good Frenchman?"

His friend said he would try to get this message through to the committee. A year and a half later, in 1930, Antonio was named a chevalier in the Legion of Honor. But he stayed on in Paris as a citizen of Italy; and this would continue to be his policy even though Paris would remain his primary residence throughout his lifetime, and be the locale of such added laurels as the Legion of Honor's third highest rank of commander.

It was not really nationalism that he saw binding him to Italy. It was something less patriotic, but more deeply rooted. It was his connection to his village, the place of his birth, the source of his energies and dreams. Although he had left it bodily, he could not replace it in spirit as his true home. He was a village Italian from the south, and the gravitational pull of that place had been felt strongly when he had decided back in 1925, just before turning thirty-one, that he wanted to be married. He had lived alone long enough.

The demands of his business had made a stable and loving relationship seem far preferable to the exciting but frequently lonely bachelor's life he had led since the war—even though he imagined he would miss the varied pleasure and some of the freedom that had also been his privilege. *But whenever I think of marriage, and having children,* he wrote in his diary, *I'm aware of how different my mentality is from the Frenchwomen I've known. I don't know if they're too frivolous, or if I'm too responsible, or if I'm just in the wrong place for finding a wife I can trust. Paris is a crazy place now. . . .*

The Frenchwoman he had gotten closest to had been Mademoiselle Topjen, the attractive and lively owner of a boutique who was also a frequent partygoer and a bit of a socialite within the fluid world of postwar Parisian society. Since the Versailles Peace Conference, Paris had reestablished itself as the international center of gaiety—late-night soirees under the sway of Elsa Maxwell; stage entertainment by such new sensations as Josephine Baker, sometimes wearing only a banana skirt; and nocturnal alliances negotiated among diplomats, bankers, *grandes dames,* and *grandes cocottes.*

Mademoiselle Topjen had first entered Antonio's shop on the arm of a Spanish embassy attaché who was on his way back to Madrid; and three days later, she had returned alone. She and Antonio became lovers before they became friends; and when they became close friends, their love life began to deteriorate. But they always enjoyed being of help to one another in their respective careers. As a designer of costly dresses and suits that were produced in her atelier by Algerian seamstresses whom she paid poorly, and who did shoddy work, Mademoiselle Topjen often found it necessary to have her merchandise resewn and sometimes completely remade before she could display it for sale—and this corrective effort was provided gratis by Antonio and his tailors. She in turn went out of her way to see that Antonio, her most frequent escort at social events, was introduced to the ambassadors, ministers, and wealthy American visitors who cared most about clothing and who would greatly enrich him as their tailor. She confided in him fully. He knew about her sad childhood—her mother had died young, her father drank heavily and had lost his job as a Métro conductor. He knew about her financial status—she had nothing in the bank, her earnings squandered on luxurious living—and her other love affairs—one with a married woman, another with the elderly Monsieur Sabate, who had made available the funds to launch her boutique. *She is a free spirit, but clever,* Antonio wrote in his diary, and *I've learned a lot from being around her. She's one of many couturieres in this city who envies Made-*

moiselle Chanel, but at least she's smart enough to know she cannot rival Mademoiselle Chanel. Lots of couturieres are fooling themselves these days into thinking that they're second best only to Chanel. But not Mademoiselle Topjen. She knows she's not second best, or third best. That's one reason she's smart. She knows what she's not. She also knows what she wants, and how to get it. . . . If I have any quarrel with her, it's probably with the way she talks about some of her men friends behind their backs. She makes them sound like fools. Even Monsieur Sabate, who had been so helpful. This bothers me. But I say nothing. I only wonder what she'll be saying about me someday. . . .

There had never been any discussion of marriage during the three years they had been seeing one another regularly. She had always made it clear that she was as yet unready to commit herself exclusively to any one individual; and when Antonio decided to go on a sojourn to Italy in 1925, there had been no question of her joining him, nor had she seemed upset—on the contrary, she had seemed pleased, if also amused—when he admitted that the main purpose of this trip was for him to be introduced to a young Italian woman who might become his wife.

The trip had been prompted in part by letters from his father in Maida. Francesco Cristiani had acknowledged receiving a number of indirect inquiries about Antonio's marital status from some prominent men in the Maida area who had marriageable daughters. Even Antonio's contemplating the *possibility* that he might find a wife through the contrivance of his elders marked him as a man who, with all his exposure to Parisian sophistication, remained intrinsically a true son of the old south. For centuries the marital bonding of young couples in this region had been consummated first by the fusion of their families, particularly their fathers. Emigration had of course tampered with this tradition. But in Antonio's case, his heart had not emigrated.

Entrusting his Paris shop for a month to his most senior tailor, and leaving during the mid-January lull that followed the holiday season, Antonio boarded the Paris express that got him into Naples on the following day. Once there he transferred to a southern-bound Italian *"rapido"* that stopped twenty-three times and took fifteen hours to get from Naples to Maida. Antonio knew in advance the names of some of the young women he would meet, but his father's last letter had also reminded him that all the arrangements were subject to last-minute changes—which, Antonio did not have to be told, might include outright cancellations if the elders could not agree on the terms of the dowry and other unromantic issues that would have to be resolved before there could be any thoughts of romance. Antonio also knew that his father had been in contact with the fathers of prospective brides who resided at some distance from Maida—one was more than forty miles away, and a visit to her might involve a trip in the company of armed guards, for highway bandits with access to town gossip were often on the alert for these courtship calls. They knew that aspiring grooms and their fathers would be eager to present the best *bella figura* to their potential in-laws, and this might mean not only wearing their finest clothing, but also packing their pockets with noticeable wads of cash, and hanging gold watch chains across their vests, and adorning their fingers with diamond rings.

Antonio knew finally from his father's last letter that in two cases he would *not* initially be introduced to the bridal candidates under the direct chaperonage of their parents or other family members. One father had explained to Francesco Cristiani that his eighteen-year-old daughter, Emanuela, was shy, incredibly shy; she was a maiden so sheltered and estranged from the wicked ways of the world that even a cloistered convent might not meet her standards of privacy and propriety—for which her father proclaimed his gratitude, because his daughter did not belong in a nunnery. "Emanuela is even more *beautiful* than she is shy," he revealed in a tone of voice that was reverentially hushed; there followed by a wink, a nodding of his head, and finally the crossing of his heart—gestures he hoped Cristiani would somehow relay to his son in Paris so the latter would realize that Emanuela was one of Italy's great undiscovered beauties as well as a peerless challenge for stalwart unmarried men.

"But in order for your son to meet my daughter," her father then emphasized to Francesco Cristiani, "he will have to be patient. Emanuela cannot be expected to immediately come face to face with a stranger of the opposite sex, even with her entire family gathered around her, unless she first has a chance to see and familiarize herself with him *without him seeing her.*" Emanuela's father next suggested how this might be done. On arriving in Maida from Paris, Antonio should come directly to Emanuela's family village of Polia, several miles south of Maida. It was, however, a bit difficult to reach. The single, rocky road leading up to Polia was too narrow for carriages. Should Antonio come by carriage, it would be necessary for him to abandon it at the base of the hill and proceed for a half-mile up to the town gate on foot or by mule.

Never pausing to allow Antonio's father a moment to doubt that the trip was surely worth the inconvenience, Emanuela's father went on to say that Antonio, after passing through Polia's gate, should cross the square and enter the town's only café, and announce his name to the proprietor,

Emanuela's oldest brother. He in turn would send word to summon Emanuela's other brothers and her father, who resided farther uphill. After they had all come down to meet Antonio, and had treated him to lunch, they would walk with him in the midafternoon *passeggiata,* traversing the square perhaps dozens of times so that Emanuela, observing him from her shadowed balcony, would come to regard him as less of a stranger, and would herself gradually become—in the words of her father—"less shy than beautiful."

The other bridal candidate whom Antonio would not immediately meet through a parental introduction was a young noblewoman in Maida named Olympia Bianchi. She had been described by her baronial father to Francesco Cristiani as unfortunately *not* shy or in the least bit old-fashioned. She was so modern in her thinking, in fact, that she automatically rejected any potential suitor whom her parents would allow in the palazzo. The whole idea of parental involvement in the garnering of suitors she decried as primitive, exploitative, and, in her case, completely unnecessary. She had more suitors than she could count. Which *was* the problem, according to her father. She had received so much attention from men through the years that it gradually became the attention, not the men, that she loved. "My daughter Olympia," concluded the baron with feigned anger, "is as spoiled as she is beautiful."

But soon she would be twenty-seven, her father admitted with sincere concern to Cristiani one day in the back of the tailor shop; and since she was the lone survivor of the baron's three children, his sons having died in the war, he and his ailing wife feared that they would never see Olympia standing at the altar as a bride; and they feared even more the possibility of her entering old age as a spinster, abandoned by her suitors—should her suitors outlive their frustrations—and of her ending up impoverished, and evicted from the palazzo because of her inability to pay taxes on it.

Francesco Cristiani was already aware of the declining fortunes of the Bianchis and similar aristocratic families in the south. It had been years since he had received an order of clothes from any man within the Bianchi family. It had also been years since the Bianchis and Maida's other nobility had hosted one of the "open house" nights that had been traditional during the Christmas season; nowadays these families could no longer afford to open their palazzos to the entire town and offer the finest in food and musical entertainment to everyone who entered. The doors and windows of some palazzos remained closed throughout the year, the owners having moved to Naples or Palermo to occupy the servants' quarters in the palazzos of their less destitute noble kinsmen. The nobles who had remained in Maida, such as the Bianchis, lived, ironically, with more exclusivity in their relative poverty than they had in their days of power and glory. They closed social ranks, retreating with inverted pride from the town's commoners, bartering only among themselves. They released many old family retainers who had been the source of high-level gossip. Their gilded carriages bearing their coats of arms no longer pushed through the streets on shopping days; and at night, even on warm evenings, the shutters of their palazzos were closed to prevent outsiders from glimpsing the candled chandeliers that glowed with less and less frequency over the social gatherings of the town's dwindling elite. Given the matchmaking possibilities, it was not surprising that Maida had been without a titled wedding since the end of World War I. And given the fact that the baron was a realist, it was not surprising that he would visit Francesco's shop in late 1924 and tactfully inquire about the latter's prospering son in Paris.

Antonio's success was no secret to anyone in Maida. His father often displayed in the window of his shop some of his son's advertising that had appeared in French newspapers and magazines (although Francesco's motive in doing this had less to do with boosting his son than with suggesting that the Cristiani shop on the Rue de la Paix was really a branch of the one in Maida). Few people in Maida, however, knew anything about Antonio's relationship with women. He had not been home since a brief visit following his discharge from the army; and during his earlier years in Maida, Antonio had kept his distance from every young woman in the village and beyond.

Antonio's father, on the other hand, was just as unknowing about Olympia Bianchi's personal life until her father had begun visiting, for she had come of courting age during the time of the social withdrawal of the nobility and after her family had ceased having their clothes made at Cristiani's. But what Francesco *was* learning about her from her father convinced him that Olympia was exactly the kind of woman Antonio should *not* marry. She was very intelligent, her father had said; and worse, she had opinions and was eager to express them. She was probably licentiously inclined, too, because as her father admitted, she liked reading French novels in the original. Francesco Cristiani could only speculate darkly, although he could never bring himself to ask, just *how* freely Olympia had been relating to those admirers who supposedly never tired of pursuing her.

As for financial gains coming to the Cristiani family if Antonio were to marry Olympia, financial gains being second to none in Francesco Cristiani's order of priorities, he could foresee absolutely nothing of material value. Her family's feudal estate in the countryside was unproductive. Their palazzo in town was crumbling. What hope was there of a dowry coming from a family who for years had owed the Cristianis the cost of a cape? Social climbing in Maida at this time was definitely along a downward economic curve.

There also seemed to be little in the way of social prestige for his son's future offspring as a result of a marriage into the Bianchi family—nothing beyond a frayed link to their threadbare title. In conclusion, even though Francesco did not boldly state it to the baron, a marital union between Antonio and Olympia did not on first reckoning appear to be a favorable deal for the Cristiani family, and on second reckoning it seemed worse— and made so by the supposition that such a union would be followed by the return of the large Bianchi family as patrons of Cristiani's tailor shop, patrons who would come in often, would select the most expensive fabric, would demand the finest in workmanship, and would assume a kinsmen's prerogative in ignoring all bills.

As if the foregoing assumptions and facts were not sufficient to mark Olympia as an undesirable marital catch, her father often repeated in his talks with Francesco that she would be very difficult *to* catch; and the baron made such statements in tones of commiseration, as if there were nothing in the world that Antonio in Paris might want more than the hand of Olympia in marriage, if, alas, she were not virtually beyond reach. Poverty did not rob the nobility of their presumptuousness. But neither did this presumptuousness affect Francesco's pragmatic nature. He knew a bad deal when he saw one. And yet he remained respectful as the baron spoke, never entirely unaware of the flowered white royal rosette on the baron's lapel, and the heavy row of old Bourbon medals pulling down on the breast of his faded frock coat. Francesco also felt a certain empathy toward the baron, who after all was a caring father like him, a man wishing only that his daughter find love and happiness. And since there seemed no threat of the daughter's finding love and happiness with Antonio, Francesco relaxed as the baron rambled on in the circuitous way that is common in the south, using many words to say very little, rhapsodizing on the joys of having grandchildren, lamenting the brevity of one's lifetime on earth, quoting a line from Dante's *Purgatorio,* pondering the price of keeping peace in the postwar Balkans, and then circling back slowly but surely to the subject of Antonio and Olympia.

"It is truly a pity that those two cannot be brought together somehow," the baron reflected with a sigh, shaking his head slowly as he leaned lightly on Francesco's showcase and gazed out the front window toward the road uphill, where the old shepherd Guardacielo was leading a flock of mangy-looking sheep.

"Yes, it is a pity," Francesco lied, standing on the other side of the counter.

"Wouldn't you think that the two of us, loving our children as we do, could come up with a solution?"

Before Cristiani could think of a reply, the baron snapped his fingers and turned with sudden enthusiasm toward the tailor.

"I think I have an idea!" he announced, as Cristiani stiffened. "Yes, I think I know how I can help your son get to know my daughter, although he must go about it cleverly, as I'm sure he'll be capable of doing—with a little help from me. When he gets to town, the two of us will get together in some secret place where I'll be able to point out Olympia to him, as she takes her daily walk to the post office. Every day after the siesta, at four o'clock or thereabouts, she goes over to unlock her little steel box and collect her mail—most of it, I don't doubt, from out-of-town admirers. And all that Antonio would have to do would be to cross her path, once or twice, *and pay her absolutely no attention!* He should appear to be very aloof or conscious only of himself. He should be wearing one of his fancy French suits, and maybe have a French novel tucked underarm, and as he walks along he should be looking at the ground, or staring at the sky, as if his mind were contemplating universal questions. While she is approaching the post office from one direction, he is walking toward it from another—and then, briefly, their shadows blend together—*but he keeps walking!* Eyes straight ahead, he never looks back, *never,* just in case she's hiding somewhere to see if he does!

"If Antonio will follow this advice for three or four days," the baron went on avidly, somewhat bewildered but in no way discouraged by the blank expression on Francesco's face, "a magical thing will happen. Take my word for it, a magical thing *will* happen! It will be a subtle thing, done with all the subtleness that a vain and beautiful woman is capable of when she realizes that she has gone unnoticed by an important and worthy man. She will *find* a way for him to take notice. Without his becoming aware of it, she will begin courting *him!*"

Although Francesco could imagine nothing he wanted less, he did not want to insult the baron with even a hint of demurral, for paternal meetings over matters such as this were typically complicated by fragile egos—and especially so in this case. A baron without money was more sensitive to slights than a baron who was rich. In either case, he was still a baron; and yet here was a baron practically humbling himself in Cristiani's tailor shop with a plan designed to make the younger Cristiani his son-in-law—an act that in another age would have more than flattered any family of tailors. Indeed, even now a certain flattery was evident, for among the noble ancestors of the Bianchis had been cardinals and bishops, one of them a delegate to the Council of Trent in the sixteenth century, and such spiritual enrichment in a family was beyond the measure of mere property and coins. Francesco's devout wife, Maria, and her equally devout father, Domenico Talese, would undoubtedly gain added strength in their faith from the knowledge that through Antonio's marriage to Olympia they might claim a retroactive relationship with men who were surely in heaven.

As he was berating himself for his mercenary tendencies, Francesco heard the baron's raised voice, repeating the question: "So we are in agreement, then?"

"Yes," Francesco tentatively replied.

The baron extended his right hand over the counter and Francesco took it, forcing a smile.

"We are now Cupid's messengers," the baron announced cheerfully, "and if we are lucky in our work—if Olympia and Antonio fall in love and marry—you and I will become relatives. And if we are not lucky, well . . . we'll remain as we are—fellow villagers and good friends. So how can we lose?"

"Yes, how can we lose?" Francesco repeated, trying not to give the matter more thought.

"And as soon as your son arrives, you'll send me word so that I can meet with him and point out Olympia?"

"Yes," Francesco said.

"And you'll get a letter off to him right away so he'll be advised of my ingenious strategy?"

"Yes," Francesco said.

True to his promise, Francesco began composing a long letter to Antonio as soon as the baron left the shop. He spent two hours working on the letter, uninterrupted by any profitable visits from customers, or chats with his fellow tailors, who had been reduced to working only in the mornings. Before addressing the envelope, and gluing to it six express-mail stamps, and then posting it, Francesco reread his letter three times. With each reading, the baron's scheme seemed more preposterous.

Francesco could not believe that his son would ever be able to take the idea seriously.

But after Antonio read the letter, he thought the idea was fascinating. It was creative and logical. Carrying out the baron's plan would also be *fun!* All that Antonio would have to do was walk around Maida like a narcissist, which for him would not be entirely out of character. If he played his part well, he would soon be vulnerable to the seductive intrigues of a beautiful young noblewoman. What could he lose? And if she won his heart, he could cancel those less convenient appointments that his father had arranged out of town—notably the one requiring that Antonio climb on foot up to Polia in the interest of igniting the passions of a shy maiden who probably *did* belong in a nunnery; and also the long trip down the coast to Bovalino that might subject him and his traveling companions to the raids of highway robbers—and for what? For the chance to dine at the table of a respectable local family and make furtive eye contact with yet another heralded daughter whose beauty and other assets might well exist only in the imagination of her adoring or conniving father.

No, Antonio decided, the baron's daughter definitely topped the list of possibilities. She would be the first stop—and, he hoped, the last. A man as ambitious and busy as he was deserved a woman who would court *him,* saving him valuable time and energy; yes, he had time only for a woman who wanted him *desperately,* who would lose all pride in claiming him as her own. Now Antonio closed his eyes and fantasized about the aggressive female who would soon make him her prey, a victim of her desire. Fatigued though he was from the interminable, putrid ride on the southern train that ran counter to all of Mussolini's strong-armed demands for railroad reform, Antonio could barely wait to make himself available to this shocking new proposal of courtship in reverse.

But as he swung his suitcase onto the platform, he was grabbed from behind and embraced by an older woman. He recognized her immediately—mainly because of what she was wearing: an elegant blue dress that Mademoiselle Topjen had designed for last year's Paris collections but had been unable to sell even though Antonio had resewn it completely. So he had mailed it to his mother in Maida as a birthday present; and as she wore it now at the station, he was pleased that it fit her so well, although he was upset on seeing the tears in her eyes.

"Antonio," Maria cried out, "Antonio . . ." It was all she could bring herself to say, resting her head on his shoulder until Francesco pulled her away to give his son a paternal kiss on both cheeks. He held Antonio by the shoulders and stood looking at him in silence for several seconds. It was presently so noisy along the platform that conversation was impossible. There were the whistles and hisses of the train, the shouting and shoving of other passengers greeting those who had met them. Glancing behind his father's back, Antonio studied the townspeople and was bewildered by the proletarian style of dress that so many people seemed to have adopted. Women as well as men were wearing peaked caps, and overalls, and ankle-length boots, and they covered their upper bodies with several layers of sweaters. The Socialist workers had dressed this way in the cities of industrial Europe in an attempt to cushion the blows they received from right-wing strikebreakers; and the abundance of sweaters also made factory floors softer when strikers staged overnight sleep-ins. But Mussolini had long since checked the strikers in northern and central Italy, and in places like Maida there had never been any factories to strike against; and yet this proletarian fashion had somehow filtered down to the rural south, belatedly and incongruously, or perhaps, on second thought, quite properly.

His father was now gently pushing him back, trying to be heard, but Antonio still could not make out clearly what he was trying to say. Antonio felt his mother's soft hand on the nape of his neck, and he turned toward her, smiling. She had stopped crying. Her face was flushed, but as always she was pleasant to look at, especially since her habitually serene expression—which Antonio associated with how she used to look at Mass when returning to the pew after Communion—was restoring itself to her countenance.

The Paris-made dress that her aura of gentility imbued with an enduring fashion unintended by Mademoiselle Topjen, and the brocaded silk shawl that she now drew more closely around her slim shoulders against the cold wind sweeping across the platform, allowed Antonio to imagine his mother as ideally attired to attend any public event that was worthy of her presence, be it a High Mass, or an opera, or a grand banquet held in his honor, or, yes, his wedding.

Not quite so pleasing were Antonio's impressions of his aging, though still dapper father, whose surety and strength Antonio had grown up expecting to be eternal, since they had once seemed so abundant and natural: he remembered Francesco's upright posture and unflinching manner, his energy as a worker and his shrewdness as a businessman (a shrewdness that usually dominated whatever kindness existed in his heart, although he *was* capable of much kindness, Antonio quickly amended in behalf of this man on whom he had largely modeled himself). But Antonio's father on this day at the station was more slope-shouldered than Antonio had ever expected to see him, and he had forgotten to wear his fedora, which he never used to forget in wintertime, and as a result Francesco's once wavy gray hair was revealed to be less gray than white, less wavy than frizzy, and noticeably thinning at the crown. His father's face, which Antonio had remembered as a lean and alert façade in search of opportunities, was now sagging, in particular under the eyes and beneath the chin. Antonio was grateful that his success in Paris had allowed him to send generous amounts of money home each month; and he was also pleased to note that his father's blue pin-striped suit was newly made, and that its waistcoat was so expertly cut as to nearly conceal his father's middle-aged paunch. It occurred to Antonio that the tailoring business in Maida had declined to such a degree that his father's best customer was probably none other than Francesco Cristiani himself.

Finally, as the noisy train moved beyond the station and most of the crowd dispersed from the platform, Francesco could make himself understood.

"I'm very sorry about what's been happening," he began, facing Antonio. "I owe you an apology."

Although Antonio was not exactly sure what he was referring to, Francesco's words surprised him nonetheless. Antonio had never before heard his father accept the blame or apologize for anything.

"But I promise you one thing, my dear Antonio," his father went on, with some of the old force returning to his voice, "I'll straighten out this mess. I tried to deal sensibly with these madmen in Maida, but it was a mistake from the start. That crazy baron is the worst of them. But somehow I'll get us out of that trap he's trying to set for us, and . . ."

"*Please,* Father, don't," Antonio interrupted, wanting to be firm without sounding firm.

"Don't worry—leave everything to me," his father said, waving him away as Antonio tried to stop him from picking up the suitcase. Antonio again grabbed for the suitcase handle, but his father held on to it firmly and began walking toward the exit while Antonio was being held back by his mother.

"Oh, Antonio," she said, "I've missed you." Again she embraced him, and once more there were tears. As his father continued on, talking to himself and assuming his son and wife were right behind him, Antonio put his arms around his mother and patted her gently on the shoulders, the pressure and rapidity of his touch increasing slightly as he wished that she would stop crying so he could release her. Then, suddenly, Antonio felt a sharp rap across *his* shoulders; and before he could disengage himself from his mother, he felt another rap, harder this time.

When he turned around, he saw a white-bearded man holding a cane overhead, threatening to hit him again. The man wore a gray caballero hat and a cape of matching color, its collar so high that Antonio had only a limited view of his attacker's face.

"Hey, what's the meaning of this?" Antonio yelled, glaring at the old man. He broke away from his mother and held his clenched fists in front of him, then slipped them under the upraised cane.

"Don't touch him! don't touch him!" Antonio's mother raised her voice. *"That's your grandfather Domenico!"*

Stunned, Antonio unclenched his fists and stood facing the scowling, ruddily complected eighty-six-year-old man, who was his oldest living relative.

"You are indeed a fool!" Domenico snapped, slowly lowering his cane. "You're such a fool, Antonio, that it takes a whack of my cane to call your attention to the fact that I've come all the way out here to greet you, and then you try to punch me!"

"Grandfather, I'm so sorry," Antonio said, "I didn't recognize you."

"No excuse," Domenico responded.

Antonio tried to step closer to embrace his grandfather, but Domenico held out his cane. "Stay away—until you learn better manners," he said. "You've been in Paris too long."

Then Domenico turned his frowning face toward Antonio's mother, who, though fifty, suddenly appeared to be transformed under her father's gaze into a guilt-ridden young daughter who knew without being told that she had displeased her father. Yes, she *had* violated one of his cardinal rules by displaying her affections in public; and even though these affections had been directed to her son, she knew this made little difference to her father.

"What a spectacle you were making of yourself," Domenico commented, seeming to know that a further explanation was unnecessary.

"But I didn't think you'd be here," Maria said meekly.

"No excuse," Domenico repeated, "and what's worse, you didn't want me to be here."

Turning toward Antonio, who had witnessed the exchange between his mother and grandfather with even more embarrassment than he had felt after almost hitting his grandfather, Domenico explained: "Your mother and father *thought* I didn't see them sneaking out through the back of the house and getting into that carriage parked down the road! All to prevent me from being here!"

"I thought you weren't feeling well," his daughter protested.

"You thought I was too old to make the trip to the station, is what you thought!" Domenico insisted, adding: "And look who gave me a ride!" With his upraised cane Domenico directed their attention across the tracks toward the shriveled figure of a man who wore a conical cap and sat holding the reins of a two-horse wagon positioned near the terminal. Antonio recognized the man because of the conical cap, a medieval heirloom kept in practical use by only one man in Maida—the venerable Vito Bevivino, Domenico's ninety-four-year-old foreman and the sole surviving off-spring of the old soldier who had fought in Russia under General Murat.

Antonio waved toward the old soldier's old son who sat holding the reins, and Vito Bevivino waved back, doffing his conical cap.

"And since it's been years since you've come here to visit us," Domenico resumed his harangue toward Antonio, "do you think you can find the time tonight to come to my house and *properly* greet the rest of your family?"

Before Antonio could reply, Domenico said: "I'll expect you promptly at seven o'clock."

Then, after pointing the cane firmly on the platform, Domenico shoved himself off in the direction of the exit, moving swiftly ahead of his billowing cape that all but covered his slight limp.

"We must be there," Antonio's mother said, still sounding more like a daughter. "He's been very angry with your father these days. He's felt insulted about being kept out of your father's negotiating with these other men, and he's insisted that he wants to accompany you and the others on your visits out of town."

"I may not be going out of town," Antonio said.

"Yes, that's another problem your father is having with him—they can't seem to agree on the baron's daughter. Your father doesn't want her, but your grandfather likes the idea. And I guess you can imagine why."

As they walked slowly arm in arm, giving Domenico plenty of time to climb up on his wagon and ride on ahead of them, Antonio could not help noticing his father sitting on the suitcase on the far side of the termi-nal, out of sight of Domenico. Antonio waited for his mother to explain what she meant; but she did not, apparently out of respect for her father, or maybe out of a conditioned fear that whatever she said behind his back would somehow find its way to his ears. Antonio could only assume that his mother was referring to his grandfather's abiding respect for, and perhaps envy of, the town's nobility, and maybe also his lingering hope that, were Antonio to marry Olympia, Domenico would finally be accorded the respect that had always eluded him in his townsmen's resistance to addressing him as *Don* Domenico.

Riding in the carriage uphill to Maida, Francesco said nothing; he was preoccupied with this unaccustomed position as the driver, and the task was made no easier by the dust flying in his face from Domenico's wagon up ahead—clouds of dust that made Francesco's white hair seem whiter. But once they had arrived home, and Maria hastened to grind fresh beans for coffee, Antonio's father took him aside and said: "I assume we're going to your grandfather's tonight?"

"Yes," Antonio said.

"He's really been making a pest of himself around here," Francesco said. Then he elaborated in a whispered voice that he was sure his wife could not hear in the other room.

"Did your mother tell you about the young woman you were supposed to see in Curinga?" he asked, referring to a village just southwest of Maida.

"No," Antonio said.

"Come closer," said his father. "This you won't believe. In Curinga there is a nineteen-year-old girl named Nina, who is very rich and very pretty. I can guarantee her looks because I saw her myself. Her father stopped in at the shop with her one day and introduced us. Her father, whom I'd met earlier through the local magistrate who is his cousin, apparently made a fortune in the cement business in America. He went there as a young laborer, and years later he was a big contractor, stuffing money each night into his mattress. He then sent back to Curinga for his wife, who was his third cousin. In America their daughter Nina was born. Nina probably speaks English better than Italian, because I could hardly understand her Italian. But they've been back in Italy only a short while. Her father sold his business and house in America about a year ago to come back to Curinga. With all his American money I don't doubt he lives in Curinga in the grand style of the old *signori*.

"He's a little rough around the edges," the elder Cristiani conceded, "and shaking hands with him is like rubbing against sandpaper—but who cares? It was Nina I was interested in, and after I'd met her I thought she came very close to what you're looking for. Not only because she was nice to look at, and dressed well, and seemed to be well mannered, but she'd also been to the New World, and I thought she'd fit into your life in Paris fairly quickly. But then I made the mistake one night of mentioning

Nina's family to your grandfather, saying that you were going to meet her, and he asks: 'Is that the family that just moved back to Curinga?' I tell him it is. He says, 'She's off the list.' Finally I ask him: 'Why do you think she should be off the list?' 'I knew her grandmother,' he says. 'Her grandmother was from Maida. She was a fast woman.' 'Her *grandmother* was fast!' I say. 'What's that have to do with Nina?' 'It's in her blood,' says your grandfather.

"I almost laughed in his face," Francesco went on, "but your mother was there, and you know how she hates it when anyone suggests that your grandfather doesn't know what he's talking about—especially if that person is me. So I held my tongue, and let time pass, and assumed he'd forget all about it. Days later Nina's father comes into the store and we discuss the dowry, and let me tell you, he is a very generous man. But shortly after he left the shop, your grandfather walks in and says, very indignantly, 'I thought I asked to have the young woman from Curinga dropped from the list.' I ask him: 'What are you doing, spying on me?' He doesn't answer that question but instead tells me a little more about Nina's grandmother. She had a husband and two children in Maida, but one day she met a young captain of the Carabinieri who'd been transferred in from Rome, and the next thing people knew, she'd run off with the Carabiniere for a whole weekend in Catanzaro. 'When was this?' I asked your grandfather. 'In 1884 or 1885,' he said. 'That's forty years ago,' I reminded him, 'and besides, we're talking here about Nina.' 'It's in her blood,' he said again, and there was no way I could convince him otherwise. Later that night, when I returned home, I realized that your mother was talking the same way; her father had already convinced her. And she pleaded with me to break off the negotiations, saying if I did this she'd see that her father would stay out of my talks with other men. We'll see if he does. But anyway, I felt I had to remove Nina from the list. I explained it all very delicately to her father. I lied and told him that *you* are not sure anymore that you're ready to settle down. Her father said he understood the feeling, and he was very nice about it. But I'm really sorry you'll not be going to Curinga to meet Nina. I think she would have been perfect."

"I'm sorry, too," said Antonio.

(Six years later, after Antonio and his wife had moved into a larger apartment in Paris with their infant daughter, Antonio would receive a letter from his mother mentioning that Nina—who had married a local man a few months after Antonio's marriage—had recently left her husband and run off with her lover to Bologna.)

39.

THE DICTATES OF family courtesy being what they were in Maida—requiring that Antonio, after greeting dozens of relatives and friends at his grandfather's reception, would then be expected to have lunch or dinner in the days ahead with each family individually—meant that nearly a fortnight would pass before he could concentrate fully on the main reason he had returned to Italy, his quest for a wife.

With the cancellation of the trip to Curinga, Antonio's list of marital candidates had been narrowed to five: there was the baron's daughter in Maida; the shy damsel in Polia; a monsignor's niece in the nearby countryside of Jacurso (a candidate proposed by Domenico); a reputedly comely contralto whose father was a concertmaster in Catanzaro and, more important, whose godfather-uncle controlled the region's property assessments and tax rates; and finally a maiden named Adelina Savo about whom Antonio knew very little, except that she was the pride and joy of a substantial family who lived far to the south of Maida in the coastal town of Bovalino, a trek through brigand-infested roads at the end of which even the prospect of meeting Italy's most desirable virgin failed to stir within Antonio much enthusiasm for the trip.

No, the baron's daughter, Olympia, still soared above the others insofar as Antonio was concerned; and while the elder Cristiani in the meantime had received a curt note from the sire of the shy lady in Polia inquiring exactly *when* Antonio planned to visit, Antonio insisted to his father that he first be allowed to try his luck with Olympia.

Her father was very friendly and encouraging during his first meeting with Antonio, which was at the baron's suggestion held behind a cluster of mangled palm trees across the road from the entrance to the post office. They met there one afternoon shortly before four. If Olympia conformed to her usual routine, she would be coming up the road in a matter of minutes. As they stood slightly crouched behind the trees, the baron speaking more softly than he had earlier, Antonio lit up one of the Turkish cigarettes he had bought in Paris, his third since he had been with the baron.

"Relax, my dear boy, *relax,*" the baron whispered with paternal concern. "She's on her way, she's a creature of habit. . . ."

It was not the uncertainty of Olympia's arrival that had Antonio on edge, but rather his having to hide behind the trees with the baron. It was an unusually mild and bright winter afternoon, with many people walking back and forth, not a few of whom Antonio recognized; and he could not imagine what they might think if they caught a glimpse of him lurking like a voyeur with the baron behind the drooping, worm-encrusted palms. He listened as the church bells signaled the fourth hour after noon, and he stomped on his cigarette. Then he felt a slight jabbing in his ribs.

"There's *Olympia!*" the baron announced softly and with apparent pride. "Coming up the road, prompt as always—she's a woman you can count on. . . ."

Antonio leaned forward between the leaves and saw a stocky woman wearing a hooded gray cape and holding a rope on the end of which was a frisky baby goat. Antonio winced.

"Is that her pet?" he asked.

"No, *no!*" the baron scoffed, "you're looking at the wrong woman. Olympia's the one on the left. She's wearing the red shawl, and with nothing over her head. . . ."

Antonio now observed a willowy brunette who moved uphill with an energetic, long-legged stride. She wore sandals with straps tied above her ankles. Her skirt was immodestly short, hanging just a few inches below the knees. Her face, what little Antonio could see of it, was angular and fair-complected, but obscured mainly by her long hair, which was blown forward by sudden gusts of wind that also kicked clouds of dust uphill around her. Olympia kept walking, seemingly unmindful of the slight turbulence. She appeared so preoccupied with her thoughts that she did not even once pause to brush away the hair that now completely covered her face and extended in front of her. As Antonio watched her in the swirling dust, it looked for a moment as if she were walking backward.

"Isn't she beautiful," the baron remarked. Antonio nodded, but what impressed him was the strength of her stride, the long muscular legs revealed under her billowing skirt. If she wanted to catch someone, he thought, she could do so with ease.

After she had disappeared into the post office, the baron stepped out from behind the trees and held on to his homburg, waiting for the wind to settle down.

"All right, my young knight, I'll be running off," he said. "I think you should begin your little stroll now, too, but slowly as you please. She'll be coming out in a second. All I can say is, Good luck."

Antonio bowed slightly and watched the baron move toward the courtyard of the church, where his carriage driver awaited him. Antonio lit up another cigarette with much difficulty in the wind, pressed his gray bowler more firmly on his head, and proceeded in the direction of the square with a sense of abandon he hoped would mark him as a true Parisian boulevardier—one whose only worry in Maida was to avoid stepping into the droppings that farm animals and horses had left scattered along the cobblestones.

Before reaching the café, where he saw some of the boyhood friends with whom he had drunk coffee and anisette the afternoon before, he quickly turned back toward the post office, as if he had forgotten something, and then remembered that he *had* forgotten something. The books of French fiction that he had brought along to carry under his arm as an added lure for the French-reading Olympia—two novels by Balzac that Antonio had brought home after the war but had never finished reading— had been left on the ground behind the trees. As he headed toward the side of the road where the trees were, however, he caught a peripheral glimpse of the spry Olympia leaving the post office, several envelopes in hand that she seemed in no hurry to open. In almost no time at all, the speedy young woman was directly in his path, regarding him with curiosity— or so he chose to imagine. Ignoring her completely, Antonio moved smoothly to his left; and then, with the nonchalance of the toreador he had seen performing in a bullring the year before during a week's visit to Spain, Antonio turned his back on his potential attacker and strolled on in the opposite direction, going where he had not intended to go: away from the town and to an uninhabited field of brambles and high weeds that led uphill through a winding path to the hillside creek where Antonio and his boyhood friends used to play on Sunday afternoons in summertime, hurling sticks and stones at the large lizards and water moccasins that lingered there.

It was already getting dark before he reached the site of the creek, and he decided to turn back, having heard behind him neither the pattering feet of a pursuer nor even the scurrying of the usually omnipresent squirrels and rabbits. By the time he had left the leaf-strewn path and reentered the cobblestone clearing leading back to town, it was close to five, and the square ahead was nearly vacated. Antonio returned to where he had left the books behind the palm trees, then blinked twice before he accepted the fact that they were gone. And so, of course, was Olympia.

That evening Antonio said nothing to his parents about his afternoon's experience with the baron's daughter, and he was glad they did not ask, for he was in no mood for talking.

The following afternoon, however, after he had again crossed paths with her, ignoring her as before, Antonio *did* hear footsteps behind him; but clearly they were not the sounds of her limber, loping strides. They were heavy-footed, very masculine sounds that became somewhat unsettling to Antonio when, midway across the square, they multiplied and gave him the impression that perhaps three men were now deliberately tailing him at a distance of no more than ten yards.

Refusing to turn around and permit them to think he was intimidated, *if* that was their intention, he maintained his casual pace until he had crossed the square, and then he quickened it a bit as he reached the narrow street where his father's shop was located. He could see the lights in the windows of the tailor shop, and in the adjacent shops as well, but the street itself lay in the shadows of buildings that blocked what was left of the late-afternoon sunlight. In the near distance he could vaguely see the outline of a cloaked woman walking toward him, a slender woman accompanied by a one-legged man who swung himself forward with the aid of crutches. Antonio heard coming from behind him the murmurings of the men, but there was no longer the sound of their footsteps. He walked on until, as the couple neared him, he moved to one side to let them pass. The woman nodded with a smile and continued, while her companion concentrated on Antonio for a moment, and then, after another vigorous thrust with his crutches, stopped and shifted his weight forward on his one good leg and tilted his head sideways.

"Cristiani?" he called back over his shoulder. "Antonio Cristiani?"

Antonio paused and then turned to see the profile of a large-nosed man with a full beard and hardly any hair on the top of his head, a head that glistened in the reflection of the light from a window behind him. Antonio also looked down the street toward the square; but he saw no sign of the men who he thought had been following him.

"I'm Capellupo!" the bearded man announced, while the woman also stopped and turned. "Mario Capellupo from Cosenza! We were together in the barracks at Catanzaro. . . ."

Antonio had been with several hundred men during his first weeks as a recruit, ten years before, and seeing Capellupo now, and hearing his name, made him no less a stranger. But Antonio nonetheless moved at once toward Capellupo and embraced him with all the signs of familiarity and the sincere sense of fraternalism that he felt whenever he greeted a fellow veteran.

"You sewed up my pants after I tore a hole in them on the wires of the cot," Capellupo laughingly recalled, tightening his grip around Antonio's neck as one of the crutches fell to the ground.

"Oh, *yes,*" Antonio said, as if he remembered, and at the same time he watched the woman stepping quickly to pick up the crutch.

"They were the pants to my dress uniform," Capellupo went on, "and I had to wear it an hour later in that parade they made us march in before they sent us up to Austria to get shot at."

Antonio certainly remembered the parade, and the train ride up the coast, and the white cans the soldiers threw out the windows. Now the woman was beside him, pushing up Capellupo's left arm with her raised elbow and, with one knowing motion, shoving the handle of the crutch into an upright and steady position under Capellupo's armpit. As Antonio stepped aside, Capellupo introduced the woman as his wife, Bettina. She greeted him with a smile that was less restrained than before.

"Bettina's grandmother lives around here," Capellupo explained. "She lives alone. We've come to visit for a few days."

"You know the Mancuso family?" Bettina asked.

"I know a Giuseppe Mancuso," Antonio said. "He's a tailor with my father."

"That's my hardworking cousin," she said. "I hardly ever see him." Antonio wondered if she knew that her cousin was now reduced to working just two mornings a week.

"And how's *your* cousin getting along?" Capellupo asked Antonio. "The one who was at Caporetto."

"You know *Sebastian?*" Antonio asked, surprised.

"Sure, we served together for a while, and he used to talk about you," Capellupo said. "Then his section got transferred up the river, and then I heard about the terrible thing that happened."

Antonio, who days before had visited the bedside of Sebastian at the Rocchinos' farmhouse in the valley—where Sebastian's mother was now living almost permanently—said that he had regained some mobility, and that on occasion he was strong enough to move around slowly with a cane. Antonio added that one of the army doctors who regularly passed through the area and had Sebastian as a patient predicted that his condition might improve in the near future.

"Sounds like my kind of doctor," Capellupo said. "An optimist, a man of hope in this gloomy world. When my legs got all shot up, I'm told, one of the doctors wanted to cut them both off. But the other doctor, thank God, outranked him and overruled him. And look at me today. I can move around faster than Bettina—right, Bettina?" His wife, who was not much taller than the crutch she stood next to, looked up at him and laughed, nodding. "And don't think I'm planning to have this ugly stump of a leg the rest of my life," Capellupo went on. "It's going to grow out and form a perfect foot with perfect toes *before* I'm middle-aged, and *then* watch me move!"

"You'd better not move too far from me!" Bettina said, smiling as she grabbed hold of a crutch and threatened to pull it out from under him.

"No fear of that," he said. "Nobody else would put up with me."

"That's right, nobody else *would* put up with you."

Bettina then turned her round and cheerful face toward Antonio, her contentment shown clearly through the faintness of the light. It seemed that she was about to ask Antonio a question. He waited, but then she slowly turned away and faced her husband.

"Mario," she said, "I'm afraid Nana is waiting for us with the horses."

"Oh, yes," Mario said, explaining to Antonio: "Bettina's grandmother has the wagon near the square. She lives in the valley and doesn't like being on the road after dark. But I'd like to stop in and see Sebastian someday before we return to Cosenza."

"He'd want to see you, too," Antonio said, "and he can't be far from where you're staying."

"Yes," said Bettina, after Antonio had described the Rocchinos' farm. "I know exactly where it is."

"So tomorrow we'll go," Mario said, "and we'll have that old soldier Sebastian marching again in no time. Or at least we'll cheer him up a little."

"I'm sure you will," Antonio said. "Thank you, Mario."

Capellupo steadied himself on his crutches, preparing to move forward; but first, with some difficulty, he pressed up on his elbows and reached out to embrace Antonio once more. Antonio stepped in between the crutches and placed his arms around Capellupo's powerful shoulders and back, feeling his weight swaying heavily, and the coarse curly beard covering his cheeks. He saw Bettina edging in beside him and, after a moment's hesitation, turned away from Mario and faced her. Her arms were already raised, and she and Antonio exchanged kisses. Then she returned to her husband's side and waited as he took the first step.

"*Ciao,* Antonio," Mario said, with a little wave of his right hand over his shoulder.

"*Ciao,* Mario," Antonio said. "*Ciao,* Bettina."

Antonio watched them move together through the dark street toward the twilight of the square. Then he headed on to his father's shop, feeling his eyes moisten slightly. But he was hardly unhappy. Indeed, he had found warmth in the presence of a couple in love, and he had not felt more cheerful and hopeful since returning to Maida.

After skipping up the steps and entering the shop, Antonio greeted his father with a smile and then, doing something he had never done before, removed his bowler and flipped it through the air across the room toward the wooden head of a mannequin in the corner. His father, who had been studying the patterns spread out on his desk near the fitting room, looked up in wonderment as the hat sailed past the mannequin and hit against a fabric shelf before falling to the floor.

"Well," said Francesco, "*you* seem to be in high spirits. You must have had a good day."

"Who knows?" Antonio said, picking up the hat and placing it on the mannequin's head, then tilting it at a rakish angle. "I had my little strut past Olympia."

"Nothing good can come of that," said his father, again looking down at the patterns.

"I think she saw me," Antonio said, "but I'm not sure I made any impression. The only people I probably impressed today were some *male* admirers. They practically followed me here from the post office."

His father looked up and stared across the room at Antonio.

"You say men were *following* you?" he asked with concern.

"Yes, I think so."

"Did you recognize any of them?"

"I didn't turn around."

"You didn't turn *around!*" Francesco repeated in a loud voice. "Well, that's typical of you—always carefree in the presence of danger. . . ."

It was not typical, but Antonio said nothing, not wanting an argument. A one-legged man might walk contentedly and optimistically through the streets of Maida, Antonio thought, with concealed sarcasm, but *not* the son of this tailor who remains constantly aware of every possible peril. Antonio was sorry he had mentioned the men to his father. He was sorry mainly because now, after thinking more about it, he believed he might have been mistaken. And the very idea that he could be unnerved by anyone along the streets of Maida, *he* who had served at Verdun and along the Marne, belatedly struck him as absurd. Taking his hat off the mannequin, he prepared to head home.

"Where are you going?" Francesco asked, frowning.

"I have letters to write, I'll see you later."

"No," said Francesco. "Wait for me. I'll be closing early. We'll go together."

"Look," Antonio said softly, with his hat in hand, "I'm afraid I gave you the wrong impression. I'm quite sure I *wasn't* being followed. I was probably just getting some attention from a couple of pederasts admiring my suit. Maybe this town has finally gotten a touch of Parisian sophistication, and now has a few pederasts. . . ."

"Pederasts are the *least* of your worries around here," his father interrupted. "You'd better get serious, Antonio. We have some dangerous characters drifting around here now. You've been away a long time. Things have changed. . . ."

Francesco stood up. He remained quiet for a few seconds but appeared to become more emotional. Then he pointed across the room toward a chair, his bony white hand shaking slightly, his expression quivering but insistent—a face Antonio knew well from his youth here as an apprentice.

"Sit down, Antonio," his father said firmly. "Sit down over there and listen to me."

Antonio shrugged but walked over and sat down, his hat in his lap.

"Since the Fascists took over," his father began, "the police around here have been forced to do things they didn't do in the old days. In the old days they didn't go up in the mountains to raid the headquarters of hijackers and ransomers. In those days, as you probably know, the police used to be the go-betweens. They'd negotiate between the gang leaders and their victims, and everybody got something in return for something else, and people rarely got hurt. But now with these raids, the organized gangs are being broken up, and the police are locking up everybody they catch, even without evidence, and it's made things worse. The runaways from these gangs are now operating on their own. They're fighting with one another for the right to rob and kidnap. Things are out of control. Nobody knows who to deal with. And the economy has made some criminals so desperate that they'll kill you for your watch. That's what happened recently one night in Catanzaro. A man got shot to death during a struggle for his watch. This could happen in Maida. It could happen to you—you with your little jokes about Paris sophistication and pederasts."

"What do you want me to do, go back to Paris?" Antonio asked, unable to repress his impatience.

"No, I just want you to keep your eyes open around here," his father replied. "And if you hear people breathing down your neck, for God's sake, why don't you turn around and see who they are?"

"*Nobody* was breathing down my neck!" Antonio insisted, about to get up.

"Sit down, Antonio," his father said, holding up his hand. "I'm not finished yet. There's something else I want to say." Antonio sighed but remained seated. His father continued: "We also have some American-born men who've come back to these parts. They're the sons of immigrants who worked hard over there, but most of the sons didn't want to work and live like their fathers. They wanted to get rich, quick and easy. So some of them drifted into bootlegging. And they travel back and forth between around here and Sicily, and then back to the United States, involved with their secrets. They carry guns. I don't doubt that some are killers. *And* listen to this: Today I heard that one of the people who's been hanging around Olympia is a guy from America."

"Oh my God, you really want her off the list, don't you?" Antonio said, standing.

"I didn't say that," his father replied. "That's just your hasty conclusion."

"Well, then, what *are* you saying?" Antonio asked, facing Francesco directly. "Are you saying that she's connected with a gangster?"

"I'm not saying that, either. I'm just passing on what I heard."

"Where'd you hear it?"

"From the regional prefect, Don Vincenzo, who stopped in today. He's a cousin of the baron, and he doesn't like this man from America."

"Did the prefect say the guy is a gangster?"

"No, he just thinks he's not the type that should be hanging around Olympia."

"I assume I *am* the right type?"

"The baron thinks so."

"And you?"

"You know what I think. I think you can do better."

"In Polia?"

"Oh, that reminds me," said his father. "There may be a little difficulty with the Polia trip. The shy young lady up there apparently is insulted by your delay in getting there, and her father sent word to me hinting that even if you two should get to like one another, he's not sure she would want to leave Polia for Paris. But I think he's just using the delay as an excuse to reduce the dowry."

"This is all getting pretty complicated, if you ask me," said Antonio, shaking his head and thinking how simple things had been in Paris with Mademoiselle Topjen. "Well anyway, where do we go from here?"

"Would you like to go down to Bovalino?"

"I thought you said the roads were dangerous, that the crooks were running wild!"

"That's what I said, but your mother and grandfather think differently," Francesco explained in a matter-of-fact manner that only confused Antonio further. "They went down to Bovalino last week, in the monsignor's carriage, which has crosses on the sides, and they're very impressed, and want you to go down very soon—using the monsignor's carriage."

"I thought the monsignor had a niece we were to see in Jacurso," Antonio commented in a weary tone, indicating his declining interest in continuing the conversation.

"The monsignor *does* have a niece in Jacurso," his father said, "but he's somehow also related to the young lady in Bovalino. And the young lady in Bovalino comes with a handsome dowry."

"Look," Antonio said, "I *have* to get home. I have to get off a letter to the man who's taking care of the shop in Paris. I also want to spend a little time alone and think a bit more about all of this."

"I understand," said his father, sounding reasonable for the first time.

"Maybe I'll take another stroll past Olympia tomorrow, maybe a *final* stroll, and then we can decide where we go from there, is that all right?"

"Fine," said his father.

"So I'll be going on home," Antonio said softly, pushing his hat down hard on his head. "And I'll see you a little later. . . ."

"Wait a second," his father said. "I'll go with you."

40.

THE NEXT AFTERNOON, a few minutes before four, Antonio crossed the square and headed toward the palm trees near the post office. It was much colder than it had been earlier in the week, and dark clouds were floating down from the mountains, and the atmosphere contained a bone-chilling mistiness and a slight musky scent that in Maida portended rain.

Midway across the square, after turning up the velvet collar of the chesterfield he had brought from Paris and was wearing for the first time in Maida, Antonio paused to allow Guardacielo's homeward-bound herd to pass in front of him. The herd consisted of nearly two dozen sheep, three goats, and two watchdogs wearing steel-spiked collars. Antonio waved spiritedly with both arms in the air and called out Guardacielo's name, having not seen him in years, but the old shepherd kept walking with the aid of his wooden pole, not looking up, seemingly deaf and blind. The trotting watchdogs, however, turned their spike-ringed faces toward Antonio and glared.

This afternoon's chilling dampness was typical of the hill country in late January; and as Antonio proceeded across the square—nodding along the way to some elderly but unidentifiable pedestrians who wore hooded capes and greeted him by name—he found the weather strangely refreshing, clearing his head a bit after two hours in the smoky local café, having a heavily liquored lunch with his boyhood friends Basile and Paone. The lunch had in fact been enjoyable, with much laughter and reminiscing. Antonio had been with both of them for a time at the barracks in Catanzaro, until their units went on ahead of his own toward the Austrian front. After the war, Basile and Paone had returned to Maida to live, if not to work, on their parents' neighboring farms, and each had married the other's sister. Both men received disability benefits from the army, but at the café neither showed any signs of disability, not even after all the grappa, wine, and anisette that Antonio had abundantly provided, along with his packs of Turkish cigarettes that were chain-smoked and finished before the arrival of the food.

While seated at a rear table warmed by the kitchen and convenient to the bar, Antonio learned much from his talkative friends about the trends and thinking of the town; and to a degree they confirmed most of what he had heard earlier from his father—although *not* to the degree that would prompt him to credit his father with great perspicacity. His father and his friends, after all, had merely seen the same things, and had interpreted them similarly—through the eyes and understanding of fellow villagers. Whereas Antonio knew, all modesty aside, that he saw and understood things with a more worldly view, and, indeed, this broader and deeper insight was saddening to him at times, for it tended to diminish in his eyes some of the people he wanted to look up to—particularly his father. Antonio *finally* understood the profundity of the old village saying that his grandfather Domenico used to quote often: "Never educate your children beyond yourself."

Antonio's father, for example, and his village friends as well, seemed to be offended by many of the well-to-do Italian families who had recently returned from the United States, labeling them as spoiled by their affluence and having an attitude of arrogance and superiority that probably came as a result of living in the young nation made vainglorious by all its postwar prosperity and power. But Antonio regretfully saw in the critical reaction of his father and his friends, and undoubtedly also in their fellow villagers who had *never* risked going to the United States, a certain enviousness toward those townsmen who had gone abroad—and, worse, had *returned* with enough money to buy whatever they desired in Italy.

It had also been suggested by his father and his friends that the rich returnees from America had often been harmed by the living conditions overseas, and were now bringing back to Italy many New World maladies and mischievous inclinations. Tuberculosis was often mentioned, as was an advanced form of alcoholism supposedly unknown to the nontraveling villagers. But Antonio recalled as a boy hearing old-timers in Maida attributing these same ailments to an earlier wave of emigrants who had returned from Argentina; and as for the drinking problems, Antonio wondered how Maida's staunchest boosters could explain the inebriated presence of such village regulars as the red-eyed undertaker, Rombiolo; and that tumbling wine vat of a veterinarian Pepe Volpe, the illegitimate son of Don Marco, the grappa-guzzling *avvocato;* to say nothing of the village's distilled barber, Pasquale Riccio, and his ever shaky scissors and razor.

And finally, if Antonio were to be limited by the thinking of his father and friends, he would accept their theory that the returning Italians also were afflicted with an inherent American propensity for violence. To hear them tell it, a man guilty of nothing more than stealing a chicken or a pig in Italy could quickly become subverted in America to a career in gangsterism, especially now when he could become rich overnight by catering to America's thirst for the tasty thrill of illegal spirits.

America was a land of cowboys, Indians, showgirls, sugar daddies, and mobsters—according to these isolationists in Maida, who also made much of the fact that, in 1924, Mussolini's Socialist nemesis, Giacomo Matteotti, had been murdered in Italy by an *American*-born Italian gunman named, appropriately, Amerigo Dumini. But making such a point was yet another manifestation of narrow-mindedness, as Antonio interpreted it; although he *did* recall hearing a similar anti-American bias expressed with reference to the Matteotti murder by some of his Italian friends in France—friends who years before had resented President Wilson's efforts at the Versailles Peace Conference to "mutilate" the territorial gains promised Italy by its British and French wartime allies. None of this carping about America's negative influence, however, made much of an impression on Antonio. Again, because of his broader perspective and awareness of history, he concluded that the Fascists' use of the murderer Amerigo Dumini had nothing to do with the reputedly violent atmosphere of postwar America; he remembered, in fact, that his grandfather Domenico had made references to American violence long before World War I: Domenico saw the nation as a spawning ground for killers in the context of the 1900 assassination of Italy's King Umberto I, a crime also committed by an Italian gunman who had sailed over from America. Domenico, of course, conveniently ignored the fact that the Mafia had been functioning in southern Italy and Sicily two hundred years *before* Columbus had discovered America.

Apart from whatever criminal behavior might be indigenous to rural Italian society, Antonio saw little to refute the historical documentation that depicted southern Italians as traditionally resentful toward invaders, and hardened in their resentment during centuries in which they had been made to feel like second-class citizens on their native soil; and therefore, Antonio wondered, why should it be surprising now, in the 1920s, that Maida's ensconced villagers might have visceral feelings of resentment or enviousness toward this latest group of "invaders," those from the Italian ghettos of North America. Was this most recent intrusion of privileged people into Maida any less envy-provoking merely because the arrivals had Italian names and spoke the local dialect (albeit datedly, and blended with American vulgarisms), and because, having bettered themselves abroad, they now were ready to return and make those who had remained feel worse about *themselves?* Granted, many among those who had earlier escaped Italy had been very generous in sharing their foreign-made earnings with the kinsmen they had left behind (Antonio thought of himself as a primary example of this generosity), but many other travelers had shown no such altruism. Therefore some resentment in the village was in order. And yet, as Antonio crossed the square and headed toward his hideaway behind the palm trees, it gave him no pleasure to identify resentment and enviousness as strong native Italian characteristics, even if the great Italian patriot Garibaldi had once reluctantly admitted that it was indeed so.

———

Arriving behind the tree, *Antonio could not believe it!*

There, at his feet, leaning against the base of a tree trunk were the books by Balzac!

They had been stolen from there two days before—*who* had returned them? Who *ever* returned stolen merchandise in Italy voluntarily? What was the meaning of this? Antonio stared down at the books, not daring to touch them. Suddenly he imagined a sinister aspect entering his courting adventure, and the sweetness of the anisette that lingered in his mouth began to agitate the exposed nerve in one of his lower molars.

From his position behind the tree he cautiously edged forward for a better view of the post office. But there seemed to be no one afoot watching him. The only people entering the post office now, moments after the four-o'clock church bells had stopped ringing, were two nuns who crossed themselves before pulling open the heavy doors with ease. Still very tense, Antonio again looked down at the books. He closed his eyes momentarily and breathed deeply, trying to regain his composure, to think with clarity. He cursed Basile and Paone for smoking all his cigarettes. He opened his eyes again; the books were still there. They looked the same as they had two days earlier; at least the book on top appeared no more wrinkled or bent than when he had last seen it, and the tiny part that had been torn off on the lower tip of the cover had gotten no larger.

Within a few seconds he had calmed himself somewhat, for it occurred to him that he was aggravating himself unnecessarily. What was there to worry about? *Surely,* Olympia had taken them—and *not* one of her jealous suitors—for, as the baron said, she read French. If she had read both books in two days, it indicated that she was a fast reader, and that she stayed home a lot (a good sign in a potential wife). Her having returned the books indicated, of course, that she was on to his little game. But so what? Maybe a love note, or a pressed flower, awaited him between the pages. If a *vindictive suitor* were involved, however, there might be the dreaded imprint of the Black Hand society; and then what? At lunch Basile and Paone had confirmed that Olympia had many admirers, including the one from America to whom Antonio's father had alluded.

Basile said his name was Raffaeli. Bruno Raffaeli. He was said to have been born in Philadelphia. Basile, who had many relatives there—and not a good word to say about any of them—had seen Raffaeli sporadically in Maida, and was convinced he was an individual of dubious character. Raffaeli's parents had operated a restaurant in Philadelphia, but they had sold the place before returning to Italy a year and a half before and acquiring the cliffside manor beyond Maida that had belonged to the late marquis of Botricello.

Antonio was told nothing more by his friend about Bruno Raffaeli, except that he was big and broad-shouldered, and that he was in and out of Maida frequently, but never predictably, and that, like the majority of trans-Atlantic travelers who made guest appearances in the local *passeggiata,* he eschewed the proletarian fashion adopted by most hometown bachelors in favor of the wide-brimmed fedoras and sharp-lapeled double-breasted overcoats preferred by gang leaders in America—overcoats with a white handkerchief in the outside pocket, and most likely a pistol in the inside pocket.

Impatiently, Antonio reached down, picked up the books, and flipped through the pages, prepared for anything—love notes, flowers, or threatening messages from the Black Hand society. He found none of these. Everything about the books seemed the same as when he had last touched them, except that his page markers were missing, which was the least of his concerns—for now, looking up, he saw Olympia walking along the road. It was four-ten. She was late. Her head was covered by the hood of her cape, which she held close to her body on this frosty day. But he recognized her instantly from her walk, and especially her long legs. If she was cold in her upper body, she was apparently warm below: her skirt today seemed shorter, exposing her legs above the knees, and, as usual, she wore sandals.

She did not look in his direction before entering the post office, which surprised and also disappointed him. The game was still on, although now there were renewed doubts about the players. Still standing behind the trees, Antonio glanced backward, then turned toward the front and peeked through the leaves. A few harmless-looking elderly couples were coming and going along the road, but no stalwart figures in fedoras. So Antonio tucked the books under his arm and stepped out of what he assumed to be his obscurity. Summoning whatever stoicism was within him, he stood ready to confront the vicissitudes of his village.

Boldly he walked toward the post office, half tempted to enter. But what would he do in there? Confront her directly? Confront her about what? No, he thought, that would be forcing the issue, and it might make him appear foolish. While he believed it had been Olympia who had taken the books, he could not be absolutely certain. It *might* have been Raffaeli. Or some other possessive deviant awaiting the right moment to ambush Antonio. Suddenly, serious thoughts of danger rose within Anto-

nio, much as he tried to repress them. For the first time in years he recalled the fate of his late uncle Gaetano. Antonio remembered hearing the
tale of how young Gaetano, standing in the shadows beneath the balcony
of the woman he would eventually marry, had been jumped from behind
and slashed across the temple with a knife. This had occurred in Maida
thirty years before. Was Maida today any more advanced? The town today
might be even *more* backward!

In any case, Antonio decided not to enter the post office. Olympia
would be coming out any second. At once Antonio turned away from the
front door and, with the books underarm, ambled on toward the square,
reminding himself, as he had earlier, that there was no reason to panic. He
should remain calm; alert but calm. He should continue for at least another day to play the baron's game: play hard to get, if that *was* what Antonio had lately been doing with his time-consuming, possibly ill advised,
masquerade of coquettishness.

Antonio saw Basile and Paone approaching. As Antonio waved, Basile
left Paone behind and ran toward Antonio. He staggered before he reached
him, and gasped for breath, seeming indeed disabled.

"Antonio," he blurted out, holding on to Antonio's shoulder for support, "I saw Raffaeli!" Basile then began to cough, and appeared on the
verge of choking until Paone rushed forward to revive him by pounding
him on the back.

"Raffaeli walked past the café with another man just after you left,"
Basile went on haltingly, as Paone rubbed his back and looked upon Antonio with an expression of Maidese gloom that Antonio found irritat-
ingly similar to the agonized face displayed in paintings of Saint Francis.

"Antonio," Basile concluded, almost in a whisper, "I think we should
stay with you."

"No, no, my friend," Antonio said, placing his hand on Basile's
shoulder, "I'm grateful, but that won't be necessary."

"Please, I think we should stay," Basile insisted, "this man might be
dangerous. . . ."

Antonio's first instinct had been to welcome his friends as bodyguards, but then he saw this as a sign of cowardice, and also a capitulation
to the philosophy of pessimism that had persisted in his village for centuries. Were he to be guided by the thinking of his friends—and, alas, his
father—he would in spirit be back with them in the hills. No, Antonio
believed that he and his father were cut from different cloth; the metaphor
displeased him as much as the paternal disrespect it implied, but it was
nevertheless the truth. Antonio had not returned home to reenter the

Middle Ages. He was in southern Italy in search of an idealized woman of old-fashioned values whom he considered timeless and priceless. And in his quest for such a woman he would not be discouraged by any reputed gangster from America, or by some local cutthroat who might exist only in the imagination of these kindly but fearful villagers who seemed at home only in a secluded place of oppression and frequent earthquakes.

"Well," Basile said, finally breathing normally, "maybe you're right. Raffaeli, when I saw him, wasn't headed toward the post office. He was walking down toward the fountain, and maybe to his horses, and maybe he was off to see his parents."

"Yes," agreed Paone, sounding quite relieved that Antonio would not be needing them as bodyguards.

"But let me thank you both again," Antonio said, shaking their hands and waving them off. "I'll just be stopping at my father's shop, and there are plenty of people around, and anyway I'm not concerned about Raffaeli, or anyone else."

After his friends had departed, Antonio continued with an added spring in his stride, his feelings of pride and self-confidence renewed. He whistled as he walked, recalling a flamboyant musical revue he had seen in Paris at the Folies-Bergère; and while he remained on the alert, aware of the pedestrians in front of him as well as those along the edges of the square, there was in neither his look nor his manner any anxious expectation. Frankly, he was feeling good. He had outgrown his town, was above its petty grievances, but was not unmindful of the positive things about this place and its people. The offer of help from Basile and Paone, fearful as they undoubtedly were, had touched Antonio, and they certainly could not be held accountable for what this land of misfortune had done to their souls. And Maida, for all its antiquation and its occasional primitive passions, retained a quality of simple beauty and familiar intimacy that he missed in Paris. This square itself, rather large for a village so small, had been planned centuries before by people who thought *big,* and there *was* a largeness to be found even in these townsmen whom he may have ungraciously thought of as narrow-minded.

As Antonio walked on in his heightened state of awareness and forgiveness, he heard things he had not heard before—the genial sounds of birds in the gray winter sky, and what sounded like the polite applause of palm leaves in the wind, and what clearly was the sound of a choir at practice in the monastery near the cemetery. His thoughts of Olympia, his wondering about where she was exactly since leaving the post office—she *had* to have left it by now!—and the thoughts of warning carried his way by Basile and Paone, had receded in his mind and were being replaced by thoughts more conciliatory and felicitous now that he was again at peace with himself.

When he reached the edge of the square and turned toward the narrow street leading to his father's shop, Antonio heard at first imprecisely, and then more definitely, the hurried tapping of female feet along the cobblestones well behind him. Not turning around, not even when he vaguely heard his name called out eagerly by a female voice, Antonio entered the street that was heavily darkened in shadows. He kept walking, his pace quickening, as the onrushing woman gained ground while pleading with him to stop. He almost did stop, hearing in her voice a tone that was oddly compelling and that brought to mind his classroom readings about the legendary Calypso every young southern Italian boy is regularly warned about by his mother and priest—the beseeching voice, both sympathetic and insistent, that induces procrastination, dalliance, and ultimately ruination. The fact that this was an exaggeratedly negative interpretation of Calypso mattered little in the rural south, where nearly all of Greek mythology was instilled with touches of Italian tragedy and iniquity. Antonio had almost reached his father's tailor shop when the woman caught up with him and, throwing her arms around his back, forced him to turn and embrace her.

"*Mother!*" Antonio cried out, as she wept in his arms. "Mother, what's wrong? What are you doing here?"

"Oh, I was afraid I'd never see you again, Antonio!" Maria said, trembling and holding him close. "I've had premonitions for days, Antonio, that you were being followed by evil men. These premonitions became so strong an hour ago that I ran out of the house to your father and told him we *had* to stop you from getting killed. He said you wouldn't listen to him, so he sent me through the back road to the post office to convince you myself to leave town. I couldn't find you, but thank God you're here now."

"Mother, Mother," Antonio said, sounding more stern than he intended, "you've got to get control of yourself. . . ."

"No," she interrupted, trying to push him away, "we must leave! The monsignor's carriage is waiting. I've packed an overnight bag for you. Your father and the monsignor's driver are all set to go."

"To go where?"

"To Bovalino," she said. "*There* awaits the woman of your dreams."

"I can't, Mother, I can't," Antonio said.

"You must!" she demanded. "If you don't, something horrible will happen—not only to you, but to me."

The street was empty, and her tearful urgings had brought some neighbors to their second-floor windows. The sounds of their shutters opening, and their inquiries about her well-being, embarrassed her.

"I'm sorry, Antonio," she said, more quietly, "but you must trust me." Then she said something that Antonio heard perfectly, but in his surprise he exclaimed, *"What?"*

"I saw her," his mother repeated.

"You saw *Olympia?*"

"Yes," she went on, "I saw her in the post office. I had a good look at her." After a pause, his mother continued: "Oh, Antonio, she's *not* much to look at. Her face is long and bony, the kind of face you see on so many noblewomen, and it always reminds me of horses. And she's tall, Antonio. She is a head taller than you are. Oh, my dear Antonio," she intoned with forbearance but finality, "she's not for you. She's just *too tall!*"

Antonio said nothing. His arms were still around his mother, but he was staring out into the shadows of the lonely street, shaking his head slowly. Yes, he thought, his mother really knew how to get him. So, Olympia was too tall. What else was there to say? That just about ended it. Antonio could not picture himself walking arm in arm with a woman noticeably taller than himself down the aisle of a church, or indeed up the Avenue des Champs-Élysées.

Antonio turned to his mother. He smiled slightly. Neither said anything for a few seconds. But they both knew that he would soon be off to Bovalino to meet the woman of his dreams.

Not only did the monsignor's carriage have large white crosses painted on both sides and on the back, but the horses wore steel rosary beads around their necks that jingled through the night, creating sounds apparently familiar to the monsignor's plundering co-religionists in the hills, none of whom charged down to mount an attack. The monsignor's guard nonetheless remained posted on the upper bench next to the driver, while Antonio sat in the warmth of the cabin with his father, who informed him about their itinerary. They would be spending the night at the home of the prospective bride, Adelina Savo. Her mother and Antonio's mother were old friends, having been introduced years earlier by the monsignor. What Antonio did not know until now was that the monsignor and grandfather Domenico had been together at the seminary. Adelina's family was a major contributor to the monsignor's diocese, and the main source of the family's wealth was derived from productive landholdings in the region and a number of small but solvent businesses in and near the town of Bovalino. In a meeting held there between the Savo family and Antonio's mother and grandfather, before Antonio's arrival from Paris, the terms of the dowry had been discussed and agreed to.

"This dowry is by far larger than anything offered by other families," Francesco told his son during the journey. "Of course, money is not the important thing," he continued with as much conviction as he was capable. "What's important is that you and Adelina meet and get to like one another."

"When do we meet?" Antonio asked.

"Not tonight," his father said. "We won't be there until near midnight, and Adelina will have retired to bed long before that. Her parents and relatives will be waiting up for us, the monsignor told your mother, and tomorrow morning we're expected to attend the seven-o'clock Mass. You won't meet her then, either. She'll be in the front pew praying next to her mother—they do that every day—and we're to sit near the back with her father, who wants to leave early and give us a tour of the town, and show us his land. Later we'll have lunch at his home. That's when you'll meet Adelina."

Things went according to schedule that night. The Savo family owned a spacious home and, although in the darkness of his arrival Antonio could not see it, the home was said to overlook the Ionian Sea. Far south into the currents was the alleged lodging place of the nymph Calypso, but what remained of her corruptive magnetism was probably too distant and faint to penetrate the Savos' thick-walled residence, where apostolic statuary stood guard at the gate and a cross was carved into the front door, and whose interior hallway was lined with niches containing stone figures representing Christ and his followers as they progressed through the Stations of the Cross.

After a brief but cordial late supper, presided over by Adelina's white-moustached father, who wore a black suit a bit tight for his expanded girth, Antonio and his father were escorted to separate guest rooms in the west wing of the house, away from the sea; the carriage driver, who had often stayed overnight at the Savos' with the monsignor in the past, occupied his usual quarters in the carriage house.

In the morning Antonio and his father were awakened by a single forceful rap of Signor Savo's knuckles against each of their doors, accompanied by his announcement that breakfast was being served. Adelina had already left the house with her mother for confession when Antonio and his father arrived at the table; but within an hour, from his vantage point in the rear of the chapel, Antonio had his first view of her slender figure as she stood and approached the altar for Communion. He had no sense of her facial features, hidden as they were behind her flowing gray veil; but what mattered most to him at this time he noted with relief and satisfaction. Adelina Savo was not tall. She was definitely not taller than he; Antonio was in fact confident that she was a bit shorter. Before the end of the Mass, as Antonio turned to leave with Signor Savo, who would escort him on the obligatory tour of the town and the family holdings in the countryside, Antonio took a furtive glance at the kneeling figure of Adelina, and he looked forward eagerly to meeting her at lunch.

If all such meetings between prospective brides and their suitors could fulfill the couples' highest expectations, as did this one involving Antonio and Adelina, the history of arranged marriages in southern Italy would be a repetitiously blithesome chronicle devoid of the disappointments, the bitterness, the angry departures, and the bloody vendettas that have characterized this ancient custom first inspired in a cave during the Stone Age by a nameless couple's scheming tribesmen. But no matter; the luncheon at which Antonio was introduced to Adelina, and the impression she made during that occasion, left little doubt in his mind that his mother had been right when she had heralded Adelina as the woman of his dreams.

Although her father did most of the talking, being on rare occasions interrupted by her uncles, who were in his employ, Adelina managed while saying very little to communicate her intelligence and modest charm during those moments when she was called upon to comment. Antonio was surprised to learn that mathematics had been her main interest at the convent school, and it pleased him to no end to learn that she had a degree that qualified her as an accountant. A woman who worked with figures, he reasoned, was likely to appreciate the price of things, and therefore practice frugality as a wife; and a woman who was a qualified accountant was definitely needed in his shop in Paris, where the *unqualified* accountant (and outright thief) whom Mademoiselle Topjen had recommended three years before had, in addition to misappropriating business funds, guided Antonio into tax difficulties with the French government.

The unexpected bonus that Adelina brought with her accounting abilities was complemented by her attractive appearance and social poise, which Antonio saw as traveling well to the French capital and, together with her dowry, contributing greatly to the advantaged life he imagined for himself there as a married man (Antonio was nothing if not practical); and when, after the luncheon, her father suggested that she show Antonio their greenhouses in the rear yard, she surprised him further by introducing him to her hobby of growing exotic flowers from seeds she imported from the Italian colony of Somaliland. Adelina had a green thumb as well as a head for money—and an impulse toward romance, too, as she showed when she snapped off a long-stemmed white rose as they left the enclosure and, standing in front of him, deftly pinned it to his lapel. It was then that he knew for sure that she was at least a half-inch shorter than he; and it was also then that he became fully aware of the momentum that seemed to be making him altar-bound, and of his own diminished desire to resist it. It was as if he was an insignificant factor in a process headed toward an inevitable conclusion. He had begun to sense this the night before, shortly after meeting Adelina's mother. Although she was a friend of his mother's, Antonio himself had never met her; and yet she assumed an immediate familiarity toward him that struck him as utterly natural, and her presumptuousness oddly put him at ease—she *was* his future mother-in-law, she seemed to be intimating without saying a word. There was nothing that he could do about it, so he might as well become happily resigned to it. She later made passing references to the earlier meeting held in Bovalino—the one attended by his mother, the monsignor, and Domenico. This second meeting was obviously looked upon by his future mother-in-law as pro forma, a ceremonious occasion whereby Antonio could meet his future bride and father-in-law, the latter a bit stodgy toward Antonio at first, but soon falling in line. Signor Savo's wealth and position, Antonio later learned, had come from his *wife's* side of the family, although the Savo family was old and respected among bourgeois Catholics of the south (and it would claim added status in future generations when an emigrant cousin's son, Mario Cuomo, would be elected governor of New York State). As to what Francesco was doing here in Bovalino, Antonio could only conclude that he had come along for the ride.

With the generous terms of the dowry having no doubt been signed, sealed, and made ready for delivery after the consummation of the marriage, Antonio further took for granted that Adelina's mother had resolved whatever problems might exist with Adelina's other possible suitors in or around Bovalino. Still, it was a nagging question; and after Adelina had taken the liberty of pinning the rose to his lapel, he took the liberty, in the most discreet way, to ask if there were any cutthroats in the vicinity waiting to attack him, or if Bovalino had a local version of Bruno Raffaeli.

"There might be a little something you'd like to explain about your recent past before we go in?" he asked, wishing he could have been more explicit as they walked side by side back to the house.

Adelina turned toward him with a modest smile indicating that she understood perfectly.

"No," she said, "nothing at all."

Inside, the others were standing and waiting, forming what Antonio thought was a receiving line. But his father stepped forward, took Antonio by the shoulder, and said, "Well, my son, I think it's time for our farewell. We'll all be seeing one another again in the near future."

As the elders smiled, Antonio kissed in turn Adelina's mother and aunts, and another older woman whose relationship to the Savo family was unclear to him; and then, after shaking hands with Adelina's father and uncles, he exchanged awkward bows with her. He told her in a voice that everyone could hear that he would write her from Paris. Adelina thanked him, and gave him her post office box number.

The horses had now arrived, and the monsignor's coachman took the Cristianis' bags and placed them in the carriage. Adelina's mother came forward with a gift package for Antonio to give to his mother. She kissed him on the cheeks and lightly squeezed his left arm. Antonio and Francesco turned to board the carriage, and, after their final wave from the window, the black vehicle with white crosses headed through the iron gates toward the coastal road along the Ionian Sea, beginning the ride back to Maida.

Antonio saw no reason to spend more time in Maida. He had found what he had sought, and it seemed wiser that he return quickly to Paris and avoid further complications in his village. His father agreed. The Savo family and the others could proceed on their own with the nuptial agreements, as they had been doing behind his back all along; and when a wedding date had been set, Antonio knew that he would receive adequate notice as to when he should reappear in Bovalino to marry Adelina. Until then, Antonio had much to do in Paris. He had to get back to his business, to arrange for the indictment of his accountant, and to locate an apartment that would be large enough for a wife and the young family that would inevitably follow.

His bachelor apartment was small, and located up five flights of steps. While he at first thought it would be adequate for Adelina and himself until they were expecting a child, he would soon learn that under no circumstances was Adelina to set foot in the place. This pronouncement would come from Adelina's father, who, a few months after Antonio had returned to Paris, had himself traveled to the French capital on what he insisted was primarily a courtesy call.

Signor Savo had strolled into Antonio's shop on the Rue de la Paix shortly before closing time one day in early April 1925. At first Antonio failed to recognize him; and although he quickly compensated for the oversight with effusive cordiality, Antonio was mildly irked that Savo's suspicions about him had been so strong that he had come all the way from Bovalino to see with his own eyes that Antonio did *indeed* own a shop on the Rue de la Paix. Apparently satisfied with what he saw, Savo then proposed that they dine together that evening and review the guest list for the August wedding. Antonio suggested a restaurant where the maître d' had yet to pay him for a tuxedo delivered before Christmas; and he also suggested that Savo come to his apartment for an aperitif before dinner. Two hours later, having climbed the five flights of stairs, the stout Signor Savo arrived at Antonio's door red-faced and breathing irregularly; and on entering the apartment, and seeing on the walls a few large oil paintings and pencil sketches of women entirely in the nude, he collapsed into a chair with his hands covering his eyes, and in a quivering but wrathful voice he exclaimed: "Oh my God, how disgusting!"

"Signor Savo, *please,*" Antonio asked, "what's wrong?"

"Disgusting!" he repeated, his eyes still covered. "Where did you get such disgusting pictures?"

Antonio turned to look at the paintings with all the tolerance of a man who had been living with them for five years, and then turned again to his guest. "These are works by some of France's most promising young artists," he explained.

"They make me sick," said Savo.

"I'm sorry," said Antonio.

"Then get rid of them."

"Get rid of them?" Antonio asked. "When, tonight?"

"No," Savo said, "after I leave town."

Antonio stood looking down at Savo slumped in the chair, his hands now resting on his knees but his crimson-colored head and walrus moustache still tilted toward the floor, away from the surrounding display of blatant immodesty.

"All right," Antonio said, finally.

"And you'll not have these pictures, or others like them, in the place where you'll be living with Adelina?"

"No," said Antonio, seeing what was left of his bachelorhood turning to autumn even before the arrival of spring.

"And another thing, Antonio," Savo continued more softly, looking up at Antonio and breathing normally for the first time. "Do you think, after you and Adelina are married, that you can find room on your walls somewhere for a crucifix?"

In a tone of voice tailors reserve for important customers, Antonio nodded and said: "Yes, but of course."

41.

MUCH AS JOSEPH was pleased by Antonio's cheerful letter describing the wedding in Bovalino, and proud as he continued to be of his pace-setting cousin in Paris, Antonio's good fortune and constant progress tended to make Joseph feel left behind, more detached than usual in this Methodist-ruled resort in New Jersey where he sewed throughout the day and rarely saw the sun, and where his interaction with people was limited largely to standing to greet the customers at the counter whenever the tiny bell on the front door of his shop jingled.

Joseph's isolation, to be sure, was primarily of his own choosing. Ever since arriving in Ocean City in the spring of 1922 and soon purchasing his tailor shop—mainly with the promissory notes provided by the asthmatic owner desperate to leave town for the drier climate of Arizona—Joseph had comported himself with formality and caution, always concerned that one injudicious act, be it social or professional, consciously intended or inadvertent, could ostracize him from the community and perhaps even lead to his deportation. In the summer of 1925, not yet twenty-two, and having barely mastered the language, Joseph was two years away from becoming an American citizen, and he was without powerful friends in the local political system or the Catholic Church who might alleviate any difficulties he might have.

Paris had lost some of its appeal now that Antonio was married; and in any case, Joseph doubted that he could earn in France, and surely he could not in Italy, anything close to what he was now earning in the United States. The national prosperity of the mid-twenties was evident throughout the island, prompting a building boom along the bay, the beachfront, and the business district, and bringing to the town not only more vacationers and year-round settlers, but also residential commuters—men who left for Philadelphia each day wearing suits, and soiling them with train soot, and later, on the homeward-bound club car, staining them with bootleg whiskey and wine, so that the suits required a deluxe dry-cleaning at twice the regular price.

Joseph's thriving "French dry-cleaning" business, which brought him three times more money than he earned from his tailoring—*until* he had introduced his customers to his ingenious Suit Club—was located within a carless four-car garage on a weedy lot behind the shop. On one side of the garage's interior were two pressing machines and three tables with brushes, sponges, and bottles of strong acidic solution prescribed for removing from the clothing those stains that had remained after a routine cleaning. On the other side was a six-foot-high oblong-shaped metal dryer that looked like a roofed carriage without wheels, and a circular dry-cleaning tumbler, three feet high and nine feet in diameter that, while rotating like a collapsed Ferris wheel, spun the clothes around in interlocking containers filled with mild dosages of naphtha believed adequate for the removal of ordinary smudges caused by grease or soot, but not ink, liquor, or rust stains. The supervisor of the three-man plant, who like his colleagues was black, was the sixty-six-year-old deacon and choirmaster of the black Baptist church located on the west side of the railroad tracks two blocks behind the garage.

A benign and small-boned gentleman with lined, leathery skin and pale blue eyes who wore high rounded starched collars and three-piece black wool suits in summer as well as winter, he was known to one and all as "Mister Bossum." No one knew his first name, or even whether he had one, including the minister who provided him with a room in the church and the privileges of its pantry in compensation for his efforts as the deacon and choirmaster. Currently unknown to Joseph about Mister Bossum, whom he had acquired with the business from the previous owner, was that he functioned after hours as the town's leading bootlegger, receiving the merchandise before dawn along the bay via a clam boat from Atlantic City, and then distributing it to his clientele in the white community with the assistance of select members of his choir—who were either female domestics employed in the homes of the town's wealthier imbibers, or the black men who worked as porters or kitchen helpers in hotels and restaurants.

Still, Mister Bossum was always sober and punctual when he appeared for work every morning at the dry-cleaning plant, strolling in cheerily at nine-fifteen or earlier, and usually whistling if not humming the gospel music he carried in his head across the tracks from the eight-o'clock church service. Working under him were two pressers, who were rarely the same pressers three days in a row, and a part-time spotter who helped out in the busy summer season but who worked mainly as a boat mechanic along the bay. Mister Bossum reserved for himself all the major spot-removing chores, particularly the liquor stains—gingerly anointing the material with the cleansing solution, with an almost pleading expression on his face, perhaps reflective of the responsibility he felt in having provided the source of such blemishes.

The dry-cleaning business during busy weeks grossed in excess of five hundred dollars, which, after the deduction of the pressers' salaries and other overhead expenses assumed by Mister Bossum, resulted in a net profit to Joseph in excess of two hundred dollars. He was nearly embarrassed by his wealth. He would be embarrassed in another way, however, after he began to succeed financially with his Suit Club—an endeavor that unavoidably brought him into close physical contact with females whenever it was a woman who won a free suit. Holding a tape measure around a mature woman's bust and hips while gathering vital statistics before cutting a pattern might, in the mind of a lecherous tailor, represent an occupational pleasure. But to a young man as cautious and sexually inexperienced as Joseph, this was hardly the situation.

Joseph had never so much as held hands with a member of the opposite sex, except perhaps in the case of relatives such as his mother, although he could not specifically recall doing even that. Joseph's upbringing had prepared him to believe that the nearness of women more often than not augured evil temptation and attendant scandal, to say nothing of the bodily harm that was frequently inflicted by unseen suitors. Despite Joseph's growing confidence in himself as a prospering proprietor, he believed he could not afford the risk of indulging in the freedoms of the New World, especially in such a relatively prim part of that world as this small island founded by reformist ministers. Joseph had too many people to support overseas—and not only the daily needs of his mother and siblings: he had also taken on the responsibility of establishing a worthy dowry for his sister, Ippolita, who was now seventeen. In the three years he had lived in Ocean City, he himself had seen a growing looseness and laxity among its people—even before his Suit Club would accentuate this impression. He recalled how unspoiled and refined the island had seemed to him during his Sunday-afternoon strolls throughout 1922, and he particularly remembered pausing one Sunday to watch a memorial service conducted by the town's elders under a cedar tree near the Methodist Tabernacle building. There had been hymn-singing by white-gloved ladies and men of steely gentility, accompanied by young evangelists with French horns; then an elderly dark-suited man wearing a straw hat stepped forward to the polite applause of the crowd and implanted his cane securely in the lawn before lightly tipping his hat. He was the last surviving founder of the town—the Reverend James E. Lake, who nearly a half-century before, accompanied by his ministerial brothers, had stood under this same cedar tree and proclaimed the presence of God on the beach. Although there had been no Catholics among the early settlers, and were few enough on the island by the time Joseph arrived, he felt himself in harmony with these two hundred or so Methodist memorialists advocating order and propriety in these prosperous postwar years that were marked also by a carnal indulgence as obvious as the stains on the garments brought into his shop.

There was not only the residue from the spilled whiskey and wine, but also the whitish spots on the fly fronts of young men's trousers that, while usually eradicated after a regular cleaning in the tumbler, revealed even more than liquor stains the loose lives of many of these unmarried couples whom Joseph greeted at his counter: the flappers with bobbed hair who often walked into the shop smoking cigarettes, and their flask-hipped boyfriends who left their roadsters double-parked in the street with the motors running. And not only was it the postdebutantes and university men from Philadelphia who were departing from the restraining traditions of the town elders; it was also their parents, who had bought up most of the beachfront for their second homes, and had built an impressive yacht club on the bay from which motorboats sped all day and in which whiskey flowed through the night. There were, in addition, several native residents who were drawn to the leisurely style of these city people—residents who had served them as real estate brokers, lawyers, and bankers, and who now aspired to membership in the yacht club and looked forward to the day when they, too, might afford the ultimate in seashore status symbols—a sailing boat with masts tall enough to require that the town's principal drawbridge be raised in its behalf.

Less than two dozen people possessed such vessels, but whenever one of those boats approached the little rainbow-shaped bridge flanked by the tiny houses of its watchmen—the boat's horn blasting, its colorful flags and ribbons whipping in the wind from soaring ropes, its white-capped skipper standing on the back deck surrounded by his guests hoisting highball glasses—every motorist en route was stalled to a stop, was perhaps halted for nearly a half-hour in the glaring heat rising from the marshlands, along with mosquitoes and odors of stagnation, *unless* the motorist was lucky enough to be stuck in a higher and breezier elevation that edged within the shadows of the bridge's saluting sections. Although Joseph's shop was more than four blocks east of the bayfront, he could hear the sounds of the impatient motorists and could picture them, too, because he had witnessed the scene often during his Sunday outings along the piers. There would invariably be cars and trucks lined bumper to bumper on the two-mile causeway that linked the island to the mainland—and the sight of jitney drivers sitting on the fenders of their vehicles, with their beach-bound day-tripper passengers from the mainland poised along the railings watching the high white sails cutting slowly behind the uptilted steel-grilled roadway with its yellow-painted center lines crossed by circling sea gulls. Halted also were many farm trucks from the hinterlands, loaded with fresh vegetables and fruit, and garbage trucks from the island followed by beach flies and other insects that would shift their attention to the nearby farm trucks *if* the latter contained any watermelons or other fruit that had been split open during the earlier ride on the bumpy back-country roads.

Joseph had overheard truck drivers complaining about such things as he sat at the counter of the corner restaurant across from City Hall, where he nearly always had his breakfast and dinner; and while he could sympathize with the truckers and car owners who had to contend with a drawbridge in a town where the major taxpayers often owned big boats, he was also aware that the yacht club crowd, and particularly the younger members between their twenties and forties, were becoming his best customers, in both his dry-cleaning business and his tailoring and alteration trade. It was mainly *their* money that was going toward the well-being of his family in Maida and his sister's dowry.

The clientele he had inherited from the previous owner had consisted primarily of older business and professional men from the local area, and their counterparts among the commuters—men generally in their late forties through sixties. Occasionally the wives of these men would accompany them to the shop, bringing in clothing of their own to be altered. Joseph's growing up under his grandfather Domenico had prepared him well for extending deference toward those reserved, serious, and rather frugal people. They wore suits until the material was threadbare, and would not pay the price of a cleaning unless their garments were noticeably soiled, insisting for the most part that their suits merely be pressed. And most often, that was all they needed. These were sober, careful men. The clothing they left in the shop showed no signs of liquor. Joseph doubted that any of them would set foot in the yacht club; he had certainly never overheard them, or their wives, making references to the club when they came into the shop, and he could not picture them as being compatible with the loud music and laughter that he often heard coming from the triple-decked building that he passed during his late-night walks along Bay Avenue. Joseph's clientele then was more in tune with Tabernacle music; he had recognized many of their surnames among those listed on the town plaque that identified the first families, and he had no doubt seen some of his customers in the distance when he had paused to watch the introduction of the town founder the Reverend Lake, and had heard the singing of the Doxology by those assembled under the cedar tree. They surely embodied the power behind the signs currently posted on the beach warning that it was no less illegal for men than women to appear without bathing tops; and from such people Joseph had intuited a sense of what God-fearing small-town America might have been like before World War I.

And yet with all their modesty, thriftiness, and standoffish manner, many of them had taken a personal interest in Joseph after becoming better acquainted with him through continuing visits to the shop. Often they asked him questions about where he had come from, why he had chosen to settle in Ocean City, what his goals were for the future; and, when he sought it, they had gladly offered their advice. In responding to their questions, Joseph himself realized that much of what he had left behind in Maida was what he had found appealing on this island; he had a natural affinity for small towns with old-fashioned values. And while these people had initially seemed cool to him as a stranger, this hardly was unusual to him as a native of Maida. He chose to believe that with such people an acceptance now withheld was, once attained, an acceptance that lasted.

If there was anything that had surprised him about these Americans who were so much older than he, it was probably that a majority of married couples who patronized his shop had retained much open affection for one another, revealing traces of romance he had never observed among late-middle-aged couples in Maida. For example, he often saw the Americans holding hands as they entered his shop (he had never seen the same along the streets of Maida or even Naples); and while he was kneeling or standing at the side of a woman with his tape measure and notebook, conducting a fitting as she posed rigidly on the pedestal, he would often catch a glimpse, in the three-sectioned mirror, of her husband watching proudly with an appreciative gleam in his eyes.

If this represented a positive side of married life to Joseph, he also became privy to its darker sides during his first years in business—marriage being a subject about which he had learned very little in his homeland of white widows and distant men. In America, where even the elderly couples expressed themselves more freely than people half their age in Maida, Joseph at times stood listening with embarrassment as couples argued openly in front of him, differing as to what Joseph should do, or should not do, with the garments they had brought in to be altered—but even Joseph, as naive as he then was, guessed that their feuding was based on something less visible than their clothing. He could almost feel their mutual hostility, and was amazed by the passion some of these older people could generate as they stubbornly insisted that Joseph do this or do that; and not infrequently they tried to draw him into the argument. Wary of exacerbating things by offering his opinion, he reacted with equanimity until he had guessed who was the stronger partner in the marriage. In Italy he would have almost automatically deferred to the men; but in America he was becoming acquainted with the forceful personalities of women. Whenever it seemed that the husband was about to yield, Joseph would quickly side with the wife; and if it was she on the pedestal being fitted for clothes, he would proceed to place the pins with special care, reassuring her constantly that she would be pleased with his final workmanship. Often by this time the husband had retired to a chair and sat with his back to the fitting, pointedly paying no further attention to his wife, engrossed in his newspaper, or blowing smoke rings across the room. At such moments Joseph sometimes felt the woman's tension rising through his tape measure.

But by 1926, after Joseph had begun his Suit Club, he started to have closer contacts with younger people who were more representative of postwar America. These were people who liked taking chances in his weekly raffle, and who indulged in social life at night, which provided many occasions for dressing up. Now, for the first time, Joseph saw women in the driver's seats of automobiles that pulled up to the curb near his shop. Unaccompanied by men, they often walked in with an armload of new dresses or coats they had purchased in Philadelphia that required alterations; or they came in to buy one-dollar weekly chances at a free suit.

When Joseph had first installed the sign in his window announcing the establishment of his Suit Club—through which, after paying a five-dollar initiation fee, members could spend one dollar to print their names and addresses on cards and place them, in unmarked envelopes, in a vase from which a winning envelope was drawn at week's end by an alternating member—he had made no reference to gender; it had not occurred to him that a woman might want to win a suit that she herself would wear. He assumed the woman with the lucky number would then order that a suit be made for her husband, father, or brother. Tailors did not make suits for women on the island. Some women with dressmakers in Philadelphia occasionally appeared on the island wearing skirts and jackets of matching fabric, but the skirts were usually full and the jackets often puff-sleeved, and they hardly imitated what Joseph would define as a man-tailored suit. In Paris he actually had seen a few women wearing masculine-styled attire—indeed, he had even seen women's suits with trousers instead of skirts—but Antonio said that these had been cut by couturieres, not tailors, and that the trouser-suited women in France were probably lesbians.

The first female to win the Suit Club raffle did so a few weeks before Christmas in 1926. She was a cigarette-smoking woman in her late twenties or early thirties; she had short dark hair that she seemed to have dyed with a reddish tint, a confident manner and spectacles that suggested an almost professorial air, and a voluptuous body about which she was not in the least self-conscious. Her posture was very erect and her shoulders were held back as she stood for the first time at Joseph's counter during the late summer, having brought in cocktail frocks to be cleaned and made ready for the Labor Day weekend; and although Joseph had no reason to believe she had seen him previously around town, she nonetheless assumed almost immediate familiarity with him, and by her second visit to his shop she was calling him Joe.

Her name was Elizabeth Townley. She had divorced her husband in Philadelphia and recently had taken a year-round residence in Ocean City, a bayside address near the yacht club. After she had bought three chances for the first week's raffle in December, she smiled as she left the shop, saying, "I hope you've brought me luck, Joe." When she received Joseph's postcard announcing that she had won, Mrs. Townley returned to the shop gleefully and asked to be shown some green wool fabric that might be flattering on her. She removed her topcoat and tossed it across the counter, and stood in her tight-fitting skirt and silk blouse waiting in an unhurried and pleasant manner.

"Mrs. Townley," Joseph asked awkwardly, "are you really planning to have a suit made for yourself?"

"Of course," she said. "You can make a woman's suit, can't you?"

"Certainly," he said. "I just thought you'd like a gift for your brother, or another man."

"None of them are worth it," she said. She leaned closer to the counter and pointed toward a bolt of green herringbone material stacked on the shelf behind him. "That's rather nice, Joe," she said. "Let's have a look at that." After he had placed it on the counter, Mrs. Townley began to stroke it softly, as if she were petting a cat; then she pinched it between her left index finger and thumb, and rubbed it briskly. "Yes, very nice," she said. "This will be fine. But you'll have to be quick about it, Joe, because I'll want the suit before I go away for Christmas."

Before he could respond, Mrs. Townley had walked toward the fitting room and stepped upon the pedestal. Joseph watched uncertainly as she stood waiting with her hands on her hips; the outline of her brassiere, supporting her prominent breasts, showed through her sheer silk blouse. Although she was fully clothed, she seemed more naked than the open-shirted Amazon lady Joseph had once seen working in the fields during the olive harvest. Blocking the memory from his mind, he took his tape measure and notebook and moved to a position behind Mrs. Townley, who, standing a foot above the floor, was dauntingly statuesque. Inhaling the fragrance of her perfume, and hearing her soft breath in this now very quiet room, he reached high with his left hand and placed the metal-tipped edge of the tape on the back of her neck. He held it there for a moment while the rest of the yellow tape, hastened by the lightly tapping fingers of his right hand, unfurled down her back and rested against her rump. He pinched the lower part of the tape at the point where he thought the bottom of the jacket should be, recorded this figure in his notebook, then paused before taking the next measurement. Had he been dealing with a man, Joseph would now have been standing in front of him, wrapping the tape around his chest and asking him to inhale and exhale. But Joseph had never taken such liberties with a woman—most of his previous experience with females had been in readjusting hemlines, sleeves, and the shoulders of their coats—and he had no idea about the rules of etiquette. But he certainly knew he could *not* face Mrs. Townley while looping the tape around her back and then pulling it forward to measure her bosom. So he remained behind her; and, in what he hoped was a professional tone of voice, he asked, "Mrs. Townley, would you mind raising your arms, please?"

She raised her arms over her head, reminding him of the drawbridge. He leaned forward and, trying not to bump his nose into her back, reached around her waist with his arms, then brought his hands together in front of her stomach momentarily while he secured the tape between his fingertips; and finally he raised the tape until he felt it grazing against her sturdy, silk-covered breasts. He arrived at what he thought was the farther point on both sides, and waited for Mrs. Townley to exhale, and then pulled back on the tape and placed the metal-tipped end he held in his left hand against the lowest number on the tape he held around her with his right hand. The tip practically touched the number 44. Despite his lack of experience in these matters, Joseph deduced that Mrs. Townley was enormous. Granting the physical differences between men and women in that area, Joseph was nonetheless aware that her chest size was nearly double his own. The tape slipped from his fingers and fell across her ankles. "Sorry," Joseph said, bending to pick it up. Mrs. Townley said nothing, and did not move.

With slightly less tentativeness, Joseph now extended the tape to measure her waist (38); then her hips (42). But his hands were perspiring, and he felt slightly dizzy. He had never really been alone with an American woman. In fact he could not remember being alone with *any* woman except the Amazon lady, and that had been in an open field where there had been ample room for his escape after she had caught him looking at her. In the shop he felt trapped. Mrs. Townley's body was definitely affecting him in a way he knew was sinful.

"May I lower my arms now?" she asked, softly.

"Of course, Mrs. Townley," he said, having forgotten about her arms. "I'm sorry."

"And how much longer will this be?" she asked, although she did not seem to be impatient.

"Just a few minutes," he said, kneeling to measure the width of the skirt she wore, deciding to use the same dimensions for the skirt of her suit. He wrote slowly in his book, not yet ready to stand and take the measurements for the sleeves. The room was so quiet and still that he could hear a fly buzzing within the front windows. It was probably the last survivor from the summer. Then he heard the welcome sound of the doorbell jingling and, leaning his head beyond Mrs. Townley's hips, he saw Harry Smith, the Ford dealer, standing in the doorway.

"I'll come back later, when you're not busy," Smith said, tilting forward and balancing himself against the outer doorknob that he held in hand.

"Come in, come in," Joseph said, relieved, "I'm just finishing."

A heavy, red-faced man in his forties wearing a plain brown fedora and a thick wool mackinaw of matching color, Smith almost stumbled in and then tipped his hat to Mrs. Townley, who stood with her back to him, but whose profile he saw reflected in a mirror.

"I see you're putting this young man to work," Smith said, settling himself in the chair nearest to the pedestal, placing his hat on his knee.

"Yes," she said flatly, not making eye contact.

"Is that *your* pretty Flint Six touring car I see parked in front?" he went on, watching closely as Joseph now stood alongside her, measuring an arm.

"No," she said.

"I'm trying to get our friend here to buy a car," Smith said with a grin. He pointed toward Joseph with his right hand shaped like a pistol, but his eyes remained on Elizabeth Townley.

"I told you, I need a license," Joseph said, with the tape around one of her wrists.

"Yes, I'll take care of that," Smith said. "But I'm here to say I've found the perfect car for you."

"You have?"

Joseph was actually interested. He had been thinking of buying a car for more than a year, but until Smith had come in a fortnight before, he had never discussed it. Smith had been in twice already this week. Each time he offered a car at a lower price. He was new in town, and very eager to make a sale.

"This is only five hundred," Smith said. "It's a handsome little Ford coupe. It's only a year old, and not a thing wrong with it. The guy who owns it needs a bigger car. He's leaving for Florida this week and wants to sell the coupe right away, and so I thought of you."

Five hundred dollars was an amount Joseph could afford. He had deprived himself of most comforts since arriving on the island. He lived in a small room behind the shop in order to avoid the cost of an apartment; and the more money he had earned in recent years, the more he had sent home to Italy. By now he had paid off his debts to the Rocchino uncles in Ambler, and had made the final payment to the shop's previous owner in Arizona. He had by now also taken so many trolley rides across the bay that he finally felt adequate to the challenge of steering himself through what was left of his hydrophobia.

Mrs. Townley stepped down from the pedestal, holding Joseph's hand momentarily. Smith lit up a cigarette and watched as she moved across the room to the counter. She immediately picked up her coat and put it on.

"I'll have the pattern cut for you by tomorrow night, Mrs. Townley," Joseph said, taking his place behind the counter, lighting a cigarette, and completing his notations in his book. "You can come in Monday for a first fitting. Then another fitting by Thursday, and within two weeks from today you'll have the suit."

"I appreciate that, Joe," she said, and with a smile she turned to leave. Joseph hurried around the counter to open the door, blocking Smith's view of Mrs. Townley as she went down the steps, moved in front of the window, and hurriedly walked up the street.

"Good-looking woman," Smith said.

Joseph ignored the comment as he closed the door.

"When can I see the car?" he asked.

"I can get it now," Smith said, quickly rising. "I'll be back in an hour. You can look it over and we can take a little ride. If you like it, we can go to the bank tomorrow. I'll get the papers ready for you, and give you a few driving lessons on Sunday. By the next weekend, you should be driving on your own."

Joseph said nothing, seeming hesitant, worried that things were moving too quickly.

"Look," Smith said, with sudden urgency, "if you don't take this car, somebody else will. You'll never find a car like this for five hundred, believe me. It's a fine car. The owner took care of it."

"All right," Joseph said. "Let me see it."

It was a navy blue coupe that had obviously been well maintained. Its silver bumpers glistened in the sunlight of this clear wintry afternoon, and its tires were not mud-splattered like those of the other cars parked on the street. Harry Smith sat in the driver's seat but leaned out the passenger-side window and he beckoned with a wave to Joseph watching from the store. As Joseph approached, Smith gunned the engine, honked the horn, and opened the door. Joseph already felt strangely possessive of the car that was his for the asking.

Five minutes after Smith had begun to drive him around in it, singing its praises while moving the gear stick like a baton, Joseph said, "All right, I'll take it. But let's get back to the shop." In his excitement for the ride, Joseph realized, he had left his shop unlocked.

"Oh, you're going to be happy with this car," Smith reassured him, pulling up to the curb. "It'll change your whole life."

The next morning, Joseph gave Smith the five hundred dollars he had withdrawn from the bank; and after placing the ownership document and bill of sale proudly in the drawer of his counter, he stood watching as Smith drove the car back to the agency's garage—where, three days hence, on Sunday after Mass, Joseph would appear for his first driving lesson.

Even before this much-anticipated event, Joseph sensed the truth in Smith's comment—Joseph's life *had* changed. Just *owning* a car opened up a world of possibilities, extending the dream that had driven him across the sea. Recently he had read that the Ford company in Detroit, which had produced as many as two hundred thousand vehicles in a month, had sold its ten millionth car, and that someone had driven it from New York to San Francisco. No less thrilling to Joseph would be his motorized maiden voyage two miles across the bay to Somers Point.

Joseph attended the ten-fifteen Mass the following Sunday. There were fewer than twenty people in the church, which was not unusual for the parish in wintertime; but the Christmas decorations around the altar, and the wood-carved Nativity scene, served as a happy reminder of the holiday ahead. It would mark the sixth anniversary of Joseph's arrival at Ellis Island. He remembered how distressed he had been at not being met by his uncles, who had not been able to come; but he would surely not forget the kindness of the interpreter who had escorted him through the stations at Ellis Island, and had finally put him on the train that had carried him into Philadelphia. But all that and Ambler now seemed as far away as Maida.

After Mass, Joseph had been offered a ride uptown by a retired fireman whom he knew from church. But Joseph preferred to walk. It was a brisk, sunny day. He was wearing for the first time a brown tweed overcoat he had recently made. After many months of parading around town, a solitary figure in his private *passeggiata,* he saw ahead of himself the end of his dependency on shoe leather.

He walked more than a mile through the center of town toward the Ford garage at the north end of the island, passing rows of boarded-up houses and closed shops, including his own. East toward the ocean, on the corners of Central and Wesley avenues, where the Methodist and Presbyterian churches were located, he saw crowds gathered on the sidewalks and cars moving slowly in search of parking spaces. Four blocks beyond the grounds of the Tabernacle, on a residential street of white Victorian rooming houses and bungalows, stood a two-story tan brick building with a fan-shaped façade and a Ford emblem in the brickwork. Despite the Sabbath restrictions, the large sliding doors were wide open, and as Joseph entered, he saw a mechanic leaning under the open hood of a truck, and the feet of another man sticking out from beneath the bumper of a vehicle with its motor idling. The glassed-in office in the corner was unoccupied, and there was no sign of Harry Smith. But as Joseph paused and looked around, he thought he recognized his car parked among the models that were lined along the wall of the garage. In the rear he heard two male voices engaged in an argument; one man was dressed in gray overalls and a peaked cap, and the other wore a jacket and tie and was smoking a cigar. Joseph hesitated before approaching. But the cigar-smoking man stopped arguing as he noticed Joseph, and with a smile he came forward and asked: "And what can I do for you, young man?"

He had a jowly face with a pencil-thin moustache and black shiny hair combed straight back, and on the lapel of his jacket was pinned a card bearing his name in bold lettering: *Jack Ward, Mgr.*

"I'm here to meet Mr. Harry Smith," Joseph said.

"He left," said Ward.

"Left?" Joseph repeated with surprise and disappointment. "Well, when will he be back?"

"He won't," Ward said. "He left for good. Picked up his salary last night and quit. Said he was off to Florida."

Stunned with disbelief, Joseph shook his head.

"But may *I* show you something?" Ward asked eagerly with raised eyebrows. "We've just received some terrific buys."

"I already *bought* a car from you people!" Joseph cried out, pulling from his coat pocket his sales receipt and registration document, and handing them to the manager. Ward studied the papers momentarily, and looking back at Joseph he nodded and said, "Yes, indeed, you got yourself a terrific buy. You bought Harry's old car."

Joseph frowned.

"But I can't drive it!" he said. "Harry Smith promised to teach me, and now he's gone."

"Yes," said Ward, "and if that bastard ever returns, we won't take him back. I can promise you that."

"What do I care?" Joseph asked, becoming angrier. "I'm stuck with a car I can't drive. Now what am I supposed to do?"

"That damned Harry Smith!" Ward exclaimed, wanting to be a commiserator, not a problem solver.

"Mr. Ward," Joseph demanded, "you must help me."

"But what can *I* do?"

"Help me drive it."

"But you don't have a license or permit," Ward said. "You'll need a driving instructor, and he'll make the arrangements. I *do* know some instructors, and tomorrow I'll give them a call and see what they can do."

"I work tomorrow," Joseph said. "I want to start today."

"They don't work on Sundays."

Joseph felt the adrenaline rising in his body.

"Look," Joseph said firmly, "this *is* my car, isn't it?"

"Oh, yes," Ward said. "It's fully paid for, and you're the registered owner."

"So why don't you just start it for me, and I'll learn by myself?"

"But you might kill yourself, and I can't be responsible."

"*I'll* be responsible," Joseph said. "You just start the car, and I'll get in."

"But if it's on our property, I'll *still* be responsible."

"So drive it across the street, and leave it there. I saw how Harry Smith moved the gear stick and the pedals, and it didn't look hard."

"You know," Ward said, reflecting in a wistful manner, "that's how *I* learned to drive. Back in the boonies behind Somers Point, where nobody ever drove with a license—and *still* doesn't—I took my brother-in-law's tin lizzie one day when he was away, and I learned in a half-hour."

"Fine," Joseph said, "so let's get going."

Ward hesitated for a moment, then turned toward the mechanic with whom he had been arguing.

"Hey, Billy Bob," he yelled. "Take that coupe parked there in number eight and leave it across the street for this young man."

The mechanic glared at Jack Ward and muttered under his breath; but after taking a rag from a truck fender, and wiping his hands, Billy Bob slowly made his way toward Joseph's coupe and did as he had been told. Joseph walked behind the car as Billy Bob drove it out, while Jack Ward, with a farewell wave, headed toward the rear of the garage, beyond view of what might happen in the street.

"You know where first and second is?" Billy Bob asked Joseph, after he had pulled the car against the curb and left the door open.

"Yes," said Joseph. "First is up, and second is back, right?"

"Yep," said Billy Bob, "and you know where the clutch and brake is?"

"I think so," said Joseph.

Billy Bob then waved Joseph into the driver's seat, closed the door behind him, and returned to the garage without turning back.

Joseph sat momentarily behind the steering wheel, feeling the vibrations of the engine, looking out the windshield toward an empty two-lane macadam road that seemed to extend to infinity, but actually led toward the Coast Guard station along the sandy tip of the island. He also looked through his rearview mirror and out both sides of the vehicle to be certain there was no one in sight to witness his initiation into the motorized age. Resting his feet lightly on the pedals without applying pressure, and reminding himself that he had to push the clutch pedal to the floor and then let it up slowly as he stepped down on the gas pedal—fortunately Harry Smith had illustrated this before fleeing to Florida—Joseph quickly said a prayer and then accepted the challenge of trying to imitate his truant teacher.

The car bolted forward jerkily, choking and sputtering. Joseph slammed his foot down on the clutch and shifted to neutral while holding tightly to the wheel with his left hand, watching wide-eyed as the vehicle rolled on and on for nearly half a block on its own momentum. He sat expectantly until the car came to a halt, idling. After waiting several moments to regain his composure and review the routine, he again stepped down on the clutch pedal and applied the gas—and once more he felt himself being bounced as the car bucked itself forward indecisively. He gave it more gas, and, instead of choking, the engine gurgled as it ingested into its finicky funnels what sounded like the bubbly soda pop he saw squirted from the fountain behind the counter of his favorite restaurant. The engine, soothed by the liquid, hummed with a mellowness similar to what he had heard when Harry Smith had been driving.

Proceeding at a speed he believed equal to Smith's, he looked up into the rearview mirror and saw the empty road behind him, and parts of white houses, and he realized that the Ford garage was now so far behind it was nowhere in sight. Redirecting his attentions to the road ahead, Joseph saw in the distance a little black box kicking up clouds of sand as it sped toward him. With a tingling sensation shooting up through his spine, Joseph braced himself, felt his palms moisten on the wheel, but did not slow down, for he feared he might slide on the sandy road if he applied the brakes at his present speed.

Not daring to look again at the oncoming car, but sensing its swift advancement from the rising sounds of its rattling engine, Joseph kept his eyes focused on the road's center line; and except for veering slightly toward the shoulder to leave maximum room for the other vehicle, he left his fate in the hands of Saint Francis and the operator of the oncoming car, hoping that the latter was a licensed and qualified driver who had enough sense to stay on his own side of the line.

After a streaking black shadow, a great *whoosh* and a buffeting gust of wind, and the lash of sand across his windshield and hood, Joseph realized that he again had the road to himself. Except for his surprise at being blown a bit closer to the shoulder—he quickly adjusted by taking aim behind his left fender and steering selfishly to the center of the road—Joseph felt himself fully in control; and with renewed confidence he proceeded northward along the road flanked by dunes and now over-looked by the skeletal steel tower of the local Coast Guard station. As Joseph followed the curved road that directed him west of the tower, passing along the way a wall of brown rocks being splashed by waves, he came upon a paved and abandoned circle, a recently completed roadway apparently built to accommodate a cluster of new homes perhaps already sold from the developer's drawing board. Joseph adopted this as his train-ing ground, and, in the splendid isolation invaded only by the swooping sea gulls, he practiced every aspect of motormanship. He abruptly stopped, started, and stopped again, getting the feel of the brakes. He learned to shift the gears back and forth with a minimum of grinding. And he also shifted into reverse, and moved slowly backward and parked along the wayside weeds between imaginary rows of vehicles.

Time passed quickly as he deepened his acquaintanceship with his automobile on this remote edge of the island; and as the light above the distant Coast Guard tower became visible in the early darkness of the wintry afternoon, Joseph discovered his own light switch on the dash-board, flipped it, and proceeded to test himself. He drove around the cir-cle again and again, each time taking the turns faster, more sharply. Finally he continued on without turning and headed back to the main road and the more populated part of the island. He felt very daring, very illegal, very American.

42.

EACH FRIDAY AT noon, Joseph entrusted his shop to Mister Bossum for at least an hour so that he might enjoy the leisurely lunch he allowed himself only once a week at the same small restaurant across from City Hall where he nearly always ate his breakfast at seven a.m. and his dinner at nine p.m.—except on Friday nights, when he did without dinner be-cause of the demands of his business. On Friday nights the customers who entered his shop represented seventy percent of his weekly income. Many were Suit Club members who waited until then to bring in their clothing for cleaning or alterations because at the same time they could wager a few dollars on the weekly drawing, which was held promptly at eight. On some golden Fridays in August, when the town overflowed with vacationers, Joseph's glass vase was stuffed with about three hundred dollars' worth of envelopes awaiting a vigorous shake and then the pick for a free suit that Joseph would have retailed for less than fifty dollars. In addition to club members, on Friday nights his shop was frequented by weekend visitors carrying in clothing to be cleaned and/or pressed by the following day—an overnight process for which most of them uncomplainingly paid twice the cost of the normal two- or three-day service. On Friday nights Joseph usually went to bed late, feeling very hungry but rich.

One Friday, as Joseph sat in a booth having lunch, he was surprised to see Mister Bossum hastily crossing the street and heading toward the restaurant.

"Who's minding the store?" Joseph called out, as Mister Bossum entered.

"Your cousin," Mister Bossum said. "He came in, and he's waiting to see you."

"My cousin from Paris?" Joseph asked with astonishment, not believing that Antonio would have traveled so far unannounced.

"No, your cousin from Brooklyn," Mister Bossum said. "He's a tall, good-looking guy with his hair slicked back. Can't remember his name, but he said he's traveling with a band, and they played last night at some club across the bay. He said he's gotta see you, it's urgent, and he's gotta catch a train."

Joseph guessed that the visitor was his trombone-playing cousin Nicholas Pileggi, the son of one of his mother's sisters in the valley, the sister who married the butcher who ran a card game in the back of his shop. When Joseph was last in Italy, the butcher's son was a member of a concert orchestra in Catanzaro; but Joseph had heard from his uncles in Ambler that Nicholas had since moved to New York, and was traveling around the country playing in dance bands and also working in the orchestra pits of Broadway theaters. Joseph had followed up with a letter to Nicholas's boardinghouse in Brooklyn, and Nicholas had replied with a postcard from Buffalo, and then another from Scranton, and then a third from Pittsburgh, all promising that he would soon be visiting him in Ocean City. Two years passed and, except for an exchange of Christmas cards, the cousins remained out of touch; in fact, the last time Joseph had actually spent time with Nicholas was during their boyhood days as Young Socialists in Maida, while marching in antiwar rallies more than a decade before. Joseph recalled in particular the night when they had joined the mob that destroyed the village streetlights, smashed the windows of the municipal building, and torched the town records in an effort to thwart the military conscriptors.

World War I had ended before Joseph and Nicholas had reached draft age, and their respective apprenticeships in clothing and music had carried them in different directions during their late teens; but Joseph nonetheless felt closer to Nicholas than to his other contemporaries on his mother's side of the family, and he only hoped that Nicholas was not bringing bad news. Joseph had never before had a kinsman visit him in Ocean City, and while he walked with Mister Bossum toward the shop he remained quiet and expectant.

But his cousin was all smiles as he rushed out of the shop to embrace Joseph on the sidewalk, kissing him on both cheeks to the wonderment of a few local pedestrians, and pounding him heavily on the back.

"I'm getting married," he announced, "and you have to come to Brooklyn for the wedding. I'm marrying a terrific girl, but her father thinks I'm a worthless vagabond, and I need you to convince him I'm better than he thinks, even if I'm not."

Nicholas apologized for the suddenness of his visit, and the fact that he had to take the next trolley back to Atlantic City to make the late-afternoon train to New York with the band. But being so close to Ocean City, he had seized the opportunity to express in person how much he was relying on Joseph's attendance at the wedding. "You're the only cousin I have in this country," he said, "and the girl I'm marrying has a very large family, and also a father who's a sonofabitch. He came over from Maida as a carriage driver, and now he's a chauffeur for some rich guy in Brooklyn. He also operates a garage with lots of trucks. His name is Dominic di Paola, but everybody calls him Rosso because of his red hair. I think he had somebody else in mind for his daughter, but she told him it's me or nobody. 'Then it's nobody,' he tells her, but she doesn't care what he thinks. She's as determined and stubborn as he is. She's also a redhead. Her name is Susan."

Susan di Paola was the second of six children born in America to Rosso and his second wife, Angelina. Angelina was a matronly dark-eyed brunette who at nineteen had been left a childless widow in Maida after her husband's death from malaria; but three years later, in 1902, Angelina was brought to America by a matchmaking uncle in Brooklyn who wanted her to marry his friend Rosso—a self-proclaimed widower who had been married in Maida in 1884 to a woman named Rosaria. Rosso and Rosaria had two sons and the added expense of caring for her ailing father—which necessitated Rosso's coming alone to America to earn more for their support. But during the year Rosso expected his wife and sons to join him in America (her father having since died), she became pregnant with the child of a middle-aged bachelor, a member of one of Maida's last noble families. That she and the sons would thereafter remain in the village, very much alive if discontent in the household of a destitute nobleman, did not deter Rosso from imagining them dead, indeed, *more* than dead; he convinced himself that Rosaria and his sons had hardly ever existed.

And yet Rosso contradicted his emotions by bearing on his clothing black symbols of mourning for his "dead" family in Italy. The suit he wore when he was introduced to Angelina in 1902 had a black ribbon on the lapel. There were black bands around the sleeves of the shirts and sweaters he wore in the garage. His manner, however, was always lacking in grief. The cuckoldry that would have inflamed most Italian men had left Rosso cold, very cold; his dispassion toward his first wife more than matched her passion for the nobleman. Rosso did not even trouble himself to divorce her legally. His marriage to Angelina in America was sanctified by a priest to whom a substantial bequest to his church was apparently sufficient atonement for bigamy.

Rosso considered himself religious, although he rarely attended Mass; he saw priests as little better than their penitents—an impression confirmed by the unconfessed and secret priest who had married him to Angelina. Rosso identified his religiosity in his fancied exclusive alliance with a fellow sufferer, now in heaven, the ascetic monk born in the southern Italian village where Rosso's own forebears had originated, Paola. Saint Francis of Paola had understood and preached against sexual sin throughout his long lifetime—as a young monk he had once jumped into an icy pond rather than stand close to an alluring woman—and if the nobleman in Maida had done likewise instead of seducing Rosso's wife, or most likely being seduced *by* his wife (Rosso could *not* forget her lustful nature), Rosso's subsequent distrust of females might have been less obsessive. In any case, he came to see women as born seductresses—the instigators in nearly all the extramarital affairs of which he would become privy as the coachman, and later the chauffeur, of many well-to-do men and their mistresses. In Rosso's world, women were soon perceived as existing either on a pedestal or in the gutter. *Puttana*—whore—was the word he came to use in referring to his first wife, on those infrequent occasions when he referred to her at all. And the main reason why Rosso felt he could speak so boldly toward his boss, the otherwise proud and authoritarian Prussian millionaire Frederick Ochse—owner of rental residences and garages in lower Manhattan and Brooklyn—was Rosso's knowledge of Mr. Ochse's infidelities with New York showgirls and other women who conformed to Rosso's definition of a *puttana*.

This moral superiority that he assumed over his boss, and the fact that Ochse tolerated Rosso's curt and sometimes abusive manner so benignly that Rosso believed he probably enjoyed it, convinced Rosso that he would never be fired from his job, no matter what he said to his employer (so long as he said it privately, as he invariably did), and so long as he continued to serve Ochse in two other ways: by managing Ochse's main garage in Brooklyn with honesty and efficiency (Rosso never stole a penny, never lost a customer), and by remaining promptly available to drive Ochse wherever he wished to be taken, including to the Brooklyn apartment of a blonde whom Ochse began to visit regularly during the early years of Rosso's marriage to Angelina.

Although Rosso loathed this duty more than any other, and always filled Ochse's ears along the way with tirades against the latter's predilection for tarts, Rosso went where he was told to go, and he waited alone in the car parked two stories below the lowered shades of the woman's bedroom window (her husband was conveniently on night duty as a waterfront warehouse guardsman), until her stocky little Prussian lover made his meek exit down the staircase to the street, adjusting his bowler as he entered the car, smelling of perfume, knowing from experience that on such voyages he would be expected to open and close his own door. Then Rosso would start up the engine and drive with a particular recklessness that he reserved for these outings, racing through Brooklyn's Prospect Park section toward the brownstone manor where Ochse lived with his wife and children, and brooking no criticism en route about the handling of the car. During such rides Rosso would in fact look into the rearview mirror and stare at Ochse, waiting for some backseat comment that would afford him the opportunity to respond with renewed invective; but Ochse usually sat quietly with his head lowered, seeming appropriately contrite.

Rosso lived two blocks away from Frederick Ochse's home, on a narrow street, Sterling Place, in an old Irish neighborhood into which a few Jewish and Italian families had recently moved. Rosso dwelled rent-free in an eleven-room apartment above Ochse's forty-car garage. None of Rosso's other children could sneak down the squeaky staircase that extended between the apartment and the sidewalk, via the interior wall flanking one side of the garage, with the quiet cunning of young Susan. She knew precisely the location of the spots on the staircase that did *not* squeak, and thus she choreographed a route through which she could tiptoe to freedom whenever she wished, always unheard by her father in the garage—a man whose sensitive auditory organs, heightened by his suspicious nature, usually allowed him to hear each drop of oil that dripped into the metal pans beneath all the cars and trucks parked under his care.

It went without saying that *if* Susan returned home directly from school, which she did infrequently, she would soon sneak out again, most often going to the neighborhood cinema to enjoy a double feature. As a countermeasure against such transgressions, Rosso insisted that she take a job after school folding boxes at a pastry shop across the street, owned by a baker friend whose two trucks were parked overnight in the garage (where the baker's nephews often borrowed them for predawn bootlegging deliveries); but Susan soon quit the job *and* school, accepting at the age of sixteen a full-time job as a trainee with the Bell Telephone Company in Brooklyn, a position she acquired with the help of her loud and penetrating voice.

Since the telephone lines during the 1920s were often feeble and charged with static, Bell's personnel department was always in search of young women with strong vocal cords to compensate for the frail cords of the company; and any candidate who was in the least bit shy, or who communicated in an understated manner, or who was otherwise indistinctive with vowels and consonants, was usually rejected after a one-day test; but seconds after Susan had opened her mouth, she was welcomed into the bosom of the Bell branch in Brooklyn—and it mattered little that her father ranted and raved for weeks, protesting that the women hired by the telephone company were without exception *puttane.*

Susan became an information operator. This demanding assignment required not only vocal strength but also sharp eyesight and nimble fingers which, covered with rubber tips, had to flip quickly through the alphabetized lists of names in the master book; then, after the desired number had been located, the operator was expected to relay it to the customer with such clarity that it could be immediately understood even when the lines were scrambled with static. The operators were trained to speak in staccato sound bites, to enunciate, ee-*nun*-cee-ate, the numbers in such a way that "four" sounded like "fo-wer," and "five" was "fy-yiv," and "seven" was "sev-ven," and "nine" was "ny-yen." Not only numbers, but the language in general was enunciated in this exaggerated manner by the operators, even when they were off duty at home with their families; and the di Paola family in Brooklyn, thanks to the syllabicating Susan, had another dialect added to the household, the Bell-induced dialect that she passed on to her younger sisters and brother, who began calling her "Su-Zand."

Susan was promoted rapidly, becoming an assistant supervisor after one year, and *the* supervisor of the daytime switchboard in Brooklyn after two and a half years, with two assistants reporting to her. Her salary increased to a degree that even her father could not quarrel with her weekly contribution to household expenses, although he had no idea that she was privately pocketing a third of the cash that was originally contained in the envelope she turned in each Saturday as her total salary. But morals were more important than money to Rosso; and when one day in 1927 his baker friend across the street reported that Susan had been seen walking home from work accompanied by a young man—a man identified by one of the baker's bootlegging nephews as a trombone player employed at a nightclub the nephew serviced (this same nephew, incidentally, had been rejected by Susan after he had made advances in the back of the bakery when she had been employed there folding boxes)—Rosso angrily decided to station himself outside the telephone building the next day in hopes of catching Susan with her consort, and terminating instantly their relationship before they became more involved. On the following day, however, Susan had no plans to meet the trombonist, Nicholas Pileggi, on the sidewalk after work; but before leaving the building she *had* caught a glimpse of her father standing behind his car three stories below, the limousine parked at the curb across from the telephone company's main door. So instead of leaving for home through the front door, as she normally did, she exited through a service entrance in the rear of the lobby, and followed an alternative route back to her neighborhood, her father meanwhile lurking behind his car for another hour, a stranded and frustrated spy.

When he returned to the apartment, Rosso screamed on seeing his daughter seated at the kitchen table reading a tabloid.

"Where were *you?*" he demanded. But she immediately jumped to her feet, pointed an accusing finger, and spoke in a tone so strident that it brought the rest of the family rushing into the room: "You were *spy*-ing on me!" she said. "And that is dis-*gust*-ing."

Rosso stared at her uncomprehendingly for a moment, while his wife and children stood between them, looking at one another in silence. Finally Rosso turned toward Angelina, saying some curse words in dialect, and then with a shrug left the kitchen and headed back down to the garage.

"I'm getting married," Susan then announced to her older sister, Theresa, who had been keeping her distance in the corner. "And *he* is not in-vite-ted."

Theresa interpreted the news to her mother, who removed a handkerchief from her apron pocket and began to cry. Susan's younger sister Catherine, who was twenty, also began to cry, while fifteen-year-old Julia and thirteen-year-old Lena jumped up and down, cheering.

"Am I invited?" Julia asked.

"Cer-tain-ly," Susan replied. "Everybody is *in-vite-ted,* except *him!*" She pointed down toward the floor. "*Him,* he stays home!"

"Oh, you can't do that," Theresa said, imploringly.

"*Ha!*" replied Susan.

The marriage of Susan di Paola and Nicholas Pileggi was set for December 4, 1927, at a Catholic church in the Park Slope section of Brooklyn, a few blocks from Rosso's garage. The couple had accumulated enough money between them to pay for the wedding, and the cost of the reception would be minimal: a nightclub owner friendly to Nicholas would donate the food and beverages, and Nicholas's colleagues in the band would provide the music. After considerable pleading from her mother and sisters (the older two threatened to boycott the wedding if Susan persisted in excluding their father), Susan finally relented. But since initially she had not sought his permission to get married, thereby depriving her father of an opportunity to deny it, he coolly rebuffed her.

So she decided to ask her only brother, John, a robust young man of seventeen, to escort her to the altar. John di Paola was never known to deny a favor to any of his sisters, although outside the family he had a reputation for being brusque and bellicose. As a boy he had tied his mother's heaviest flatirons to the ends of a broken broomstick to form a piece of weightlifting equipment, and then had built up his body for the combative days that he foresaw for himself, and that he would help to provoke. His formal education at Brooklyn's P.S. 9 had ended with his punching a seventh-grade teacher who had called him "dago"; after his expulsion he had spent most of his time at Stillman's Gymnasium on Eighth Avenue in Manhattan, working with a trainer who believed he could become a leading welterweight or middleweight contender. Although John appeared to be fulfilling his potential as a knockout puncher in Golden Gloves competition, and in his early professional bouts in small arenas where he was billed as "the Kid from Park Slope," the nasal surgery that he underwent after his bloodiest triumph left him with the option of retiring from the ring with his profile preserved, or continuing his pugilistic career and risking the possibility that the plastic bridging within his nose would become shattered in such a way as to induce retinitis and vision impairment.

John chose to retire, but reluctantly, because now he had fewer excuses for absenting himself from his father's garage, where his presence was demanded as an attendant, a car washer, and his father's replacement to drive Mr. Ochse two nights a week to the *puttana*—to say nothing of having to drive *her* on occasions when she had heavy shopping to do in Brooklyn or across the bridge in lower Manhattan. More dangerous if less boring to John was having to drive one of the bakery trucks late at night to deliver cargo to a pier on the Brooklyn side of the East River—substituting for the baker's nephew while the latter recovered from gunshot wounds in the legs. John would learn that the baker's trucks were intruding into the bootlegging territory of the gangster Dutch Schultz and, before he resettled himself full-time in Chicago, of Al Capone.

In an effort to escape the drudgery, the servitude, and the bullets that came with working in Rosso's garage, a month before his sister's wedding John had applied to Bell Telephone for a job as a lineman. One of the business executives who parked his sedan in the garage said he could get John hired, and did; and had it been necessary, Susan stood ready to use her influence within her division of the company as a means of returning John's favor in escorting her to the altar. But days before the wedding, and without explanation, Rosso abruptly changed his mind: he would be attending after all! So after Angelina had sponged and pressed her husband's coachman's morning coat and striped trousers, which he had last worn to their wedding twenty-five years before, and after he had loaded up the limousine with his wife, the four bridesmaids, and the bride, Rosso drove them to the church—where he later accompanied Susan up the aisle, two incongruous redheads impelled by circumstances briefly to follow the same path.

There were nearly two hundred people in attendance, most of them Brooklyn Italians with ties to Maida, but there were also a number of young women from Irish and Jewish families who were Susan's coworkers at the telephone company, in addition to several of Rosso's customers from the garage, who provided the enthusiasm that Rosso lacked on witnessing the first marriage of his five daughters. The baker was there with his wife and her widowed sister (the mother of the baker's nephew who got shot); and also present was Angelina's uncle who had introduced her to Rosso in 1902, and the uncle's thirty-year-old son, who had provided the bridal party with flowers from his floral shop and who had already gained distinction within the family for his habit of wearing steel-lined black hats.

Near the front of the church, behind the bridal party, sat Mr. and Mrs. Frederick Ochse, who initially had *not* been invited by Susan (how could she invite *them,* and not their *driver,* her father?); but after Rosso had invited himself, Susan had dispatched her sister Catherine to the Ochses' manor to urge them personally to attend while at the same time apologizing that their invitation had gotten lost because of brother John's carelessness while posting it earlier—to which Mrs. Ochse responded: "Yes, that sounds just like John." She had been recently upset with him when, shortly before dinner guests of hers were to arrive, he delivered a box of groceries to her home that she had *not* ordered. She would have been *more* upset had she known that what she had ordered had been mistakenly left by John at the apartment of her husband's mistress.

Mrs. Ochse's opinion of John was in contrast to the affection she extended to his sister Catherine, who was the prettiest and most shy of the five di Paola sisters, and the one whom Mrs. Ochse most often welcomed into the manor to play with her two daughters who were close to Catherine's age. Catherine happened to be in the manor when Mrs. Ochse received the tragic news that her two older children, a son and daughter, had both drowned off the Irish coast while traveling with their guardian to Liverpool, after the passenger ship they were on, the *Lusitania,* was sunk by a German submarine on the assumption that the British liner was armed and heavily loaded with explosives. The incident had occurred in early May 1915, shortly after Catherine's eighth birthday; and although the tearful Frederick Ochse had repeatedly read aloud in the living room the sad telegram he had received from the Cunard office in Britain, and despite the radio announcements and newspaper headlines that continuously publicized the disaster, Mrs. Ochse refused to acknowledge the loss of their children, insisting that they had somehow escaped the fate that had taken the lives of nearly twelve hundred others on board.

In the years that followed, Mrs. Ochse would always tell Catherine that the missing children would surely be discovered alive and well; and although she once pleaded with Catherine to take home the doll that had been her dead daughter's favorite—a large, beautifully dressed china doll that Catherine would cherish for the rest of her life—Mrs. Ochse would never part with any of the two children's clothing, even while conceding that they had long before outgrown everything. Often while Catherine played in the manor with the younger daughters, she would notice the elegant gray-haired Mrs. Ochse sitting alone in the parlor knitting large-sized sweaters that, she let it be known, she was hastening to finish before her two older children's return. Sometimes Catherine would see Mrs. Ochse sitting with her eyes closed, and with no ball of wool in her lap; and yet her hands were still busy, knitting now with imaginary needles.

After witnessing Susan's church wedding, Mrs. Ochse said she did not feel well enough to attend the reception, whereupon Catherine accompanied her home with Mr. Ochse, with John doing the driving. Then Catherine and John joined the other celebrants at a rented hall for dinner and dancing. It was there that Catherine met the groom's dapper cousin, the tailor from New Jersey.

43.

JOSEPH TRAVELED TO the wedding in a secondhand Buick roadster in mint condition that he had purchased for $975 after junking his exhausted and disfigured Ford, which he had sideswiped against a stalled trolley. The Buick had a turquoise body with black fenders, a new set of tires with mahogany-spoked wheels, a rumble seat that the previous owner had furnished with a fur blanket and a flask, and a Rolls-Royce hood ornament that had somehow come into the possession of Mister Bossum, who had screwed it on the day before Joseph's departure for Brooklyn.

Delighted with the gift, Joseph motored northward with his eyes peering over the upraised wings of the silver statuette, feeling airborne throughout the five-hour journey—gliding over the misty marshlands, hovering below the clouds through the north Jersey highlands, swooping down into the newly opened Holland Tunnel, then soaring up again between the steel cables of the Brooklyn Bridge. His spirit was still soaring as he made his way back on the following day; but the reason now was Catherine, with whom he had danced almost exclusively throughout the reception, to the chagrin of the saxophone player who had met her a month earlier through Nicholas Pileggi and had greatly fancied her. But she had already agreed to see Joseph again on the following weekend, which was all Joseph had thought about during the 135-mile journey back to the island—not noticing until he had arrived that someone in Brooklyn had stolen the winged figure off the hood.

Joseph mourned it briefly and replaced it with the plainer ornament that had come with the Buick, and traveled no less blithely to Brooklyn on the next Sunday in time to meet Catherine at noon outside the church where Susan had been married. He and Catherine took a slow ride through Prospect Park and had lunch at a small restaurant overlooking the East River, and thus began a series of Sunday meetings that would continue throughout 1928. Each rendezvous ended before late afternoon, as both Joseph and Catherine had to be up early for work on Monday (Catherine was in her third year at Abraham & Straus's dress department in Brooklyn, and had recently been promoted to assistant buyer), and the couple also preferred to keep their Sunday arrangements private and beyond the criticism of her father.

But perhaps Susan's earlier confrontation with Rosso had resigned him to the futility of trying to regulate romance; and if he had any knowledge that Catherine was seeing Joseph, he never questioned her about it, nor did he indicate anything but indifference to her announcement within the household during the Christmas holidays of 1928 that she and Joseph planned to marry in the following June.

"Do you know what you're doing?" Rosso asked her in the same tone of voice he might well have directed to a stranger threatening to jump off a cliff.

"Yes," Catherine said.

"Then do it," he said somberly, in what passed for his permission.

Catherine married Joseph on June 8, 1929, in the church where Susan had been married, and in front of many of the same people—except instead of telephone company personnel, there were A&S employees who two evenings earlier had given Catherine a farewell party after work in the store. Rosso escorted Catherine up the aisle as stiffly as he had Susan, and later he placed in Joseph's car a gift-wrapped short-wave radio, which was the same wedding present he had given Susan, and would give to his son and three other daughters when they too would marry.

When Catherine said good-bye to her family and friends after the reception, there was no doubt in her mind that she was distancing herself most likely forever from all that had been familiar, but she showed no signs of regret. She welcomed the chance to escape the claustrophobic feelings she had long known as one of six children in an oppressive Italo-

American family—she was the third born, but always the first to close her door, often preferring the company of her gift doll from the manor to that of her sisters above the garage.

Mrs. Ochse had convinced her that the world was larger than Brooklyn, but Catherine had not ventured much beyond her borough until the twilight of her wedding day, when she rode next to her husband in the roadster as it passed the gleaming tiles of the Holland Tunnel, then rumbled through small rustic towns with Indian names, the automobile's headlights flashing now and then on stray dogs and deer ambling along the tree-lined roadside, and later illuminating the fog that floated across the last bridge leading to the island that would become her home and retreat. Here everyone spoke English; the Protestants were predominant; the grocer sold only sliced white bread; women drove cars and were as socially forthright as the men. It was the New World to Catherine, and for the first time she felt more like a United States citizen than a resident of an ethnic neighborhood. She soon learned to drive. She registered to vote. And she applied for a bank loan so that she could open a dress shop next to her husband's tailor shop, and she was prevented from getting it only because the local bank suddenly closed in the wake of the financial crash of 1929. And yet she remained optimistic during the Depression years, so that when her first child, a son, was born in February 1932, in a small white house that she and her husband fortunately had paid off without a mortgage, she insisted that their son not answer to the name of his Italian grandfather Gaetano, but should be known instead by the more American and cheerful-sounding "Gay."

When she accompanied her husband and child to Ambler, however, which she did every few months so Joseph could visit his maternal uncles, the Rocchinos, who worked at Keasbey & Mattison, her optimism and contentment as a young mother were jarred by the grim effects of the Depression on the factory workers and their families. Catherine saw bread lines along Ambler's sidewalks, saw workers in dusty overalls carrying picket signs outside the Keasbey & Mattison headquarters building, saw women and children gathered around the iron gates of the castle screaming at the guards and barking dogs within. The town was on the brink of bankruptcy, Joseph told her, and during each visit to his uncles' boardinghouse—which was now only half occupied—the news seemed to worsen.

Nearly half of the two thousand asbestos workers had been laid off before Christmas 1933, and hundreds more would be dismissed within the following year. Those still on the payroll received salary reductions;

and even though Joseph's uncles were senior employees, their jobs too were taken away. One disgruntled countryman from Maida who was out of work had sent word to immigration authorities in Philadelphia that the Rocchino brothers had illegally reentered the United States after World War I, in order to bypass the restrictive postwar quota on Italians coming through Ellis Island. The Rocchinos had indeed slipped into the United States via Canada, and after being summoned before an immigration board they were both found guilty of illegal entry and marked for deportation to Italy. Although they were now without work, the Rocchinos were too proud to accept financial help from Joseph, but they did welcome his offer to appeal their eviction to the Italian consul general in Philadelphia and to a United States congressman whose district embraced South Philadelphia's Italian ghetto. Joseph's efforts, however, were unsuccessful. His uncles were given a month to settle their affairs in Ambler before surrendering to the agent who would ship them back to where they came from.

Dr. Richard V. Mattison himself was in the process of being forcibly relocated from his castle and losing control of the company as a result of a series of economic and other misfortunes visited upon him even from within his own family. Although it occurred many months before the Depression, the death in 1927 of Dr. Mattison's first son, Richard Jr., at forty-six, would signal the start of the doctor's financial nightmares, burdening him in 1928 with a very costly equity suit prompted by his son's vengeful widow, forty-four-year-old Georgette, who attributed her late husband's alcoholism to his father's overbearing nature, and who further charged the doctor with deliberate executive mismanagement that denied large profits to the stockholders (she being one of them), and with misappropriation of company funds for his own use in the amount of several million dollars.

Even before her husband's death, which had been preceded by periods of hospitalization, Georgette Mattison had privately communicated her misgivings about the doctor to his expatriate partner in the south of France, Henry G. Keasbey. Keasbey at first paid no attention to her complaints, for it was generally known that she drank nearly as much as her husband, and that her opinions regarding Dr. Mattison were tainted by a personal malice she had often expressed about him in public during her thirteen years of marriage to his son. Georgette, in marrying, saw herself as entering into a nouveau riche industrial family headed by a social-climbing physician whose first son, her husband, was his father's senior vice-president and heir apparent. Only after her wedding did she realize that her husband, despite his title, was little more than his father's errand boy; and that while she lived in splendor on a seventy-acre estate abounding with servants and had access to several elegant automobiles with or without chauffeurs, everything at her disposal was legally listed in the doctor's name, and would remain so throughout her years of marriage to his son. Her wrath toward Dr. Mattison was hardly assuaged when, a week into her widowhood, she learned of his intentions to evict her from her marital estate.

The doctor saw no reason to continue subsidizing a hostile daughter-in-law who had no children of her own to support, and who apparently had nothing better to do with her abundant leisure time than to pry into his personal affairs and malign his character. He had heard from his old friend Keasbey about her allegations; and although he believed he retained Keasbey's trust after deluging his partner with indignant cables and letters of refutation, he nonetheless ordered the destruction of all corporate records in Ambler that might embarrass him should they come to the attention of lawyers hired by people bent on causing trouble. He commanded that all such data be tossed into a bonfire.

In 1927, Keasbey finally reacted to Georgette Mattison's criticisms by hiring a team of investigators who uncovered sufficient evidence against the doctor to warrant an equity suit filed in early 1928 at the Montgomery County Courthouse in Norristown, Pennsylvania. The allegations against the doctor included mismanagement and deceit—using company funds to create profit-making corporations under his own name without feeling obliged to share the wealth with the K&M stockholders, to say nothing of withholding dividends on their K&M stock; and, similarly, using K&M capital toward the construction of the town's homes and mansions while maintaining discretionary control over these properties by listing himself as the proprietor. In his turn the doctor denied any intent of wrongdoing; if he was guilty of anything, it was perhaps his expeditiousness, his promptness in responding to business problems and opportunities without prior consultation with Keasbey—but then how could he consult with Keasbey, when the latter refused to serve with him on the board of directors and spent all his time overseas? Mr. Keasbey, the doctor rightly pointed out, had not contributed an honest day's work to the firm since 1892, the year Keasbey had left Ambler for France. Mr. Keasbey, having come to America, was not disposed to a drawn-out feud with his old friend. He just wanted a financial settlement so he could extricate himself from the complex web the doctor had spun around Ambler; and when the judge suggested that Mattison buy out Keasbey's interest in K&M for four million dollars, Keasbey agreed. Had he been a less wealthy or a hungrier man, he might have haggled for a much higher price; but Keasbey eagerly anticipated leaving behind forever the polluted skies of Pennsylvania for the Côte d'Azur—a journey the doctor just as eagerly wanted him to take. And as an indication of the doctor's eagerness, he severed all connections with Keasbey in a single day—a gray afternoon in the autumn of 1929, when he surrendered four million dollars to Keasbey in one lump sum, denying himself the option of paying off his partner in several installments that could have been spread over many years.

Shortly after Keasbey had pocketed the money and returned abroad, the Crash of late October 1929 arrived to reduce the doctor's liquidity to a trickle, making him damn the day he had allowed Keasbey to escape the industrial debacle richer than ever and leave the doctor alone with the problem of saving the company from bankruptcy. Four million in cash would not have been an overwhelming sum in the prosperous twenties; but the absence of that money after 1929, in a period of declining asbestos production made worse by the fact that the doctor was already mightily mortgaged because of expansionist decisions he had made years earlier, left him cash-poor and vulnerable to being taken over by the banks. He had invested heavily in building a new asbestos brake-lining branch in Wyndmoor, Pennsylvania; an asbestos textile division in Hoboken, New Jersey; and in Saint Louis, Missouri, an asbestos shingle, slate, and sheathing plant that was to manufacture products for the western half of the United States and thereby avoid the increased railroad delivery costs from the East, while also undercutting the cost of Belgian-made asbestos that began substantially invading the American market during the mid-twenties. But these and other of Mattison's decisions that had seemed so wise in the pre-Depression years now, after the Crash of '29, merely hastened his departure from the helm of K&M.

By 1931 the bankers had officially replaced him as president of K&M with an executive named Augustus S. Blagden. Dr. Mattison was now eighty years old, losing his eyesight, but still proud and bold enough to believe that he was out of power only temporarily. Under the auspices of the cost-cutting Mr. Blagden, K&M functioned for three years on a modest scale, reducing jobs continuously in Ambler while gradually closing most of the firm's out-of-town sales offices and subsidiaries, and, of course, eliminating all the frills and privileges to which Dr. Mattison had long been accustomed. Although the doctor did vacate his castle, which was immediately put up for sale, he moved no farther away than across the street—beyond the castle's main gate into a corner mansion at No. 1 Lindenwold Terrace, a three-story twin-turreted Gothic edifice that years before he had prudently placed in the name of his second wife, the crippled Mary Mattison, who now nonetheless lost her lofty perch in the castle tower from which she had previously enjoyed a wide-ranging view of community life through her binoculars.

Mr. Blagden did fulfill the doctor's desires in banishing Georgette Mattison from her bosky retreat west of the castle (determinedly keeping her late husband's Packard roadster, she resettled in Philadelphia, where in subsequent decades she would outlive two other husbands before retiring to a nursing home in the Chestnut Hill section of the city, where she died at seventy-six in 1961). The doctor's other daughter-in-law, Florence—wife of his wayward younger son, Royal—would retain the mansion at No. 8 Lindenwold Terrace, which had been the doctor's wedding gift on the occasion of her marriage to Royal in 1914.

The bankers finally sold the firm to a leading British asbestos-manufacturing enterprise (Turner & Newall, of Rochdale, England), which foresaw a profitable future for asbestos in America beyond the bankers' expectations. (The public outcry against asbestos as a health hazard was yet decades away, and the cautious medical advice that *was* being disseminated was largely ignored not only by management but also by workers, much in the way that the risks in cigarette-smoking long went unheeded in a later period; indeed, during the 1930s many K&M factory workers refused to wear a face mask because it *interfered* with their smoking.)

Dr. Mattison lived until a few minutes after his eighty-fifth birthday, victimized by a fatal heart attack on November 18, 1936, at No. 1 Lindenwold Terrace, where his poor eyesight for many months had prevented him from having a clear view from his window of the castle that loomed in the near distance on the other side of the street. Earlier in the year, after a prolonged period of vacancy, the castle and a bit more than seventy-five acres of surrounding land had been sold by the bankers for $115,000 to a Catholic charitable order on the outskirts of Philadelphia, the Sisters of the Holy Family of Nazareth. So many homeless children had been taken in by the nuns during the early years of the Depression that the order was forced to find a larger center with more land, and the nuns saw the castle as a blessed discovery.

After they had demanded the removal of the voluptuous nude female statue that had stood boldly in a sunken garden (it was sold to a local artist), and gotten rid of the Civil War cannon that the late Mr. Devine, while Dr. Mattison's aide, had positioned near the front steps, the estate was renamed Saint Mary's Home for Children. The doctor's eyesight notwithstanding, he was fully aware of what was transpiring behind the gates of his old domain, but he had no comment to make except to request that certain possessions he had left behind now be delivered to him. His list included the cannon, which was rolled onto the doctor's front lawn; the framed motto that had hung in his castle office (in Gothic letters, *Sans souci*—Without worry); and countless pieces of valuable glassware and silver he had brought back from his many trips abroad. Although the doctor's residence at No. 1 was the most spacious of the eight mansions that lined Lindenwold Terrace (it would be converted into an eight-unit apartment building after his death), it was hardly large enough to accommodate all the Oriental rugs he had bought for the castle. He nevertheless ordered them returned to him, and after this had been done he instructed that most of the floor space be covered with *three* levels of rugs, which produced such soft-footed unsteadiness throughout the mansion that those within (including the doctor himself) were frequently losing their balance and toppling almost soundlessly to the floor.

During most of his five years in retirement at No. 1, Dr. Mattison shared the mansion with his wife, who spent much of her time in a wheelchair in a large upper-floor solarium that the doctor had had built for her, overlooking a garden of roses and daffodils, and with two English servants, a married couple of whom the husband had formerly worked as a K&M plant manager until the bankers had eliminated his job. The doctor also employed a caretaker who lived in the Gothic carriage house in the rear of the property, where there were also hundreds of square feet of soil devoted to vegetable gardens and fruit trees, and chicken coops as well, that provided much of what was consumed at the doctor's table. The caretaker not only tended to the farming and gardening but also served as the doctor's chauffeur. He was a lanky, ruddy-skinned Virginian named Bayne Girthious Rowe, popularly known as "Gus"; a widower for many years, he lived with his teenaged daughters, Clara and Elsie, who attended the local schools. They were questioned regularly by Dr. Mattison about their homework, and were often asked to show him their report cards. Much of the doctor's tender remembrances of his lost daughter were enacted in the affection and attention he bestowed upon Gus Rowe's girls; and they in turn came to see a side of Dr. Mattison that went beyond the self-centered authoritarian figure most people assumed was his full embodiment.

At night, from their windows in the carriage house, the girls could glance across the courtyard into the rear windows of the mansion and see the doctor seated in the library, white-bearded, dark-suited, radiant in the light flashing down from the tall tableside lamp that also reflected across the pages of the book he was reading to his wife, and that illuminated as well her expression of contentment. The girls were aware that each morning he placed a flower next to his wife's breakfast plate, and that under the plate was a love poem he composed to her every day. After Mary Mattison died in the late summer of 1935, fifteen months before his own death, Dr. Mattison was never remiss in bringing fresh flowers to her gravestone to replace those close to withering; and as depressed as he was by her absence, he remained cheerful toward Clara and Elsie Rowe, and he also succeeded during the final weeks of his life in helping his late brother's adopted children, who were then residing on the old family farm in Bucks County, where the doctor himself had been brought up as a barefoot farm boy in the 1850s.

The children adopted at the turn of the century by the doctor's childless older brother, Asher, and Asher's wife, Hulda, had been part of the neighboring Ely family, who had been struggling to support the offspring of one female relative who had died in childbirth after producing twelve children. A male child from this family, Reuben P. Ely, was raised in Asher and Hulda's home, and he remained on the property as their adopted son after he himself had married and had two children of his own. But with Hulda's death in 1935 (Asher had died in 1922) there was some question as to the legal entitlement of the Ely family to the Mattison farmland, since the doctor and *his* heirs in an earlier will had also been recognized as having proprietary claims to the Bucks County land. During Hulda Mattison's lifetime, the doctor had ignored this matter, knowing how much she disliked him—she had never forgiven him for allowing his guards to block her and Asher at the castle gates that day when they tried to visit. But on the morning of October 6, 1936, he told Gus Rowe to dust off and gas up the old Packard, which had not been driven in weeks; they would be taking a few hours' drive out to Bucks County to see what was left of the thousand-acre tract that in 1682 a maternal ancestor from England, the Quaker yeoman George Pownall, had acquired from William Penn.

Only eighty-two acres were still under family control in 1936; and while the stone house and the porch furniture looked exactly the same as when he had sat at the feet of his aunt Martha while she read him Gothic tales, he was somewhat saddened by the endurance of its simplicity, and he wished that somehow more had been made of the place, that the walls of the house and the porch deck had been spruced up with fresh paint and a few new floorboards, and that the soil had been better cultivated, and that perhaps some of his own energy and vision had flowed through the veins of his late brother. But as the doctor strolled around the property, accompanied by Reuben and Virginia Ely, and their children and visiting nephews, who respectfully called him "Uncle Doctor," he suspected that the only hope for improving this land lay with these young people who now occupied it—people who, *if* they owned it outright, would take personal pride in developing it beyond the limitations of tenant farmers and squatters. So he impulsively turned to his traveling companion and one-time castle employee, Charles Hibschman, whom Gus Rowe had also brought to Bucks County, and discussed the idea of bequeathing the whole estate to the Ely family for a single dollar. Hibschman conceded that this was a most generous act, and Reuben and Virginia Ely—and the inheritors nearby—could barely express their gratitude.

In the car on the way back to Ambler, the doctor was clearly a happy man; the old homestead would remain in the "family," it would remain true to its original intentions, enriching the earth while nourishing its cultivators—it would not fall prey to land developers who might pave it out of existence and destroy its natural function. (Which is what *did* happen; the Ely offspring would one day sell the property to developers, who would in turn pave it in anticipation of the population growth that might make the land suitable for a shopping mall.)

But Dr. Mattison went to his grave never thinking this likely—no more than he could have thought, after he had purchased the Mattison family burial land within the Laurel Hill Cemetery in North Philadelphia, selecting a scenic spot overlooking the Schuylkill River, that this would in future years be blocked by a grand highway bordering the river below.

44.

BEING AN ITALIAN in Paris had been a pleasurable and profitable experience for Antonio Cristiani, but in the fall of 1937, during the week in which various examples of his tailoring had been placed on display at the Paris International Exposition of Arts and Technique in Modern Life, he was uncharacteristically morose. He had recently had premonitions of disaster; the light autumnal breezes that whipped the flags atop the exposition's many pavilions carried a touch of eerie calm that reminded him of the atmosphere in Maida hours before an earthquake.

Early in the week, feeling chest pains and vertigo, he had hastened to his doctor; but after an examination, he was pronounced in good health for a man of forty-three—and that opinion only made him feel worse. Either he had been struck by a malady that was eluding detection, or, like so many of his Italian countrymen whom he had mocked in the past, he *too* had fallen victim to the curse of southern pessimism, to his village's time-honored habit of inventing illnesses about which to complain.

But there was nothing imaginary about his nightmares. They invaded his sleeping hours and sent him bolting out of bed, waking up not only his wife but their three children; and yet in the morning he was reluctant to discuss with Adelina what was bothering him, partly because he himself was not entirely sure, and partly because what awoke him was too alarming to reveal.

In his nightmares she was always dead, along with their children and dozens of other people and animals, all of them piled in a pyramidal heap cluttered with skeletons, with a few squirming arms and fingers reaching toward the sky; and always Antonio was separated from them, prone, powerless, but alive. In his diary he had tried to describe it, each time crossing out what he had written; and then, one afternoon, while walking around the exposition grounds, Antonio was stunned to confront his nightmare in a painting. He recognized and identified with the artist's rendering of a man who lay at the bottom of a pile of people victimized by calamity: the fallen man's arms were outstretched, his eyes and mouth were open, and he held a broken sword in his right hand next to the hoof of a horse and near the bare feet of a stumbling figure whose posture resembled that of one of the bleeding penitents Antonio had seen decades earlier in Maida. What Antonio saw was Pablo Picasso's *Guernica* in the pavilion of the Spanish Republic, the painting named in memory of the Basque village that had recently been bombed by Hitler's fliers in the civil war in Spain. Hitler was allied with the Spanish dictator, General Francisco Franco, as was Mussolini; and some of Antonio's relatives were now soldiers in Spain, including his twenty-three-year-old cousin Domenico Talese, Joseph's youngest brother.

As an Italian citizen in Paris, where every day demonstrators in the streets protested the war and condemned Franco, Hitler, and Mussolini, Antonio felt uneasy about his future, but he managed to repress these fears until he saw them boldly presented by Picasso. Antonio felt again the sweat and terror of that day long before when he and thousands of others had fled Paris on the eve of the Great War, but that was in 1914, when he had been a young bachelor with few possessions and few cares beyond his own welfare. Now, he was a father of three children born in Paris, the youngest less than five months old; and if he were forced to go he would have to leave behind his spacious apartment, his business, and the many associates and friends he and Adelina had collected during a decade of married life in Paris.

Although a Francophile for more than twenty years, Antonio would not renounce his Italian citizenship, much as he might disagree with some of the contemporary policies of Fascist Italy. World opinion had begun to sour on Italy after Mussolini's troops had invaded Ethiopia in 1935, but Mussolini's joining Hitler in 1937 had further damaged Italy's relationship with its World War I allies France, Britain, and the United States; and while these nations had remained officially neutral during the Spanish Civil War, there was antipathy among their citizens toward the Spanish, German, and Italian dictators. Nowhere was this more prevalent than in Paris, where left-wing factions had asserted themselves within the labor unions and the national bureaucracy, and on the boulevards and side streets of the city, waving red flags as they denounced the dictatorial triumvirate and fomented strikes protesting the French government's resistance to joining the fight in Spain against the forces of Nazism and Fascism.

The French people's hostility toward Mussolini at times grew into an anti-Italianism that touched Antonio and other Italian residents of the capital as it challenged their loyalties and dared them to choose between the two nations they loved. The French customers who now avoided Antonio's shop, and the French veterans who had become uncharacteristically cool to their aging former Italian trenchmates who stood next to them at commemorative ceremonies honoring the battle victims of World War I, were in Antonio's opinion hardly representative of the friendship that a majority of ordinary Frenchmen felt toward Italians. But he could not avoid the fact that the strong French–Italian bonds that had been forged on the frontlines were now in jeopardy of being buried with their wartime comrades *unless* the leaders in both nations quickly altered their policies and restored the harmony that had once existed between these two Catholic nations.

In the privacy of his fitting rooms, Antonio diplomatically urged both the French and the Italian statesmen who were part of his clientele to strengthen the weakening ties between the two countries; and in his role as president of the Italian Economic Federation of France and leader of the Paris-based Italian war veterans' association, he reiterated this theme in the presence of other nations' ambassadors and ministers with whom he came in contact as a frequent guest at official dinners and receptions. Antonio saw Mussolini as a man with more bark than bite, an egotist with a perhaps neurotic need to gain other people's attention; yet he thought that the Duce could be reasoned with, *must* be reasoned with before he embraced Hitler as his single strongest ally. Mussolini was a dictator, but, Antonio believed, only a dictator could have restored order in Italy during the strike-ridden 1920s, perhaps saving the country from Communism; and to excoriate Mussolini for invading Ethiopia, as the French and British were doing, seemed somewhat hypocritical when one considered these two nations' own history of colonial conquest. Worse, insofar as French–Italian relations were concerned, was France's compounding its disapproval of Italian colonialism in 1936 by removing its ambassador in Rome, an individual who enjoyed Mussolini's friendship and trust, Count Charles de Chambrun, and replacing him with Count René de Saint-Quentin, who on behalf of France refused Mussolini's demand that he acknowledge Victor Emmanuel III as King of Italy *and* Emperor of Ethiopia. The Frenchman was unwilling to do so, for it would indicate official recognition of Italy's recent African acquisition, and that prompted Mussolini to block Saint-Quentin's transferral. Consequently, from October 1936 through October 1938, the years in which Mussolini and Hitler were engaged in foreign policy discussions affecting Europe and the Mediterranean, the French government was without the benefit of an ambassador in Rome. Not only Antonio but many Frenchmen saw this as a major diplomatic blunder—one made worse when Mussolini followed by pulling *his* ambassador out of Paris in 1937.

The French official most identified with the rift with Mussolini was a onetime customer of Antonio's who, in early June 1936, had ascended to the premiership of France. He was Léon Blum. At sixty-four, Blum became the first Socialist and first Jewish premier in French history. Coming two months after Hitler's militarization of the Rhineland—at a time when pacifism and the emancipation of the working classes seemed to represent a higher political calling in France than the clamorings by Colonel Charles de Gaulle for more tanks—the election of a nonmilitaristic, left-wing Jewish intellectual was infuriating to the French radical right; and even some Jewish leaders in France were discomforted by Blum's success. They saw in his ascent a possible rise of French anti-

Semitism to the level it had attained in the previous century during and after the Alfred Dreyfus trial, in which the Jewish French army officer had been unjustly accused of spying for Germany. An important rabbi in Paris urged Blum to resist the honor of leading the French government, and the rabbi's concerns were perhaps realized when, on the very first day Blum was installed as premier, the right-wing deputy Xavier Vallat declared in the national assembly: "Your arrival in office, *Monsieur le Président du Conseil,* is incontestably a historic date. For the first time this old Gallic-Roman country will be governed by a Jew." Immediately called to order by the supervising official, Vallat would not be silenced. "I have a special duty here," he insisted, ". . . of saying aloud what everyone is thinking to himself: that to govern this peasant nation of France it is better to have someone whose origins, no matter how modest, spring from our soil than to have a subtle Talmudist." Again Vallat was admonished by the official and others in the chamber, none of whom was more enraged than Blum himself.

But Blum had experienced far worse in Paris earlier in the year. In mid-February, while riding with Socialist friends along the Boulevard Saint-Germain during a week when he and his party colleagues had held publicized pre-election meetings with their Communist associates, Blum was recognized by a group of right-wing ruffians who, after smashing the windows of the car, pulled him into the street and beat him so badly that he had to be taken to a hospital. Photographs of the battered Socialist leader that appeared in the press, and the public outcry against such violence, were generally believed to have influenced many voters to shift toward Blum's Socialist–Communist coalition, the Popular Front; but the sympathy and concern for Blum's well-being quickly subsided after he had moved into the premier's office at the Matignon Palace.

Antonio Cristiani's opinion of Blum had nothing to do with the latter's religion (despite whatever failings might be attributed to the Italian people, their inherent individualism seemed to guarantee that anti-Semitism would not flourish in Italy); it had more to do with the fact that Blum had ceased being his customer. Exactly why he stopped ordering suits remained a mystery to Antonio, who recalled the many compliments Blum had paid him in past years, and Antonio could now only wonder, in the privacy of his diary, if Blum's disenchantment with the expansionist colonial policy of Italy's increasingly aggressive right-wing regime might have influenced his attitude toward his Italian tailor. Antonio continued to mail his brochures to the premier, but he received no more business from Blum.

In this Depression era, when many of the wealthier Frenchmen were taking their money out of the country—and when the franc, which had slipped from fifteen to twenty-one francs to the dollar, was expected to slip further, along with industrial production—Blum's coalition of Socialists, Communists, and bourgeois Radicals had demonstrated an unprecedented tolerance for strikes and work stoppages. It had committed itself to a workers' wage increase averaging twelve percent, and the right of collective bargaining, and it would limit the work week to forty hours, with compensation for overtime. Workers were now entitled to a two-week annual vacation with pay, and Blum's coalition would also allow the unionization of plants that employed more than ten workers.

Antonio employed nine men in his workroom, and should he hire two more his shop could fall under the control of a union, with his employees electing a shop steward who could challenge Antonio if he wished to dismiss or reprimand a tailor for inferior craftsmanship or an insubordinate attitude. Not only did Antonio worry that this might lessen his authority over his personnel, but he feared a decline in the standards of his craft. How could he insist that his men meet his highest standards with each stitch, and strive for perfection with each suit, if they knew that he lacked the power to punish them for deviations from his instructions? The shop steward, and not Antonio, would be setting standards. And what if the shop steward supported the men's wish to work primarily on sewing machines, which involved less time and tedium than sewing every stitch by hand—what could Antonio do? If he said no, they could impose a work stoppage or a strike, and possibly put him out of business.

Strikes and work stoppages had proliferated throughout the nation; there had been revolts against management by French metalworkers, public utility workers, fuel oil deliverers, agricultural workers, bakers, and employees of hotels and department stores, restaurants and cafés. In excess of one million Frenchmen were on strike in early June 1936, and Léon Blum's reaction was to sympathize with their demands, to condone their forceful takeover of factories as part of the class struggle, as a step toward an egalitarian society—giving the impression that he believed publicly, even if he did not privately, that equal rights and opportunities would produce equal results. If Léon Blum was so naive as to believe this, Antonio thought, the premier might have benefitted from knowing old Domenico Talese in Maida—who believed that some of God's creatures were incorrigibly lazy, and that the proper way to wake them up in the morning was the method he used, slashing his whip against their bedroom walls. Antonio was not *really* sure that Léon Blum was privately any more democratic than Grandfather Domenico, as he noted in his diary:

Léon Blum is a wealthy descendant of a family of silk merchants. I knew him and his brothers from the time I began making their suits at Damien's, and later at Larsen's. Léon Blum became the family Socialist. He liked making speeches for workers' rights and higher pay. But in his own household I know he was tough with his servants. He worked them hard and paid them little. I remember the messenger boy who used to deliver his suits saying that Léon Blum seemed to be changing his cooks, waiters, and other servants almost every week.

It was finally not Blum, but his Communist colleague Maurice Thorez, who managed to convince the French strikers to evacuate most of the factories they had seized during the spring and early summer of 1936, and to accept the gains the Popular Front had negotiated in return for the restoration of labor peace and the workers' resuming their jobs. At the Bastille Day celebrations of 1936, in the second month of Blum's premiership, Antonio watched Parisians crowd the streets singing the "Internationale" as often as the "Marseillaise," and waving what seemed as many red flags as tricolors of the French Republic. Antonio stood among the spectators as Premier Blum acknowledged the marchers' salutes and their signs reading *"Vive Blum!"* and *"Vive le Front Populaire!"* and for the first time he thought seriously of Communist influence in the city.

Antonio had continued to think of Paris in these terms throughout the period of the Spanish Civil War, which began four days after that Bastille Day celebration and lasted until Barcelona fell to Franco in January 1939; and while the war was conducted on the Spanish side of the Pyrenees, hundreds of miles from Paris, its ramifications surrounded Antonio daily in the French capital. There were the red-bannered recruitment booths with posters urging men to enlist in the left-wing ranks of the Spanish Loyalists; the myriad events held to raise money and collect supplies for the Loyalists' welfare; the rallies and revived strikes protesting the French government's continuing failure to enter the war and assist their Popular Front *confrères* in Spain against the mutinous Spanish generals and their Fascist and Nazi friends in Italy and Germany. A work stoppage among Paris bus drivers and Métro workers in 1937, along with a strike at the Goodrich tire plant, were cited as the deeds of Paris-centered Communist union leaders who felt betrayed by the queasiness of Popular Front leaders in meeting the challenge of saving Spain from right-wing militants.

Antonio and other businessmen in Paris, few of whom believed that France had anything to gain by becoming entangled in the Spanish crisis, but who kept their thoughts to themselves (Paris abounded with spies, eavesdroppers, partisans unhesitant about smashing storefront windows), went about their duties and errands each day striving to conceal their inner feelings about the raucous speeches they heard all around them: from the left against the Fascists, from the right against the Communists, and sometimes the more squeamish voice of a centralist interrupting to ask (before being booed): Had France not shed enough blood in World War I? Should it not concentrate on defending its eastern borders, or building more tanks as de Gaulle had suggested? Loudly represented within the French right-wing rallies were middle-class Catholics who had loathed Blum from the start, and who saw the Popular Front leaders as the bastard offspring of Robespierre and those other godless revolutionaries who had tried to cut out the heart of the Church from the body of the nation; now in the 1930s these leaders had unleashed a workers' reign of terror and an economic crisis, and had all but delivered the French nation into the arms of Soviet Russia. Given the choice of Spain's being run by the Communists or the Fascists, the Catholics overwhelmingly favored the Fascists. Some Catholics would go even further than that, as was clear from the signs they brandished at right-wing rallies bearing the words: "Better Hitler than Blum!"

Antonio had no idea what Mussolini's true relationship with Hitler was during 1937 and 1938, since he read conflicting opinions on the subject almost every week in the French and Italian press. But from his regular visits to the Italian embassy in Paris, together with frequent trips to Rome (where he continued to receive recognition and medals from the Italian government as an achieving emigrant), Antonio deduced that Mussolini was at most flirting with Hitler, although at times the Duce seemed to be emulating Hitler. Antonio was concerned in November 1938 when Mussolini broadcast a speech expressing the Fascists' desire to expand the Italian empire at France's expense into Tunisia, Corsica, and Nice. But at a reception at the Italian embassy in Paris, to mark the return of the Italian ambassador after a year's absence, the latter privately reassured Antonio and other business leaders that Mussolini was *not* being serious, that he was just venting some of his frustrations toward the French Socialists and the Paris press for failing to give him sufficient credit for his peacekeeping role two months earlier at the Munich conference.

The Duce had been magnificent at Munich, the ambassador reminded his guests; Mussolini had convinced the Führer to settle for a small piece of mostly German-speaking Czechoslovakia in return for a vow of no further aggressions in Europe. The French representative to Munich in September, joining Hitler, Mussolini, and British prime minister Neville Chamberlain, was Edouard Daladier, a Popular Front figure who had stepped in as premier after Blum's second cabinet had fallen in April 1938. When Daladier returned from Munich he was greeted enthusiastically by most Frenchmen for his efforts in maintaining world peace. In his cheering section was Blum, who, ignoring Mussolini's participation, commented: "There is not a woman and not a man to refuse Messrs. Neville Chamberlain and Edouard Daladier their rightful tribute of gratitude. War is avoided."

Antonio was unconvinced by Blum's optimism, and was even less convinced in the following months as Mussolini became palpably more belligerent, unnecessarily provoking anger in Paris with such observations as: "The French respect only those who have defeated them." When Chamberlain visited Mussolini in January 1939, no doubt trying to convince the Duce that Italy could have friends other than the Germans (Hitler had visited Rome the previous spring), Antonio was in Rome with his wife, en route back to Paris after spending the Christmas holidays with Adelina's family in Bovalino. They had decided to leave their three children under the care of Adelina's family in southern Italy, for they were unsure that Paris would be safe for them much longer.

I must take every precaution, Antonio wrote in his diary on January 26, shortly after returning to Paris. *I don't feel right about what's going on. I don't trust any of these people in government. I wouldn't trust Mussolini, Hitler, Chamberlain, Daladier, Blum, or any others. I don't trust the crowds around them. The crowds in the streets of Rome gave Chamberlain a tremendous reception. I'm told they also did that for Hitler. I remember hearing them cheer for President Poincaré as he waved from his carriage after returning from Russia in 1914. You should never trust people when they are enthusiastic.*

In mid-March 1939, disregarding the promises made in Munich, Adolf Hitler invaded and conquered all of Czechoslovakia, while other nations protested but did nothing militarily. The Nazi army was now operating unchallenged; and Benito Mussolini, as if envious of Hitler's success as an aggressor, sent Italian soldiers into poorly defended Albania a month later. Satisfied with this easy triumph, Mussolini in May 1939 signed a cooperation agreement with Hitler; Antonio saw this as a sign that Italy was beyond being courted by the Allies.

Soon after, Antonio left Paris for two weeks, entrusting his shop, as he always did when he went away, to his most senior tailor, and escorted Adelina back to Italy by train to rejoin their children. Despite her tearful and persistent pleading, Antonio refused to remain with them in Bovalino, and he returned to Paris alone in early June. He was not yet ready to abandon all that he had built and owned in the French capital. Paris had seemed oddly festive all spring, crowded with tourists and well-dressed people jamming the hotel lobbies and sidewalk cafés, speaking various languages and seemingly unconcerned about the things that had long been tormenting Antonio. French and foreign journals no longer featured Czechoslovakia and Albania in the headlines; and not only had the Spanish Civil War come to an end, but the French government quickly recognized Franco's Fascist regime and appointed as ambassador to Spain the most famous and respected general in all of France—eighty-two-year-old Philippe Pétain, the hero of Verdun. Although Antonio was lonely at night in his large apartment and did not enjoy having all his meals in restaurants and bistros, he was encouraged by the revival of trade and energy in the city, and the fact that he had just received an order to make fifty tuxedos for the Folies-Bergère.

I must stop this obsessive worrying, he reminded himself in his diary in early July 1939, as he looked forward to closing his shop for two weeks in August and rejoining his family at the seaside home of one of his wife's relatives along the Strait of Messina. *I must accept the fact that life goes on, that what seems so bad today may change tomorrow. Remember, nobody has declared war! All this hysteria that I've had might just be my overactive imagination when I'm not busy at night. But even in the sunshine of the day I see things that make me worry about the future. I see that the Fascist officers, with their black shirts and arrogant manners, have moved into the Italian Consulate. I'm not sure this is a good thing. Do they want to aggravate our relationship here with the French who want peace? I read in the Italian press that French anti-Fascist gangs are extorting money and harassing Italian businessmen here, but I know this isn't true. The Fascists are just trying to stir up new problems between the French and Italian people, and I must contact Ciano about this and object in the name of our Federation.*

Count Galeazzo Ciano was the Italian foreign minister, and although he was only thirty-six and relatively inexperienced in international affairs, he was tremendously influential because he was the husband of Mussolini's daughter Edda, the Duce's favorite child. Antonio had met Ciano on a number of occasions in Paris and Rome, the first when Ciano stepped forward to greet Antonio in 1935 when the latter had received the title of Grand Officer of the Crown of Italy for his craftsmanship and civic leadership. After consulting with his fellow officers in the Italian Economic Federation in mid-July 1939, Antonio drafted a communiqué to Ciano and wired it at once:

> I bring the greetings of the Italian Economic Federation of France, of which I am the president, and I also bring my personal greet-

ings . . . and would like further to offer my modest contribution to increasing the Italo–French relationship that at this moment is hindered by misunderstanding.

I have lived and worked in France for most of the last thirty years, and I feel qualified to interpret the thinking of most merchants, artisans, and industrialists toward the Italian nation . . . and I can assure you, for example, that it is *not* true that Italians are being harassed or discourteously treated by French officials or French citizens. The Italian people who live honestly in France and who respect, as the Duce has ordered, the laws of France, are allowed to continue to remain here as always, in the spirit of mutual understanding and respect. I hope that you share my hope that nothing is done, or falsely reported as being done, to disturb these many years of fine relations between the French and Italian people.

The communiqué went unanswered. After three weeks had passed, this concerned Antonio, for the count's replies to Antonio's earlier cables had always been prompt and cordial. Perhaps the count was away from his Rome office on a short vacation, Antonio thought, all but dismissing the matter from his mind; but late in the second week of August, days before he was to leave for his vacation in Italy, Antonio's shop was visited by a black-shirted colonel and two Italian civilians who said they were from the Foreign Ministry and were investigating reports that Antonio's life had been threatened by French anti-Fascist hoodlums to whom he had refused to hand over a large sum of money.

Antonio had been called out of one of the fitting rooms by a clerk, leaving behind an important French banker who had been a customer for years. Antonio stood staring at his visitors momentarily, his face reddening, and wondered what was really behind this so-called investigation. The colonel was an erect, broad-shouldered man in his forties, who wore a peaked cap forward and down over his eyebrows, and displayed on the chest of his well-fitted gabardine jacket a double row of ribbons and the winged gold medallion of an air force unit. Flanking the colonel on the other side of Antonio's glass counter were a stout man in his thirties, wearing a beige suit and a straw hat, and a younger, thinner man who had on a white shirt and a brown silk tie, and who combed his thick, heavily pomaded black hair straight back in the style favored by the late film star Rudolph Valentino.

"This report is false," Antonio said finally, placing his hands on the counter, next to an ashtray and a pack of his Turkish cigarettes.

"But it comes to us on good authority," the colonel said, addressing Antonio in a cultivated but aspirated Italian accent that Antonio identified as Florentine.

"Please believe me, Colonel, it is false," Antonio repeated. He now stood with his arms folded across his chest, over which was draped his tan pleated tailor's smock; a small rose stuck through the buttonhole of the left lapel, while the rest of the lapel flickered with the reflections of dozens of needles and pins.

"This is your shop?" the colonel asked.

"Yes."

"And you are a citizen of Italy?"

"Yes," Antonio answered, a bit sharply, noticing that the straw-hatted civilian had removed a pen and pad from his jacket and was taking notes. Turning to the civilian, Antonio said: "I assume you know that all this information about me, and a lot more, is documented in your files."

The man looked up and said nothing, while the colonel cleared his throat. Antonio was tempted to ask if these men were acting on direct orders from Ciano, but he decided against it until he knew exactly what was going on.

"We do not mean to upset you," the colonel said, trying for the first time to seem pleasant. But the straw-hatted man was still writing in his little book, and the younger Valentino type was gazing around the shop, studying the stacks of material on the shelves and the other people in the room. He had already helped himself to a couple of Antonio's business cards that lay in a silver tray on the counter, and tucked them into the breast pocket of his shirt. "You realize, of course," the colonel went on, "that we're required to look into these reports, even if you believe they lack merit."

"I have not been threatened," Antonio repeated, "and I'm just trying to understand what you want from me."

"Your cooperation," said the colonel.

"I'm giving it to you," Antonio said.

"When will you be leaving Paris?" asked the straw-hatted man, speaking for the first time. He had a bold Milanese accent, and Antonio now resented his questioner's accent as much as the fact that these people were possibly aware of his travel plans. Feeling his perspiration flow as he stared into his questioner's eyes, Antonio knew that he was definitely alienated from the Italy of these Milanese and Florentine trespassers—the Italy of the Piedmontese dynasty, the Italy of the northern bankers and industrialists who had financed the Risorgimento, the Italy of the ex–Milanese newspaper publisher who was now the Duce. Antonio had fled the worsening poverty the northerners had brought to the south, and now they had the audacity to hunt him down in Paris and make further claims upon him!

"Who said I was leaving Paris?" he demanded, almost shouting. He realized too late that he had lost control, but he no longer cared. He saw the colonel and the two men suddenly turn around as the other people within hearing distance now seemed to be paying full attention. Three customers (including the French banker) poked their heads out from the velvet curtains of the fitting rooms; four tailors walked toward Antonio and stood not far from the counter; and two apprentices came out from the workroom. The colonel, raising his hand in a gesture of conciliation toward Antonio, said, "No offense was intended."

"I think I've heard enough impertinent questions for one day," Antonio went on, heatedly. "And now, with your permission, I'd like to return to my work."

"Very well," said the colonel, nodding with understanding toward him and the others around the room. "We shall be going. I may have to ask your assistance again in the future, but meanwhile let me express our thanks for the time you have given us."

Watching them leave, Antonio was still shaken with anger; but on his way home from the shop that night he felt only sadness. He had sent a wire to his wife, now in Bovalino, explaining that he had to postpone his visit. He blamed it on business, a lucrative order placed by a very important person who required delivery within the month. But in his diary he wrote: *This is no time for a vacation. I cannot leave my shop and the apartment unguarded. Once more, I feel like a soldier.*

Antonio remained in Paris alone through the summer and fall of 1939 expecting that every day might be his last, that at any hour the alarm would be sounded and the government would announce (as it had in the late summer of 1914) that all foreign civilians were to return immediately to their homelands and leave to the French the task of fighting a war. Antonio would always remember the bravery of those Parisians as they banded together to save the city—the older citizens manning the interior, the younger ones rushing to the front in military vehicles, municipal buses, and even taxicabs. Never was the word *camaraderie* more nobly defined than during the summer and autumn of 1914; and Antonio left Paris then with all the love and regret that he felt now, twenty-five years later, at the thought of having to abandon once more his chosen home during a perilous time. But he also sensed that there was a considerable difference between the prevailing sentiments within the capital today and those in 1914. Then, the city was filled with the drum sounds of patriotism and a passion for challenging the Kaiser; now, the city was factionalized and quarrelsome, and even as the Hitlerian hand that held Austria and Czechoslovakia was reaching toward Poland, the rallying voices of the pacifist crowds in view of the Arch of Triumph were asking: "Why die for Danzig?"

On September 3, 1939, the French and British governments declared war on Germany, two days after the Nazi invasion of Poland, but the French and British showed little determination to pursue the battle. A large portion of the French military was at that moment underground, assuming defensive positions along the French–German border inside a two-hundred-mile subterranean installation called the Maginot Line. Begun in 1929 and named in memory of France's late minister of war, André Maginot, the fortification extended along the eastern edge of France, northward as far as Belgium and southward toward Switzerland. In its final form it would be spacious and deep enough to hide multiple substratums, triple- and quadruple-decked constructions connected by steel beams that held floors and roads that supported the weight of a covert army of men moving about under the footprints of the trench fighters of the previous war. While the Maginot Line was not completed by 1939, enough had been done to deem it impregnable.

And thus troops were massed there on the day France declared war. They remained there for half a year without any sign of the enemy. It was all quite surrealistic: war had been declared after the Nazi invasion of Poland, and French soldiers and civilians waited expectantly, but the autumn of 1939 became the spring of 1940 without a French bullet's being fired at the enemy. Many French citizens began to relax, believing that the fighting would never come, that the impregnable Maginot Line had already diverted Hitler's war plans toward less potent targets along the North Sea or perhaps west of Poland into Russia.

If the Communists in Paris were less noisy than usual, it was possibly because they were too embarrassed to speak after Hitler signed a nonaggression pact with Russia—a pact permitting Russia to share in the partitioning of Poland. Two weeks after the Nazis had entered Poland, the Soviet troops joined them, arousing such outrage among anti-Communist political leaders in France that the government banned the party and declared illegal the distribution of Communist newspapers and other literature.

Fortunately for Antonio, Mussolini's government remained neutral during and immediately after the conquest of Poland, and Antonio kept his business running in an atmosphere of perpetual twilight. What he lacked in clarity was balanced by his resolve to see the situation through, to not panic and desert the city, to honor his training as a soldier. Enough of that remained within him, along with his pride as a proprietor, that his shop became his command post, and he would not surrender it by choice.

His reassuring letters to Adelina and his children in Bovalino, and to his parents in Maida, stressed that everything appeared normal in Paris despite Hitler's ominous ambitions, and Antonio urged them not to fear for his safety or become alarmed by what they might read in newspapers about the fate of France. *Paris is as beautiful today as when you last saw it,* he wrote Adelina during the early spring of 1940, *and it will be even more beautiful when you return.* He truly believed these words when he wrote them, for nothing that he could see in the streets of the city, or on the faces of its people, would justify his worries about another war on French soil. People strolled at their normal pace every day along the Champs-Élysées; they dined unhurriedly in restaurants and cafés; they attended the opera and fashion shows; they went to the Louvre to see paintings, to the Folies to see showgirls, to Notre-Dame to speak to God. Antonio told Adelina about the springtime arrival of tourists, their wandering pleasantly about the city while news vendors screamed out headlines that predicted rising gloom in distant places; but in Paris the sun was shining, and most people felt very safe and secure far behind the mighty Maginot Line.

But before the end of spring, much of the gloom reflected in the headlines became horribly real: the invading Russians overcame Finnish resistance in March; the Germans broke into Denmark in early April, taking Copenhagen in twelve hours; and in late April, the Nazis were supreme in Norway. By May, Hitler had taken Holland and Belgium, violating the neutrality he had often reaffirmed with those countries in the recent past; and as the massive German attack smashed through Belgium, flanking the Maginot Line to the south, the French people learned to their distress in mid-May 1940 that Nazi armored divisions had crossed the Meuse River, and were rolling unimpeded toward Paris—which they would enter and control by mid-June, unfurling a swastika flag high up on the Eiffel Tower.

I cannot believe what I'm hearing on the radio! Antonio wrote in his diary a few days before the city yielded to General Georg von Kuechler's Eighteenth Army. *The French government is leaving Paris for Tours! Everyone else is being urged to leave. All the roads south are jammed. I'm packed and have a ticket for Rome but don't want to go. Italy's still neutral, thank God, but everything's a mess. Daladier's government has fallen, Reynaud is Minister but they've brought in Marshal Pétain and General Weygand, two very old men, to help keep order. Thousands of English soldiers have escaped back to England from Dunkerque, and the French are scattered all over. What happened? What caused the collapse of France? . . . An army that cost millions and it couldn't resist even a week! . . . All that suffering and sacrifice between 1914 and 1918 for THIS!*

A day later, Antonio visited the Italian embassy, where he was met in the corridor by one of his customers who was an adviser to the Italian ambassador, Raffaele Guariglia.

"Antonio," he said, taking him by the arm and speaking softly. "Get out of here, and get out of Paris as fast as you can! Don't ask me any questions. I'm doing you a favor. . . ."

That evening, after bolting the door to his shop, Antonio boarded the train for Rome. He had not left a note in his shop for his tailors; all of them had left two days before, as had the superintendent and custodian in his apartment building on the Avenue Rachel. *I'm too stunned to know what I'm thinking now,* he wrote as he sat in a crowded but quiet railcar moving slowly toward the Italian border. *I'm still not sure I'm not dreaming all this. . . .*

The train pulled into Rome the following day. Antonio saw hundreds of people running up and down the platform and heard the cries of news vendors coming through the open windows of the car. He bought a newspaper as he transferred to a train bound for Naples.

The nightmare continues. Mussolini made an announcement at twelve o'clock. Italy is now at war with France. . . . This page of my diary is wet with my tears. . . .

45.

IHE NEWS OF Italy's declaration of war on France brought disappointment and disgust to the American White House, and as President Franklin D. Roosevelt arrived at the University of Virginia to deliver a commencement address, he announced to his audience: "On this tenth day of June, 1940, the hand that held the dagger has struck it into the back of its neighbor." The president was frustrated that his appeals in recent months to the Rome government and to Pope Pius XII had failed to prevent the Italian army from following Hitler's forces into France, and his anger at the Duce was applauded now by his listeners and echoed the following day on the editorial page of *The New York Times:*

> With the courage of a jackal at the heels of a bolder beast of prey, Mussolini has now left his ambush. His motives in taking Italy into the war against the Allies are as clear as day. He wants to share in the spoils which he believes will fall to Hitler, and he has chosen to enter the war at the precise moment when he thinks that he can accomplish this at the least cost and risk to himself. This is the end of all these weeks of hesitation, all the eager watching, all the cautious sniffing of the air, all the splendid courage held in the leash so carefully for some sign of the weakness of its victims. Fascismo marches when it thinks that it smells carrion.

Suddenly signs of anti-Italianism were heightened in the United States: "dago" and "wop" and similar insults were heard more frequently in the nation that contained five million residents of Italian ancestry; the Duce was burned in effigy in many American cities; and the Italo-American members of several "Italian" clubs in the country changed the names of their social organizations to "Columbus" clubs, seeking to link their Mediterranean roots to the laurels of the fifteenth-century sea captain from Genoa.

Many American diplomats and businessmen who had accepted honors from the Italian government in the past now returned their medals and scrolls; and when New York's Mayor La Guardia was asked if he would do likewise with the combat medals he had received as a World War I ally of Italy, the ex-officer in the United States air force shook his head and said he would save them to wear during future bombing missions—leaving no doubt that, if the United States joined France and Britain against Mussolini and the Nazis, he was ready to attack his ancestral homeland.

This was the public position of nearly all Italo-American politicians and celebrities after Roosevelt's speech; they were Americans first, Italians second. And yet in the privacy of their homes, away from the newspaper reporters and the grandstands of Columbus Day parades, many hoped and prayed that the United States would remain neutral in this latest conflict in Europe. Not only did they have close relatives and friends living on the other side, but they were also less disenchanted with the Duce privately than they pretended to be in public. Mussolini had achieved much in Italy, bringing ethnic pride to Italians throughout the world. In a nation of weak political leaders and sycophants he had symbolized boldness and strength, posing bare-chested and muscular with bathers and fishermen at the beach, and guiding his horse over the hedges at Villa Borghese in Rome, and helping peasants, bricklayers, and blacksmiths do their jobs (boasting that as a blacksmith's son he had grown up a manual laborer); and simultaneously he showed no humility toward the pin-striped statesmen of Britain, France, and the United States, those ungrateful nations which had "mutilated" Italy's share in the spoils of World War I, and against whom he was now prepared to mobilize as well as bargain, for as his mentor Machiavelli had written and as the Duce often quoted: "armed prophets won and the unarmed perished." Mussolini at the same time had made peace with the Church, which his political predecessors in Italy had been unable to do since the Risorgimento; and in the once disorderly streets of the capital and other major cities, he had restored order and public safety—cracking down on beggars and thieves, squelching the striking unions and disruptive Communists, and exiling or incarcerating the subgovernment of the Mafia by giving carte blanche to the enforcers of Fascist law, who cared little about fair trials.

If Mussolini did not get all of Italy's trains to run on time, he certainly improved the rail system, which had previously been geared to the convenience of conductors; and another domestic accomplishment was his vast reclamation programs, his conversion of such areas as the malarial Pontine marshlands south of Rome into habitable new towns such as Littoria. At a ceremony that celebrated the completion of that project, he announced: "Once, in order to find work, it was necessary to go beyond the Alps or cross the ocean. Today the land is here, only half an hour away from Rome. It is here that we have conquered a new province." Driving from Turin to Milan, leading a column of five hundred cars, Mussolini opened the *autostrada*. Riding on horseback in Rome along a road lined with pine trees and the ruins of the caesars, Mussolini inaugurated the Via dell'Impero. Earlier on the same day he had presided over the opening of a sports complex with a stadium surrounded by sixty marble statues of athletes and a fifty-five-foot-high gold-topped obelisk.

To the semiliterate farm boys and urban drifters who were unable to avoid conscription, and whose lack of loyalty to anything larger than their families had long contributed to Italy's reputation for producing many of the world's worst soldiers, Mussolini delivered impassioned speeches, exhorting them to emulate the Roman warriors—to forget what they might have heard about Caporetto, and to focus instead on the monument builders who had turned stone into marble and had founded an empire that the Fascists stood ready to revive by following the Duce's dictum: *Credere, Obbedire, Combattere!*—Believe, Obey, Fight! These words were displayed in military barracks and recruitment centers around the nation, and were stenciled on public buildings large and small in cities and towns from Milan to Maida; and Mussolini heralded the invasion of Ethiopia in 1935 as the first step toward the restoration of the once great Italian Empire. Married couples in Italy and the United States donated their gold wedding bands to the Duce to help defray the cost of his quest, and an Italo-American rally at New York's Madison Square Garden in support of the Ethiopian invasion drew a crowd of more than twenty thousand, including such prominent Italo-Americans as Mayor La Guardia. This was five years *before* Roosevelt's stab-in-the-back speech, and Mussolini's popularity in the United States at this time (except among blacks and left-wing organizations opposing Italy's entry into Africa) was high not only among La Guardia's Italo-American voters—and thus it was politically expedient for him to join them at Madison Square Garden—but among average Americans across the country as well. The Duce's name, in fact, had been featured in a 1934 hit tune by Cole Porter: "You're the top— you're Muss-o-li-ni. . . ."

Among those attending the Madison Square Garden rally in 1935 was Joseph Talese. He had brought his wife, Catherine, and their three-year-old son to visit Catherine's family in Brooklyn for a few days, and he left them there on this evening while he took the subway alone into Manhattan. When he told his wife's parents where he was going, there had been some demurring within the large family gathering at the di Paolas' dinner table—not from Catherine's father, Rosso, who was apolitical, but from Catherine's brother-in-law the Maida-born musician Nicholas Pileggi. As boys in the village, Joseph and Nicholas had marched together as Young Socialists; but since Joseph's immigration to America, and his assimilation into the conservative community of Ocean City, he had left all traces of his Socialism on the other side of the ocean. Pileggi, on the other hand, had become even more committed to Socialism in the United States: in his musicians' union in New York he had solicited financial support and recruited followers for the Socialist leader Norman Thomas; and as a frequent employee of the Empire Shoe factory in Brooklyn (where Pileggi and other Italo-American musicians supported themselves between jobs with the band) he had formed a small but active anti-Fascist workers' group that attended the speeches and distributed the left-wing pamphlets and newspaper of one of Mussolini's archenemies in America, the Italian publisher and anarchist Carlo Tresca.

Tresca, a tall, gray-bearded intellectual, was born into a prominent family in the central Italian town of Sulmona, seventy-five miles east of Rome. Sent as a boy to the seminary by his mother, Tresca would emerge (as had his hero Garibaldi decades before him) with a loathing for priests that would last a lifetime. When Tresca later became a newspaper publisher, it was his priest-baiting more than his radical politics that would bring him into conflict with Italian law. Not only did he believe that many priests were obsessed with sex, but also he believed he had the right to print the clergymen's names and the condemning evidence that supported his view—a journalistic service that led to enough libel suits and prison terms to prompt his immigration to the United States.

First as the editor of *Il Proletario,* and finally as the publisher of *Il Martello,* Tresca intended for his words of warning and rage to arouse the Little Italys of America. His editorials condemning the moral hypocrisy of the Church, the venality of the *padrone* system, the prejudicial verdict of the Sacco-Vanzetti trial, the brutality of the strikebreaking goons in the railyards of the Midwest and the sweatshops of the East became the manifesto of a new Italo-American Risorgimento to such readers as Nicholas Pileggi. After hearing Tresca speak at an anti-Fascist rally in Manhattan's Union Square in the early 1930s, Pileggi became a devoted follower—and a nuisance to his cousin Joseph whenever they were reunited at the di Paolas' dinner table for Christmas or other family gatherings in Brooklyn. Here, until dawn, over bottles of wine and bowls filled with cracked walnut shells, the merits and demerits of Mussolini were debated by these native sons of southern Italy and their kinsmen and friends, just as happened around tables throughout the United States. Mussolini had divided these Italian immigrants as their craggy villages and towns overseas had been divided for centuries, finding common ground only during earthquakes and other disasters. Mussolini was Italy's newest disaster, Pileggi argued, while his cousin said that it was too early to tell. Embarrassed by the lowly status of Italians in America, Joseph had found comfort in the Duce's identity with ancient Rome, and with Italy's preeminence in classical music, poetry, and art.

"The Italians were bringing art and culture to the world when the damned Anglo-Saxons were living in caves like savages and painting their faces blue," Joseph shouted one evening, angered because his cousin and one of his anarchist friends seemed to be debunking Italy while praising the cultural achievements of the British Empire, unhampered by the repressions of Catholicism and the Fascist state. The English were Joseph's least favorite people. He blamed the English for double-crossing the Italians at the Versailles Peace Conference in 1919—the English and their Anglo-Saxon kinsman in the American White House, Woodrow Wilson (who had once referred to Italians in America as a "cursed rabble"); and now as Mussolini was expanding into Ethiopia, it was the English, of *all* people, who were decrying colonialism as they welcomed the imperious Haile Selassie into London as a deposed hero.

Joseph of course kept such thoughts to himself when he was in Ocean City, where they might not be appreciated by his Anglo-Saxon clientele. But during these nocturnal quarrels in Brooklyn, after Rosso and Angelina had gone to bed, and while the younger wives were washing dishes in the kitchen with their children slumped drowsily in high chairs, pieces of cake and fruit resting on the floor beneath their feet, Joseph spiritedly and single-handedly defended Mussolini against Nicholas's left-wing cabal, most of them disgruntled strong unionist musicians with their fingernails blackened from working in a shoe factory, *all* of them apostles of the atheist and anarchist Carlo Tresca, who, in Joseph's view, was probably no less a Fascist than that other product of impassioned journalism, Benito Mussolini. Whether it was from the far left or the far right, these two leaders were after the same thing—control of the masses. Joseph was neither a devotee of nor an authority on the Fascist movement in Italy, having left the country two years before Mussolini's takeover in 1922; but he doubted that Italy in the interim could have become worse than it was. In any case, Joseph's pride and defensiveness about his Italian origins made him resentful of those who debunked Italy—which, at long last, was now trying to rise above its reputation as an unmilitaristic nation of bad soldiers, retreaters, and *imboscati,* shirkers. What a relief to have an Italian leader who invaded *other* nations for a change, as opposed to remaining at home and hiding in the hills waiting to surrender to yet another conqueror of Italian soil. If Joseph was not a Fascist at heart, his cousin and the other turncoat Italians made him sound like one whenever he came to Brooklyn.

Each time he arrived it seemed that his cousin had packed the room with even *more* soiled-fingered Socialists and anarchists who were eager to shout down Joseph's every pro-Italian statement. Being pro-Italian now was unfortunately construed as being pro-Fascist, but Joseph firmly expressed what he felt. Sometimes he wondered how he and Nicholas had become so different politically. Though born and reared in the same place as Joseph, and under the same guiding light of Saint Francis, Nicholas had become an atheist, had refused to baptize his infant son, had regretted marrying Susan di Paola in church. He had recently admitted this to Joseph, who was shocked into silence; and Joseph was quite sure that Nicholas would *never* acknowledge his Catholic wedding to his Jewish and Protestant friends in Union Square, those proponents of Emma Goldman, John Reed, Norman Thomas, and others who joined Tresca in denigrating Mussolini and the Italians—no doubt contributing to the self-loathing that many Italians such as his cousin felt about themselves these days. Joseph would never tell Nicholas this to his face, but he truly believed it. And if the Italo-Americans were still the most undesirable immigrant group in the United States, as an opinion poll had recently announced, then Joseph blamed his countrymen. Instead of supporting one another like other minorities, trying to combat prejudice by channeling their energies into a strong national organization such as B'nai B'rith, or the NAACP, the Italo-Americans squabbled among themselves; and *if* they formed organizations, they formed so *many* organizations—Garibaldi clubs, Mazzini clubs, Columbus clubs, Sons of Italy lodges, and dozens of others, each headed by a leader who was jealous of the other leaders— that the Italians in America could barely agree on the rules for playing *bocce*. What could be done with such people? Mussolini in Italy was trying to beat some sense into them, to bind them in *fasces* as the great caesars had done—to elevate them, to educate them about the glories of their past. If this was an integral part of the Fascist credo, Joseph saw no reason to oppose it. He had always been responsive to monument builders, miracle workers in heaven, strong leaders on earth. Joseph, like many men who had not grown up around their fathers, tended to idolize.

Roosevelt's speech in June 1940, however, made Joseph circumspect about defending Italy openly. He had been an American citizen for more than a decade, and he was not responsible for the situation in Italy. Since leaving his homeland in 1920 he had never desired to return, even for a visit—contrary to what he professed in letters to his mother. He had sent money and care packages back to Maida every month. He had sent enough money to his old parish priest to have his family remembered at each Sunday Mass. He had tearfully mourned the passing of his grandparents Ippolita and Domenico, who died of old age, and his history teacher Don Achille, who died in a rock slide that crushed his carriage and killed his horse. Joseph sent wedding gifts, christening gifts, grants, and loans in response to every announcement and request from abroad. He thought constantly of Maida. But once he had landed in America, that is where he wanted to stay. In his nightmares he often saw himself as middle-aged in Maida—unable to get back to America, imprisoned in the village for some undefined offense, or bedridden next to Sebastian. If Mussolini and Roosevelt were now on a collision course, which, sadly, appeared to be the case, Joseph knew where he stood—indeed, he had already declared it when he became an American citizen. Still, he was inwardly tormented and guilt-ridden by the turn of events. He now invented excuses to avoid going to Brooklyn, unwilling to face what he assumed would be much overweening smugness on the part of his cousin and other I-told-you-so Italians. Joseph despised Roosevelt for stirring up added animosity toward Italians in America and vowed he would never again vote for him. In November 1940, Joseph switched everlastingly to the Republican Party, backing Wendell L. Willkie in the presidential election race.

Other Italo-Americans were similarly upset with Roosevelt, as was evident in the press that carried statements by some *prominenti* accusing the president of being anti-Italian; but whatever consolation this brought Joseph was lost in his sadness and even bitterness over the fall from grace of the one man he was counting on to restore power and pride to the Italian people. Now with the Duce deemed no better than Hitler, who was there left to admire among contemporary Italians? Joseph could think of very few. And of those few, even *he* had reservations.

Perhaps this explained why Italians collectively could admire only those who had been dead for centuries. Only saints could survive Italian scrutiny and jealousy. Only when they named saints were the Italians the most generous and magnanimous people on earth. As for himself, Joseph was shamefully disappointed to admit that the Italians he most admired on earth were invariably products of northern Italy. Why was this true now in 1940, a half-century after the mass immigration of southerners to the United States? Were his southern countrymen really so dim-witted and insufficiently ambitious to rise quickly in America—except through the Mafia? Or were the honest, earnest southerners held back by the prejudicial Anglo-Saxons who controlled the nation and were more favorably disposed to the usually fairer-skinned immigrants from Piedmont and Tuscany? In Argentina, for example, the southern immigrants had gained legitimate power within one generation. And consider the progress made by his cousin Antonio in Paris. But here in the United States, where the overwhelming majority of Italy's five million settlers were refugees from the old Bourbon kingdom that stretched between Naples and Palermo—a number that would have been much larger if one counted the many southerners who concealed their heritage by changing their names, or by lying to, or hiding from, the survey-takers—the fact remained that it was the small fraction of northerners to whom Joseph turned for a confirmation of Italian worthiness in America.

Prominent among these was the California-based financier Amadeo P. Giannini, who expanded from a small Italian neighborhood banker in San Francisco to the founder in 1930 of the powerful Bank of America, which would soon have branch offices throughout the nation. Giannini's ancestors were from Genoa—hardly within range of a southern Italo-American's search for prideful regional identity; but, as in the case of Christopher Columbus, Joseph took what he could get. The NBC Symphony Orchestra was headed by another northerner whom Joseph looked up to: Arturo Toscanini, who was a native of Parma, southeast of Milan—although Toscanini *had* by 1940 installed as his first flutist a southern Italian, a future composer and conductor named Carmine Coppola. Coppola had an infant son who would grow up to become a Hollywood director, of such films as *The Godfather.* But as in the case of the younger Coppola—named Francis *Ford* Coppola because he was born in Detroit—the famous offspring of the Bourbon kingdom (offspring that would also include the 1984 vice-presidential candidate Geraldine Ferraro, the New York senator Alfonse D'Amato, the architect Robert Venturi, the artist Frank Stella, and the feminist leader Eleanor Cutri Smeal) were at least a generation away from success and recognition. More typical of the occupation of southern Italo-Americans between World Wars I and II in America were such unheralded figures as Nicola Iacocca, who worked variously as a shoemaker, a short-order cook, and a seller of auto tires in Allentown, Pennsylvania (his son Lee would become president of Ford Motor Company in 1970); and Andrea Cuomo, who dug sewers in northern New Jersey (his son Mario would be elected governor of New York in 1982). But in 1940 the only well-known Italian name in American politics was of course that of New York's Mayor Fiorello La Guardia, and if the popular politician was not unduly sensitive about the origins of his bandmaster father, Achille (a native of the southern town of Foggia), he most likely *was* about the origins of his Trieste-born Jewish mother, Irene. When her background was revealed in a New York Yiddish newspaper during the mayor's first term, La Guardia initially refused to discuss it.

Insecure and factionalized as the Italians in America seemed to be—especially after Roosevelt's stab-in-the-back comment in 1940—there was one politician who believed he could take advantage of this situation and swing great numbers of unhappy Italian voters to his side. He was the

Republican candidate for president, Wendell L. Willkie. And during his campaign against Roosevelt, he often dared the president to repeat his reference to the Italians as back-stabbers. But Roosevelt avoided doing so. Although the race was close—with Willkie carrying most neighborhoods heavily populated by Italo-Americans—Roosevelt won an unprecedented third term with a popular vote of 27 million to Willkie's 22 million. After this, as far as Italians in the United States were concerned, things only worsened.

Roosevelt's declaration of war against Japan after the latter's surprise air attack on the American naval base at Pearl Harbor, on December 7, 1941, meant that Japan's Axis allies, Italy and Germany, were obliged to take sides against the United States; and thus Americans of Italian descent were now officially at war with their families in Italy. Joseph's situation was typical: while he was parading his patriotism by volunteering for patrol duty along the boardwalk with other members of his Rotary Club, his brothers and other relatives overseas were dressed in Fascist uniforms strutting to the goose step that Mussolini had introduced in the hope that his soldiers might look and act more like the bellicose Nazi troops whom the Duce envied and revered.

But unfortunately for the Duce, he could not turn Italians into Germans; and their battlefield performances from the outset of the war most often embarrassed him. His forces had hardly gained enough mileage against the weakened French in 1940 to be worthy of an armistice—France's yielding to Italy had more to do with Hitler's strong desires than with Mussolini's timid invaders—and the Italian army proved equally inept after attacking Greece in 1940 (where the Italians again needed German help). And Italy was no more persevering in the African campaigns that followed from 1941 through 1943; every Italian advancement in the desert was followed by military blunders and setbacks, including one in Ethiopia, which allowed the British to transport back to his palace and his throne the deposed emperor, Haile Selassie. While an exasperated Mussolini could only conclude that Italy's generals and soldiers were unworthy of his leadership, a more plausible explanation was perhaps offered by *The Christian Science Monitor*'s correspondent in Rome, Saville R. Davis, who observed: "It is not possible to fight modern battles with an army of conscientious objectors."

The national Italian persona, individualistic in the extreme, simply could not be regimented into a war machine by Mussolini or probably anyone else. At this point in their history, the people of Italy were beyond regimentation. Anyone who doubted this had merely to watch Italian soldiers marching in a parade: they were rarely in step. The average Italian conscript saw no reason to fight in World War II. In World War I, there had at least been the longtime animosity toward Austria, dating back before the Risorgimento. But whom could they be convinced to hate in World War II, especially after Italy had gained so little after the costly triumph of World War I? The Italian people had no real quarrel now with the French, or even with the British, whose country had long enriched Italy with friendly tourists and admiring travel writers; and *certainly* no quarrel with the United States, the locale of myriad Little Italys generating the income that kept multitudes of Italians from starvation. It was also true that Italian men, by their very nature, are averse to impersonal killings, which was what a soldier was expected to accomplish, and what most countries' conscripts adapt to doing quite readily. But as triggerhappy as the average Italian male might be in avenging a *personal* affront— some other man's winking at his girlfriend; seducing his wife; stealing his sheep: three offenses that many hotheaded Italian men would punish with equal vigor—the same man would instinctively absent himself from the *impersonal* bloodletting that was endemic to battlefields occupied by clashing infantrymen, machine-gunners, and tankers. If he had learned anything from Italian history, it was that today's enemy will be tomorrow's friend; and that in conflicts fought at the behest of kings, or dictators, or politicians, there was very little that was worth dying for.

There were, to be sure, Italian males who were exceptions to the norm, and many of these were employed by the Mafia—in which perhaps most of Italy's natural-born "soldiers" were enlisted, and in which there still might exist the residue of the predatory blood that once flowed through the veins of Roman warriors. The *mafiosi* were, if nothing else, the Italians most capable of "impersonal" killings—bringing death to absolute strangers if need be to fulfill an order from a *capo mafioso,* who routinely passed it down from above. Many of the better Mafia soldiers had immigrated to America after their civil rights in Sicily and southern Italy had been curtailed by the frequently lawless raids of Fascist lawmen. But when Mussolini required a reliable gunman, as he did in 1943, he was, ironically, obliged to purchase an expensive contract killing via a Fascist deputy to a Sicilian-born Mafia boss in Brooklyn, whom the Duce's law enforcers had banished from Italy as an undesirable citizen. Shortly after the boss had reviewed the contract, and received a lucrative down payment, he approved the order and relayed it down the ranks to be carried out by one of his soldiers, a sharpshooter of Sicilian origin named Carmine Galante—who efficiently did his job. After stalking for a few days the man whom Mussolini had come to abhor as a political nemesis in the United States, and wanted to have eliminated, the *mafioso* Galante finally confronted the man on a dark street in lower Manhattan and pumped bullets into one of his lungs and his brain.

Carlo Tresca died almost immediately.

46.

ADOLF HITLER'S CONTROL over France from the spring of 1940 into the summer of 1944 meant that Antonio Cristiani, as a citizen of Italy, was free to travel back and forth across the French–Italian border; and he often arrived in Maida with bundles of gifts that brightened the spirits of the melancholy townspeople, who greeted him sometimes with outbursts of cheering that, whether he deserved it or not, he thoroughly enjoyed.

With each visit home the number of his greeters increased, no doubt because the train station's indiscreet telegrapher, after receiving Antonio's wired time of arrival from Paris and relaying the message to the elderly Cristianis by donkey express, then shared the information with the station's carriage drivers, who in turn circulated it throughout the village and persuaded a growing number of local dignitaries and bureaucrats (each seeking favors from Maida's most distinguished native son) to book carriage reservations to the terminal in time to welcome their potential benefactor. Although Antonio lacked the financial resources and political influence in either Paris or Rome to achieve most of his countrymen's desires, he never rejected their requests or hinted that it was beyond his power to fulfill them; for what his countrymen most needed he felt compelled to encourage—the notion that anything was possible. This notion was fundamental to their religious faith, to their belief in miracles, to their strength and stoicism in times of natural and manmade upheavals. Southern Italy was a fountainhead of dark fantasies, turmoil, and hope.

Submerged but reachable by a true and probing touch, every southerner's sense of hope was tempered by the rock-hard reality that nature progressed slowly in this part of Italy, where the planters of olive trees never survived to see the fruits of their labor, and where individuals seeking favors from high places anticipated a *very* long wait. But the average needy southerner found comfort in the familiarly slow process by which all requests for special treatment were lobbied by aspiring benefactors up through the hierarchy of influence-peddling bureaucrats and *prominenti* (people not always corrupt, but rarely incorruptible); and then further up to the levels of Machiavellian ministers and magistrates renowned for their pondering and vacillation, and their expectation that with every favor they dispensed they would receive one in return—if not today, then tomorrow; if not on earth, then in heaven.

The legacy of broken promises being what it was in this village where everything was remembered and tardiness was a venerated tradition, Antonio felt less reluctant to represent himself to his townsmen as a problem solver. It was an honorable calling in the south, one in which he really never had to solve a problem but had only to convey the impression that he was *trying* to solve one. Being a social-climbing tailor, well practiced in the cloaked art of appearances, made him ideal for this role; and whenever he arrived at the Maida train station he gave a command performance.

Hardly did he embrace his mother and father before he would turn to the crowds pressing around him: people who whispered into his ears, and to whom he nodded encouragingly; people who shouted reminders of past requests, which he now jotted down for the first time in his notebook, pausing to slip a few hundred-lire bills into the pockets of others as they pretended not to notice. Such gestures of kindness and hope, repeated whenever he came to town, brought merriment to this terminal most often pervaded by the gloom of black-ribboned trains bearing coffins of war victims as well as injured soldiers returning from Italy's ill-fated campaigns in Africa, or Greece, or, more recently—as Mussolini had backed Hitler's turnabout on their onetime ally Joseph Stalin—the bloodstained steppes of Russia. What a contrast Antonio's arrivals were to such reminders—his leaping onto the platform with a two-handed wave after doffing his homburg, his clothing remarkably unwrinkled and his jacket lapels rouged with rosettes; his tan-and-white semibrogue footwear, buffed minutes before with a dinner napkin he had purloined from the dining car, shining as brightly as his lacquered leather valises, which two huffing porters carried behind him, along with his gift packages for his family, his friends, and a few favored bureaucrats and *prominenti*. After reassuring his entire constituency, and devoting more lines in his notebook to their wishful thinking, Antonio would be escorted by the town's left-wing mayor and right-wing monsignor toward Maida's only motor vehicle, a four-door Fiat touring car owned by the municipality and used on such special occasions as Saint Francis's feast day procession, the most important funerals and weddings, and Antonio's quarterly sojourns to his native village. The driver of the vehicle on all occasions was the prefect of the province, a white-haired, blue-uniformed man bearing a pistol and sword whose oldest son was currently serving with the Italian air force in Albania. When the prefect had once complained of his son's distant assignment, Antonio had hinted that arrangements might be made to transfer him closer to home—to Cosenza perhaps, or better yet to Catanzaro. The prefect knew that this was impossible, there being no air bases located in Cosenza or Catanzaro; but appreciating Antonio's good intentions, he made no mention of this. He also hoped he might use Antonio's influence in other ways, for he had studied the photographs and news clippings in the window of Francesco Cristiani's tailor shop, accounts of Antonio's receiving many honors, including one that pictured him shaking hands with the Duce's son-in-law, Count Galeazzo Ciano.

When this was first sighted by the baron of the Bianchi family, it brought tears to his eyes as he remembered his hopes years before to have Antonio for *his* son-in-law, and it might have happened if the baron's beautiful daughter Olympia had not been too narcissistic to court, and wiser than to end up in Argentina owning a bankrupt boutique. As a sign of his enduring esteem for Antonio, the baron was always on hand at the station to greet him, expecting nothing in return except that Antonio dine on occasion at the crumbling palazzo and regale the doddering baroness and himself with amusing tales and comments about modern life beyond the surrounding mountains.

Another habitual attendee of Antonio's arrivals was the local leader of the Fascist Party, a cement mixer by trade who was born of a Sicilian mother and was therefore viewed with grave suspicion by party leaders in the north; he believed Antonio could swing a lucrative road-building contract his way on the Maida marina through influence with the Duce's son-in-law. When the cement mixer sought Antonio's intercession in this matter, the latter patted him on the back, gave him a hearty smile, and said he would see what could be done—knowing as he spoke that he would do absolutely nothing. As Antonio remembered well, the last time he had tried to use his influence with the Duce's son-in-law, the graceless Count Ciano had reacted by sending three intimidating Fascist henchmen to visit his shop in Paris. *One of my friends in the Italian Embassy confided that Ciano's office thinks I'm too pro-French and therefore an enemy of Italy,* Antonio noted in his diary during the spring of 1942. *But in Paris many French people think I'm too pro-Italian, and naturally a Fascist. . . . I must remain very, very careful these days,* very *careful. . . .* And very careful he remained throughout the year. So long as Ciano was Mussolini's son-in-law, and so long as

Mussolini was the Duce, Antonio's image in Maida as being close to Italy's ruling family would continue as a myth he would neither affirm nor deny.

The local order of mendicant friars, from whom some people kept their distance because the friars rarely took a bath, were also regularly part of Antonio's receiving committee. They anticipated the day when he would serve as their fund-raiser—if there again came a day when the people of Maida had funds. The village had been on the barter system for years; and with the wartime rationing laws restricting everything except what was traded secretly on Italy's flourishing black market, the mendicant friars claimed they were close to starvation, although there was rarely one among them who was not grossly overweight. It was truly impossible to starve in Maida, where vegetables and fruit grew miraculously out of rocks whenever there was the slightest whiff of famine in the air, which was discernible with the first sky battles between buzzards. But it was also true that, except for enough to eat, few people had enough of anything else.

The petrol to operate the municipality's Fiat had to be procured periodically from the ferryboats that docked on the coast at a port where the prefect had nefarious connections. And the charcoal that burned in the braziers of the villagers' homes came largely from the state railway, which was unaware of the generosity of its local stationmaster. Since all wool and other fabric had been requisitioned by the army for making uniforms, tents, and other military articles, Antonio's father, Francesco, would have lacked the material to make suits even *if* he had had the customers with the money or sufficient tradable commodities to afford them. Francesco, now in his middle seventies, was reduced to patching people's worn-out clothing, or to exchanging with tailors in distant villages and trying to resell locally the unneeded garments of customers who had died before trying them on, or who had tried them on, taken them home, and died at some later date—leaving to their next-of-kin the dismal but traditional duty of returning the wardrobe to the "dead storage" rooms that existed in every tailor shop. Even in these modern times of the 1940s, with the Germans inventing rocket ships that flew over England without pilots, it was considered dangerous and disrespectful for a villager to don the clothing of the dead, whose eternal and omnipresent spirits would surely avenge such insults. It was also deemed disrespectful to profit from dead people's clothing, either through sale or barter.

But now that fabric was so scarce even scarecrows had been divested, many tailors felt no compunctions about trading and reselling buried men's bespoke clothing, although the tailors took care to sell only clothes of men buried far away. The term "far away" in the mountainous south usually meant any distance of more than twenty miles.

Antonio grabbed one of the gift packages from the stack the railroad porter was carrying, and handed it to a friar, saying, "Here, I've brought you a present from Paris." Before the friar could say thank you, Antonio allowed himself to be shoved forward by those pressing behind him, a crowd that included the mayor, the monsignor, and the prefect, all of whom were eager to board the awaiting Fiat and proceed toward the village. If Antonio had handed the friar the correct present, and he prayed that he had, the friar would find in it the robe of a Franciscan monk who had recently died in Paris, and had earlier served as the chaplain in Antonio's veterans' association. The mayor's present, which the prefect had just placed in the car trunk along with other packages, was a brand-new suit Antonio had made nearly three years before for a French deputy minister who had fled Paris days before the German invasion of 1940. The deputy minister had neither paid for the suit nor subsequently written asking Antonio to save it, and Antonio assumed that he had joined France's other fleeing political figures in Vichy, the town in central France earlier known for its spa and health-giving waters, but presently known as the refuge for the ousted French government led by Marshal Pétain and others who had collaborated with the Germans. Many of these people had left behind in Antonio's shop not only new suits and overcoats but also older garments that had been remodeled or altered. After storing them for so long without a word from their owners, Antonio was quite sure they would never be reclaimed. He became doubly convinced of this before Christmas 1942, when the Germans—who had hitherto limited their occupation to north central France and the coastal areas along the Atlantic Ocean and the English Channel—suddenly ordered their troops throughout central and southern France, thus occupying the entire country, including Vichy. Seeing no bright future for the forgotten French menswear that was crowding his shop, Antonio packed much of the new and used clothing into boxes and brought it to Maida to distribute to the townspeople.

As the Fiat carrying Antonio pulled to a stop on the edge of the Piazza Garibaldi, the afternoon *passeggiata* was already in progress. It was four p.m. on an unseasonably mild and almost windless day, with the sun dangling like an orange under the trees that reached out over the cliffs and shaded the valley. Church bells were ringing and the town band, seated along the stone base of the fountain, played an aria from Verdi's *Rigoletto*. A large group of slow-moving walkers, most of them elderly men—some accompanied by the young widows of soldiers (few white widows now resided in Maida)—paused and stared across the square as they spotted the Fiat, then nodded respectfully when they recognized the monsignor, the mayor, and Antonio stepping from it. Antonio waved and tipped his hat toward them, and also up at the baroness, whom he spotted watching him from behind the curtains of her palazzo; but he remained close to the car, waiting as the procession of horse-drawn carriages that had followed him from the station made its way up the winding cobblestone road. Piled high on the racks of the carriages, held secure by leather straps or lengths of hemp, were the gifts that Antonio had brought from Paris. He had never before brought so many parcels as on this occasion, and at the station it had taken fifteen minutes (and a gratuity in the form of four packs of Turkish cigarettes) for the porters to unload them from the baggage car and hand them, under Antonio's direction, to the drivers of the carriages bearing the passengers to whom the boxes were inscribed.

Antonio was sure that his father would be pleased when he unwrapped his gift. It was a bolt of excellent English herringbone material that Antonio had acquired on the French black market, and out of which it would have been imprudent of him to make a suit or coat to be worn in Nazi-occupied Paris. Antonio had brought for his mother a black dress he had purchased at Galeries Lafayette, a simple but well-made frock similar to the others he had been bringing home for several years, since the sudden death of her nearly one-hundred-year-old father; her stunned reaction to his death suggested that she had assumed Domenico would live forever. Now approaching seventy, with her long white hair arranged in a bun under an ebony silk veil that flowed out from under her black lace mantilla, Maria Talese Cristiani spent most of her daylight hours in prayer either at the cemetery or in church, a routine she varied only when she accompanied her husband to the station to meet Antonio. Antonio had often asked her to ride back to town with him in the Fiat, but she had always refused. She seemed to know that the Fiat was powered by petrol of questionable origin.

After assisting his mother down from the carriage in the Piazza Garibaldi, Antonio escorted her and his father toward the crowd now gathered around the fountain. The mayor was already there holding a megaphone. The monsignor stood next to him ready to give the benediction. The prefect remained in the Fiat, keeping an eye on it and also on the extra packages that had not fit into the trunk and had had to be roped to the roof. A group of teenaged boys, too young for conscription, were standing nearby along the road, one of them holding a chained leash attached to the leather collar of a goat. A few mangy-looking sheep wandered around near the edge of the square, having gained complete independence since the death of the village's unsucceeded shepherd, Guardacielo.

After the band had stopped playing, and the monsignor had offered a prayer for the safety of Italian servicemen at the front, the mayor, a short moustachioed man wearing a leftover French frock coat that Antonio had given him the year before, mounted the bandmaster's wooden box and began to speak into his megaphone. There were almost three hundred people gathered in the square and standing in the surrounding balconies, among them the late arrivals from the station—the baron, the Fascist cement mixer, the head mendicant friar. Sooner or later the mayor intended to introduce Antonio, but now, holding the megaphone in the air to the height of his flat-crowned black hat, the mayor was magnetized, unable to pull the trombone-length cone away from his mouth, even though it seemed to become heavier with each platitude and caused him to switch it constantly from one hand to the other.

Antonio could not understand much of what the mayor was saying, for he stood directly behind him and heard mostly sounds echoing off the nearby buildings, interrupted occasionally by municipal employees applauding in the front row. Antonio made use of his waiting time by trying to pacify his mother, who had expressed irritation after greeting him, because he had once again come to Maida unaccompanied by his wife and children.

Since the Germans had invaded France, Antonio had preferred that Adelina and the children remain with her family in Bovalino, which was well south of Maida on the Ionian shoreline facing Greece, and which Antonio considered a less likely spot for military invasion than that part of the toe that practically touched upon Sicily, and *especially* that most narrow part of the toe on which Maida protruded. He and his mother had quarreled often in the past year over his insistence that there were safer places in the world than Maida, notwithstanding her conviction that it was under the constant and personal protection of Saint Francis. What Antonio did not have the heart to tell his mother at this time, a day prior to his going on to Bovalino, was that he planned to take his wife and children out of Italy altogether and bring them back with him to Paris. If the Axis forces failed to halt the Allies in North Africa, it was reasonable to assume that the Allies might soon cross the Mediterranean into Sicily, and ultimately invade southern Italy. With all due respect to Saint Francis, Antonio now preferred Paris.

As the mayor droned on behind his megaphone, Antonio shifted his attention out to the people in the crowd who were also looking around, talking among themselves, and sometimes yawning. More than a few of these people wore articles of clothing that, before the success of the friars, had been restricted to his father's dead-storage vault; and Antonio began to notice some garments that he himself had brought earlier from Paris, most of them now looking rather old-fashioned. The frock coat that Antonio studied on the back of the mayor, for example, dated back to World War I and might well have been worn by a diplomat attending the signing of the Treaty of Versailles. But then Antonio reasoned that *nothing* was really out of fashion in Maida, a village that had been out of fashion for centuries, and had nearly made a fashion of timelessness. The old palazzos that faced the square—these outdated domains where as a boy at Christmastime he had feasted with the likes of this crowd at the musical open houses the aristocrats used to sponsor—had themselves played host to receiving lines linked to the distant past and faded fashions of Baroque Bourbons, Lord Nelson's admirals, and the effulgent reign of Joachim Murat. But there were signs of the New World too on the backs of those gathered around the bandstand—clothing that Antonio recognized as clearly American-made, some of it no doubt sent to Maida by his cousin Joseph. He recognized, on the shoulders of one of Joseph's Rocchino uncles who had been deported from Ambler during the Depression, a raglan tweed topcoat with extrawide lapels that Joseph himself had been wearing in a snapshot he had once sent to Antonio in Paris. He spotted one of Joseph's Rocchino nieces, an unmarried woman in her early thirties, wearing a fur coat Antonio had never seen before; but it, too, had probably come from Joseph, who had recently written that he was clearing out abandoned garments from his fur storage vault in Ocean City and shipping some furs to Maida. This particular coat was of leopard skin.

Finally the mayor stopped talking and turned the megaphone over to Antonio. Antonio refused it, as he always did, for the crowd moved in closely whenever he spoke, and he was known to be mercifully brief.

"Thank you for your warm welcome," he began, nodding as they applauded, "and please know that I'm doing everything I can to remain worthy of your trust. As I look around, I see that some of you have honored me by wearing the clothing I have provided. And as you're probably aware, I've come here today with many more things from Paris. There's a limit to what I'm allowed to carry on the train, so please forgive me if I've been unable to bring something for you. The next time, I assure you, I will. . . ."

Antonio went on to thank the mayor for his generous introduction, and the monsignor for his benediction, and the prefect for guaranteeing to deliver personally the parcels to those addressees who were not in the crowd. Then he gave a final wave and made a quick exit with his parents down a narrow road behind the fountain, before the portly head friar of the mendicants could catch up with him.

That night, in the home of the late Domenico Talese, Antonio had dinner with many of his Maida relatives. Joseph's mother, Marian, was there, and so were her two brothers who had been deported from Ambler, as well as Joseph's next-to-youngest brother, Nicola. A trim, lean, fine-featured man in his mid-thirties, Nicola bore a striking physical resemblance to Joseph—so much so that Antonio (who had seen very little of the soldiering Nicola in recent years, and whose impressions of Joseph now came from photographs) had at first believed that it was Joseph who stood waiting to greet him on this occasion from behind the tottering gate of their grandfather's property. Nicola's dark wavy hair was beginning to gray in the same places as Joseph's, and in addition to their deep-set dark eyes and their erect postures, the brothers shared a pride in their appearance: Antonio noted that Nicola, who had been trimming the wall vines when Antonio arrived at the gate, was wearing a jacket and tie and cotton gloves, presumably to protect his hands from scratches. But what Antonio had noticed most was Nicola's tempered manner of greeting, his tentative touch as he had embraced Antonio, his kiss on each cheek so slight as to be hardly felt. This sense of unfamiliarity even within the family was one of Joseph's qualities that Antonio remembered well and had always accepted as part of his uncertain upbringing, his absent father and the presence of a mother who favored her son Sebastian. Antonio had no explanation to offer about Nicola, who had been only six years old when Antonio had run away to Paris. And during Antonio's subsequent visits to Maida, it seemed that Nicola had always been elsewhere—on military duty in northern Italy, or Africa, or Albania. Or if he *was* in Maida during Antonio's visits, Nicola for some reason had kept his distance, as he had earlier on this particular day, not coming to the station or the square, and apparently feeling no obligation to explain why.

"Come," Nicola had said, lightly taking Antonio's arm after placing his gardening shears and gloves on the ledge of the wall. "They're all inside waiting for you." Antonio would have liked to spend a few private moments with Nicola outside, but his cousin clearly shared no such desire. Somewhat troubled, Antonio let Nicola guide him into the house.

Antonio's parents were already with the other guests—Francesco was talking to one of Antonio's elderly uncles, from the nearby town of Nicastro, who stood with the aid of a cane, while Antonio's mother, having removed her black veil and gloves, was in the kitchen with the other women preparing dinner, among them Joseph's mother and only sister. Now thirty-four, with her husband a prisoner of war of the British in North Africa, Ippolita nonetheless looked as youthful and pretty as Antonio remembered her; she lived in a house nearby with her three young children, and they frequently accompanied Antonio's mother to early-morning Mass. Antonio's mother had written him often in Paris urging him to do what he could for the captured soldier, whose name was Francesco Pileggi (he was a distant cousin of the Brooklyn musician Nicholas Pileggi), and Antonio's return letters to his mother and Ippolita promised that he was doing everything possible and was in contact with the Italian Foreign Ministry. What he withheld from his letters was an unconfirmed report from the ministry that Corporal Francesco Pileggi was dead.

When he heard his name called by the elderly uncle and others who had spotted him with Nicola, Antonio hastened toward them and embraced them; and for the next several minutes he made his way slowly around the room, greeting people whose surnames were mostly Cristiani or Talese or Rocchino or Pileggi, and whose first names he readily recalled except in the cases of some of the children—who remained shyly in the background, or ran gleefully around their tolerant elders. The guests stood close to the flaming fireplace, where Nicola was now placing more logs; or they sat on the old threadbare brocaded chairs in the far corner of this anteroom, which was between the dining room and the open door to the kitchen, misty with steam rising from the cast-iron caldrons that released an aroma of blended sauces and herbs that was a pleasant contrast to the damp and chilly breezes sweeping through the drafty stone house. It seemed to Antonio that, despite the heat from the kitchen and fireplace, the room was no warmer than it was outdoors; indeed, most of the guests kept on their coats, their capes, and, in the instance of the talkative Rocchino spinster, her leopard-skinned gift from America.

But the uncomfortable conditions inside were understandable; except for occasional reunions such as this, the house was rarely used and obviously had not been properly maintained since the deaths of its last full-time occupants—Antonio's grandparents Domenico and Ippolita Talese. It was not merely a lack of materials and labor that caused deterioration, but also a reluctance on the part of family members to touch or change in any way what had brought contentment and familiarity to the departed couple. And so except for the deepening dust that had now settled over Ippolita's objets d'art on the shelves, and on her mauve-colored draperies, and on the wall painting that had once clearly identified the cliffside manor built in Vibo Valentia by Ippolita's ancestors in the Gagliardi family, Antonio saw this place as completely unchanged from the time of his boyhood visits—when he would occasionally slip away from the adults and indulge his curiosity upstairs in the room with the four-poster bed and the moving-eyed statuette of Saint Francis lodged in a candlelit niche above his grandfather's bureau. During Antonio's last visit to Maida, he had peeked into that bedroom to see if the eyes still moved, but they were so laden with dust it was impossible to tell. Curious, he moved toward the statuette with his handkerchief in hand, then paused as he recalled from childhood his mother's admonishments against his ever touching a holy object—or any object, for that matter—in this house. She herself had grown up here, and had no doubt been similarly warned by her devout and dictatorial father. But in fact one thing *had* been touched and even removed from the house since the death of his grandparents. It was the ornamental bronze jewel box that Antonio always used to see resting on his grandmother's bureau, the one that held the Gagliardi jewels remembered from the story of Domenico and the gypsies. Antonio's father had first told him the story during his days as an apprentice in Maida, and Antonio had enjoyed retelling it to his friends in Paris; but after his grandfather's death, Antonio's mother begged him to cease repeating it, for Domenico's spirit would not be amused by reminders of that devout Christian's greed. And the day after Domenico's death, Antonio's mother had taken the bronze jewelry box and, without opening it, gave it to the church.

Antonio now saw his mother coming in from the kitchen, followed by his aunt Marian, who pointed out where everyone was to sit at the long table in the dining room. As Marian's daughter, Ippolita, and daughter-in-law Angela, Nicola's wife, carried in plates of pasta and vegetables, Marian urged everyone to begin eating immediately while the food was hot. Marian was a petite, handsome woman in her late sixties; her softly braided gray hair was still thick and shiny, and with her maroon shawl tossed back over one shoulder and her arms akimbo, she struck a pose that Antonio saw as both feminine and commanding. Her posture was as erect as those of her sons on whom she had imposed it; and in all the years that Antonio had been in her presence, she had never appeared to him more composed and self-assured. Of course the family-rearing responsibilities forced upon her during her youthful years as a white widow, and her subsequent years as a true widow, had developed her capacities as a decision maker; but even so, Antonio was especially impressed by her as he took his honored place at the far end of the table, and then watched as his aunt sat down at the other end, in the high-backed chair always reserved for Domenico.

Dinner lasted until midnight, with the conversation centered around the war, the subject of increasing anxiety if not fear. Antonio tried to assure the family that southern Italy would not become a major battleground, arguing that it lacked the industrial centers and key military targets that would justify the Allies' difficulty in trying to penetrate mountains even now controlled by Axis artillery. The Rocchino brothers disagreed, saying that the Allies would invade along the indefensible southern coastlines, and that whatever Axis artillery was perched on the upper cliffs would soon be negated by the Allied aircraft that already flew freely over Sicily and much of the Mediterranean. Antonio's mother interrupted the discussion once to ask them all to pray for Ippolita's husband in the POW camp in Africa, and for Marian's youngest son, twenty-eight-year-old Domenico, who was now believed to be with the Fascist–Nazi forces on the Russian front. Then the youngest of the Rocchino men added a prayer on behalf of his nephews in the *American* army. The two nephews, both born in Ambler, had reached draft age and been conscripted.

Marian's oldest son, the almost forty-four-year-old veteran of World War I, was not at dinner tonight. Though dependent on his mother, Sebastian occasionally asserted himself, and on this night, as his mother explained to the others, he would not get out of bed. Sebastian now lived in his mother's house next door, occupying a room on the ground floor that opened into a yard where some farm animals grazed—a few of them the offspring of animals Sebastian had cared for as a teenaged foreman on old Domenico's farm. Sebastian was well enough to wander through the village on his own, although many villagers, often failing to understand his garbled speech, thought he was demented, a hopeless victim of shell shock and poison gas. But on previous visits Antonio had found him quite lucid as they spoke about the childhood experiences they had shared. Sebastian would not, however, speak of the war, and he spent many solitary hours whittling wood into delicately carved figures, not always separated, of animals and humans. There were times when Antonio wondered whether Sebastian's possible madness had not freed him from a life of drudgery and given him the chance to use a gift he otherwise would not have discovered.

Now that Nicola had returned to Maida, Marian had help in caring for Sebastian. Nicola, who became more cordial and comfortable with Antonio as the evening went on—keeping Antonio's wineglass filled, and sitting next to him after Antonio's mother had vacated her chair to help in the kitchen—asked Antonio if he thought Joseph would come back to Maida after the war. Joseph had never once indicated any intention of doing so in the letters he wrote regularly to Antonio, although their correspondence had of late been interrupted by the war; Joseph might send his clothes to Maida, but that was as close as Antonio guessed Joseph's presence would be felt.

Joseph's father had left Maida more than fifty years before, and even though Gaetano's bones rested in the nearby cemetery, he had never intended to remain in Italy. Joseph had once written Antonio from America that he wished his mother had followed Gaetano to that wonderful country; it was a wish that Antonio knew Joseph would have expressed only to him. Antonio also knew that Joseph wanted his brother Nicola to join him in America; but Nicola was destined to be a victim of bad timing. Just as he was old enough to set out on his own, the United States' immigration restrictions became all but insurmountable. In 1925, Nicola was drafted by the Fascists, and he had been liberated from military service only in 1940, by which year he was the father of four children. Nicola's marriage to Angela Paone, whose family in the valley was close to the Rocchinos, had been arranged by his mother when he was home on leave. Marian wanted to root him to the village, and to the position of head of the family, since Sebastian was incapable of that role. As Antonio now heard Nicola express his relief on being away from the battlefield, he thought sadly that his cousin had most likely not escaped at all; even as dinner was ending, the Allies were probably preparing to cross the Mediterranean Sea and bring the war home to Nicola and the rest of his family on their native soil.

Antonio returned to Paris in mid-January 1943 with Adelina and their three children; he enrolled the children in an Italian school, and brought his wife into his business—both to make use of her accounting abilities and to have at his side the only person in the city he knew he could fully trust. Paris was now a city of intrigues and duplicity, and everywhere Antonio went, he assumed he was surrounded by spies and double agents. Nazi officers came into his shop more to browse than to buy, and civilians Antonio had never seen before often seemed to be eavesdropping along the counters where the Germans stood. The cafés were filled with military officers speaking German to blond-haired women, perhaps their wives or mistresses, but there was no touristlike informality in their manner; they spoke solemnly, rarely laughed, and said nothing at all when the waiters were nearby. *But from what I can tell, there are still some French people who don't mind the Germans' being here,* Antonio wrote in his diary. *A few French people continue to stress the good things the Germans have supposedly brought to Paris during these years of occupation. The Germans have disallowed smoking in the movie theaters, for example, which used to be polluted. They have made the traffic patrolmen, who used to be* stracciati *[raggedy], put on neater uniforms, and enforce the road rules and regulations. At night, there are fewer aggressions and robberies in the streets. Many criminals have emigrated. The concierge in our building on the Rue de la Paix, who used to hate the Germans—and hated me, because I'm Italian, in spite of all the good things I did for him—now sometimes sounds like a German propagandist. This is also true of the superintendent at our apartment on the Avenue Rachel. He used to curse the Germans, but now he speaks of their impeccable uniforms, and how they've cleaned up the city. The streets* are *cleaner. There are no strikes. . . .*

A number of high officials in the prewar French government, among them the onetime premier Léon Blum, had for months been confined as prisoners of the French state. Although the Vichy government had tried to convict him of treason in a court trial that had ended inconclusively in 1942, they had recently surrendered the seventy-year-old Socialist to the Germans (under whom he would barely survive the war at Buchenwald and Dachau). The Nazi collaborators in Vichy, a group whose most notable citizen continued to be Marshal Pétain, had instituted a French version of the Gestapo during the winter of 1943; called the Milice, it was headed by Joseph Darnand, and it immediately began to wage an anti-Semitic campaign rivaling that of the Nazi masters. Numerous French Jews were rounded up on false charges by the Milice and turned over to the Germans, who transported them long distances to labor camps and often to extinction. The anti-German resistance movement in France was thus greatly enlarged by Jews hiding from the Milice, joining underground Communists who had been increasingly active since Hitler's betrayal of Stalin in 1941—a betrayal that Russia would avenge in February 1943 by beating the German army at Stalingrad. Still, the conviction that

Germany would win the war was not openly questioned by Nazi allies and collaborators in Paris, and if Antonio was beginning to have doubts, as he was, the Italian ambassador who summoned him in the spring of 1943 sternly emphasized the inevitability of Hitler's triumph. *The ambassador was hostile to me for the first time,* Antonio wrote. *My name had gotten on a list of anti-Fascists, and he warned me that I had important enemies in France, and had better watch my step. He said I should never doubt that the Hitler–Mussolini victory is a sure thing, and it was necessary for me to believe it, and to obey. I think he was embarrassed to be so rude to me, but I thanked him for his warning. As I left the building I was shaken, mortified. The guards, who always used to greet me pleasantly, now looked at me in a different way. I'm suspected of something. . . . Yes, I must be careful. But how can I be more careful than I am? The whole city is nervous. Everybody suspects somebody. The German officers who come into the shop have lost their confident and relaxed manner. The war in Russia has not helped German prestige. And the United States is helping Russia. It's another case of strange bedfellows in wartime. The United States entered the First World War to destroy German imperialism. But after the war, the United States and Britain helped Germany to revive itself. What was the use of that war that claimed so many victims? Can the same thing happen again?*

47.

BY MID-MAY 1943, the German and Italian armies in North Africa had been defeated; by July, the Allies were ready to invade Sicily. The Allied plan was to transport its troops across the Mediterranean Sea from North Africa to the southern shores of Sicily, and attack one hundred miles northward, against 240,000 Axis defenders, toward the ancient port city of Messina, nestled along a narrow channel at the northeastern corner of the island. Messina had been seized from Carthage by the Romans in the First Punic War, which ended in 241 B.C. Now in the first week of July 1943, at his advance headquarters near Carthage in North Africa, the Allied commander, General Dwight D. Eisenhower, was scheming to take it. (The military importance of Messina, which had a population in excess of a hundred thousand, was its nearness to the toe of the Italian boot. To possess Messina was to have access to its twenty-four-mile-long channel, the Strait of Messina, which in some places separated Sicily from the mainland of Italy by only two miles.)

The best-known among the celebrated American officers under Eisenhower's command was General George S. Patton; but the most renowned of all the generals was Britain's Bernard Montgomery, an Anglican clergyman's son who, as commander of England's Eighth Army in North Africa in 1942, had defeated Field Marshal Erwin Rommel's Afrika Korps at El Alamein. Rommel had since been reassigned to northern Europe, where Hitler foresaw an Allied invasion coming from the English Channel; and Sicily's defense was entrusted to the Italian Sixth Army, under the command of General Alfredo Guzzoni, a portly officer of unheroic credentials who wore a black wig. But a quarter of General Guzzoni's 240,000-man contingent were highly trained, well-equipped, and motivated German soldiers, and these were Eisenhower's main concern. The Allies would at first be outnumbered, having only 150,000 in the early wave of invaders. But they would be supported by battleship artillery lobbed in from the Mediterranean Sea behind them, and by swarms of bombers and fighter planes; the Allied infantry planned to fight its way across the island, and finally to converge upon Messina from different directions simultaneously.

Field Marshal Montgomery's army, composed largely of British and Canadians, would strike from the southeastern tip of Sicily and move up toward Messina via the eastern edge of the island, a scenic route through cliffside towns abundant with classical ruins and vacant tourist hotels, past such cities as Syracuse and Catania, and, beyond the fuming crater of the ten-thousand-foot Mount Etna, through the lofty aesthetic community of Taormina (known in peacetime for its cultured international travelers and its beautiful native boys) and the town of Bronte, with its ducal estate that had been granted by the grateful Bourbons to Lord Nelson for his efforts against Napoleon. Nelson and Lady Hamilton had used the estate as a love nest.

General Patton's army, whose American majority would be joined by multinational units, including some from Free France, would depart from the southern coastline west of Montgomery's landing site and head toward Messina via the center and western areas of Sicily, a less picturesque, more rugged, and very parched landscape of sun-bleached villages that rarely saw tourists, and where the minimum of existing government was frequently under the control of organized crime. And yet Allied intelligence agents were predicting considerable support in these areas from the civilian population; indeed, once the shooting began, the agents expected pro-American support from most of Sicily's five million inhabitants throughout the island. The Sicilians, whose often brutal and always condescending treatment under Mussolini's regime was characteristic of what the islanders had come to expect from Rome, were decidedly anti-Fascist, if not outright anti-Italian. Often they had campaigned for autonomy from the Italian government; and during World War II and the postwar period, Sicilian separatist sentiments would be vigorously kept alive by a young folk hero named Salvatore Giuliano, the enterprising leader of a gang of bandits who stole from the landowners and shared with the poor, and who urged that Sicily bolt from Italy and annex itself to the United States.

There were now two million residents of the United States with blood ties to Sicily (a group that included the singer Frank Sinatra; the writer, teacher, and anti-Fascist Jerre Mangione; and the future author of *The Godfather,* Mario Puzo); and while it was not publicly known during the war years, the godfathers of Sicily had volunteered their services to the American military even before the island had been invaded. In contributing their skills as intimidators, cutthroats, saboteurs, and underground escorts for advance patrols, the Sicilian *mafiosi* were respecting the wishes of a Sicilian-born Mafia boss in America, Charles ("Lucky") Luciano. In 1943, Luciano was serving a thirty-to-fifty-year prison term in New York State for his profiteering in the prostitution industry; and, quite apart from whatever American patriotism might have motivated his secret appeals relayed to his Sicilian friends by Allied intelligence agents, he also believed his cooperation with the Allies might shorten his jail term; and he would be right. After the war, Luciano's sentence would be commuted by New York's governor, Thomas E. Dewey; and the deported Luciano would be observed in 1946 at a Palermo hotel, along with other leading *mafiosi,* attending yet another Sicilian separatist rally.

Having Sicilian gangsters as cobelligerents against Nazi and Fascist soldiers did indeed contribute to an American military success on the island—or so was the conclusion of writer Norman Lewis, who served with British intelligence during the war, and who would subsequently write a book about the Mafia's role in Sicily entitled *The Honoured Society.* As Lewis would point out in his book, the Sicilian Mafia worked closely with the American-led, not the British-led, units; and as a consequence, the path followed by General Patton's charges would be traversed more swiftly and safely than that of General Montgomery's men, who had to fight without local gangster support.

—

General Patton's invasion of Sicily began on July 9, and, after minimal op-position, part of his forces had linked up with the *mafiosi* eleven days later; from then on they overcame the Fascist–Nazi opposition with amazing ease. As Norman Lewis would explain in his book, certain forward ele-ments of Patton's army, which included American military personnel of Sicilian heritage, arrived on July 20 in the town of Villalba, the home base of the island's top Mafia chief, sixty-six-year-old Calogero Vizzini, known to his colleagues as Don Calò. Six days before, an Allied fighter plane with a yellow flag on its cockpit bearing the letter L had circled over Don Calò's town; and inside a packet dropped by the pilot—which fell near the town church and was delivered by a villager to the home of Don Calò—was a smaller replica of this yellow L flag.

According to Lewis, the L referred to Lucky Luciano; and while the Allied military would never know what Luciano had communicated to Don Calò, the arrival of the message to Don Calò set in motion a series of events that would help weaken the Axis hold over Sicily. Italian soldiers began to defect from their units in increasing numbers. Many Italian POWs later admitted that their ranks had been infiltrated at night by *mafiosi* who convinced them that the Fascist cause was lost, that the Allies would absolutely overwhelm them (indeed, the Allies had by now landed four hundred thousand troops on the island); and these *mafiosi* frequently provided Italian deserters with civilian clothing, concealed them tem-porarily in private houses, then smuggled numbers of them off the island.

Don Calò in the meantime was touring Sicily in an American tank, surveying the frontlines with a subdued confidence that was almost blasé. He said nothing to the tank crew as he squinted through the peep-hole; and if a shell exploded nearby, he registered little emotion and certainly no fear. Although some GIs called him "General Mafia," his ap-pearance was less commanding than comic: fat and ungainly, dressed in shirtsleeves and suspenders fully stretched to hold up his voluminous trousers, Don Calò had required the strong-armed assistance of many men to lift him into the tank that had come to fetch him near his home in Villalba on July 20—a tank that displayed a yellow L flag on its turret. After the tank and the rest of the American convoy rumbled out of Vil-lalba, Don Calò's townsmen would not see him again for an entire week. But it was during this week—from the twentieth to the twenty-seventh of July—that the Americans seemed to advance without deterrence through the towns and villages in central and western Sicily where Mafia influence had traditionally been strong (such places as Corleone, Castelvetrano,

Termini Imerese, and Cerda); and while Don Calò did not travel farther than Cerda—the land beyond presumably fell under the jurisdiction of a fellow *mafioso*—it was a fact that by July 27 the morale of the Axis command in Sicily was lower than it had been since the start of the invasion, and the prestige of the Mafia had probably never been higher.

Shortly after his return to Villalba, the Allies would install Don Calò as the town mayor. A ceremony marking his appointment was held in the barracks of the town's Carabinieri; and later that night, the new mayor hosted a party honoring some of the Allied officers. Don Calò wore a jacket for the occasion and seemed mildly embarrassed on hearing the cries of the crowd: "Long live the Allies! Long live the Mafia!" Laconic as he was in manner and speech, Don Calò was highly sensitive and alert—his eyes, wrote Norman Lewis, "moved like lizards"—and he was sufficiently opportunistic at this time not only to grasp political power for himself, but to convince the Allies to install several of his *mafioso* friends as mayors and administrators of other Sicilian cities and towns. His friends were ardent anti-Fascists, he reasoned earnestly, adding that many had suffered for years in dark prisons and dungeons on orders from the Duce—neglecting to mention that many had previously been convicted on charges of mass murder.

Still, the American officers endorsed most of Don Calò's appointments; and the Mafia that Mussolini had quelled for more than twenty years, suddenly, in a matter of days, gained revenge against the Fascist leader. Except by this time Mussolini was no longer the leader. Word had arrived in Sicily on July 26, 1943, that Mussolini had just been dismissed from his position as prime minister by the Italian king, Victor Emmanuel III. On the previous day—and a few days after Rome had been bombed for the first time by Allied planes—the Fascist Grand Council had met and expressed limited confidence in Mussolini's abilities to rule over the nation's army and economy. Among those voting against him was his son-in-law the count, Galeazzo Ciano.

The king's appointed replacement was Marshal Pietro Badoglio, a career officer with a reputation for reliability, if not battlefield panache. The Fascist Party was dissolved, and a constitutional monarchy was restored with the promise of a democratic parliament. But the war against the Allies would continue, according to an announcement by Badoglio, and Italy would maintain its alliance with Nazi Germany.

Benito Mussolini, stunned and indignant over the king's decision to dismiss him, was escorted out of Rome by armed guards and transported to the isle of Ponza, off Naples to the north, and then shipped farther out to sea to the island of La Maddalena, near the northern tip of Sardinia—close to the private island retreat where Garibaldi had died a half-century before in a state of disillusionment equal to his fame. At La Maddalena on July 29, Mussolini would mark his sixtieth birthday, an occasion unattended by his wife, his children, or his mistress, Clara Petacci, a woman less than half his age, with whom he had been secretly cavorting for nearly a decade. Belatedly, Mussolini received a birthday gift from Hitler, with the Führer's warm inscription: a special edition of Nietzsche's works in twenty-four volumes. These would become part of Mussolini's summer reading, along with a book on the life of Christ, which moved him very much. He let it be known that he could well identify with a savior surrounded by unworthy apostles.

There was remarkably little protest among the people of Italy over the ouster of the man who had led them majestically for almost twenty-one years, and who had received their thunderous applause whenever and wherever he had appeared before them. Even the four million Fascist Party members, and the countless leaders of youth groups who used to honor him with one-armed salutes, failed to express condolences over his political demise, nor would they identify with his downfall—nor refrain from burning their black shirts. Many of his erstwhile loyalists in fact hastened to congratulate his successor, Badoglio, and to pledge their services to the new prime minister. Badoglio, no stranger to Italian political history, was hardly surprised; and if there were ways he thought he could make use of them, he was not remiss in availing himself of their counsel and companionship. Mussolini's newspaper in Milan, *Il Popolo d'Italia,* accepted the Duce's exit without editorial regret. Mussolini's name was removed from the masthead, and where the newspaper had formerly displayed a photograph of Benito Mussolini, it now displayed one of Marshal Pietro Badoglio.

In the United States, the overthrow of Mussolini in July 1943 received a standing ovation from baseball fans reacting to the announcement over the public-address system during a game at Yankee Stadium; and when the news was communicated to a musical audience at an NBC studio in Rockefeller Center in New York City, interrupting an all-Verdi concert conducted by Arturo Toscanini, the people also stood and applauded, and the maestro was described in the next day's *Times* as having "clasped his hands to his head, and gazed heavenward, as if his prayers had been answered." The city's Mayor La Guardia used the occasion to denounce

Mussolini as "the betrayer of Italy," while the ex-dictator was depicted as a "Sawdust Caesar" in *The Washington Post*. The *New York Herald Tribune* lauded the deflation of Mussolini's "Napoleonic egoism," and *The Christian Science Monitor* welcomed the end of his "balcony braggadocio."

But *New York Post* journalist Samuel Grafton, who also did radio broadcasts for the Office of War Information, reminded his listeners that there was little to cheer about; Italy was still in the war, and "the moronic little King, who has stood behind Mussolini's shoulder for twenty-one years, has moved forward one pace. This is a political minuet, and not the revolution we have been waiting for. It changes nothing; for nothing can change in Italy until democracy is restored."

In August 1943, Mussolini was moved from La Maddalena to a place Badoglio believed would better guarantee his isolation: a vacated hotel at a ski resort perched seven thousand feet up on the Gran Sasso d'Italia, a range of the Apennines northeast of Rome. Mussolini was permitted to keep up with battle reports on the radio and to read the newspapers that came with the supplies toted through the mist each day by cable car from the fogbound cliffs below. One day he heard that Milan had been bombed heavily, including the Church of Santa Maria delle Grazie and its refectory. Only one wall of the refectory had withstood air attacks. On this wall was painted Leonardo da Vinci's *Last Supper*. Mussolini was demoralized, anxious, and in physical pain from liver ailments and stomach ulcers. He had recently lost much weight, and he lacked energy. Fearful of being poisoned, he had eaten little since his imprisonment.

At two p.m. on Sunday, September 12, 1943, Mussolini heard the heavy droning sounds of several planes flying over the hotel, and he was surprised to see gliders swooping toward the mountainside, and finally landing softly in a pasture about one hundred yards from where he stood. Suddenly a German colonel, a commando of Austrian birth named Otto Skorzeny, appeared before him, saluted, and explained that he had come on direct orders from Hitler to liberate the Duce. Mussolini shook hands and said pleasantly, "From the beginning I was always convinced that the Führer would give me proof of his friendship."

Mussolini was flown to Rome, then in a larger plane to Vienna. On the following day, in Munich, he was met by his wife, Rachele, and the youngest two of their five children, the teenagers Romano and Anna Maria. "I did not think that I would see you again," said Mussolini as he received his wife. Their thirty-three-year-old daughter, Edda, wife of Ciano—with whom she had been stopped by the Germans from escaping to South America—was not part of the Duce's greeting party; nor was the oldest Mussolini son, Vittorio, a twenty-seven-year-old military pilot. (The couple's other pilot son, Bruno, born two years after Vittorio, had died in an air accident in Italy in 1941.) But Vittorio Mussolini would show up to greet the Duce a day later at Hitler's headquarters near Rastenburg, in eastern Prussia. Here the Duce would embrace not only Vittorio but Hitler as well, and with them he would pose for photographs, and make cordial comments to the Axis-controlled press. He would also spend private hours with Hitler in the latter's underground shelter, exchanging views in German without the presence of interpreters or stenographers; Mussolini would emerge from the lengthy dialogue with a sullen expression on his face that was appropriate to the terms he would henceforth be obliged to live by. He would be reinstalled as the Fascist leader of his homeland—Hitler thought it would have a stabilizing effect on the Italian population—but in actual fact he would be serving as Hitler's puppet in Italy.

What was left of the Fascist army, and the subsequent additions to it drawn from northern and central Italy, was subservient to German authority. Mussolini's government center was shifted from Rome to the northern Italian town of Salò, along the shores of Lake Garda, in the vicinity of alpine peaks and ski slopes; and here, throughout the winter of 1943–1944, he would not make a move without German instruction or supervision.

He made very few speeches in public, and when he did, even his Italian supporters remarked that his voice lacked timbre. His qualities as an actor declined along with his vocal powers, and while his health improved under the German doctors Hitler specifically sent to him, his once robust jaw and chest had clearly shrunk in size, and all the medals dangling from his newly tailored uniforms failed to resurrect his former image as Duce. It was suggested by some Fascists in his circle that Mussolini, almost desperate to seem decisive, was now receptive to partaking in a level of cruelty that was not truly in his heart. Edda, always his favorite among his five children, appealed to him repeatedly during this time to forgive the father of her three children, Ciano, for his concurring with the Fascist Grand Council when it had moved during the previous summer, nineteen votes to seven, to restore to the king and parliament the power and prerogatives that had for so long been assumed by the Duce.

The Grand Council, which had not criticized the Duce by name and which was functioning within its legal rights to circulate motions and respond to them, had not committed an act of treason against Benito Mussolini, in his daughter's opinion, and she saw no reason why her husband should be detained by the new Fascist regime as a prisoner of Italy. Most of the other Grand Council members were now in hiding, or had fled the country; five were currently in jail in Verona awaiting trial, one of them Ciano. Because of his marriage into Mussolini's family, most Italians believed he would ultimately be pardoned, even though Rachele Mussolini and her son Vittorio did not support Edda's appeals; to them, Ciano *was* a traitor of the most ungrateful sort imaginable, to say nothing of his alleged accumulation of illicit wealth during his time in government. But Edda was indefatigable and threatening in her father's presence; she warned that should harm come to her husband she would see to it that his diaries be made public, making it clear that they contained much that was politically embarrassing and harmful to Mussolini.

On January 10, 1944, the Duce received a similar threat from Edda in writing. The letter had come from Switzerland, where she had escaped with her children. Her husband had not been pardoned, nor had the four other imprisoned Grand Council members; all had been convicted of treason by a court in Verona. Mussolini was outraged by the letter, and to his secretary he conceded that publication of Ciano's diary could have "irreparable consequences." But the Duce did nothing more at this point than he had done in the past to liberate his son-in-law.

On the morning of January 11, Ciano and the four others were taken before a firing squad and shot. Mussolini sent his secretary to witness the execution.

The Germans tried to defend southern Italy, but the Allies gradually overpowered them on the ground, in the air, and from ships that hugged the shorelines and bombarded German-occupied seaports and villages that had known war for centuries. On the west coast, Allied dive-bombers attacked Panzer divisions as the latter crossed Roman viaducts or sought cover behind Norman walls and the thirteenth-century buttresses built by the last German ruler of Italy, King Frederick II. On the east coast, the Allies targeted the ancient and once fearsome city of Crotone, which in 510 B.C. had invaded, torched, and buried forever its neighboring town of Sybaris. Allied amphibious battalions drove back Nazi machine-gunners along the beachfront of Pizzo, where in 1815 Joachim Murat had tripped over a fisherman's net and was hauled before a Bourbon firing squad; and countless Italian towns and villages that had been depopulated through emigration were now depopulated further by Allied weapons often fired by the emigrants' children and grandchildren. Italo-Americans served with

Allied units that conquered the ancestral hometowns of American families named Iacocca and Cuomo, Ferraro and D'Amato and Auletta, and of a future rock singer surnamed Ciccone who would become known as Madonna. The birthplace of Mayor La Guardia's father was strafed and cannonaded—while the mayor's sister, Gemma Gluck, who had been living in Budapest at the start of the war with her husband, a Jewish bank clerk, was now imprisoned in a Nazi concentration camp. She would survive the war; her husband would not.

Among the Allied bomber crews with orders to strike Maida, which was then surrounded by German tank units and infantrymen, was an Italo-American from Ambler, Pennsylvania, whose father was employed by Keasbey & Mattison but whose grandfather and other kinsmen still resided in Maida. In the interest of greater safety, the bombardier's relatives in Maida had recently moved downhill to the open fields of the valley, and were now living in tents located as far as possible from the crossfire of the warring soldiers in the highlands. A vast tent city had already been formed along the plains of the valley—hundreds of Maida families, virtually the entire village, had relocated there, including Joseph's mother and the rest of his family. His brother Sebastian had at first refused to leave the village. "I'm staying right where I am," he had insisted, as two of his uncles and his brother Nicola had arrived with a stretcher in his ground-floor room that opened on the yard with the animals.

"Come on, Sebastian," Nicola had pleaded, "the planes might come any minute."

"I'm staying," repeated the gray-haired veteran of Caporetto, who, after his losses in the first war, perhaps felt he had little to lose in the second.

But one of his Rocchino uncles grabbed hold of Sebastian's thin arms and tried to pull him from the cot, provoking screams from Sebastian. His mother then rushed into the room, carrying his freshly laundered clothes and an overcoat Joseph had sent from America.

"Get away from Sebastian, and wait for me outside!" she demanded. As the three of them turned to leave, she added, "And take that stretcher with you."

Ten minutes later, fully dressed and with his hair combed, Sebastian walked slowly out of the house toward the carriages, with an arm around his mother.

The family lived for more than a week in the outdoors, dwelling in such close proximity to their townsmen that they were always surrounded by recognizable voices, by the familiar smells of their neighbors' cooking, and by the sounds of the *passeggiata* which went on throughout the day in pastures edged by wheat fields and olive groves. Throughout the night the valley softly resounded with the litanies led by priests kneeling in front of wagon-wheeled altars; and from the churches in the hills came the sounds of bells, uninterrupted by the distant droning of planes and the occasional thunder of artillery. Many brave parishioners had remained in the churches, where they took their turns in the towers, ringing the bells at the appointed hours, and carrying the statue of Saint Francis through the vacated streets, praying that he would save the town from destruction. Maida's police chief and its baron, together with the mayor and his megaphone, also remained; and thrice daily after the Angelus, the mayor stood along the edge of the Norman wall bellowing messages of reassurance to his constituents in the valley. But the clouds hung low, and there was so much fog during these days that the mayor could not see much farther than his megaphone, and at no time was there sufficient sunlight for anyone in the valley to see the outline of the town. Nor could Maida be seen by the Allied bomber pilots above, who were so thwarted by the clouds that enshrouded the mountain peaks that they dared not dip their wings in descent, for fear of turning the rocky highlands into their gravestones.

For three days and nights, while the bells rang and the litanies continued, the clouds hung heavily over the town, and during this time the Germans moved their defenses farther north, shifting the focus of battle closer to Naples.

48.

THROUGHOUT THE WINTER of 1944, Joseph prayed several times each day in the living room of his home, kneeling on the red velvet of the priedieu under the portrait of the saint, ignoring the store bell below and leaving the operation of his business largely to his wife. He did this at Catherine's suggestion, for he had been hospitalized after the Christmas holidays with appendicitis, and after returning to work he had become so uncharacteristically curt with the customers that he realized the business would be better served by his absence. A high percentage of the clientele now were American servicemen on shore leave, young men demanding quick service, often insisting that their uniforms be pressed or their newly earned chevrons be sewn on while they waited; and among such customers, many of whom had returned from triumphant tours in Sicily and Italy, Joseph could not always conceal the humiliation and divided loyalty he felt as an emotional double agent.

He had dutifully attended the memorial service for the town's first war victim—Lieutenant Edgar Ferguson, a customer's son who had died in Italy (Joseph had hesitated only briefly before approaching the victim's family to express his condolences)—and Joseph had punctually participated in his daily shore patrol assignments along the boardwalk, on the lookout for German submarines with his fellow Rotarians, until his hospitalization had interfered; but since his release from the hospital in early February 1944, he had tried to isolate himself from his friends and business associates on this island that had become increasingly jingoistic as the war's end seemed to be nearing and victory for the Allies seemed inevitable. He had stopped having lunch as usual at the corner restaurant near his shop because he was weary of the war talk at the counter, and tired of hearing such tunes on the jukebox as "Praise the Lord and Pass the Ammunition." He ceased attending the ten-fifteen Mass on Sunday mornings and went instead to an earlier one, at seven, which was less crowded and fifteen minutes shorter; it came without the sermon, which tended to be patriotic, and without the priest's public prayers that singled out for blessing only the servicemen of the Allies.

Joseph continued to keep up with the war news in the daily press, but now he bought the papers at a newsstand beyond the business district, a six-block trip instead of the short walk to the corner cigar store, because he wanted to avoid the neighborhood merchants and his other acquaintances who lingered there and might try to draw him into their discussions about the war in Italy. The last time he had gone there, during the summer before his illness, Mussolini had dominated the headlines (he had just been imprisoned by the Italian king) and as Joseph left with his papers underarm, he heard a familiar voice calling out from the rear of the store: "Hey, Joe, what's gonna happen to your friend now?"

Joseph glared at the men gathered around the soft-drink stand, and spotted his questioner—a thin, elderly man named Pat Malloy, who wore a white shirt and black bow tie and had worked for years behind the counter of the corner restaurant.

"He's no friend of mine!" Joseph shouted, feeling his anger rise as he stepped down to the sidewalk and went quickly up the avenue with his papers folded inward so that the headlines and the photographs of the

jowly-faced interned dictator were covered. Joseph did not make eye contact with the soldiers and sailors he saw among the strollers, although he
could hardly avoid the American flags that flapped across the sidewalk
in front of every shop on Asbury Avenue, including his own; and it was
never possible at night to forget the ongoing war: the town was completely blacked out—all the streetlamps were painted black; lowered
shades and drawn curtains hid the lighted rooms within houses; and few
people drove their automobiles after dark, not only because there was a
gas shortage but also because the required black paint on their headlights
induced automobile accidents and collisions with pedestrians and wandering dogs.

Although there had been no new German submarine attacks in the
area since an American tanker had been torpedoed ten miles south of
Ocean City a year before, the island's continuing blackout had introduced
new problems: gangs of hoodlums from the mainland regularly ransacked
vacant summer homes during the winter months; they also operated a
flourishing trade in pilfered cars, having an abundance of parked vehicles
to choose from during the nocturnal hours, when it was more difficult to
drive cars than to steal them.

Joseph secured his dry-cleaning trucks each night in a garage, and he
chained the bumper of his 1941 Buick to a stone wall in the lot behind his
shop. Before driving it he often had to hammer the ice off the lock, but he
accepted such delays as by-products of the war and the blackout—a blackout which, in his case, extended well beyond the boundaries of his island.
He had been cut off from communication with his family in Italy, and his
cousin in Paris, for many months. Antonio's last letter, received in the
spring of 1943, before the Allies had attacked Sicily, described the Maida
relatives as sustaining themselves but expecting the worst, and added that
the POW husband of Joseph's sister (captured by the British in North
Africa) might have been shot while trying to escape; in any case, no official word of his whereabouts had been received. Whether Joseph's
brother Domenico was dead or alive was also questionable; he had not
been heard from in more than a year. Antonio had passed on the report
that Domenico was possibly with a German-led Italian infantry division
near the Russian front—Antonio had received this information from a
contact in the Italian Foreign Ministry—but he had emphasized to Joseph
that the report was unsubstantiated. Since the arrival of Antonio's last letter, the Allied invasion of southern Italy had begun; Mussolini had been
rescued from prison by Germans to serve as Hitler's puppet; and Joseph

was now trying to recuperate on this island where he had lived compatibly for almost twenty-two years but on which he currently felt estranged as never before.

While his withdrawal was voluntary, having not been prompted by flagrant personal slights or expressions of ostracism toward his business, Joseph felt powerless to free himself from his remoteness and the hostile emotion that too often erupted within him after such remarks as Pat Malloy's. It was possible that Malloy's referring to Mussolini as Joseph's "friend" was a casual remark, made without ill intent. Joseph was, after all, the town's most prominent Italian-born resident, one who had delivered lectures on Italian history and politics to community groups on the island and the mainland; and there had also been no derisive tone in Pat Malloy's voice, to say nothing of the cordial informality he had always shown toward Joseph in the restaurant. Furthermore, to be linked with Mussolini in Ocean City was not necessarily insulting, for the anti-union, Communist-baiting policies of the Duce had long been popular among the staunch Republicans who governed the island; and even in recent years, as the Fascist and Nazi regimes had closed ranks, Mussolini gained from whatever *was* to be gained in the United States by being identified as less odious and murderous than Hitler.

Still, during this winter, Joseph dwelled in a state of exile, adrift between the currents of two warring countries; he would read the newspapers at the breakfast table until nearly ten a.m., his children having already left for school and his wife gone down into the shop, and would then exit down the side stairwell of the building and out the back door, wearing his overcoat and homburg and with a heavy woolen scarf wrapped around his neck, and proceed across the lot to the railroad tracks, and then onward through the black ghetto toward the bay—in the opposite direction from the ocean and his binoculared submarine-searching friends and acquaintances who were lined up with their feet on the lower railings of the boardwalk and their eyes squinting toward the sea. The bayfront district was the most desolate section of town during the winter months; a few black men and women ambled through the bungalow- and shack-lined streets and the weedy fields cluttered with rusting car parts and other rubble, but there was no other sign of human life back here, save for the motorists driving along Bay Avenue, and the white workmen who sometimes scraped the bottoms of overturned dinghies and sloops in the boatyards, and repaired the docks in front of the vacated yacht club. There were hardly any sea gulls around the bay, where the scavenging possibilities could not compare with those offered by the ocean; and never during Joseph's excursions did he meet pedestrians whom he knew well enough to feel obliged to pause and converse with, and explain why he was off by himself traipsing about on the broken concrete sidewalks and frosty fields of this black, backwater part of town. His doctor had not suggested that daily walks would be beneficial to the restoration of his health, although Joseph had said so in explaining to his employees his comings and goings from the store; and it also became the excuse his wife gave to those regular customers who inquired, as some did, why he was constantly out of the shop and spotted frequently by them as they motored along Bay Avenue. Joseph had full confidence in Catherine's ability to make whatever he did seem plausible and proper, and meanwhile to carry on the business without him. She was assisted of course by her saleswomen, and by the old retired tailor from Philadelphia, who now worked a six-day week on the island; and she was supported as well by the reliable Mister Bossum, the black deacon and bootlegger who supervised the dry-cleaning plant and had taken over the responsibilities for the punctuality of the irresponsible pressers, especially the one presser everybody called Jet, the flat-footed, carbuncled ex–jazz musician who even on snowy days arrived for work wearing sandals and short-sleeved silk Hawaiian shirts.

Joseph passed close to Jet's boardinghouse each morning en route to the bayfront, and he was sometimes tempted to stop in and see if Jet had left for work yet; but Joseph resisted, having more urgent concerns. His mother was rarely out of his thoughts during his walks, although he found himself chiding her as much as praying for her. If only she had followed his father to America, Joseph told himself again and again, all the family would now be better off. They would be living with Joseph, or near him, somewhere in America, sparing him his present anxieties about their welfare, and his nagging suspicion that he had somehow abandoned them. If only he had some confirmation that his mother and the rest of his family were alive, that the Allied troops had skirted Maida and left the village undestroyed, he believed, he would no longer be the reclusive and petulant man he had become.

But the war news from southern Italy was scant and inconclusive as far as Maida was concerned. From the Philadelphia and Atlantic City papers he purchased each morning, and from *The New York Times* he received each afternoon in the mail, sometimes two days late, he knew only that the Allies were pushing back the Germans from several locations in the general vicinity of Naples. But Maida was too small, or too insignificant militarily, to warrant mention in the reports; and whatever damage had occurred there, or was occurring now, was left to Joseph's ever-darkening imagination.

When he returned from his walk, by noon if not sooner, he would unlock the rear door on the north side of the building and ascend to the apartment by the walled-in staircase without being seen by anyone in the shop. He would then press once on the wall buzzer near the living room door, signaling to his wife at her desk downstairs that he was home; and usually within seconds she would acknowledge his message with a return signal, and would press twice if she wanted him to pick up the phone extension to discuss something she thought he should know before she closed the shop at five-thirty and came up for the evening. Only on rare occasions did Catherine press twice, however, for there was hardly anything about the business that she could not handle at least as well as he could—a fact that they were both aware of, but that neither discussed. Catherine felt herself sensitive to his every mood and vulnerability, particularly at this point in the war, and in the aftermath of his illness. Having lived under the same roof with him virtually every hour of their almost fifteen years of marriage, except for the recent fortnight of his hospitalization, she thought she knew his strengths, his weaknesses, and his daily routine perhaps better than she knew her own. She knew that when he returned from the bayfront walk, he would first hang up his coat and hat in their bedroom closet in the rear of the apartment, then walk through the corridor back into the living room to kneel briefly at the prie-dieu. A quick lunch would follow in the kitchen, invariably consisting of a plain omelet with crisp unbuttered toast, and a cup of reheated coffee left over from breakfast. He ate little during the day and preferred eating alone. He washed and dried his dishes, but never put them away, leaving this chore for his daughter, Marian, when she came home from school.

Catherine did not leave the shop at lunchtime; instead she had the saleswomen who had their lunches at the nearby five-and-ten soda fountain bring back a milk shake for her. If it was relatively quiet in the shop at midday, as it nearly always was in wintertime, Catherine could hear her husband walking through the corridor after lunch to the mahogany Stromberg-Carlson console in the far corner of the living room, near his record collection. By this time she had already turned off the two particular neon lights in the front of the shop that caused most of the static upstairs on the radio; and if she did not hear him pacing the floor as he listened to the war news, she assumed Joseph was seated in the faded velvet armchair next to the set, leaning forward while twirling his steel-rimmed glasses. He would usually switch stations every three or four minutes, turning the console's large brown asbestos knob slowly and cautiously, as if fearing what the next broadcast might bring. At night she had often observed the intensity with which he listened to the news, awaiting each battlefront bulletin with his face so close to the set that his soulful expression varied in color as the console's green "eye" fluttered in and out of frequency. The children were asleep at this time, these nightly reports often being broadcast well beyond midnight; Catherine herself usually retired shortly after closing the children's bedroom doors, having earlier helped them with their homework. But for hours afterward she lay awake restlessly, not because of the softly tuned radio that continued to absorb her husband's attentions in the living room, nor because of the pink light from the corridor torchère that was reflected forty feet away on the ceiling above the L-shaped ten-foot-high mirror-faced divider that masked the marital bedroom. She was disturbed instead by her husband's pacing back and forth in the living room *after* he had turned off the set, pacing that continued sometimes until dawn, to end only when he had fallen asleep on the sofa, fully clothed. In the morning, hoping not to wake him, Catherine would whisper as she alerted the children for school; but he was always up before they had finished breakfast, and before shaving he would come into the kitchen in his rumpled suit to greet the children formally and then address his wife more gently, usually speaking to her in Italian so the children would not understand.

Except when disciplining them, Joseph paid a minimum of attention to the children during this troublesome winter. Each had been assigned daily chores, both in the apartment and in the store. Even when the chores were performed punctually and competently, Joseph regularly found things to criticize. His complaints were expressed as assertively to eight-year-old Marian as to twelve-year-old Gay. Of the two, only Marian was bold enough to defend herself against his accusations; she alone had the nerve to defy him. While she agreeably carried her mother's shopping list to the neighborhood grocery store, where the family had a charge account—it was actually a barter arrangement dating back to the Depression, when her father and the grocer began exchanging goods and services, making up the difference with gifts at Christmastime after the annual tallying—Marian was far less cooperative in her parents' store. She dusted the glass cases carelessly, swept the floors of the fitting rooms grudgingly when she did so at all, and reacted to her father's reprimands sometimes by dropping the broom or dustpan and stomping out of the shop, ignoring her father's promises of punishment.

"You're more stubborn than my mother," he once shouted at Marian, whom he had named in honor of his mother, although physically she clearly favored his wife's side of the family. Marian had her mother's fair complexion and the red hair of her mother's father, Rosso. She did not appear to be the sibling of her olive-skinned, dark-haired brother, who, while more tractable and less defiant than she, was also more capable of remaining out of their father's sight. Only during his father's illness and self-imposed exile from the shop did Gay enter it without feeling tense and apprehensive—and return to it after school without fear of being late, for his mother was not a clock-watcher; and thus in the winter of 1944 he began taking a more leisurely route home each afternoon, stopping first at the Russell Bakery Shop on Asbury Avenue, where a friend, the baker's grandson, could be counted on to bring a few éclairs out to the alley for a delicious, hastily consumed treat, and then play catch for a few minutes with the rubber ball that Gay always carried in his schoolbag.

Later, in the pressing room, after delivering to Jet and the other presser, Al, enough hangers-with-guards to fulfill their needs for at least a half-hour, Gay had the option of exiting through the back door via the steam screen provided by the pressers, and practicing his pitching form in the lot behind the shop—hurling the rubber ball against the brick wall of the neighboring hardware store's annex, and at times letting it carom off the roof of his father's chained Buick before catching it. He was secure in the knowledge that his father spent the afternoons up in the apartment on his knees, or sitting in the living room listening to operas or news broadcasts, and so he was stunned one afternoon to hear the thumping sounds of his ball punctuated by the urgent rapping of his father's knuckles against the rear window that overlooked the lot.

Gay ran back into the safety of the pressers' steam and quickly resumed the task of affixing guards to hangers, and also sandpapering and unbending those rusty and crooked hangers that customers had provided in response to the store's advertised appeal, and its promise to pay half a penny for each wire hanger, because of the wartime metal shortage. As he worked, he feared the appearance of his father and some form of retribution that might well be overdue. In recent weeks, he had received a failing report card after the midterm examinations; and he had been warned repeatedly by his father to discontinue making his prized model airplanes, for the glue used in sealing their parts cast a hypnotic and possibly toxic odor throughout the apartment. His father had furthermore charged that the glue was most likely the cause of his son's daydreaming and general dim-wittedness in school, the lack of scholarship that had been noted, in kinder terms, by the Mother Superior on the bottom of the recently received report card.

Gay anxiously worked at the hangers, still awaiting his father's arrival in the workroom, knowing that he could expect no protection from Mister Bossum, or Jet, or Al, or the old tailor. But as the minutes continued to register on the misty-faced clock that hung on the workroom wall, and he sandpapered one hanger after another without interruption, he lost track of the time until he saw in front of him his mother's high-heeled shoes and heard her consoling voice suggesting that he was working too hard. It was also closing time, she said, as she extended a hand to help him up from his crouched position.

He was surprised to see that the tailor and the pressers had already left; now only slight sizzling sounds rose from the valves of the machines. Marian also stood waiting, holding a light bundle of groceries in the cloth sack their mother had made because of the paper scarcity. Gay walked up the interior staircase behind his mother and sister, then entered the living room and saw his father seated near the console with his back turned, leaning forward with his head in his hands. The radio was off. He could hear his father softly crying.

His sister, who seemed unaware of it, headed toward the kitchen with the groceries. Gay followed her. Catherine hastened toward her husband and placed a hand on his shoulder. For several minutes they could be heard speaking quietly in Italian. Then she left him and went into the kitchen to prepare the children's dinner; she explained to them that their father was feeling worse than usual, and added that after they had finished dinner they were to go to their rooms and close their doors, and, as long as they kept down the volume, they could listen to their radios. There was no homework to worry about. It was Friday night. Tomorrow a more leisurely day was in the offing, the always welcomed Saturday that brought no school bus or any chores in the shop until after ten a.m.

Joseph spent Friday night on the sofa, having hardly touched the dinner on the tray Catherine had placed on the coffee table in front of him. She had remained in the living room with him until midnight, continuing to speak in Italian. English was heard only when Catherine went to warn Marian that her radio was too loud, and to remind her that she should soon turn off the bed lamp because the following morning she would be picked up by the parents of one of her classmates, with whom she would be attending a birthday party on the mainland.

On Saturday morning after nine, when Gay got up, he saw that his sister had already left. Her door was open, her bed unmade. His parents' bedroom door was shut, as usual, but he knew his mother was downstairs, opening the store for the busy Saturday trade. He could hear the bell downstairs as customers opened and closed the shop's main door on Asbury Avenue. It was a sound he associated with Saturdays, and he always found the tones reassuring, signals of his family's financial stability. In the kitchen, as he poured himself some orange juice, he noticed that there were newspapers on the table that had not been there the night before. Returning to the front of the apartment, he saw no sign of his father. He found it odd to be in the apartment by himself and uniquely exhilarating to be able to walk around freely and privately, answerable to no one. As he approached the console, he noticed that its usual gleaming mahogany exterior was now smudgy with fingerprints. He then saw his father's bathrobe lying on the floor behind the sofa, and the ashtray filled with cigarette butts, and sections of newspapers that had been crumpled up and hurled in the other corner, and had come to rest near the piano. Since his father had always been the family's enforcer of tidiness and order, Gay could not even venture a guess as to the cause of this laxity.

Back in the kitchen, sitting in front of a bowl of dry cereal that his mother had left for him, he looked at the headlines and photographs on the front pages of the newspapers. One was an Italian-language paper that he of course could not read; another was *The New York Times,* which he refused to read because it did not have comics. But on this day he was drawn to the front pages of these and other papers because most of them displayed pictures of the devastation left after recent air raids—smoke was rising out of a large hilltop building that American bombers had attacked in Italy, and had completely destroyed. The headlines identified the ruins as the Abbey of Monte Cassino, located in southern Italy, northwest of Naples. The articles described the abbey as very old, dating back to the sixth century. They called it a cradle of learning throughout the Dark Ages, a scholarly center for Benedictine monks, who had occupied it for fourteen centuries; it was built on a hill that Nazi soldiers had taken over during the winter of 1943–1944. The raid on February 15, 1944, had involved more than a hundred forty of America's heaviest bombers, the B-17 Flying Fortresses; these, together with the medium-sized bombers that followed, released nearly six hundred tons of bombs on the abbey and its grounds. It was the first time the Allies had deliberately made a target of a religious building.

After breakfast, while brushing his teeth in the bathroom, dressed and ready to go down to the store, Gay heard strange noises in the apartment, a pounding on the walls and the cursing of an angry male voice. When he opened the door, he saw his father, in overcoat and hat, swatting down the model airplanes suspended from Gay's bedroom ceiling by almost invisible threads.

"Stop it, they're mine!" Gay screamed, horrified at the sight of his carefully crafted American bombers and fighter planes, framed with balsa wood and covered with crisp paper, being smashed into smithereens by his father. *"Stop, stop, stop—they're mine, get out of my room, get out!"* Joseph did not seem to hear, but kept swinging wildly with both hands until he had knocked out of the air and crushed with his feet every single plane that his son had for more than a year taken countless evening hours to make. They were two dozen in number—exact replicas of the United States' most famous fighter planes and bombers—the B-17 Flying Fortress, the B-26 Marauder, the B-25 Mitchell, the Bell P-39 Airacobra fighter plane, the P-38 Lockheed Lightning, the P-40 Kittyhawk; Britain's renowned Spitfire, Hurricane, Lancaster; and other Allied models that until this moment had been the proudest achievement of Gay's boyhood.

"I hate you, I hate you," he cried at his father before running out of the apartment, and then down the side staircase to the first landing, where he grabbed his roller skates. "I hate you!" he yelled again, looking up toward the living room door, but seeing no sign of his father. Crying, he continued to the bottom of the staircase and out onto the avenue, then thrust his skates around his shoe tops without bothering to tighten them; and as quickly as he could, he headed up Asbury Avenue, thrashing his arms through the cold wind and sobbing as he sped between several bewildered people who suddenly stepped aside. As he passed the Russell Bakery Shop, he lost his balance and swerved toward the plate-glass window. People were lined up in front of the pastry counter, and two women screamed as they saw the boy, his hands outstretched, crash into the window and then fall bleeding with glass cascading down on his head.

Unconscious until the ambulance arrived, and then embarrassed by the crowds staring silently behind the ropes that the police held in front of the bakery's broken window, he turned toward his father, who was embracing him in bloody towels, crying and saying something in Italian that the boy did not understand.

"Non ti spagnare," Joseph said, over and over—don't be afraid—using the old dialect of southern Italians who had lived in fear of the Spanish monarchy. *"Non ti spagnare,"* Joseph went on, cradling his son's head with

his bloody hands, and closing his eyes as he heard his son repeating, tearfully, "I hate you."

Joseph then became silent, watching the ambulance crew arrive with a stretcher as the police ordered the people in the crowd to keep their distance. When Joseph next spoke, he did so in English, although his son found him no less bewildering than before, even as Joseph repeated: "Those who love you, make you cry. . . ."

THIS BOOK, BEGUN in 1981, took ten years to complete. At least half of that time was devoted to research—interviewing people in Europe and the United States; reading about emigration from Italy and about the rulers the emigrants escaped—while the rest of the time was spent trying to portray on paper the quaintly mythified but pragmatic clan of village spiritualists and opportunists who populate my Italian ancestry.

An invaluable source of information about these ancestors was my father's cousin and mentor in Paris, the late Antonio Cristiani, whose retentive memory I tapped often and at length prior to his death in 1986, when he was in his nineties; and I profited as well from his diary, which preserves much of the history of his native village and of our family as it was related to him by his maternal grandfather, Domenico Talese. I was also able to enhance my knowledge of the lore of the village and my forebears by reading some outstanding privately published local chronicles, which are cited below.

Still, my efforts to keep my own book within the boundaries of "nonfiction"—that is, to remain factually verifiable—do not meet the strict standards I have always followed in my previously published work. For the first time in my career as a nonfiction writer, in this latest book I have altered some of the personal names. These name changes do not apply to any of the major characters, including members of my own family, but I have deliberately falsified the names of some minor characters—either to avoid undue embarrassment and pain to their survivors or for legal reasons.

BIBLIOGRAPHY

The chronicles of the history of Maida that I refer to are Giuseppe Barone's *Maida;* F. DeFiore's *Monografia di Maida;* and Antonio Parisi's *Il Feudo di Maida.* These three works, translated into English by Kristin Jarratt, to whom I am indebted also for her talents as an interpreter, served as my first guides in exploring the area and its ancient culture during my many sojourns there in the early and middle 1980s.

Other works that have been helpful to me are listed below:

Acton, Harold. *The Bourbons of Naples, 1734–1825.* London: Methuen, 1956.

Atteridge, A. Hilliard. *Joachim Murat: Marshal of France and King of Naples.* London: Methuen, 1911.

Banfield, Edward C. *The Moral Basis of a Backward Society.* New York: The Free Press, 1958.

Caldora, Umberto. *Calabria Napoleonica, 1806–1815.* Naples: Fausto Fiorentino.

Cateura, Linda Brandi. *Growing Up Italian.* New York: William Morrow, 1987.

Colton, Joel. *Léon Blum: Humanist in Politics.* New York: Alfred A. Knopf, 1966.

Cordasco, Francesco, and Bucchioni, Eugene. *The Italians: Social Backgrounds of an American Group.* Clifton, N.J.: Augustus M. Kelley, 1974.

Crawford, Francis Marion. *The Rulers of the South: Sicily, Calabria, Malta* (2 vols.). London: Macmillan, 1900.

Croce, Benedetto. *History of the Kingdom of Naples* (trans. Frances Frenaye). Ed. H. Stuart Hughes. Chicago and London: University of Chicago Press, 1965.

De Conde, Alexander. *Half Bitter, Half Sweet: An Excursion into Italian-American History.* New York: Charles Scribner's Sons, 1971.

Di Donato, Pietro. *Christ in Concrete.* New York: Pocket Books, 1977.

Diggins, John P. *Mussolini and Fascism: The View from America.* Princeton, N.J.: Princeton University Press, 1972.

Douglas, Norman. *Old Calabria.* New York: Harcourt, Brace, 1956.

Fermi, Laura. *Mussolini.* Chicago and London: University of Chicago Press, 1961.

Fernandez, Dominique. *The Mother Sea* (trans. Michael Callum). New York: Hill & Wang, 1967.

Gallagher, Dorothy. *All the Right Enemies: The Life and Murder of Carlo Tresca.* New Brunswick, N.J.: Rutgers University Press, 1988.

Gambino, Richard. *Blood of My Blood: The Dilemma of the Italian-Americans.* Garden City, N.Y.: Anchor Press/Doubleday, 1975.

Gibson, Hugh, ed. *The Ciano Diaries, 1939–1943.* Garden City, N.Y.: Doubleday, 1946.

Gissing, George. *By the Ionian Sea: Notes of a Ramble in Southern Italy.* London: Chapman & Hall, 1921.

Hapgood, David, and Richardson, David. *Monte Cassino.* New York: Congdon & Weed, 1984.

Hare, Augustus J. C. *Cities of Southern Italy and Sicily.* London: George Allen, late 1800s.

Hibbert, Christopher. *Garibaldi and His Enemies: The Clash of Arms and Personalities in the Making of Italy.* Boston: Little, Brown, 1966.

Hutton, Edward. *Naples and Southern Italy.* New York: Macmillan, 1915.

Johnson, Colleen Leahy, *Growing Up and Growing Old in Italian-American Families.* New Brunswick, N.J.: Rutgers University Press, 1985.

Johnston, R. M. *The Napoleonic Empire in Southern Italy and the Rise of the Secret Societies* (2 vols.). New York: Da Capo Press, 1973.

La Sorte, Michael. *La Merica: Images of Italian Greenhorn Experience.* Philadelphia: Temple University Press, 1985.

Lewis, Norman. *The Honoured Society: The Sicilian Mafia Observed.* New York: Hippocrene Books, 1984.

Liddell Hart, B. H. *History of the First World War.* London: Pan Books, 1972.

Mack Smith, Denis. *Cavour.* New York: Alfred A. Knopf, 1985.

———. *Mussolini.* London: Paladin/Granada, 1983.

Mangione, Jerre. *America Is Also Italian.* New York: G. P. Putnam's Sons, 1969.

Marshall, S. L. A. *World War I.* New York: American Heritage Library, 1985.

Masson, Georgina. *Frederick II of Hohenstaufen: A Life.* New York: Octagon Books, 1973.

Moquin, Wayne, with Charles Van Doren, eds., and Francis A. J. Ianni, consulting ed. *A Documentary History of the Italian Americans.* New York: Praeger, 1974.

Murat, Inès. *Napoleon and the American Dream* (trans. Frances Frenaye). Baton Rouge and London: Louisiana State University Press, 1981.

Murray, John. *A Handbook for Travellers in Southern Italy.* London: John Murray, 1878.

Nichols, Peter. *Ruffo in Calabria.* London: Constable, 1977.

Panella, Vincent. *The Other Side: Growing Up Italian in America.* Garden City, N.Y.: Doubleday, 1979.

Ramage, Craufurd Tait. *Ramage in South Italy: The Nooks and By-Ways of Italy. Wanderings in Search of Its Ancient Remains and Modern Superstitions* (Introduction by Harold Acton; abr. and ed. Edith Clay). London: Longmans, 1965.

Ridley, Jasper. *Garibaldi.* London: Constable, 1974.

Rolle, Andrew F. *The Immigrant Upraised: Italian Adventurers and Colonists in an Expanding America.* Norman: University of Oklahoma Press, 1968.

Sowell, Thomas. *Ethnic America: A History.* New York: Basic Books, 1981.

Taylor, Henry Osborn. *The Classical Heritage of the Middle Ages.* New York: Frederick Ungar, 1957.

GAY TALESE began work as a reporter at *The New York Times* in 1956, where he worked until 1965. Thereafter he wrote often for *Esquire* magazine; his piece "Frank Sinatra Has a Cold" was named by the magazine's editors the best it ever published. He is the bestselling author of *Thy Neighbor's Wife, Honor Thy Father,* and *The Kingdom and the Power.* His most recent work is *A Writer's Life.*

He lives in New York City.

Printed in the United States
by Baker & Taylor Publisher Services